The Favourite

Ophelia Field

The Favourite

Sarah, Duchess of Marlborough

Hodder & Stoughton

First published in Great Britain in 2002 by Hodder and Stoughton
A division of Hodder Headline

A CIP catalogue record for this title is
available from the British Library

ISBN 0 340 76807 X

Typeset by Palimpsest Book Production Limited,
Polmont, Stirlingshire
Printed and bound in Great Britain by Clays Ltd, St Ives plc

Hodder and Stoughton
A division of Hodder Headline
338 Euston Road
London NW1 3BH

For my mother

Contents

List of Illustrations

List of Illustrations

Acknowledgements

I was introduced to Sarah Churchill, Duchess of Marlborough, through one of my closest friends, whose *Debrett*ish knowledge of the British aristocracy I used to mock but have come to envy in the course of writing this book. I will always be grateful that Kirsty Fowkes knew both Sarah and me well enough to make the match.

As I began to understand Sarah's similarity to several women I have admired (all of whom would be surprised, embarrassed, and perhaps even insulted by the comparison), I became fascinated by her. For the impetus to turn this fascination into a book, and for the courage to invest in an unpublished writer, I must thank my editor at Hodder & Stoughton, Roland Philipps, and my agents, Ed Victor and Lizzy Kremer, for all their work on my behalf.

In one letter, Sarah says she wants to convince the recipient of her cause 'without sending you such volumes as, without retiring, you could never read'. She was referring to the enormous stacks of her own correspondence and memoirs, which today are mostly kept, exquisitely catalogued, in the British Library. I could not have attempted to master this subject were it not for the patient assistance of the staff in the Manuscript Department there. Similarly, I thank Charles E. Pierce Jnr, Director, and Robert Parks, Curator, at the Pierpont Morgan Library, New York; Mr John Rathe and his colleagues at the New York Public Library; Gerald Wager and his colleagues at the Library of Congress, Washington DC; Mary L. Robertson at the Huntington Library, Los Angeles; Stephen Parks and his colleagues at the Beinecke Library, Yale; Clare Brown and her colleagues at the Bodleian Library, Oxford; Dr Patrick Zutshi and his colleagues at the University of Cambridge Library; J. van Wandelen at the Gemeentearchief in The Hague; Madame Docnot and Madame Simons at the Archives de la Ville Bruxelles; Allison Derrett at the Royal Archives, Windsor; David Pearson and his colleagues at the Wellcome Library, London; as well as the helpful staff at Britain's National Registry of Archives, the Public Record Office, and the National Trust.

I am hugely indebted to previous scholars who have painstakingly combed through other, more peripheral and opaque manuscripts for references to the Marlboroughs. In particular, I must thank Dr Frances Harris, who laid the first truly reliable, factual groundwork in her 1991 biography, and who generously assisted me with her time and advice in the course of my research.

What I hope to have contributed to the historiography of the first Duchess of Marlborough is a sense of how her character has been tarnished, distorted and diffused by repeated handling, just as many portraits of her have been recopied and misattributed beyond recognition. Sarah believed posterity's judgement would be truer than that of her contemporaries, but this has proved a misplaced faith. I have been continually conscious of how much historical biography is a matter of our willingness to believe one piece of hearsay over another, and have tried to make the reader equally conscious of each story's frequently dubious sources.

I have quoted literary sources extensively to convey a sense of the times in which Sarah lived, of the pressures that provoked her to act as she did, and to trace the origin of the mythology surrounding her. Daniel Defoe, a strangely recurring figure in the background of her life, wrote: 'We fight with the poison of the tongue, with words that speak like the piercing of the sword, with the gall of envy, the venom of slander, the foam of malice.' If Sarah's own tongue became poisonous, it was because she understood the power words had over her reputation better than most. Like a favourite monopolising royal patronage, she sought to monopolise truth with her own version of her life's events – as we all do to some extent. In many instances, I have given Sarah's narrative voice a status and sympathy above others, without, I hope, being overly credulous.

Unpublished doctoral theses by Dr Richard Brown (University of Rochester, 1972), Dr Kathleen Szpila (Temple University, 1997) and Dr Rachel Weil (Princeton, 1991) have been cited as sources throughout the book. The author also wishes to thank Oxford University Press for their kind permission to quote from Dr Harris' *A Passion for Government* and from *The Marlborough–Godolphin Correspondence*, Snyder, Henry L. (ed.).

I would also like to thank those who read and commented on the book in its various drafts including Hazel Orme, Lizzie Dipple, Tom Weisselberg, and especially Dr Eveline Cruikshanks; Frances Wilson and Adam Smyth for their advice and assistance with research; Kathy Lette for opening doors; Katrin Herbst and Juliet Brightmore for their assistance with picture research; David Onnekink for discussions on Dutch sources and royal favourites; Robert Ketteridge for assistance with video research; Lucy Moore for advice on Lord John Hervey; Friso Roscam Abbing for my own experience of political lobbying; Earl Spencer, Dawn Conchie, Diane Springett and especially Joyce Coles for their help and hospitality at Althorp; Anthony Griffiths, Deputy Director, the Commonwealth Secretariat, and Harold Jecksley, retired Keeper of the Royal Palaces, for assistance with my research at Marlborough House; the present Duke of Marlborough and Mr John Forster for facilitating my visits to Blenheim Palace; Clare Baxter, Collections Manager of the Northumberland Estates, for assistance with my research at Syon House; Michael Prodger for advice on Wren; James Mulraine for his advice on the portraits by Jervas; Lady Heald for information on Chilworth Manor; Canon Jim Richardson for a missing clue; and my grandmother, Arlene, for providing a quiet haven while I was writing the final chapters and for giving me empathy with Sarah in her eighties.

Above all, I hope that my own favourite, Paul Laikin, will

accept my thanks here in lieu of an accreditation more befitting the time and energy he has spent helping me with this book.

Ophelia Field, March 2002

NOTE ON MODERNISATION: Spellings (and some punctuation) in quotations have been modernised, except in certain verses or where otherwise specified. Capitalisation has been modernised in quotations from manuscripts, but not from printed texts. Dates have been given according to the Old Style (Julian) calendar, including for letters sent from the Continent where the New Style (Gregorian) calendar was in use. However, the year has been taken to begin on 1 January instead of 25 March.

But what are these to great Atossa's mind?
Scarce once herself, by turns all Womankind!
Who, with herself, or others, from her birth
Finds all her life one warfare upon earth:
Shines, in exposing Knaves, and painting Fools,
Yet is, whate'er she hates and ridicules.
No Thought advances, but her Eddy Brain
Whisks it about, and down it goes again.
Full sixty years the World has been her Trade,
The wisest Fool much Time has ever made.
From loveless youth to unrespected age,
No Passion gratify'd except her Rage.
So much the Fury still out-ran the Wit,
The Pleasure miss'd her, and the Scandal hit.
Who breaks with her, provokes Revenge from Hell,
But he's a bolder man who dares be well.
Her ev'ry turn with Violence pursu'd,
No more a storm her Hate than Gratitude:
To that each Passion turns, or soon or late;
Love, if it makes her yield, must make her hate:
Superiors? death! And Equals? what a curse!
But an Inferior not dependent? worse.
Offend her, and she knows not to forgive;
Oblige her, and she'll hate you while you live:
But die, and she'll adore you – Then the Bust
And Temple rise – then fall again to dust.
Last night, her Lord was all that's good and great;
A Knave this morning, and his Will a Cheat.
Strange! by the Means defeated of the Ends,
By Spirit robb'd of Pow'r, by Warmth of Friends,
By Wealth of Follow'rs! without one distress
Sick of herself thro' very selfishness!
Atossa, curs'd with ev'ry granted pray'r,
Childless with all her Children, wants an Heir.
To Heirs unknown descends th'unguarded store
Or wanders, Heav'n-directed, to the Poor.

Alexander Pope, 'Epistle to a Lady'

Prologue

There is an apocryphal anecdote about Sarah, Duchess of Marlborough, and the poet Alexander Pope. Pope went to visit the old dowager one day, as he did throughout the 1730–40s, and read aloud to her the description of Atossa that appears on the preceding pages. He told her it was based on the Duchess of Buckingham, but Sarah 'spoke of it afterwards and said she knew very well whom he meant'.[1]

What of herself might she have seen in Atossa? The internal conflict? Probably not. She got along with herself reasonably well. But throughout her life she had been caricatured as prone to rages, so she would have assumed that lines such as 'No Passion gratify'd except her Rage', 'So much the Fury still out-ran the Wit', or 'By Spirit robb'd of Pow'r, by Warmth of Friends' were arrows aimed at her.

Sarah had been the companion of Anne, as Princess and Queen, for twenty-seven years, and a powerful political force in Britain for 'full sixty'. Her life had defined both the extent and limitations of a woman's influence in public affairs during the late-seventeenth and early-eighteenth centuries. She chose to marry a man who, with her support on the home front, would change the course of European history through his military victories. She gave him seven children, of which four survived to adulthood, and dedicated much of her widowhood to celebrating the immensity of his achievement. As Anne's favourite, she had played a small but vital part in the Glorious Revolution of 1688, been courted and spurned by politicians, suffered allegations of treason and public disgrace, and was twice exiled to the Continent.

She was made a celebrity and a scapegoat by journalists of the first modern newspapers – to which she responded with more instinctive understanding of the press, and more courage, than most of her contemporaries. Opponents commonly portrayed her as her own worst enemy, as having caused her own and her husband's fall from the pinnacle of their careers, and the collapse of the Whig government she championed, through her tactless handling of Queen Anne's favour. 'By the Means defeated of the Ends' might therefore have seemed a fitting epitaph.

She did not have an 'Eddy Brain', any more than any woman was deemed intellectually inferior to a man, but her writing style, which Pope knew well, reads in places like a whirlpool. She was an indefatigable self-dramatist, casting herself, in her memoirs and unpublished writings, in a variety of heroic roles and prejudicing history for ever against those who opposed her. Her surviving letters appeal as much to posterity's good opinion as to their beleaguered recipients. Her records of seemingly petty conflicts at Court are indicative of far greater forces competing for control of Britain during her lifetime.

Largely through her own efforts and investments, she became the richest woman in England and probably the western world, worth over £1 million – roughly equivalent to £82 million today. She oversaw the building of Blenheim Palace and Marlborough House, and became the sole owner of twenty-six other estates. She held a controlling interest in the national debt, and the fate of the Bank of England lay in her hands on more than one occasion.

But the most apposite lines in the Atossa passage may be those that refer to her being 'whate'er she hates and ridicules', for Sarah had a knack, particularly in her sexual slanders of those who succeeded her in the Queen's affection, of implicating herself whenever she insulted others. As she was well aware, this was what gave her attacks their force.

Despite her lifelong Whiggery and Pope's Tory Catholicism, Sarah and he became friends through their shared opposition to Prime Minister Robert Walpole. In 1739, when she was seventy-nine and he fifty-one, he wrote to Jonathan Swift that '[t]he Duchess of Marlborough makes great court to me, but I am too old for her, mind and body'.[2] At one level the poet was fond of her. He wrote jokingly to their mutual acquaintance the young Earl of Marchmont: 'There are many hours I could be glad to talk to (or rather to hear) the Duchess of Marlborough . . . I could listen to her with the same veneration, and belief in all her doctrines, as the disciples of Socrates gave to the words of their master, or he himself to his Demon (for I think she too has a Devil, whom in civility we will call a Genius).'[3] Sarah was not so flattering about him behind his hunch-back, allegedly writing that 'Lord Fanny [the camp Lord Hervey] has my best wishes for the success of her attack on that crooked perverse little wretch at Twickenham.'[4]

The suggestion that Sarah cultivated Pope's friendship only to prevent him writing satires against her and her dead husband is appealingly cynical, but cannot be proved. Lord Bolingbroke spread the story that she once bribed Pope with a thousand pounds not to publish the Atossa verses. In revenge for a literary theft he believed Pope to have committed, and perhaps remembering a time when he had been a prominent target of Sarah's animosity, he related the story of the bribe in a footnote to the Atossa verses when he arranged for their posthumous publication under the title *Verses Upon the late D[uche]ss of M[arlborough]* (1746). This ensured that Atossa, whether or not based on Sarah, remained the prevailing image of her throughout the eighteenth and nineteenth centuries.

However, the specific detail of the verses fits more exactly the life of the Duchess of Buckingham, with whom Pope had quarrelled in 1729. On the other hand, an earlier, quite different version, written before Pope made Sarah's acquaintance, was nominally about someone else: Princesse Marie-Anne de la Tremoille (Princess Orsini) who rose to power in Spain at the same time as Sarah did in England through an intimate friendship with the young queen of Philip V and was then, like Sarah, dramatically dumped. This was Pope's way of writing about Sarah, without libel, as a public figure. Pope also liked to joke that the militant Thalestris, who cut Belinda's hair in *The Rape of the Lock*, was based on Sarah.

So this is one of the first things we know about Sarah: she can be read into places she does not belong, overlooked in other places where she should be seen, and accused of actions (such as bribery) that she probably never even considered.

In Pope's *Epistle to a Lady* the antithesis of Atossa is Martha Blount. According to Pope, Martha was the epitome of female modesty and obedience, staying housebound in her 'godly garret' to 'spill her solitary Tea'. To a greater or lesser extent, Sarah's life has always been judged against this standard: a temperate, demure model of correct female behaviour, which involved staying away from worldly business. The thirty or so biographies of her life have been a little like the autobiography of John Dunton whose *Life and Errors* (1705) contains alternate chapters telling the events of his life, first as he had lived them, and then as he believed he should have lived them. Many biographers have passed judgement on Sarah based on an alternative personality they think she should have had. Even when her energy and vivacity have been admired, they have also been presented as her fatal flaws.

Sarah knew how hard it would be to get a good word out of posterity, especially as a woman. Among papers found after her death was a piece called 'A Character of her Highness the Princess * * * * attempted by Richard Hollings MD'.5 The author claimed to have known the Princess of Wales 'almost from the hour of her birth' and so to be well qualified to assess her character. He complimented the Princess on the fact that 'she seems to be the only person ignorant of that superiority [of birth]', on not having an enemy in the world, and on showing only sincere smiles of happiness and tears of grief, never those caused by disappointed ambition. She apparently lived within her means, spent only what she needed and was 'free from the ostentation of little or sordid minds'. She was congratulated on staying out of politics, on not being vain or frivolous, and on never having told a lie or even disguised a truth. Hollings added that '[h]er silence, considering her sex, is not the least admirable of her many qualifications . . .'

The joke was that this character portrait was of a newborn baby girl, not yet christened. It underlines the foolishness of other eulogies on the infantile virtues of women in this period, and the general biographical folly of looking for a blameless life. Sarah wrote a scribbled memo on it: 'This paper makes me laugh, for I think there is a good deal of humour in it, and two very exact characters.'[6] By this she probably meant that the baby princess's perfect character was an inverted satire about her enemy, Queen Caroline, wife of George II. But it is also, whether she knew it or not, a reflection on Sarah's own character – a reversible catalogue of all the accusations made against her during her lifetime and repeated time and again by historians and biographers. On the one hand there is the innocent babe, on the other, the monstrous Atossa.

I

Miss Jennings

Sarah Jennings (or Jenyns) was born on 5 June 1660, the week after Charles II returned from exile and was installed on the restored throne. Her mother was Mrs Frances Thornhurst Jennings, married to Mr Richard Jennings of Sandridge, near St Albans. They were minor gentry with property in Somerset, Kent and Hertfordshire. There were many men like Sarah's father, who had been a supporter of John Pym, an architect of the revolt against Charles I, but then subsequently a member of the Convention Parliament that had recalled Charles II.[1] Most of the gentry had greeted the monarchy back with relief and even jubilation, but also with a new sense that its authority was dependent upon their support. Some men, like Sarah's father, expressed no clear enthusiasm.

Sarah recognised the snobbishness of genealogies and disapproved of them in biographies. In 1736 when she read Thomas Lediard's biography of her husband, she noted: 'This History takes a great deal of pains to make the Duke of Marlborough's extraction very ancient. That may be true for aught I know; but it is no matter whether it be true or not in my opinion, for I value nobody for another's merit.'[2] This might have been a convenient view to take when her own extraction was not particularly grand, but Sarah never tried to disguise this. When asked, she said simply that her father's family background 'was reckoned a good one'.[3]

Nor need much be said about her early childhood. In this post-Freudian era we tend to think we cannot know someone properly unless we are aware of where he or she came from. In Sarah's era, where character was considered a fixed thing carried around like a suitcase, childhood was viewed as an irrelevant period before one did one's packing. People kept little record of their own or others' childhoods, and in the absence of facts, biographers used to invest their subjects with precocious qualities that foreshadowed their adult characters or actions. In the *History of Prince Mirabel* (1712), a fictionalised biography of Marlborough, he is shown reviving a schoolfriend struck by lightning as a precursor to his later military heroism. The biographer Frank Chancellor was doing the same thing in 1932 when he imagined Sarah to have been something of a 'spitfire'4 as a child.

Sarah was the youngest of five children, with two brothers and two sisters. Her eldest sister, Barbara, died at twenty-seven, leaving a widower who would later pester Sarah for financial and political favours until, as she put it, he 'turned her head'.5 Both brothers, John and Ralph, were also to die relatively young, leaving little on the historical record but property disputes with their mother. The other sister, Frances, lived to a ripe old age like Sarah, but made very different choices.

When Sarah was five, London was overwhelmed by the plague. Another child living in Cripplegate, Daniel Defoe, later wrote a vivid account of this catastrophe as though he had experienced it as an adult. Sarah was less exposed to the horrors – the recorded death toll in St Albans was only 121 – but her parents would have known many people who died in London, and she might have witnessed the crowds of displaced people living in 'great extremities in the woods and fields' of Hertfordshire.6 The following year, 1666, the Great Fire of London lit up the sky 'like the top of a burning oven'.7 The conflagration was visible as far north as St Albans and the smoke cast a pall over the countryside for fifty miles.

If we look for major events that might have affected Sarah as a child, we must include the separation of her parents when she was eight. Divorce was rare, but private deeds of separation could be arranged and informal separations were not uncommon. In 1668 Sarah moved to London with her mother and sisters just as the city was being frenetically rebuilt. Why her parents separated is unknown, but it probably had to do with her father's financial problems and the fact that her mother had started legal proceedings against him to reclaim her dowry. By the time Sarah was born her father was insolvent, thanks to inherited debts and having to support his many younger siblings.[8] So while Sarah did not grow up poor, she must have felt that the family was close to the edge, living always on the credit of an affluent appearance. Her financial prudence in adulthood has usually been traced to this early insecurity.

In late 1673, Sarah followed her sister Frances to Court and became one of four Maids of Honour to the Duchess of York, Mary of Modena, second wife of James, the King's Catholic brother. Frances had served James's first wife Anne Hyde, who had nine children, among whom only Princesses Mary and Anne survived. Anne Hyde had died of breast cancer in March 1671, and Margaret Blagge described the event in her own notebook rather matter-of-factly: 'None remembered her after one week, none sorry for her. She smelt extremely, was tossed and flung about, and everyone did what they could with that stately carcase.'[9]

The fifteen-year-old Mary of Modena was a Catholic, which alarmed an Anglican nation. She probably had little idea of the religious tensions and the unfaithful husband with whom she had climbed into bed. She did not get on well with her stepdaughters, who were her own age and had been raised, according to Charles II's orders, as fervent Protestants by their mother.

Sarah was fortunate to find this job serving the new Duchess, though it paid little. Parents sometimes paid patrons to find such places for their daughters because of the contacts and opportunities for advancement they afforded, including a decent-sized dowry paid by the Crown. Royalists who sought compensation or gifts of gratitude from the restored King, which he could not afford to pay, received instead Court employment for their family. Sarah's parents had been such petitioners.

When Sarah's father had died in 1668, he had left Mrs Jennings as a single mother with debts. Mrs Jennings moved with her daughters to St James's Palace where her creditors could not come knocking. When Sarah's brother John inherited much of the family property in 1674,[10] their mother started a new series of legal proceedings to regain control of her share.

The fact that the alternative to St James's might have been Newgate debtors' prison makes it genuinely shocking that, at sixteen, Sarah attempted to have her mother evicted from Court, or at least did not seek to prevent this happening. In a letter from Lady Chaworth to Lord Roos in November 1676 there is gossip about the fight between mother and daughter: 'Sarah Jennings has got the better of her mother who is commanded to leave the Court and her daughter in it, notwithstanding the mother's petition that she might have her girl with her, the girl saying she is a mad woman.'[11] Sarah, as we shall see, was in the middle of courting John Churchill at this time and perhaps the argument with her mother had related to the chance of the relationship ending in marriage or, alternatively, an illegitimate pregnancy. If Mrs Jennings had talked publicly about the danger of the latter, Sarah would have been seriously embarrassed. She was probably referring to her mother when she wrote to her sister Frances in around 1675 that '[t]oday I will constrain myself as much as is possible but sometimes she would provoke a saint'.[12] The command for her mother to leave Court does not seem to have been carried out.

There is something mysterious about the figure of Mrs Jennings. She did not leave many historical traces, except as a disappointed, litigious woman in need of money. What remain are mainly fictional incarnations of her, which feature in the anti-Marlborough satires of the 1700s and mostly represent her as a witch or procuress. In March 1712, for example, a pamphlet called *The Perquisite-Monger; or the Rise and Fall of Ingratitude* depicted 'Zaraida' as 'a Person of a mean Extraction, but who had by the Subtlety of her Mother, that was a noted humble Servant to the Pleasures of certain Great Men and her own Inclinations, so wormed herself into the Confidence of her Mistress as to be in the highest Esteem with her . . .'[13]

In another poem, which survives in manuscript and is undated but likely to be from Mrs Jennings' lifetime, she is referred to as King Charles's 'bawd' when 'whoring was no crime'.[14] And in 1682, the year in which Sarah's husband received his first title, the anonymous 'Satire to Julian'[15] mocked Sarah by a reference to her mother as an infamous whore-mistress. There may be a link between this slander and the letter Nell Gwynne wrote in 1684 from Windsor to one Mrs Frances Jennings living 'over against the Tub Tavern in Jermyn Street'. In it, although Nell addresses the lady in question as 'Madam' and signs with respectful affection ('I love you with all my heart & so goodbye'), she also gives orders for her correspondent to arrange for her shopping.[16] They obviously had a close relationship, as if Mrs Jennings were both Nell's servant and guardian. We cannot be sure that this is the same Mrs Jennings, but it would seem a great coincidence for two women of this name to have been linked to the Court at this time.

There is a famous portrait by Sir Godfrey Kneller, painted some time between 1685 and 1690, that is believed to be of Mrs Jennings. It is remarkable for showing an old woman with warts and all, contrary to conventions of the time by which respectable women were invariably painted as youthful.[17] Either Kneller was influenced by Dutch realism, a turning point in English convention, or the sitter's morals were dubious. It is hard to see why Mrs Jennings would have chosen to sit for such a portrait. Even today it is a slightly disturbing image: her face is dark and threatening under her widow's hood.

Combined with the scraps of evidence that Sarah left behind – her perhaps flippant comment that her mother was mad, and her later letters, which imply that she was both annoyed and aggrieved by her mother's behaviour – it is difficult not to feel that there was something behind the slanderous attention that Mrs Jennings received. This sense of no-smoke-without-fire, however, is also derived from Sarah's own Atossa-image – the assumption that a woman like her must have had a mother of strong or unusual character.

On 16 February 1675, Shrove Tuesday, Sarah was on stage at the Great Hall of Whitehall Palace,[18] performing in a masque called *Calisto* as the male figure of Mercury. The rest of the cast consisted of her young aristocratic friends. They were caught by, among others, the diarist John Evelyn at a moment when they were unaware of the extraordinary lives in store for each of them. The title role of Calisto ('a chaste and favourite Nymph of Diana') was played by Princess Mary, aged thirteen, to whom the play was also dedicated. Thirteen years later she was on the throne of England. Her ten-year-old sister Anne, another future Queen, also played a nymphet. This 'lymphatic, pasty-faced child-Princess'[19] had not yet become, as Sarah would bluntly put it, 'exceedingly gross and corpulent'[20] and she was still two years away from the smallpox that would permanently disfigure her face, but the 'perpetual squinting',[21] which caused a 'sullen and constant frown', was already in evidence.

The Chief of the Dancers was the young Duke of Monmouth, the illegitimate Protestant son of Charles II, whose uncle, James II, would execute him for treason after Sarah's future husband had helped put down his rebellion in 1685. Beside Monmouth, playing Jove, was Lady Henrietta Wordsworth, who would become his mistress and die shortly after his execution.[22] The goddess Juno was played by the Countess of Sussex, Charles II's daughter by his mistress Barbara Castlemaine. She had recently been ordered home to England and married off after escaping from a convent in France and starting an affair in Paris with the English ambassador, her mother's other lover, Ralph Montagu. Another nymph, Psecas, was played by Lady Mary Mordaunt, later Duchess of Norfolk: she was fated to become a byword for scandal when her equally faithless husband divorced her by Act of Parliament in 1700 for adultery with a Dutch gambler.

The chaste goddess Diana was played by Margaret Blagge. Disliking the flirtatiousness of the rehearsals, according to Evelyn, she preferred to sit backstage in 'the Tiring-room' and read a devotional book. She was the only leading cast member apart from Sarah who was not a 'lady', and in May of that same year she secretly married a page to the King, who later became First Lord of the Treasury and Sarah's lifelong friend, Sidney Godolphin.

He was a short Cornishman with, according to Matthew Prior and several portraits, a long horse-like face. Sadly, Margaret died young, of an infection caught during the birth of her first child and was not helped by being treated with 'the pigeons' (live birds tied to her feet, believed to reduce fever).

Watching the performance of the masque, at the front of a huge audience on two tiers, were the King, with spaniels on his knee, his brother and their wives, all snacking on wine and fresh olives. Red, white and blue curtains draped the stage dangerously lit by wax and torch staves, oil lamps and candles. The curtains drew back and a musical prologue opened with the characters of Peace and Plenty attending the River Thames, a part sung, to the Queen's embarrassment, by Moll Davis, a mistress the King kept in a house in Suffolk Street. The set was a wood-and-silk replica of Somerset House with a Temple of Fame perched on top, amid painted clouds. Personifications of Europe, Africa and America joined the Thames, turning to the King and Queen in the audience and throwing tributes at their feet. Then the play proper began, set in Arcadia and 'the Duration of it, An Artificial Day'. The ladies in the cast were supposed to be playing scantily clad classical characters but were loaded down in costumes of gold and silver brocade, coloured feathers and real jewels worth hundreds of pounds.

Sarah's character, Mercury, is the confidant of Jove (Lady Wentworth). Mercury is in love with the nymph played by Princess Anne. The plot centres, however, around Calisto (Princess Mary) who is the royal favourite of the goddess Diana (Margaret Blagge). Both were witty reverse castings of mistresses and their serving ladies. Jove decides to transform himself into the shape of Diana to trick and rape Calisto. Taking advantage of the chastity assumed to exist in same-sex relationships, Jove declares:

> 'A sure and pleasant Ambush I will lay;
> I'll in Diana's shape the Nymph betray:
> My wanton Kisses then she'll ne'er suspect . . .
> Disguis'd like her, I'll Kiss, Embrace, be free.'

In Act II he puts this plot into action and, disguised as Diana, declares to the other woman that 'your merits breed/ In my last Heart, a strange uncommon flame:/ A kindness I both fear and blush to name'. Calisto is disturbed by the sudden eroticism of her mistress and asks, 'What kindness can I show? What can I do?/ Stand off, or I shall be infected too.'

Having escaped this trap, Calisto is almost displaced by Psecas spreading sexual slander against her. Thwarted, Psecas denies that she aims to be a royal favourite and makes a declaration of independence which is both condemned and applauded: 'I'll hunt alone, and in myself delight,/ And be my own most dear-lov'd Favourite.'

A musical scene, involving for no apparent reason a chorus of women blacked-up to be African, closed the masque.

In this silly performance, which Sarah rehearsed and performed over several weeks, many themes of her life were prefigured – favouritism and jealousy, public disgrace and slander, opposition to a monarch and attempts at self-justification, sexual ambiguity and role reversal, ingratitude and pride.

Maids of Honour were not servants in the sense that they performed manual chores. Rather, they were paid companions for Court ladies and 'public-relations girls' for the Court itself. Later, when Sarah herself was in charge of selecting the Queen's Maids of Honour, she wrote that the main qualifications for the post were beauty and a good education, meaning polite manners.[23] They were also intended as a steady supply of virgins for male courtiers. Pepys wrote that the 'Duchess's maids of honour and a hundred others bestow their favours to the right and to the left and not the least notice taken of their conduct'.[24] It is certainly true that James, both as Duke of York and later as King, took a number of them as mistresses. He liked the clever, witty ones, not caring if they were ugly.

It is easy to be carried away by descriptions of moral laxity set amid idyllic surroundings, with the young ladies enjoying picnics in the park of 'Tarts, Neats-tongues, Salacious Meats and bad Rhenish',[25] water parties on the Thames, and staying out till after midnight. Mrs A. T. Thomson, Sarah's Victorian biographer, remarks that '[t]he female sex, in all ages responsible for the tone given to morals and manners, were in a state of general depravity during the whole period of Lady Churchill's youth'.[26] Modern historians' efforts to revise the picture with more realistic details, such as people scraping their teeth and spitting at table, do not make this 'general depravity' sound any less inviting. The dark side of the late seventeenth century, however, was not its hygiene standards but the narrow-mindedness of a world that, for example, educated Sarah in how to walk backwards out of a room and curtsy without falling over, but not to do sums or speak even basic French.

Sarah later approved a ghost-writer's account of her life, which said: 'I came extreme young into Court & had the luck to be liked by many in it.'[27] There is independent verification of her popularity and also of her beauty: one friend, Mary Fortrey, imagined her as a kind of proto-media celebrity, radiant and unattainable. In a letter from Paris addressed to 'Miss Jennings, Maid of Honour', she wrote a flatteringly detailed fantasy about having met an old man on a terrace who was looking through a telescope bequeathed to him by an enchantress, which let him see all around the world. At Miss Fortrey's request he turned it to England and 'hit about St James' park' where he saw hundreds of beautiful girls milling about in the early evening. 'I see, said he, a young beauty coming down the great walk which has rays about her head like a sun, but tis impossible for me to distinguish at this distance whether tis the lustre of her complexion or of her eyes that produces them. She is in a crowd that follows her wherever she goes, but there is a people that never quits her one minute.' Miss Fortrey grabbed the telescope from the old man's hands and 'Like a thing transported, I shouted and hollowed after you. I called you by your name a hundred times as loud as I could hollow: "Miss Jennings, Miss Jennings!!!"'[28]

Despite her popularity with both sexes, Sarah later wrote that 'at fourteen I wished myself out of Court'. Though such worldly disdain was widely affected, her claim to early disillusionment sounds credible: of Court frivolities she said, 'for my own part I never was young enough to like any thing of that sort'.[29] Perhaps she had grown up too quickly.

Sarah's sister Frances, some eleven or thirteen years older, was described as one of the great English beauties. Evelyn called her 'a Spriteful young Lady'[30] and Philibert Comte de Grammont compared her appearance to Aurora, a nice compliment if he had not added that 'there was something lacking in her hands and arms' and that 'her nose was not the most elegant and her eyes left something to be desired'.[31] A portrait shows her as having had curly blonde hair, styled to stick out at the sides like giant earmuffs.

The most famous story about Frances is of her dressing up as a poor orange-seller outside a playhouse to taste life among the common people. The costumed girls were propositioned like prostitutes by two gentlemen they knew until they were recognised by another gentleman because of their expensive shoes.[32] Samuel Pepys was amused at the girls' becoming indignant when treated as exactly what they pretended to be. In fact, there was a popular fad for dressing-down under Charles II, whose wife Katherine once dressed herself and her ladies as peasants and went to a country fair where they were easily discovered 'by their gibberish'.[33] This fad was less dangerous than the pose of false humility in which Queen Anne was later to indulge, only to be cast off indignantly when her subject, Sarah, like the unwitting young gentlemen with the orange-girls, crossed the line.

Frances married Sir George Hamilton and, by 1676, was already left widowed and in debt. In March 1677 she returned to the English Court with her three children, begging for a pension and desperately in need of her younger sister's assistance.[34]

Sarah's future husband, John Churchill, came from a background not unlike her own. If anything, it was rather more modest. Like Sarah, he had followed his elder sister into a place at Court, where at sixteen he became a page to the Duke of York. Sarah described him as 'handsome as an angel though ever so carelessly dressed',[35] and even at fifty-six he was described by one of his male contemporaries as having 'a clear red and white complexion which could put the fair sex to shame'.[36] If Camille Paglia is right to define charisma as 'the radiance produced by the interaction of male and female elements in a gifted personality',[37] then Sarah and John both had it.

Arabella Churchill, John's sister, became James II's lover and had four children by him, including James FitzJames, later Duke of Berwick. The Comte de Grammont told of Arabella falling from her horse while hunting, and winning the love of the King by accidentally revealing her thighs: 'She was so stunned that her thoughts were far from occupied with questions of decency, and those who first crowded around her found her in rather a negligent posture.'[38] However, military historians and biographers of Marlborough, out of respect for his later career, find it offensive that Arabella should be credited with obtaining her brother's first army post through her liaison with the King. John's strenuous early soldiering makes it seem unfair to account for his promotion solely in this way, but it may well have been that he took his first step up the ladder thanks to his sister.

After Marlborough's death, Sarah instructed his biographers to begin in 1688, when his career was already under way. She told one prospective biographer that she wanted no mention of his sister. In 1736, she commented on Thomas Lediard's unauthorised biography:

I want to say something more . . . to show how extremely mistaken Mr Lediard was in naming the Duke of Marlborough's sister and her train of bastards. Because they had titles he seems to think that was an honour to the Duke of Marlborough. I think it quite the contrary. For it seems to insinuate that his first introduction was from an infamous relation, when the whole truth of that matter was as follows: His sister . . . had at least two or three Bastards by the Duke of York or others . . . Now I would fain have any reasonable body tell me what the Duke of Marlborough could do when a boy at school to prevent the infamy of his sister, or why Mr Lediard could have any judgement in mentioning King James' favourite.

Sarah does not deny the link between Arabella's 'infamy' and

John's later appointment, only that he was too young to have encouraged his sister's liaison to serve his own interest.

Why should it matter so much to Sarah? In part, because Arabella remained an irritant even in old age. After James II discarded her she had married Charles Godfrey, Clerk Comptroller of the Board of Green Cloth, and became the 'Aunt Godfrey' whom Sarah's rebellious daughter Henrietta would befriend to annoy her mother. Arabella's son, Berwick, also symbolised everything against which Sarah and John later fought. After accompanying his father James II into exile, he became a commander in the French army and at only nineteen commanded James's forces in Ireland against his uncle who was fighting for King William. Yet John Churchill often negotiated with the French and the exiled Jacobites (adherents of James or his son after the Revolution of 1688) through Berwick. To Sarah, Arabella and Berwick were reminders of her pre-Revolutionary life – and of just how closely related the Marlboroughs were to the Jacobites she always tried to demonise. More importantly, Sarah hated the suggestion that John became Duke of Marlborough through the influence of women. Not only Arabella's affair with James was at stake, but also, by analogy, the suggestion that the Marlboroughs' meteoric success after 1702 was dishonourably dependent upon Sarah's relationship with Anne.

She had another reason, too, for wanting to suppress the details of her husband's life before 1688: his pre-marital affairs. The best known was with his second cousin once removed, Barbara, Countess of Castlemaine and later Duchess of Cleveland. She is often referred to as the 'superannuated' mistress of King Charles II, but she was just over thirty when she met John. She was famous for her promiscuity, which the King tolerated, and for her generosity to her lovers – grants from the Post Office and Customs – in an otherwise impecunious Court.

The main source of the story that she had an affair with the younger John Churchill before he married Sarah was Mrs Delariviere Manley (1663–1724), a Jacobite who wrote so-called scandal-histories, although John's father also referred to it in letters, bemoaning his son's folly. Mrs Manley had been the confidante of Barbara, who thought that she brought her luck at the gaming table and sheltered her after she was deserted by her first husband. Mrs Manley wanted a post as a Maid of Honour, but her hopes were thwarted by the 1688 Revolution. She wrote about Barbara from the perspective of the bad fairy not invited to the party, and was understandably jealous of those, like Sarah, who profited from the Whig party's ascendancy after 1688. She did not write her tales of Court scandal from any moral high ground or out of a prurient sense of disgust; she herself had an unconventional life. First she was the lover of a lawyer named John Tilly, and then of a publisher, John Barber: he, Mrs Manley and their lovechild lived together openly at his printing house on Lambeth Hill.

John Churchill's sexual history first appeared, disguised as fiction, in Mrs Manley's *Secret History of Queen Zarah and the Zarazians: Being a Looking-glass for S[arah] Ch[urchi]ll in the Kingdom of Albigion* (1705); the French translation included the subtitle *La Duchesse de Marlborough démasquée*. In *Queen Zarah* Barbara Castlemaine, renamed Clelia, becomes bored with Charles II and takes the John Churchill character as a lover, who then betrays her with Zara.

The book tells us a great deal about political propaganda during Queen Anne's reign, and the insult to John was less the account of his sexual peccadilloes than of his ambition for advancement, and the deceit and disloyalty into which this led him. The message is that he was politically unfaithful. Like all who served James II and deserted him to join William III in the Revolution, John swapped one king, one master, for another. In 1688 he rode out of London at the head of one army but returned with another. Mrs Manley's book records him swapping Barbara Castlemaine for Sarah Jennings, a subtle reference to this more important betrayal.[39]

The historian Bishop Burnet relates the story of King Charles catching Barbara in bed with a courtier who had to jump out of a window, Don Juan style, to escape.[40] Barbara gave the courtier

£5,000 as a reward, which was a sixth of her annual income in the 1670s and the equivalent of around £375,000 today. Burnet probably allowed the 'party concerned' to remain anonymous because of his and his wife's friendship with the Marlboroughs. A variation on the story, where John is discovered hiding in Barbara's cupboard and the King says to him 'I forgive you, for you do it for your bread', was related in the report of the French ambassador Barillon. Both versions have the familiar quality of stage farce and echoes of Joseph and Potiphar's wife. The insinuation is that John was a Joseph: a soldier of favour rather than one who had raised himself by his own endeavours. Again, the mysterious source of the Marlboroughs' immense fortune, and how much it depended on Sarah's helping hand, was the subtext of these slanders, reflecting general anxieties in an age where the *nouveaux riches* and newly designated peers were gaining power and influence.

By 1676 the affair between Barbara and John was over, and in March of that year, Barbara's departure from Britain was marked by the publication of a 'Lampoon':41

> Churchill's delicate shape
> Her dazzling eyes had struck
> But her wider cunt did gape
> For a more substantial fuck . . .
> . . . now she must travel abroad
> And be forced to frig with the nuns
> For giving our sovereign lord
> So many good buttered buns.

One of her 'buttered buns' was a daughter christened Barbara after her mother. Charles II accepted her as his and she took the surname Fitzroy, but she was also rumoured to be John Churchill's. Today John's paternity is often cited in indexes, picture catalogues and dictionaries of biography. She followed her mother's career path in becoming mistress to the Earl of Arran, later the Duke of Hamilton, by whom she had a son. She then went to a convent in France under the name of Sister Bernadette, and eventually became the head of a priory in Pontoise, Normandy.

In a variant of the story of John's affair with Barbara, contained in Manley's *Secret Memoirs and Manners of Several persons of Quality of Both Sexes. From the New Atalantis . . .* (1709) he was criticised for failing to lend money to Barbara after she fell on hard times – supposed proof of his stinginess. Perhaps, in his failure to own his illegitimate daughter, if indeed she was his, John Churchill did behave dishonourably, at least according to today's standards. In the seventeenth and eighteenth centuries, however, illegitimacy was casually accepted among the aristocracy; if anything, it was the status symbol of a rich man, proof that he had money to spare for mistresses and their offspring. But Sarah and John, who prided themselves on having made a love-match, would have taken a more bourgeois view of his early sex life. Certainly the existence of Barbara Fitzroy and the rumours surrounding her paternity, though never mentioned by Sarah, throw light on Sarah's rant against her sister-in-law Arabella's bastards and her warnings to her own children about extra-marital affairs.

Barbara Castlemaine was not Sarah's only romantic rival. Another, easier to perceive historically because less distorted by contemporary slanders and fictions, was Catherine Sedley, a fellow Maid of Honour and an heiress picked as a match for John by his parents. Her story shows that while Sarah was an unusual character for her period, she was not uniquely so. Indeed, although Sarah called Catherine 'a shocking creature', John seems to have chosen between two similarly strong women. A contemporary poet depicted her cruelly as swaggering 'like a batter'd bully/ To try the tempers of men's hearts'.[42] And Catherine, too, had a mother who was considered out of control (had delusions, in fact, that she was the Queen and was locked away in a Benedictine nunnery in Ghent). It is as if the previous generation of women were condemned for personalities that their daughters only just managed to carry off.

John was enthralled by Sarah but came close to marrying

Catherine. As their letters show, Sarah did not care for his plan to have one girl as a wife and another as a mistress. A French ambassador's letter reported that on 27 November 1676 Sarah had been seen crying at a ball because of John Churchill's possible engagement to Catherine. Then it was thought he might run away from both girls and join Barbara Castlemaine in France. However, in 1677, Sarah and her sister inherited the family property in Hertfordshire when their brother Ralph died,[43] and John Churchill's decision became easier: he chose Sarah.

Catherine had an illegitimate daughter by the Duke of York some time before March 1679. This child was named Catherine Darnley, and was to grow up to look creepily like the twin of her half-sister, Queen Anne.

The early love letters of John and Sarah are, respectively, mouthfuls of syrup and salt. If John's to her are read in conjunction with the adoring letters she received from Princess Anne in the 1680s, three conclusions are inescapable: Sarah must have been an extraordinarily alluring personality; she seldom indulged in the romantic posturing of those who fell in love with her; and she was not put in the easiest of positions by either of her admirers.

John's *billets doux*[44] are written in strong black ink, with no second thoughts or crossings-out. They appear to have been dashed off in the heat of the moment, yet are monotonously repetitious, with catchphrases ('you who is much dearer than all the world'/ 'sure never any body loved to that height I do you'/ 'when will you bless me with your light?') and complaints that Sarah never wrote to him or allowed him to see her. In an early letter he wrote, 'for my soul there is no pain so great to me as that when I fear you do not love me' and that 'I will, by all that is good, love you as long as I live.' He said that 'every time I see you I find new charms in you' and, significantly in light of all the rumours surrounding his sexual liaisons, begged her not to be 'so ill-natured as to believe any lies that may be told you of me'.

Though the letters are undated, the courtship was under way by

1676 when the French ambassador, who hosted various entertainments that summer, reported that John had refused a post in the French (at that time allied) army because he was too lovesick: 'Mr Churchill prefers to serve the very pretty sister of Lady Hamilton [Frances] than to be Lt Colonel of Monmouth's Regiment.' A week later he said that Sarah had asked John to marry her but his parents had refused their consent.[45]

John's declarations were often courtly, even to the point of submission: 'I am resolved to take nothing ill but to be your slave as long as I live', or that Sarah had 'made for sure a conquest of me, that had I the will I have not the power ever to break my chains'. In one letter (to which his wax seal, bright green silk and grains of sand to dry the ink still cling), he wrote to say that he was hoping to see her in the drawing room of the Duke and Duchess of York. In the next he told of how she left the room as soon as he entered, showing 'as much contempt as is possible'. He continued: 'I can't imagine what you meant by your saying I laughed at you at the Duke's side for I was so far from that, that had it not been for shame I could have cried. And for being in haste to go to the park, after you went I stood near a quarter of an hour, I believe, without knowing what I did . . .' and finally, 'If I may have the happiness of seeing you tonight pray let me know and believe that I am never truly pleased but when I am with you.'

Sarah's note back to him, one of the few to have survived, contained a clear message: '[Y]ou would find out some way to make yourself happy; it is in your power.' It is a covert refusal to have sex with him until or unless he married her. Years later, Mrs Manley insinuated in *Queen Zarah* that Sarah's mother tried to push her daughter into bed with him so that she could catch them in a compromising situation and force him to marry Sarah, and the slander had an element of truth: Sarah had to twist John's arm to make him propose – but to do this, she held on to her chastity.

John, however, pretended that he did not know why she was refusing to see him and covered his evasion with more romantic declarations: 'give me leave to do what I can not help, which is to adore you as long as I live'/ 'from henceforward I will approach and think of you with the same devotion as to my god'. Sarah saw through all this. Her position was like that of the historian today trying to decipher what is real feeling amid all the conventional romantic language. You try, she told John, to 'make me think you have a passion for me when in reality there is no such thing', and she refused to go on seeing him 'if it be only to repeat these things which you said so often'. While his contemporaries described John Churchill as the epitome of charm,[46] Sarah found his intentions slippery. His first lover, Barbara, was just moving her household to Paris. He might well have been looking at Sarah more as a replacement mistress than fiancée.

At the same time, Sarah herself was being disingenuous by not recognising the financial burdens which, until 1677, prevented John from choosing her over Catherine Sedley. He had a responsibility to his parents, who needed money. When he repeated his plea to meet Sarah without an offer of marriage, Sarah became cold. She told him that he might see her only so that 'I may be freed from the trouble of ever hearing from you more.' This letter is recopied in Sarah's elderly handwriting. It is interesting that she undertook this act of preservation on a letter that shows her pushing him into marriage so unromantically. She did not hide this side of her personality, probably because she was not ashamed of having saved her reputation by tough negotiation. John replied: 'My soul: I go with the heaviest heart that ever man did . . . If you are unkind, I love so well that I can not live, for you are my life, my soul, my all that I hold dear in this world . . .'

Finally, in a letter that probably dates from 1677, when Sarah had come into her inheritance, John told her that he had made an appointment with the Duchess of York to ask for Sarah's hand in marriage. It is interesting that Mary of Modena, rather than Sarah's mother, was approached for consent. Perhaps John thought she would provide a larger than usual dowry to help clear the debts on Sarah's inheritance. And far from entrapping John into marrying Sarah, it seems likely that Mrs Jennings at first tried to drag Sarah away from Court to prevent her seduction by him. The wedding has sometimes been described as 'secret', but it was not an elopement: it was only unofficially announced so that Sarah could keep her place as a virginal Maid of Honour. However, neither Sarah nor any other witness has left a description of it.

Sarah filed John's early letters in a bundle labelled 'Copies of letters to Mr Churchill before I married' to which she attached a note, testifying that she had tried to destroy them several times, but could not bring herself to do it. Instead she left instructions with a maid for them to be destroyed after her death, which – luckily – were disobeyed. Perhaps she reasoned that Sarah would not have left a memo to a future archivist about her struggle to preserve her privacy unless some part of her wanted the letters to survive.

On 5 April 1678, almost as soon as they were married, John had to go to Brussels. In parallel to being a successful soldier, appointed a colonel in February, he had impressed the Duke of York with his diplomatic tact during the previous three years. Along with Sidney Godolphin and Prince William of Orange, he was entrusted with negotiating a new alliance between England and France. Sarah remained at Court and continued to use her maiden name. Later she moved into the house of her parents-in-law in Minterne, Dorset, which cannot have been an easy start for the young bride, given their previous opposition to the match.

John was considered almost sinfully uxorious throughout his life, and his earliest letters to his new wife continue to sound like those of a suitor.[47] In July he wrote begging her not to doubt his love and sending her a ring as a memento. He hoped for peace so that he could return to her, but was still not back by September. He reiterated his devotion to her, 'but I find you are not of the same mind, for when you write you are afraid to tell me that you love me'. In another letter he remonstrated that even though he had such a 'great cold' he could hardly see the paper, Sarah had not written to him for three weeks.

2

'Flames of Extravagant Passion'

In August 1679, Sarah and John went to Brussels to join their employers, the Duke and Duchess of York, who had been exiled there since March. They travelled via The Hague, described by Pepys as 'full of English'. For the past two years Princess Mary had been living there with her husband, William of Orange, receiving diplomats and other noble travellers at the start of their European tours. She took her cousin the Duke of Monmouth ice-skating on the canals, her petticoats tucked up to her knees, and the previous autumn had received her stepmother, Mary of Modena, and her sister Anne, then aged thirteen, for a three-week visit.

Pregnant with her first child, Sarah travelled several days in advance of Princess Anne with whom she was to spend much time in the coming months. In Brussels, the royal household occupied the Hôtel des Hornes, or the Haureanum – today the Collège Jan Berchmans – on the rue des Ursulines. Behind the Haureanum was a large garden into which turreted conservatories protruded, and around which the ladies could stroll; etiquette dictated that if Sarah was walking with Anne she could not stop to admire a flower or pick a piece of fruit without the Princess doing so first. Other ladies in attendance included Lady Peterborough, Groom of the Stole, and Lady Belasyse, the third wife of a distinguished royalist general who had just been impeached. Sarah's sister Frances might also have been there. With the young Anne, Sarah was dependent on these women for company while John was sent on various diplomatic missions to Paris and back to London.

On the opposite side of the street they could see the Sainte Chapelle Catholic Church, which remains standing today. While she was in the Spanish Netherlands (modern Belgium and Luxembourg), Sarah formed strong opinions about Catholicism. She later wrote: 'I had seen so much of the cheats & nonsense of that religion abroad that it gave me a greater prejudice to it than is possible for anybody to have that has never been in a Catholic country'.[1] Her friend, Margaret Godolphin, by contrast, admired the meditative seclusion of the nunneries when she toured France.

The royal household's exile was a direct result of the 'Popish Plot' crisis of the previous year. In 1678, in the middle of a scorching summer, London had been thrown into turmoil over the allegations of a disaffected Anabaptist preacher, Titus Oates, that he had uncovered an international plot to assassinate King Charles and place his Catholic brother James on the throne. The story played on national paranoia about Jesuit conspiracies, and gained credibility after the brutal murder of one of the investigating judges and the coincidental discovery that the Duke of York's secretary had been in correspondence with Louis XIV's Jesuit confessor. Roadblocks were set up, travellers were interrogated at ferry ports, and 'all people were furnishing themselves with arms'.[2] Practising Catholics were prosecuted and Parliament passed a Test Act, which forced all public-office holders to renounce the doctrine of transubstantiation as a test of their Anglican faith. It was ironic that Charles, in whose defence the whole hysterical investigation had been mounted, was himself making secret deals with Catholic France.

As the Duke of York's Catholicism became apparent, a strong faction insistent upon his exclusion from the throne developed under the first Earl of Shaftesbury's leadership and defined a constitutionally radical 'Whig' agenda. Charles II was forced to send his brother into exile at the insistence of Parliament, upon which he was dependent for funds. From the outset, Sarah was a staunch Whig supporter, yet she was personally and financially tied into the centre of the Duke of York's household. Later she emphasised the precocity of her Whiggism and thereby her lifelong consistency of principle. One version of her memoirs starts with the ringing claim:

I was born with an imbued love of my country. I hated tyranny by nature, before I could tell why & long before I had read a line upon the subject: I thought mankind was born free, & if Princes were ordained to make their subjects happy; so I had always in me an invincible aversion to slavery, & to flattery. I also hated popery before I had ever looked into a book of divinity . . .3

Words such as 'tyranny' and 'slavery' were vague enough to be used by those at either end of the political and religious spectra, but to Sarah the equation of popery with these evils was self-evident. In her vehement anti-Catholic stance, she was more in tune with the majority of the English people than with the ambivalent aristocratic circles in which she moved.

Whether we view Catholicism and Jacobitism as merely late-seventeenth-century bogeys or accept Sarah's fears of repressive occupation as realistic determines how she appears to us. If Sarah was an anti-Catholic bigot, then so were many of the greatest minds of the century. Isaac Newton, for example, thought of nuns as whores for monks' use, and approved of the Vandals having tortured them 'with heated plates of iron applied to several parts of their bodies'.4 To her credit, Sarah was always against such rabid religious persecution; she was anti-Catholic precisely because she believed Catholicism was persecutory. Like Andrew Marvell in his *Account of the Growth of Popery and Arbitrary Government* (1677), she equated Catholicism and French rule with political oppression, infringement of public liberties, idolatry, economic exploitation and indolence.

She came from a London that was rapidly expanding in size, wealth and confidence, and probably saw more evidence of destitution in continental Europe than at home. Yet popery and slavery were considered separate threats: the Danish move towards absolutist monarchy in 1660, for example, was unrelated to religion. Sarah saw in the Duke of York an heir to the throne who was doubly dangerous: as both born-again Catholic and, she believed, as a harbourer of absolutist ambitions. As the daughter and the wife of Members of Parliament (John held a seat for a short time in 1678), Sarah feared that James would abolish Parliament and replace it with an unelected chamber, as in France. Above all, she disliked him for his hypocrisy, which she was in a privileged position to witness at first hand: she wrote that he 'sent a man to prison for saying that he was a Roman Catholic' yet she watched James himself 'go twice a day to mass'.[5]

Soon enough, on 9 October 1679, the Duke's entourage, including Sarah and John, was rushing back from Brussels to England. News had reached them that the King was ill, and it was therefore urgent that they contest the Whig Exclusion Bill, which would have barred James from the throne on the grounds of Catholicism. Between 1679 and 1681, a series of Exclusion Bills were advanced by Lord Shaftesbury's faction at each new session of Parliament, and defeated with difficulty by Charles II while his brother was in exile. Finally, in March 1681, Charles would dissolve the Oxford Parliament and force Shaftesbury into exile to bring the matter to a close, at least for the duration of his lifetime.

Charles's mortal illness was a false alarm, and the Duke returned to exile at the end of October, this time in Scotland. The party stayed in houses vacated by their noble owners who wished tacitly to express their sympathies with the Whigs. John accompanied them, but Sarah stayed behind in London to have her first baby.

She was unconventional in her habits during pregnancy, listening to her own body rather than the prescriptions of doctors or society. Years later, while advising her granddaughter, she recollected that 'When I was within three months of my reckoning I could never endure to wear any bodice at all, but wore a warm waistcoat wrapped about me like a man's.'[6] On 8 November 1679 John was still ten days away from Edinburgh when he wrote to advise her on who might be godfather. Six days later he wrote again, worried that she was in labour while he had had no word. By 3 January 1680, a day after he had hoped to be home, a girl, named Harriot, had arrived. He wrote with great fondness: 'Pray let Harriot know by some very intelligible sign that I am very well pleased with her hair and that I long to see her, hoping that since she has her mother's coloured hair that she may be also like her.'[7] (Sarah's hair was strawberry blonde, washed every day in honey-water to maintain its glow.)

Sarah's letters to John during these separations have not survived, but on 13 January 1680, John's letter to her shows that she suspected him of having affairs in Scotland that had kept him away during the birth.[8] He protested: 'I have not a greater pleasure in the world than in doing what I think would be acceptable to you, for on my faith you are dearer to me than all the rest of the world together', and 'you are both unjust and unkind in having a suspicion of me'. Later, he reassured her again: 'I swear to you the first night in which I was blessed in having you in my arms was not more earnestly wished for by me than now I do to be again with you.' (It was such declarations that gained him the reputation for once having come home from war and immediately 'pleasured' his wife 'in his top-boots'.[9])

Sarah was blessed with a strong constitution, a characteristic that her first baby did not inherit. By the time John arrived at Jermyn Street in March, accompanying his returning master James, Harriot had died.

There is no record of how Sarah was affected by the death of her first child. The modern assumption that because infant mortality was common in those days mothers bore such losses stoically is belied by poetry written in the latter half of Sarah's lifetime. In 'To an Infant Expiring the Second Day of its Birth' (1733) Mehetabel Wright begged to die with her baby, and certainly Sarah would not bear the later deaths of her children with anything approaching stoicism.

When the Duke of York was exiled for a second time to Scotland in October 1680, John again went with him and spent the next year commuting between Edinburgh and Sarah in London. She was living at their lodgings in Jermyn Street, five doors down from St James's Street. This western area of town, recently built by Henry Jermyn, Earl of St Albans, was advertised as convenient for all the best London coffee-houses and as having the use of Thames water before the rest of the population had polluted it. It was separated by countryside from the suburb of St Giles to the east, and from workshops and shanty towns to the north. Just to the south of Jermyn Street, St James's Palace overlooked long walks of elms and limes, where the wealthy local residents promenaded on most days of the week but which was taken over by the London populace for recreation on Sundays.[10]

John was at home to witness the christening of his second daughter, Henrietta, in July 1681, at which Sarah's sister and her mother stood as godparents. Two months later, Sarah had to leave her baby 'in the country', with servants, friends and relatives such as Edward Griffith to check on her,[11] in order to attend the Duchess of York and Princess Anne in Scotland. It was customary for ladies to pass on their babies to wet-nurses; nevertheless she must have been conscious of the tension between her roles as courtier and mother when she left Henrietta behind. Early modern biographers have been critical of her decision to do so – as if she had a choice.

On 6 September 1681, John wrote to Sarah while impatiently awaiting her arrival, reminding her to bring supplies of coffee and wax lights.[12] Living standards in Edinburgh were primitive in comparison to those in London, although the exiled Duke of York undertook public building projects to modernise the city. He was titled Commissioner of the Estates, but ruled the region from Holyrood Palace as a *de facto* king, and 'vast numbers of nobility and gentry . . . flocked around the Duke and filled the town with gaiety and splendour'.[13] Holyrood was where the twenty-one-year-old Sarah and the sixteen-year-old Princess Anne were to spend the next eight months together. John reported that a running race at the Scottish Court was won by a man who carried another on piggy-back; the Duke of York spent time playing an early form of golf or going hunting; and Sarah and Anne attended various theatrical entertainments. However, behind the festive scenes, the Duke's programme for Scotland was far from enlightened.

James was determined to eradicate Presbyterianism, and during his years in Scotland he orchestrated several phases of persecution. Bishop Burnet, the Scottish historian who had acquired religious tolerance while living in Amsterdam, recorded stories of people having their hands cut off, or being tortured with 'the boot' and thumb-screws.[14] To these, the Whig historian Macaulay added the apocryphal detail that James himself watched the tortures with relish. Sarah witnessed some executions of Scottish dissenters, whose martyrdom made a deep impression on her: 'I have cried at some of these trials, to see the cruelty that was done to these men only for their choosing to die rather than tell a lie.'[15] In her 1715 memoir, written in the third person, she applauded her pity for the victims as 'an aversion to all such arbitrary proceedings very uncommon in so young a courtier', and contrasted it with Princess Anne's alleged indifference to the same scenes.[16]

In her published memoirs, Sarah explained that her husband, Princess Anne and Lord Godolphin were all 'educated' to be Tories, while her natural instincts, she claimed, had turned her against those politicians who expressed a 'persecuting zeal' and therefore towards the more religiously tolerant Whigs. She confessed:

The word CHURCH had never any charm for me in the mouths of those who made the most noise with it, for I could not perceive that they gave any other distinguishing proof of this regard for the THING than a frequent use of the WORD, like a spell to enchant weak minds; and a persecuting zeal against dissenters and against those real friends of the Church who would not admit that PERSECUTION was agreeable to its doctrines.[17]

Throughout her life, Sarah's tolerance of dissenters was attacked as quasi-atheism. She did not see it that way, and prided herself instead on a stringent rationalist scepticism, like that of the Marquess of Halifax who said he could not 'digest iron as an ostrich [n]or take into his belief things that would burst him'.[18] Sarah believed religion was a matter of conscience and told one friend that 'I would always rather do my devotions where I could meet no one of my acquaintance.'[19]

Her repulsion at the methods of repression used in Scotland might be admirable to us, but she expressed her opinions only from the safety of hindsight. As the persecution went on around her, she kept her head down, and in the winter of 1682, John was created Lord Churchill of Aymouth, in recognition of his loyal service to the Duke of York.

Meanwhile Sarah's relationship with her mother, who was now living in St Albans, continued to be marked by friction. Only one letter from Sarah to her mother survives from this period. It is, characteristically, more of a post-quarrel vindication than an apology:

[I]f I thought I had done anything that you had reason to take ill I should be very angry with myself, but I am sure I did not intend anything but to pay you the duty I ought, & if against my will and knowledge I have committed any fault I hope you will forgive it . . . I will ever be your most Dutiful Daughter, whatever you are to me – Churchill

The young Princess Anne had her own admirers, such as John Sheffield, Earl of Mulgrave. He was in his thirties, an exact contemporary of his friend Lord Rochester, and also a poet, though much less talented. He had served, like John Churchill, as a soldier in the French army under Marshal Turenne and, also like Churchill, had been posted to Tangiers to defend the English garrison against the Moors. He is described as arrogant, sour and of a dark brown complexion. An official note from November 1682 states: 'Lord Mulgrave, for writing to Lady Anne, is discharged from Court.' Mulgrave claimed he had been 'only ogling'[20] but the public thought he had gone 'so far as to spoil her for marrying to anybody else, and therefore the town has given him the nickname of King John'.[21]

Sarah did not mention the flirtation between her mistress and Mulgrave in her memoirs, and it does not surface in the surviving letters between them, the earliest of which date from the following year. But Edward Gregg, Anne's biographer, writing in the 1980s, believed that the episode 'marked the flowering of the friendship between Lady Anne and Sarah Jennings'[22] because it gave them something to gossip about. He assumes that the girls needed this impetus, rather than crediting Sarah with her own attractions.

The story that it was Sarah who revealed a secret correspondence between Anne and Mulgrave, thereby causing his banishment from Court, can be traced again to the fiction of Mrs Delariviere Manley. In *The New Atalantis*, Sarah's character intercepts letters from 'Count Lofty' to the 'Princess of Inverness' to keep the Princess's affections to herself. Again, the resonance of this story is political: Sarah is shown as a scheming monopoliser of affection, and, by association, her Whig friends are labelled monopolisers of the government and of the nation's wealth.

Later Mulgrave returned to England and a successful political career. When Anne became Queen he was made Lord Privy Seal, though Anne wrote to Sarah in June 1703 that 'nobody can have a worse opinion of him than I have'[23] and he was dismissed in March 1705. By this time he was styled Duke of Buckingham, and had built his grand home on the site of today's Buckingham Palace. He married three times, and when he died in 1721, he left money to an impressive collection of illegitimate children. His third wife was Catherine Darnley, the illegitimate daughter of Catherine Sedley and half-sister of Princess Anne. By this marriage Catherine Darnley became the Duchess of Buckingham – the other model for Pope's character of Atossa. Sarah's character was therefore to be conflated for ever in the public imagination with the daughter of her old romantic rival.

In 1683, Sarah became Princess Anne's Lady of the Bedchamber, and stepped into a role already defined by the former post-holder. Sarah described Mrs Mary Cornwallis as Anne's 'first favourite'.[24] After three or four years of service, she was dismissed in October 1682. Sarah recorded that Anne's letters to Mrs Cornwallis were censured by Anne's father and stepmother for being too passionate.[25] She wrote suggestively in one version of her memoirs: 'K[ing] Charles used to say, "No man ever loved his Mistress as his niece Anne did Mrs Cornwallis." '[26] She commented sardonically, too, on how little time it took Anne to recover from the loss of her beloved servant: 'What became of her afterwards I could never learn ... Thus ended a great friendship of three or four years' standing in which time Lady Anne had written, it was believed, above a thousand letters full of the most violent professions of everlasting kindness.'[27] The overly close nature of the relationship seems a far more likely explanation for her dismissal than the one often cited, that Mrs Cornwallis was a Roman Catholic. Perhaps Charles II wanted his niece's companions to be Protestant, but there is no evidence that he ordered Mrs Cornwallis to leave, and Sarah says that her Catholicism was only 'the popular reason given out'.[28] It was rumoured elsewhere that Mrs Cornwallis had been dismissed for acting as go-between in the affair with Mulgrave. George Legge, 1st Baron Dartmouth, a cousin whom John had supplanted in the Duke of York's favour and who therefore held a grudge against the Churchills, accused Sarah of ruthlessly displacing her predecessor by revealing this to Anne's parents.[29] Sarah claimed, on the contrary, that it was she who, out of pity, found a job for Mrs Cornwallis as 'keeper of a madwoman, as she requested',[30] and letters survive from a Mrs Cornwallis to Sarah petitioning for charity after 1703 and referring to Sarah's former kindness to her.[31] This would seem, however, to contradict Sarah's statement that she could never find out what happened to the woman. Sarah's version of events should be viewed with the suspicion that when she was writing her memoirs she had reasons for portraying Anne as inherently prone to love affairs with female favourites to whom she was heartlessly unfaithful. On the other hand, we have no cause to doubt Sarah's claim that a romantic correspondence between Mrs Cornwallis and the Princess existed.

Another young woman who had just left Princess Anne's service, at least temporarily, was Frances Apsley, daughter of the Duke of York's Treasurer. Frances, nicknamed 'the Nag's Head' by Sarah and Anne, wrote and received amazing letters from both of the Duke of York's daughters. Mary called Frances her 'husband', leading generations of historians to mistake them for love letters addressed to William of Orange. A drawing tutor, a dwarf named Mr Gipson, carried the letters between the pair.[32] Mary wrote to Frances that:

I have sat up this night . . . to tell my dear dear dear dearest dear husband . . . that I am more and more in love with you every time I see you, and love you so well that I cannot express it no way but by saying I am your louse in bosom and would be very glad to be always so near you.[33]

Or again, where it is worth preserving the original spelling and absence of punctuation to convey the letter's strangeness:

What can I say more to perswade you that I love you with more zeal then any lover can I love you with a love that ner was known by man I have for you excese of friendship more of love then any woman can for woman & more love then ever the constanest lover had for his mistress . . . to kis the ground when once you go to be your dog in a string your fish in a net your bird in a cage your humbel trout . . .[34]

These letters were exchanged by young women, not children. Though they started their correspondence in childhood, Mary was eighteen, an adult by the standards of her times, when she wrote: 'In all your letters you complain of me as if I were a cruel mistress instead of a kind wife as I look upon myself to be . . .'[35] and, three years after her marriage to William, she was urging Frances jealously to 'take heed . . . for tis dangerous to vex a lover and a woman'. Anne also wrote love letters to Frances, but she took on the male role. They used the nicknames 'Semandra' (Frances) and 'Ziphares' (Anne) – the lovers in Nat Lee's version of *Mithridates* (1678) in which the sixteen-year-old Anne had acted while staying in Edinburgh in November 1681.[36] In 1683 Anne wrote to Frances: 'Do not have so ill opinions of your Ziphares for, though he changes his condition, yet nothing shall ever alter him from being the same to his dear Semandra that he ever was . . .'[37] In the play, Ziphares is a prince committed to an arranged marriage but in love with Semandra, the daughter of one of his father's advisers. Frances was the daughter of James's adviser, and by the early 1680s Anne had begun to view her father as a religious tyrant; the two girls dramatised themselves, according to the plot, as star-crossed lovers, separated by their parents' politics and their disparate ranks.

Further evidence of love affairs among the Maids of Honour and their mistresses at Whitehall does not mean that this was commonplace and therefore insignificant. Comte de Grammont,[38] whose unreliable memoirs were written by his brother-in-law Anthony Hamilton, mentions a certain Miss Hobart, the eldest of the Duchess of York's Maids of Honour, who was ridiculed in ballads for loving women and being a hermaphrodite, and 'upon the faith of these songs her companions began to fear her'. She is described as having been 'susceptible only to the charms of her own sex' and, sure as stereotypes are stereotypes, as having 'a sharp tongue, a bold air and an abrasive temperament'. Apparently public mockery did not deter her from posing as a rival to a male suitor, Lord Rochester, for the affections of another Maid of Honour, Miss Stuart (or Stewart). Miss Hobart was said to have persuaded the innocent Miss Stuart to take a bath with her, having tempted her with confectionery and liquor, then trying to persuade her to renounce men.[39]

Anne's early relationship with Sarah has often been dismissed as a schoolgirl crush. David Green, for example, wrote in 1967 that their relationship was only evidence of a 'manless world' and of 'interminable evenings when all the girls could think of was to play at mothers and fathers or husbands and wives and to write more or less imbecile letters to their friends'.[40] In fact, Sarah and Anne continued to write to each other in the same terms long after they were married. In 1692, when Sarah had been married for about fourteen years, she still received letters from Frances Apsley that were only slightly less romantic than those Frances had sent to the Princess. With hindsight, Sarah dismissed Frances's romantic professions, but she never doubted the sincerity of Anne's.

One of Sarah's biographers, Louis Kronenberger, writing in the late 1950s, relegated the whole issue to a footnote, describing the tone of such letters as 'no more than adolescent transferences coupled with period romanticism'. Yet he admitted that even '[a]llowing for the current tendency to ferret out and stress sexual abnormality, one still has a sense of something in Anne's emotions that suggests the abnormal'.[41]

Normal or abnormal, Anne's relationship with Sarah took place in the midst of many other intense, semi-erotic female friendships, but that did not make their relationship necessarily immature, imbecilic or artificial. It can never be certain what unlabelled feelings – which Sarah would manipulate skilfully in later life – existed between the two. For now, it is enough to emphasise that Sarah and Anne were not entirely innocent of what their words might mean if history happened to eavesdrop.

Only one side of the early correspondence between Sarah and Anne now survives in the Blenheim Papers.[42] Anne destroyed almost all of Sarah's letters, as instructed, but Sarah preserved many of Anne's. They are mostly short notes on cream paper, tightly folded for delivery within London or the south-east of England. The ink is now pale brown and sometimes blotched. There are so many letters that it is hard to believe they date from only 1683, ten years after the pair had first met, and that a large number were lost during the 1688 Revolution. In the bitterness of old age, Sarah called them 'very indifferent, both in sense & spelling, unless that they were generally enlivened with a few passionate expressions, sometimes pretty enough but repeated over & over again without the mixture of anything either of diversion or instruction'.[43] She summed up these early years of serving the Princess in equally scathing terms: 'Though it was extremely tedious to be so much where there could be no manner of conversation, I knew she loved me, & suffered by fearing I did wrong when I was not with her; for which reason I have gone a thousand times to her, when I had rather have been in a dungeon.'[44]

As Anne was uneasy in social gatherings, they probably spent most of their time together in her chamber, with embroidery or fringe work, or with Anne playing her five-stringed, lute-like Italian guitar. Religious instruction had formed the bulk of Anne's education, while Sarah claimed to have 'never read or done anything but play at cards in my life'.[45]

Even when they were grown women, Sarah remarked, in a note on her correspondence: 'I do solemnly protest that if it were in my power I would not be a favourite, which few will believe . . . I fancy anybody that had been shut up so many tedious hours as I had been with a person that had no conversation & yet must be treated with respect, would feel something of what I did . . .'[46] It is as if Anne were Sarah's equivalent of a repressive husband to whom she had been matched by thoughtless parents. Certainly their friendship was skewed because the one who wanted to emulate the other was also the one who had all the advantages of birth.

Anne's first surviving letter from 1683 concerns Sarah becoming a Lady of the Bedchamber, responsible for assisting her at mealtimes and when dressing, for introducing guests then standing beside the Princess in their presence. The letter shows the first reversal of the mistress/servant roles, which Anne continued for the next twenty-five years: '[Y]ou see that tis no trouble to me to obey your commands.' In a later letter Anne must have been upset by a disagreement with Sarah, perhaps concerning a delay or difficulty in arranging the promotion: '[L]et me beg you once more not to believe that I am in fault, though I must confess you may have some reason to believe it' and 'My eyes are full. I cannot say a word more but I hope you will come to me at six o'clock.' In other letters Anne issued commands disguised as requests. In one, she begged Sarah not to go from Whitehall to Windsor until Sunday, 'in mere pity and compassion to poor me (who you say you love) you should not go yet, for this cruel disappointment is too much to be borne'. She mentioned some 'unkind thought' that Sarah had had of her and signed off with a fairly explicit exclamation: 'Oh come to me tomorrow as soon as you can that I may cleave myself to you.' The word 'cleave' is heavily scratched out then rewritten. (It has sometimes been transcribed as 'clear', but this seems incorrect from the manuscript.)

In 1683, John was sent to Denmark to escort Anne's fiancé, George, to England. Prince George was described by John Evelyn as having 'the Danish countenance, blond; a young gentleman of few words',[47] and that is about as three-dimensional as his character has ever become. There has always been a slightly comic aspect to the marriage of George and Anne, with his wheezing asthma and her dropsy, his thick accent and her sentimentality. The stock image of the couple, described by Sarah, is of Anne sitting on her couch, fondling her lapdogs, while George 'used to employ himself agreeably all day either in standing upon a stair-head or in looking out of a window to make malicious remarks upon people that passed by'.[48] In June and July of 1683, Sarah acted as chaperone during their short courtship and attended her mistress's wedding. In February she had given birth to her second daughter, Anne, named after the Princess, who stood as her godmother.

English politics continued to simmer with conspiracies. The Rye House Plot, to murder Charles II and the Duke of York, was detected in June 1683 and led to the execution of the first Whig martyrs, and to Monmouth fleeing for his life to Holland. This episode, as a kind of retaliation for the anti-Catholicism that had followed the Popish Plot, boosted James's popularity and temporarily discredited the Whigs by making them appear regicidal extremists.

Bishop Burnet recorded the Whig Lord Russell's trial and execution at Holborn for his alleged part in the Rye House Plot when Prince George arrived in England, and honoured Russell's willingness to die for his belief that Popery was an 'idolatrous and bloody religion'.[49] In Sarah's memoirs co-written by Burnet, she noted: 'I remember nothing that happened in K[ing] Charles' time worth mentioning, only the many executions upon that which was called Ld Russels plot . . .' She described her 'horror' at this persecution, but confessed that she herself was not yet brave enough to speak up for the Whig cause under such dangerous circumstances: '[A]ll I could prevail on myself to do was to say nothing . . .'[50]

As a woman, it was not for Sarah to express political opinions but to serve the Princess and her husband, each of whom demanded her full attention and craved her company. Despite her recent marriage, Anne continued to address Sarah as a dejected lover: 'I have been in expectation of you a long time but can stay no longer without desiring to know what you intend to do with me, for it is most certain I can't go to bed without seeing you. If you knew in what a condition you have made me I am sure you would pity . . .'[51]

In the summer of 1684, Sarah had to attend Anne in Tunbridge,[52] leaving her husband to look after the two children. 'Having nobody but their maid,' he wrote, 'they are so fond of me that [when] I am at home they will be always with me, a-kissing and hugging me . . .' Henrietta was pulling on his arm as he wrote the letter, asking him to send her love 'to her dear mama'. The surprising modernity of this joint parenting does not mean that the Churchills' early marriage was unconventional. John believed that he alone was the head of his family, and Sarah agreed. Circumstances merely dictated that they shared domestic responsibilities while they built the family's fortunes in a divided Court. It took both of them to bridge the gulf between the Catholic Duke and his Protestant daughters, so insuring their family against every political eventuality. John was astute in encouraging his wife's friendship with Anne, even if it meant that the time she could spend with him as a wife and mother was limited. In 1683, he had prompted her gently: 'Lady Anne asks for you very often so that I think you would do well if you would write to thank her for her kindnesses in enquiring after your health.'[53]

The image of John with the children climbing all over him 'a-kissing and hugging', however, is notable in an age where most young children of noble families bowed or curtsied to their parents when entering or leaving rooms. As a General he would later gain a reputation as a softie (Lord Ailesbury said that '[h]e could not chide a servant . . . and in command he could not give a harsh word, no not to the meanest Sergeant, Corporal or Soldier'[54] and Defoe described him as 'courteous, mild, affable, humble'[55]), so it is a fair guess that at home Sarah was the family disciplinarian. There are a few sad little letters to her from her infant children, begging her not to be so angry with them. Young children who are frightened or awed by their parents are usually reliable character witnesses, and this is some of the surest evidence that Sarah indeed had a fiery temper.

She also had to take the lead in the family's financial management. In one version of her memoirs she explained why she was unable to wait more frequently on Anne:

Soon after my Marriage, when our affairs were so narrow that a good degree of frugality was necessary, Ld Marlborough, though his inclination lay enough that way, yet by reason of indulgent gentleness that is natural to him, he could not manage matters so as was convenient for our circumstances. This obliged me to enter into this management of my family.[56]

Her underlining shows her trying to counter the common slur against her husband that he was miserly. Elsewhere she explained that her management of the household accounts was preceded also by her own financial independence: 'Till he made me an executor, I never had anything to do with his fortune, nor he with mine . . . [T]his is a very uncommon thing to give to a wife, but he had experience enough of me to know that I would make no ill use of the power.'[57] Yet it is misleading for Sarah to imply that she had sole management of the household accounts: many exist in her husband's handwriting, and later letters from the war front told her there was no need to rush to send him the household accounts for inspection.[58]

In the early 1680s, a letter from a female friend testified to Sarah's marital bliss, which none of her female relationships could equal.[59] The friend complained that it was useless to write because if Sarah received a letter from anyone but John when she was expecting one, she lacked the patience to read it, and if it arrived alongside one from her husband she was too 'transported' to pay attention. Many years later, when Sarah observed to her granddaughter that 'nothing is more terrible than to be married where either sense or virtue is wanting',[60] it was understood that she was not speaking from personal experience. In a letter from the early days of their marriage, John wrote that he not only loved but esteemed Sarah.[61] The marriage contained many of the qualities of a friendship, while Sarah's relationship with Anne was developing those of a fraught romance.

In old age, Sarah warned her granddaughter against whipping the horses of her chaise while pregnant. She had once done this herself and, she believed, miscarried her first son as a result.[62] 1683–4 has been suggested as the most probable period for Sarah to have had this miscarriage, in between her other, virtually annual pregnancies. It is from this date that Anne regularly urged her to take care when travelling in unsprung coaches: '[Y]ou should take more care of yourself than you do till you are quick, for you go up & down as much as you were not with child.'[63]

Without Sarah beside her when she moved with the seasonal migrations of the Court, Anne complained of loneliness and boredom: 'I must tell you I am not as you left me . . . I long to be with you again and tis impossible for you ever to believe how much I love you except you saw my heart.' Seeing into another's heart is a recurring theme in Anne's letters. In one note, possibly from 12 September 1684, after they had arranged a secret rendezvous during the night in Salisbury, Anne vowed: 'Whatever my letters are, my heart shall be still the same.' A few days later Anne wrote from a royal yacht, anxious to catch the post while she was in port. She apologised for speaking some 'nonsense' when they last parted and hoped Sarah would forgive her for it. She insisted that Sarah should not call her 'Your Highness' and should speak and write to her with complete freedom.

Most commentators have suggested that the hyperbole in Anne's letters to her friend was merely stylistic. In fact, the overwhelming impression is not of overstatement but that Anne was repressing what she really wanted to say. Her dramatisation of herself as a submissive courtly lover was certainly a pose, but this does not mean that her underlying feeling was less than real. In the first year of her marriage, she wrote to Sarah: 'I am sure you cannot write to one that is more sincerely yours than I am and I hope that next to Ld Churchill I may claim the first place in your heart. I know I have a great many rivals . . .' On the back she scribbled, 'Pray let nobody see this.' In another she reassured Sarah that she did not regard John as a rival: 'I hope you don't think me so unreasonable as to take anything ill that you do when on your Lord's account.'

The winter of 1684 was the coldest in living memory. The sea froze for two miles from the English coast and a Frost Fair was held on the Thames with booths of amusements, including a press where people could have their own names printed. Hackney coaches plied their trade up and down the river, and huge bonfires failed to melt the ice on which they stood.[64] During this winter, Sarah and her family moved into new lodgings at the Cockpit. This was a section of old Whitehall Palace, a Tudor building that stretched from Westminster Bridge to St James's Park. It had been the home of George Villiers, the favourite of James I, so it was a nice coincidence that after Charles II gave it to Princess Anne as a wedding present, she chose to house Sarah there. The Churchills were to be the last private residents before it became the Treasury and later the offices of the Privy Council.

In the same year, thanks to Sarah's frugal management, the Churchills bought Sarah's sister's share in the St Albans house where Sarah had been born.[65] Holywell nestled in a picturesque setting at the bottom of a hill near the Abbey, with a summer parlour on the lower ground floor that opened on to the gardens.

In early 1685, the Princess was still asking Sarah in her letters why she did not come to her more often: Sarah's absence 'be it never so short, it will appear a great while to me'. She repeated that other female friends, 'though maybe they can express themselves better', were not so sincere in their love for Sarah. Later the same day, in another letter, Anne wrote: 'Just as I had writ thus far I received your dear kind letter which I have kissed a hundred times' and 'I would say more, but if I writ whole volumes I could never express how well I love you nor how much I long to see you.'

Among those in the early 1680s whom Anne might have perceived as rivals for Sarah's friendship was Lady Sunderland. This was Anne Digby, wife of Robert Spencer, 2nd Earl of Sunderland. She wrote often to Sarah from Althorp, avowing that 'I covet very few things more than to have you kind to me, which I shall endeavour to deserve by all the ways within my poor power and persuade you by all the actions of my life that you have none in the world more faithfully and sincerely yours . . .'[66] Sometimes when Sarah was away attending on Anne, Lady Sunderland would care for Henrietta, her goddaughter, and report that the three-year-old 'has cut three great teeth since you went', or that she is 'so kind to me that she left her dinner to sit in my lap today'. After such domestic cheer, she would end: 'I long to embrace you . . . I love you beyond expression . . .'

Unfortunately such professions of love did not appeal to Sarah. She was annoyed that Lady Sunderland's daughter, whom Sarah had placed in the Princess's household to ease her own burden of attendance, had been off sick, so that Sarah was still working like 'a slave'. Lady Sunderland stated that 'I am sure my daughter and I shall fall out irreconcilably if she is not as much at your service as mine' and, in 1686, begged that this matter should not spoil their friendship.[67]

The survival of only one half of the correspondence exaggerates the tone of unrequited love in both Princess Anne's and Lady Sunderland's letters. It is as if they are shouting into a void. Yet whenever Anne refers to points from Sarah's letters, they seem to concern practicalities that Sarah wanted Anne to sort out for her: arrangements for lodgings or excuses for not visiting. Anne begged her constantly to come to visit, and wondered whether the absence of more letters from Sarah was due to some offence she might have committed or just the unreliable postal system. Sometimes the pleas were mixed with requests to Sarah as her dresser: an order, for example, on 3 August 1685 for some thick-soled shoes so that she could take muddy walks in Windsor, or others to buy her gowns with extra petticoats, a velvet scarf or patches for her face. In another from Windsor she told Sarah: 'If the whole castle was mine I would not dispose of any of it till I knew what you had most mind to.'

In one letter Anne ordered a pair of coloured gloves. In the next she complained that they had been delivered by messenger rather than by Sarah. In the same letter she explained that she could not write for long because of her 'waters': lowering her head apparently made her face overheat. As if this had given Sarah an idea, Anne was soon enquiring whether Sarah's own headache, which prevented her writing more often, was any better. For her own part, she claimed to be too carried away to stop, despite the obvious absence of reciprocation: 'If I could tell how to hinder myself from writing to you every day I would.'

One of Sarah's achievements was to determine history's view of Queen Anne. Not even twentieth-century efforts to rescue her reputation have managed to deny that she was a bore, as Sarah implied throughout her memoirs and in other unpublished writings after the friendship ended. Anne herself admitted to Sarah, in a letter from 1691, that 'for my humour, I know I am morose & grave',[68] and many other contemporary writers agreed that Anne was socially gauche. But it was Sarah after the relationship had soured who turned Anne into the caricature of 'insipid heaviness' that makes her appear a minor figure beside, say, Elizabeth I or Queen Victoria. To illustrate Anne's stubborn irrationality, she told an anecdote about Anne and her sister Mary when children:

[W]alking in the park together, a dispute was started between them, whether something they saw at a great distance were a man or a tree . . . When they came so near that their eye-sight could convince them it was a man, the Lady Mary said, 'Now sister, are you satisfied that it is a man?' But Lady Anne, after she saw what it was, turned away, & persisting still in her own side of the question, cried out, 'No, sister, it is a tree!'[69]

In the 1711 version of her memoirs, Sarah wrote:

I confess it was not so very agreeable to my temper, that was always cheerful, to be so much with her as she desired me to be. Her conversation was not so entertaining . . . [but] she loved me to a passion and often said it was <u>a constant joy to her</u> to see me & as constant an uneasiness to let me go from her. We were for many hours shut up together daily & when I made my escapes & was with other company she said she envied them & <u>desired to possess me wholly</u> . . .

Her Court was so oddly composed that it was no extraordinary thing for me to be before them all in her favour & confidence. This grew upon me to as high a degree as was possible and <u>to all that was passionately fond & tender</u> . . .[70]

Rewriting four years later, she gave even more explicit emphasis to the depth of Anne's feeling for her. To create a certain distance from these insinuations, they are narrated in the third person by her co-author, Bishop Hoadly:

This favour quickly became a passion; and a passion which possessed the heart of the Princess too much to be hid. They were shut up together for many hours daily. Every moment of absence was counted a sort of tedious, lifeless state. To see the Duchess was a constant joy; and to part with her for ever so short a time, a constant uneasiness, as the Princess's own frequent expressions were. This worked even to the jealousy of a lover. She used to say <u>she desired to possess her wholly</u>: and could hardly bear that she should ever escape from this confinement into other company.[71]

While this version admitted that Sarah took some pains 'to fix that favour' of Anne – meaning that she made conscious efforts to cultivate royal favour that would benefit herself and her family – it also argued that Sarah had not pursued the 'extraordinary & almost unparalleled friendship' in a cynically manipulative way. The memoirs explain clearly to us that Sarah did feel a fondness for Anne, maybe even a protective pity, but could not help it if the love was one-sided. She did not reject Anne's love outright because it would have been unkind to do so, and difficult to tell a princess and employer to leave her alone.

This version of her memoirs also made clear that love and friendship were not synonymous:

But though there was this passionate <u>love</u> on the one side, &, as I verily believe, the sincerest <u>friendship</u> on the other, yet their tempers were not more different than their principles and notions . . .

Hoadly tried to prove that it was Anne who loved spontaneously 'to excess' by inserting in the memoirs long quotations from her private letters to Sarah, followed by the comment that 'there were some full of much higher expressions which ought not to be omitted; & which yet I hardly care to repeat' because they give one 'a sort of horror' about Anne's later inconstancy. The manuscript is so scarred by crossing-out at this point that perhaps he also felt another sort of 'horror'. It is the kind of scoring-out that is not just editorially indicative but obliterates the words underneath. The Bishop wrote that '[t]hese few transcripts are sufficient to show the sentiments which the Queen, at her time, <u>either</u> had or <u>pretended to have</u> about the Duchess'. Sarah's pen has crossed out the underlined words, which shows that she acknowledged Anne's feelings were genuine, at least at this stage of the relationship. However, she did not remove the narrator's wider conclusion that Anne's close friendships with women when 'compared together' show 'that she still kept her heart untouched and unpossessed by any one but herself [Anne]'.

By the time Sarah's memoirs appeared, the perfervid element in the depiction of Anne's love for her during the 1670s and 1680s had been toned down because it no longer served any political purpose. Gradually Sarah's sense of personal injustice had healed, so the terms 'love' and 'friendship' had become innocently synonymous. Sarah merely referred to Anne's 'inclination for me'[72] and their 'unreserved intimacy of friendship',[73] adding that '[h]er friendships were flames of extravagant passion, ending in indifference or aversion'.[74] Then, sarcastically, she suggested that even this idea might offend her most royalist readers: 'Friendship is an offensive word; it imports a kind of equality between the parties.'

* * *

Charles II died in February 1685. Sarah was among those who believed that he had been poisoned by conspiring Jesuits – or, at least, she was among those who enjoyed spreading this kind of anti-Catholic rumour.[75] To celebrate the new reign of James II, it was advertised that on 24 April the Thames would turn into a river of fire. Sarah would have been among the crowds of spectators who watched lurid, German-designed fireworks swimming in the water and giant straw manikins burning on the banks.

Only two months later James faced the insurrection of his Protestant nephew, the Duke of Monmouth, backed by Lord Shaftesbury. While, as a Whig, Sarah might have wished to see the misjudged attempt of Monmouth and his seven thousand ramshackle peasants succeed, this was overridden by her husband's having been sent to command the King's defence force. At the battle of Sedgemoor in July, John Churchill sent the rebels running for the woods and ditches, and witnessed the capture of Monmouth and his grovelling before the King as he begged for his life.

Lady Sunderland was the first to tell Sarah that Monmouth had been routed.[76] She gushed about 'how glad, how wondrous glad, am I to have this good news to send my dearest . . . I wish the man had wings to fly to you . . .' Shortly afterwards, Sarah could feel proud that John hurried home from the battle and did not stay for the reprisals, known as the 'Bloody Assizes', in which 233 men were hanged, drawn and quartered in Somerset, and over 800 condemned to transportation to the West Indies. John wrote asking her to meet him in London 'for I shall be at no ease till I am in your arms'.[77] Their time together was brief, but he was made Baron Churchill of Sandridge in recognition of his loyal service.

After the Monmouth rebellion, James II increased the size of his army to dissuade Londoners from any future attempt at insurrection. He had invited Catholic Irish troops to take on this task, which provoked huge resentment, and rumours were widespread that the soldiers bullied and robbed innocent locals. However, he felt confident enough now to commence his programme of relieving English Catholics from the social and legal discrimination they suffered. This meant promoting those considered socially marginal throughout the country, and gradually the tensions that would culminate in the Glorious Revolution of 1688 began to mount.

In September 1685, Sarah and Anne's letters are those of two happy, gossipy wives, comparing notes on their husbands' health and exchanging scandal, yet in Anne's the old strain of unrequited love is still discernible. While Sarah seemed increasingly interested in other company, such as that of Lady Sunderland or Barbara Berkeley (Lady Fitzharding), Anne was exclusively interested in Sarah and forced to spend time with courtiers she disliked, in particular the Countess of Clarendon, her Groom of the Stole, 'who grows more and more nauseous every day'. Bishop Burnet's version of Sarah's life emphasised that Anne's repulsion was primarily physical: Lady Clarendon 'had an awkward stiffness and greatly disgusted the Princess'.

Anne's refrain was always that Sarah must keep writing to her, even if the letters were short. She asked Sarah to write 'with less ceremony' and complimented her superior style: 'You are pleased to have a very humble opinion of yourself about writing in which I cannot agree.' When she did not hear from Sarah for two days in a row, she concluded something was terribly the matter or that 'I am quite forgot'. She guessed it was because Sarah's husband was at home: 'I hope the little corner of your heart that my Ld Churchill has left empty is mine.'

Anxieties about pregnancy, childbirth and menstruation (referred to as the comings and goings of 'Lady Charlotte'[78]) are another leitmotif throughout Anne's letters. She endured twelve miscarriages, one stillbirth and had five children who died in infancy of encephalitis (inflammation of the brain). It has been argued[79] that some of her pregnancies might have been phantom, a theory supported by Sarah's reference in her memoirs to Anne 'thinking herself with child'. The pressure on Anne to produce a healthy royal heir was enormous, and the contrast between her obstetric problems and the robust good health of Sarah and her children put an unspoken strain on their friendship. Sarah later observed matter-of-factly that Anne should never have expected another child after 'she had had before seventeen dead ones'.[80]

Anne's ailing infants were often left in Sarah's care, and although Anne worried about them (Should one be weaned? Is another peevish? Should her daughter join her in the fresh country air?), she was frustrated by Sarah's reticence about herself: 'You give me an account in every letter of my children for which I thank you, but I desire you would tell me how you are yourself.' After a lecture to Sarah on the faithfulness of true friendship, Anne reproached her for having made the 'great journey to Althorp' to visit Lady Sunderland, even though Sarah was pregnant and had been using this as an excuse not to visit Anne. Sarah promised to visit her shortly afterwards.

In January 1687, Sarah gave birth to her son John (Jack), having suffered during the pregnancy with toothache ('a very common thing with anybody who is with child'[81]). The perpetual cycles of 'breeding' were useful because the women could keep themselves tactfully out of the way while Anne's father, James II, intensified his efforts on behalf of English Catholics. In November 1685, his Ministers had tried to challenge him legally and, in response, he had dissolved Parliament. In June 1686 his divine right to dispense with the law was confirmed in the case of Godden *v.* Hales. James brought four Catholics into the Privy Council and pushed for Catholic appointments in the magistracy, the county militia, the treasury and the universities.[82] Bishop Compton of London, a militant Protestant who had been Princess Anne's childhood tutor and was a friend of Sarah, was suspended in September. This was the first major attack on the Anglican Church.

In 1679 Sarah's widowed sister Frances had remarried a man nicknamed 'Lying [or Mad] Dick' Talbot. He was Lieutenant-Colonel and Groom of the Bedchamber to James II, had been imprisoned as a result of Titus Oates's allegations, and exiled to France during the crisis over the Duke of York's exclusion from the throne. Now, under James, Talbot became Deputy Lord

Lieutenant of Ireland. Talbot drove forward a harsh pro-Catholic programme motivated by bitterness over his brother's death in an Irish Protestant prison. His actions in Ireland – purging the Irish army of non-Catholics and the confiscation of Protestant lands – belied the King's oft-repeated claim that he wanted only to emancipate English Catholics, not to undermine Protestantism. The 1641–2 massacre of Protestants in Antrim and Derry had not been forgotten, and refugees voiced fears that Catholics would reclaim their lands. As Sarah watched them arrive, or as she put it 'when the design of Popery was bare-faced', her brother-in-law Talbot 'took pains on me, but without any effect, to persuade me to bring over the Princess [Anne] to their [Catholic] purpose'.[83]

Following the revocation of the Edict of Nantes in 1685, which had guaranteed freedom of conscience to French Protestants, thousands of French Huguenot refugees also arrived in England. To Sarah's mind, they were living evidence of papist barbarism and their plight confirmed her every prejudice. The Huguenot silk manufacturers settled in Spitalfields, and French became the commonest language on the streets of Soho.[84] Sarah's friend Bishop Burnet would later record that in France the Protestant women 'were carried into nunneries where they were starved, whipped, and barbarously used'[85] and Sarah no doubt saw various tracts describing the persecution in wildly embellished terms. Evidence that James II had grave doubts about both the wisdom and Christianity of Louis XIV's policy of persecution has now come into the historical light, but this was not what the French ambassador reported and Sarah was not alone in believing the King to approve of the revocation.

In early 1687, shortly after the birth of her first son Jack, Sarah attended on Anne where she had retired to Richmond in order to avoid association with her father's unpopular policies. They then stayed at Windsor over the summer, while London was focused on the trial of seven bishops who had refused to read out King James's Declaration of Indulgence in their pulpits. Bishop Burnet's *History of His Own Time*, which sought to portray the Glorious Revolution as the result of a popular uprising rather than a *coup d'état*, described the 'fermentation' in the city as these seven bishop-martyrs were taken by barge to the Tower. Despite a jury stacked against them at the trial, their barrister, the brilliant Whig Lord Somers, managed to have them acquitted. On the same day, seven lords, both Whig and Tory, sent an invitation to William of Orange to land with Dutch troops.

Sarah and John signalled their own awareness of the shifting political wind by choosing Lady Lumley, a known supporter of William of Orange, as godmother for their third baby daughter Elizabeth, born in March 1688.[87]

Indicating James II's weakened position after this public-relations disaster, and the correspondingly increased importance of his two Protestant daughters, we find in this same month the first mention of Anne's relationship with Sarah in an official diplomatic report. Louis XIV's special envoy, Bonrepaux, wrote to Seignelay on 4 June that Anne had 'a passion without measure' for her friend Sarah Churchill.[88]

Among Sarah's papers at the time of her death was this quotation, copied from Francis Bacon: 'It was prettily devised of Aesop the fly sat upon the axletree of the chariot wheel and said what a dust do I raise.'[89] As Sarah's memoirs move into the period of her public influence, it is difficult to assess how important she was to the course of events. The part she played in the Glorious Revolution is symptomatic of this problem: she is at once proud of her involvement in these seismic events, yet well aware that a woman would be most admired by contemporary readers if she denied responsibility for initiating political action or manipulating the decisions of those considered above her in both gender and rank.

John Churchill was part of an army grouping which supported William's intervention, and he therefore sent a separate pledge of allegiance in August 1688, rather than signing that of the large landowners and Bishop Compton in June. This shows that the Churchills had decided to desert James II at least three months in advance. In her memoirs Sarah tried to deny this premeditation:

she claimed that her decision to side with the revolutionaries was 'a thing sudden and unconcerted'.[90] In fact, while he was in London over the summer, Churchill took various precautions. Sarah wrote that, as the Revolution was so hazardous, before he 'entered into the design, he made settlements to secure his fortune to his family'.[91] At this point his account at Child's Bank contained £1,201 (approximately £99,106 in today's money), which although modest in comparison to his later fortune was a great deal to lose.[92]

Meanwhile, William had his own reasons for invading. By 1688, the French had built a fleet which had almost attained parity with that of the Dutch, and William saw control of the English navy as the simplest solution to this threat. He was also able to rely upon a growing international coalition against France. In September he issued a declaration, laying out his intention to invade. James started to backtrack desperately on the pro-Catholic domestic policies that had alienated so many powerful men, and by the day of the invasion, the only significant point in William's declaration on which James had not caved in was his refusal to summon a free Parliament. But it was too late.

The final trigger to the invasion was the birth of James's son, James Francis Edward. Despite the sworn deposition of a Whig midwife, Mrs Wilkins, that this baby was the true child of Mary of Modena, and therefore half-brother of Anne and Mary, the King's opponents spread the story that the pregnancy had been a hoax. A rumour grew that a child had been smuggled into the delivery room inside a warming pan. *A Brief Discovery of the True Mother of the Pretended Prince of Wales* (1696), for example, alleged that the baby was an illegitimate son of Dick Talbot, Sarah's brother-in-law. Sarah wrote later that '[i]f it was a true child, it was certainly very ill ordered, but if it was not I don't see how it could be better.'[93] The news of her stepmother's pregnancy must have been a devastating blow for Anne – and all those who hoped for a Protestant heir. She absented herself from the birth so that she could choose to disbelieve it, and for many years would only refer to her brother as 'it'.

Many years later a close friend of Sarah said that he agreed with her 'with respect to the legitimacy of the Prince of Wales', and that the warming-pan myth 'can't go far with thinking people, but then I beg leave to ask how very few there are who think; and useful prejudices should not be taken off the minds of the people till you are sure you succeed in putting into them something better . . .'[94] While it lasted, however, the dispute about the royal birth was significant because it placed the tension between Anne and her stepmother centre-stage in the public imagination, shifting the guilt of treason and deceit from the male conspirators to the shoulders of the women.

On 5 November, William and his 15,000 troops invaded; for a fortnight both sides established themselves in the western counties and tried to gather and consolidate their forces, until, on 17 November, the King rode out to meet his army at Salisbury, accompanied by men of mixed and hidden loyalties. By the twenty-fourth, John Churchill and Prince George had deserted the King, along with 400 men, sparking a wider mutiny within the army. Churchill and the Duke of Grafton together presented themselves to William of Orange at Axminster. The following day an order was sent from the King to London for the seizure of the traitor Churchill's possessions, and guards were placed outside Sarah's door. Luckily, however, as Sarah recorded it: 'In all this trouble I got out, for the guards were very easy, & went to a house in Suffolk Street where I found the Bishop of London. He told me he would go to his friends in the City to advise what would be done, & that he would come to the Cockpit at twelve that night & carry the Princess where she would be private.'[95] In the published version of her memoirs Sarah makes it the Princess who 'sent me to the bishop' and insists that she was only 'obeying my mistress' orders'.[96]

Sarah presented the episode as a matter of rescuing the Princess, but she herself was in far more immediate danger. Had the Revolution failed, both Churchills might have ended up in the Tower of London awaiting execution for their part in it, whereas James was unlikely to harm his own daughter. In the first draft of her memoirs, Sarah recalled Anne as terrified, telling her that 'her father was coming back [to London] and rather than see him she would jump out a window',[97] but in a version written in the 1730s she admitted: 'And I was very frighted myself; all the Roman Catholics in the Court having behaved with great insolence to the Protestants.'[98]

Many contemporary critics of Sarah's memoirs pointed out to her that the escape with the Princess was 'not so much a Piece of Chance-Medley-Work as it has been represented',[99] while Lediard's 1736 biography of John Churchill claimed that some time in advance Anne and Sarah had ordered the building of a secret back staircase out of Anne's chambers.[100] This image fits neatly with the idea that the Churchills did not just climb a metaphorical ladder to the top but built their own. Lediard's literal building of the stairs symbolised the influence Sarah exerted over Anne before the Revolution, prejudicing her against her father and galvanising her resolve to desert when the time came.

At midnight on 25 November, Sarah and Anne, with Lady Fitzharding and a servant, left the Cockpit. They met the Bishop of London and the Earl of Dorset where they were waiting with a hackney coach near Charing Cross and fled initially to the Earl's house, Copt Hall in Epping Forest. They had escaped in the nick of time: before dawn an order arrived confirming that the women should be kept under house arrest. When the Princess's absence was discovered at 7.30 a.m., they were already on their way to Nottingham to join the other revolutionaries. In her first draft memoir Sarah wrote that '[t]he Princess going to Nottingham was purely accidental'[101] and even in the final published version complained that it was 'maliciously imputed to my policy and premeditated contrivance'[102] that Anne should be dragged towards William's invading forces. Pepys quipped: 'Hardly anything can be thought more natural than that ladies should think it time for them to withdraw as soon as they have received tidings of their husbands having done the same.'[103]

The question of who decided that Anne should flee and where she should go had behind it the more serious question of whether

Anne had been unduly influenced by Sarah, her Whig favourite, to send encouragement for William's invasion. Bishop Burnet wrote that 'it was probably by her [Sarah's] prevalency that both the Princess and her husband, the Prince of Denmark, were induced to encourage the expedition [of William]'.[104] It is more likely that Sarah's influence was on her husband, who might not have betrayed King James had it not been for his wife's Whig sympathies and her intimate relationship with Princess Anne.

When Anne and Sarah arrived in Nottingham, they were entertained at a victory banquet in a court improvised by Lord Devonshire. The teenaged Colley Cibber, later Poet Laureate, happened to have a job as a waiter there that evening because his father, a sculptor, was working at Chatsworth. Later Colley described his attraction to the beautiful Sarah Churchill: 'So clear an emanation of beauty, such a commanding grace of aspect struck me into a regard that had something softer than the most profound respect in it' and he wanted 'no better amusement than of stealing now and then the delight of gazing on the fair object near me'.[105] However, he wrote this in 1740, perhaps hoping for some legacy from the eighty-year-old Duchess of Marlborough.

Sarah did not want to be remembered just for her looks. On the 1715 draft of her memoirs, her pen deleted her co-author's sycophantic references to her beauty.[106] She also crossed out descriptions of her 'wit', 'vivacity' and 'accomplishments'. The only compliment she let stand was to her 'spirit'. Unless she was stunningly self-conscious about the fate of these manuscripts as historical documents, this little piece of editing tells us more about Sarah's character than any number of contemporary reports.

From Nottingham, the party went on to Oxford, where Sarah watched the emotional reunion of Prince George and Princess Anne in the middle of Christ Church quadrangle. Amusingly, Anne's first letter back to the Palace, addressed to Benjamin Bathurst, contained orders that the backstairs, which presumably she had never seen before her escape, should be repainted.[107] Sarah had to wait a few more days for reunion with her husband, who had been sent ahead by William to London when the news of King James's intended departure reached them.[108]

Anne's escape with Sarah had demoralised James to the point that his own flight from the country seemed the best option. By 18 December William was in control of government, while Protestant mobs exploded into violence against Catholic chapels throughout London. James sailed from England on 22 December (his second attempt) and headed for Saint-Germains, one of Louis XIV's surplus châteaux.

In a letter to Bishop Burnet, Sarah tried to explain what motivated her entry into politics: 'You ask what were the schemes proposed. I had no scheme of any kind but to get honest men into the service [government] & such as would not give us up to France.'[109] Sarah has usually been represented as what she sometimes pretended to be: politically naïve, interested in nothing beyond her own family, and failing to comprehend the meaning of the historical events in which she became embroiled. Yet in many ways she shared the idealism about government accountability that made the rebellion of Whig lords in 1688 the forerunner of eighteenth-century, rights-based revolutions. She was probably among the least conservative of the Revolution's participants, although like others she tried to downplay its radicalism.[110] She vowed famously: 'As to what is called the Whig notion, that I will never part with.'[111] That 'Whig notion' has been defined as a view of 'the monarchy as a convenience rather than an institution for reverence'.[112]

Retrospectively the Whigs portrayed the 1688 Revolution as a much more high-minded affair than it had felt at the time, citing the contractarian theories of John Locke's *Second Treatise of Civil Government* (1690). Sarah had always been more comfortable with progressive beliefs about the 'contract' between government and people than had her husband or friends like Godolphin. In her first draft memoir, written in 1704, she wrote: 'I must confess I was born of a principle never to have any remorse for the deposing of any King that became unjust.'[113] Towards the end of her life she approvingly quoted an 'old Castile oath': 'We, that are as good as yourself and more powerful, choose you to be our King upon such conditions . . .'[114]

No one would claim that republican ideas exerted any positive influence over the course of the 1688 Revolution, and Sarah always disassociated herself from 'rank republicans'.[115] Yet there was a tradition,[116] dating back to the fifteenth century, of opposition to the venality of royal courts, their standing armies and abuse of privilege, which Sarah expressed increasingly vocally with age. The Whigs were caricatured by their enemies as republicans who would erase 'all distinctions . . . all ranks and degrees of men',[117] and Sarah was tarred with this same brush.

Sarah was important to the Whig leaders as Princess Anne's agent. Her first role as lobbyist for the Princess's interests after the Revolution arose in relation to the settlement of succession to the throne. It was a fundamental premise of the hereditary monarchy that the throne could never be vacant, yet after James went to France, it clearly was. In January 1689 intense negotiations took place between groups in Parliament. Essentially three options were considered: a regency (in James's name); the accession of Mary with William as her consort; or the accession of William with Mary as his consort. Anne opposed the third option because she had a better hereditary claim to the throne than William, and Sarah supported her. There was a four-day impasse as the House of Lords debated the issue, during which Sarah kept Anne advised. She personally lobbied Members of Parliament and took 'a great deal of pains (which I believe the King and Queen [William and Mary] never forgot)'[118] to push forward Anne's claim. Sarah described herself in her memoirs as 'so very simple a creature'[119] that she never imagined that the invading Dutchman would want to stay and rule, but it soon became clear that William was not going home and would not accept a place merely as Mary's consort.

On 6 February, what Burnet called the 'double-bottomed monarchy' was finally agreed in the House of Lords: William and Mary would rule together until one died, to be succeeded by the survivor and then by Anne or her heirs. Following consultations

with Dr Tillotson, the future Archbishop of Canterbury, and with
Lady Russell, the widely respected widow of the Whig martyr,
Sarah advised Anne to accept the settlement. It was difficult for
Anne to accept that William's much weaker claim to the English
throne, through his mother Mary Stuart, would precede either
her sister's or her own. The debate was essentially about the
authority of women to rule, and so it was appropriate that the
princesses' claims were defended by another woman.

In 1886, *Memoirs of Mary, Queen of England (1689–1693)*[120]
claimed to be based on a copy of an original manuscript discovered in Hanover. The 'Queen Mary' narrator wrote of '[m]y
opinion having ever been that a woman should not meddle in
government . . .' and admitted to her friends that thinking about
State business gave her a headache. Mary's denial of personal
ambition was important to her own family conscience and to
the Whig efforts to relaunch themselves as rulers rather than
rebels. Male authors who wrote treatises on whether women
were capable of governing effectively, such as William Walsh
in his *Dialogue Concerning Women, Being a Defence of the Sex
– Written to Eugenia* (1691), always complimented Mary on her
submissive character while concluding that, on the whole, regnant
queens were better avoided.

While Sarah privately considered Mary and Anne unworthy
of the power they stood to inherit, she argued on their behalf
with envious vehemence. In the first draft of her memoirs, she
confessed that 'I could not endure to have the Princess do anything
that I would not have done if I had been in her place.'[121] This is
one of the most revealing statements she ever made: implicit in it
are her own repressed desire for power and her impatience with
characters weaker than her own.

William and Mary were crowned on 11 April 1689 in Westminster
Abbey. Anne and Sarah were both too pregnant to play active
roles in the coronation (Sarah with her fourth daughter, Mary,
and Anne with her one son to survive infancy, William, Duke of
Gloucester).[122] Though Sarah once wrote that she could never
observe any scruples in Queen Anne about wearing the crown,

the Princess Anne must have felt guiltily conscious, as she sat and watched her sister's coronation from their private box, of the letter she had received that morning from her exiled father, in which he had cursed them both.

Under William's first Parliament, Sarah again played Anne's agent when the issue of the Princess's revenue arose. In the memoir she wrote with Bishop Burnet she made herself sound like the initiator of this matter: 'I tried to get a provision of £50,000 a year to be settled on her by Act of Parliament.'[123] In fact, against her Whig principles but out of loyalty to her mistress, Sarah allowed herself to be used by the Tory opposition, who saw in Princess Anne a potential figurehead if they could separate her interests from those of William and Mary. William offered Anne £50,000 on the understanding that the issue was not brought into Parliament, the Tories having first pressed for £70,000. Later satirical works would suggest that Anne only needed such a large income because Sarah had made her into a compulsive gambler.[124]

One of the Secretaries of State, Lord Shrewsbury, was sent to talk to Sarah. He offered to resign if the King's promise was not kept. Sarah remarked drily that in that event his resignation would not be much use to Anne. Similarly, when Lord Rochester said that Anne should have been grateful to take her income from the King rather than from Parliament, Sarah reflected 'that he would not have liked that advice in the case of his own four thousand pound a year to him & his son, but I was not so uncivil as to make that reply'.[125] On Anne's behalf she refused the offer on the grounds that a Parliamentary grant would be far more secure than the charity of the Privy Purse.

Eventually Anne received her grant through Parliament and always felt she owed this to Sarah. She rewarded her friend in 1691 with an increase in her salary from £400 to £1,000 a year, a token of favour that she shyly asked Sarah to accept and never mention again.[126] She declared: 'I believe you in all things as the Gospel, & could you see my heart you would find I have not one thought but what I ought of that dear woman who[m] my soul loves.' Sarah wrote later that she was pleasantly surprised by the reward, as she had 'thought it satisfaction enough that she should have so great a part in making the Princess free & independent'.[127] In old age, she inserted some notes between the pages of her 1691 correspondence, stating that William and Mary's antagonism towards her dated from this active role in the settlement negotiations, and justifying her acceptance of the salary increase by claiming that she was only reluctantly persuaded to it by Lord Godolphin.

Whether or not Queen Mary's alleged memoirs are authentic, they contain a version of events as seen from her perspective that is psychologically plausible. The author writes of Mary's 'very sensible affliction' that Anne was 'making parties to get a revenue settled and said nothing of it to me'. In this account, Shrewsbury was sent to talk not to Sarah but to John Churchill, who apologised that his wife was 'like a mad woman' in insisting on the full amount. The breach between the royal sisters opened, according to Mary, thanks to Sarah's influence, when Anne started taking her Sunday sacrament separately from the King and Queen and 'doing little things contrary to what I did'. Mary said that these slights did not matter in themselves but were significant because they gave the public an excuse for 'making a party' of opposition against William. She claimed that Sarah advised Anne to demand £50,000 because she found 'it could be carried no other way' and so 'with much ado, rather than lose it, brought herself to give my sister this advice'. Similarly, an astute critic of Sarah's memoirs suggested that her early strategy had been simply to demonstrate that she exercised power over Anne to as many people as possible.[128]

Sarah's behaviour suggests that she was indignant about William's automatic assumption that he could control a woman who had a far better claim to the Throne. Just as Sarah valued control of her own fortune, she associated Anne's freedom with the possession of an independent income. She also perceived that William and Mary were interested in keeping Anne dependent on them for reasons of political consolidation rather than familial love, so cast herself as Anne's only true friend. As she did brilliantly in later life, she shifted the accusation levelled against her – of being Anne's friend only for the sake of personal gain – onto others, in this case the King and Queen. When Anne told Mary that 'her friends had a mind to make her some settlement', Sarah quoted Mary replying 'with a very imperious air: "Pray what friends have you but the KING and ME?"'[129]

As a writer, Sarah had a talent for selecting such anecdotes. Her description of Mary showing unseemly joy when she entered Whitehall Palace after the Revolution, 'turning up the quilts upon the bed, as people do when they come to an inn', is ten times more cutting than John Evelyn's similar observation that Mary came into Whitehall 'as to a wedding'. To Bishop Burnet, Mary was the model of womanhood, yet Sarah remarked in her memoirs: 'I cannot forbear saying that whatever good qualities Queen Mary had to make her popular, it is too evident in many instances *THAT SHE WANTED BOWELS*.'[130]

As for William, Sarah remembered a hilarious story of him eating a plate of peas, 'the first that had been seen that year', in front of Mary and Anne without offering any to either lady. When they arrived home later, Anne confessed to Sarah that 'she had so much mind to the peas that she was afraid to look at them and yet could hardly keep her eyes off them'.[131] While ostensibly about William's gluttony (a stereotypical Dutch trait) and vulgarity, this anecdote also tells us about Anne's own appetite – for peas and for power.

However, in 1689 the King and Queen were on good enough terms with the Churchills for Queen Mary to stand as godmother to Sarah's baby daughter, christened Mary in her honour. Churchill, meanwhile, was rewarded for his part in the Revolution with the extinct earldom of Marlborough.

Although fairly conservative forces had driven the Revolution, it led to a series of innovations very much in the spirit of Sarah's faith in the superior moral conscience of Protestantism and in the English Parliament as the protector of the people's property and liberty. The Declaration of Rights secured the English Throne against Catholic succession and stressed that the rule of law would henceforth be based on the consent of Parliament rather than on royal discretion. It also forbade the monarch to raise funds outside Parliament, to keep a standing army without consent or to establish special courts or tribunals, and guaranteed the English gentry free elections, and the right to petition. At the same time William passed a Bill of Toleration, which ended the persecution of many Nonconformists and had the unintended consequence of freeing people from the obligation to attend church. Finally, there was a general relaxation of constraints on the press – even when hostile satirists besieged her, Sarah always championed free speech as a basic and distinctively English right. But the single biggest step towards the democratisation of the constitution was the frequency and predictability of Parliamentary sessions after the Revolution. This produced a new breed of politician and shifted the emphasis away from power struggle by armed rebellion into a realm where, indirectly, women could wield far greater influence.

In 1690, Louis XIV attacked the English forts and settlements in New York and the Hudson Provinces of America. By the summer, there were fears of an invasion, and William III was fighting in Ireland against the deposed James, who was still technically King of Ireland, and his Jacobite troops. There is a story, perhaps apocryphal, that James complimented Sarah's sister Frances on the speed with which the troops of her husband Talbot, by then Duke of Tyrconnel, had deserted at the battle of the Boyne. Frances replied boldly that 'His Majesty had the advantage of them.'[132] Meanwhile, John Churchill was left in command of the army in England until August, when he, too, sailed to Ireland to fight on William's side.[133] He wrote to Sarah that 'as ambitious as you sometimes think me, I do assure you I would not live in this place to be emperor of it' if it meant being away from her any longer.[134]

Sarah and her sister now found themselves married to opposing Generals in a war that William and Marlborough were to win. The 1691 Treaty of Limerick, which concluded the war, marked the beginning of the Protestant ascendancy in Ireland. Frances's estates in Ireland were confiscated and she was forced to join other Jacobite exiles in Saint-Germains, a fate for which she could not help but hold her sister partially responsible. Other prominent families were split by the Revolution, but few so dramatically.

From some undated letters to her mother's brother, Martin Lister, we know that Sarah kept an eye on the material advancements available to her own family through her position in Anne's household. She was dutiful and respectful to her uncle – a talented scientist, Fellow of the Royal Society, friend of John Evelyn, and author of books on conchology, travel and cookery. Now Sarah wrote: 'Dear Uncle – Though you have not heard from me, I have not been negligent in your business, but I doubt I can't make an interest enough to get you [a post as] one of the four physicians to the King because I believe he will take the same that was to the last King . . .'[135] She referred to money that her uncle had told her he would be willing to offer as bribery but added: '[I]f it is in my power to do it, there is no need of that.' She ended by admitting that obtaining a place for him near the King would help her own career. She was unsuccessful, however; Lister did not become a royal physician until Anne became queen.[136]

A week before Marlborough left for the Irish war, Sarah had given birth to their second son, Charles, and she was still 'lying in' on the day he left. On the eve of the birth, at the age of thirty, Sarah made her first will. In it she left the bulk of her personal fortune (some £7,000 – approximately £577,000 in today's money) to her husband, and some money to Lady Fitzharding to buy herself a ring and act as godmother to the coming child. She bequeathed rings to her mother and to Lord Godolphin as tokens of affection. She also left a gift to her favourite waiting woman, Betty Moody, and £500 'to release poor people out of prison'. Her father's bankruptcy made this her charitable cause of choice throughout her adult life. Finally, she drafted a provision that her daughters should forfeit any inheritance if they married without their father's consent, but at the same time each should receive the interest from their inheritances 'into their own hands' from the age of fifteen. This document[137] tells us what she omits from her memoirs: which personal relationships she valued, and which eventualities she most feared.

It was around 1690[138] that Sarah undertook an act of familial duty that verged on extravagance and was later to have serious repercussions. She was upset to hear that she had cousins on her father's side who were living in relative poverty: the Hill family. She had never heard of them before because her father had had twenty-two brothers and sisters.[139] Mr Hill, a merchant in the City, was married to one of her aunts, who had a portion of only £500. Marlborough's cousin, Anne Chudleigh, brought them to her attention, and Sarah was probably motivated in part by social embarrassment when she discovered that the eldest daughter, named Abigail, was working as a servant to Sir John and Lady Rivers in Kent. Soon after, Sarah heard that the four children had been orphaned and decided to take them under her wing. In 1711 she wrote an account of how she had 'relieved them all manner of ways': getting one boy a place in the custom house, and the other a place at St Albans School, a job as a Court page, and then in the Bedchamber of Anne's son.[140] In her published memoirs, she adds that she also found the younger daughter, Alice Hill, a job as Court laundress, a pension, and then a fixed annuity from the royal funds that supported her until her death.[141] As for Abigail, Sarah said, 'I used her in all regards as a sister.' In an earlier version[142] she mentions nursing her through smallpox.

The tradition that a woman's weak character is represented in her appearance has continued into the twentieth century, during which Abigail has almost always been described as pale and 'red-nosed'.[143] One of Sarah's more malicious friends referred to her as 'fair-faced Abigail';[144] such sarcasm would have been pointless unless she was indeed rather plain.

Abigail left no record of any resentment she might have nurtured against her cousin. Like so many of those who surround Sarah, she has suffered in posterity for her silence.

3
The Cockpit Circle

A friend was what [Anne] most coveted . . . It was this turn of mind which made her one day propose to me that whenever I should happen to be absent from her, we might in all our letters write ourselves by feigned names, such as would import nothing of distinction of rank between us. MORLEY and FREEMAN were the names her fancy hit upon; and she let me choose by which of them I would be called. My frank, open temper naturally led me to pitch upon Freeman, & so the Princess took the other; & from this time Mrs Morley and Mrs Freeman began to converse as equals, made so by affection & friendship.[1]

In her memoir, Sarah located the adoption of the nicknames some time before the Revolution, but in the surviving letters they do not feature until 1692.[2] In that year James Tyrrell published his *Bibliotheca Politica, or An Enquiry into the Ancient Constitution of the English Government* in which the character named 'Mr Freeman' is the voice of pure Whiggism while 'Mr Meanwell' is his Tory, crypto-Jacobite opponent. Sarah's choice of name might not have been a deliberate literary reference, but 'Freeman' had precise associations.

The nicknaming was part of the same fad for playing among the working classes as the young Frances Jennings' escapade as an orange-seller. The women's alliance with the 'middling sort Mrs' whose husbands worked in the City or at a trade, was considered charmingly ironic, but also mildly subversive. Bishop Hoadly's version of Sarah's memoirs emphasised that 'from this time, Mrs Morley and Mrs Freeman are to converse as <u>equals,</u> made so by <u>love</u> . . .'[3] The tension between their respective ranks and love as a social leveller lay behind the nicknames each time they were used, for, as Defoe wrote in a book enticingly titled *Conjugal Lewdness*,

'Love knows no superior or inferior, no imperious Command on the one hand, no reluctant Subjection on the other . . .'4

Their husbands were included as 'Mr Morley' and 'Mr Freeman'. The use of the nicknames therefore defined the core of a new faction, which came to be known as the 'Cockpit Circle'.

During the Nine Years War Marlborough both fought the French under William's command on the Continent and, whenever he was in England, sat on the Council responsible for assisting Mary with government. Although William's campaigns were not dramatic victories, they were depleting the French military machine and therefore laying the groundwork for the victories Marlborough would one day win in Queen Anne's name.

Despite the very limited trust placed in him by the King, Marlborough was dissatisfied with the new regime (he was denied the post of Master-General of the Ordnance and the Knighthood of the Garter, which he felt he deserved for services rendered in the Revolution and in Ireland). He is believed to have communicated secretly with Saint-Germains during the early 1690s, pledging his repentant loyalty to James II and requesting written pardons for himself, his wife and his closest colleague Godolphin.[5] Jacobite reports state that Marlborough privately received their emissaries in England. James's pardon was sought by most of the Revolution's leaders as insurance against the possibility of his restoration, and Winston Churchill argued convincingly in the 1940s that William regarded them with a tolerant eye.[6] The split in the royal family had made duplicity an almost unavoidable feature of the age and Marlborough was one of many to maintain contact with both sides.

Despite her devotion to 'Revolution Principles', Sarah too remained friendly with several Jacobite women, such as Lady Dunmore. This lady had snubbed Sarah under James II 'without any sort of provocation' but came to see her in London after the Revolution 'in a very low condition'. Sarah took pity on her and helped her son get a job in the army.[7] However, these kindnesses did not prevent Lady Dunmore from dropping Sarah again when she later fell from favour. Other Jacobite ladies, like Elizabeth Wilmot, now Lady Sandwich, wife of the 3rd Earl of Sandwich, attempted to turn Sarah's personal dislike of William and Mary into support for James, but none succeeded. In old age Sarah said that many Jacobites and Roman Catholics were misguided, 'simple people',[8] which speaks for her own intellectual self-confidence.

Sarah had some respect for the logical consistency of the Jacobite 'Compounders', who believed that James II could be returned to the throne on trust 'without asking any terms', as opposed to those 'Non-compounders' who argued that his son, a Catholic, should be returned only as a Protestant ruler.[9] But her family's interest became so bound up with Anne's claim to the throne that both categories of Jacobite, and even the more moderate Tories, became objects of Sarah's paranoia. Her fears focused on the machinations of secret agents, however, far more than on her own acquaintances.

It is unclear how much Sarah knew of her husband's dealings with the Jacobites and whether she was as tolerant of them as King William. If she knew of them, they were probably presented to her – or she presented them to her own conscience – as counter-espionage rather than as self-interested double-dealing.

On 20 January 1692, Marlborough was summarily dismissed from his posts. Count Stratemann, the Austrian ambassador, wrote that this had occurred for a combination of reasons: Marlborough had been stirring up resistance to William's promotion of foreigners within the English army and the peerage; he had publicly accused William of ingratitude towards those who had placed him on the Throne; he 'had tried, by means of his wife, who is Chief Lady in Waiting to the Princess of Denmark, to cause discord between the Queen and the Princess'; and, finally, he had renewed communication with the exiled James.[10] The last of these offences was obviously the most serious (Marlborough had been in touch with the French and Jacobites via a certain Captain Lloyd), but William was also concerned by Sarah's creation of 'discord' – shorthand for the opposition circle forming around Princess Anne.

In her memoirs, Sarah attributed her husband's dismissal to

her relationship with Anne. In the first draft she wrote that 'my stubbornness in all that concerned the Princess did prejudice to the Duke of Marlborough'. In the 1730s version she explained further that 'nobody can doubt that the occasion of his being removed from all his places was not only from the desire of many in hopes of dividing the spoil, but from their dislike that anybody should have so much interest with the Princess ... And it was plain that my Lord Rochester [Anne's uncle and William's adviser] was desirous to have me removed . . .'[11] Then finally, in the published version, she imputed his dismissal to the influence of other enemies – the Earl of Portland, who was the King's favourite, and also William's mistress, Elizabeth (Betty) Villiers.[12] Changes in the masculine government were driven, she claimed, by backstage battles raging among Court ladies and homosexual lovers. She was, she believed, the scapegoat for Mary's malice against her sister, and her husband suffered only as 'a plausible reason' for removing Sarah from Court: 'The disgrace of my lord Marlborough therefore was designed as a step towards removing me from about her.'[13] This narrative was shaped by Sarah's romantic wish for Marlborough to have fallen on his sword for her sake, and by her tendency to place herself at centre-stage, like the fly on the axle-wheel.

Sarah's response to her eviction from Court was to ignore it. She said it was not to her taste to be 'turned out' or 'put away', and claimed that she took advice from Godolphin before deciding to appear at Court following her husband's dismissal. She pretended that she did not foresee the scandal this would ignite. While citing the example of the Marchioness of Halifax, who apparently remained at Court after her husband had been sent away, Sarah knew full well that she was flouting Queen Mary's wishes.

A coldness had been apparent between the royal sisters since the previous year. In a letter from 1691 Anne promised Sarah that she would spend more time with Mary, especially when William was overseas,[14] but complained that 'tis very hard I may not have the liberty of following my inclinations and being kind as much as lies in my power to those I really dote on, as long as I do nothing extravagant. But if it will be any satisfaction to you I promise you I never will take any more notice of you before folks than I do of Lady Charlotte [Beverwaert, a Lady of the Bedchamber]'. In later life, Sarah noted that this letter showed she had been innocent of stirring up discord between the sisters: it proved, on the contrary, that she was urging reconciliation, and that 'I did beg of her not to take so much notice of me as she did in public.'

Sarah spelt out why she thought Mary had developed an antipathy towards her sister: 'Mary grew weary of anybody who would not talk a great deal; and the Princess was so silent that she barely spoke more than was necessary to answer a question.'[15] In other words, Mary shared Sarah's opinion that Anne was dull company. Why she disliked Sarah's relationship with Anne, on the other hand, is less straightforward. There was Anne's intrinsic value, both as a figurehead for political opposition and as eventual heir to the Throne, but perhaps Mary also understood the true strength of Anne's feelings for Sarah. She herself had renounced sentimental friendships of the kind she had had with Frances Apsley and perhaps felt her sister should do the same.

In February 1692, the morning after Sarah's audacious appearance at Court, Mary wrote to Anne that it was 'very unfit Lady Marlborough should stay with you since it gives her husband so just a pretence of being where he ought not'. In her memoirs, Sarah jeered that 'No-one, I think, can be so foolish as to imagine that the Queen's dislike of me was only on account of my being the wife of Lord Marlborough.'[16] Instead she wondered why her 'friendship and sincere affection' for Anne were now labelled 'crimes'.

On receiving her sister's letter, Anne wrote to Sarah: 'I had rather live in a cottage with you than reign empress of the world without you.' To the Queen she replied: 'There is no misery that I cannot readily resolve to suffer rather than the thoughts of parting with [Sarah].'[17] Mary's response was a direct order via the Lord Chamberlain for Sarah to leave the Cockpit. Anne dashed off an urgent note to Sarah saying that they needed to meet to plan their response.[18] Sarah must have helped Anne compose her next defiant letter to the Queen, explaining that she would be 'obliged to retire' from Court rather than part with her friend. In notes from 1704[19] Sarah described the argument with William and Mary as 'so uneasy to my own temper that if I could have known it would have lasted so long I am confident I should have gone to the Indias rather than have endured it.' She listed her many offers to resign, and Anne's weeping refusal to hear of it. Anne wrote that if Sarah should ever resign her post she would 'shut myself up and never see the world more'.

Anne relished the fact that their friendship could now be tested by adversity, but Prince George's friends and servants were concerned as to how the Princess's self-banishment might affect them, and urged her to give up her favourite for the sake of better relations with the King and Queen.[20] However, George himself had suffered various snubs at William's hands and was sympathetic to his wife's loyalty to Sarah. He told one of Lord Rochester's servants that 'he had so much tenderness to the Princess that he could not desire to make her so uneasy as he knew that [giving up Sarah] would do'.[21]

When casting about for a place to move to from the Cockpit, Anne asked William for the use of Richmond Palace where she had stayed in early 1687, and he refused. Elizabeth, Duchess of Somerset, stepped in. She was a redheaded heiress who, by the age of sixteen, had been twice married and widowed and now, married to her third husband Charles Seymour, Duke of Somerset, was a close friend of Sarah and Anne. Elizabeth persuaded her husband to offer the Prince and Princess, the Marlboroughs and their children, the use of Syon House in Brentford.

The offer was gratefully accepted and the two couples moved there in February 1692. As the heavily pregnant Anne left her lodgings at Court, Sarah noted that Lord Jersey, Betty Villiers' brother, 'had not so much manners as to offer the Princess his hand to open a Door'.[22] She was shocked, too, by the behaviour of a servant named Mr Maul, whom Sarah had asked Anne to make a Bedchamber Man to Prince George and for whom she had 'invented an employment [. . .] of overlooking the Princess's accounts to mend his salary'. At Syon House, Maul spied on them for the Rochesters, and 'avoided as much as he could ever to make me a bow', Sarah observed. He would hurry the food from the dinner table and never speak to either Sarah or Anne as he served, 'but looking as if he was so weary of them that the Princess said she took a sort of pleasure to sit at Dinner the longer'.[23]

Syon House was then, in structure, much as it is today. It had valuable landscaped gardens dating back to the Renaissance and an area called 'The Wilderness' was being built on the west side. The Marlboroughs spent nine months commuting between Syon and their Jermyn Street lodgings. On one occasion, when Anne herself was travelling between Brentford and London, her coach was attacked by highwaymen, which led to a public outcry that the King and Queen were denying the Heir Apparent a proper escort.[24]

William's popularity was fragile following February's Glencoe massacre in Scotland. As the rift with Anne became public, his opponents turned to her as a prospective figurehead. On 27 April, Anne sent Sarah a copy of a letter from Lord Rochester, which again demanded that the women stop seeing each other, with a note from herself to reassure her friend that 'tis not in the power of man to make me ever consent to part with you'. She averred that not only would she brave the hardship of living in a cottage, but would 'live on bread and water within four walls', rather than lose Sarah.

On 20 May (according to a copy made in Sarah's hand around 1710) Anne wrote: 'After having read and kissed your dear kind letter over & over, I burnt it much against my will and, I do assure you, you need never be in pain about your letters, for I take such care of them tis not possible any accident can happen that they should be seen by anybody.' Her caution might indicate that Sarah's letters contained dangerously free observations on the King and Queen's characters (she referred to them as 'Monsters'[25] and 'Calibans',[26] while according to Macaulay, Anne and Sarah referred to the King as the 'Dutch

Abortion'[27]), rather than because they were incriminating as love letters.

The Villiers family had a long tradition as royal favourites, and for being 'as plentiful as blackberries and their relationships as tangled as the vines'.[28] Lady Frances Villiers had been governess to Princesses Mary and Anne, and her own eight children had grown up playing in the royal nursery. In 1683 Anne asked Sarah not to bring the witty Lady Fitzharding (born Barbara Villiers, and a distant relation of Barbara Villiers, Countess of Castlemaine) with her on visits so that the two of them could speak more freely. Lady Fitzharding was, of course, godmother to two of Sarah's children and had accompanied Anne and Sarah in their dramatic escape on the eve of the Revolution. Over the years, she became a focus for Anne's jealousy because she was Sarah's closest friend – a friendship based on choice rather than duty. As Sarah explained in her memoirs: 'I loved . . . [Lady] Fitzharding when I was but a child & living with all the intimacy imaginable with her.'[29] Elsewhere she wrote of Lady Fitzharding that '[t]is certain I had more fondness and inclination for her than anybody I ever knew in my life'.[30]

In 1691 Anne wrote cattily to Sarah that Lady Fitzharding, whom she nicknamed 'Loupa', was the 'spleenatickist, out of humour creature that ever was seen'.[31] She wrote later that Lady Fitzharding 'made me more uneasy than you can imagine', but then seemed to apologise: 'Seeing every day more and more how little reason I had for my fears, I should be the unreasonablest creature in the world if I gave way to them any longer, and what is past I beg may be both pardoned and forgot, for I am ashamed and angry with myself that I have been so troublesome.'

Anne justified her jealousy by claiming she feared Lady Fitzharding was a Jacobite who would betray their secrets. She begged Sarah to 'have as little to do with that enchantress as is possible' and to stay at home 'out of the way of temptation' since 'the Lady's friends will endeavour to bring you together as often as they can in hopes by degrees they may insinuate her again into that great blessing of my dear Mrs Freeman's friendship'. She excused herself for having to give such orders, 'but remember what the song says (to be jealous is the fault of every tender lover)'.

In April or May 1692, Anne's jealousy of Sarah's 'singular affection'[32] for Lady Fitzharding resurfaced. She contrasted the sacrifices she was willing to make for Sarah's sake with Sarah's refusal to give up her other female friends for Anne. When Sarah and Lady Fitzharding had previously fallen out, she remembered, they slowly made up again 'till at last you were as much bewitched by her as ever'. Anne portrayed Sarah, in other words, as if she were the royal innocent who was being led astray by a manipulative, evil favourite.

Sarah came eventually to distrust Lady Fitzharding, not as a Jacobite but as a Williamite, and had her own cause for jealousy in another direction. Lady Fitzharding, she wrote, 'had a great deal of wit but was [self-]interested. And Queen Mary showed more inclination for her than anybody. I loved her extremely, though I found at last her morals were not good.'[33]

After Marlborough's dismissal, the atmosphere of distrust and espionage intensified. Sarah believed, correctly, that the primary informant in their midst was not Barbara Fitzharding but her sister, Betty Villiers, subsequently Lady Orkney and Duchess of Hamilton.[34] Yet Sarah prided herself on never taking revenge on Betty Villiers after Anne came to the throne. Her reply to a 1704 letter from Betty, pleading her innocence in the matter of Marlborough's dismissal during the 1690s, belies the caricature of Sarah as unable to drop a grudge: 'As for what is past,' she wrote, 'whether you or I were in the wrong, I hope it will make no difference in what is to come. If it were myself I ought to be & am very sorry for it, & if it were you, I have wholly forgot it, & shall never revive any remembrance of it to hinder me from being very much yours . . .'

When Princess Mary had first gone to Holland to marry William in 1677 she had taken Betty and her younger sister Anne with her as English company. There, Anne Villiers became the lover and later wife of Bentinck, William of Orange's favourite Guelderland courtier, and Betty became William's mistress. The relationship continued until Mary, who had always known of it, asked her husband on her deathbed to break it off. William did so, and in 1695 arranged for Betty to marry Hamilton.

Anne Villiers died in 1688, leaving Bentinck free to devote himself to serving William, who gave him the English title of Earl of Portland. Sarah came to see herself as both counterpart and adversary to Portland. While she had lobbied in 1689 for the right of the two princesses to sit on the Throne when their turns came, Portland had spoken up for his friend William's right to do so, declaring that 'A man's wife ought to be his wife, in subjection to him.'[35] Sarah later believed that Portland was among those behind Marlborough's dismissal. He served the traditional purpose of royal favourite in becoming a scapegoat for opposition to the King, and was criticised for the wealth he amassed during William's reign, though he actually spent a lot of it on charitable schemes for the English peasantry. Finally, in 1698, he was supplanted, for personal more than political reasons, by another Dutchman, Arnold van Keppel, created Earl of Albemarle, who was more sympathetic to the Marlboroughs.

Several historians have suggested that there are 'the strongest indications that William was homosexual',[36] and it is notable that this interpretation of the King's relationships with his male favourites is commonly accepted by those who dismiss similar suggestions about Queen Anne's feelings for her female friends. It is true that the accusation of William's homosexuality is mainly to be found in Jacobite sources (such as the verses 'His Majesty's gracious speech to both houses of parlement' found among Sarah's papers). Jonathan Swift, writing history with a Tory bias,[37] repeated gossip that William was both 'male and female' and a lover of Portland. Those who wished to attack the monarch indirectly exploited the ambiguity surrounding close same-sex friendships in this period. But just because there were party political – and xenophobic – reasons for branding William as bisexual, we cannot assume that these accusations were without foundation. As we see from Anne's letters to Sarah, considerable ambiguity existed even within the privacy of these relationships. The fact that no man ever tried to become Anne's favourite, as Essex or Raleigh were to Elizabeth I, and that everyone used Sarah rather than Prince George as the main channel of influence to Anne, tells us more about the unspoken assumptions of the day than any amount of satires.

Part of the confusion for modern readers arises because of the changing use of language. The word 'passion' may set bells ringing before one realises that Sarah also wrote of feeling 'passions' for her mother and for her daughter Mary. On the other hand, it may be naïve to assume that the rapture of certain same-sex relationships was just talk. In a poem entitled 'The Toast' (1736), for example, the female narrator promises to cover up her sexual sins with sentimental explanations:

> I'll deny that thou art taught
> How to pair the Female Doves,
> How to practice Lesbian Loves . . .
> I will swear 'tis Nature's Call,
> 'Tis exalted Friendship all.

Sarah's adult life coincided with the growth of a distinct male homosexual subculture in London. Female homosexuality, on the other hand, continued to be regarded as an action rather than an identity – hardly even a vice, merely a *faute de mieux*. In a book called *Plain Reasons for the Growth of Sodomy in England* (1728), it was called 'the Game of Flats' and identified as a new fashion 'among the W[ome]n of Q[ualit]y' – something naughty, but not legally punishable, like sodomy, by being burnt alive.

In *Les Vies des Dames Galantes* (first published 1665–6),[38] Pierre de Bourdeille Brantome presented lesbianism not as a sexual but as an emotional perversion and supported the widely held opinion that it flourished only where women were left cloistered alone too long in harems or nunneries. He described it as 'merely the apprenticeship to the great business with men', and, significantly in the light of public anxiety about Queen Anne's failure to produce an heir, suggested that its only danger was that it might cause permanent infertility. The belief that impassioned same-sex love was on a higher plane than heterosexual love meant that a woman such as Katherine Philips (1631–1644) – who if she were alive today would be called a lesbian – was then, at the height of Puritanism, admired as a model friend and noble soul. If occasionally this platonic ideal slipped over into physical expression, it did not seem to matter.

Lesbianism, by its unverifiable nature, is an awful subject for historical research and, inversely, the best subject for political slander. The question is ultimately of less biographical importance than that of what was experienced emotionally by those concerned. On this count it seems fair to say that, while her marriage to Marlborough was the most important relationship in Sarah's life, the friendship with Sarah was the most important in Anne's.

Before asking whether Anne had latent lesbian feelings for Sarah, however, we need to acknowledge the extent to which, at the beginning of the twenty-first century, we denigrate friendship. Biographies seldom devote the same attention to a friend as to a spouse; Freud hardly bothered to discuss friendship because he did not consider it a primal enough relationship; and most us have been culturally conditioned to deny any great depth of emotion for those who are not part of the mating game. Above all, society today generally regards romantic partners as consecutive while friendships may be simultaneous and therefore non-exclusive. To understand the relationship between Anne and Sarah one needs to perform a mental shift and listen to Jonathan Swift when he wrote, 'Believe me that violent friendship is much more lasting, and as much engaging, as violent love',[39] or to Madame de La Fayette when she told her friend Madame de Sévigné in 1691: 'Believe me, you are the person in the world I have most truly loved.'[40]

A shift was also occurring in the meaning of the word 'friend' from primarily an associate, patron or backer to the meaning given in Dr Johnson's *Dictionary*: someone 'with whom to compare minds and cherish private virtues'. Private friendships among literate women were valued precisely because – as with Anne and Sarah's nicknames – they existed independent of economic or social hierarchies, and were a way for these women to cope with, or briefly escape, a society based on female subservience. They were no threat to marriage or motherhood because most men had little interest in intense relationships with those they considered their intellectual and moral inferiors. They were also meant to be monogamous and faithful relationships, to last until death-do-us-part.

Among Sarah's papers[41] there is a handwritten extract from a poem tying this kind of sentimental friendship back to an older classical idea of friendship's political role:

> A Generous friendship, no cold medium knows
> Burns with one Love, with one resentment glows
> One must our interest, one our passions be
> My friend must hate the man that injures me.

Among the same papers there is a mysterious letter which Sarah has labelled: 'Letter of the woman that died for love'. It is addressed to 'Dear A—', but with no explanation of how it came into Sarah's possession. The writer bemoans her melancholy, says that she is unable to divert her mind in the city or in the countryside or, significantly, to find comfort in another woman's 'soft bosom', and is now growing physically sick with love: 'nothing pleases my mind but indulging the fatal passion . . . the disease returns'.

In short, an understanding of friendship as something encompassing what we would nowadays class as romantic or erotic feeling is required. There was, it seems, a female equivalent to the eighteenth-century phenomenon, which has sometimes been labelled 'sentimental sodomy',[42] and even if they were somewhat in denial about their own sexuality, these women must have enjoyed and understood the frisson involved in casting their friendships in erotic language. What is still shocking is that the Queen of England's letters should supply so much evidence of this.

*　　*　　*

On 4 May 1692, Marlborough was staying alone at Jermyn Street. As dawn broke, the streetlamps (the first in London, recently installed by the Co-partnership of the New Invention of Lights) were extinguished by the watchman and the bells of St James's Church rang out the hour. The servants rose to begin their round of morning chores: slopping out, opening the shutters, lugging in the sea-coal, and the tradesmen's and milkmaid's deliveries. Suddenly, their routines were rudely interrupted. Two officers arrived at the door and informed the footman that they had come to arrest his master on charges of high treason.

A disciple of Titus Oates, named Young, had accused Marlborough and Godolphin, among others, of participating in a Jacobite conspiracy to kill King William, and had forged a document to prove it. Young hid the document under a flowerpot at the Bishop of Rochester's house where it was discovered. In William's absence, the Council, chaired by Queen Mary, had taken immediate action. Marlborough was driven straight to the Tower. He was placed in a room at the top of the building, which probably had a fireplace, windows and servants. The costs of imprisonment were paid by prisoners, so conditions were as comfortable as they could afford.

When Sarah heard, she rushed from Syon to London, but was not allowed to see her husband for five days.[43] When Anne discovered that Marlborough was in the Tower, she wrote to Sarah that 'I can't help fearing they should hinder you from coming to me, though how they can do that without making you a prisoner I cannot imagine.' During the following weeks she sent many more letters of support and concern to her.[44] When Sarah went to St James's Palace to petition William, she was sometimes kept waiting for up to an hour and a half among the other common petitioners before she was admitted to his presence. She wrote: 'Some of our friends, who had lived in our family like near relations for many years, were so fearful of doing themselves hurt at Court that in the whole time of his confinement they never made him or me a visit, nor sent to enquire how we did, for fear that it should be known.'[45] Lady

Fitzharding was one such coward, and Mr Maul avoided her at this time, 'apprehending, I believe, that I should ask him to be Lord Marlborough's bail'.[46] In another draft, she pays tribute to Lord Bradford who visited Marlborough when others were too scared for their own careers.[47] Sarah's idea of history is a score-sheet of such little heroisms and moral failures.

After only one visit, Sarah was not allowed to see her husband again for six weeks, and feared that Young's plot would end in Marlborough's being sent to the scaffold. Her energy began to wane for the first time in her life. It was this period that she had in mind when she would later refer to the 'long persecution'[48] she suffered under King William. She was then struck by another blow: the death of her two-year-old son Charles. On 21 May, Anne, who had also just lost a newborn baby for the seventh time, sent Sarah her condolences, 'knowing very well what it is to lose a child', then quickly went on to report a failed reconciliation with Mary and to complain that she is 'sure never anybody was so used by a sister'. Two days later, having not heard back from Sarah, she wrote again, expressing concern for Sarah's health and saying that she would come to visit. Sarah was too grief-stricken to cope with the Princess, and refused her kind offer. It seems she always excluded Anne from such personal crises.

Meanwhile Marlborough wrote to Lords Danby and Devonshire, protesting his innocence and invoking his right to release on bail under the Act of Habeas Corpus. Having paid surety of £6,000, he was released. On 15 June, his case was brought before the King's Bench, and Young's forgery was exposed with relative ease.

During Marlborough's imprisonment, while Sarah was in London, a scene took place between Anne and Mary in a bedroom at Syon House, which Anne recounted to Sarah, who included it in her memoirs. Anne was lying, still clammy-browed, in her curtained box-bed after having given birth to another stillborn child. Her sister, accompanied by two ladies, came in but 'never asked her how she did, nor expressed the least concern for her condition, nor so much as took her by the hand. The salutation was this: "I have made the first step, by coming to you, and I now expect you should make the next by removing my Lady Marlborough."'[49] When Anne refused, Mary 'rose up and went away'. Soon afterwards Anne contracted a fever, which Sarah blamed on the quarrel. Sarah recorded the incident partly to show herself as symbolising the voluntary bond of friendship – like the voluntary contract between the People and the Parliament – in contrast to Anne's inescapable kinship with Mary. The story was reminiscent of Mary's heartless cheer as she entered Whitehall after deposing her father, suggesting that she lacked family feeling. Sarah thereby justified her refusal to obey her sovereign's order and resign from Anne's service.

During the summer of 1692, the Marlboroughs retreated to Holywell to recover from John's imprisonment and their son's death, while, in September, Anne and her husband moved from Syon to Berkeley House in Piccadilly, where they would live until King William's death. To attend on Anne, Sarah had to travel between this residence and her home in St Albans. She wrote of her sadness at seeing her daughter Henrietta watching from the window of Holywell House as she drove off to London.[50]

Sarah and the royal couple did not have an easy time while they were at Berkeley House because they were still out of favour at Court. At least once they ordered boats to go to the playhouse, but in general they lived 'in a very quiet way' and regularly attended St James's Church across the street. Several times the couple's son, the Duke of Gloucester, was sent to Hampton Court to wait on his aunt and uncle, where Sarah's sharp eye for spin saw that they 'made a great show of kindness to him, and gave him rattles and several play-things, which were constantly put down in the *Gazette*'. When he was ill, representatives of the King and Queen were sent to visit him but told to ignore his mother. Even if she were in the same room they took no more notice of her, said Sarah, 'than if she were a rocker'.[51]

Mary continued to snub and punish her sister and Sarah. In September 1692, for example, they travelled to take the waters in Bath and found that the Lord Mayor was under orders not to receive Anne as royalty. In the archives today, the ornate document containing the orders (for which Sarah claimed her old enemy Lord Rochester, Anne's uncle, was responsible)[52] is juxtaposed with the scrappy notes sent by Anne to Sarah saying that they must learn to laugh off such insults.[53]

Throughout 1693, Anne's letters continued to flow, but although 'one kind word . . . would save me if I were gasping', Sarah did not write back with any regularity. Anne was also disappointed when a hoped-for visit was cancelled and referred to 'your dear company which the more one knows you the more one must covet'. Her loneliness screams from the page: '[M]y happiness or unhappiness depends wholly on my dear Mrs Freeman, for as long as I have possession of the second place in her heart I can never be the last . . .'

Since the Revolution, Robert, 2nd Earl of Sunderland, an infamous apostate who had served James II as a Catholic, had been gradually working his way back into political favour to the extent that he had become one of William's advisers and retaken his seat in the House of Lords. In August 1693, Sunderland organised a 'Meeting of Great Men'[54] at Althorp. It aimed to reconcile Anne's rival Court with that of William and Mary.

In her memoirs, Sarah called Sunderland 'a man of sense and breeding'.[55] Despite her claims to be immune to flattery, she overlooked qualities in him that she despised in others, solely because of his charm and the cultural kudos of Althorp with its elegant layout and impressive library. It might have been on his advice that Sarah retired to St Albans in early 1693 and, uncharacteristically, avoided politics during this period of reconciliation. On 11 January, Anne wrote that 'Mrs Freeman can do nothing that is so much for her faithful Morley's service as to continue her kindness and never have the least thought of leaving her', but in effect Sarah had already left. 'I cannot help envying everybody's happiness that can go to St Albans,' Anne cried and signed off, 'Farewell my dear dear life. I am, if it be possible, more than ever yours . . .' In February Anne wrote again, saying that though her life in exile from the Court was dull she did not regret her actions. Sarah's temporary absence seems to have benefited Sunderland's initiative, which ended the King and Queen's slights against Anne's circle.

Meanwhile Sarah had been preoccupied with nursing her mother, who had been ill for several years and was living with another widowed friend, Elizabeth, Countess of Anglesey, at Newport Street in south London. In earlier dutiful notes she had promised to do favours for her mother, such as obtaining some money for Lady Anglesey from the Treasury. In October 1691 she wrote to say she had been able to obtain a hundred pounds but no more.

By 1693 the frequency with which Anne offered consolation in her letters to Sarah indicates that Mrs Jennings, who had moved to St Albans to live with the Marlboroughs, was dying.[56] Anne offered to supply doctors and send milk from the ass in St James's Park, believing this to 'cool and sweeten' the blood. She urged Sarah neither to neglect her own health nor to forget to eat and drink.

On 27 July 1693 Mrs Jennings died. Sarah had received a malicious penny-post letter from an anonymous enemy referring back to when she 'got your mother turned out of your lodgings'.[57] Anne wrote to reassure her that, despite the public arguments with her mother before her marriage, she had nothing with which to reproach herself: '[Y]ou have shown yourself the best and tenderest daughter that ever was.'

For her part, Mrs Jennings's will[58] is testimony that she loved and trusted her youngest daughter. Sarah was its primary beneficiary, but her mother included the unusual injunction, which harks back to Sarah's father's improvidence, that she should manage her legacy without Marlborough's interference. In the event, all Sarah received was debt.

In August 1693, John Closterman began a portrait of Sarah's children; perhaps the deaths of her mother and little Charles had prompted the desire for a family memento. This picture is almost certainly the large portrait of Sarah and her five living children, Elizabeth, Mary, Henrietta, Anne and John, that hangs today in the entrance hall at Blenheim. Sarah sits centre-stage in a lavish satin gown, while her daughters, their faces almost as careworn as hers, hold their usual symbolic fruit baskets and sprigs. The Duke was added later, in an extension to the left-hand side of this picture. He alone looks relaxed, amused and fresh-faced, perhaps because he was painted by John Riley, who finished the picture for Closterman in 1697. The result is that his rather incidental, advisory role in family life during these years is emphasised by the picture's unintended composition: he could afford to be detached and beloved, while Sarah played matriarch in the centre.

The death of Mrs Jennings marked the start for Sarah of a long-running argument with her sister when Frances discovered that she had not been 'so much as named' in their mother's will. In 1694, Frances reproached Sarah for not having secured the return of her husband's property, as had happened with other Jacobites through the help of their families. Sarah's long reply, one of the few letters written in her thirties that survives, opened with the hope that 'I shall be in better temper to answer . . . than I believe you were at the writing,' and she answered Frances's accusations systematically. Far from being 'careless' in helping her sister to regain her Irish property, Sarah said she had done everything in her power to help – even, in 1693, petitioning Queen Mary despite their bad relations. She remarked impatiently that if Frances had renounced her Jacobitism sooner and come to plead for forgiveness, she might have been luckier, and emphasised the unique strength of the opposition felt by the Lord Justices of Ireland to Frances as widow of the repressive Lord Tyrconnel.

Of their mother's will, she wrote: 'I know nothing but debts you are excluded from.' This is an interesting insight into Sarah's own financial anxieties at a time when John remained effectively unemployed, with five children to support. Sarah emphasised that she had not influenced her mother in making it and went on to detail the costs attached to the inheritance. She concluded with words that sealed the end of their communication for several years: 'I must own with the same plainness you express in yours,

I am much more indifferent as to what you think of me since I had your last letter than I thought I could ever have been.'

The historian Macaulay accused Marlborough of disclosing to the French, in May 1694, William's intention to destroy the French fleet in the harbour of Brest, which led to the catastrophic defeat of the English expedition. A handwritten note in James II's memoirs indeed confirms that Churchill was the traitor. Sarah requires defence on a similar charge. Several early historians implied that Sarah's gossiping with her sister Frances led to the French discovery of William's expedition to Dunkirk, which, like Brest, had ended in disaster. Their sources were fictional: Mrs Manley's *The Secret History of Queen Zarah* (1705), for example, or Defoe's pamphlet *No Queen: or, No General* (1712). In *The Other Side of the Question* (1742) James Ralph repeated the story, adding a mercenary motive, that Sarah sold the Dunkirk plans to her sister Lady Tyrconnel 'for what she could get' – implausible given that Sarah's assets were so much greater than her sister's. But as usual the slander related to an uncomfortable truth: Sarah's tie to an exiled sister whose husband had been accused of high treason in 1689.

While vindicating herself on lesser accusations, Sarah must have thought it beneath her to refute this charge of treason in her memoirs, leaving others to defend her. Henry Fielding, for example, in *A Full Vindication of the Duchess Dowager of Marlborough* (1742) asked why, if it were true, William never made the accusation public even when he was most opposed to the Marlboroughs' influence over the Princess, or when Marlborough was in the Tower, or even during his trial regarding Young's forgeries.[59]

In the winter of 1694, the Marlboroughs enjoyed a dramatic reversal of fortune. Queen Mary had smallpox. Anne, despite the risk to her own health, wrote to her estranged sister offering to visit her.[60] Mary refused curtly. She died on 28 December, leaving William as sole monarch. A reconciliation between William and Anne, his heir, was therefore prudent and, Sarah noted in her memoirs, opposed by none but William's favourite, Lord

Portland. Sarah also wrote cynically of the Court returning to flock around Anne after Mary's death and the 'half-witted Lord Caermarthen' saying to her that he hoped she would remember he came to wait on her when no one else did.[61] Lady Sandwich was among those quick to resume contact with Sarah: 'I have at this time but one wish in the world which is that you may know how much I value you', but the real point of her letter was the postscript: 'I don't know whether I may presume to present my humble duty to the Princess or no?'

Sarah described how Anne made her first political decision under these changed circumstances. She was advised by Ministers to write William a very deferential note of condolence, which would pave the way for closer relations.[62] In view of the treatment Anne had received from her brother-in-law over the past three years, Sarah objected strongly to these insincere expressions. Anne, however, was afraid to take the advice of an uneducated woman over experienced men, who were beginning to impress the weight of her responsibilities upon her. She therefore sidelined Sarah, whose ignored advice was, in the event, fully vindicated: William did not reply.

In December 1695, Sarah moved with Anne into lodgings at the south-east corner of St James's Palace: they were back in the corridors of power. Above St James's Gate, someone scrawled: 'Here Reigns Queen Sarah and K(ing) John . . .'[63]

By this time, Anne had become too lame to climb the Palace stairs. She was only thirty, but already riddled with gout, morbidly obese, and strangely resigned to this. Although he was at war with England, Louis XIV sent her a newfangled invention called a 'wheelchair', which she loved, but Swift's image of the invalid Queen driving her hunting chaise through Windsor Great Park 'furiously like Jehu' must have been flattery. Although Sarah was five years Anne's senior, her health and stamina were far stronger, so if she had felt bored and claustrophobic when closeted alone with Anne as teenagers, she felt doubly so now.

Anne's gout was a subject of public horror when she later became queen: her opponents commonly used images of diseased putrefaction as a metaphor for the country's political ill-health.[64] 'Gout' was then a catch-all term applied to many kinds of inflammation that were not properly understood, but Anne probably had it in its true sense: it was known to be caused by uric acid in the blood that left deposits in the joints. Gout seems to afflict societies undergoing a transition from simple to rich diets, and is therefore as common today in westernising, third-world countries as it was among the upper classes in eighteenth-century England. In several letters Anne asked Sarah to supply her with drinking chocolate, and Daniel Defoe, in his newspaper *The Review*, wrote a semi-serious editorial on the increasing weight of English women and speculating that it was due to the fashion for drinking chocolate.[65] Considering the excruciating pain of gout, it was truly a declaration of love for Anne to write to Sarah that 'I swear I could with pleasure endure ten thousand fits of the gout or any rack in the world if it could but be a relief to my dear Mrs Freeman when she is in trouble.' Anne's invalidism is reason enough to believe that her relationship with Sarah was no longer, if it ever had been, physical.

Politically, the years 1695 and 1696 were plagued by Jacobite intrigue, with the Duke of Berwick, Marlborough's nephew, planning an invasion of England supported by the French. In June 1695, on the birthday of James II's son, revels in the Dog Tavern had turned into a full-scale riot in Drury Lane. The mob, probably a mixture of ex-soldiers and Irishmen, had clashed with a pro-Williamite group, the latter proving the tougher. There was no widespread popular enthusiasm for Jacobitism, but the violence was real enough.[66]

With hindsight, Sarah's fears of a Jacobite invasion might seem like hysteria. However, each conspiracy on English soil was mirrored by French troop movements and naval preparations, about which, in her privileged position, she would have heard. On 22 February 1696, William uncovered what became known as the 'Fenwick Conspiracy', in which Marlborough and Godolphin were, again, implicated. Sir John Fenwick, a genuine Jacobite, tried to embarrass the government by revealing the dealings of prominent Ministers with the exiled James, and in July testified that Marlborough and Godolphin had received pardons from Saint-Germains, which, of course, was true. William may not have regarded this as treason in itself, but he would have been publicly embarrassed if it was proven to be true and no action was taken. Luckily Fenwick also named Lords Shrewsbury and Russell, and William did not want to sacrifice these two leading Ministers. The government discredited the confession, and Marlborough and Godolphin were cleared alongside the others. Only Fenwick was beheaded in January 1697.

The Fenwick Conspiracy did, however, create a setback in Marlborough's professional rehabilitation, and Godolphin was dismissed from the Treasury. In the summer of 1697, he moved in with the Marlboroughs at Holywell House, and thereafter kept his own set of rooms in all their houses. Whenever her husband was away at war, Sarah turned to Godolphin for advice and company.

So far Godolphin's career had paralleled Marlborough's. He had been elected to the Cavalier Parliament as MP for Helston.[67] He had served as Groom of the Bedchamber to Charles II (who described him as 'never in the way and never out of the way'), as an ambassador for James II, and then in William's Treasury. By nature he was an accountant, not always courageous or creative but his skill at managing the Treasury was consummate.

On Sarah's instruction, Burnet immortalised Godolphin as 'the silentest and modestest man that was perhaps ever bred in a court. He had a clear apprehension and dispatched business with great method, and with so much temper that he had no personal enemies.' Jonathan Swift, on the other hand, described him having 'tears at his command, like a woman, to be used either in an intrigue of gallantry or politics'.[68] Sarah grew to respect Godolphin, and he was unfailingly loyal to her. She said that Godolphin 'was no way concerned in making the Revolution & disliked it very much', yet despite this she was responsible for his rise, alongside her husband, when Anne became queen.

Their friendship stands out, along with certain other friendships between men and women of the late seventeenth century, such as that between Godolphin's wife and John Evelyn, or that between John Locke and Lady Damaris Masham, as a tribute to individual common sense overcoming custom in a sexist society.

It was probably during their period of retirement from Court following the Fenwick Conspiracy that Sarah and Godolphin arranged the marriage of their two eldest children. Godolphin's son Francis, a tepid young man, was married to Henrietta Churchill on 28 April 1698, when she was seventeen and he was twenty. In the first years of their marriage, they lived with Sarah at St James's and St Albans.

With one daughter down and three to go, Sarah arranged a courtship between the second eldest, Anne Churchill, and the young widower Charles Spencer, son of her old friend Lady Sunderland, who wrote a long letter welcoming their children's proposed engagement.[69] With this idea, Sarah can be credited with the foundation of the Spencer-Churchill dynasty. She hesitated over the match, however. Politically, Spencer was close to her: he was already, at twenty-four, a rising Whig star in Parliament, and she described him to Queen Anne as 'very warm in his temper but very honest and very firm in the true interest of his country, very diligent in business & very disinterested'.[70] She might almost have chosen the same words to describe herself, and in many ways Charles Spencer was the man Sarah might have been. On a personal level, however, she found him lacking: he had 'no more genteelness than a porter'[71] and his face, she said, was one giant smallpox scar. The courtship between him and her strikingly attractive daughter dragged on for almost two years before Sarah decided on it.

Anne had offered to help the Marlboroughs pay Henrietta's dowry.[72] Sarah wrote a note on the Princess's letter, explaining that she would accept only half of the £10,000 offered, and no more than £5,000 for each of her other daughters. Depicting herself as the most virtuous of royal favourites, she observed that 'in all the time that I lived at Court I can't give one instance of any person that ever refused any bounty', an observation mocked by one of her memoirs' reviewers who sarcastically described accepting the £5,000 as '[t]he bravest, noblest Thing alive'.73 Anne wrote back on 23 October 1697 saying that she was reluctant to give Henrietta only £5,000, but would agree if that was what Sarah wanted, and added 'where one owes so much one can never get out of debt'.

In 1697 Sarah was responsible for preserving Anne's money in other ways. She spotted that Sir Benjamin Bathurst, Frances Apsley's husband, was paying Anne her income incorrectly after the recoinage in 1696.74 By 1698 she had helped the Princess to uncover the extent of Bathurst's extortion from cooks and other servants at St James's and together the women wrote a letter confronting him with it.75 It was these little services to Anne, while greater political service was not open to her, that moved Anne to write to Sarah: '[S]ince there is nobody perfect but dear Mrs Freeman I must have patience with the rest of the world and look as much into all my affairs as I can. If I were not satisfied with you I should be the greatest monster that ever breathed, for as I have often said, I do really believe there never was nor will be such a friend as dear Mrs Freeman.'

During the 1690s, whenever she was at leisure in St Albans, Sarah began to read: she tried political, philosophical and religious tracts and even some fiction, but concentrated, like her male contemporaries, on classical authors. She had decided she must be an educated mother to her son, the main rationale offered by the feminist Mary Astell in her 1697 tract on women's education. With her husband so often overseas, it was up to her to monitor his tutoring, and how could she be sure that he was being properly educated if she did not know the authors he read?

She read Burton's *Anatomy of Melancholy*, Seneca, Montaigne, the first book of the *Aeneid*76 and the poems and essays of Abraham Cowley. Anne asked Sarah to send her her thoughts on reading Seneca, a philosopher who dealt with how to live a moral life in the midst of wealth. Sarah also read Francis

Bacon's essays, no doubt finding much in 'Of Followers and Friends' (1597) and 'Of Friendship' (1612) that was relevant to her own situation.

Many of her friends were baffled by Sarah's interest in books. Lady Scarborough, one of the few friends who had continued to visit her when she and Anne were expelled from William and Mary's Court, wrote to Sarah that she would turn out 'so wise and learned that you will despise us poor mortals and a pack of cards, and will sit reading in your chamber all day. But I hope you are not so changed.'77

While Sarah oversaw the education of their son, Marlborough was appointed in 1698 to be a governor, alongside Bishop Burnet, to Anne's one surviving child, the nine-year-old Duke of Gloucester. This was part of the general easing of relations between William and Princess Anne's circle as memory of the Fenwick episode faded – his first Court appointment since his stay in the Tower.

After the treaty of Ryswick in September 1697 had brought French recognition of William as King of England and Anne as his rightful heir, William felt able to relax his monitoring of Jacobite activities. They were permitted to travel freely between London and Saint-Germains, for example, and it was amid this atmosphere of toleration that Sarah appears to have made the first move to re-establish contact with her sister. Frances wrote gratefully from France:

Your letter made me wet it more than you could have done when a-writing and if you can in the least remember the real passion and inclination I ever had for you, tis what you will easily believe, and I must again affirm that in my whole life I never did love any thing better than yourself . . . Your pure and honest heart is a comfort to find when one sees so little in anybody one imagined would be counted upon.

In the following year, 1699, Sarah received a number of notes from Frances thanking her for small gifts. Sarah had sent her a 'magnificent parcel of cheeses', for example, bought at her favourite cheese shop by the Three Horseshoes in Newgate Street next to St Martin's. She also sent furniture as ordered, but Frances often complained about mistakes in the deliveries.

During 1699, Princess Anne's monotonous letters continued to arrive while Sarah was at Althorp with her friends Lord and Lady Sunderland, supervising her daughter's courtship. Anne confessed her insecurities: 'I hope you will pardon my uneasinesses since they proceed from the humble opinion I have of myself and the great passion I have for you.' The litany of minor ailments and other misfortunes that apparently stopped Sarah from writing 'mortify me extremely because I think it would look like growing cold; I know you hate writing & so do I & to people that are indifferent to me I have been three hours writing a dozen lines, but methinks when one's heart goes along with one's pen tis no difficult matter to write half that number . . .'

The marriage of Sarah's daughter Anne – nicknamed 'The Little Whig' by her mother's Whig friends[78] and 'Eyelashes' by Godolphin[79] – to Charles Spencer went ahead on 2 January 1700. Despite Sarah's misgivings it proved a singularly happy match: Anne made an excellent wife to a husband every bit as uxorious as her father. Unlike Henrietta, she did not have to start her married life living at home; Charles soon made her mistress of St Albans House in St James's Square, and then of Clarges House in Piccadilly, later renamed Sunderland House, across the street from Mr Fortnum's new grocery store.

In the summer of that year, while the Marlboroughs were with the Sunderlands at Althorp, they received news that the young Duke of Gloucester, who had suffered from encephalitis since birth, was dangerously ill. They rushed to London to be with Anne who, according to Burnet, nursed her son herself 'with a grave composedness that amazed all who saw it'. On 30 July, however, the boy died. Sarah comforted Anne, while facing the fact that Marlborough was again without an appointment and an avenue of lucrative employment had been closed to her other relatives. Sarah's remark concerning William's overly hasty dismissal of the Duke of Gloucester's servants without further pay, showing 'a diligence of frugality which was surely not very decent in a king',[80] no doubt reflected some of this personal disappointment, though Marlborough remained on the Privy Council and one of the nine Lord Justices.

The death of Gloucester also left in doubt the continuation of a Protestant monarchy, and prompted the House of Lords to seek an Act of Settlement whereby after Anne the Throne would pass to her cousin the Princess Sophia, Electress of Hanover and granddaughter of James I, or to her descendants. However, the Act passed in June 1701 went further: in implied criticism of the way William was ruling, it decreed that a monarch could neither make war using English troops merely to defend his or her foreign possessions, nor appoint foreigners to English offices, nor give them land – as William had to his favourites, Portland and Albemarle. It also detached, to some extent, control of the judiciary from the Crown.

With the Act of Settlement in place, William could concentrate on his chief concern: containing Louis XIV's expansionist ambitions. Charles II of Spain ('The Sufferer') had died childless in 1700, and the terms of his will undermined the first and second Partition treaties between England and France, which had agreed on compromise partition of the Spanish empire for the sake of maintaining the balance of power in Europe. Charles bequeathed Spain in its entirety to Louis XIV's grandson, which was too much of a temptation for Louis. He accepted the offer and, knowing that this would provoke war, immediately pounced on Dutch garrisons.

If the French succeeded in securing the Spanish throne by force, their commercial power would be unassailable and the buffer zone of the Spanish Netherlands between France and England would be removed.[81] More cynically, the resumption of war with France was desired by England because it wanted to keep the world's markets open for its cloth and other trade.

In June 1701, William appointed Marlborough Commander-in-Chief and Plenipotentiary in treaty negotiations to form a new Grand Alliance of European powers to prevent French succession to the Spanish throne. This was recognition not only of Marlborough's proven military ability but also of the fact that, with Anne now certain to succeed, Marlborough would be her key adviser – thanks to his wife's personal bond with her.

In July when Marlborough left for The Hague, he wrote to Sarah apologising for not having said a longer goodbye to her at the docks because he had been 'so little master of myself that I should have exposed myself to the people in the street' by weeping. Sarah wrote him a tender note in return: 'Wherever you are whilst I have life, my soul shall follow you, my ever dear Ld Marl; & wherever I am, I shall only kill time, wish for night that I may sleep, & hope next day to hear from you.'[82] William himself accompanied Marlborough to The Hague, but also with him were two professional associates who were to be by his side for the next twenty years: William Cadogan, a burly Irishman who had fought as a boy in the Battle of the Boyne, and Adam de Cardonnell, the son of a French Protestant refugee, who acted as Marlborough's secretary.

When Sarah wrote asking to join him, Marlborough told her it was safer, with a world war brewing, for her to remain in England. Apparently she wore down his objections, for on 7 September she was in The Hague to witness the ceremonial signing of the second treaty of Grand Alliance against France, which Anthonie Heinsius, Grand Pensionary of Holland, and the Hapsburg representatives, Count Wratislaw and Count Goëss, had negotiated. Sarah travelled there with her two unmarried daughters, Mary and Elizabeth, and stayed with her husband at the Mauritshuis. This was the grand home built in 1634 by Pieter Post and Jacob van Campen for a wealthy sugar merchant, which had stood empty since William and Mary had left for England in 1688. It was an amazingly eccentric house, full of rich Brazilian woods and exotic imports such as stuffed crocodiles. The walls were covered in frescoes of life in Brazil and Africa. The ceiling of the banqueting hall had a glass dome in which musicians could sit and play unseen behind a gallery so that it seemed as if music were descending from the heavens. Outside, to the rear, a garden full of grottoes and Indian water birds was reached from the house by an underground passage.[83]

All this Golden Age splendour, which must have been enjoyed by the Churchill ladies in 1701, was destroyed by one of their servants three years later. Adam de Cardonnell's servant got drunk while lighting fires in advance of Marlborough's arrival. The entire house and its contents went up in smoke, though without any injuries.[84] Today all that remain are the house's classical exterior and its front view over the Vijver lake.

While in The Hague, Sarah and her daughters were entertained with excursions to Amsterdam and Antwerp. Sarah paid a thousand guilders to Mr Michel of Antwerp for some Flemish lace.[85] In October they visited Het Loo, William's hunting lodge, with Lord and Lady Albemarle, and Sarah felt disadvantaged because she spoke no Continental languages. She told the anecdote that while she was at Loo, William asked what she thought of Lady Albemarle and added, as if trying to ingratiate himself, 'Don't flatter her.' Sarah pointed out that she held her tongue but wanted to reply by asking, 'Why he should think I would flatter her since I had never flattered him?'[86]

Marlborough astutely realised that William was creating resentment by returning to England only when he needed to extract money from Parliament, and that for the war effort to succeed it was necessary for a wider circle to feel responsible. However, on 5 September 1701, James II died in exile and Louis XIV violated the treaty of Ryswick by recognising his son as James III of England. This led to a wave of outraged Protestant patriotism in England and forced the Tories in Parliament to accept that war was now unavoidable to secure not only the Spanish but also the English succession. Stretching the point, William told the House of Commons that it was 'an inevitable necessity in our defence'.[87]

While Anne and Sarah differed in appearance, energy, sense of humour, political leanings, level of emotional neediness, manner and temper, they were identical in ambition. In Anne's case this had shown itself in her hostile attitude towards the Prince of Wales's birth, and towards her sister Mary when she had tried to give Anne orders. Therefore, when William died suddenly on 8 March 1702 after a fall from his horse, Anne and her favourite were both more than ready to assume power.

On the evening of 10 March, Marlborough, Godolphin and the Speaker of the House of Commons, Robert Harley, had held a secret meeting at Godolphin's house to plan the course of the new government. On the following day, Anne arrived to make her first speech to the House of Lords, accompanied by the Marlboroughs. On 23 April, she was crowned at Westminster Abbey.

Sarah was in charge of the spectacle of the coronation. She dressed Anne in red velvet lined with ermine, to resemble a famous portrait of Elizabeth I.[88] This patriotic costume matched her famous declaration that day that her heart was entirely English. One observer, Narcissus Luttrell, recorded that 'Her Majesty was carried in an open chair of state by four Yeomen of the Guard, under the royal canopy supported by four dukes.' With her enormous bulk and gouty legs, Anne must have struggled to carry off the glamour and dignity of the occasion. As her subjects had to demonstrate their loyalty to her in compliments, many chose to remark on her voice and gestures. The Bishop of Rochester read the service and the Tory Archbishop of York, Dr Sharp, preached a sermon to which Sarah later made a scathing reference.[89] Finally the Archbishop of Canterbury read the coronation oath, and Anne was carried home to Westminster Hall for a six o'clock supper with Sarah.

It was then believed that, on assuming the Crown, a queen should become metaphorically masculine, or at least androgynous. In her speech at Tilbury Elizabeth I had boasted that she had 'the heart and stomach of a King', and throughout Sarah's correspondence we find references to Queen Anne as England's 'Prince'.[90] People, it seemed, were not worried about having a queen, as long as she was not too womanly. Queen Mary's behaviour had frequently been depicted as too submissive to her husband, which did not make it easy for Anne subsequently to assert her authority.

Sarah, regarded as a transgressively ambitious wife who wore the trousers in her family, was therefore a real asset to Anne at this point in her career. Just as she shaped history's image of Anne, she was the impresario responsible for projecting the living Queen's public image. Precisely because she herself did not see the nimbus around the throne, Sarah could help to create it.

The stage-management worked. In *The Prerogative of the Breeches* (1702) Anne was complimented for having a 'masculine spirit beneath the softer body of a woman',[91] and when she went on her first royal tour, she entered Bath to be met by a performance of 'two hundred maids richly dressed and carrying bows and arrows like Amazons'.[92] In this context of attempts to emphasise Anne's manlike characteristics, the fact that she was a bit too fond of her female favourites was not yet treated as problematic.

Sarah still thought of Anne as a puppet to which she was lucky enough to hold the strings: the Queen, she said, 'would not go to take the air unless somebody advised her to it'. Bishop Burnet wrote in his *History* that when Anne came to the Throne, Sarah 'had an ascendant over her in everything'. From Anne's piles of sentimental letters we can understand how Sarah herself had formed this impression, and so share her surprise when the ascendancy proved short-lived.

4

The Glass Ceiling

A posthumous satire addressed to Sarah observed that it dated 'your throwing off Indolence and Cards and commencing the British-female Machiavel'[1] from the moment Anne became queen. A critic of her memoirs described this as the point at which she changed from being 'merely the Princess of Denmark's FAMILIAR to your being held the evil GENIUS of the whole State'.[2] Sarah put it less dramatically: after William III's death, 'I began to be looked upon as a person of consequence. Hitherto my favour with her ROYAL HIGHNESS, though it sometimes furnished matter of conversation to the public, had been of no moment to the affairs of the nation.'[3]

That Sarah's 'favour' might affect the nation's affairs was not as inevitable as she supposed. Determined to be taken seriously, Anne was not prepared to be seen running her government on the basis of a female friend's opinions. On the one hand, Sarah was the lynchpin in the alliance between Marlborough, Godolphin and the Queen, which gave the highest positions of government a uniquely personal cohesion, yet on the other, as a woman untransformed by the power of sovereignty, she was the most dispensable of the four. Many years later, writing to her friend Captain Humphrey Fyshe, Sarah recalled, with some bitterness: 'In the late Queen's time, though I was a favourite, without the help of the Duke of Marlborough and Lord Godolphin I should not have been able to do anything of consequence, and the things that are worth naming will ever [only] be done from the influence of men.'[4] From a modern perspective, it is this glass ceiling, on which she almost immediately cracked her head, that overshadows Sarah's life after 1702.

Meanwhile, her husband benefited at once from being Mrs

Freeman's spouse. He was made a Knight of the Garter and Captain-General of the army, and was promptly dispatched to The Hague to reassure the continental allies that William's war aims would be pursued by Anne's government. In May, Sidney Godolphin similarly received his reward for having stood by the Freemans and Morleys when they were out of favour at the court of William and Mary: he was appointed Treasurer.

Sarah was now Groom of the Stole, Mistress of the Robes and Keeper of the Privy Purse. These were three of the top posts in the Queen's household, and certainly the most lucrative that could be awarded to a woman. They gave Sarah a personal income of £5,600 per annum, which was paid into an account in her own name. Since the 1680s, the royal bedchamber had come under the Groom of the Stole's jurisdiction, the only department in the Queen's household that was not under the control of the Lord Chamberlain.[5]

The Groom of the Stole was given ten rooms at Kensington Palace and was responsible for the Queen's bedchamber staff, which consisted of the ten Ladies of the Bedchamber, who were permitted to touch the Queen's body, four Bedchamber Women, who did most of the work, six Maids of Honour, and various lower offices including six pages, a 'Necessary Woman', a seamstress, a starcher, a laundress and two coffer-bearers. As Mistress of the Robes, Sarah also appointed and oversaw the 'Robes staff', consisting of a yeoman, two grooms, two waiters and a handful of tradesmen. The Court, though rigidly hierarchical, was unusual among early modern institutions in that it contained this wide range of people from every social stratum, all living and travelling together. Sarah's posts were not sinecures and her managerial skills needed to be more polished than those of the mistresses of great estates. To assist her, she brought to Court her favourite servant from St Albans, a country girl named Rachel Thomas,[6] and found a new young man to attend her when she went out in public; she selected him for the very good reason that he was 'the handsomest boy that ever I saw in my life'.[7] She also wasted no time in appointing three of her daughters – Henrietta, Anne and Mary – as Ladies of the Bedchamber.

As Keeper of the Privy Purse, Sarah prided herself on her bookkeeping, prompt payment and minor economies. Apart from pensions and other debts inherited from previous reigns, Sarah supervised Anne's supply of pocket-money, play-money, and charity-money, as well as other gifts to royal godchildren, such as their travel expenses, party costs and various 'Indian Things'.[8] Sarah defended her simple taste in dressing the Queen, which deprived the royal dressmakers of certain customary profits: 'Some people to be revenged of me for not letting them cheat have said she was not fine enough for a queen, but it would have been ridiculous with her person & of her age to have been otherwise dressed.' Although she kept tight purse-strings, Sarah insisted that nothing was ever found wanting in the royal household.

Initially, Sarah handed the Privy Purse accounts to a goldsmith for double-checking: her own banker, John Coggs, whose offices were 'over against St Clement's Church' in the warren of alleys south of Threadneedle Street. Later she sent them to a comptroller at the Exchequer to certify that there were no deductions for fees or poundage (a duty of so much per pound, payable on merchandise, which she might have pocketed on each of the Queen's transactions). It had been customary for the Keeper of the Privy Purse to note down sums of money given to the monarch, but Sarah introduced the practice of making Anne sign for every amount she received, no matter how small. She explained how, on the advice of the Duke of Montagu, she sometimes managed cash flow by transferring funds between the Privy Purse and the accounts for the Robes and the Wardrobe, but was adamant that she never borrowed from them for her own purposes.

The symbol of Sarah's power in the household, representing her unique access to the Queen, was the Gold Key. It opened the doors of the bedchamber, other private rooms and galleries, State and reception rooms, and all the garden gates. Several portraits of

Sarah can be dated conclusively post-1702 because this key hangs from her dress pocket.

Having grown up in Hertfordshire, Sarah appreciated the countryside, and was particularly pleased to be awarded the Rangership of Windsor Great Park. This not only enabled her to enjoy the herds of deer and long elm-lined vistas of the park itself, but to turn the Earl of Portland out of the Great Lodge, a beautiful house with high roofs and a façade twelve windows wide, which once sat at the end of the Long Walk. To observers, the hand-over of royal favourites was as obvious as the change in Cabinet Ministers.

To gain a sense of Sarah's influence, or at least the influence that was potentially hers to exert, it is necessary to define the powers Anne acquired when she became queen. Most significant was that no meeting of the Cabinet could take place without her, and its membership depended on whom she summoned to attend. The Cabinet had overtaken the unwieldy Privy Council as the main government decision-making body, and usually met after dinner on a Sunday evening. Traditionally the Lord Chancellor was the most senior member, but under Anne, thanks to her tie with Godolphin through the Marlboroughs, power shifted to the Treasurer.

Outside the Cabinet, Anne had the right of veto in the Houses of Parliament. The key debates took place in the House of Lords, which the Queen regularly attended 'on a bench at the fire' and subtly influenced by ignoring some speakers and taking notice of others.[9] Technically she was head of the executive, the legislature, the judiciary and, of course, the Church of England. She was responsible for the appointment of judges, but was also, herself, the final court of appeal.

It is inaccurate to date the decline of modern royal power to Anne's reign: her successor George I made himself into a figurehead because he did not attend Cabinet meetings and was unable to speak to his Ministers in English. Anne, by contrast, was so fearful of being treated as if she were simply keeping the Throne warm for the next king that she performed her duties with extraordinary diligence. As she wrote to Godolphin in 1707, 'Whoever of the Whigs thinks I am to be hectored or frighted into compliance though I am a woman, are mighty mistaken.'

A fortnight after the coronation, on 12 May 1702, the Marlboroughs set out together for Margate, from where John was due to sail for the Continent. After her husband's departure Sarah lingered in Kent, where she received letters from Anne.[10] She was told that 'whatever hurry I am in (which indeed is every day very great) I shall never forget the least service that lies in my poor power to do for my dear Mrs Freeman that I love more than words or actions can express . . .' But by July Anne was so busy with government business that Sarah must have felt her influence was slipping. In a letter in which their emotional roles seem for the first time reversed, Anne told Sarah to 'banish all your fears for there is, nor never will be, any cause for them. Oh no, your poor unfortunate faithful Morley has a constant heart, loves you tenderly, passionately and sincerely & knows the world too well (if I were of a fickle temper) ever to be charmed with anybody but your Dear Self.' She made plans to visit Sarah and added: 'I hope I shall get a moment or two to be with my dear Mrs Freeman that I may have one dear embrace, which I long for more than I can express.' The Queen now needed their friendship as an escape from her royal duties.

Marlborough, too, had plenty to keep him busy. He reported to Sarah on the campaign's progress, on overtures from his Jacobite nephew Berwick, on befriending the Elector of Hanover's brother, and on his efforts to unify his disgruntled allies. He complained, 'I am a-horseback or answering of letters all day long', which was hard because 'you know of all things I do not love writing.'[11] He claimed he would be happier if he had Sarah's quieter life in the orchards of St Albans, unconsciously soothing her repressed envy of the responsibilities Anne and he now both possessed.

Sarah made a point of letting them both know that *she* was the busy one. When Marlborough sent a petition from one of his men to the Queen via Sarah he wrote that he knew it was an unworthy one 'but twas impossible to refuse the sending of it, so that you will excuse it. It is not that I am unsensible [*sic*] of the trouble you have, for I do assure you I apprehend it so much that I would be very glad to give the only time I have to myself to ease you.'[12] At the same time, however, he seemed to rebuke Sarah for not having taken care of all his recommendations for patronage and because his friend James Craggs, 'a very honest man' who had joined with him during the Revolution, had not been named in the Ordnance. He ended, perhaps with too much qualification for Sarah's liking: 'Nothing can equal the happiness of my being with you when you are kind.'

The next day he continued the letter, asking Sarah for her 'account of what had passed between the Queen and Dutch Ambassadors concerning the Prince'. This was the important question of whether Marlborough or the militarily inexperienced Prince George was to be given overall command of the allied armies. Marlborough's enemies in London had tried to make the Queen suspicious of his personal ambition, suggesting that he was pushing himself forward at the expense of her husband.

The Dutch Envoy in London, René Saunière de l'Hermitage, wrote to Heinsius on 21 March 1702:

It is said that Holland must make the Prince of Denmark Captain-General of its armies in order to cement the alliance between the two States, and it is also said that this Prince will go to Holland to command the English troops and will have under him the Count of Marlborough, who will not trouble himself about leaving the Queen because the Countess his wife will always be near her, which is the same thing.[13]

When the allies finally gave Marlborough rather than Prince George their command, the Dutch ambassador informed Sarah personally.

Marlborough had already had cause to complain of the Dutch that he had been 'obliged to take more pains than I am well able to endure'.[14] He told his wife that the Queen must be persuaded to call an early Parliament to prove her commitment to the war, and suggested that she persuade Godolphin to lobby Anne. In this he was exerting influence at three removes and appearing to keep his soldier's nose out of domestic politics.

When Sarah complained that he did not appreciate her letters or answer them promptly, he reminded her gently that he had other preoccupations: 'I do assure you that your letters are so welcome to me that if they should come in the time I were expecting the enemy to charge me I could not forbear reading them.' If nothing else, he depended on them to monitor the 'envy and malice' which he felt was undermining him back at Westminster since his appointment.

The result of the July–August 1702 general election showed a shift away from the Whig bias of William's reign, and Sarah's lack of influence was immediately apparent from the composition of Anne's first Cabinet. The leading Tory, Lord Rochester, Anne's uncle, whom Sarah believed to have been behind the persecution of her husband under William and Mary, was given the Lieutenancy of Ireland (though he resigned within a year when Anne ordered him to actually live there). The Earls of Nottingham and Jersey, the Duke of Buckingham and Sir Edward Seymour were likewise brought into the Cabinet, and old Tory administrators like Francis Atterbury returned. Meanwhile, Anne purged the Court of all but the most moderate Whigs.

In her memoirs, Sarah explained her frustration at this initial rise in Tory power.[15] Suddenly forced to compete with Rochester for Anne's ear, Sarah dismissed his blood relationship with the Queen as 'a sort of accident' in contrast to her own elective affinity with her. She called it an 'amazing thing' that a man 'should imagine he is to dominate over the Queen . . . as he does in his own little family'.[16] Cunningham's 1742 review of Sarah's published memoir later turned this on its head and depicted it as a battle between honest claims of kinship and those of an unhealthily close friendship now turned mercenary: 'For the Queen's own relations being kept at a distance, all things were managed by the sole authority of one woman, to whom there was no access but by the golden road; and it was to no purpose for the Earl of Rochester to set forth his own duty, affection and the rights of consanguinity.'[17]

In fact, it was simply a battle between a Whig and a Tory, and two equally strong wills. Sarah claimed that she had never given the Rochesters 'any just cause of being angry with me' but that they simply could not endure her 'because I had the honour of serving the Princess against their will'.[18] The anecdote about Sarah chopping off her hair in a fit of rage is said to relate to an argument at around this time that erupted because Marlborough invited Rochester to dinner without asking Sarah first. He informed her of the extra guest only as she was sitting at her dressing-table. When he tried to placate her by complimenting her on her hair, she cut the long golden coil that usually hung over her right shoulder clean off.

Usually recounted to smirk at Sarah's self-defeating petulance, what this story actually tells us is that her temper was almost always a protest against a sense of powerlessness. When treated like a child-wife who could be flattered into submission, she simply cut away that part of herself. On the other hand, this story would never have come to light if Sarah herself had not given it a postscript with an altogether different meaning. In old age she told Lady Mary Wortley Montagu that Marlborough had secretly picked up the shorn tresses after the argument and put them into his chest as a keepsake, which Sarah only discovered while sorting through his belongings after his death. Suddenly a story about Sarah's childishness, or her frustrated feminism, becomes a love story about Sarah's value to her husband overriding both of these traits.[19]

The guides at Althorp and the present Earl Spencer[20] refer to an oval portrait of Sarah (catalogued as by Kneller) that supposedly shows Sarah still 'in a temper' after chopping off her hair. In fact, if it is Sarah, she looks unhappy rather than angry. Then, on closer inspection, it seems that the hair cupped in her hand is not severed at all, but just an extremely long strand that disappears in part under the darkening varnish. Other tourist guides sometimes relate the anecdote to another beautiful sketch in the Picture Gallery at Althorp, also said to be of Sarah by Kneller, which shows a young woman with apparently short hair. When this is inspected, however, it seems more probable that it was only half-completed, the hair not coloured in by the artist. As with the unflattering portrait of Sarah's mother, it remains entirely unclear why Sarah would have rushed to Kneller to have either image of herself after self-mutilation captured for all eternity.

It worked in Marlborough's favour that the French high command believed he had only gained his position thanks to his wife's relationship with the Queen: they were thus unprepared for the victories in the Spanish Netherlands he swiftly secured, including the successful sieges of Kaiserwerth, Venlo, Stevenswaert, Ruremonde and Liège. These triumphs were impressive, but that Anne chose to offer him his reward in a letter to his wife shows that her relationship with Sarah remained just as important a factor in the family's advancement. In October 1702, Anne wrote that although she knew 'my dear Mrs Freeman does not care for anything of that kind', she would like to offer Marlborough a dukedom when he returned.[21] Sarah recorded in her memoirs that 'if there be any truth in a mortal' the offer made her uneasy: 'I let it drop out of my hand & was for some minutes like one that had received the news of the death of one of their dear friends.' She presented herself as almost a parody of indifference ('I fear you will think what I say upon this subject is affected'), and wished to distance herself in her readers' minds from those who failed to conceal their craving for ennoblement ('I have no taste for grandeur'). She went on to explain, however, that her unease was not motivated so much by modesty as by, more plausibly, the practical fear that a dukedom would place too great a financial strain on her family. The growing prosperity of the 'middling sort' during this period was inflating the cost of demonstrating one's nobility through conspicuous consumption, and Sarah worried that if her husband died at war, their son Jack would be ruined by the lifestyle a duke was obliged to support.

In early November Marlborough wrote to his wife from The Hague, 'I do agree with you that we ought not to wish for a greater title till we have a better estate', but two days later, having taken advice from Pensioner Heinsius, who had become a close friend, he had changed his mind. He wrote that they ought to accept the dukedom now, immediately after his military victories, because at another time the gift might be 'thought the effect of favours, which would not be so great an honour to my family'. (Still mocked for his affair with Barbara Castlemaine, he had learned the cost of having his promotions viewed as dependent on personal relationships.) He ended his letter, however, by saying that he would be governed 'by you two', meaning Sarah and Godolphin, on the Queen's offer.

Sarah must have spoken to Anne about their qualms. There is also evidence that she persuaded Godolphin to talk to Anne on their behalf, for the Queen made a further offer: a pension of £5,000 was attached to the title. Marlborough pushed for this to be settled by Parliament on his heirs in perpetuity – which John Evelyn was not alone in thinking greedy[22] – but the private Bill was defeated by Rochester. To compensate, Anne offered the Marlboroughs £2,000 per annum from the Privy Purse: 'I think the richest Crown could never repay the services that I have received from you,' she wrote.[23] Sarah said they could not possibly accept the money and later boasted of her refusal. She knew that such ostentatious gifts would only attract criticism, and preferred to drop hints concerning her remaining two daughters' dowries. However, she did not forget the £2,000 offer and kept a copy of the Queen's letter. So, on 2 December 1702, Anne publicly proclaimed the new dukedom and Sarah became a duchess, though she would never be able to overcome her sense of inferiority to those like the Duchess of Ormonde who boasted of the ancient bloodlines behind their titles.[24]

At the end of her life a literary attack dated Sarah's antipathy to the Tories from their defeat of the Bill regarding the Marlboroughs' ducal income.[25] Similarly her friend Francis Hare later confessed to her that, as things looked to him 'who only saw the outside', Sarah had seemed a natural Tory when Anne first came to the throne.[26] By rights Sarah should have had an aversion to the Whigs, 'confirmed by the ill usage she had met with' under William and Mary, while the Tories had 'paid her more than usual civilities' as a means of expressing their opposition to the King and Queen while the Cockpit Circle was exiled from London.[27] But Sarah continued to claim that her Whig zeal was innate and that it 'could proceed from nothing but conviction of the goodness of the cause I espoused. For, as to private interest, the Whigs could have done nothing for my advantage more than the Tories.'[28] It is certainly more likely that the Tories defeated the Bill because Sarah was already known as a Whig sympathiser and opponent to Rochester, rather than that her loyalty to the Whigs sprang from this disappointment.

Since Parliament had acquired enhanced powers in 1688, there had been a notable growth of lobby groups, mostly based on regional interests and guilds. Increasingly hired agents went to Parliament to monitor legislation and liaise with the clerks, or visited Ministers of State between nine and eleven each morning. Those who wished to influence the Queen looked to Sarah as their best intermediary.

The nature of Sarah's own lobbying can be guessed from Anne's replies to her letters. Some time in late 1702 or early 1703 Anne wrote: 'I am entirely of my dear Mrs Freeman's mind that the heat & ambition of Church men has done a great deal of hurt to this poor nation, but it shall never do it any harm in my time . . .' This is presumably an answer to Sarah having warned that the High Anglicans, or 'High-Flyers', were as dangerous to religious pluralism as the Catholics. (Unrelated to today's 'High Anglicans', this was an essentially political movement of the lower clergy against their superiors, appointments of William.)

Sarah recalled in her memoirs that, in those first years of Anne's reign,

I used to pass many hours a day with her and always endeavoured to give her notions of loving her country, of justice, & governing by the laws & making herself be beloved rather than feared . . . & I ever told her that nothing was so great & honourable as to govern upon the conditions that a crown was taken, nor no way so certain as that to keep it as long as she lived.[29]

Which reminded Anne – tactlessly – that the crown could be taken from her head as easily as it had been from her father's. Such lectures were already beginning to irritate as Anne struggled under new responsibilities.

In early October Godolphin was entertaining Sarah's son Jack at his house at Newmarket. He wrote to her at Bath complimenting her on how well the lad had turned out: 'very lean, like a young greyhound, but in extreme good health . . . and good humoured . . . and has lost a great deal of that impatience of diverting himself all manner of ways which he used to have'. When back in London, Godolphin repeatedly asked Sarah to return as soon as she could as he had 'no other support in your absence'. He needed her help to receive visits from 'all your acquaintance of Scotland', meaning friends-cum-petitioners like James Douglas, Duke of Hamilton, who had written to Sarah to say that he wished to do the Queen some service.[30] In one day, 17 October 1702, Godolphin wrote Sarah three separate letters: they contained a mixture of family and Court news, and referred to the idea of union between England and Scotland: 'The Queen is pestered out of her life with these Scotch lords. She says five of them came to see her together this morning and in the afternoon she was to have the Duke of Queensberry.' Strikingly, Sarah was now privy to affairs of State mainly through Godolphin's letters rather than Anne's.

Sarah has often been called uncompromising, yet one of her early political intrigues involved trying to persuade the Whigs to drop their opposition to a Tory-backed Bill, the 'Prince's Bill', concerning the financial settlement on Prince George. So soon after the gift of the dukedom and its pension, she could hardly do otherwise than support Anne's wish to increase the income of her husband's household. She was therefore horrified to discover that her own son-in-law, Charles Spencer, was leading the Whig attack on the Bill.

Charles, though he had become 3rd Earl of Sunderland in September, considered himself a republican. He opposed the Prince's Bill first because he opposed all further enrichment of the Crown, but more importantly because it came in the form of a 'tack': the Tories made their support for another piece of legislation dependent upon its being passed. Charles rightly predicted that tacking would prove a dangerously divisive trend and made a speech to this effect in the House of Lords. However, as Sarah feared, the Queen took his opposition as a personal affront. Before the vote, Sarah lobbied energetically against her son-in-law, persuading as many Whigs as she could that this was not the issue on which to take a stand. In January 1703, after the Bill had got through, Anne wrote to Sarah, 'I am sure the Princes Bill passing after so much struggle is wholly owing to the pains you & Mr Freeman have taken.' Her efforts had not gone unnoticed.

Sarah's daughter Anne stood by her husband over the Prince's Bill but was pained at his disagreement with her parents. In a letter from Althorp to her mother in January 1703 she tried to explain that it was only the excessive amount requested by the Prince Consort that had outraged Charles, and that otherwise he was for the Queen's interest.[31] She told Sarah that she and her husband fully appreciated how much the Marlborough family owed to the Queen and that she would suffer any punishment if she believed for one moment that her husband had behaved ungratefully. On the other hand, she observed that, like Sarah herself, 'Ld Sun would never do anything against his conscience, for any obligation in the world, or for the dearest father . . .'

Anne's devotion to her mother and her tendency to play peacemaker shine through their correspondence, as does her fear of Sarah's high standards. Her love, she wrote, was 'more than I can ever show, and [I] can never be happy but when I think you are satisfied with me'. Sarah seemed to look more gently upon the mild-mannered Anne than on her other, stronger-willed children. On one letter from Anne in 1704 Sarah noted that she was 'always reasonable and trying to do good'.

Sarah opened all the correspondence between the Captain-General and the Lord Treasurer as if by right. Letters from husband to wife, or from friend to friend, were often written with the intention that Sarah should show them to the Queen to prove what the Ministers 'privately' believed. At this time letters were frequently considered more like newspapers, for general consumption. While Marlborough's letters to the Queen were often a blend of maudlin and chivalric devotion to his monarch, he wrote less formally to his wife and could therefore convey more critical opinions to Anne at one remove. Opening official correspondence between the other three, meanwhile, must have made Sarah feel both included in the nuts and bolts of politics and frustratingly separated by the glass divide through which she was an observer.

Sarah admitted that Anne had only taken Marlborough and Godolphin into the Cabinet because they were 'reckoned in the number of the Tories': the only sense in which the two men were not essentially Tories at the start of Anne's reign was in their internationalist, pro-Dutch perspective, inherited from William. Both men shared with the Queen a certain nostalgia for pre-Revolutionary days, while Sarah had no such ambivalence. She foresaw that only the Whigs, who controlled 'the trade and money of the nation', would provide lasting support for the war.

Except for the Queen's personal dislike of the more radical Whigs like Sunderland, and the fact that the Tories were electorally stronger, there was no real reason for Marlborough and Godolphin not to ally with them. Eventually, when there was no alternative, first Godolphin and then Marlborough would grasp this. Swift wrote in his history of Anne's reign that Godolphin's 'alliance with the Marlborough family & his passion for the Duchess were the cards which dragged him into a party whose principles he naturally disliked & whose leaders he personally hated as they did him'.[32] Sarah, by contrast, was more modest, seeing it as inevitable that an astute Treasurer should begin to pay the wealthy Whigs 'as much regard as the times and the Queen's prejudices would permit him to do'.[33]

The Queen's dislike of the Whigs was sharpened because they were a highly organised force and, as such, a threat to her prerogatives. Her greatest fear was 'though I have the name of Queen, to be in reality their slave'.[34] Their leaders, the 'Junto', consisted of what Anne called the 'five tyrannising lords': John Somers, Charles Montagu (Baron Halifax), Thomas Wharton, Charles Seymour (Duke of Somerset) and Edward Russell, Earl of Orford. Charles Spencer (the Earl of Sunderland), despite his radicalism, was increasingly regarded as a sixth, junior Junto member.

Somers was the brilliant barrister who had secured the acquittal of the seven bishops under James II, and was widely respected as the principal author of the Bill of Rights. Halifax would mastermind the development of a modern credit economy during Anne's reign; an important artistic and literary patron of men like Congreve, he was the first to suggest a national library. Wharton, who lost his place on Anne's accession, was a master of party organisation and electioneering, and a historian of some repute. Somerset, with his Revolutionary credentials and ancient lineage, would be appointed Master of the Horse, a Minister of imprecise portfolio, in Anne's first government. Finally, Lord Orford was an experienced Lord of the Admiralty, who had signed the original letter of invitation to William and had accompanied the invading forces to England.

Although Edmund Burke's picture of the Junto as defenders of constitutional freedom was romantic when set against the reality of pocket-boroughs and personal ambition, it is true that these men together rewrote the nature of Westminster politics by their belief that it was their right to force their way into government, regardless of the Queen's wishes. All were men of Cavalier tastes in their private lives: they flaunted their mistresses, and Somers lived openly with another man's wife. This was further reason for Anne's distaste: she was the first monarch to insist on having her naked shoulders covered when she appeared on gold coins and, like the Tory satirists, she prudishly associated the Junto's attachment to constitutional freedom with their moral laxity and atheism. Sarah, though far from a libertine, did not hold their personal conduct against their political characters.

Under William and Mary, several of the Junto had been in favour of the Marlboroughs' expulsion from Court. With Marlborough classed as a Tory, most did not question that his devoted wife followed his politics. In 1702, the Earl of Sunderland's marriage to her daughter was Sarah's only link with the Whig leadership. On the other hand, she had a large number of friends among Low Church clergy and Whig MPs. Now that Anne was Queen, Sarah aspired to serve the Whigs' interests more fully, just as they hoped to utilise her position as royal favourite. The Junto's mistake was to overestimate Sarah's influence as a royal favourite, and foreign diplomats made the same error: the Electress Sophia's unofficial London representative, Pierre de Falaiseau, for example, described Anne as a cipher dominated by Sarah.

They were literally listening to the word on the street in making these assumptions. A ballad sung by pedlars in the West End to the tune of 'For He's a Jolly Good Fellow'[35] mocked the Marlboroughs' humble origins:

> It is what must move both spewing and laughter
> To see a great Duchess in Old Jenning's Daughter
> And little Jack Churchill a Knight of the Garter
> Which nobody can deny . . .

> No Child ever stood in more awe of the rod
> Than Nan doth of Sarah's wry looks or a Nod.
> It were well if she stood as much in fear of her God
> Which nobody can deny . . .

> She [Sarah] ransacks her pockets as well as ranges her [Anne's]
>   parks
> Like Jack-in-a-Lantern she leads her in th'dark
> And vows she'll ne'er leave her while worth but a spark
> Which nobody can deny . . .

The same accusation was levelled against her in an anonymous poem entitled 'Upon a Great Lady's Visiting the Tomb of Humphrey the Good, Duke of Gloucester, at St Alban's',[36] which depicted Sarah going to visit the grave of that old royal favourite.

As though to answer such satires, Sarah wrote to a friend that she had 'never seen any condition yet that was near so happy as twas thought. When I was a great favourite, I was railed at and flattered from morning to night, neither of which was agreeable to me; & when there were but few women that would not have poisoned me for the happiness they thought I enjoyed, I kept the worst company of anybody upon earth.'[37]

On a day-to-day level Sarah's main role was to act as clearing-house for petitions to the Queen, and she made a new enemy each time she turned one down. It was also inevitable that she was constantly seeking 'favours' from Anne: as she explains very reasonably in one letter, her job 'unavoidably forces [me] to be often troubling Mrs Morley upon the account of others'. She wrote to Bishop Burnet to vindicate herself against the accusation that she did not spend enough time with her royal mistress: 'I did constantly write abundance of letters in answer to the petitions and applications that were made' and she spent too much time with Anne in private to also be seen playing a 'diligent waiter in public'.[38] In fact her preference for attending on Anne in private was precisely what irritated her Tory enemies. The historian G. M. Trevelyan, who had derived his view of Anne's character from Sarah, wrote: 'Anne's mind was slow as a lowland river, Sarah's swift as a mountain torrent. Sarah kept her sharp witty tongue in constant use. Anne, though she could read a speech well in public, could not carry on a conversation . . .' That disability, together with her ill-health, prevented her from keeping Court to the same extent as previous monarchs.[39] As the Court's social gatherings became less important for political lobbying and cultural patronage, the private favourite gained a correspondingly greater advantage.

Sarah claimed that her criteria for accepting or rejecting petitions were needs-based: 'I could not imagine that people could have so little shame as to ask money of a Prince without personal kindness, merit or want (which, though I have ranked it in the last place, I think the argument first for anything of that nature)'.[40] This charitable fair-mindedness did not prevent her putting forward the petitions of her own family and securing appointments for them: a Bill restoring part of her sister's Irish estates was passed as soon as Anne came to the Throne. Aside from her own daughters' appointment to the bedchamber, her eldest sister Barbara's husband, Edward Griffith, was made Clerk of the Greencloth, and Colonel Charles Godfrey, who had married Marlborough's sister Arabella, also received promotion. Anne's wish of 1697 that she could have 'a Mrs Freeman in every post of my family [household]'[41] looked like coming true.

In February 1703 Sarah's third daughter Elizabeth, aged fourteen, was married to Scrope Egerton, the Earl of Bridgwater. Sarah obtained a place at Court for this young man she described as 'no Solomon' but 'young enough to improve',[42] replacing the mentally ill Lord Sandwich.[43] A childish note from her daughter declared: 'I don't know how to thank my dear mama enough for the kindness she has showed in my Lord Bridgwater's being Master of the Horse to the Prince . . .' and ended in a strangely insecure formulation: 'my dear mama has always given me so much reason to hope you loved me'.[44]

Sarah's contemporaries were quick to complain. John Evelyn recorded that the Marlboroughs were 'engrossing all that stirred and was profitable at Court'.[45] However, it was not the nepotism *per se* that was resented: nearly half of Anne's appointees were related to those already in post, and in an age when marriages were so often made as political manoeuvres, family connections were not necessarily to be regarded as purely 'private' anyway. Sarah's clan perhaps took more places than others, but the Russells and the Cavendishes also did well. However, the Marlborough connections were bringing into Court a less noble element, and this attracted hostile attention.

Those Court places Sarah did not fill with her family were disposed of only with her express approval. In the same letter in which Anne said she was 'more & more sensible of the great blessing God Almighty has given me in three such friends [Marlborough, Godolphin and Sarah] . . . a happiness I believe nobody in my sphere ever enjoyed before',[46] she apologised for having given away a post in the Commission of the Sick and Wounded without consulting Sarah. In her memoirs, Sarah claimed to have achieved the introduction of Lady Frescheville, the preferment of the Duchesses of Ormonde and Somerset, Lady Burlington, Lady Hyde and Lady Scarborough, and the appointment of several Maids of Honour.[47] She wanted both to deny the accusation of monopolising the distribution of patronage and at the same time to take the credit for everyone's careers. Thank-you letters exist from Lady Hyde and Lady Scarborough to suggest that Sarah indeed pulled strings for them. She remembered, with particular pleasure, securing a post in the bedchamber for Lady Hyde, Rochester's daughter-in-law, 'for in my life I never saw any mortal have such a passion for anything as she had to be in that post' and 'she could not speak to me about it while it was in doubt without blushing.'[48] She recognised that granting the favour to a woman Sarah and Anne both found disagreeable demonstrated her power as favourite just as effectively as refusing it.[49]

Petitions for charitable cases also arrived in bundles on Sarah's desk throughout the first year of Anne's reign.[50] They ranged from Lady Thanet's request for a pension, to letters from the middling classes, such as the unemployed Robert Lundie, who hoped she did not find it 'monotonous to help the distressed'. Her old Jacobite friend Lady Sandwich wrote in 1702 to say that she had finally forced herself to 'recommend myself to your favour and intercession' to obtain a place at Court. Sarah replied that as Lady Sandwich had repaid her earlier kindness by snubbing her after she was expelled from Court by William and Mary, 'I am not naturally much inclined to the Christian virtue of returning injuries with patience.'[51]

The important distinction to be made was between ordinary patronage and venality. In one draft of her memoirs, Sarah stated that she did not sell places and 'that if there is any man or woman upon earth that can give the least proof to the contrary, I am contented for the future to be looked upon both by friends and enemies as one of the vilest of women'.[52] She gave the example of one Mr Cook (grandson of the Duke of Leeds) who offered £6,000 to her if she could get him a peerage, which she turned down flat. Also in her draft memoirs is a response to a libel that 'in the time of her favour, no employment at court was disposed of, not so much as that of a beefeater, for which she had not a gratuity'. Her co-author of that time testified: 'I can assure you from my own observation that whenever any persons offered money for a peerage or were earnest with the D[uches]s of M[arlborough] to get them the favour of selling a Scotch or an Irish title, she constantly refused them.'[53]

When pushed on the facts, however, Sarah admitted to having sold three very minor places for Pages of the Backstairs – 'for in those times,' she wrote, 'it was openly allowed to sell all employments in every office . . . and in short everybody that had the disposal of places looked upon it as their right to sell them, and were no more ashamed of doing it than of receiving their salaries or their rents out of the country'. She claimed the credit for having partially reformed this practice. It is more likely, however, that the Treasurer was the real reformer, whose lead was followed by Anne and Sarah. She observed that places were 'generally purchased by people that have more money than wit' and that 'nobody that was poor and deserved well could ever be provided for whilst places were got by those that would give most for them'.

Over time, the war on bribery and corruption became one of Sarah's hobbyhorses and the main reason for her opposition to Prime Minister Robert Walpole in the 1720s. One anecdote about Sarah as an old dowager has her returning five guineas Henry Fox had given as a tip to her servants with a note saying such bribes were not acceptable in her house, but 'if I were a First Minister, perhaps I might have other sort of notions'.[54]

*   *   *

During 1702 Sarah experienced difficulty in handling her now fifteen-year-old son. Jack was studying under a tutor at Cambridge, but wanted to join the army.[55] Sarah begged Marlborough to dissuade him; she had already lost one son. Her husband promised to write a stern letter and to check it with Sarah before dispatching it to the boy. '[I]f you do not like it, send me such a letter as you would have me write.' By February 1703, however, Jack, now styled Marquess of Blandford, had somehow won over his father and was packing for Flanders. Sarah, whose posthumous papers included the scribbled homily 'a horse not broken becometh head-strong and a child left to himself will be wilful',[56] must have felt her maternal control was slipping away.

Unable to stop him, Sarah sulked, the last refuge of the powerless, and therefore had not communicated with him for several days when she received news from Cambridge that he had caught smallpox. Sarah had always feared losing her children through this disease – Godolphin had had to reassure her only the previous October that Jack would not visit any other houses to protect him from an epidemic in Newmarket.

She travelled to Cambridge to nurse her son, taking her own doctors with her, while Marlborough stayed in London. At nine in the morning of 18 February, Marlborough sat down to write to his wife while she was still on the road: 'I have no thought but what is at Cambridge.'[57] Later that day he wrote again, begging for news, telling her that he had sent to the royal apothecary for medicines, and adding, 'I pray God enable us both to behave ourselves with that resignation which we ought to do.' Godolphin wrote too, urging Sarah to let 'the whole world see that God Almighty has blessed you with a Christian patience and fortitude as eminent as the reason and understanding by which you are most justly distinguished from the rest of your sex'. The Queen's letter of the same day expressed the hope that Blandford would recover and 'once more to beg you for Christ Jesus sake to have a care of your dear precious self'.[58]

The following day, Marlborough joined Sarah in Cambridge, just in time to see his son die in his mother's arms.

The Queen received the news almost immediately and was the first to send a note of condolence, in which she told Sarah that she was 'too sensible of your condition' to expect a reply. She referred back to her own grief for the death of her son, which she had borne with all the religious piety she now wished upon Sarah: 'Christ Jesus comfort & support you under this terrible affliction.' Later Sarah wrote scornfully of Anne's tearless response to the deaths of both young Gloucester and her husband George. Such stoicism was not her idea of virtue.

Two days later Anne apologised for her inability to 'be with you as any other friend might' but promised soon to come for a day-visit to St Albans, if invited. Marlborough could not stay with his wife either – he had to return to the war – so Sarah's only company as she mourned at Holywell was the faithful Godolphin, who stayed with her for three days.59 He promised Marlborough that he had not been encouraging Sarah in her bereaved delusion that she could accompany the Captain-General to the Continent, but admitted that 'if she had asked me to fly, in the condition I saw her, I would certainly have said I would try to do it'.

Anne had written to Sarah in March begging her – 'which I would do upon my knees if I saw you' – not to go alone to the Lodge at Windsor but to come to Kensington as soon as Marlborough had departed. Sarah's note on the back calls this 'a very kind letter' but Anne's next letter suggests that Sarah was again shutting out her friend at a time of personal crisis. Anne asked to see her as much as possible before she went to Windsor, though she knew herself poor company – 'for believe me, my dear dear Mrs Freeman, you'll never find in all the search of love a heart like mine, so truly, so sincerely, so entirely without reserve, nor so passionately yours'.

Having spent the spring alone in the countryside, Sarah moved back to St James's as soon as the Court shifted in the reverse direction for the summer. She still could not stand being in society. In one of her letters from exile years later, she recalled that in times of trouble, 'I used to run from the Court and shut myself up . . . in one of my country houses, quite alone.'60

Despite all her husband's and friends' advice, Sarah ignored the convention by which the death of a child was regarded as a test of faith. She gave full vent to her grief. As late as May 1703, the schoolboys of Westminster said they saw the Duchess wandering like a madwoman through the cloisters of the Abbey, among the vagrants.[61] Godolphin wrote to Marlborough that he feared Sarah was losing her mind, and she certainly seems to have become paranoid about her husband's state of health. He had to write asking her to 'look upon sicknesses as you used to do, by knowing I am sick one day and well another'.[62] In a way she was also grieving for a life that had, so far, been lived entirely for the sake of others. Half of her political and social ambition had been ambition for her children and, above all, for her last surviving son.

Sarah's grief was immortalised by Congreve in a poem written for her daughter Henrietta. In *The Tears of Amaryllis for Amyntas* (1703),[63] a hysterical Sarah throws herself on to Blandford's grave and begs to die alongside him. She weeps and

> Her loosely flowing Hair, all radiant bright,
> O'er spread the dewy Grass like Streams of Light.
> As if the Sun had of his Beams been shorn,
> And cast to Earth the Glories he had worn.

She begs Nature for some response to her loss, and a sympathetic storm promptly whips itself up. As usual, Sarah is depicted as the centre of the whirlwind. Then at last there is a sudden calm, and flowers burst out of the grassy knoll. The real Sarah knew that such sunny acceptance of God's will was superficial balm. In a letter to her friend Lady Elizabeth Longueville, she stated realistically that '[t]ime, one sees by experience, lessens people's grief, when nothing can repair the loss'.[64]

In the summer of 1703, as if trying to bury her grief, she threw herself back into the political scene. In one version of her memoir,[65] Sarah made a rare reference to how her private emotions affected her public life: at the time that the Queen was appointing four Tory peers, 'I happened to be in the country in great affliction upon the death of my only son,' and so was unable to influence this political move of which she disapproved strongly. When she heard about it, however, she was in time to persuade Anne, through interventions by Marlborough and Godolphin, to add at least one Whig peer to the list: John Hervey, a man to whom she had promised a barony as though it were hers to give away. Sarah kept a letter from Hervey's wife to prove that she had not sold him the title.

In April, preparing for the siege of Bonn, Marlborough had written from Cologne that he had witnessed a religious procession through the town and thought how much Jack would have enjoyed it.[66] '[T]he greatest pleasure of my life will be the endeavouring to make you happy,' he told Sarah.[67] He also remarked that he hoped his wife had not had 'the visit I so much fear' which may imply that Sarah thought she was pregnant again. This was unlikely as she was now forty-three and it was twelve years since her last pregnancy. Mostly, though, Marlborough's letters to his wife concerned business – coded references to their suspicions that Anne (referred to as 85) was dealing, behind the Cabinet's back, with Rochester (19), who had recently been forced to resign – or advice on the buying and selling of East India Company stock.[68]

Marlborough was anxious to make a new will before he launched his next offensive, to take account of his son's death and because, if he died intestate, 'I might be deprived of letting the world see the kindness and esteem I have for you'. He wrote to his lawyer at Lincoln's Inn making Sarah his sole executor, recipient of his plate, jewels, furniture, a jointure of £2,000 a year and sole owner of her family's homes, the houses at Sandridge and Holywell. In the event that they had no further sons, he left £20,000 to Mary, so long as she married with her mother's consent, £2,000 to Henrietta, and £2,000 to each of the Countess of Sunderland's two children.

The dowry-sized inheritance for twelve-year-old Mary – the child who most resembled Sarah – looked likely to be spent before Marlborough's death: Sarah had received a proposal from

Ralph, Earl of Montagu, on behalf of his thirteen-year-old son, Lord Monthermer. Marlborough instructed Sarah to consult with Godolphin; his own view was that Mary was too young to marry. He still saw her, reasonably enough, as a little girl for whom he was bringing home a pet bird that 'whistled very finely' (but which was killed in his army tent by Lord Albemarle's dog).[69]

Sarah viewed Mary as a more mature character, who might offend or amuse as much as the next person – not exactly unconditional love. As she wrote in her unpublished memoir of family life, Mary 'had always a great deal of harshness in her nature, & from a child she would often snap me up, though I spoke to her with ever so much kindness. However, as she had a great deal of wit, & (as I thought) beauty, it was a vast while before she would wear out my passion for her . . .'[70]

Mary's letters to her mother from around this time[71] bring to mind the old saying that the children of lovers are always orphans: '[M]y dear mama can't imagine how much I long to see her, but [I] won't desire to come to St Albans yet, for I know you can't be enough alone when Papa is with you to care for me, but I hope if you stay there longer than Papa, you will be so good as to let me be with you, for you can't think how happy that would make your most dutiful daughter.' Once, when departing for a visit to her sister Anne at Althorp, Mary had received so fierce a glare from her mother that she had begged to know the sin for which she should try to make amends. Sarah often punished her for some perceived misdeed by turning a cold shoulder and waiting to see how long it took her daughter to notice: 'I have been afraid for these two days that my dear mama was angry with me, but being very willing to believe it was only a fancy of mine I never spoke of it till now that I see it is so plain . . . ,' Mary wrote, 'I can neither eat nor sleep when you are angry, so if you would have me live, you will believe I never intended to do anything that you could take ill.'

At this time Sarah was also cold-shouldering the Queen. In late April, Anne became anxious that Sarah must be angry with her: she begged her to write, so that 'I may justify myself if you have any hard thoughts of me'. But in early May she was still tormented by Sarah being 'so formal and cold' without giving the reason: 'For Christ Jesus Sake, tell me what's the matter, lay all the faults you think me guilty of before me, that I may vindicate myself . . . [Y]ou told me once I was changed, I am sure I am not so in the least . . .' Anne continued to beg for an answer, adding that Sarah should send it 'neither by the coach nor post . . . for I would not have it light into anybody's hands but my own'. She asked Sarah to tell her any gossip she might have heard that had upset her, so 'that nothing of that kind may ever lie festering in your dear heart'.

The cause of Sarah's coldness, as Anne should have guessed, had more to do with politics than gossip. As the Tories became publicly critical of Marlborough's war, Anne had to write to Sarah justifying her continued preference for them.

In May 1703 Marlborough wrote to Sarah that '[I]f I did not flatter myself that in some short time I should live quietly and happily with you I do not think I should be able to bear the loss [of Jack] we have made.'[72] A few days later, Anne despatched a letter to Sarah in which she begged the Marlboroughs not to think of retirement: '[W]e four must never part, till death mows us down with his impartial hand.' The country would be 'ruined' and she would 'but make another abdication, for what is a Crown when the support of it is gone?'.

The theme of rural retirement, a rhetorical pose for any ambitious statesman of the time, was also code for the battle between Anne and Sarah for Marlborough's time and attention. Marlborough owed the Queen his patriotic duty, which drew him away from his family and might cost him his life. Yet despite his troubles with the risk-averse Dutch generals, Marlborough enjoyed soldiering, and the implication in several political satires that he found the front line more peaceful than his home life with Sarah probably contained a grain of truth. His expressed desire to retire was a kind of protestation of fidelity, in which the Crown and the national interest were Sarah's rivals. He told Sarah that he had 'no ambition but that of living with you and, whilst I am in the world, endeavouring to lessen the power of France'. Unfortunately these two ambitions were mutually exclusive, and Anne's claim on him was winning at the moment over Sarah's.

Alongside the rhetoric of retirement, there was the rhetoric of political neutrality, meant to show the speaker as above the undignified 'rage of party'. Party allegiance was seen as bourgeois: aristocrats might deign to lead a party but should not belong to one. And party politics was seen as a temporary aberration that would disappear one day in a spirit of national unity. The Queen, Marlborough and Godolphin all shared the delusion that the Whig/Tory divide was a distortion of true government – as dangerously arbitrary as the whim of an absolute monarch. Appointments based on party were feared to lead to incompetence, an anxiety that led eventually to the development of a nominally apolitical civil service. Marlborough was particularly concerned that party bias in army appointments might undermine the quality of his officers.

Today we would assume that the Queen at least was right to aspire to this neutrality, but in an age where she was, in effect, actively leading the Cabinet, this position was not very constructive. Solidly parked by the fireside in the House of Lords, she tried to act as a kind of ballast, balancing and moderating through a policy of non-alignment. In practice this meant that she had to veer from one side to the other.

From the siege of Bonn, Marlborough wrote to his wife: '[M]y dearest soul, when we come to live together my happiness will depend upon our having but one thought, in order to which we must renounce all parties and content ourselves in praying for the Queen's long life, and that France may never have it in their power to impose laws upon England.'[73] He declared he would 'meddle with neither party' and that Sarah should share the same temper.[74] Sarah, however, was unapologetically partisan and did not regard pleasing her husband as a higher cause.

Though she instinctively understood the new style of politics, she was not blind to the need for compromise. In June 1703, she told Marlborough that 'either of the parties would be tyrants if they were let alone'. She also respected independence of conscience above party loyalty, so long as she agreed with the conscience: '[T]is no matter what men are made use of if they are but such creatures as will, right or wrong, be at the dispose of two or three arbitrary men that are at the head of them.'[75]

The Tories and Whigs were not political parties in the modern sense, but what they lacked in party organisation they made up for in propaganda. Society became polarised as never before: everything and everyone, from coffee-houses and shops, to newspapers, academia, architects and artists, had to decide which political heart to wear on its sleeve – and there was no secrecy at the ballot. Factionalism was condemned on a personal level as a form of prejudice. It was how people judged one another at first meeting – knee-jerk reactions that would have been considered more acceptable if based on some other distinction, such as social rank. This was why Anne blamed Sarah, in a letter of June 1703, for being 'fixed in the good opinion you have of some & the ill opinion you have of other people' so that it was 'to no manner of purpose to argue anything with you'. Sarah, as historian, would later try to fix this stubborn, irrational personality on to Anne (the little girl who would not accept that a tree was a tree) while portraying herself as comparatively open-minded.

In early June, Marlborough travelled on to Hannef. He did not need Sarah's updates on Westminster shenanigans because Count Wratislaw, the Austrian envoy to London, was passing through on his way back to Vienna. All he needed from his wife were supplies from their estates: ten dozen Palm Wind and ten dozen Piper Cider apples to be shipped over as soon as convenient. In return he sent Sarah a set of horses and a replacement bird for Mary.

The Queen, too, had little need of news or advice from Sarah and wanted only to place orders for more quilted petticoats. She urged Sarah to tell her what was on her mind, but disagreed with her on affairs of State: 'I have read & heard read all the accounts that are come from Scotland . . . I must beg my dear

Mrs Freeman's pardon for differing with her in that matter as to the succession, for certainly if the union can ever be compassed there would be no occasion of naming a successor, for then we should be one people, & the endeavouring to make a settlement now would in my poor opinion put an end to the union . . .' A few days later she explained that she was not acting without advice: she had guidance from the Scottish Ministers and the Duke of Somerset, who wanted an Act of Union to be proposed to Parliament. She would take Sarah's advice on the settling of a private estate, she said, but only because 'I forgot to ask Ld Treasurer when he was here'. In another letter she asked Sarah to pass on some business letters to Godolphin, and to report back on his opinion. She did not ask Sarah's.

On 11 June 1703, Anne began a letter with an injunction to Sarah to speak freely 'though we differ' and continued, 'I am very sorry you think I can treat anything you say as if it came from Mrs James [presumably a servant].' The Queen went on to state her position clearly: many Tories took part in the Revolution, which meant that no one party was solely responsible for safeguarding the Protestant succession, and 'I dare say there are millions that are called Jacobites that abhor their principles as much as you do.' In another letter, in answer to Sarah's list of the troubles Marlborough was facing at Tory hands, Anne repeated: 'I can see as well as anybody all the faults and follies of others, except that great one [Jacobitism] you think them guilty of, & that I must own again I want faith to believe . . .' Anne wished that there were more 'good reasonable people' in both parties, and replaced her usual declaration of love for Sarah with: 'I will answer for myself that by the Grace of God I will ever be sincere & true to my religion, country and all my friends & inviolably yours.' It was no coincidence that this letter mirrored so closely what Marlborough was writing to Sarah at around the same date; he and Anne were colluding to appease her.[76] He agreed with his wife that the Tories in the Cabinet, such as Rochester, were not serving the war effort very well, 'but who is fit for their places? I do protest before God I know of none.'

By the middle of the month, Sarah was writing long political diatribes to Anne almost every day. She wrote later that Anne urged her to do it so 'I did therefore speak very freely and very frequently to Her Majesty upon the subject of Whig and Tory.'[77] Anne's resentment of these lectures began to surface in her replies – no longer the blotted scraps of the 1690s but now regal gilt-edged stationery – yet she was still the one doing the apologising. Exhausted one evening, she wrote to Sarah to 'beg your pardon again from the bottom of my soul for anything that I ever said that occasioned that formal cold letter'.

Marlborough was trying to race the French army to Antwerp. His men did not set up camp until midnight each evening, in fields made muddy by heavy rain. From his tent pitched at Tielen, he wrote to reassure Sarah about their daughter Henrietta. Sarah was worried that she was keeping 'bad company', by which she meant the playwright William Congreve and his friends, and saw her eldest daughter growing close to women she considered morally dubious: 'I wished she would not go often to my Lady Fitzharding, for though she had a great deal of wit & humour and was diverting, her house was a dangerous place for young people.'[78] Marlborough informed her that he had followed her wishes and written to urge his daughter to avoid this social circle.

Sarah tried to impress upon Henrietta the importance to the Marlborough-Godolphin families of keeping her reputation intact. Godolphin handed Henrietta her mother's letter one evening while she was in waiting at Windsor. She took herself aside from the tea table to read it by candlelight then returned to the company, looking troubled. At the same soirée, Godolphin passed an equally troubling letter to the Queen – another political complaint from Sarah.[79]

Sarah and the Queen were finally reconciled over whether the Scottish succession or the union of the two kingdoms should come first: Anne vowed to follow the advice of the Lord Treasurer, whom Sarah felt she could influence.

*　　*　　*

While Anne had finally given up hope of another child, Sarah continued to believe throughout the spring of 1703 that she was pregnant. That she allowed herself to be bled in early June, however, suggests that some of her doctors had other ideas about her 'cessation of flowers'. Anne wrote that she was sorry to hear that Sarah was 'more out of order than I knew'; she herself was in relatively improved health and was able to walk with the help of two crutches. Marlborough, too, wrote tenderly to his wife: 'It is very true that I have a great desire you should have more children, but it is as true that you are so dear to me that I would not have them at the expense of your health . . .'[80] – an unusual order of priorities for a husband in these times.

Sarah's confidence in the pregnancy lasted until mid-July, almost four months after her husband had left England. From Vorselaar, he wrote that her letter confirming it 'gave me so much joy that if any company had been by . . . they must have observed a great alteration in me'.[81] Ten days later, however, another letter indicated that her hopes had been misplaced:

It was a great pleasure to me when I thought that we would be blessed with more children; but as all my happiness centres on living quietly with you, I do conjure you, by all the kindness I have for you, which is as much as ever man had for woman, that you will take the best advice you can for your health and follow exactly what shall be prescribed you.[82]

A few days later, from the siege of Huy, Marlborough wrote anxiously to her, having heard from Godolphin that she was unwell.[83] Her disappointment at discovering she was not pregnant after all must have brought back the depression that had followed Jack's death in February. Though they both knew he could not, Marlborough told Sarah he would leave his command immediately if she wanted him at her side. In another long, stoical letter he advised her to count their blessings and 'I would endeavour to persuade you to think as little as possible of worldly business.'

But Sarah always met disappointments in her personal life

with fresh bursts of worldliness. Two days after her husband had sent that letter, she was lobbying the Queen to appoint a Whig, John Methuen, as ambassador to Portugal. Since her success with Hervey's peerage, the Whigs had turned to her with increasing frequency: by September she had secured the governorship of Guernsey for a Whig and was pressuring the Queen over the appointment of a certain Welsh judge.

Those who have not blamed Sarah's supposed low spirits on her son's death, have found another, more speculative diagnosis: an early menopause.[84] It was a tidy explanation for Sarah's increasing outspokenness and self-righteousness. To Sarah's contemporaries, menopause was seen as the result of mysterious 'uterine furies'. Like menstruation, it was considered an illness to be cured by bleeding – leeches were placed on the genitalia – purging, or, less drastically, a cooling diet of melons and ices.[85] Since the majority of older females were those who had not risked their lives in childbirth – in other words, spinsters – menopause was associated with independent-minded women. Sarah suffered from hot flushes, which she self-diagnosed as 'St Anthony's Fire' (erisypelas),[86] and the cessation of menstruation would explain why she thought she was pregnant. Nine years later, a Tory writer linked Sarah's St Anthony's Fire with her 'raving' temper, adding that 'It is probable the Distemper only changed its Situation' – that is, from her genitals to her face.[87]

In September, Marlborough wrote from Alderbeesten explicitly asking Sarah not to intercede with politicians on his behalf 'for all parties are alike' and he did not want 'to be a favourite to either of them'. Then, contradicting this, he expressed his alarm at a letter from Speaker Robert Harley, who appeared to have taken the hardcore Tory line, advised by Admiral George Rooke, that England should only be fighting a defensive war, with a maritime strategy, leaving the Dutch to defend themselves. (There was a widespread public misperception that the navy gave better value for money than the army, because it also had a commercial use, and a traditional suspicion about standing armies, both of which

Marlborough had to counter in order to keep receiving funds for his campaigns in Flanders.)[88] On the same day, he sent an identical message to the Treasurer, hoping that one way or the other, through Godolphin or Sarah, the Queen would hear of his anxieties: 'If it be true that the heads of both parties are resolved that an offensive war must not be made in this country . . . the Dutch would not think themselves safe,' and 'when they are ruined, we are undone'.

Still ailing from the mistaken pregnancy, Sarah was persuaded by Godolphin and the Queen to spend September taking the waters in Bath. Sarah could not help but feel that the Queen was trying to keep her out of the way while continuing to deflect her political complaints with protestations of love.

On the night of 26 November 1703, a violent hurricane hit south-east England. It stripped roofs and chimneys from London's houses, smashed boats in the Thames and toppled several church spires. Defoe wrote that it killed more than the Great Fire, and 'many thought the end of the world was nigh'.[89] The novelist Jean Plaidy would one day depict Sarah and Anne awake together in the bedchambers of Kensington Palace during the nine long hours of the storm, fearing that it was divine retribution for their illegitimate power.[90] This was continuing a tradition started, as London picked up the pieces, by contemporary Tory wits who were quick to equate this Great Storm with the ill-wind of the Marlboroughs' rise. One poem entitled 'On the Duchess of Marlborough' (1703)[91] ran:

> No wonder winds more dreadful are by far
> Than all the losses of a twelve years war
> No wonder prelates do the church betray
> And statesmen vote and act a different way.

The reference to the treacherous prelates concerned Low Church opposition to the second Occasional Conformity Bill. High Churchmen had just introduced this Bill to Parliament after the first had been defeated in January 1703. It aimed to ban the practice whereby dissenters were allowed to take communion in the Church of England, and so fulfil the legal requirement for holding public office, while not giving up their religious beliefs. Occasional conformity was a pragmatic tolerance of those who paid religious lip-service to Anglicanism, but High-Flyers suspected that it was merely a smokescreen for the ambitions of the dissenters, just as Sarah believed that James II had preached religious freedom only as a cover for imposing Catholicism. The political significance of an official end to such toleration was that this would reduce the number of dissenters in many government offices and in the corporations, and hence the number of Whigs. One of the greatest strengths of the Whig party was that it united people as diverse as Daniel Defoe, raised a dissenter, and the Anglican Duchess of Marlborough. The Bill's aim was to sunder this broad base of Whig support.

Defoe had published jeremiads against the practice of occasional conformity to persuade his fellow dissenters that it betrayed the ideals of earlier nonconformist martyrs. In July he had stood trial as the author of *The Shortest Way* and ended up with his hook-nosed face poking through a pillory hole. Now the High-Flyers turned these denunciations to their own ends, ignoring Defoe's basic message of religious toleration and stirring up anti-dissent feeling. Henry St John was the young, fine-featured and eloquent Tory Member of Parliament, originally a protégé of Marlborough, who most notably latched on to the issue as a means of furthering his own career.

Sarah lobbied furiously against the Bill and the 'zealots' promoting it, berating both the Queen and Marlborough on the subject during the months before it went to the House of Lords. Marlborough told her that he had to avoid voting against the Bill and thereby playing into the hands of Rochester, who wanted the chance to label him a Whig, but he promised her that he would 'speak to nobody living to be for it'. He regretted that 'As you are the only body that could have given me happiness, I am the more troubled we should differ so much in our opinions.'[92]

Perhaps he was being shrewd in maintaining an appearance

of unity with the rest of the Cabinet by voting in favour of the Bill that December, or perhaps Sarah was the only one to see the danger of such complacency and to stick out her neck for the occasional conformists and the principle of religious conscience they represented. But Marlborough had once told Godolphin that 'I do not love to be singular', and it was this tendency to maintain consensus, despite private misgivings, that made him so different from his wife. She enjoyed flaunting her indifference to what others thought of her.

After the Bill was shelved, the grateful Whigs were determined not to let Sarah retire from Court, and her friend Elizabeth Burnet begged her not to give up politics for charitable work:

I am sensible you would gain quiet and be more happy, but surely now you do more good & how would the Duke struggle with so many difficulties without your help? . . . You will be a great benefactor to the world though you should only employ your interest to assist the distressed, or defend the innocent when wrongfully accused, but I hope to see your Grace before you take any resolution . . .93

Feeling threatened, the Tories overplayed their hand. In April 1704, Lord Nottingham threatened to resign if Anne did not form an all-Tory ministry, but the Queen called his bluff, and wrote to Sarah to tell her that there would be further forced resignations soon that 'will not be disagreeable to Mrs Freeman'. Sure enough, Sir Edward Seymour and the Earl of Jersey followed Nottingham. Yet she replaced the three not with Sarah's Whig recommendations but with more moderate Tories. Marlborough and Godolphin were behind this centrist policy, and pressed for Robert Harley to succeed Nottingham as Secretary of State for the North (of England and the known world). Exasperated, Sarah reproached them all for taking only half-measures.

When Marlborough set sail from Harwich for the Continent on 8 April 1704, his marriage was in trouble. He and Sarah were not sleeping together and barely speaking. Being one of the first celebrity families, however, they put on a good show for the cheering crowds and kissed goodbye on the quayside.

He had been meeting with various Jacobite agents to try to glean information about the enemy, and at this time was concealing from Sarah – indeed, from everyone except the Queen – his plans for a daring march into the German states. Perhaps Sarah's suspicions that she was not fully in his confidence politically had become mixed up with other suspicions which had been growing in her mind over the previous couple of weeks. At the last minute, before he boarded ship, she slipped a letter into his hand.

A number of undated letters from Marlborough to Sarah answer accusations of infidelity, but it is unclear whether they all relate to the same episode. The first sign of Sarah's suspicion comes in a letter from Marlborough, probably written in early April 1704, some weeks before he was due to depart: 'I do to my great grief see that you have fixed in you so very ill an opinion of me that I must never more think of being happy. If the thought of the children that we have had, or ought else that has ever been dear between us, can oblige you to be so good natured as not to leave my bed for the remaining time I shall be in England, I shall take it kindly to my dying day . . .'[94] He hinted that he might not return from this campaign, and made reference to having given 'my poor dear child to a man that has made me of all mankind the most unhappiest'. This led Winston Churchill to suppose that their son-in-law Sunderland had informed Sarah of her husband's infidelity. However, despite their crossed swords over the Prince's Bill, it is hard to see why Sunderland would have wanted to cause a rift between his in-laws.

Marlborough's next letter to his wife suggests that the quarrel was simply about politics: 'I know of no design carrying on that makes it necessary for me to impose upon you; nor have I myself any other but that of serving the Queen to my best understanding, without being biased or afraid of either party . . .' But the one that followed it makes it clear that the infidelity in question was also personal:

Your carriage to me of late is so extraordinary that I know not how to behave myself. I thought you used me so barbarously that I was resolved never to send nor speak, but I love too well to be able to keep that resolution. Therefore I desire that you will give me leave to come to you tonight so that I may know in what it is that I have thus offended. I am sure really in thought [emphasis added] I have not, for I do love you with all the truth imaginable.

After Sarah had confronted him with the grounds for her suspicions, he wrote from London: 'You say that every house since I came from St Albans has given you fresh assurances of my hating you, and that you know I have sent to this woman.' He was miserable, he said, because he was never so glad to be with her as in the last four or five days and, he repeated over and over, 'May I and all that is dear to me be cursed if ever I sent to her, or have had anything to do with her, or ever endeavoured to have.' His protestations are so violent that either he was wrongfully accused or, caught out, guiltily desperate for a reconciliation. His last letter to Sarah while he was in England told her that 'your suspicion of me as to this woman, that will vanish', but he mourned the loss of trust between them.

Biographers have often linked 'sexual paranoia' to Sarah's menopause – Iris Butler, for example, wrote that '[e]xtreme sexual jealousy and suspicion of a greatly-loved partner are well-known neurasthenic symptoms in women of middle age'.[95] But although Marlborough wrote her such devoted letters, he was not necessarily faithful. His pre-marital affairs, the large portions of each year that they spent apart, and the general allowances made for male promiscuity in the period, all seem to count for nothing when weighed against the image of Sarah's volatile personality.

The identity of the alleged mistress in 1704 is unclear. One candidate is Elizabeth Cromwell, wife of Lord Southwell, a Joint

Commissioner of the Privy Seal, who wrote an undated reply to what must have been an accusatory letter from Sarah: '[T]hough in your letter you proclaim your lord an ill husband as I often heard you do everywhere, [you] are willing to discharge the cause of it upon anybody but yourself. Give me leave to tell you (with the same frankness you use to me) that . . . what you call your misfortunes have proceeded wholly from yourself.'[96]

Six years later, a letter from Lady Wentworth to her son reported that in the 'next pew to me there sits a young lady very genteel and very fair, but I think far from a beauty, but it's said she is kept by the Duke of Malberry [Marlborough]; his Duchess, for all she is many years older than this, yet she is ten times handsomer'.[97] This is just one titbit of gossip that has filtered down the centuries, but the idea that Marlborough might have meant every loving word he wrote to Sarah yet also have kept mistresses should not be too far-fetched.

After their farewell at Harwich, Marlborough wrote Sarah a long letter from The Hague.[98] In it, he asked her 'what alterations you would have me make as to yourself and the children', which suggests that Sarah had demanded a new will from him. Sarah had told him that she would not live at Blenheim, but he 'should be always welcome to see me at my houses' (the Lodge at Windsor or Sandridge).

Next he wrote a short note to say he was not sure where the forthcoming campaign would be fought, but '[w]hatever becomes of me, I wish you with all my heart, all happiness'.[99] He referred to the letter she had pushed into his hand at Harwich: 'I do own to you that I have had more melancholy thoughts and spleen at what you said in that paper than I am able to express, but was resolved never to have mentioned it more to you . . .'.[100] He signed himself contritely her 'faithful servant, though loaded with many faults'.

Three days later he confided to Sarah his secret strategy to march to the Danube.[101] Three days after that, it seems that the tension between them broke.[102] He had received a letter of via Amsterdam, and in relief and gratitude burned the letter she had given him at Harwich. He was under instruction to burn all her letters anyway, but begged permission to keep this latest 'kind' one in his strongbox until the day he died. It is impossible to tell from the letter whether her forgiveness related to a true trespass or whether he was simply happy that she had calmed down – either way, he declared, 'I do this minute love you better and with more tenderness than ever I did before.'

Marlborough was so cheered by their reconciliation that he almost agreed to Sarah's request to join him on the march, but despite the home comforts provided for officers, this was not feasible. He knew it would be a particularly gruelling race against Marshal de Villeroi's troops. Even their usual channels of communication would falter: 'I reckon I shall be about a month in a continual march, so that I shall not have your letters so regularly as I could wish . . .'

From Godolphin's letters to Sarah after the reconciliation, we can infer that she was deeply anxious about the risk to her husband's life, and was sad that during their last days together in England they had been on bad terms.[103]

Tactfully Godolphin had made no mention of the Marlboroughs' marital problems in his correspondence with them during early April, but it is likely that he was more worried about Sarah's neglected and increasingly uncomfortable relationship with the Queen. On 24 April, as various Cabinet ministers resigned, he warned her that she should not abuse 'that great indulgence of Mrs Morley' by staying away from Court any longer.[104]

5

'Driving the Nail'

On 29 April 1704, Sarah stood at Anne's side in the great banqueting hall at Windsor as a procession of poor and afflicted subjects trudged past. It was the ceremony called 'touching for the evil' in which Anne gave pieces of 'healing' gold to those suffering from scrofula. Sarah had to ensure that the Queen was kept supplied with gold, and while she probably disapproved of the ceremony's associations with Roman Catholicism and divine rule, she would have appreciated the public-relations value of the Queen's conspicuous charity. Most of those who received the money valued their coins more for their intrinsic worth than because of any royalist superstition, yet the old practice, discontinued by William and Mary, was symbolic of the return with Anne to a more hereditary style of monarchy – and the Queen's half-brother, the Pretender, was also 'touching' his followers on the other side of the Channel.

During the ceremony Sarah may well have pondered Anne's Tory proclivities and her own position at Court. At precisely the time that she confronted Marlborough with accusations of infidelity, she was also harbouring suspicions that she was losing the Queen's affection. In May, Anne wrote to assure her that 'It is not in my nature to say I am tenderly fond of you (which is as true as Gospel) if I were not so.'[1] But even if that were true, it did not mean that Anne would govern according to Sarah's advice. She warned Sarah that although she would take her advice on the disposal of a certain church living to Benjamin Hoadly, she must not take offence if Anne double-checked the candidate with the Archbishop of York. This is the first reference we have to Sarah's support for the prominent latitudinarian Hoadly, who became her close friend and co-author. Hoadly was described by an opponent as a 'thin, meagre, sour fellow'² but Sarah liked him and his view that religion was a matter of conscience and social mission, not forced obedience to the Church.

On 24 May, Anne wrote to inform Sarah that, contrary to her earlier promise, she had given the living in question to a High Churchman named Dr Waugh.³ The following evening, the women apparently argued about the Queen's effrontery in ignoring Sarah's wishes.⁴ Sarah was probably embarrassed that she had promised Hoadly something she could not deliver, and hated being patronised by the Queen's pretended compliance while all the time Anne had intended to select another candidate. But Sarah's wishes were not merely personal interest, nor expressed solely to test her control of Anne: it was a genuine championing of religious free-thinking and opposition to the reactionary political role played by the Anglican priesthood. In Anne she faced a woman of a staunch conservative nature. She did not underestimate the Queen, but made the mistake of allowing her to feel that she did. Anne regretted, she wrote, how 'every thing I say is imputed either to partiality or being imposed upon by knaves or fools. I am very sorry anybody should have either of those characters given them, for any fault in my understanding, since all I say proceeds purely from my own poor judgment, which though it may not be so good as other people, I'm sure is a very honest one.'⁵

At the same time, Sarah watched Tory opposition strengthen against a large English military presence on the Continent: Nottingham, Jersey, Buckingham and Seymour were all now publicly critical of Marlborough's policy. Sarah had to lobby the Dutch envoy in London on her husband's behalf for the reinforcements needed to outnumber the French.⁶ At the beginning of May, she wrote to Godolphin to warn him that Nottingham now had nothing but malice for the Ministry and could not be trusted. She knew Godolphin and Marlborough always thought that the reports from her Whig friends about Tory conspiracies, which she believed, were exaggerated.

Marlborough, meanwhile, was in the middle of his march to

rescue the crown of the Habsburg emperor from the French. Along the way people welcomed him and his troops as their saviours, and he confided to Sarah, 'If I have success my name here will not die for some time, which is a pleasure to me, though I should be ill-used by my own country.'[7]

Even before the campaign's culmination in the battle of Blenheim, Marlborough received news that the emperor wished to make him a prince of the Holy Roman Empire, in gratitude for his speedy march to defend Vienna. Characteristically, he did not accept until the Bavarian principality of Mindelheim was created to support the title's dignity. He told Sarah that he would accept the princedom without changing his title in England,[8] but after he was formally invested with it in 1705 we find letters from Continental correspondents addressed to Sarah as 'The Princess and Duchess of Marlborough'.[9] Meanwhile, kings began to write to Marlborough as if he were minor royalty, calling him 'Mon Cousin' – an extraordinary example of a former page and Gentleman of the Bedchamber having pulled himself up by his own army bootstraps.

On the morning of 10 August, Sarah was in London, conspicuously avoiding attendance on Anne at Windsor, when Marlborough's aide-de-camp, Colonel Parke, came galloping to her door. He had with him a message from Marlborough, scrawled after seventeen hours in the saddle, informing her of his victory at Blenheim. The news of the greatest military victory in living memory, which had saved the Habsburg empire and snatched the initiative from the French, came first to her, to be forwarded to the Queen only after she had taken a copy. Marlborough was now not just a respected Captain-General but one of the most famous men in the world, who had decisively altered the balance of power in Europe. The next day he wrote again to make sure that she had understood: 'I can't end my letter without being so vain as to tell my dearest soul that within the memory of man there has been no victory so great as this.'

In the eyes of the public, the news of the victory at Blenheim further cemented the relationship between the Queen and the

Commander who had delivered her reign unprecedented security. As Sarah put it in her memoirs, with her usual anti-Catholic bias, 'The liberties and peace of Europe were in a fair way to be established upon firm and lasting foundations.'[10] However, she also remembered the 'visible dissatisfaction of some people on the news' and, indicating how closely her husband's campaigns were related to her own Westminster battles, remarked that from the reaction of the Tory party, 'one would have imagined that instead of beating the French, he had beat the Church' (in other words, defeated the Tories' third attempt to pass an Occasional Conformity Bill).

The victory should also have bound the Queen closer to her Groom of the Stole, yet Anne continued to deny Sarah the political influence that Sarah's intelligence and ambition demanded. In one of her most revealing complaints, Sarah told the Duke of Montagu that the Queen plied her only with 'common questions about the linings of mantoes, & the weather, instead of talking with that entire freedom & confidence that she used to do'.[11]

Throughout August, both women tried to play the jilted victim of the other's indifference. Sarah wrote to Anne: '[H]ow can you imagine it is possible for me to be persuaded of your kindness only by a kind word or an expression now & then in a letter, when that tone & sincere kindness of heart is wanting & that confidence & reliance which always attends it is gone from me?'

In her replies, meanwhile, the Queen defended herself from Sarah's jealousy of other Court ladies, especially Tories, who might be gaining her trust, such as Lady Sandwich, Lady Frescheville and Lady Fitzharding. As with Sarah's accusations of infidelity to Marlborough, the personal and political were inextricable. In the same letters Anne defended her Tory friends from the accusation that they were secretly thwarted by Marlborough's victory at Blenheim and offered their congratulations through clenched teeth.

Sentimental friendship among women was supposed to be immune from the political splits that sundered society and families, and Anne told Sarah in a letter that she did not want their political differences to come between them: '[D]o not nurse up any hard thoughts of me because I can not enter with you into some notions as other people can.' On 1 September 1704, Godolphin wrote to Sarah, 'I am sorry to find Mrs Morley and Mrs Freeman can not yet bring things quite right. I am sure they will do it at last, and when this case happens between people that love one another so well, it is not impossible but that both may be a little in the wrong.' Though he himself had a good deal of respect for Sarah's political judgement and discussed most matters with her as though she were a fellow Minister, he believed that Sarah should accept the Queen's wish for their friendship to be merely romantic and for her job to consist of maintaining Anne in a pliable humour.

The two women's mutual distrust, however, had gained too much momentum. At some point Sarah quoted to Anne a maxim she had picked up from her favourite author, Montaigne, 'that it was no breach of promise of secrecy to tell such a friend anything, because it was no more than telling it to oneself'.[12] Anne agreed that complete honesty was vital to their friendship.[13] In Sarah's published memoir, however, she said that Anne had introduced and liked to repeat the quotation from Montaigne. They often tried to trade rhetorical places in this way, each wanting to claim an openness of heart that the other failed to reciprocate. Again, what is remarkable is the way that friendship was conceived as an intermingling of souls – the kind of imagery only used at weddings these days.

Six days later the crowds lined the streets to watch Anne and Sarah ride together in an open carriage to the thanksgiving service for Blenheim at St Paul's, and had no inkling of the mounting tension between them. To outsiders the old Cockpit Circle seemed intact, with Harley, Godolphin and Marlborough managing Commons and Cabinet while Sarah managed the Queen. Sarah concealed the extent of the estrangement even from her husband, who was at this time winding his victorious way back to London via the capitals of Europe.

She was in poor health during the autumn of post-Blenheim

celebration. She did not stay in London to revel in everyone's compliments but, before Marlborough's return, went to stay with her daughter Anne at Althorp, where her doctrinaire Whiggism could find better company. The Queen worried that Sarah was again contemplating retirement: 'I can not live without you, & though I wish you and Mr Freeman everything your own hearts can desire, you must not think to live out of the world as long as I am in it'. She persuaded Sarah and Anne Spencer to return to the Lodge at Windsor, where Sarah embarked on the first draft of her memoirs.

With the exercise of riding in the park every day, Sarah's health improved, and during the last week of September she was well enough to dash off a series of political letters to Marlborough, urging him to demand the dismissal of the Lord Keeper, Sir Nathan Wright, whom she described as 'a man despised of all parties, of no use to the Crown, and whose weak and wretched conduct in the Court of Chancery had almost brought his very office into contempt'.[14] She also remarked that Marlborough and Godolphin were playing a fatal game with the Tories, to which her husband replied that 'my pretending to be of no party is not designed to get favour or to deceive anybody.'[15] He would, he said airily, only 'endeavour to leave a good name behind me in countries that have hardly any blessing but that of not knowing the detested names of Whig and Tory'.

On 19 October Sarah wrote to the Treasurer: 'I find I might have won a good wager when I said 17 [Nottingham] would keep his winter quarters in the Queen's house to cabal with all her enemies . . . Why the Queen should accept of such services from people that have no reputation, Lord Marlborough and you will find it a pretty hard thing to give a good reason . . .' (The words 'cabal' and 'clique' were both coined during Sarah's lifetime – an age of parties, clubs and 'closeting'.)

Marlborough begged her not to involve him in driving the Queen towards Whig appointments, but he agreed to write to Godolphin about the threat to the present Ministry posed by the Duke of Buckingham, the Lord Privy Seal.[16] Sarah knew that she could only lobby Godolphin directly with regard to minor Court appointments, and that any suggestion of major Ministerial changes would sound better coming from her husband. Letters from Godolphin to Sarah in November 1704[17] refer to him having complied with her wish that a certain Whig Mr Meredith be created an equerry. Meanwhile, her strategy with regard to Buckingham proved successful: she persuaded Marlborough to persuade Godolphin to persuade the Queen to dismiss him and replace him with the Duke of Newcastle, a Whig.

The same old debates about party prejudice echoed through the correspondence between Anne and Sarah, but with a marked change of tone. As Sarah continued to send the Queen Whig reading materials for her self-improvement (Bishop Burnet's writings, for example), Anne was telling Godolphin that she did not think she and Sarah could ever be true friends again. A copy of a letter from Sarah to Anne, written in late 1704, gives us some idea of how Sarah's well-intentioned advocacy probably left the Queen feeling: at a time when Lady Russell described her as being so ill with gout that she could not set her foot on the ground,[18] and when Godolphin observed that the gout in her knuckles left her hardly able to hold a pen, she received only lectures on history from Sarah. Sarah argued that Charles I had provoked the Civil War and went on to query what Anne meant in saying that there were only a few Jacobites in England when Sarah saw the Tory majority in the Commons obstructing the war effort at every turn.

When she reread her letter in 1711, Sarah did not regret her forceful remonstrations, noting only that 'I really think I have one merit that is not common' – the avoidance of sycophancy. By then she had discovered the personal price to be paid for this merit, but also, and to her mind more importantly, seen many of her predictions about Tory intentions realised. Jonathan Swift's later history of Queen Anne's reign blamed Sarah's fall from favour on her inability to grasp why the frankness of her relationship with her friend should be altered by Anne's sovereignty: 'The Duchess . . . who had been used to great familiarities could not take it into her head that any change of station should put her upon changing her behaviour . . .'[19] In other words, Sarah refused to know her place.

Marlborough was forced to spend longer than planned in Berlin obtaining pledges of troops to defend Savoy. Sarah continued to write to him 'freely of the parties',[20] and during December 1704 her letters kept him informed of developments with the third Occasional Conformity Bill. Since April, the Tories led by Nottingham had been threatening to tack this Bill on to the Money Bill[21] – which meant, in effect, that they would only vote supplies for Marlborough's army if the Whigs permitted the persecution of dissenters. Once again, Sarah gave Godolphin the backbone to join with those who opposed it.

She also lobbied her husband, repeating carefully selected Tory insults until he gradually began to see that, like it or not, the war effort had become dependent on a single party issue: occasional conformity. For the first time he resolved to abandon his ostensible party-neutrality and publicly break with the Tories. Anne, who had written to Sarah in December 1703 that she saw 'nothing like persecution' in the idea of occasional conformity,[22] was also ultimately persuaded to oppose the Bill because it would have formed a serious barrier to union with Scotland. It was defeated in the House of Lords in mid-December. Marlborough received the welcome news, as usual, from his wife's pen.

Marlborough did not arrive back in London until Christmas, bringing with him, alongside fine tapestries from the Electress Sophia for Sarah, several prominent French prisoners-of-war. It was said that the French prisoners were stunned by the extent of English patriotism displayed at Marlborough's victory parade through London on 23 January, and for the first time understood that he was no longer merely a 'general of favour', thanks to his wife, but a national hero.[23]

After the battle of Blenheim, the English were exhibiting a new smugness from having led Europe's resistance to French hegemony. Marlborough's victories directly fed the flames of this national pride, and his wife could hardly be blamed if she increasingly conflated her own family's destiny with that of England. When the Queen made it known that she wished to reward Marlborough for his latest military services, someone proposed that a statue of him should be placed, with one of the Queen, inside a square of townhouses to be built near Charing Cross and called Blenheim Square. However, Godolphin thought this idea imprudent: 'I am not fond of the proposal of two statues, one for the Queen and th'other for the Duke of Marlborough. What merit soever a subject may have, I am doubtful that may set him upon too near an equality with one upon the Throne.'[24]

On 17 January, after some debate, Anne suggested granting the royal manor of Woodstock, a wilderness of 15,000 acres, to the Marlboroughs, and that the State coffers should pay for the construction of a magnificent house there. Unfortunately, in view of future quarrels, this commitment was not officially recorded.

It is not certain how the playwright-turned-architect Sir John Vanbrugh was introduced to the project. According to Sarah, it was their mutual friend Mr Craggs who introduced him.[25] Vanbrugh's taste for monumentality had been influenced by the mausolea and palaces he had seen on his travels as a young man on the west coast of India where he had dealt in silks and cottons. Marlborough admired Castle Howard, which Vanbrugh had recently completed for Lord Carlisle, and Sarah must have approved of his Whig credentials. On 17 June 1705, therefore, together with his assistant Nicholas Hawksmoor, Vanbrugh signed the warrant that put him in charge of the works at Woodstock, to become known as Blenheim Palace during the nineteenth century.

The following day, at dusk, there was a ceremonial laying of a foundation stone by the Marlboroughs' daughter Anne. All the locals, who would benefit enormously from the work involved in building the great house, were invited. They enjoyed several kinds of music and three groups of morris dancers: one of men, one of young girls, and one of old women. About a hundred buckets, bowls and pans filled with wine, punch, cakes and ale were laid on.[26] Sarah played hostess in the Oxfordshire countryside, while her daughter Mary stopped in at St James's to check that her mother's pet nightingales were being properly fed and watered by the servants.[27]

Sarah's choice of Anne to lay the stone was indicative of the tensions that persisted between Sarah and her more glamorous daughter Henrietta. Henrietta continued to bridle at her mother's censoriousness over her friendships. Godolphin had tried to bring about a reconciliation between them in late November 1704, but the resulting truce had proved fragile. As with Jack, therefore, mother and daughter were not speaking when, in February, Henrietta fell ill with smallpox. She was attended by Dr Samuel Garth, soon to become a trusted friend of her mother's, who prescribed drinking of possets (hot milk with liquor, spices and other ingredients such as sage or pippin apple seeds) but did not immediately inform the patient of his diagnosis.[28] Sarah wrote later that upon hearing the news of her daughter's illness she 'flew from Woodstock without sleeping or eating'[29] and nursed her day and night. Henrietta eventually recovered, but was left permanently disfigured.

The following month saw the marriage of Mary, Sarah's youngest daughter, to John Montagu, Lord Monthermer, son of the 1st Duke of Montagu, and a cousin of the Junto member Charles Montagu, Lord Halifax. In the summer of 1704, after over a year's consideration, Marlborough had reluctantly agreed to accept the offer on condition that they wait until the groom turned sixteen. Another proposal from Lord Peterborough's son, Lord Mordaunt, had been rejected the previous summer because Marlborough thought him a 'rascal' and warned that if Mary did 'not esteem the young man, it is neither title nor estate that can make her happy'.[30] From this we can presume that Mary had some say in her betrothal to Monthermer and hence to one of the most politically important families in the country. For Sarah the marriage was another useful tie between herself and the Junto.

The marriage took place on 20 March 1705 at St James's Palace in the presence of the Queen. After the wedding the fifteen-year-old bride continued to live with her mother, the expense of which Sarah considered a favour to the Montagus. When her husband wanted her to join him, she moved to live at Montagu House, on what is today the site of the British Museum. Sarah had obtained a Court post as Master of the Wardrobe for her new son-in-law as part of her daughter's dowry.

After Mary moved out, Sarah was angered to hear that she was complaining about her allowance being cut from £800 to £500 a year, especially given that Mary's husband continued to bill Sarah for Mary's dresses for some years into the marriage.[31] However, to be fair to Mary, her complaints were only about the cost of keeping up appearances as the lady her parents had raised her to be. And perhaps they could have been more generous: the joint annual income of the Duke and Duchess of Marlborough, as calculated by one pamphleteer, was around £65,000.[32] This was more than Anne's income before her accession, and compares to an average annual income for a nobleman at that time of £3,000, or for a milkmaid of just £2.[33]

Though Mary came to visit her mother at her lodgings in St James's Palace often enough, relations between them were strained. Sarah took offence at her daughter's manner: 'One of her fancies was when she was first married, that if she met me in any visit or public place, she would not make me a curtsy . . .'[34] Mary explained, 'I am so unfortunate that you take so many things ill of me without saying what, that it comes at last to make you so angry that then I must own I do not know how to behave myself to you, nor what to do of any kind,' which further offended her mother who hated, above all, to be called irrational.

The following spring, when Mary was pregnant with her first child, Lord Monthermer went to join the war. Apparently neither that experience nor any of his subsequent careers matured him. Many years and many arguments later, Sarah dismissed him cuttingly: 'All his talents lie in things only natural in boys of fifteen years old . . . to get people into his garden and wet them with squirts, and to invite people to his country houses and put things into their beds to make them itch . . .'[35]

In April 1705 Marlborough returned to The Hague, where he met Sarah's sister, now living in Delft having fallen out with the other Jacobite exiles at Saint-Germains. He told Sarah that Frances 'was very full of expressions of your goodness and my civilities, but not one word of politics, which I am extreme glad of . . .'[36]

We know that Frances was in England again some time during the winter of 1704 and wrote to Marlborough, who checked with his wife as to whether her presence had been sanctioned by the Queen before he replied.[37] She and Sarah are likely to have met in September 1702, when Frances passed incognito through Bath, *en route* to Ireland, and 'Lady Marlborough went that same day to see her and returned that night'.[38] It is very probable that the sisters met again in 1704 and in 1708, but only briefly and as discreetly as possible.

During the spring of 1705, however, Sarah's main preoccupation was neither her daughters' nor her sister's welfare: it was the forthcoming general election. She prolonged her absence from Court, and focused on campaigning for the Whigs through male agents, such as Mr Craggs, and by means of strategic correspondence with contacts wherever the Marlboroughs owned property. In April Marlborough wrote to her from The Hague to tell her that he wanted William Cadogan, his Quartermaster-General and unofficial Chief of Army Intelligence from 1701 to 1712, to be his candidate in Woodstock.[39] He asked Sarah to work on it and to take advice from Lord Halifax and the Tory Henry St John.

Sarah concentrated her efforts elsewhere: she went in person to St Albans to canvas for Mr Henry Killigrew who was opposing a Tory 'Tacker' named John Gape,[40] who had been elected in 1702 alongside Marlborough's brother George Churchill. Sarah made use of the Queen's name and of what most patriotic voters assumed was her continuing knowledge of the Queen's wishes. She also asked her friends to support Mr Killigrew's election, observing, 'I dare say tis what the Duke of Marlborough would recommend if he were here.'[41]

In 1705 the Whigs won a sizeable majority, making effective

government dependent upon their support, as Sarah had long foreseen. Now Godolphin and Marlborough were forced to the same conclusion. Godolphin wrote to Sarah to express his disappointment that his son, and her son-in-law, Francis had been defeated in the contest at Cambridge.[42] High Tory churchmen had campaigned energetically against the Godolphins and this seems to have played a significant part in persuading Godolphin to move closer to the Whigs, with whom he had already started working during the winter session.

Sarah's own electioneering efforts were rather more successful: Killigrew won in St Albans. However, after Sarah encouraged him to take a case to the Committee of Elections and Privileges, alleging that the Tories had tried to rig the vote, the Tories retaliated by claiming that Sarah had placed undue pressure on her tenants – in other words, had dined, intoxicated, bribed, bamboozled or threatened them beyond the usual measure. The case was heard in the Commons on 14–16 November 1705, but the best evidence the Tories could muster was a gift of twenty guineas given to one Thomas Crosfield, an old servant of her mother's, which Sarah was able to show had been only to get him out of gaol – albeit conveniently in time to vote.[43] Other interesting evidence includes testimony that Sarah had systematically called prominent local voters to see her and forced them to listen to political lectures in which she alleged that Mr Gape was a Jacobite and a papist.[44]

Sarah wrote a note on some of the relevant correspondence, referring to the 'noise the Tories made against me in the House of Commons where Mr Bromley said a great many very unhandsome things & compared me to some strong woman in a history I have forgot'.[45] This 'strong woman in a history' was Alice Perrers, the favourite of Edward III. Even more pointedly, in the final Committee Report of 24 November, Sarah was compared to James I's lover, the Duke of Buckingham. So although she won the case, Sarah had been publicly attacked for exploiting a romantic relationship with the monarch for party-political ends.

It was not unusual for ladies in this period to campaign behind the scenes on behalf of male family members. Sarah placed her husband's reputation at the top of her list of priorities. She never campaigned in a borough where she did not have a direct family or property interest, and she never appeared in person at the hustings. Such actions were not to be taken by a woman until the 1780s when her great-great-grand-daughter, Georgiana, Duchess of Devonshire, carried on the family tradition of Whig electioneering with a vengeance. Yet Sarah's involvement in politics was far more independent, more based on her own opinions, than that of any female contemporary. In an age where only one in five adult men had the franchise and where she herself had no vote, Sarah's belief in her right to act as her husband's proxy, but ignoring his instructions, was radical.

The core of her career coincided with a decade in which politics were unusually pervasive in England (ten general elections in the twenty years since 1694) and the freedom Sarah gained from Marlborough's absence at war was indicative of a wider social and economic, if not political, freedom enjoyed by English women of all classes during the War of Spanish Succession. There was also a great deal less commercialised leisure on offer to divert bored duchesses than in the second half of the eighteenth century or subsequently. But Sarah's political ambitions went beyond a hobby. Genuinely enamoured of Whig principles – we know she had been reading Locke in 1705 – and driven by a streak of personal ambition, which was then considered a uniquely male prerogative, she later reflected: 'I am confident I should have been the greatest hero that ever was known in the Parliament House, if I had been so happy as to have been a man.'[46]

During the first two or three years of Anne's reign, as piles of petitions spilled across her desk every morning and both Godolphin and her son-in-law Sunderland confided in her about government business over dinner, Sarah's confidence in her own political judgement grew. She considered herself as well qualified and as legitimately 'in power' as Ministers who almost all owed their posts to accidents of birth. She was later to boast to Bishop Burnet that she had 'a great deal of experience of the men on both sides' and 'a certain knowledge of a great many facts which Her Majesty could hear from nobody else'.[47] Unfortunately Anne did not share this confidence in Sarah's abilities.

A young man who had just left Cambridge wrote to Sarah hoping to secure patronage for his writing:

Your Grace has asserted the liberty of your sex & convinced the other of their unjust usurption . . . your extraordinary talents have equalled the greatest examples upon record, two of them crowned heads: Queen Elizabeth & Queen Christine of Sweden were your illustrious predecessors in this glorious enterprise . . . Your Grace is intimately acquainted with the whole fabric of government & can with inimitable skill play the springs that will set in motion the mighty pageant of State . . .

He went on to describe the Duke of Marlborough as laying the spoils of war before her feet as if she were queen.[48]

We do not know if the young man's rather brazen bid for patronage was successful, but Sarah preferred to patronise anonymously. In this spirit she had forwarded a gift to Daniel Defoe in recognition of his support for the Whigs during the 1705 elections: letters from Lord Halifax to Sarah in May refer to a sum of £200 (equivalent to just over £15,000 today), which she asked him to pass on to the author without disclosing the source.[49] She had probably been prompted directly by Defoe's poem *A Hymn to Victory*, which celebrated Marlborough's military achievements and tried to cast the Duke as a moderate Whig rather than a Tory, or perhaps by *The Double Welcome* (1705), which celebrated Marlborough's return to England.

In the previous year Defoe had begun to publish his Whig newspaper, *The Review*, and what he wrote publicly in it Sarah wrote privately in her letters to her husband, the Treasurer and the Queen. With common targets – for example, Nottingham and Sir George Rooke – Defoe and Sarah were a pair of powerful voices speaking, coincidentally, in unison. Marlborough was ambivalent about both, and slow to appreciate the value of the press in modern politics: 'I do not know who the author of "*The Review*" is, but I do not love to see my name in print; for I am persuaded that an honest man must be justified by his own actions and not by the pen of a writer.'[50]

It was a bitter irony for Sarah to reflect that the satires against her as a royal favourite only started to come thick and fast just as she was losing the Queen's trust and affection. In 1705, as Tory election campaign literature, Mrs Delariviere Manley published *Queen Zarah*. It describes Sarah's lowly birth and how she 'received the breath of life common to all other creatures ... but which none has improved to her vast advantage'. Jenisa, Zarah's pimping mother, is described as willing to compromise her own daughter for the sake of engineering the family's social rise, but the real target of this accusation of gross ambition was Sarah and the Whig party. At the same time, the accusation of pimping may have been a swipe at Sarah as a mother notorious for arranging the marriages of her own children to secure specific political alliances.

Queen Zarah was the first satire to tell the full story of Marlborough's pre-marital affair with Manley's old patron, Barbara Castlemaine. By 1705 Barbara was back from Paris and living in St James's. She had married a gambler, Major-General Robert 'Beau' Fielding, who, like Mrs Manley's first husband, turned out to be a bigamist. It is possible that there is a link, perhaps only of association, between Barbara's presence in the neighbourhood and Sarah's reawakened suspicions about Marlborough's fidelity during the previous year (although Barbara was now sixty-three, and would die several years later from something that made her swell to 'a monstrous bulk').[51]

Mrs Manley's history *à clef* extended the eroticism of the Restoration Court into William and Mary's reign, then Queen Anne's. She claimed that the Duke of Shrewsbury (Salopius) once raped Sarah, who was surprised by this but had the presence of mind to ask him about politics when he had finished. In a way it is as if Manley cannot help delighting in the energy and audacity of Zarah even as she sets out to vilify her. Women who were thought to dominate their husbands were often referred to as 'queens', equating their domestic revolutions with political ones, and in *Queen Zarah* Marlborough is criticised for handing the reins of power to his wife, who is depicted as an emblem of the Whore of Babylon in her chariot, or mounted on the back of Faction, a monstrous beast.

In 1709 Mrs Manley wrote *The Secret Memoirs and Manners of several Persons of Quality of Both Sexes. From the New Atalantis*, an even more exuberantly slanderous fiction. It went further than *Queen Zarah* and suggested that Sarah's mother was not only an immoral old bawd but also a sorceress able to foretell the future: 'The public would have it that she knew more than the common race of mortals; in short, that she was conversant with the Demon, who gave her to understand the future.'

Another bestseller of 1712 included Sarah's mother, by now dead for nineteen years, as a witch-like ghost. *The Story of the St Alb[a]ns Ghost, OR The Apparition of Mother Haggy* has sometimes been attributed to Jonathan Swift, but usually to William Wagstaffe (1685–1725). It states that 'Mother Haggy' was not born of human flesh at all. At Sarah's birth she sees omens of her daughter's life: a coronet appears in her crib and then shatters. 'Such,' cries old Mother Haggy, 'will be the fortune of my daughter, and such her fall.' What comes across is anxiety that Sarah, a girl from a landed but not particularly noble family, was able to rise until she sat alongside Queen Anne and, indirectly, controlled the British government. Supernatural parenthood was the only explanation; the Macbeth story was somehow less threatening to their enemies than the truth of the Marlboroughs' social mobility.

In an earlier political poem from around 1703, 'The Witchcraft', Sarah is described as the incarnation of her dead mother's magical influence, undermining the national interest:

No wonder Magic Art surrounds the Th[rone],
Old Mother J[enn]ings in her Grace is known;
Old England's Genius rouse, these Charms dispel,
Burn but the Witch, and all is well.[52]

And a mock-prophecy, written after the victory at Blenheim, has Sarah as a witch turned usurping princess:

When a Church on a Hill to the Danube advance,
Then's near to his Ruin the best cock in France,
Then Three shall beat five, being Angered in Spain,
And Five out of Eight run to Paris again,
Then the Witch of St Albans a Princess shall be . . .[53]

Politically rebellious women were, like witches, still threatened with being burned alive. An ecstatic letter of thanks survives from one Anne Merryweather,[54] for whom Sarah seems to have arranged a pardon in July 1702.[55] In a note Sarah explained that 'this is from a woman of a great age that I got out of prison, where she had been kept many years & had been brought out several times to be burnt for having dispensed treason, but she would never confess who employed her.' Witch-hunting had always blossomed at times when women had inherited or claimed positions of govern-mental power – under Elizabeth I and Mary I, for example – and anophobia – fear of old women – was rife in the early eighteenth century. Witches in English folklore were thought to be perverted mothers, and those accused were often old beggarwomen who demanded support aggressively from their children or villages.[56] This resonance, combined with the gossip that Mrs Jennings had supplied Charles II with mistresses, explains why she suffered the same satirical treatment as her daughter.

Sarah never answered these slanders: she said that there was a class of Grub Street story too ridiculous to refute. Neverthe-less, somewhere in all her writing, out of sheer duty, she might have been expected to leave us a portrait of her mother's true character. She did not, partly because men like Bishop Burnet, Lord Dartmouth or Lord Bolingbroke did not degrade their political memoirs by speaking about their mothers. In the version co-written by Burnet, she declared: 'I do not think the world ought to be troubled with impertinent stories; I shall only insist on what was public & fit to be known . . .' Perhaps, in fact, the truth about her mother was not.

In the summer of 1705, when Marlborough returned to war, his son-in-law Lord Sunderland travelled with him as a special envoy to Vienna. The fact that Sunderland's entourage of Whigs rode alongside Marlborough's own caravan was symbolic of the Commander's shift of loyalties after the election and after the conflict over occasional conformity.

In his letters home, he railed as usual against the negligence and stubbornness of the European princes he was trying to help,[57] but he also referred constantly to the building works at Woodstock: 'Pray press on my house and gardens,'[58] he wrote, and asked Sarah to supervise the killing of rabbits in the areas of the grounds to be planted by their head gardener, Henry Wise.[59]

Sarah was constantly concerned about her husband's health during the 1705 campaign. He wrote to her about loss of weight, headaches and that his blood was 'so hot I can hardly hold my pen'.[60] He had been forced to abandon his strategy on the Moselle earlier that summer to defend the city of Liège after Marshal Villeroi had pounced on Huy, and his Imperial allies were transferring their troops from the Rhine to Italy. 'My dearest soul, pity me and love me,' he wrote to Sarah at this his lowest point in the war so far. Most of all he feared that the Dutch generals' refusal to fight offensively indicated that they were engaged in peace negotiations with the French behind his back. To divide the Allies, Louis XIV had offered terms that satisfied the Dutch but meant letting Philip V, his grandson, take the Spanish throne, thereby abandoning one of the central aims of the war. 'No Peace Without Spain', which meant no peace without Charles III, the Allied candidate, on the Spanish throne, became the Whig motto.

That July Charles III wrote to Sarah from his ship, *The Remela*, choosing to pay his respects to Queen Anne through her favourite's 'most pleasing hand'.[61] This was a reference to an incident in 1702 when he had visited London *en route* to taking up the Spanish throne and had publicly slipped a ring on to Sarah's finger while she held a fingerbowl for him at a banquet, as an acknowledgement of her influence and in allusion to the ring given in the sixteenth century by the Holy Roman Emperor, Charles V, to the mistress of the French King, Francis 1.

Meanwhile Sarah continued to receive Marlborough's exaggerated accounts of how each strategic failure resulted from Allied indecision. On 17–18 July, he had executed another bold plan: the crossing of the Lines of Brabant, which were fortifications that ran from Namur to Brabant, by tricking the French as to where he would cross. Whether due to his own flagging energies or to excessive Allied caution he was not able, however, to capitalise on this achievement.

On 15 August, Marlborough's troops had reached Corbaix, near Brussels, where they encamped. In those days armies could only march until they needed to bake fresh bread, which was about every fourth day.[62] As usual the bivouacs were arranged in the centre of the camp, the guns and munitions stored a safe distance from the foot-soldiers' ridge-tents, the standards prominently displayed to the fore, and Marlborough's own spacious tent pitched safely to the rear. Through its entrance, with the flap pinned back to let in the evening breeze, he could smell the baking and watch his men settling down to cook their rations around campfires. The horses were being watered and the foraging parties were returning from the woods with what they had trapped and shot.

Lying back on his azure camp-bed, Marlborough finally had time to turn his attention to Sarah's letters, and in particular a satirical Tory pamphlet she had just sent him, entitled *The Memorial for the Church of England*. He called this pamphlet 'the most impudent and scurrilous thing I ever read', and wrote to Godolphin that he wanted the anonymous author (one Dr James Drake) found and punished.[63] Sarah also sent Marlborough copies of another newspaper she admired, *The Observator*,[64] edited by a vehement Whig survivor of the Bloody Assizes named John Tutchin. Marlborough regarded this paper as Whig extremism, and an unsubstantiated source tells us that he later threatened to 'find some friend that will break his and the printer's bones'[65] This was shortly before the editor was beaten up by a street gang and died of his injuries in September 1707.

While Marlborough's claim to feel no concern for the opinions of the reading public at large might have been a noble stance when it concerned his reputation alone,[66] there was something a little ungallant about it when Sarah was the surrogate victim of attacks on him. In the summer of 1704, she had sent him a poem entitled *Faction Display'd* (November 1703–January 1704) by William Shippen that he said was so far beneath them that it 'does not deserve the title good or bad.'[67] In it, Sarah was depicted as Sempronia, born of 'a lewd procuring race, / The Senate's grievance, and the Court's disgrace'. The other female character in the poem was also, obliquely, an image of Sarah: Faction herself, 'a restless and repining Fiend' who curdles the blood of men and 'gnaws upon their Mind'. Faction was clearly a Whig, and the poet was only thankful that England was not a republic where the monster would grow to become a 'Hydra-State, / Whose many Heads threaten each others Fate.' She sat smiling approval in the corner as the Whig Junto and her disciple Sempronia caballed at the Duke of Somerset's house.

The poem's 'Club that gave Direction to the State' was a reference to the Kit-Cat Club, which had been founded as a non-partisan meeting of literati at the tavern of Christopher Cat in Shire Lane, but had now grown distinctly Whig. In 1710, when his Whig allegiance was better established, Marlborough would join the Kit-Cat. As a woman Sarah was not allowed to be a member but often found reason to be in the room when the club met, so that when the Whigs fell from power Lady Hyde would gloat that Sarah would have to 'forget all the joys of the Kit-Cat'.

Sarah apparently believed that Matthew Prior was the author

of *Faction Display'd*. In retaliation she was responsible for the poet losing his position on the Commission of Trade, his main source of income. Prior wrote in his diary that he had declared his innocence to Godolphin,[68] and that the Treasurer had promised to act as intermediary with Sarah. Prior tried to prove his loyalty to the Marlboroughs by writing several adulatory poems about the Duke's military victories. When he sent them to Sarah she returned them unopened, 'declaring that she should not receive anything of [Prior's] writing for that she was persuaded that he could not mean well to her or her family'.[69]

The fact that Sarah had to defend herself against her attackers without assistance was shown when Prior sent a similar poem directly to Marlborough and the Duke not only wrote back a note of appreciation, indicating that he had no knowledge of his wife's grudge, but also procured a pension of £500 for the poet. Marlborough later had to write an apology to Sarah for undermining her vendetta in this way.[70] Four years later, still unable to gain reappointment to the Commission thanks to Sarah's prejudice against him, Prior wrote to the Duke that he desired 'no more of my lady Duchess than that she would not think me a villain and a libeller'[71] and also to Sarah, 'averring that he had ever esteemed her as one of the best of women & would justify that esteem with his life'.[72] But it was of no use. Prior would have to wait for the rise of other, Tory patrons to restart his career.

On 20 June 1705, Godolphin wrote to Sarah: 'I did read last night to Mrs Morley my letter from Lord Marlborough . . . I thought the best way was not to make any comment at all upon it, but to leave that to her own reflections; and I believe it will have a better effect, and make more impression that way, than by all the labour and endeavour one could use to enforce it.' This was a subtle hint to Sarah to stop lobbying Anne, and perhaps she took it, for on 22 August Marlborough wrote that he was pleased to hear things were easier with the Queen and that he was 'very confident by 72 [Godolphin's] letters it would be of great use to him'.

The Queen had been forced to take Sarah's side in an argument with Lady Frescheville, whom Sarah accused of having been impertinent to her while the Court had been in Winchester.[73] Marlborough described Lady Frescheville as one to whom malice was 'as natural . . . as eating', and Sarah branded her a kleptomaniac. Sarah noted that although she had given Lady Frescheville her post, she could only interpret the woman's rudeness as ambition to replace her as Groom of the Stole. That another Lady of the Bedchamber should entertain such an idea and dare to insult Sarah was an indicator of Sarah's uncertain standing with the Queen, and it was for this reason that Marlborough, in the middle of his campaigning, took some interest in the ladies' spat. Sarah told him that 'a great change' had come over Anne, who was now writing to her less frequently. She had told Anne that she could no longer stand to live with her 'infatuation' for the Tories when it was clear that they were not true supporters of the war effort. She concluded: 'I hope you will pardon me for not waiting upon you, for tis not possible to love you and your interest as I do & not say a great many things that I know (by sad experience) is [*sic*] uneasy to you . . .'

However, Sarah's influence was far from at an end. In late September, Anne reluctantly dismissed Sir Nathan Wright as Lord Keeper and on 11 October appointed the Whig William Cowper in his place – a 'Cabinet reshuffle' for which Sarah gave herself primary credit.[74] The Whigs believed Sarah had been responsible for persuading Anne to accept Cowper even though the Keepership controlled a great deal of Church patronage and the Queen was suspicious of Whigs, even moderate ones, when it came to protecting the Church. (Wright had been what Sarah called 'a warm stickler'[75] for it.) Sunderland wrote to his mother-in-law from Vienna to thank her on behalf of the Junto, adding that 'If England is saved it is entirely owing to your good intentions, zeal, and the pains you have taken for it.'[76]

Godolphin enlisted Sarah's help in several more minor matters. On 19 September, for example, he wrote asking her to talk to her friend Lady Grandison and thereby secure the vote of her son, John Fitzgerald MP, for the government. He also thanked Sarah for letting him know about an anti-government sermon that had been preached. As Sarah and Godolphin grew increasingly united (he had even promised Sarah never to speak to the Queen about any petition without first notifying her),[77] Anne appealed to Marlborough not to take his wife's side against her as well.

The more bloody the war became, the more the now fifty-five-year-old Duke invoked his dream of the house and garden at Woodstock as a pastoral retirement paradise. At this point he limited Sarah to following his instructions with regard to the interior: 'I know you will not like the house till it be furnished, which must be your business, and I will make it mine that the stables may be so well filled that you have pleasure in riding.'[78] The number of alterations to the original designs was already alarming, and Sarah wrote privately to Godolphin about her fears for the 'expense and unwieldiness' of the project. In July she had had the sensible idea of asking Sir Christopher Wren to give an independent estimate, based on Vanbrugh's designs, of the project's estimated cost. Wren came up with a figure of more than twice what Vanbrugh had suggested. At his instigation, and with Sarah's encouragement, Marlborough therefore instructed Vanbrugh to make a model so as to limit the number of further alterations.[79]

Godolphin told Sarah to try to think of the house more as a national monument than a private home.[80] It was sage advice, which Sarah could never quite accept – and indeed, if a national monument had been the intention behind the gift, that it should take the form of a private house was odd. The confusion between public and private interests could not have been more clearly illustrated than by the rising foundations at Woodstock, which Sarah went to survey in the company of what the Oxfordshire Tories described as 'a parcel of Whiggish, mobbish people'.[81]

In Vienna, after having toured Europe to reunite faltering Allies, Marlborough was formally invested with the principality of Mindelheim by the new Habsburg Emperor Joseph I. He travelled home via Berlin, where he smoothed relations with

Frederick I of Prussia, and then via Hanover – his second visit to the heirs to the English throne.

When Anne's second Parliament opened in October 1705, the Tories, led by Nottingham, Rochester and the mischievous Lord Haversham, made a serious miscalculation: they introduced a motion to the House of Lords pressing for the Electress of Hanover to be invited to reside in England. This move was intended to usurp the Whig claim to be the party of Protestant succession, but the Queen was appalled at the idea: she feared that the presence of a foreign heir would only prove to be a rallying point for opposition factions. In a draft memoir Sarah explained how it 'came to be accounted a great piece of rudeness to mention the House of Hanover in addresses to the throne; & to be interpreted as no better than presenting the Sovereign with a death's head . . .'[82]

The 'invitation crisis' reached a climax in November. Sarah advised Anne against inviting the Electress and recommended inviting the young Prince of Hanover instead.[83] Had Anne taken her advice and extended such an invitation to George, the British people may not have found themselves later ruled by a king with little knowledge of their country. But Anne was equally offended at this suggestion, as it meant admitting that she would never have another child, and because it reminded her conscience that she had disowned her half-brother.

The Whigs, adroitly, swapped their usual colours for the purposes of helping the Queen fend off this Tory Bill. In doing so, they won more of her favour than they had so far enjoyed. It was their opportunism, rather than Sarah's letters or lectures, that made Anne write to Sarah after the crisis had passed, 'I believe dear Mrs Freeman and I shall not disagree as we have formerly done . . .'[84]

On 12 April 1706 Marlborough sailed again from Greenwich. He left Godolphin to try to meet the Whig demand that Lord Sunderland should replace the Tory Sir Charles Hedges as Secretary of State for the South (of England, Europe and the known world). Before the year's end, this ministerial battle would exhaust Sarah's last supply of influence over Anne.

Halifax, who had first suggested it, imagined that Sunderland would be a more palatable candidate for the Queen because he was the Marlboroughs' son-in-law. Sarah recalled one of the Whigs telling her that it would be 'driving the nail that would go'.[85] In reality, however, as Godolphin glumly put it in a letter of April 1706: 'That matter goes so much uphill with her [the Queen] that she will hate one for endeavouring to persuade her to half of what is really necessary for her own good.' At least now the Treasurer was sharing the same frustrations as Sarah, even if only to pacify Whig MPs and bankers rather than out of conviction. At first Sarah did not intervene with the Queen over Sunderland. She feared that to do so would look too much as if she was seeking only family advancement and knew that her own influence had lately been less effective than the Junto supposed – perhaps even counter-productive.

Anne objected to Sunderland's advancement because he was what she called 'a party man'[86] and because she believed he had the same temperament as his mother-in-law.[87] Furthermore she objected, as a matter of principle, to being forced to make any change in her Cabinet against her wishes. To do so would be to set an irreversible precedent in terms of the power of the House of Commons. Sarah and Godolphin sought a more personal explanation – a rival favourite who might be strengthening Anne's resolve against the appointment. They cast around for suspects.

As far back as February 1704, Marlborough and Sarah had discussed whether Marlborough's own younger brother, Charles, was feeding the Queen with Tory opinions through his intimate relationship with the Prince Consort.[88] Then Sarah had suggested that Marlborough's other Tory brother, Admiral George Churchill, might be the rival favourite, but by the summer of 1706, Marlborough told Sarah he feared somebody else was making the Queen 'uneasy'.[89] Although he was too far away to judge properly, he wrote to Sarah that 'I can't but think you lay a great deal more to 49 [George Churchill's] charge than he deserves, for 83 [Queen Anne] has no good opinion nor never speaks of him.'[90]

When he told Sarah he was unable to give Sunderland's appointment his full support, because he preferred the Queen's centrist policy to that of the Whig Junto, Marlborough remarked ironically that he knew 'very well you rely on other people's judgement in this matter', as if his wife were the monarch with secret advisers. He believed that everyone would be happier if the Whigs backed off and Sunderland settled for a lesser post.[91] Knowing how Sarah would receive this opinion, he concluded the letter affectionately: 'Writing this by candlelight, I am so blind that I can't read it, so that if there be anything in it that should not be, burn it, and think kindly of me who loves you with all his heart.'[92]

Sunderland had returned from his 1705 trip with his reputation for diplomacy much enhanced. He had previously been distrusted as the kind of radical (educated at the University of Utrecht) who was always running down his own country in comparison to the Venetian or Dutch republics. With the exception of their row over the Prince's Bill in 1702, he and Sarah had usually seen eye to eye. In contrast, she thought Secretary Hedges had 'no capacity, no quality, no interest', being only the flunky of Lord Rochester.[93]

Surprisingly, Sarah made no bones about the gap between her own and her husband's wishes when it came to Sunderland's appointment. In her memoirs, she quoted a long letter from Marlborough in which he voiced his doubts. But even if Marlborough was predisposed to agree with Anne's preference for a bipartisan government, he was also aware that her rejection of his son-in-law would reflect badly on his own standing. It was remarkable that he was so sensitive about it. On 16 May 1706, his army had erased the ignominious memories of the previous year's abandoned strategy by winning the battle of Ramillies, which forced the French to surrender most of the Spanish Netherlands. He wrote to Sarah that he had not told her about the battle in advance so as not to worry her.[94] Indeed, he had come so close to being killed that an equerry had been shot dead while holding Marlborough's stirrup for him.

The victory occurred while, as Sarah put it, the appointment of Sunderland was still hanging in suspense.[95] For Sarah, who saw the pleasing of the Whigs as essential to the continuation of the fight against French tyranny, these matters were inextricably bound together.

Throughout the long, sweltering summer Anne felt besieged. One observer remarked that she appeared like a pauper with 'a poultice and some nasty bandages' tied to her gouty limbs: 'Nature seems to be inverted when a poor infirm woman becomes one of the rulers of the world.'[96] Sarah still did not speak directly to her about the appointment, yet constantly implied her displeasure, and Anne's letters from early summer 1706 are confused and emotional, begging Sarah to tell her what the matter is, complaining of Sarah's unkindness: 'I must thank my dear Mrs Freeman for the kindness she expresses in her letter to Lord Treasurer for her poor unfortunate faithful Morley, but had much rather have received two lines from yourself in the style which you say is very unfit. I am very impatient to know the reasons why you would not see me last Saturday . . .'[97]

Sarah, too, was suffering from 'fits', for which she was taking a medicinal 'course of steel.'[98] In late July, perhaps encouraged by the increasingly desperate Godolphin, she and Anne nursed their respective ailments together at Windsor. Sarah had always said that London was disagreeable to her when she had nothing to do there,[99] and at least in Windsor she could keep an eye on who else met with the Queen. In public their behaviour together must have appeared frosty. When Anne later referred back to these times and described Sarah's looks as full of 'disdain', Sarah called it a 'mighty ridiculous' term to use since: 'I never looked upon [Anne] at all, but talked always to other people when I waited upon her in public places . . .'[100]

Nor are there any records of their conversations over the weeks that Sarah waited on the Queen in her boudoir, a polygonal room in a turret over the Norman gateway of Windsor Castle. One day, however, sitting at a tea-table laid with ratafia biscuits, and all the condiments for Bohea tea – orange brandy, aniseed, cinnamon, citron or Barbados water – as she listened to Anne talk about her wardrobe, her lapdogs and her husband's asthma, Sarah must finally have lost patience and raised the subject of Lord Sunderland's promotion. The conversation made Anne so 'uneasy' that Sarah had to excuse herself from Court and move back to St Albans on 27 August. She left behind, however, a long letter that expressed the hope that 'Mr and Mrs Morley may see their errors as to this nation before it is too late.'[101] She received no reply but heard that the Queen had been much offended by this. Godolphin told her: '[The Queen] complained of a letter she had received from Mrs Freeman which she said with a great deal of stiffness and reservedness in her looks was VERY EXTRAORDINARY in her opinion . . .'[102]

Sarah begged Anne to show the Treasurer which phrase had offended her, and when the Treasurer saw the manuscript he tried to convince the Queen that what Sarah had written was 'errors as to this notion', rather than 'nation'.[103] However, a copy of the original letter, which Sarah must have made at a later point for her own files, clearly shows the word to be 'nation'.

Anne was prepared to view it as a misunderstanding and asked Sarah to return to attendance, 'for though you are never so unkind, I will ever preserve a most sincere and tender passion for my dear Mrs Freeman'. Sarah's reply was not so conciliatory, 'I cannot for my life see any essential difference in the meaning betwixt these two words [notion/ nation],'[104] but she obeyed the summons.

In September, when Godolphin returned to press Anne for a decision about Sunderland's appointment, he said she had broken his heart with weeping. Sarah merely chided Godolphin for being taken in by a woman's tears, to which he sent an affectionate rebuke that might serve as an answer to so much of Sarah's life: '[Y]ou are much better natured in effect than you sometimes appear to be.'[105] He also wrote to let Marlborough know, as he had put it to Sarah, that he had only been getting 'coldness and constraint' from the Queen since this 'hurly burly' over Sunderland had started.[106] He added, significantly: 'There is no room to hope for the least assistance from Mrs Freeman in this matter.'[107] At this stage, Sarah's only role was as an intermediary between Godolphin and Sunderland and, most importantly, as a lever on Marlborough himself. Alarmed by Godolphin's description of the situation and his tone of defeat, Marlborough impressed upon Sarah that if Godolphin resigned everything would fall apart:[108] the war would be starved of English funds and the Dutch would make a separate and premature peace with France.[109] Finally Sarah brought her husband to write a letter of unequivocal support for his son-in-law's appointment and hence for Godolphin.

Spending what credit he had left with the Queen, Godolphin tried to assist Sarah in repairing her relationship with Anne. When he suggested to Anne that Sarah felt badly treated, 'she said, as she has done 40 times, "How could she show her [Sarah] any more kindness than she did, when she would never come near her?"'[110] The 'kindness' that Sarah wanted was not, after all, a kiss on the hand, but the appointment of a Secretary of State.

Until this point Sarah, Marlborough and Godolphin believed that Queen Anne's uncle, Lord Rochester, was whispering in her ear against the Whigs, assuming there was no other favourite. Then, on 18 October 1706, Godolphin reported to Marlborough that their friend Mr Craggs (now Postmaster General and MP for Grampound in Cornwall) had accused Robert Harley of working behind the scenes to strengthen Anne's resistance. Godolphin said that Craggs only mentioned it in passing 'as taking it for granted it was what I could not but have heard of before'.[111] He was at first incredulous that this old associate, who had himself been a Shaftesburian Whig during the Revolution (to the extent of being labelled a republican in the 1690 elections)[112] and who owed many political favours to the Duke of Marlborough, was at the root of their trouble. He wondered whether Harley might simply be dealing with the Tories as a kind of precaution. Godolphin had just received a supportive letter from him, 'but at the same time,' he mused, 'I doubt so much smoke could not come without some fire . . .'

Marlborough had worried about Harley's loyalties with regard to war policy during the long summer of 1705.[113] Now, given the cue from Craggs, Sarah fixed on the villain of the piece: '[T]he difficulties raised by her Majesty against parting with Sir Charles Hedges were wholly owing to the artifice and management of Mr Harley,' she concluded.[114] Her theory was that Harley felt able to manipulate his current fellow Secretary, Hedges, and she feared that Sunderland would not be so malleable. More simply, having formed her political opinions in the days of James II, she saw Harley's claims to want a moderate bipartisan Cabinet as a smokescreen for darker, crypto-Jacobite aims.

Marlborough did not share these suspicions, still believing Harley to be a genuine moderate, who was only against Godolphin because he saw the Treasurer as controlled by extremist Whigs. Not so personally loyal as his wife, Marlborough would perhaps have been willing to abandon Godolphin and join forces with Harley if he had looked likely to triumph in gaining the Queen's favour. For the moment, therefore, he sat on the fence. Only Sarah faced the fact that no Parliamentary majority would support the Ministry without the backing of the Junto, so their endorsement now mattered almost as much as the Queen's. Harley's bipartisan strategy, genuine or not, was unworkable.

Robert Harley is not an easy man to know across the centuries, although he was the nearest in his generation to our modern idea of a politician, skilled at handling the House of Commons and the press. Sarah had never liked him: she was repelled by his stuttering Welsh accent, his jowly, thick-lipped face and bluff, often drunken manners. She referred to him in various narratives as 'always showing his small learning out of season',[115] as having 'an excessive vanity',[116] and as 'a little, shuffling wretch'.[117] Even the pro-Tory Alexander Pope satirised his speech as being as devious as Milton's serpent: 'everything was in the epic way for he always began in the middle'.[118] A later description of 'Honest

Robin' written by a friend of Sarah's makes him sound almost physically handicapped by bad character: 'He was a cunning and a dark man . . . This mischievous darkness of his soul was written in his countenance and plainly legible in a very odd look, disagreeable to everybody at first sight, which being joined with a constant awkward motion or rather agitation of his head and body, betrayed a turbulent dishonesty within . . .'[119]

History gives us the chance to read the evidence of Harley's 'artifice and management' for ourselves, proving that this was not just a figment of Sarah's imagination. In 1704 he was still on the warmest of terms with the Marlboroughs, writing to congratulate Sarah, for example, on her husband's victory at Schellenberg that July.[120] By August 1706, however, at the same time as he wrote to Sarah that he had been 'provoked to see so much public and private ingratitude exercised toward the Duke', he had been meeting secretly with Daniel Defoe at an inn called the Vine and prompting him to publish anti-war, anti-Marlborough views in *The Review*.[121] After Ramillies, for example, he pushed Defoe to take the line that 'England strives best by peace'.[122] What stuck in Sarah's mind as even more hypocritical was his letter of condolence to Marlborough on their son Jack's death the previous year. She quoted it in her memoirs to emphasise his subsequent disloyalty amid 'the most nauseous professions of affection and duty'.[123]

Two days after Craggs's revelation, Sarah drafted one of the long letters to the Queen that caused Winston Churchill to observe in his biography of his ancestor that '[s]he sought to win by argument, voluble and vociferous, written and interminable, what had hitherto been the freehold property of love'.[124] The nicknames allowed her to write in the third person and take a bold tone: 'I must in the first place beg leave to revive the name of Mrs Morley and your faithful Freeman because without that help I shall not be well able to bring out what I have to say. It is awkward to write any thing of this kind in the style of an address . . .'[125] She presented it as her duty to tell Mrs Morley a few hard truths: 'I do solemnly protest I think I can no ways return what I owe her so well as by being honest and plain.' And in a line that contains the essence of how Sarah saw herself, martyred to the cause of truth, she stated, 'I have more satisfaction in losing Mrs Morley's favour upon that principle than any mercenary courtier ever had in the greatest riches . . .'

Sarah enclosed a letter addressed to her from her husband so that Anne could see what the Ministers were saying in private about the temptation of retiring, and she asked for both papers to be returned after Anne had read them, in case she should ever need them for her own vindication. Then, undoing any pity or guilt that may have been prompted by the enclosed letter, she reminded the Queen that the Stuarts had always suffered from 'an obstinacy in their tempers' and marvelled that Anne had the confidence to do any business 'upon your head' alone, without the experienced advice of her two key Ministers.

In another similar letter ('It's hardly possible to write anything but repetition upon this subject'), Sarah accused Anne of driving Godolphin towards resignation. For the first time she made reference to the influence of 'somebody artful' whom she could not believe Anne would prefer over the victorious Commander and careful Treasurer. '[T]his perhaps will be thought by Mrs Morley too much for me to say' but she only wrote it because the Queen was 'very near bringing all her affairs into disorder'. She claimed that she was only worried about what 'the world' would say when it discovered Anne was abandoning her friends. Finally, ironically, she told the Queen that 'Tis not enough to mean well.'

On 30 October Anne responded to these two letters. She observed that unless she agreed entirely with Sarah's political views 'what I say is not thought to have the least colour of reason in it' and asked whether Mrs Freeman could really think she was so stupid. She stated her wish to keep Marlborough and Godolphin in her government and suggested that it was Sarah's intransigence rather than her own that would be to blame if they went: 'I beg you would not add to my other misfortunes of pushing them on to such an unjust and unjustifiable action.'

Now it was Anne who had to lobby Sarah not to turn Marlborough against her. As she later complained to a royal physician: 'The Duchess made my Lord Marlborough and my Lord Godolphin do anything, and that when my Lord Godolphin was ever so finally resolved when with Her Majesty, yet when he went to her [Sarah], she impressed him to the Contrary.'[126] This mirrors a self-aware remark Sarah made to her friend Bishop Burnet: 'I never, or very rarely, succeeded in any endeavour . . . till the Ministers themselves [Marlborough and Godolphin] came into it at last.'[127]

The impasse continued for several months, until the Queen realised she could not drive a wedge between Godolphin and Sarah, and Marlborough realised he could not continue the war without Junto support. On 18 November he told Harley that he had to choose Sunderland's appointment over his preferred scheme for a moderate Cabinet. Marlborough had already given Anne a promise that he would not support his son-in-law within the Cabinet if, as Anne regally put it, 'he ever did anything I did not like'.[128] Still Anne did not budge and the crisis would have continued, had not Sir Charles Hedges volunteered to resign on 3 December. In return for a promise of the next available appointment, he tactfully helped the Queen disguise the fact that an irreversible constitutional precedent had been set.

In her published memoirs, Sarah summed up the episode with deceptive neutrality and understatement: 'It was not till after much solicitation that her Majesty could be prevailed with so far to oblige the Whigs as to make my Lord Sunderland Secretary of State . . .'[129] She had allowed herself to be the instrument of Whig ambition, achieved the desired goal and opposed her husband to do so. But as Anne had taken at least five months to capitulate, the limits of Sarah's influence had also been revealed to many Court-watchers. She herself had been aware of these limits for some time and did not squander the limited resource of Anne's favour, as most historians have argued; rather, she spent it to secure what she believed to be the most important Whig appointments.

Every biographer agrees that this episode was not just a constitutional turning point but also marked the death of any romantic feeling on Anne's side for Sarah. She could never forget having been bullied so relentlessly. And Sarah could not escape the knowledge that, though politically she had triumphed, she was no longer loved.

6

'Raised from the Dust'

During the wet autumn and winter of 1706, Sarah lived at Woodstock and supervised the Blenheim site. She told Marlborough that she had pointed out a 'good many errors' to Vanbrugh and his men, and complained repeatedly about their slow progress. As Vanbrugh continued to underestimate costs and promise unrealistic completion dates, Sarah often turned to Hawksmoor for the truth. In August Marlborough had agreed that Godolphin should no longer be bothered with the particulars of the project because he already had enough on his plate.[1]

Mary II had viewed the collapse of new extensions at Hampton Court as God's punishment for faults in her own character. Sarah tended to blame the workmen. In the spring of 1707 she directed that the whole garden façade be pulled down (around 100 feet of wall) and that the basement windows be enlarged to let in more light.[2] A fondness for natural light was one of Sarah's most unshakeable architectural views. Her other was that a house's interior should be convenient. Everything she saw at Blenheim seemed grotesquely impractical: it would take, for example, about forty minutes to carry warm food from the kitchens to the dining room. Opulence was all very well, but she was going to have to live in this monument. Though she later conceded that Vanbrugh's stubbornness was due to his artistic sensibilities ('I know that what I did not like, as well as what I did approve of, you intended for the best . . .'),[3] she was also confident of her own good sense when it came to buildings.

Vanbrugh was vexed and offended by interference from a woman in such matters. During the summer, however, Sarah tried to be on better terms with him for her husband's sake, and was promised that one wing would soon be habitable. Throughout the next two to three years, however, her relationship with Vanbrugh remained fraught as he continually failed to deliver and as Sarah came back time after time to make tours and alterations. She took a meticulous interest in every detail. There are records of her deciding on the placement of windows, the types of stone, the designs of iron railings, chimneypieces, wainscoting, doors and cornices and – most dramatically – cancelling some orangeries because they obstructed the views from the main gallery. This last order was given despite Vanbrugh's determined opposition and her husband's instructions.[4]

Meanwhile she continued to keep a finger in the party-political pies of various ecclesiastical appointments. Godolphin wrote to her in November 1706 with news of the Bishop of Winchester's death, whose place was sought by both Sir Jonathan Trelawny, Bishop of Exeter, and Burnet, Bishop of Salisbury. He remarked: 'I will endeavour to keep the Queen from coming to any resolution upon it till we have advised with all our friends.'[5] But, as Sarah complained in her memoirs, the Queen did not wait to take either Sarah's or Godolphin's advice. Her head filled with 'notions of the high prerogative . . . & of being Queen indeed',[6] she wished to fill the bishoprics with appointees of her own choosing. The tension between the old Stuart and new consultative style of monarchy was clearly illustrated by the arguments between Sarah and Anne on this issue. In July 1706, Anne had told Sarah that disposing of Church livings was 'a power I can never think reasonable to part with & I hope those that come after will be of the same mind.'[7] Later she complained to Marlborough that it was as plain 'as the sun at noonday' that the Whigs wanted 'to tear that little prerogative the Crown has to pieces'.[8] The dispute dragged on throughout the following year until Anne appointed the Bishop of Exeter to Winchester in April 1707. There were similar heated arguments about the appointment of a new Bishop of Ely, and of an Oxford Professor of Divinity. For the latter, the Duke of Marlborough backed the Whig candidate, Dr Potter, using this to test his own standing with the Queen after the battle over Sunderland. When his candidate met with opposition, he complained of Anne's ingratitude. Sarah was employed to write 'to the same purpose'. It was not Anne's fault that she had anti-Whig prejudices, Sarah wrote, but '[y]ou are like people that never read but one sort of book . . . [B]esides, everybody in your station has a great disadvantage in not conversing freely as others do in the world, & tis not so easy for you to come at truth as those that see with their own eyes all that passes . . .'[9]

These letters, in which Sarah represents herself as so much more in touch with reality than Anne, coincided with her own near-ascendancy to a quasi-royal position. At the end of 1706, Emperor Joseph, in the name of his candidate for the Spanish Throne, offered Marlborough the Governor-Generalship of the Spanish Netherlands as a reward for his military services. This would have provided him with additional income of £60,000 a year and a position independent of English party feuds. Anne was happy for him to accept, but the Dutch were offended that the Habsburgs had not consulted them. In 1709, Marlborough refused the offer for the sake of maintaining harmony within the Grand Alliance. The episode, however, created further suspicion in England of his ambitions to govern. It is also a reminder of how contingent Sarah's achievements were upon her husband's career. As 'First Lady' of the Spanish Netherlands she would have had a very different, perhaps happier biography, in which her more imperious traits would have been seen as appropriate.

A smaller, yet still significant favour was granted to the Marlborough family during the winter Parliamentary session of 1706–7: it was established by law that the dukedom could be inherited by the female line. On the assumption that Sarah was too old to have more sons, Henrietta Godolphin would become Duchess of Marlborough on her father's death and also inherit the £5,000 pension Marlborough had been granted after the battle of Blenheim. For his ministerial services, Godolphin was given an earldom.

The bishoprics' crisis and her suspicions of Harley preoccupied Sarah far more than the political issue that, with hindsight, seems of much greater significance during 1706–7: the union of England and Scotland. However, it is unfair to say, as Iris Butler did, that the issue 'does not appear to have interested or involved Duchess Sarah',[10] for the desire for union was intrinsic to Sarah's Whig ideals. Without it, sufficient taxation for the war could not be secured and, as Burnet put it, union was only 'shutting the back door' against invasion.[11] Sarah told Burnet that Anne had 'often said to me that there were no Jacobites in England, but acknowledged there were some in Scotland'.[12] Nothing could have interested Sarah more than this.

Since 1704, the union had also been the central preoccupation, next to the war, of Godolphin. During 1706, he laid the groundwork for the Treaty of Union with Scotland in collaboration with James Douglas, 2nd Duke of Queensberry, Anne's Commissioner thanks to a £20,000 bribe. Queensberry opposed the Duke of Hamilton's nationalist movement, which was funded by French money and by Pope Clement XI.

The union was, as Defoe put it, one of policy and not affection.[13] In return for the loss of their independence, the Scots would be permitted to jump on the back of England's valuable overseas trade and commerce. The negotiations took place at Sarah's old Whitehall home, the Cockpit. As usual Sarah played the role of informal intermediary between the members of the Junto, especially Sunderland and Somers, and the Ministry – that is, Godolphin.[14] She also had to deflect visits from Scottish lords hoping to secure one of the sixteen newly created seats in the House of Lords through her husband's nomination or the Queen's influence. In July 1706, Godolphin had complained to Marlborough that 'great preparations are making by the angry party here [the Tories]' to oppose the treaty in Parliament. '[I]t begins to be preached up and down that the *church is in danger* from this union,' he wrote.[15]

In March 1707, a Jacobite invasion from Scotland was daily expected. A repelled attempt caused a dramatic fall in stock prices and the Bank of England had to be rescued by its Whig investors, ranging from Sarah to various Huguenot refugee merchants. Marlborough and Godolphin proved their reliability to the Junto by repelling this invasion, and the Tory party was discredited as a bunch of Jacobite conspirators in the run-up to the 1708 general election.

Marlborough left England on 21 March to visit Sweden where he met with King Charles XII and dissuaded him from tipping the balance in the war by allying with Louis XIV. As he sailed from Margate, Sarah reminded Anne once again that she was saying goodbye to her husband 'perhaps forever & for [Anne's] service'.[16]

Under a newly strengthened Whig ministry, the Act of Union was passed quickly by the last English Parliament on 1 May. Sarah distrusted many of the principal players in this initiative. On a letter from the Treasurer to Marlborough on 25 May 1707, she added her own note, a rare glimpse of the kind of observation that must have filled her other letters to Flanders, all presumed destroyed by Marlborough:

I remember in Mr Montgomery's last letter he writ something to you of the great desire of 220 [Queensberry] to be in 85 [the Cabinet], which I can't but wish may not be, for I think nobody should go there that is not in all respects what one would desire, unless there is a necessity of it; and I have known several things of him that I do not like, besides that he is so near relation to 31 [Rochester], and I believe he has been sufficiently gratified for any service he has ever done. God send good news from you, my dearest life.[17]

Letters from a friend in later years also refer to Sarah having felt some ambivalence about the sixty-one new Scottish peers coming into Westminster politics: 'As for your Scots,' her friend wrote to her, 'it is impossible for you to think worse of them than I do, or to apprehend more mischief from them; and I think your being against the Union should always be remembered to your everlasting honour . . .'[18] This was probably retrospective opinion, however, formed during 1710–11 when many of the Scottish peers were opposing the Grant Bill for war supplies. In 1708 Sarah had written with irritation that the Queen would not 'consider fairly and coolly' how the Whigs 'did her such real

After the Kneller portrait at Althorp dated 1702. Sarah wears the symbol of her power in Queen Anne's household: the Gold Key.

Two portraits, attributed to Kneller, both said to depict Sarah after cutting off her hair in a fit of rage. In fact, in the portrait on the left she could be merely touching her long locks.

A selection of Sarahs: with a bulbous nose (*this page, top left*), by Gascars; a miniature by Lens (*this page, bottom left*) in which she wears a likeness of her husband on her armband; Kneller's Petworth portrait (*opposite page, top left*) showing her in coronation robes; a Kneller (*opposite page, top right*) painted from life after she was forty-eight and likely to be the one in which Sarah described herself as 'clotted all over with powder, when I fancy the best thing I had was the colour of my hair'; and a Jervas (*opposite page, below*) where the hand touching the head symbolises intellect.

Double portrait of Sarah in mourning with her beloved granddaughter
Lady Diana Spencer. Painted by Maria Verelst following the death of
Marlborough, copying an earlier Kneller portrait of Sarah in mourning
for her son Jack.

Above: Sarah and one of her best friends, Barbara Viscountess Fitzharding, playing cards, by Kneller dated 1691.

Below: A copy by an unknown artist, in which the cards are replaced by a letter – ironically mirroring Sarah's own progression from 'ladylike' to literary pursuits.

The Marlboroughs with their children (*from left to right*: Elizabeth, Mary, Henrietta, Anne and Jack), started by John Closterman in 1693 and completed by John Riley in 1697. Riley added Marlborough by means of a canvas extension, unintentionally emphasising his peripheral role in family affairs during these years.

and acceptable services in the Union with Scotland'[19] and Sarah's encouragement of Godolphin towards conclusion of the Treaty of Union does not fit with her having had strong reservations at the time.

In the middle of May 1707, Sarah mentioned to her husband that she suspected Abigail Hill, the penniless cousin she had adopted and employed in Anne's household, of speaking to the Queen about politics. In 1704 Sarah had promoted her to a position in which she came into direct contact with the Queen. When Sarah discovered that Abigail was becoming a favourite, she was dismayed, but neither she nor Marlborough yet had any presentiment that the woman would become a significant adversary. They thought they could warn her to keep to her place and that would be that: 'I should think you might speak to her with some caution, which might do good,' wrote Marlborough, 'for she certainly is grateful and will mind what you say.'[20]

Presumably Sarah followed her husband's advice, and at the end of the month the two women were still on cordial terms, when Abigail asked for her sister, Alice, to be promoted to housekeeper at Whitehall. 'I must own it may seem very confident after so late an instance of your Graces' generosity, to solicit for a new favour,' Abigail began humbly.[21] With hindsight, Sarah would later regard this request as calculated to hide the fact that Abigail was already on intimate enough terms with the Queen to apply for Alice's promotion herself.

Some time during that spring, when Kensington Palace was 'a perfect solitude'[22] and nobody waited on the crippled Queen but some guards in the outer rooms and a few lowly serving women, Abigail was married to one of Prince George's servants, Colonel Samuel Masham. It was a private ceremony held at Dr Arbuthnot's lodgings, and Sarah was not invited. Perhaps Abigail had some small but infected wound, inflicted by Sarah many years ago, which motivated her to exclude and deceive her cousin. Most likely it was not conscious malice on Abigail's part so much as realising her good fortune in being liked by the Queen and –

having seen Sarah alienating herself – she made a pragmatic decision to side with the infinitely more powerful patron. Sarah observed that Abigail 'was grown more shy of coming to me, and more reserved than usual when she was with me; but I imputed this to her peculiar moroseness of temper, and for some time made no other reflection upon it'.[23]

Sarah was not told of the marriage until the summer or early autumn,[24] while Colonel Masham was away in Ireland. When Abigail begged her pardon for having concealed it, Sarah claimed she quickly forgave her, thinking it had only been a case of 'bashfulness and want of breeding'. She embraced Abigail 'with my usual tenderness', wished her well, and then, still believing that Abigail was dependent on her, 'entered into her concerns in as friendly a manner as possible, contriving how to accommodate her with lodgings'. During this conversation, Sarah offered to tell the Queen about the 'secret' marriage, and Abigail 'answered with an air of unconcernedness that the bedchamber women had already acquainted her with it'. When Sarah later chided Anne for failing to pass on this gossip about one of her own relations, the Queen made a slip. She replied: 'I have a hundred times bid [Mrs] Masham tell it you, and she would not.'[25]

Despite her own claim to have 'that native openness & generosity of soul which doth not easily give into jealousies & suspicions',[26] Sarah was troubled by the discrepancy between the two accounts and started to cross-examine other servants in the Queen's household. Within a week she discovered that Anne had attended the marriage ceremony, given Abigail a dowry of two thousand guineas from the Privy Purse,[27] and, as Sarah suggestively put it in her published memoirs, that 'Mrs Masham came often to the Queen, when the Prince was asleep, and was generally two hours every day in private with her . . .'[28] In addition, she discovered that Abigail was not only her cousin but a distant relative of Robert Harley. The Ministers' political rivalry suddenly acquired a precise parallel among the Court women.

In early draft memoirs, Sarah wrote that Abigail's concealment of her marriage from her was as wrong as if Abigail had been her own daughter.[29] In later drafts the emphasis shifts to the Queen's infidelity. Retrospectively, Sarah could now 'decipher' all the signs of another woman in Anne's life. In a letter to Bishop Burnet, she wrote: 'An instance of which I remember, when I was with the Q[uee]n at Windsor & went in through my own lodgings, a private way & unexpected, [Abigail] unlocks the door in a loud, familiar manner & was tripping cross the room with a gay air, but upon seeing me, she immediately stopped short & acting a part like a player dropped a grave curtsy . . .'[30]

In the memoirs Burnet helped Sarah write, he omitted the theatrical simile which made it too obvious that Sarah was attempting to cast Abigail as a stage villain. He also expanded the 'private way' from Sarah's own rooms to 'a secret passage from my lodgings to the bedchamber' of the Queen.

It is difficult to reach a balanced view of Abigail's character because contemporary opinions were so biased by party loyalty. The pro-Harley Jonathan Swift described her as the embodiment of every virtue: '[A] Person of a plain sound Understanding, of great Truth and Sincerity, without the least Mixture of Falsehood or Disguise; of an honest Boldness and Courage superior to her Sex; firm and disinterested in her friendship, and full of Love, Duty and Veneration for the Queen her Mistress.'[31] The French ambassador Mesnager 'wondered much that so mean a character, as some had made public, should be attributed to this lady who seemed to me more worthy of the favour of the Queen than any I have conversed with in my life'.[32] Lord Dartmouth, another Tory but perhaps more of a snob, called Abigail 'mean and vulgar in her manner'.[33]

Sarah described her cousin as a genius of false deference, covering her 'sour ill temper'[34] with skill. With hindsight Abigail's every humble gesture as a girl, such as the way she would always offer 'to pin up [Sarah's] coat', was interpreted as deceit.[35] When one of her co-authors asked for clarification on how Sarah would like Abigail to be portrayed, Sarah responded that the woman was 'not a fool' but 'brutal' and lacking in manners, as shown by the way she avoided other Court ladies and preferred to spend time with the lower servants (including one other treacherous appointee of Sarah's, a laundress named Mrs Abrahal).[36]

Sarah's account of Anne's relationship with Abigail is certainly unreliable in terms of chronology. Once she had discovered the infidelity, she projected it back to explain every argument with Anne since the beginning of the reign, whether or not she had any solid evidence for this. In some cases this might have stemmed from the confusion of old age, in others it seems to have been deliberate obfuscation: in blaming Abigail for undermining her relationship with Anne, Sarah no longer had to blame herself.

When Anne was staying at Windsor in 1704, she had written to Sarah at the Lodge, explaining that she had not spoken to her that morning only because 'I knew if I had begun to speak I should not have been fit to be seen by anybody'. She was so upset because 'I fancied by your looks and things that you have sometimes let fall that you have sometimes hard & wrong thoughts of me' and asked Sarah to send her these thoughts in writing so that she could clear herself. Sarah's notes on the back of this letter offer another interpretation of the letter: '[T]is plain to me that she was fearful I should tax her with her passion for Mrs Hill, & therefore she would not have me speak to her but write, nor show her scrawl as she calls it . . . As to her not being fit to be seen if I speak to her, she only feared blushing if I speak upon the subject of Mrs Hill . . .' We know, however, that Sarah suspected nothing about Abigail at this date, so that cannot have been the cause of their argument or the Queen's shyness. More likely, Sarah had been browbeating Anne about the Tories.

Again, on a letter from Anne dated 1 September 1704, in which she asked to be restored to Sarah's 'favour' and wrote that 'I must again desire you would excuse my not answering some things in your letters, not for the reason you give, for it is a strange unkind one, but because I know it is better not to do it, for both our sakes', Sarah noted on the back: 'When this letter was writ she was fond of Mrs Hill, but twas then a great secret.'

Warming to the subject of Abigail as evil favourite, Sarah described a letter of 6 September 1706 as written 'under the *witchcraft* of Mrs Hill'. Sarah protested,

The Queen calls me unkind, but nobody of common sense can believe that I did not do all that was possible to be well with her . . . But it was not possible for me to go to her as often as I had done in private, for let her write what she will, she never was free with me after she was fond of Mrs Hill, and whoever reads her former letters will find a great difference in the style of them when she really loved me from those where she only pretended to do so . . .

It is tempting as a biographer to imagine, as Sarah did, Abigail lurking in the background of earlier scenes. Had she been at Windsor the previous summer when Sarah confronted Anne about Sunderland's appointment? Did she stir up Anne's indignation over the nation/notion letter? At what point did she discuss with her cousin Harley how her position at Court could be used to assist his policy?

Victorian biographers, in particular, felt the need to identify a single turning point at which Queen Anne transferred her affections. Many took the lead from an anecdote that originated with Horace Walpole, who said that Sarah started to treat Anne 'as if the Queen had offensive smells' and was once observed by the Queen to throw down the royal gloves in disgust. Agnes Strickland was the first biographer, in *Lives of the Queens of England* (1884), to repeat the anecdote to justify Anne's apparently callous dropping of her oldest and dearest friend:

One afternoon, not many weeks after the death of the Duke of Gloucester, the princess Anne noticed that she had no gloves on; she therefore told Abigail Hill, who was in attendance on her toilet, to fetch them from the next room, as she remembered that she had left them on the table. Mrs Hill obeyed her royal highness and passed into the next room, where she found Lady Marlborough seated, reading a letter; but the gloves of the princess were not on the table, for Lady Marlborough had taken them up by accident and put them on. Abigail most submissively mentioned to her 'that she had put on by mistake her royal highness' gloves' – 'Ah!' exclaimed Lady Marlborough, 'Have I put on anything that has touched the odious hands of that disagreeable woman?' Then, pulling them off, she threw them on the floor . . . The door was ajar between the two rooms and Anne heard every word . . .

Viscount Wolseley repeated it almost word for word in his 1894 biography of Marlborough. By setting it 'not many weeks after the death of the Duke of Gloucester', Abigail's role is pre-dated to 1700 – a full seven years before Sarah noticed that her cousin had Anne's confidence, and four years before Abigail reported that it became her duty as a bedchamber woman to pull on the Queen's gloves 'when she could not do it herself'.[37] Five years later, Mrs Aubrey Richardson compressed the same story in her book, *Famous Ladies of the English Court* (1899), when she said that Sarah's 'insolence and unamiable tyranny, in particular little acts of disrespect in performing such duties of her offices as handing the Royal gloves and other menial acts, which her soul loathed, were the first causes of the Queen's cooling humour'.[38]

The connotations of the glove anecdote include the obvious one of the 'gloves coming off' in the arguments between Anne and Sarah, but the story also focuses the reader's attention on Sarah's rejection of Anne's body. This faint innuendo is less present in another version of the glove story, told by the King of Prussia. He was more scandalised by the arrogance of any subject thinking herself better than a queen. In his version, their first argument arises because Sarah instructs the royal glover to make her own pair before Anne's. In a letter to one of her admirers, the elderly Sarah refers to the King of Prussia having 'writ a book in which he imputes the ruin of Europe to have happened from a quarrel between Queen Anne & me about a pair of gloves'.[39] She says it is complete rubbish, but refuses to repudiate it in any revised edition of her memoirs: 'To pretend to say anything to them is like answering all the Grub Street papers, which are only writ for people in garrets to see ... and I am as little concerned at what kings may write ...'

In June 1707, Anne wrote to Sarah saying, 'I am on the rack & cannot bear living as we do now.'[40] She denied 'that I am infatuated, that I am fond of some people (who I care no more for than I do for the pen in my hand),' but protested that 'I have the same sincere tender passion for you as ever.' She pointed out that she sent for Sarah far more than Sarah agreed to wait on her, and that it was usually Sarah who tired of her company when they were together, not vice versa. Sarah's reply to those who criticised such self-indulgent tactlessness was that whenever she resolved 'to try if by being easy and quiet I could regain any influence with her Majesty'[41] she met with no greater success.

The Queen specifically refuted whatever the servants had been telling Sarah about Abigail's long private visits: 'I hope in God you will give no credit to this cursed lie that you have heard of your poor unfortunate faithful Morley.' She made no reference to the continuing battle for power between Godolphin and Harley, and between the political parties over Church appointments, which, as much as private jealousy, motivated Sarah's anger. On 16 June, Marlborough wrote to Sarah saying that the Queen had to choose between the two men, and though he states that 'this is only to yourself', the style of the letter seems intended for the Queen's eyes.

By mid-July there seems to have been some warming of relations between the two women.[42] On the sixteenth, Anne told Sarah that she was looking forward to their meeting in the gallery at Windsor Castle. Unfortunately they missed each other. Anne claimed to have sat around waiting for Sarah, but Sarah answered this with a note on the back of Anne's letter that the Queen had been 'locked up with Abigail after dinner' while 'the Prince was in one of the rooms asleep'.

The meeting was rearranged and took place at dusk on Maundy Thursday.[43] It has become known as the 'Gallery Visit' and is supposed to have been the first occasion on which Sarah really lost her temper with the Queen. At some point during the meeting, Sarah accused Anne of getting her policies from Harley via Abigail Masham, which Anne flatly denied. Sensing she had crossed a line, Sarah wrote to her afterwards to soften the accusation: Abigail, she said, was merely strengthening Anne's prejudices against the Whigs rather than seeking to dominate her policy.

Anne's reply is a masterpiece of irony and so much more polished than her earlier letters that it is easy to imagine, as Sarah did, that she had had help in composing it. While 'not doubting but what you say is sincerely meant', she insisted that Sarah's cousin 'is very far from being an occasion of feeding Mrs Morley in her passion, as you are pleased to call it; she never meddling with anything'. Anne compared Abigail with 'others that have been in her station' who had meddled a good deal more – saying to Sarah that she was a hypocrite, or at least that she was projecting her own failings on to someone else.

Away at war, with no secure channel of communication to his wife, Marlborough remained unaware of the extent to which Sarah feared Abigail's influence. He had written to Anne on 7 July warning her in vague terms not to listen to 'anybody near your person' who might have been advising her against the Whigs. He now saw that it was necessary for her to side with the Junto because their interest in the Hanoverian succession 'obliges them to be more governed by You', and because it was they alone who would 'carry on this war with vigour, on which depends Your happiness and the safety of our religion'.

On 21 July Sarah wrote to the Queen again to say that she felt patronised by the way Anne never seemed to think that her political opinions 'deserved entering into'.[44] Once again she mentioned the pernicious influence of Abigail and her friends, whom she called Jacobites, Tories and Tackers. Around 10 August, she threatened that 'my greatest concern now is to think of the prejudice it must do Mrs Morley when the true cause of it is known, which will make her character so very different from that which has always been given'.[45]

A letter home from Marlborough on 4 August, meanwhile,

contained two clear examples of Sarah's powerlessness. He told her that he would continue working alongside Harley in the Cabinet, and that she should keep Vanbrugh happy by allowing him to work on an ornamental bridge in the grounds of Blenheim.[46] Sarah was scathing about this 390-foot-long pseudo-Rialto: she thought it a preposterous crossing for a trickle of a stream that was easily jumped over.

The summer was also blighted for Sarah by arguments with her eldest and youngest daughters. Henrietta and Mary both had the frivolity of bright but neglected children who had been roped into unhappy marriages. In 1707, Sarah blamed Mary for having failed to maintain happy relations with the Duke of Montagu, her 'very ill-natured'[47] father-in-law, and thereby failing to pull her weight in the family's political struggle. She refused to ask the Queen for a promotion for Mary's husband, remarking to her daughter that there are 'so few employments and so many to gratify' rather than explaining that her own standing at Court no longer allowed for such non-essential favours. Godolphin told Marlborough that, in the dispute between mother and daughter, Mary 'must certainly be to blame . . . for both you and I have seen a thousand times how kind and indulgent 240 [Sarah] has always been to 241 [Mary]'. The Treasurer's private opinion was that Mary was too clever for her own good and could do with 'less sense and more compliance'.[48]

At about this time, when London was hit by a plague of flies and 'many of the streets were so covered in them that the people's feet made so full an impression on them as upon thick snow',[49] Mary sent her son to visit Sarah at St James's Palace as a peace-offering. She sent a note with him explaining that it was his first day out of Montagu House since his recent illness. She herself could not come because she was weaning another infant. Mary wrote apologetically that 'I am prodigiously unfortunate in your always thinking when I do a wrong thing that I do it apurpose to be impertinent'. Her mother, for example, had thought that she had seen Mary and a servant laughing at her behind her back, and reacted as she had reacted to Abigail Hill's sneakiness – lecturing Mary on seemly behaviour and duty rather than admitting to hurt feelings.

Mary paid frequent visits to the Godolphin household where her elder sister Henrietta played hostess. Whenever Sarah invited the two of them on respectable but boring social outings, they declined, while their sister Anne usually agreed to go.[50] Anne had tried to defend Mary to their mother: she admitted that her younger sister had 'not the mildest of temper', but begged Sarah to be forgiving because she was sure nothing was meant as a deliberate snub.[51]

As his favourite child, Mary also engaged her father to speak in her defence, but shortly after she had become Duchess of Montagu in March 1709, and while he was at home in London, Marlborough wrote to tell her that he could no longer condone her behaviour: 'I observe that you take no manner of notice of your mother . . . [Y]ou can't imagine that any company can be agreeable to me who have not a right behaviour to her.' In apparently the last letter from Mary to her mother for several years, she wrote regretting their disagreements: 'I can't be tolerably easy without saying that every mark of your displeasure is a new & great trouble to me that have always loved you with a passion & I believe shall always do so, though you make me so very unhappy, which is made a double hardship upon me by your being generally so good-natured . . .' We cannot know how sincere her testimony to Sarah's good nature was, or whether it was meant only to appease a domineering mother.

For months Godolphin continued to believe the Queen's assurances that she was not taking advice against his own from Harley, and dismissed Sarah as a conspiracy theorist. By 16 August, however, Sarah seems to have persuaded him to read the situation according to her narrative. In a letter to Marlborough, carried to him by their friend and army chaplain Francis Hare, Godolphin for the first time supported Sarah's story that Abigail Masham, 'improved by' Mr Harley, was now a key influence on the Queen. He emphasised that they must put a stop to it before the winter session of Parliament and urged Marlborough to return home.

Marlborough replied to Sarah that it might be better to let it be known publicly that Harley was now the Queen's chief adviser, for if he and Godolphin had lost her confidence it would be tortuous to act as though 'it is in their power to do every-thing'.[52] This differentiation between real and perceived power was unusual: generally, when their influence was on the wane, the Marlboroughs and Godolphin struggled harder to maintain the appearance of it. In September, for example, Marlborough had complained privately to Sarah that he had lost all credit with the Queen, as shown by the length of time it had taken to obtain the Oxford professorship for his candidate Dr Potter, yet because he was keeping up the façade of having Anne's trust, he was still being pressurised by Somerset to make a clean sweep of all Tories in the government.

Anne's distrust of Sarah following their argument in the Windsor gallery is most obvious in a note in which she ordered her Groom of the Stole to present Abigail's younger sister Alice at Court. Whether or not Sarah wanted to, Anne wrote, she 'must be pleased to give yourself the trouble to do it'.[53] In another letter, Marlborough expressed his fear to Sarah that Godolphin would be dismissed, and asked her whether she thought the Treasurer should resign pre-emptively.[54] 'I do with all my heart pity 42 [the Queen], being very sure she does not know the fatal step she is going to make.'[55]

In Windsor, on 23 September, Sarah decided to open up a new front in the war against Abigail and Harley by writing directly to her cousin. Since the revelation of the secret marriage she had further discovered 'that you have made me returns very unsuitable to what I might have expected; I always speak my mind so plainly that I should have told you so myself, if I had had the opportunity which I hoped for, but being now so near parting I think this way of letting you know it is like[ly] to be the least uneasy to you, as well as to – Your humble Servant – L: Marl:'[56] She delayed her departure from Windsor to wait for an answer but, in her memoirs, remarked that Abigail had first to consult with 'her great director',[57] Mr Harley. In fact the reply came the next day; Sarah received it in her coach on the road to Woodstock. Abigail wrote:

While I was expecting a message from your Grace to wait upon you according to your commands last night, I received a letter which surprised me no less than it afflicts me. I am very confident by the expression of your letter that somebody has told some malicious lie of me to your Grace from which tis impossible for me to vindicate myself till I know the crime I am accused of; I am sure, Madam, your goodness can't deny me what the meanest may ask of the greatest. I mean justice.[58]

It is impossible to know whether there was any conscious irony in the final reference to the meanest and the greatest, now that their fortunes were reversing, or to guess at the presence of guile. What is clear is that Abigail was not an unsophisticated woman – her spelling and grammar are better than Sarah's or the Queen's. Certainly the letter was effective enough to silence Sarah for a long moment. She did not reply for several days and then only to say that, as to the 'malicious lie', 'I think the subject is not very proper for a letter, and therefore I must defer it till we meet.'[59]

When Sarah returned to London from her inspection at Wood-stock, Abigail avoided her. After twelve days when they were both at St James's Palace, Abigail merely sent her maid to ask Sarah's how her mistress did and to inform her that she was moving to Kensington. This, at any rate, is Sarah's version.[60] Abigail wrote to Harley during this period and described the stand-off between them from her perspective: '[A]s she [Sarah] passed by me, I had a very low curtsy, which I returned in the same manner, but not one word passed between us, and as for her looks, indeed they are not to be described by any mortal but her own self.'[61] There is also evidence of a conciliatory letter from Abigail promising to keep their altercation private: 'I hope nobody can imagine me so great a fool as to publish to the world my greatest misfortune, which is to lie under Your Grace's displeasure.'[62]

Sarah complained to the Queen about Abigail's discourtesy

towards her, but was shocked when Anne 'pulled up, looked very grave and answered she thought [Abigail] was mightily in the right not to come to me'. Astounded, Sarah exclaimed: 'Lord Madam, can your Majesty think so, after expressing so much trouble as she does in her letter upon the knowledge of my taking anything ill of her . . . ?' Anne responded that she thought it was 'very natural for her to be afraid to come'. Baffled by the implication that her temper might be at fault, Sarah muttered only that Abigail 'must certainly be guilty of something' to behave in that way. Though she did not record it in her memoir, it must have been during this same, unsatisfactory meeting that she mentioned the impending Whig attack on George Churchill, the Tory Admiral of the Navy, and implied that he in turn had an unnaturally intimate hold on the Queen's husband.

Sarah began to refuse to see Abigail, making her servants say she was not home. She justified this as a dislike of hearing false professions. Finally Abigail was forced to write for an appointment, and the two women met at Sarah's lodgings. Sarah laid out the charges: 'that it was very plain that the Queen was very much changed to me, that it was now come out [Abigail] being very much with the Queen in private, that she had used many artifices to hide that intimacy from me.' Abigail's answer left the Duchess aghast: '[S]he answered that the Queen who had loved me so extremely, she was sure, would always be very kind to me. These were her very words and I am sure if I could live a thousand years I could never forget them.'

In the version of her memoirs written with Burnet, Sarah described herself as shocked that a woman whom she had 'raised out of the dust' could turn on her with such ingratitude. This stock phrase was often applied to royal favourites on the stage – Sarah might have heard it in performances of Marlowe's *Edward II*, Jonson's *Sejanus*, or Massinger's *Duke of Milan*.[63] She interpreted her own situation according to historical dramas with their cautionary tales about overreaching favourites and tragic martyrs to just causes, observing in one of her letters that what she had done – speaking the truth for the good of the country, even at the expense of her own career – 'has rarely been seen but upon a stage.'[64] She nicknamed Anne and Abigail after two figures in popular plays, 'Dame Dobson' and 'Nab',[65] and latched on to Abigail's humble origins as a way to differentiate herself from her cousin. Despite her egalitarian attitude when it came to her own origins, Sarah reverted to snobbery when it suited her.

Lord Dartmouth recorded that Abigail 'slept on a pallet in the ante-room of her Majesty's bedroom'[66] and Dr Arbuthnot noted down Abigail's daily duties as a bedchamber woman: she handed clothes to the Queen as she dressed in the morning, poured water from a ewer on to the Queen's hands, and brought her bowl of hot chocolate 'without kneeling'.[67] She performed what was known as 'royal body service', which would have included changing the Queen's bandages and emptying the royal slops. Despite the absence of a modern concept of personal privacy in the 1700s, the touching of the Queen's body was highly charged with significance, and therefore open to slanderous interpretation. One 1712 satire described Abigail as one who 'buttoned on the imperial robe upon the Empress' shoulders, and, by a fawning diligence, [was] let into the most secret recesses of Palatine's [Anne's] soul . . .'[68]

In fact, as shown by satires depicting Sarah's mother as a witch and Court bawd, Sarah's origins were considered just as lowly in the eyes of her Tory enemies, and Sarah had little more education than Abigail to qualify her as an adviser to the Queen. When Sarah and Abigail confronted one another that September, Abigail had admitted to bringing Anne petitions and spending money from the Privy Purse without Sarah's oversight, but she still denied having any specific political agenda to rival Sarah's.[69]

When Abigail's marriage to Colonel Masham was made public, Sarah took her daughter Anne to pay their respects, as was polite, 'to hinder any noise or disagreeable discourse upon a change which I thought might make a great many people merry'. She pretended she was only concerned to spare the Queen this 'noise' and to prevent the political pundits from reading the change of favourites as a precursor of future changes in the Cabinet.[70]

That autumn Marlborough was kept in The Hague by stormy seas, and wrote home to Sarah about figurative storms that lay ahead: 'What you say of 256 [Abigail] is very odd, and if you think she is a good weathercock, it is high time to leave off struggling, for believe me nothing is worth rowing against wind and tide; at least you will think so when you come to my age.'[71] Sarah did not, however, 'leave off struggling' until Marlborough was home on 6 November. While he remained overseas, she wrote Anne a long letter attributing all 'the success you have had in a country that has never been thought very easy to govern' to those Ministers who had served her so well. Sarah enclosed one of her husband's letters home, without his permission, to show his fears for the government and for his own reputation, and concluded hers with the words: 'I believe in history too that for the most part the favourite of the prince has been a burden upon them & a grievance to the nation.'

Perhaps it was this line – or perhaps some other phrase Sarah had used at their interview in the Windsor gallery – that the Queen construed as meaning that her husband and Admiral Churchill were lovers. On 29 October 1707,[72] when Sarah heard that this was one cause of the Queen's anger, she wrote disingenuously protesting her innocence:

I did mean what I said of Mr Morley only as a comparison, & not with any disrespectful thought or reflection upon him, to show what a sort of friendship it was, & if I had thought, or ever heard, that he had any such inclination it would have been the last thing that ever I should have touched upon, for in my whole life I never did any thing so ill-bred, or so foolish, as to say a thing only to offend you, without doing you any service.

Taken at face value, this letter could be read as evidence that Sarah never intended her attacks on either George Churchill or Abigail Masham to sound like accusations of homosexuality. However, it also shows that she understood a word like 'inclination', which she frequently used in connection with Anne's friendships, to have a sexual meaning. And it is notable that the letter does not explicitly retract the accusation against Prince George. Sarah also refused to repent of anything she or Godolphin might have said about Abigail, emphasising that '[w]hatever freedom I have taken in speaking to you for your own service, it was when you were alone'. Anne feared that Sarah was not always so discreet: Sarah referred to Anne being 'possessed of so many false stories of me, as if I had talked strange things of her'.

The Queen did not answer either of Sarah's long letters until 30 November, and then only to say that she did not have time to write back because she was too busy combing her hair: 'If I thought anything I could say would make us live easier together, I should be encouraged to write as large a volume to you.'

One Wednesday near Christmas, Sarah tried again to speak with Anne. At the Queen's chamber she was told that Abigail was expected shortly, yet Sarah went straight in and took pleasure in watching Anne's discomfort at the possibility that the two women's paths might cross at any minute. To prevent Sarah staying, Anne did not seat herself. After a while, as Sarah was stooping to kiss her hand goodbye, she said that Anne 'took me up with a cold embrace'.[73] Today, this scene is difficult to interpret because an embrace, even a cold one, seems more affectionate than a kiss on the hand, according to modern body language. Perhaps Anne, knowing that their friendship was at an end, was trying to communicate some remnant of fondness, even pity for Sarah – or perhaps the exact opposite, a kind of snub.

Sarah herself seems to have been unable to fathom the exact significance of the 'cold embrace'. On 27 December, she wrote to ask Anne what it had meant. She complained that she felt patronised by such empty consolations, in gestures or in letters: '[T]o pretend kindness without trust and openness of heart is a treatment for children, not friends.' Whatever Sarah's other faults, or talents at self-deception, she was telling the truth when she explained that 'it is not possible for me to dissemble so as to appear what I am not.'[74] By contrast, Jonathan Swift later wrote of Anne: 'There was not, perhaps, in all England, a person who understood more artificially to disguise her passions than the late Queen.'[75] And when Sarah claimed that the loss of royal favour pained her not so much for the cost to herself or her family but because it was a betrayal of trust, she was not lying: her 'inveteracy' against Masham, as Anne called it, could never have been so extreme without an element of personal pain and jealousy. The following quotation was found in her papers after her death: '[T]here be three things that my heart feareth, & for the fourth I was sore afraid. The slander of a city, the gathering together of an unruly multitude, & a false accusation – all these are worse than death. But a grief of a heart & sorrow is a woman that is jealous of another woman . . .'[76]

Writing in a more conciliatory tone than in her querulous, pre-Christmas letters, Sarah asked to at least be treated with professional courtesy while she remained at Court. It is no surprise to discover that it was Marlborough and Godolphin who urged her to send this letter, against her better judgement. She received no reply from Anne for several days, 'and then nothing to the purpose'.

Gradually, during this winter of 1707–8, Sarah's loss of favour and Abigail's ascendancy became public knowledge. Sarah used her memoirs and archived letters to catalogue grimly how the courtiers jumped like rats from a sinking ship: Lady Ormonde, whom Sarah had given a post 'out of pure compassion', was the 'first woman of quality that owned Mrs Hill & used me very impertinently upon that account'.[77] The Earl of Kent, from whom she possessed a letter of thanks for obtaining his post as Lord Chamberlain in April 1704, was 'the first man of great quality that publicly made court to Abigail'.[78] On the back of an undated note from Lady Hyde, begging to be allowed to wait upon her at a play, Sarah writes a whole page and a half to explain that this friendliness lasted only until Mrs Masham came into favour. In this case, however, Sarah is fair enough to remark that she could not blame Lady Hyde for deserting her, as she had only ever treated the Hyde family with, at best, cold civility.

Sarah also had the misfortune to lose one of her great supports that December: her lawyer, Anthony Guidott.[79] She became increasingly distrustful of all around her, even those apparently offering support. On an anonymous note, which claims to have sympathy for Sarah against her 'upstart competitor', for example, Sarah scrawled: 'To get acquainted with me in order to betray me . . .'[80]

On the evening of Sunday 8 February 1708, Marlborough, Sarah and Godolphin went together to tell the Queen that either Harley had to go or they would all resign and the Whigs would withdraw their Parliamentary and financial support from the government. According to James Stanhope, then commander of the British forces in Spain, Anne was prepared to see Godolphin and Sarah resign, but would not part with her Captain-General. Even at this stage, had it not been for Sarah's profound loyalty to Godolphin and Marlborough's love of his wife, the Treasurer might have been sacrificed. But, as Lord Coningsby later wrote to Sarah, Marlborough and Godolphin could 'have no separate interest'[81] and Sarah would never have forgiven her husband for not standing by the Treasurer. Anne, on the other side, refused to be bullied into dismissing Harley.

When the Cabinet met the next day, Marlborough and Godolphin absented themselves in protest. Anne tried to carry on business as normal, but the Duke of Somerset interrupted to say that he did not see how the government could continue with neither the Treasurer nor the Captain-General present.[82] Both Harley and Henry St John, Secretary for War and ally of Harley, therefore offered resignations which Anne was forced to accept if she wanted Parliament to pass the army Supply Bill.

Until this point Harley's calculations had not included the overthrow of Marlborough, whom he saw as a moderate Tory by nature. In the humiliation of his dismissal, however, the explanation can be found for his later rancour against the Marlboroughs and their clique. Defoe, in *The Conduct of the Parties* (1708), wrote with pity for his patron, Harley: '[F]ar from dropping him easy or letting him fall, as a man might say, on his feet . . . they flung him from them as a stone out of a sling or as a glass or cup dashed to the ground.' In the wake of his departure, the Whigs reinforced their appointments throughout the Cabinet, and it was during this period that Marlborough promoted the young Robert Walpole.

The Queen's response was to continue taking advice from Harley and the Tories outside the Cabinet. Given that Harley's private secretary, William Greg, had been convicted and executed for secret correspondence with the Pretender that spring, Sarah viewed this with alarm. She believed Anne stayed longer than was usual at Windsor Castle that summer because she could meet easily with Harley in the gardens. When Marlborough confronted Anne with the accusation of taking advice from the dismissed minister, Sarah remembered that 'She answered: "I am sure he does not come here. It is true I never did forbid Masham seeing her relation", which was a quicker & more artful answer than she generally thinks of, but love they say makes people ingenious . . .'[83] Marlborough still found it hard to believe Anne was being so duplicitous, while Sarah 'who had had more experience of how small account words & assurances were come to be with [Anne], was little moved by such protestations'.[84]

Now that Harley was out of government, Abigail was even more useful to him. Sarah wrote in one draft of her memoirs[85] that when 'Mr Harley and his creatures [were] brought in to the public management of affairs it was not only acknowledged by themselves but often boasted of by them (both in their cups & out of them) that whilst Her ministers were asleep, they were frequently at Court, advising in secret . . .'

Evil favourites were an element of every national demonology in Europe. Defoe said that England was 'particularly jealous of Favourites'.[86] This means of complaint about the monarch's decisions, without treason, became increasingly important under the heat of party rivalry. For the first time, Court favourites were clearly the creatures of political parties. As one satire about the Marlboroughs, *Bellisarius, a Great Commander, and Zariana, his Lady: A dialogue* (1710), put it: 'Parties, like lovers, full of warm Desire/ Will see no Faults in Fav'rites they admire.' So Anne reversed the image of herself as a puppet controlled by her favourites and started accusing Sarah of being a puppet manipulated by the Whigs.[87]

Sarah tried to portray herself according to a different dramatic type: the virtuous favourite who reformed the system, compensated for the intellectual inadequacies of a monarch selected by hereditary lottery, then sacrificed herself for the national good. This image was promoted in the best-selling *Unfortunate Court-Favourites of England* (1695) by Nathaniel Crouch, and in a number of other hagiographies of male historical favourites published during Sarah's lifetime. They were shown as the fall-guys, who allowed the monarch to express his or her will without being directly autocratic, allowed competition for places to flourish without destabilising the Crown, and served as 'a buffer, a lightning conductor, or at worst a burning-glass interposed between king and people'.[88]

In terms of female favourites, the precedents were less honourable. They had mainly been kings' mistresses, scheming for personal gain and seldom for the sake of principle. Nell Gwynne was popular because she had stayed out of politics, or at least was perceived to have done so. Other mistresses were more obviously influential: Barbara Castlemaine, for example, had made Charles II dismiss Edward Hyde, Earl of Clarendon, and Louise de Kerouaille, Duchess of Portsmouth, was famous for her lubricious involvement in relations with France. Over the Channel, as Sarah and Abigail battled for favour, Madame de Maintenon remained influential over Louis XIV. She said she defined happiness as detachment, gained from knowing one had played one's part in the world.[89]

In her seventies Sarah concluded: 'Women signify nothing unless they are the mistresses of a prince or a First Minister, which I would not be if I were young; and I think there are very few if any women that have understanding or impartiality enough to serve well those they really wish to serve.'[90] She was determined to portray herself as the exception to the rule, a woman who had acted on the basis of principle rather than personal allegiance. '[E]verybody must see that had I consulted that oracle about the choice of a party, it would certainly have directed me to go with the stream of my mistress' inclination and prejudices' yet 'When I first became this high favourite, I laid it down for a maxim, that flattery was falsehood to my trust, and ingratitude to my greatest friend.'[91] More than gratitude, she believed that she was engaged to Anne by honour – 'a more disinterested principle of action'.[92] One of her co-authors went further, averring that Sarah 'had a soul above the slavery of a favourite'.[93]

Sarah's direct power over Anne had always been more imputed than real. Now she cast Abigail as the same sort of mock-favourite, a fictional *alter ego*. She stirred up the resentment that had dogged her for so many years and directed it towards a new victim. In fact, apart from assisting Harley in gaining the Queen's ear, Abigail achieved little of independent importance. Like Sarah she promoted her relatives to Court posts, but also like Sarah she was to be away from Court for much of her career, pregnant six times in the first seven years of her marriage and then raising this large family.

The Whigs, however, were caught up in the propaganda against Abigail, and began to threaten a Parliamentary address demanding that the Queen dismiss her bedchamber woman, the only precedent for which would have been Edward II's removal of Piers Gaveston. Over the Christmas season one of the leading Whig MPs behind this idea had formed a close friendship with Sarah. Arthur Maynwaring was Auditor of the Imprest, a friend of the Junto, a member of the Kit-Cat Club, editor of a newspaper called *The Medley*, a respected literary critic and, according to portraits of him, a handsome man with a long, high-bridged nose. His background (Christ Church, Oxford, and the Inner Temple) had been solidly Tory, and he had even flirted briefly with Jacobitism, but now he had all the zeal of a born-again Whig. The important difference between his personality and Sarah's was his stronger stomach for satire. He told her that 'a good ridicule has often gone a good way to doing a business' and Sarah's daughter Mary once wrote that she would rather not visit her mother when Maynwaring was there because 'he is so malicious that I am sure he will make a thousand disagreeable observations of me'.[94]

Maynwaring adored Sarah. He was sincere when he told her, 'I do not think you were ever in the wrong in your life,'[95] and that she was 'more capable of business than any man'.[96] His interest in her was not sexual – he kept as a mistress a famous actress named Mrs Oldfield by whom he had a son – but he fell passionately under the sway of Sarah's heroic self-image. He was one of the few men who encouraged her to act on her own principles, rather than for the good of her husband and family, even if this meant offending the Queen and, in the short term, losing her reputation. His letters convey the impression that he got a thrill from being in on the secrets of the rich and famous, and from 1707 onwards he had been happy to act, he joked, as a kind of private secretary to Sarah.[97]

In March 1708, Maynwaring and Sarah sat down to their first collaborative piece of writing: an anonymous letter (in the persona of 'an honest Englishman') to Anne on the subject of Abigail.[98] This 'humble address' fumed about how everything had gone downhill since Anne had swapped advisers:

For Heaven's Sake, Madam, what could your majesty be thinking of?! . . . Your Majesty's favour to the Duchess of Marlborough was always looked upon as a peculiar happiness to your People, because it naturally led you to put your chief confidence in the two ablest men of your kingdom. For which reason I have often heard it said that she was the only favourite that ever a sovereign was the better for.

It urged Anne to consider her reputation and, if not that, preservation of her Crown from Jacobite invasion. It referred to 'a Certain Lady' who was 'very near being publicly named' in the House of Commons, and how scandal at home would weaken Marlborough's standing abroad. Sarah was not quite so reckless as to send this letter.

At around the same time Maynwaring drafted a letter to Abigail in Sarah's name,[99] regretting that there was no hope of making Abigail give up her ambitions: 'Tis like telling a lover what ill consequences will attend a present passion, and to think that any arguments of mine will bring you to reason or moderation would be to have a better opinion both of you and of myself than I am afraid either of us deserve.' Abigail, it went on, did not even have the 'generous vices' of previous favourites. She was warned to watch out for moves against her in the next Parliament and, melodramatically, was threatened with execution as a traitor: '[Y]ou must certainly expect before Christmas to hear yourself declared a common enemy to the State and a firebrand which all men will join to extinguish . . .' It ended with a vivid rendering of the biblical Abigail showing her humility before David when he came to destroy her family, in which Marlborough is cast as 'our David and deliverer' before whom she should prostrate herself. When Sarah told him she could not send this letter either, Maynwaring replied that he did not care if he offended those he was sure he would never please and encouraged her to adopt the same attitude.

The Queen had a fright in March 1708, which pushed her back into sympathy with the Whigs. It did not come from one of Maynwaring's or Sarah's anonymous letters, however, but from her half-brother, who attempted an invasion in Scotland. Though modern historians have generally endorsed Anne's view of the Jacobite threat as overrated, Sarah's worst fears were vindicated, to some extent, by this unexpected attempt. She was, at any rate, frustrated when Anne's alarm lasted only as long as the immediate and present danger, and when the Whig propagandists failed to capitalise on the public fears it aroused.[100]

The invasion attempt was reflected, in microcosm, by a dispute that same month over some lodgings at Kensington Palace.[101] Sarah discovered Abigail was making an incursion into her rooms there 'without my knowing the least word of it'. An honest mistake might easily have arisen because, as Sarah admitted, they were formal rooms which 'though I had never lain in 'em, I had intended it'. She protested that she would have given up the rooms if she had been 'commonly' asked, but instead, as with the marriage, she only found out by chance that Abigail was using them to receive visitors.

Once again Sarah ran to Anne to complain, but Anne denied having given the rooms to Abigail, with so much vehemence that Sarah could only apologise for her mistake. Not entirely convinced, however, she went to inspect the situation and quiz the Palace servants. When she confronted the Queen with fresh evidence, Anne again denied that Abigail used them. '[B]ut Madam I have seen 'em with my own eyes!' Sarah cried. Stubbornly the Queen persisted, 'I am sure she has none of your rooms . . .' and refused to send any third party to settle the matter. Sarah complimented herself on letting the matter drop, but could not resist complaining 'aloud before several people . . . in hopes it might be carried to Mrs Masham'. When the story did reach her, Abigail claimed she had not known the rooms were Sarah's. Nonetheless Sarah asked her to move out immediately. She also went back to the Queen and argued with her about it for a quarter of an hour until she obtained an admission that she had, once again, been right.

Rereading this saga in old age, Sarah noted that she still found it disagreeable. It had been a petty dispute, but she reminds us that it had wider ramifications:

[I]t may perhaps seem not prudent in me to insist so much on my lodgings at Kensington, since I never made use of them and certainly at another time & to any other person I would not have stood so much upon it. If my friends think I was too earnest in this matter I forgive them that and every other censure, so long as they acknowledge me to have acted with an uncorrupted fidelity and disinterested zeal in everything that related to the Queen & her people, to the Crown & to the Protestant Succession. If I was not a cunning dexterous favourite, yet I was a true & sincere one . . .[102]

As disinterest was the defining quality of a virtuous favourite, Sarah took offence when even her Whig sympathisers portrayed her as a spurned favourite whose anger was mere female jealousy.

On the other hand, she couched her arguments about the public good in the language of sentimental friendship, equating the qualities of a good friend with the qualities of a disinterested adviser. Small matters had wider political meanings because a person's character might be revealed through either. Finally, she justified writing the whole story in such detail only as a form of self-defence against others: '[T]here came out soon after a scurrilous paper about it, representing me as having barbarously & insolently turned a virtuous good woman, who it seems highly deserved the Queen's favour, out of her own lodgings, whereas the truth of the case was just the contrary . . .'[103]

Just before Marlborough sailed for The Hague on 29 March 1708, the Queen wrote to him complaining of Sarah's unkindness and explaining that she dare not say anything as it will only 'inflame her more'.[104] She begged him to help bring his wife round, if only to prevent gossip over the rift. At this point, however, he was equally cowed by Sarah's displeasure and his remonstrations were useless. Some days after he had left the country, Sarah was again writing to Anne.[105] On 31 March, Anne replied in the same patronisingly patient tone that Sarah used with her, hoping that 'a time will come that you will be disabused'. She repeated her promise to give Sarah's jobs to her daughters if Sarah were forced to retire. In early April, Anne wrote a kinder letter, willing to let bygones be bygones, and wishing that she and Sarah could live together as they had seven years before. '[Y]ou are pleased to accuse me of several things in your last letter very unjustly, especially concerning Masham,' she complained, and signed with her old promise of eternal faithfulness.[106]

Sarah's reply was sceptical. Since Anne had taken so long to write, she said, she had hoped 'that you would have convinced me that I was in the wrong as to what I said of the power of Abigail'. Instead she witnessed Tories riding daily back and forth on business between Abigail's lodgings and Harley's, and observed that Lord Haversham had already used Abigail to intercede with the Queen. With commendable clarity, Sarah explained that her dispute was not about having a low opinion of the

Queen's character but about a genuine and profound difference of political opinion. As evidence that Anne was being influenced against her own interests, Sarah mentioned her recent reluctance to meet privately with Marlborough or Godolphin. '[W]ho can it be but this woman?' Sarah asked. 'For you see nobody else.' Again, Sarah shifted the source of slander away from herself and on to the outside world, against whom she pretended to be defending the Queen: '[I]f I were to ask the first ordinary man that I met what had caused so great a change in you he would say that the reason was because you were grown very fond of Mrs Masham . . .' Sarah posed as an ignorant member of the public asking Anne to disabuse her, rather as the novelist Mrs Manley claimed only to record 'what everybody fearlessly reports with their tongue'.[107] But in light of their previous intimacy, Sarah's avowal that she did not know what to believe amounted to an accusation of lesbianism.

Anne was unable to dignify these accusations with an answer or even to admit she understood the insinuations, which left Sarah free to misread her silence as guilt. Then Sarah changed tack:

I had almost forgot to tell you of a new book that is come out on the subject. It's ridiculous and the book not well writ, but that looks so much the worse, for it shows that the notion is universally spread among all sorts of people. It is a dialogue between Madame Maintenon & Madame Masham in which she thanks her for her good endeavours to serve the King of France here . . . & there is stuff not fit to be mentioned of passions between women.[108]

The book was an anonymous satire entitled *The Rival Duchess: or, Court Incendiary. In a Dialogue between Madam Maintenon and Madam M[asham]* (1708). Several scholars have nominated Arthur Maynwaring as its author. If that is correct, Sarah must have known, and her criticism of her friend's writing was probably camouflage. What is clear is that Sarah mentioned it to Anne to threaten her with precisely what was 'not fit to be mentioned'.

The *Dialogue* was a classic use of homosexuality as slander, linking it with the idea of conspiracy. In the 1710s and 1720s pornographic texts often included lesbian scenes set inside convents to suggest Roman Catholic intrigues. As Abigail was linked with the French interest and the Catholic monarchy, so she was branded with the matching set of sexual inclinations, made all the more believable by the strength of Queen Anne's attachment to her.

Maynwaring's letters to Sarah encouraged her to return to Court to bully their enemies and revive the spirits of their Whig allies. He directly contradicted her husband's orders to steer clear of the place: 'I am persuaded that whenever Your Grace appears, Mrs Abigail will lead but an uncomfortable life and hardly venture to peep abroad. May I hope your presence will turn her into a bat, and that I shall see her come into a room where my Lady Hervey is at play, and set her good ladyship acrying.'[109]

In another letter he compares Anne's phrase 'you wrong Masham and me' to James I's reference to his lover Buckingham as 'Steenie and I'. Sarah did not read the James/Buckingham correspondence until the 1730s, when she laughed heartily at the letters' absurdity and told her granddaughter that they were 'incomparable'.[110] In fact they were far more like the love letters that Anne had written as a princess to Sarah than anything known to have been sent between Anne and Abigail.

Sarah's friendship with Maynwaring served in part as an ego-boost while she suffered fresh suspicions about Marlborough's fidelity. When her husband had departed for the Continent, Sarah had not gone to see him off, and soon he wrote to her that he did not intend to return to England that winter.

On 9 April, he referred to Sarah's 'resolution of living with that coldness and indifferency for me, which if it continues must make me the unhappiest man alive'.[111] It is not known what had provoked this extreme coldness, but it is possible that Sarah had discovered his interest in an eighteen-year-old actress and dancer named Hester Santlow. She had first performed on the London stage in 1706, and was said to have won the heart of James Craggs – son of Marlborough's old friend and confidant, Postmaster James Craggs – with her 'melting lascivious motions'.[112]

Lady Mary Wortley Montagu wrote that Marlborough used the two Mr Craggses as procurers of women and cash while he was on the Continent;[113] as she and Sarah were close friends her gossip about the Marlboroughs can usually be trusted – and by 1712 Sarah had certainly discovered something about the younger Craggs that made her hate him. However, there might have been other reasons for her animosity and there is no firm evidence that Craggs passed on Hester to Marlborough. Indeed, if he were so in love with her himself, it seems unlikely. *The Dictionary of National Biography* has it the other way round, saying that Hester 'was said to have lived under the protection of the Duke of Marlborough and subsequently Secretary Craggs'.

Sarah, in her late forties, was flattered for her beauty that same month by at least one Whig poet, William Oldisworth, who included her in an execrable piece of panegyric called *The British Court: A Poem describing the Most Celebrated Beauties at St James's, the Park and the Mall* (1707), yet she remained insecure about ageing. She later remembered this stage of her life as a time 'I should have been glad to have put out my own eyes if the dear Duke of Marlborough would have done the same that I might never have been tormented with any fears of losing him . . . I think tis best for most of our sex to have blind husbands.'[114]

Whether or not Hester was the reason for Sarah's coldness in 1708, there are sufficient other rumours about Marlborough's extra-marital affairs to suggest that this might have been part of the reason for the tension between them. In *The New Atalantis* Mrs Manley referred to a character named 'Daphne', who had an affair with Marlborough and who has been variously identified as a Mrs Griffith or as a female novelist named Catherine Cockburn. The same slander is repeated in her *Adventures of Rivella* where Cockburn is called 'Calista' and is forced to have sex with the Duke in his coach when she comes to beg for charity. Manley commented, 'I think there yet wants an example of elevated generosity in him to any of his mistresses, though the world can't dispute that he has had many . . .' But, she concluded, he never talked about these affairs in his 'good correspondence with his wife' where he 'speaks only of war and state, of the camp and the cabinet . . .'

In fact, Sarah and he wrote to one another as much about the sexual intrigues of the Queen and Prince Consort as about policy. On 11 April he wrote from The Hague that 'the credit of 256 [Abigail] occasions a good deal of disagreeable discourse in this country'.[115] The Marlboroughs wrote that Abigail Masham and George Churchill were serious threats to the public interest, not just useful scapegoats. Sarah thought that she and her husband would benefit from spreading what they knew of these royal relationships, but Marlborough was eager to hush them up. Anne, meanwhile, wrote to Godolphin demanding that Sarah should come and wait upon her more often to avert any public scandal over their falling out: it would 'in a little time make us the jest of the town. Some people will blame her, others me, & a great many both,' she complained nervously.[116] Sarah saw that Anne was 'frighted out of her wits that people should discover the passion she had for Ab[igail]'. Meanwhile, Sarah and the Duchess of Somerset would 'laugh & be very free on the subject' as they drove home from Court together.[117]

From Brussels, Marlborough replied to a letter from Sarah: 'You are so good as to say you will never write of politics that may be disagreeable to me if I desire it. You know in friendship and love there must be no constraint, so that I am desirous of knowing what your heart thinks, and beg of you the justice to believe that I am very much concerned when you are uneasy.'[118] It would seem, therefore, that at least part of the tension between them was political. He probably disapproved of Maynwaring's influence over her. In another letter he told her to stop writing angry letters to the Queen because they only 'make her more obstinate and shy of speaking to you even when she changes her mind'. He all but ordered her to leave the lobbying to Godolphin and himself.[119] Sarah, on the other hand, disapproved of his passivity and was letting him feel her displeasure. '[U]pon my word,' he wrote, 'when you are out of humour, and are dissatisfied with me, I had rather die than live; so on the contrary, when you are kind, I covet of all things a quiet life with you.'[120] The first half of this statement is always quoted against Sarah's bad temper, while the second half is often overlooked.

On 27 May 1708, Marlborough asked Sarah to ensure that William Guidott, a relation of her old friend Anthony who was standing for election, would be 'for the carrying on of the war' before giving him his backing.[121] Sarah followed his instructions but was more preoccupied with other preparations for the general election. It has now been determined that she and Maynwaring together wrote an anonymous political pamphlet, titled *Advice to the Electors*, which was at first misattributed to Lord Somers and then, until the 1970s, to Defoe. The pamphlet put forward a simple argument with which Defoe would certainly have agreed: that there were reasons to suspect certain Tories of plotting with France to invade and restore the Pretender, while there were no such suspicions against any Whigs, so if you were for the Protestant succession, you were safer to vote for the latter. Whether for these or other reasons, the Whigs made significant gains in the elections.

On 1 July 1708, news of Marlborough's victory at Oudenarde reached London, along with assurances that he was safe, though the battle had 'occasioned much blood'.[122] Maynwaring reassured Sarah that the victory would give a boost to the Whigs and make it as impossible for Marlborough's political enemies to attack him 'as for the wind to blow down Mr Vanbrugh's thick walls'.[123] He was busy in London trying to prevent a split in the Whig leadership, but claimed all he wanted was to join Sarah in the country and 'be allowed to hear music with Your Grace easily'.[124] The next day he wrote again, advising her not to lend more money to Vanbrugh, who was in personal financial trouble due to his theatrical ventures. He ended with a suggestive piece of gossip from the Duke of Somerset who had 'more than once seen Mr St John with the Pr[ince] lately, but believes that there was still the servant in waiting in some part of the room'.[125]

Sarah continued to write to Anne about the threat to her reputation posed by the relationship with Abigail: '[A]ll sensible and honest people,' she wrote in one version of her memoirs, 'laughed at such proceedings or else pitied the Queen's misfortune who was thus exposed to the talk of all courts & countries for so wrong a thing as having such a fondness for a bedchamber woman.'[126] Anne replied that she did not care what the 'malicious world' thought of her, they were wrong. She asked that Sarah 'would not mention that person anymore who you are pleased to call the object of my favour'.[127] Sarah almost immediately disobeyed this order and wrote to justify the fact that she would never bother to mention someone so 'inconsiderable' were it not for the woman's links to Harley: 'I never thought her education was such as to make her fit company for a great queen. Many people have liked the humour of their chambermaids and have been very kind to them, but tis very uncommon to hold a private correspondence with them . . .'[128] Increasingly Anne left Sarah's letters unanswered.

In her letters to Marlborough, Sarah repeated Maynwaring's political gossip and informed him that the Queen was fonder of Abigail than ever.[129] They now used two different cipher numbers for the Queen as if to represent her two personalities – her true self and her misadvised-by-Harley-and-Abigail self. On 12 July he assured her that 'You may depend upon my joining with 89 [the Whigs] in opposition to 84 [the Tories] in all things', but went on to add that he would not support the Whigs if they pushed to invite the Electoral Prince to England: 'I must never do anything that looks like flying in [Anne's] face.' He also refused to do more for the Whigs than give speeches and votes to them in the House of Lords.[130] He asked Sarah, as a go-between with the Junto and particularly Sunderland, to test reactions to his view that the war required one further campaign.[131]

On 22 July, he wrote with annoyance to Sarah upon discovering that she had forwarded another of his private letters to the Queen without permission;[132] in it he had referred critically to Anne's failure to make use of the victories he had brought her. Four days later, Sarah sat down to write her longest and least circumspect letter to Anne so far:

I remember you said . . . of all things in this world, you valued most your reputation, which I confess surprised me very much, that your Majesty should so soon mention that word after having discovered so great a passion for such a woman. For sure there can be no great reputation in a thing so strange & unaccountable, to say no more of it, nor can I think the having no inclination for any but of one's own sex is enough to maintain such a character as I wish may still be yours.[133]

Her suggestion that a same-sex relationship would not necessarily be viewed as innocent was a veiled threat. But it was also an admission: for Sarah to say that Anne had 'no inclination for any but of one's own sex' was as much as to say that she knew Anne was in love again, just as she had once been in love with Sarah herself. She never explicitly accused Anne of acting on her romantic feelings for women – indeed, it is unlikely that, when alone, Anne and Abigail did more than chat and play the harpsichord – but the idea that their relationship was 'strange' was shocking enough. No other Whig writer had dared go so far. Vanbrugh once referred to Anne's love for Abigail as 'not to be expressed'[134] and that was both figuratively and literally true; Sarah's letter mentioned the unmentionable.

Double entendres were endemic in the period, so Sarah could speak of Anne's 'passion' both for Abigail and for the Tories, or her 'most real and invariable passion for that phantom which she called the Church'.[135] She could refer interchangeably to Anne's sexual and political 'inclinations', or imply, by the use of the word 'unaccountable', that the relationship with Abigail was also perverting democracy. The Queen's love for Abigail became synonymous with her maintenance of the wrong political position.

Sarah referred to having shown the Queen two ballads when they had last met and noted 'that you never see any of them but from me, though the town and country are full of them'. While pretending to share Anne's distaste for such verses, she told her friend Lady Cowper that she had learned to sing by heart 'the two ballads of The Battle & Abigail' so that she could perform them at private assemblies.[136] Maynwaring was again the likely author of the crudely scatological 'Ballad on Mrs Abigail. To the Tune of the Dame of Honour' (1708),[137] which Sarah showed to Anne. Now she posted another, similarly offensive ballad to the Queen and reminded her, either tactlessly or threateningly, that 'it is a melancholy thing to remember that your royal father was in a manner sung out of his kingdoms by this very tune of Lillyballero, especially since your Majesty seems also inclined to hazard them all rather than displease Abigail . . .' She also compared the attacks on Anne and Abigail with the attacks on Charles II and his mistress the Duchess of Portsmouth: '& I think one need not say a great deal to show how much worse it is for you . . . to be put in print and brought upon the stage perpetually for one in Abigail's post'.

However, Sarah's next letter, of 26 July, was not all threats. It contained a strain of sadness, revealing that she was motivated as much by personal loss as by political conviction: 'Your Majesty would pardon my returning so often to this odious subject if you would but once reflect on the strange mortifying circumstances that there are to me in this affair . . .' She concluded with confidence that one day her views would be confirmed by history: 'I have formerly desired your Majesty to burn my letters. Now I make it my humble request that you will please lay this in your cabinet . . . in hopes some accident or other, when I am dead, might make you remember me & think better of me than you do at this time.'

Queen Anne's biographer, Edward Gregg, states that Anne 'never regarded Abigail as more than an excellent servant and nurse'.[138] But to view Abigail as merely a scapegoat for Whig satirists who wished to complain about Anne's policies is to miss the situation's complexity and to underestimate the personal feelings of all three women. It was not just shyness, ill-health and strict morality that made Anne spend all her private time with women. And when Sarah hinted that, unless Anne dismissed Abigail, she would be left with no choice but to believe and endorse the circulating slanders, she was aware that this would be a self-implicating accusation: no one had been closer to Anne than Sarah since Mrs Cornwallis's departure almost thirty years earlier. Just as her parents had separated Anne from Cornwallis, and just as Queen Mary had urged her sister to give up Sarah in 1692, so Sarah was trying to eject Abigail.

Marlborough suggested that her threats would be better directed to Abigail than to Anne: 'I am of the opinion I ever was of, that the Queen will not be made sensible, or frightened out of this passion; but I can't but think some ways might be found to make Mrs Masham very much afraid.'[139] Letters in which he urged her to keep her temper ('by endeavouring to hurt we do good offices to 256 [Abigail]')[140] were usually followed by others that drew her back into the fray. It was too useful for him to have Sarah speaking on his behalf, and taking the flak, while he could appear respectful and moderate. On 9 August, for example, he returned a draft copy of a letter Sarah was planning to send to Anne, approving of its contents and underlining the key points for emphasis.[141] He instructed her to show the Queen his private letter in this instance, which just happened to express his loyalty to the Crown and to bemoan that he had lost his influence to 'God knows who'.

Sarah used her letter to Anne to comment on Marlborough's: 'And here I can't help reflecting,' she wrote, 'what a sad appearance it will make in the world when it shall come to be known that whilst a man is at the head of your affairs, and entrusted by most of your confederates, he has not so much credit with you as a dresser unknown to everybody but those that she has betrayed.'[142] With an insinuation that was sexual as much as social, she repeats that it is 'a strange competition between one that has gained you so many battles and one that is but just worthy to touch your limbs'.

Only days later, on Thursday 19 August, Sarah was obliged to join Anne in an open carriage to ride to another thanksgiving service at St Paul's for the victory at Oudenarde. It was a brilliant spring morning, and people hung out of their windows to see the procession. Such thanksgiving services had been the setting for some years now of Sarah's most public appearances and she was used to smiling and waving. On this occasion, however, her smile concealed humiliation.

That morning Sarah had performed her duties as Groom of the Stole by laying out the Queen's clothes and jewels 'in a way that I thought [Anne] would like'.[143] But when she sat down beside Anne in the carriage, she found she wore no jewels at all. This dramatic austerity, to Sarah, had multiple meanings: that Abigail had advised the Queen not to wear whatever Sarah prepared, and that Anne wanted to express to the onlookers a lack of enthusiasm for the thanksgiving service and hence for the continuation of an increasingly unpopular war. As Winston Churchill understood:

It was not only feminine anger which stirred her. Sarah was also a politician. She knew well that those jewels, or no jewels, would be the talk of every Court in Europe. All the ambassadors who now crowded in the greatest state upon the once-neglected Court of St James' would write that night the story of Marlborough's failing favour.[144]

As they alighted at the steps of the cathedral beside the new statue of the Queen, which faced the coaches struggling up Ludgate Hill and was already a target for street urchins' pebbles,[145] Sarah and Anne continued their argument about the absent jewels. Inside the building the congregation's voices buzzed around them. Anne started to say something and, in an unguarded moment, Sarah snapped, 'Be quiet!' Unfortunately she was overheard by those standing nearby. They sat through the rest of the service, which was conducted by Godolphin's brother, the Dean of St Paul's, in mutually offended, mortified silence.

Anne did not let Sarah forget this insult. In a seven-line note written some time later she referred to the 'commands you gave

me on the thanksgiving day of not answering you'[146] and assured
Sarah that she need never be troubled with her answers again.

Sarah replied, 'I desired you not to answer me there for fear
of being overheard,' but said that she was desperate for a proper
answer to all her complaints. 'I flatter myself that I have said
several things to you that are unanswerable,' she wrote, hoping to
provoke the Queen out of her silence, and insisted that she would
far rather not write such 'disagreeable letters' but 'nobody else
cares to speak out upon so ungrateful a subject.' Just as Anne's
early love letters read like shouts into a void, so Sarah's long
letters now seemed to fall on deaf ears.

Marlborough, in the middle of the long siege of Lille, must have
been depressed to receive reports of the escalating tension between
his wife and the Queen. He wrote to Anne, in a letter edited by
Sarah before it was sent, that he could now serve her only as a
soldier because he did not feel trusted as a Minister.[147] To Sarah
he said, 'I am in the galley and must row on as long as this war
lasts',[148] as though he were not one of its leading protagonists.
In an early version of her memoirs, Sarah suggested that the fate
of Europe depended on her ability to put a good face on things
during these months: 'I thought it advisable in all respects to
conceal as much as I could from the public [of her split with
Anne], at least till the Campaign was over.'[149]

While the Queen was receiving alarmingly suggestive letters from
Sarah, various large sums were borrowed from the Privy Purse
of which Sarah remained the Keeper. It has been calculated that
Sarah withdrew about £21,800 (approximately £1.5 million in
today's money) between August 1708 and January 1710. Just
as the Junto was blackmailing Anne to comply with its policies
by threatening to withhold five million pounds she needed for
the Treasury, so Sarah appeared to be blackmailing her on a
private level. Anne must have known that Sarah had kept all
her letters since they were adolescents, and the credibility that
Sarah's views on Anne's character – and sexuality – would carry
with the reading public if she published her memoirs. This hint

of blackmail can be inferred from a cryptic comment by Anne, quoted with pride by Sarah. When someone accused Sarah of embezzling funds from the Privy Purse, Anne replied: 'Everybody knows, cheating is not the Duchess of Marlborough's crime.'[150]

Sarah had been tempted to borrow the money because she needed an injection of ready cash to finance the building of a new property. She had been living at St James's Palace since December 1695 but now felt that the precariousness of her position at Court made it prudent to find a new London home. She also wanted to move out of her Palace lodgings to symbolise her transition from royal favourite to independent political player.

On 31 August 1708 she received from Anne a lease of four and a half acres of land in St James's on which to build Marlborough House. The first reference to the idea in her correspondence with Marlborough appeared in June 1708, when he mentioned 'the house you have a mind to build' and they made arrangements for what each of them would contribute from their separate bank accounts towards the cost, and how it would be handled in their wills.[151] Marlborough was discouraging ('you know I have no great opinion of this project') because he believed that the land was too cramped for the size of townhouse necessary to satisfy Sarah.[152] He also warned her that it would end up costing twice as much as any first estimate[153] – as though Sarah had not learned this lesson through her management of the Blenheim works.

In 1709 Sarah was granted a further two acres on which to build[154] and her plan became more feasible. Over the winter months she chose her architect – Christopher Wren, although he was a Tory MP – and her workmen, with the aim of starting in the spring. London was then Europe's largest city but still only five miles wide from east to west, and two and a quarter miles from north to south. The building of Bloomsbury, Piccadilly and Mayfair was well under way, and Oxford Street was no longer the northern border – there were a few settlements higher up in the area where today we find Harley Street. But Cavendish

Square was not yet built, and to the north-east the area of St Pancras remained green fields, the edge of open countryside.[155]

On 24 May 1709, the foundation stone of Marlborough House was laid. It was to be Sarah's 'anti-Blenheim'. In its design she wished to express a Whig aesthetic linked to her belief in plain-spoken honesty as opposed to courtly artifice, 'to have things plain and clean, from a piece of wainscot to a lady's face'.[156] The Whig mind saw architectural order threatened by the baroque, just as law and order was threatened by Jacobitism – as if curlicues on buildings were only a step away from Catholic idolatry. She expressed her ideas to Wren in terms of the convenience she desired in Marlborough House. His insistence on mathematical forms within the baroque style was in accord with her liking for austerity and, guided by Sarah's instructions, he could easily follow her wishes. The designs were also heavily influenced by Buckingham House and, in certain features, by the mansions in the Marais district of Paris. It was planned so that if it were 'set in an equal line with Her Majesty's palace, it will have a view down the middle walk of her garden.'[157]

Marlborough House would consist therefore of a simple rectangular block with unadorned façade. The central area would have two floors (today it has four) and a basement for domestic staff and wine cellars. It was flanked by two pavilions. The kitchen with its open fires was in the one on the left, connected to the central block by an open colonnade so that it could burn down without damaging the main house. The whole was to be built in red brick and Portland stone, with alcoves between the windows. The main entrance (today an inner wall) was to the north, and on the southern side were gardens with a raised promenade from which one could look down on the Mall and St James's Park.

To make the gardens, Sarah needed to uproot an oak tree planted in the grounds by Charles II in gratitude to the one that had hidden him from the Roundheads during the Civil War. When this became known, Sarah's insolence to royal history, as to her present royal mistress, provided rich material for anonymous Tory satirists:

> Be cautious, madam, how you thus provoke
> This sturdy plant, the second royal oak,
> For should you fell it or remove it hence
> When dead it may revenge the vile offence
> And build a scaffold in another place
> That may e'er long prove fatal to your Grace
> May furnish out a useful gallows too
> Sufficient for your friends, though not for you.[158]

Unafraid of such criticism or superstition, Sarah dug up the tree.

Maynwaring might only have been exaggerating mildly when he flattered Sarah that 'Sir Chris. Wren had no more hand in designing it [Marlborough House] than the bricklayers or masons' and that 'Your Grace sits at the head of the work.'[159] She was certainly busy with the interior at any rate: sending to Holland for tiles, bricks, mirrors and hangings.[160] She felt a great deal more affection for the elderly Wren than she ever had for Vanbrugh, and worked closely with him and the trusted Hawksmoor. In July 1709, Marlborough wrote from his camp before Tournai, the town to which he would lay siege that summer: 'I think every innocent pleasure should be indulged, and as I think at this time yours is building, I wish you with all my heart good weather.'[161]

Marlborough House was important to Sarah as an investment and as a status symbol, but the Marlboroughs were also aware of the need to downplay their reputation for avarice and extravagance. The grant of the land in St James's was one of the few clear examples, along with Windsor Lodge, of 'bounty' derived from Sarah's position as favourite (or, more precisely, as an ex-insider who now threatened to spill the beans), and Marlborough's investment in the property was related by observers to the perception that he was profiteering from the war.[162] Mrs Manley depicted Sarah as a female Midas, accusing her of selling places to the highest bidder, her daughters into sham marriages, and secrets to foreign enemies.[163] In fact, during 1708–9, much evidence survives among Sarah's papers to suggest the exact opposite: that she was generous to those in trouble who approached her for charity. One letter from a Mrs Cornwallis (possibly Anne's old servant but more likely the wife of a Thomas Cornwallis) begged Sarah to intercede for her brother who had been declared a lunatic and had insufficient income to keep himself like a gentleman without working. Sarah replied kindly that, if Mrs Cornwallis knew nobody else who could apply to the Attorney General for help in this case, she would gladly do so. Another letter from a Mrs Elizabeth South thanks Sarah for having helped her family to find jobs, but asks that her younger sister be given a month's training before coming into waiting at Court since 'at present she cannot stand still without tottering'. A second letter asks Sarah to help break the little sister's boisterous spirit, which might get her into trouble.[164]

Marlborough was criticised more for his reluctance to part with money. An anecdote told of how he had borrowed money from a friend for a sedan-chair ride, but was then spotted walking home with the coins in his pocket. The source for this seems to be apocryphal.[165] His relatively simple style of living in the field camps – not throwing banquets except for other Allied leaders, for example – was confused with miserliness by many hangers-on. Sarah wrote that he 'hated mortally the trouble of living in grandeur: and that was sufficient to make many think him covetous'.[166] But many years after his death, when someone tried to ingratiate themselves with Henry St John by ridiculing the Duke's avarice, the old Tory put them down by saying, 'He was so very great a man that I forget he had that vice.'[167]

The Whigs' reputation for greed was also used by the growing anti-war faction, who suggested that the English were treated like lackeys of the Bank of Amsterdam and killed for the sake of Dutch trade. This 'Hollandophobia' was not only a remnant of two recent wars against the Dutch but was also based upon an aversion for the *nouveaux riches*, both as nations and as individuals. Given that Sarah was, to some extent, snobbish and xenophobic, it was ironic that the self-made Marlboroughs found themselves susceptible to this prejudice. The Duke was mocked for 'play[ing] the Stadholder'[168] in The Hague, while at home the rising edifices of Blenheim and Marlborough House gave opponents concrete targets at which to aim their resentment. As the death toll rose in increasingly bloody battles, so did the resentment of London widows and grieving mothers against Marlborough House – which cost the Duke alone around forty to fifty thousand pounds.'[169] Yet Sarah was still alone in fully understanding how this rift with the Tories over the cost of the war would necessitate even closer alliance between Godolphin's ministry and the Whigs.

Relations between the Marlboroughs were strained through the autumn of 1708. In September he told her to 'be quiet' since she herself had admitted it was futile to try to change Anne's mind with letters.[170] A week later he thanked her for keeping to her resolution 'of neither speaking nor writing' to the Queen, and joked that if they all went silent the Tories would be so surprised that they would make a wrong move of their own accord.[171] Godolphin and Maynwaring, however, continued to encourage Sarah's interventions. Godolphin wrote from Windsor on 20 September, complaining that she had left the Court for London upon receiving the news of her old friend Lady Fitzharding's death. He reproached her like an abandoned lover, 'who can grieve myself to a shadow' whenever she showed him 'indifference'. Such strength of affection suggests that Sarah was her own worst enemy in this sense at least: she systematically arranged for the destruction of all the letters in which she was likely to have expressed kindness and love for her husband or her close friends, while preserving all those that concerned her disputes.

The Whigs were now demanding the removal from the Admiralty of not only George Churchill but also Prince George, and his replacement with the Whig Lord Orford. In this matter Sarah was still treated as being of pivotal importance by the Junto since she was the only wholehearted Whig in the confidence of the two leading ministers. Yet even she thought the Junto was pushing its luck; the Queen would never agree to her husband's dismissal.

Anne doted on George like the mother she had never really had a chance to be. Since 1702 he had suffered from prolonged asthmatic attacks. When she and Sarah had been close, Anne had written anxiously to her whenever his 'complaints' returned. Sarah had observed Anne staying at Windsor to take advice from Harley 'all that sultry season' of 1707, 'even when the Prince was panting for breath'.[172]

By the following October the Prince lay dying at Windsor. When Sarah heard the news she was in a no-win situation: if she had not rushed to Court to be at Anne's side, she would have been condemned, yet she knew her presence there was unwanted. Having been so long away from Court, she had not even been aware that George was seriously ill and had written him an offensive letter, upbraiding him for treating her badly the last time they had met.[173] This ill-timed action would have made Anne even more hostile to her when she arrived at the castle shortly after the Prince's death.

Sarah described the scene in one of her unpublished memoirs.[174] She transferred her sense of intrusion on to others, remarking that 'There were others of her servants by, which, I thought, must be uneasy to her and that made it impossible for me to speak to her.' Nonetheless, she knelt before Anne at the deathbed and 'said all that I could imagine from a faithful servant and one that she had professed so much kindness to, but she seemed not to mind me . . .' She urged the Queen to go immediately to St James's, rather than sit morbidly in 'a place where a dead husband lay'. Anne refused. Sarah wondered why she did not want to leave that 'ugly little close place' and implied that it was because of a back door that led by some stairs to Abigail's lodgings rather than to be near the Prince's body. When Sarah tried to move her, Anne pulled away and sent her out to wait in the corridor. Then she asked her to send for Abigail, which Sarah thought 'very shocking, but at that time I was resolved not to say the least [a] wry word to displease her'. She did not summon Abigail but went back into the room and pulled Anne to her feet. Later, she justified disobeying the Queen's order by claiming that she was trying to protect Anne from gossip.

Leaning weakly on Sarah's arm, Anne was led like a captive out of the bedchamber and through the public rooms. As they walked along the castle's gallery, the Queen veered nearer to where Abigail stood in line with the other servants, and swerving, as Sarah put it, 'like a sail' towards her, managed to whisper a few words in passing. This brilliant simile of Sarah's contains the suggestion of Anne's inconstancy (blown by passing winds) and makes literal her physical inclination towards the bedchamber woman.

That evening, however, Sarah realised that she 'could gain no ground' against Abigail. Having transported Anne to St James's Palace against her will, she found her there 'at table again, where she had been eating, and Mrs Masham close by her. Mrs Masham went out of the room as soon as I came in, not in the humble manner she had sometimes affected as bedchamber woman, but with an air of insolence and anger.' Presumably she and the Queen had just been discussing Sarah's shocking insensitivity.

Every detail of this memoir, which Sarah wrote a month after the event, implied its author's disparagement of Anne's grief. She described Anne's healthy appetite that evening, the absence of tears, and her petty interest in the etiquette of George's funeral. Anne's love of the Prince, she wrote, '*seemed* in the eye of the world to be prodigiously great & great was the passion of grief, *in all appearance*, when death parted them' [emphasis added].[175]

After her bereavement, Anne sent a note to Sarah asking her to provide purple sheets (the colour of royal mourning) for receiving visitors in bed, and to send a portrait of George to her at St James's.[176] She also sent a reasoned reply to Marlborough's rather precipitous request for permission to take over the Prince's stables. Sarah, meanwhile, was the only courtier to refuse to wear full mourning dress. One observer gossiped that she was 'the only one that had powder in her hair, or a patch upon her face'.[177] Perhaps this was revenge for Anne's refusal to wear jewels at the Oudenarde thanksgiving ceremony. Or perhaps Sarah simply wanted to make her doubts about Anne's love for George as public as possible, again implying that she had her reasons for this scepticism.

7
'Noise of the Town'

After Prince George's death, Sarah retreated to her country property to avoid further humiliation at Abigail's hands, while Maynwaring remained her eyes and ears at Court. She dined at Woodstock with the Duke and Duchess of Somerset, they who had once loaned Syon House to Princess Anne and the Marlboroughs. According to Sarah, Somerset's 'taste for power, which he is not fit for' led him to behave 'like a spoiled child', making demands of the Marlboroughs that they could not fulfil.[1] Later Sarah stated that, had it not been for her warning him about what was and was not pleasing to the Queen, he would have been expelled from the Privy Council long ago.[2] Maynwaring was not much exaggerating when he reflected: 'Sure 78 [himself] is under some fortunate planet at this time, for it seems to me that if he would be secretary to anybody but 240 [Sarah] he might almost hope to be so to the very Cabinet.'[3]

Godolphin felt isolated in the Cabinet and under constant pressure to conform to Whig policies. He wrote to Sarah:

6 [Sunderland] has been with me this morning, very inquisitive to know if I have prevailed on you to come to town, not doubting, as indeed he has no reason to do, but that I endeavoured it as much as I could . . . I see so many difficulties coming upon me from all sides, that unless I would have recourse to you oftener, upon many occasions, than it is possible for me to have at this distance when the ways grow bad and the moon fails, then I am afraid they must needs be too hard for me; besides that, I would not willingly make any step but what is first approved by you.[4]

It is a remarkable tribute from a Treasurer and chief minister to a colleague's wife.

The elder Mr Craggs was travelling back and forth with letters between Marlborough, who was bringing the siege of Lille to a close, Sarah and Godolphin in London. Marlborough told Sarah she should not hinder the Whigs from paying court to Abigail, as he hoped they might persuade her to change sides. His pragmatic approach did not heal Sarah's wounded vanity.[5] Similarly he told her not to worry if Abigail governed Anne's choices of Church appointments, as what mattered was whether she listened to the Cabinet 'in their affairs of consequence'.[6] Marlborough's sole concern, it seems, was continuation of the war to total victory while Sarah held a wider agenda, including defence of religious freedom. The couple's differences, both political and marital, were probably healed by a tense week in late November during which Sarah had no news of her husband. She retreated to Windsor Lodge and told Maynwaring that the uncertainty over Marlborough's safety was driving her so crazy that she felt like drowning herself.[7] Certainly she forgot about Church appointments until news of his safety and victory defending Brussels arrived on the twenty-sixth.

As many leading Whigs competed with High Tories like Rochester to ingratiate themselves with Abigail, Sarah's disillusionment with the Whig party brought husband and wife closer in opinion than they had ever been. In January 1709, on an unusual midwinter trip to the Continent, Marlborough wrote home that '[t]he assurances you give me in yours of the 14th of being of my mind as to parties has given me all the hopes imaginable of a future happiness'.[8] He agreed with Sarah that Halifax, who coveted Godolphin's Treasury, should not be brought in, and commented that their son-in-law Sunderland must be 'distracted' if he was going to back Halifax against the will of the Marlboroughs and Godolphin. Yet Sarah continued to work towards other Whig advancements. Supporting her self-image as more driven by principle than patronage, she did so even as she fell out with the party leadership.

1708–9 was the winter of the Great Frost and in London there was another Christmas ice fair on the frozen Thames. In France, the harsh weather had precipitated a famine that forced Louis XIV to consider peace on less advantageous terms. Marlborough's letters to Sarah were full of optimism about the end of the war,[9] which disproves his enemies' accusations that he wished to prolong it for personal profit. On the other hand, he had reason to tell his wife, who worried constantly about his health, that he wanted the war over in order to be at home with her: 'If I can believe 39 [himself] his real intentions are to be as quiet as is possible.'[10] He returned home in late February, reuniting with Sarah in Canterbury.

Like Marlborough, Sarah protested that she preferred the quiet of her own house to life at Court. In a letter to a friend she predicted that her persecutors would be overthrown 'because I think nothing that is both unjust & unreasonable can last long'.[11] In practice she was less philosophical. That February she complained to Anne again about an apparently trivial matter for which it is hard to find wider symbolic significance: Anne had tried to increase by a daily bottle of wine the emoluments of her starcher, Elizabeth Abrahal, a friend of Abigail. Desperation can be detected in Sarah's lectures to Anne about the limits of her powers within her own household: the bedchamber rules stated, 'All the Inferior Servants of the Bedchamber are in the disposal of the Groom of the Stole'[12], so theoretically Anne should have consulted Sarah.

Marlborough sailed again for The Hague on 3 May, having spent only a few weeks at home. Later that month he remained hopeful of peace, and instructed Sarah to let Godolphin know which Cabinet Ministers should be sent as plenipotentiaries and which should be kept at home.[13] He also answered Bishop Burnet's concerns about the French Protestant refugees and whether their right to return would be included in a peace treaty.[14]

For the moment, Anne took care not to tread further on Sarah's toes, promising not to make appointments to the bedchamber staff against her wishes, though still refusing to fire Abigail.[15] Briefly offended by Abigail, one staff member, Mrs Danvers, called on Sarah to spread salacious gossip:

that the Queen was very fond of her at the bath & that upon Mrs Hill's disliking the lodging that was marked for her, she told the Queen that she would [sell] up, upon which there was the most ridiculous scene, as Mrs Danvers acted it, that ever I saw: of Mrs Hill's sorely ill-bred manner & the Queen going about the room after her and begging her to go to bed, calling her 'Dear Hill' twenty times over.[16]

Mrs Danvers later returned to friendship with Abigail and, Sarah believed, told tales in the other direction: '[W]hen she came to me one day to thank me for a share which I had sent her of the Queen's clothes I desired her to spare her compliments, telling her that I knew very well what she said of me upon other occasions.'[17]

Sarah claimed that Marlborough shared her sense of injury at every petty slight, but was too ashamed to discuss it with the Queen. In fact, although Marlborough claimed 'I would go upon all-four to make it easy between you,'[18] he was now disinclined to interfere in the disintegration of the women's relationship. When Sarah, with Maynwaring, wrote again to Anne and sent a copy to Marlborough for his opinion, he cautioned her: 'It has been always my observation in disputes, especially in that of kindness and friendship, that all reproaches, though never so reasonable, do serve to no other end but the making the breach wider.'[19] In understanding that love is never won by argument, he was wiser than his wife. For the first time he discussed the prospect of their both being forced to resign, despite all his victories and all her years of service.

That August Godolphin saw an unusually depressed Sarah at Windsor Lodge, sitting alone in a 'dismal room . . . with one poor candle'.[20] To keep herself cheerful, Godolphin suggested she should bring a small coterie of friends with her whenever she stayed at Windsor. When she left the Court and travelled to Althorp the next day, he wrote again to persuade her to come back to wait on Anne even if it hurt her pride. Sarah's absence, he argued, gave the Duke of Somerset and others cause to accuse her of negligence. He also mentioned the 'deep designs' of a new favourite, whom he nicknamed 'Troule-It-Away'.[21] This was Sarah's old friend Elizabeth, Duchess of Somerset. The Whig party had realised that Sarah's influence had waned and needed to back another candidate for the role of royal favourite: the ambitious Somerset had put forward his wife.

Maynwaring still backed Sarah. He urged her to disturb the Queen's privacy with Abigail, appealing to Sarah's self-image as an amateur apothecary who would cure Anne of her unhealthy love: '[T]he humour must spend itself, let the object be ever so leprous; . . . And though I have so great an opinion of your Grace's skill in the science you profess of physick . . . yet I cannot but think you have far greater qualifications to cure the distempers of the body politic.'[22]

In the midst of the battle of Mons, Marlborough received a letter from Sarah that blamed him for failing to defend her honour sufficiently in her arguments with Anne. On 29 August he replied, refusing to hector Anne on Sarah's behalf, yet declaring his devotion to his wife at the high romantic pitch of a soldier facing personal danger: 'If ever I see the Queen I shall speak to her just as you would have me; and all the actions of my life shall make the Queen, as well as all the world, sensible that you are dearer to me than my own life; for I am fonder of my happiness than of my life, which I cannot enjoy unless you are kind.'[23]

The next day he wrote again, reporting on French troop movements, and concluding with what Sarah's critics have considered a subtle rebuke for her egotism in troubling him with her problems at this juncture: 'I can't hind[er] saying to you, that though the fate of Europe – if these armies engage – may depend upon the good or bad success, yet your uneasiness gives me much greater trouble.' Yet to read this as a reproof is to underestimate how closely connected the war was to Sarah's power battles at home, and Marlborough's love for his wife. Two days later he informed her, and hence England, that 'We have had this day a very bloody battle' in the woods near Malplaquet.[24] At the same time he wrote to Godolphin to assure him, with sombre relief, that it was 'now in our power to have what peace we please'. Sarah was at the building site at Woodstock when she received Marlborough's letter, and with it the alarming news that he had suffered a minor stroke due to the stress of the battle.

The victory at Malplaquet was a turning point because the carnage, though worse for the Dutch than for the English, fed anti-war opinion. No battle seemed to bring the prospect of peace any closer. Unemployed labourers were now being press-ganged, the war was blamed for the high price of corn and bread, and Defoe's *Review*[25] was not alone in noting that London seemed to be in recession, with fashionable shops turning into junk shops and overseas trade declining. Only artisans who produced luxury goods benefited from wartime protectionism, which explains why so many distinctive styles in English design flourished during Queen Anne's reign.[26] Nonconformist refugees from England's ally Austria were still fleeing to England in large numbers – between May and October 1709 14,000 Lutherans arrived from the Rhineland Palatinate, sparking xenophobic riots in Kent. The labouring men believed that the refugees had come 'to eat up the bread of the poorer sort of people & take away their work & increase the number of the parish poor'.[27] They were even accused of importing the plague. Only Whigs like Sarah and Defoe gave them a sympathetic reception, seeing their plight as incontrovertible evidence of French tyranny.

Yet to a growing number of voters, Marlborough and Godolphin appeared to be prolonging the war against the nation's immediate interest. Anne's failure to congratulate Marlborough or Sarah after Malplaquet was indicative not only of tension between the three, but also of the Queen's change of heart about the war. Sarah told her friend Lord Coningsby on 17 September that, although Marlborough had been exposed to dangers for many hours of the battle, Anne had neither sent 'the least human message' nor expressed anything to either of his two daughters who served as Ladies of the Bedchamber.[28]

When Abigail left St James's in mid-September to give birth to her second child, Sarah returned to Court aiming to prevent the

Duchess of Somerset installing herself as the next favourite. The political pressures continued: the Whigs were pushing for Orford to be made First Lord of the Admiralty now that Prince George's death had left the post vacant, and the Tories were campaigning against the conduct of the war.

Sarah gained access to the Queen with what she admitted was an 'artifice', a story about a poor war widow who needed royal charity, and proceeded to put forward her own request for a favour – a trifling matter by which to test her credit. She wanted some additional rooms in the Palace to link hers with the park. Godolphin had obtained an earlier promise of them on Sarah's behalf, but Anne claimed to have forgotten this. Sarah asked whether she had promised the rooms to anyone else, and Anne replied she had not, but that she might need to give them to one of her servants. '[A]t these words,' wrote Sarah, 'I smiled and said I found Her Majesty did not reckon Lord Marlborough nor me her servants. She looked a little out at that, as if that had been a slip, and made a show of speaking but the words were not intelligible . . .' One can only imagine what Anne must have been muttering.

Sarah went on to tell Anne that her friends had heard vicious gossip about the Marlboroughs, and she had had to vindicate herself repeatedly to others. Again she showed that she was not averse to blackmail: 'I believed it should be thought yet more strange if I should repeat this conversation: that after all the service Lord Marl[borough] had done her she should not give him a miserable hole to make him a clear way to his lodgings, and I desired to know if I might tell that to any of my friends.' Anne did not reply.[29]

Ultimately Abigail's sister was given the rooms in question, from which Sarah feared she and her family could eavesdrop and where they 'sometimes make such a noise and smoke and stink in the lodgings that it is impossible to stay in them'. Later that month Anne wrote Sarah a note agreeing to her request to remove these people. In any case, Sarah would soon be free to move out herself. Marlborough wrote to her: 'I propose to make my court to you this winter by being very much pleased with the great advance you have made in your building at London.'[30]

Marlborough also courted his wife by writing to Anne at last to complain about the way she had treated Sarah. This letter, sent on 29 September 1709,[31] was every bit as wild and insecure in tone as any of Sarah's, the only difference being that he sounded more sorry for himself, as if he believed arguing with the Queen was a waste of breath. 'In time,' he hoped, 'you will be sensible of the long and faithful services of Lady Marlborough and that God will bless you with the opening of your eyes . . .'

He followed this with a request that even Sarah knew to be unwise: in October he formally put to Anne that he should be made Captain-General for life. This idea, which smacked of Cromwellian ambition, had been on his mind since May. He wished to rise (or retire) above the violence of party politics, but he had overestimated his authority. He never forgave the Whigs, such as Somers and Cowper, for failing to support this unprecedented application for a lifetime post.

Meanwhile he wrote to Sarah about everything from the choc-olate ('jocolat') she had requested he send[32] to Orford's chances of obtaining the Admiralty appointment. 'By your last letter,' he observed, 'I fear you do not think me sincere where I tell you that I do with all my heart wish 15 [Orford] at the head of 104 [the Admiralty].'[33] His letters did not refer to Sarah's continuing correspondence with Anne, which kept up the pressure on the Whigs' behalf regarding such appointments. On 16 October, for example, she put her grievances into writing. In that letter, she called Abigail a 'low creature', and argued teasingly that if Anne was so mistaken in Sarah's character after a twenty-year friendship, she could be equally mistaken about Abigail. More darkly, she repeated her warning that 'nothing your M[ajesty] does can be a secret'. Sarah was clear here about the cause of their arguments: she remembered that her Whig lobbying 'was the first occasion of your dislike for me' but that subsequently Anne treated her coldly because 'you said it was that I believed you had such an intimacy with Masham'.[34]

Ten days later, Anne apparently replied to this letter more fully than she had ever answered Sarah before. The original seems to have been destroyed – perhaps by Sarah – so we only have her paraphrase. She wrote that Anne charged her 'with inveteracy (as her word is) against poor Masham, and with having nothing so much at heart as the ruin of my cousin'[35] and that Anne sarcastically apologised for not being able to 'see with my eyes & hear with my ears'. The final blow, quoted verbatim, was a categorical statement 'that it is impossible for me [Sarah] to recover her [Anne's] former kindness, but that she shall behave herself to me as the Duke of Marlborough's wife and her Groom of the Stole'.[36] In sum, Anne had declared their friendship dead.

A couple of days later, in the letter in which the Queen refused Marlborough the lifelong possession of his post, she also responded unambiguously to his earlier accusations about mistreating Sarah:

I do not love complaining, but it is impossible to help saying on this occasion I believe nobody was ever so used by a friend as I have been by her ever since my coming to the Crown. I desire nothing but that she would leave off teasing and tormenting me, and behave herself with the decency she ought, both to her friend and the Queen, and this I hope you will make her do . . .[37]

Sarah's immediate response was frantically to copy out, in her own hand, samples of Anne's early letters and send them to her as reminders of her old feelings. She also composed a narrative of their relationship from beginning to end.[38] It told of how the 'chiefs of the Tories had a design to bring in the P[rince] of W[ales] & in such a case nobody could be sure how far such a change might be carried . . . I feared the loss of Mrs Morley's life . . .', which was why Mrs Freeman was 'perpetually telling her' and writing 'volumes' about avoiding a Tory government. It referred to the dangerous influence of George Churchill, 'who most people believed a Jacobite in his heart', over Anne's husband before he died, and claimed that 'This was the true reason of my going seldomer to Mrs Morley, which is one of my greatest accusations, because I had not always patience to pursue her when she was strange to me.'

She described Abigail's rise from the shadows, and went on: '[W]hen Mrs Morley goes back and seriously reflects upon all the extraordinary things she has done for a woman who combs her head . . . I am confident she must think (as all the world does) that such things can proceed from nothing but extravagant passion.' She excused her own malice as a natural defensive instinct: 'I do not comprehend that one can properly be said to have malice or inveteracy for a viper because one endeavours to hinder it from doing mischief.'

In the letter that accompanied the above narrative, Sarah told Anne to read her letters as if they were sermons before she took the Holy Sacrament. Then she wrote out a list of obligations attached to friendship according to a devotional book called *The Whole Duty of Man*: '[N]eglecting lovingly to admonish a friend, forsaking his friendship for slight or no cause, unthankfulness to those that admonish, or being angry with them for it . . .'

There is a certain pathos in Sarah's continual talk of the duty rather than the pleasure of friendship. Her sense of rejection appears only occasionally from behind her logic: '[A]sk your own heart seriously whether you have ever told me of any fault but that of believing as all the world does that you have an intimacy with Mrs Masham & whether those shocking things you complain I have said was any more than desiring you to love me better than her . . .'

Sarah's final letters are fascinating because they can be read either as pained entreaties for a lost private bond or as politically motivated. Just as Locke asked what kind of behaviour merited a break with a sovereign, so Sarah asked what merited a break in a longstanding personal friendship. While she lobbied for the Whigs, she appealed at the same time to philosophical doctrines of friendship. When Anne mentioned her right to a private life, Sarah immediately turned it round to suggest that Anne had something political to hide.

After she had sent this to Anne, she waited in vain for a reply. All she received was a strange smile when the Queen passed her in the corridor on the way to take communion in St James's Chapel, which she 'found reason to interpret as given to B[isho]p Taylor or the Common Prayer Book & not to herself'.[39] Even this seems an optimistic interpretation of the smile. What else might it have been? Sarcasm? Mockery? Triumph? Myopia? We shall never know because we must rely on Sarah to read the gestures of someone who was becoming opaque to her.

That Sarah had sent a 'narrative', as well as the copies of Anne's adolescent love letters, signalled that she was ready to publish her memoirs – to 'appeal to the whole earth', as she put it, for justice. On 1 November, she received back the copies of Anne's correspondence she had loaned to Godolphin. He warned her that 'they should not be seen but by very few' but he must have had some idea of why she now wanted all of her papers in her possession. He also reported from Westminster that Sunderland and Somerset were as thick as thieves, whispering in corners. The key issue remained Orford's appointment to the Admiralty, and the party-political composition of the rest of the Admiralty Board. On 5 November, Godolphin wrote: 'You will have it that I differ with you, at the same time that I am labouring like a slave in the galleys for what you desire.' When Orford was finally brought into the Cabinet later that month, Sarah was credited by many of the Whigs with having achieved this appointment by sheer nagging.[40]

Meanwhile the peace talks in which Marlborough had placed so much hope appeared to have been sabotaged by the Junto's demands. They were united behind the 'No Peace Without Spain' slogan, which had been a lost cause since the French victory at Almanza in 1707, and demanded that France not only surrender but also, unrealistically, join the Allies in fighting against Louis XIV's grandson, Philip V, for the Spanish Throne.[41] Back in October Marlborough had sent Sarah instructions for the sewing of a 'canopy of State' to be used at the peace-treaty ceremonies[42] – he had had the foresight or the frugality to suggest it should be made so that it could also double as a bedspread. At the end of the year he returned to England, disappointed by the likely continuation of the war, to find a bittersweet political stew being stirred by Sarah. The Whigs were now fully in power and fully behind him, but the Queen had never been more estranged.

Undeterred by Anne's failure to reply to her letter containing the long narrative of their friendship, Sarah wrote to her again in early November 1709.[43] She has been called insane for doing this, but her words were never really out of control. Now that Anne had appointed all the leading Whigs to the Cabinet, as Sarah had wanted her to, Sarah felt 'a secret pride' in her own achievement. Disregarding the fact that Anne had been forced into every appointment, she concluded: '[W]e can have no differences remaining now that I know of, but about this most charming useful Lady [Abigail]. And yet my only crime, at least that you are pleased to tell me of, is that I think you have an intimacy with her.' To show she was not the only one who thought this, Sarah transcribed passages from a 'very unaccountable' book lately published 'in which I & Ld Marl & almost everybody that I know is abused'. Sarah said that she thought Abigail had 'encouraged the wretch that writ this book' in which Abigail was named as the current favourite.

The book to which Sarah referred was Mrs Manley's *The New Atalantis*. Maynwaring had sent Sarah extracts, which she forwarded to the Queen, but had begged her not to worry about reading the rest of it as ''tis all old and incredible stuff of extortion and affairs with 38 [Godolphin]'.[44] This slander of an affair between Sarah and Godolphin was repeated by Jonathan Swift in his *History of the Four Last Years of the Queen* (1712), in which the purpose was to explain how Sarah managed to persuade a man as sensible as Godolphin to work with the Junto. In an emotional sense this influence over Godolphin was true, and the average reader of Manley or Swift could be forgiven for believing that there was something more between Sarah and the Treasurer.

Mrs Manley had had a career-long obsession with Sarah,

who appeared in almost all her writings. She and Sarah held diametrically opposed beliefs, and it is highly unlikely they ever met, yet they had a great deal in common. Both had a healthy cynicism about politics and an indifference to the respect usually shown to their superiors; both were defamers and self-vindicators; both played with the lethal power of half-truths; and both betrayed their friends' secrets. Manley portrayed Sarah with all the hallmarks of an uncontrolled female (a lust for spending money, a relish for malicious gossip, a volcanic temper, a sweet tooth) and turned her into a symbol of the Whig party's overweening ambitions, but in truth Sarah's ambition fascinated the equally ambitious novelist. In Manley's fictionalised memoirs, *The Adventures of Rivella* (1714), she described Sarah with what sounds to modern ears like empathy: 'If she had been a Man, she had been without Fault.'[45]

When she went on to write the two-volume *The New Atalantis* (1709) and *Memoirs of Europe* (1710), she returned to many of the same themes as *Queen Zarah*. It was to go through six editions in ten years, becoming the best-selling fictional work of the decade. The book opens with Lady Intelligence (meaning news and gossip, rather than brains) being recruited by Mother Virtue as a spy. Intelligence, who holds Sarah's post as Groom of the Stole, watches a long procession of characters at Court – the Empress's favourite (Sarah again) rides in the procession with an emblematic companion called Virtue Pretended. True Virtue watches and remarks that she has never had any contact with this 'She-Favourite' who manages everything in the new reign.[46]

In the *Memoirs of Europe* sequel, Abigail is celebrated as Theodecta, the virtuous wife of Constantine VI (Queen Anne), who saves him from the influence of his domineering mother Irene (Sarah). Writing when the Whig Junto was at the height of its power, Manley invented a happy ending for the Tories that Queen Anne died in childbirth leaving a baby daughter to inherit the throne instead of the Hanoverians. The Whigs then fell from power and Sarah's character was urged to flee abroad. Sarah refused to leave England because it had been the 'scene of glory to her! The heaven in which she had blazed, a terrible comet . . .' Manley imagines the mob rising up to punish the Marlboroughs, plundering Blenheim and reclaiming their stolen taxes. Abigail, kindly, steps in to save her cousin's life.

Mixed with the anti-Whig propaganda of *The New Atalantis* was another, far more audacious strand of slander. Lady Intelligence describes the 'Cabal' among the ladies at Court where she has seen '[t]wo beautiful ladies joined in an excess of amity (no word is tender enough to express their new delight) innocently embrace! . . . Tis true some things may be strained a little too far and that causes reflections to be cast upon the rest . . .' but, she says uncertainly, she is sure that it was all innocent. If even Socrates can be accused of being in love with the same sex, she observes, then others should be careful with their 'unaccountable intimacies'. She describes Queen Anne's Court as a kind of lesbian commune and suggests that this corrupt Cabal of women is turning Nature on its head. In the end, the Cabal is condemned by the divinities on the basis of circumstantial evidence and the argument that provoking slander is as bad as deserving it. This was precisely the argument Sarah was using with Anne regarding her relationship with Abigail. Sarah, however, did not mention this section of Manley's book to the Queen. She was too concerned with the direct libels against herself and her family to notice the similarities between her own insinuating letters to Anne and the stories of lesbianism told by Mrs Manley.

On 29 October 1709, nine days after publication of *The New Atalantis*, Mrs Manley was arrested on libel charges. She turned herself in, in exchange for the release of her printers when she heard they were detained on a warrant obtained by Sunderland. He was not pressing this charge on behalf of his in-laws, but because of a story Mrs Manley had included about an extra-marital affair between him and a famous opera singer.

Mrs Manley was granted bail on 5 November, having been 'most tyrannically and barbarously insulted by the Fellow and his Wife who had her in keeping' for those eight days.[47] She was tried before the Queen's Bench on 11 February 1710, where Sunderland himself cross-examined her.[48] We do not know whether Sarah deigned to attend. We do know that she told Maynwaring it was better not to use Mrs Manley's as a test case to deter other Tory libellers as this would only bring the book added publicity.[49] In any case, Sarah blamed those behind Mrs Manley who were paying her and feeding her gossip far more than the woman herself. She believed Harley and Lord Peterborough were behind the book, though Manley later insisted that at the time of writing she had not yet met Harley.[50]

In the end, for reasons that remain unclear, the charges were dropped. Perhaps, as Sarah had in her letters, Mrs Manley had evaded them by claiming to be an oral historian recording gossip. Perhaps the fictionalised identities in the book made it impossible to prosecute her. Or perhaps someone in government, or even Sarah herself, intervened when it became clear that Mrs Manley would not reveal her sources or backers.

Anne never replied to Sarah's *New Atalantis* letter. She merely sent a curt note asking her to forward a hundred guineas from the Privy Purse to a Mr Gueche for the treatment of her eyesight and another five hundred to pay her household servants.[51] Abigail would manage the distribution of these amounts.

It would be naïve to think that people of the time believed everything that Mrs Manley wrote about Sarah or the other semi-fictionalised Whig characters. She was playing with her readers' knowing disregard for the truth. Yet Sarah's claim to ignore the slanders should also be taken with a pinch of salt. Maynwaring constantly referred to her as the Junto's 'martyr', and by October 1709 she was spinning in the widening gyre of relentless press exposure. Sarah later wrote that this was the time 'when the greatest clamours were raised against me'.[52] The bookstalls of London were a-swarm with penny pamphlets about her and her husband, and more genteel authors than Mrs Manley wrote for the amusement of enemies within her own social circle. Many of the satires were nursery-style allegories, such as *The Eagle and the Robin* (1709) or *The Beasts in Power, or ROBIN'S SONG:*

with An Old Cat's Prophecy (1709). The 'noise of the town' was a literal cacophony: news was bawled out on street corners, slanderous songs were sung by peripatetic vendors, and 'pinners up' fastened the broadsheets, like eighteenth-century fly-posters, on to railings around town. Apart from the famed Grub Street, there was a centre for the printing of catchpenny broadsides and ballads by the pillory at Seven Dials in southern St Giles.[53] There was also a cluster of printers and booksellers located close to Sarah's banker in the East End. She could not avoid hearing the lies being spread about her, so could only pretend that her skin was thick. One Tory pamphlet even remarked regretfully that she was 'too Wise to take particular Notice of anything that was either said or published against her, and so we were disappointed . . . for had she stirred in the Affair, the Mob would have taken everything we had said for Truth . . .'[54]

In an age when people honestly believed women more naturally sinful than men, most female victims of the post-Restoration free press had their reputations and hence their lives ruined. Sarah was probably the most continuously libelled Englishwoman of her lifetime, yet even in her husband's absence, she was never cowed by these attacks. Whether it was what she truly felt, she claimed to follow Maynwaring's belief that '[t]he kindness and good opinion of one's general acquaintance are so far from being absolutely necessary to one's happiness that they are something like fair weather which makes one's days pass a little more pleasantly'.[55]

Early in 1710 another crisis threatened the Marlboroughs' reputations. As Sarah saw it, the Queen's secret advisers outside the Cabinet had 'prevailed with her to appoint military officers without advising her General'[56] and, more specifically, to appoint Captain Jack Hill, Abigail's brother, as a colonel in Lord Essex's regiment of dragoons: '[T]hey knew that nothing could be more disagreeable to the Duke of Marlborough, or would tend more to lessen his weight and authority in the army, and consequently at home too,' Sarah wrote. If he let the appointment stand, it would be 'in effect setting up a banner for all the unreasonable discontented people in the Army to fly to'[57] – 'And on the other hand, if the Duke should not comply, or should show any reluctance in complying, this would furnish an excellent pretence for grievous complaints and outcries, *that the QUEEN was but a cipher and could do nothing.*'[58]

Sarah was personally wounded again: she had adopted Jack Hill when only a 'tall lad' and paid for his education and upkeep. He had been privately tutored at St Albans by a retired teacher from Westminster School whom she had hired; then she had found him a post as a Page of Honour and later as a Groom of the Bedchamber to the boy Duke of Gloucester. Finally, she had convinced Marlborough to employ him in the army: 'Though my lord always said that Jack Hill was good for nothing, yet to oblige me he made him his aide-de-camp and afterwards gave him a regiment.'[59] Sarah later described him to a friend as 'idle, drinking and mimicking'[60] and 'making low bows to everybody, & being ready to run to open a door'.[61]

Now Marlborough and Godolphin argued against Hill's pre-ferment, not only as an affront to them because he was Abigail's brother but also because he was, they claimed, inexperienced and undeserving. Sarah believed he was a crypto-Jacobite despite all her efforts to educate him in Whiggery. She viewed the appoint-ment as a deliberate provocation, just one of many devised behind the scenes by Harley and introduced to the Queen by Abigail in order to force Marlborough's resignation. Marlborough pleaded with Anne not to undermine his command for the sake of pleasing Abigail, but to no avail.

At Windsor Lodge, the Marlboroughs drafted an ultimatum regarding the Duke's position, including a demand for Abigail's dismissal. Sarah enlisted as many Whigs as she could to support her husband. Marlborough asked Lords Somers and Cowper whether his ultimatum should be sent. Both told him to hold off and said they would first intercede on his behalf with the Queen. On Monday 16 January they met with Anne for this purpose, although Tory insiders later suggested Somers played a double game and encouraged the Queen at that meeting to dismiss Marlborough.

On 18 January, Marlborough sent a revised draft of his resignation letter, attacking Abigail but falling short of demanding her dismissal. The language he used, however, was as forthright as Sarah's: 'I can't but think the nation would be of the opinion that I have deserved better than to be made a sacrifice to the unreasonable passion of a bedchamber woman.' Two days later a furious Anne told Godolphin that she would refrain from appointing Hill to the regiment. Years later, however, when Marlborough had left the country, she would give a pension of £1,000 to the young man as compensation, and make both him and Colonel Masham generals.

Throughout the crisis Maynwaring had been writing to Sarah, encouraging her resentment of Abigail. On 19 January he had told her, 'It is children's play for any men to hold the first posts in a government, & not have it in their power to remove such a slut as that.' He proposed that a petition should be brought by the Commons to remove Abigail. Marlborough is often blamed for coming up with this idea,[62] but in fact he could afford to leave this radical strategy to the Whigs and his wife, then deny responsibility to the Queen without technically lying. Sarah mocked Anne for her alarm when she heard rumours of the petition or Bill 'as if some great attack were going to be made upon her'[63] while knowing full well that the implications of its introduction to Parliament would be scandalous.

In February Sarah returned to Court and met with Anne. She had been sent an unsigned note ordering her to bring a thousand guineas to Abigail from the Privy Purse[64] and she knew now that her days in her posts were numbered. When they met, knowing how little she had to lose, Sarah pushed relentlessly for Abigail's dismissal, and reminded Anne that the Groom of the Stole had always been someone 'of the first Quality' and therefore that Sarah's post should not be given to her cousin. She said it was plain that Anne did not intend to keep her earlier promise of passing Sarah's offices to her daughters. In linking this to Anne's broken promises over various Church appointments, Sarah lost sight of the distinction between her own family's grip on power and that of the Whigs.[65]

Meanwhile, both Houses of Parliament ordered Marlborough back to the Continent to 'attend to the great affair of the peace'.[66] Sarah was so worried about his health at this point that she wanted him to resign if only to prevent him leaving, but he set sail once again from Harwich on 19 February.

On 27 February, from six o'clock in the morning, carriages, sedan chairs and coaches littered New Palace Yard outside Westminster Hall. The doors would not open for several hours, but queues were already forming for what was set to be the best show in town and another turning point in Sarah's political career: the trial of Dr Henry Sacheverell.

By nine, the crush in the surrounding streets was suffocating. Those who held one of the precious tickets, each printed with an ornate flower border, waved them above their heads and pushed forward. Most peers had guest tickets, so a thriving black-market had sprung up and many had paid high prices for a seat. The uninvited crowds were from every social stratum, and journalists reported in particular on the packs of rowdy working-class women who were Tory supporters of the defendant. As the peers arrived, the women hooted at the recognisable Whigs walking in order of rank. Constables had to link arms to keep the throng back so that the peers could enter unmolested.[67] Sarah was among the first to arrive.

About two thousand spectators crammed into the gothic hall, described by Defoe as 'a great barn'. Special scaffolding had been erected, on Wren's instructions, with spectator seating. Members of Parliament sat on nine terraced benches built along the left-hand side, with bishops in the front row. Minor gentry sat on matching benches to the right, with ladies in that side's front row, and the peers down the middle of the room. There was a gallery high on the right for more spectators.

Behind the Lord Chancellor and the twelve judges, to the

Commons side of this makeshift amphitheatre and near to where the foreign diplomats had been squeezed in, a special box had been built for the Queen and her Ladies of the Bedchamber. It had a canopy and could be curtained from view during the proceedings if Anne so chose. Sarah walked straight to this box and stood where she could survey the hall.

At ten o'clock, there was an audible roar outside as Dr Sacheverell arrived in his 'Chariot with large Glasses'.[68] He stood up in it and waved to his fans. In his thirties, he was a tall man with a certain sex appeal, despite his bulging eyes. Sarah remembered him as dapper, having '[a] good assurance; clean gloves; white handkerchiefs well managed'.[69] That day there was nothing defensive or distraught about his appearance. He acted 'like an Ambassador making his Entry rather than like a Criminal conducted to his Trial'.[70] His footmen in bright yellow-green liveries threw coins to the crowds, which excited them even further.[71] Wafted along on this wave of enthusiastic support, he entered and waited in the atrium to be called after the Court officials were seated.

The decision to impeach the Doctor had been taken at the end of 1709. For years his sermons had been remarkable only for the intensity of the hatred he expressed against the dissenters and Whigs. He preached the doctrine of 'passive obedience',[72] meaning the duty of loyalty to rulers divinely appointed, even when one did not believe that they deserved their power. Sarah rejected this idea outright, and she had practised this opposition on both a grand (revolutionary) and a small (epistolary) scale.

Sacheverell's sermons were not particularly well written, but his voice and manner conveyed them powerfully, dangerously. In July 1706 he had preached against occasional conformity at All Saints' Church, Leicester. In 1709, he had made two notable appearances: first in April at the Derby Assizes, and then in St Paul's, on 5 November, the anniversary of deliverance from the Gunpowder Plot and of William of Orange's landing. This second sermon had aimed to 'open the eyes of the deluded people in this our great metropolis': in it he accused the Whigs of republican tendencies, abusing Anne 'whose hereditary right to the Throne they have the impudence to deny . . . to make her a creature of their own power'. He suggested that progressives – like Sarah – were undermining the constitution and the Church: 'Schism and faction are things of impudent and encroaching natures; they thrive upon concessions, take permission for power, and advance a toleration immediately into an establishment.'[73] The sermon drew vast crowds and afterwards 100,000 printed copies were hawked in the streets; it was not wholly unreasonable for Ministers to fear that unless they acted they would soon have a popular demagogue on their hands.

Some historians have suggested that Marlborough himself initiated the impeachment process before leaving for the Continent,[74] but it is more probable that it was Godolphin, whom Sacheverell had attacked in one sermon as 'Volpone', together with the Junto. Though he had once told Sarah that censorship was 'a remedy that instead of curing the disease does most commonly make it worse',[75] he had become more defensive since the battles of recent years. The decision to prosecute had been taken at a meeting of the Kit-Cat Club on 8 December. Marlborough was present and it is believed that Sarah also attended 'to fill out their tea and wash their cups',[76] but Godolphin was not: he decided to impeach at a Cabinet Council meeting on 12 December.[77]

Since the charges against Dr Sacheverell had been brought, there had been the crisis over Jack Hill, which many interpreted as a sign that the Queen was out of faith with the Whig ministry and would welcome Tory agitation in her name. With Marlborough in retreat at Windsor, the anti-government movement whipped itself up in the City and Sacheverell became a *cause célèbre*. As one version of Sarah's memoirs put it: 'The delay of the trial & the unseasonable & pompous preparation for it gave time enough . . . The poison spread itself incredibly.'[78]

In impeaching Sacheverell, ministers had overreacted, but they had been forced into it because the law of seditious libel was so easily circumvented by careful choice of words. And when

William Bromley, the leader of the Tories in the House of Commons, proposed that the trial take place before both Houses of Parliament in their entirety, the prosecutors felt they could not object without appearing weak. The stage was thus set for the trial to act as a lightning rod for all the Tory anxiety about the speed of Whig liberalisation – or, as Sarah put it, 'the gibberish of that party about non-resistance and passive obedience and hereditary right' – and for all the Whig neurosis about the Revolution. The Whigs chose the precarious argument that if the Revolution was illegal because it defied the doctrine of passive obedience, so was everything done by the English government since 1688. It was a defining episode for Whig political theory, the first time that they had told their story to themselves with such conviction. It became so famous that Sarah's published memoirs do not describe the episode: 'Everybody knows that whole story, and the terrible cry that was raised about the danger of the Church, from the attempt that was made in a parliamentary way to punish an ignorant, impudent incendiary, a man who was the scorn even of those who made use of him as a tool.'[79]

By the time of his trial, Sacheverell had had a seven-year career as a clergyman and academic theologian at Oxford. He was a Fellow of Magdalen College and the chaplain of St Saviour's in Southwark, a 'black coat' who had no compunction about dragging party politics into the pulpit. The champion on the Low Church side was Sarah's friend, Benjamin Hoadly. On the same day in December that Parliament announced Sacheverell's impeachment, it recommended Hoadly's advancement within the Church.[80] Though the Queen ignored this, the coincidence focused public attention and anger on the party lines that now divided the Church of England.

Marlborough's departure for The Hague a week or so before the trial cost the Whigs several votes, mainly of moderate Tory peers who were personally loyal to him from before Anne's reign.[81] Sarah, however, attended the entire proceedings and reported regularly to him by letter. The trial lasted three and a half weeks, since in an impeachment the prosecution was given the chance to answer the defence. For the duration of the trial, Colley Cibber complained, the theatres of London sat empty.[82]

The audience brought picnics. Richard Steele remarked in his *Tatler* that it was a tribute to the barristers' performances that night after night so many grand ladies were prepared to eat cold chicken in their seats. Lady Rooke was seen snatching back a chicken wing she had offered her neighbour when she discovered they were anti-Sacheverell, and there were stories of catfights between ladies of opposing parties over reserved seats. Defoe's *Review* focused on the absurdity of women taking an interest in such things:

The women lay aside their tea and chocolate, leave off visiting after dinner, and forming themselves into a cabal, turn Privy Councillors and settle the State ... Among the ladies – show me a virago, a termagant, a stride-rider, that loves her cold tea, and swears at her maid; that plays all night and drinks chocolate in her bed; I'll hold five to one she's for the Doctor.[83]

Children were also allowed to watch the trial. In a letter to his grandfather Marlborough, the ten-year-old William (Willigo) Godolphin, Henrietta's son, said, 'I have been at Doctor Sacheverell's trial every day and am against him.'[84]

As the clerk of the court read the long list of articles of impeachment[85] and the prisoner's legal response, about two or three hours into the trial, Sarah was seen to leave the royal box to sit with the MPs at the end of one of the Commons' benches, next to the managers' (barristers') stand. This caused a stir of surprise among the audience. One historian has speculated that this might have been a pointed gesture 'from the *ci-devant* favourite to demonstrate her still uncompromising Whiggery and her unqualified support for the prosecution; but an embarrassing one for her friends, not least because it encouraged less notable spectators over the next few days to follow her example ...'[86] In fact, it was a much more complex gesture, containing more meanings than even Sarah herself realised.

When Anne had entered, Sarah explained, in one of her frag-
ments of draft memoir, she did not tell her ladies-in-waiting to
be seated. She drew her box's curtain around her and forgot
about it. After two or three hours' listening to the clerk droning
in the overheated hall, various women nudged Sarah, as the
senior lady-in-waiting, to ask permission to sit down. Sarah,
weary on her feet and suffering from a bad head cold,[87] did so,
and forced the Queen to repeat the permission several times in
front of witnesses so that no one could claim she had taken a seat
insolently. Yet when Sarah sat down, her recent rival, the Duchess
of Somerset, remained standing. Sarah decided that she had done
so to make it appear that Sarah had sat down without permission.
She concluded, '[M]y Gold Key was the thing aimed at.'[88]

In the context of Harley's having just drawn Somerset and
Shrewsbury from the Whig Junto to form a separate faction in
opposition to Marlborough and Godolphin, Sarah's contretemps
with the Duchess of Somerset over seating etiquette was loaded
with significance. Sarah's 'uneasiness' came not only from standing for several hours but also from the dramatic public support
being shown for Dr Sacheverell and the Tories. Her position at
Court was in question, and now she found she was literally
wrong-footed. Just as the trial was a microcosm of a wider
national struggle for power, so the jostling for places among
the Court ladies mirrored that which was taking place within the
Cabinet. It would be a misreading to think that Sarah was being
petty, ill-mannered or abrasive, as one of her biographers, writing
in 1899, believed:[89] she was too aware that she was her husband's
representative in his absence. As one Tory woman spectator wrote
in her journal, Sacheverell's trial was all about the fact that 'things
of little consequence in themselves are sometimes the Cause of
Great Events'.[90]

Whatever embarrassment Sarah felt after this incident, she must
also have felt pleasure in hearing the Whig managers, including
the Duke of Montagu, lay out her own political philosophy so
eloquently. Their speeches went on all day, the Queen retiring
to a small anteroom to take her lunch at two or three o'clock.

At the end of the day Anne left to dine with Lord Halifax, which many interpreted as a signal that she was more than ready to ditch Godolphin and the Marlboroughs.[91] Her intention, in fact, was to remain as neutral as possible. Abigail wrote to Harley that she had been to see Anne 'last night on purpose to speak to her about Dr S and asked her if she did not let people know her mind in the matter. She said, "No, she did not meddle one way or other and that it was her friends' advice not to meddle." '[92]

After the Queen's exit, most of the politicians remained in Westminster doing business late into the evening. Sarah also had canvassing to do: she met with various moderate Lords to try to 'fix' them to vote with the Ministry.[93] That evening, when she arrived at her lodgings in St James's Palace, she wrote to her husband that the trial was being managed to her satisfaction. She also confessed her enforced *faux pas*, to which he replied in his next letter: 'What 13 [Somerset] made his wife do is a confirmation of his designs.' He added: 'We have a good many disagreeable accounts come from England to this country, both as to the intentions of the Court, as well as the inclinations of the people for Sacheverell, which does great hurt'.[94] He meant that the French would prolong the peace negotiations in the hope of a change of ministry in England.

The following morning, the Queen did not arrive until eleven. Irritated by close scrutiny, she wore a hood over her face so that she could sit with the curtain open. The trial was delayed not only by her late appearance but also, more dramatically, by the Sergeant-at-Arms, who forcibly removed Sarah and a group of other ladies who had followed her to sit again in the Commons' enclosure.[95] Once again, Sarah was publicly humiliated, to the delight of the Tories in the gallery. She was put back into her place – with the women, behind the curtain.

This was the morning on which Robert Walpole made his speech for the prosecution, in which he drove home the irony that the Tories were trying to recommend themselves to the Queen by condemning 'that Revolution without which she never had been Queen . . . The greatest and most inexpressible emergencies,' he claimed, 'did justify and warrant the resistance and the Revolution,' and those who had led it – including the Marl-boroughs – should not be 'misrepresented as maintaining anti-monarchical schemes'.[96] James Stanhope and Sir Simon Harcourt also spoke well.[97] One after another the Whig speeches answered the offending sermon in a spirit of free debate – one of the very things Sacheverell detested.

At the end of the following day's proceedings, the Whig managers were attacked as they left Westminster. Dirt was thrown at Hoadly's coach and some in the crowd read out a new broadsheet that imagined a boxing match between him and Sacheverell.[98] Sarah's coach probably did not leave the Yard unmolested. That evening she was going to a great banquet hosted in her honour (and that of the Treasurer and other Whig gentlemen) by Mr de Vrijbergen, the Dutch envoy. Many foreign ministers attended and the evening finished with fireworks and the distribution of a large quantity of free wine.[99]

These ostentatious Whig festivities did nothing to dampen the violence brewing in the streets. Hired thugs, brought from Sacheverell's Southwark parish, assaulted anyone in the street who did not cheer for the doctor as he drove by,[100] and at nightfall there were attacks on dissenters' meeting houses. The Tory mob built a huge bonfire from debris in Lincoln's Inn Fields – which brought out more crowds – and danced around it as a chapel burned to the ground. Similar bonfires and attacks took place throughout east London, and Hoadly's house was threatened. Guilds of working men battled along party lines, wielding axes and crowbars. While wartime hardships during that bitter winter had something to do with the mood in the capital, economic grievances were not among the slogans shouted. That night the level of violence was worse than anything London had seen during the Civil War, and Sarah believed it had been organised by the Tories. In the version of her memoirs written with Hoadly, she remembered that 'By the help of proper officers and tools, great mobs and tumults were raised.'[101]

Lord Sunderland was working late at Whitehall when Lord Cowper and the Duke of Newcastle rode over to inform him of the rioting. He immediately obtained the Queen's permission to use her own horse and foot guards to keep the peace. The mobs were soon subdued and dispersed by these troops who lined up to face them in Drury Lane and along Long Acre. Order was restored before dawn without a shot being fired.[102]

The next day, the press had a good laugh at the Whigs, who had claimed to be speaking for the sovereignty of the people just as the mob rose against them, and at the Tories, who had proclaimed the need for passivity just as their supporters went on the rampage. It was the first day of the Tory defence and, most importantly, the day of Sacheverell's own speech. He had his platform on which to play the martyr, as many on the Whig side dreaded, though others such as Defoe wrote that they were unconcerned: 'Let this beast break wind . . . let him belch, his breath stinks so vilely it will make the whole cause smell of it.'[103] Accounts of the doctor's performance diverge along party lines: the Tory diarist Mrs Caesar wrote that he spoke perfectly, moving the audience to tears, including the Queen 'as I was told, for I could not see it'.[104] Maynwaring quipped that Sacheverell 'gained to such a degree the soft hearts of his female friends that I wonder he should continue to be in favour with any of the men'.[105] Sarah's daughter Anne said that she wept merely because she was hearing the Lord's name taken so in vain.[106] Sarah's review of the speech was scathing: it was a 'heap of bombast, ill-connected words'.[107]

After the prosecution had spoken again, the peers took ten days to reach their verdict, and Sacheverell was found guilty by a majority of only 17 out of 171 votes. It took them another day to pass sentence: he was not to be imprisoned, merely suspended from the pulpit for three years and copies of his sermons confiscated and burned. This mild sentence was what the Queen, still hoping futilely that she could lead a bipartisan government, had desired.

The closeness of the vote was viewed as an ill omen for Godolphin's government. The public was left with the impression that the trial had been a waste of taxpayers' money and that the Junto would persecute anyone who dared criticise it. Marlborough had told Sarah that how each peer voted at the trial would be 'a true weathercock',[108] and she sent him a full list of their votes when it was over. Marlborough replied that he was 'very glad to see that everything in this affair of Sacheverell has gone to your own mind',[109] yet both he and his wife must have seen how far support for Godolphin had eroded. Although the Whig 'Revolution Principles', in which Sarah believed so vehemently, had won the debate, 'James III's' hereditary claim to the Throne had been admitted and Anne further alienated from the Whigs.

Robert Harley was also examining the voting lists to see which Whigs could be swayed to join him against the Marlboroughs. Somerset had been absent on the day of the vote to avoid making explicit his new alliance with the moderate Tories, while Shrewsbury, who had 'talked so many years for Revolution Principles',[110] had boldly voted for acquittal.

Sacheverell had left the courtroom in triumph, and on the streets the Pyrrhic nature of the Whig victory was obvious from the Tory celebrations, which lasted until 23 March. Sailors testified to Sacheverell's health being toasted in France.[111] In June and July the Doctor would go on tour and be fêted by Tory sympathisers across the country. Harley knew that the only way to utilise this anti-governmental public mood was to force an early election, but Anne had given no indication that she intended to call one. Therefore the Tory party, aided by the 'black coats' among the High Church clergy, organised public addresses to flood in to her from the counties and boroughs. John Oldmixon reported that he witnessed people being bribed with free beer to sign these petitions asking Anne for a new Parliament.[112] On 5 April, she told the House of Commons: 'I could heartily wish that men would study to be quiet, and do their own business, rather than busy themselves in reviving questions and disputes of a very high nature . . .'[113]

However the press was still free, and in the aftermath of the Sacheverell trial, a number of publications continued the debate.

One of these, *Four Letters to a Friend in North Britain – Upon the Publishing the Trial of Dr Sacheverell* (1710), accused the Doctor of being part of a wider Jacobite conspiracy that had been narrowly averted. It was attributed by contemporaries to Walpole, and then to Defoe. Historians have finally determined that Maynwaring was the author.[114] On 24 May he had written to Sarah: 'I have finished this morning the tedious thing that I have been writing about Sacheverell . . . and when I have got somebody to write it [out], I will send it to you.' In it, he had expressed the belief that bound him to Sarah, that 'Monarchy is established for the good of the Subject.'[115] Another Whig writer composed a ballad of paradoxes called *The Age of Wonders – To the tune of Chivy Chase* (1710) which spoke of Sacheverell's light punishment while

> The Duke of Marlborough to requite
> For retrieving English honour
> His D[uche]ss shall have all the Spite
> That fools can put upon her.

Meanwhile Hoadly wrote *Thoughts of an Honest Tory upon the present Proceedings of that Party: In a Letter to a Friend in Town* (1710) in which he took on the persona of a disillusioned Tory. Sarah wrote to Maynwaring that '[t]he book you sent me of the Honest Tory is more reasonable and better than anybody can write except 78 [Maynwaring],'[116] and sent a copy straight to Marlborough.[117]

In reply to Hoadly, Simon Clement wrote the most brilliant piece of Harleian 'moderate' ideology titled *Faults on Both Sides* (1710), which pointed the finger not at the Whigs in general but at the Junto-Godolphin-Marlborough circle for abuse of their power. The author berated Marlborough for having 'presumed to dispute the disposal of a single regiment in the army with his sovereign', and also attacked the impertinence of his wife. Sarah received and read this work as soon as it was published and wrote her own ripostes as marginalia:

The Whigs are accused for acting against their own principles to ingratiate themselves only for places and preferment, which I think proceeded only from their want of strength to support themselves against the poison and flattery of the Tories to all Princes upon their prerogative, & I believe, besides the love of employments, they thought to do some good & hinder the Tories from doing a great deal of mischief . . .[118]

To a friend she remarked that there could not be a worse description of the Tory party 'than that it should be raised upon the account of so scandalous a man as Sacheverell'.[119]

Sarah realised that she must bite her tongue more often after Sacheverell's trial: the public outcry had given Anne the confidence to oppose the Marlboroughs. Yet Sarah would not be told to 'be quiet' like Parliament. At the beginning of April, she begged Anne for 'a private hour' with her because it was 'really very difficult if not impossible to put what I have to say in writing and,' appealing to Anne's piety, 'I can't receive the sacrament on Sunday without saying it.'[120] She wished to clear herself of some lies told about her, she explained. In her published memoirs, she recorded Anne's humiliating refusal with painful honesty.

Sarah also believed that the Somersets had been spreading stories against her. She wrote that Abigail and the Duchess of Somerset now sat so close to the Queen that she 'could hardly put her hand in her pocket'.[121] Whether or not the Somersets were responsible, the chances are high that Sarah's contemptuous view of Anne's intelligence and religious hypocrisy had been reported to the Queen by someone. Sarah claimed she never disparaged the Queen behind her back, but there is evidence to the contrary: Maynwaring mentions Halifax's criticism that Sarah 'made at Windsor an open complaint'.[122] Sarah wrote later that, throughout this time, Halifax was playing a two-faced game: sending Abigail gifts of wine and meat while at the same time entertaining Sarah at Hampton Court with 'a thousand jests and ridiculing her [Abigail] and her favour – and I believe he diverted her as much afterwards with me'.[123]

It might even be that Sarah made, in conversation, the kind of risqué remarks about the Queen and her intimate relationship with her Jacobite bedchamber women that she had made in her letters to Anne – we know that at least Maynwaring shared the joke. In the unpublished versions of Sarah's memoirs, when it comes to the precise charges against Sarah for 'saying shocking things and some other particulars', some lines are heavily blacked out, almost cutting through the paper, in the middle of texts otherwise remarkable for their scarcity of corrections.[124]

Finally, on Good Friday, Anne granted Sarah a meeting at Kensington Palace to hear her self-defence. It was to be their last face-to-face meeting. Sarah rewrote the scene in her memoirs again and again, refining and adjusting it.[125]

She remembered that a page went in to tell the Queen that she had arrived unannounced, and there was some delay before she was finally admitted. Anne was unwelcoming, braced against the confrontation she dreaded.

In one version,[126] Sarah transcribed the conversation like a play script. To everything she said, Anne replied mechanically, 'Whatever you have to say, you may write it.'

> La. Marl: Indeed I can't tell how to put such sort of things into writing.
> Queen: You may put it into writing.
> La. Marl: Won't your majesty allow me to tell it you now I am here?
> Queen: You may put it into writing.
> La. Marl: I believe your majesty never did so hard a thing to anybody as to refuse to hear them speak. Even the meanest person that ever deserved it . . .
> Queen: Yes, I do bid people put what they have to say in writing when I have a mind to it.
> La. Marl: I have nothing to say madam upon the subject that

is so uneasy to you; that person is not, that I know of, at all concerned in the account that I would give you, which I can't be quiet till I have told you.

Queen: You may put it in writing.

La. Marl: There is a thousand lies made of me, which are so ridiculous that I should never have thought it necessary to go about to clear myself of what never entered into my head, and is so unlike my manner of talking of Your Majesty, who I seldom name in company and never without respect, and I do promise Your Majesty that there is several things which I have heard has been told to Your Majesty that I have said of you that I am no more capable of than I am of killing my children.

At this point, Sarah's version of events seems to blur together with her description of an argument they had had in 1709, during which Anne turned her face away from the candlelight when Sarah was about to mention her love affair with Abigail.[127] 'When she saw I went on to tell her the thing, she turned her face from me as if she feared blushing upon something I might say to her.' Of course, Anne might have done this on both occasions. With her expression hidden, she solemnly, cryptically muttered: 'There are without doubt many lies told.'

After a tense pause, the Queen moved to leave the room. Sarah leapt to block her way but was unable to speak 'for the tears that fell down my face, at which I was sorry but could not help it'. She tried to tell her old friend that although she knew there was the appearance of neglected duties and others might think insolence the cause of this neglect, 'Your Majesty, that knows what has passed between us, must know that I have had reason not to come to you so often as others expected from me.' Anne's parrot response, apparently echoing their argument after the Oudenarde thanksgiving service, came back to Sarah: 'You said you desired no answer and I shall give you none.' Anne's cold shoulder was a precise inversion of all Sarah's own manipulative silences since 1703.

Tormented by Anne's refusal to discuss the ending of their relationship, Sarah cast around for the reasons behind it, as if wanting Anne to confirm them before she made the mistake of saying too much herself. With 'a concern sufficient to move compassion, even where all love was absent', she asked whether, as she had heard, the Somersets had been accusing her of spreading slander, or whether Anne had been upset by her 'long narrative of my past life'. Understandably, Anne refused to name those who had gossiped. Sarah could only profess the Marlborough family's loyalty, the tears still falling 'in streams'. When Anne remained silent, unmoved, Sarah drew back and made a curtsy, 'saying I was confident she would suffer in this world and the next for so much inhumanity, and to that she answered, "That would be to herself."'

In one of her draft versions, Sarah's pen crossed out the last curse she had uttered,[128] but she allowed it to appear in the published memoir where she confessed it was 'the most disrespectful thing I ever spoke to the Queen in my life'. She might also have noted that, for all her dissatisfaction with Anne's behaviour, the argument and the fact that she was so fearless of its consequences was in itself proof of the English liberties she believed she was defending. Sarah knew that whatever she said to Anne she would not end up in the Tower.

She concluded her description of the scene by saying, 'I shall make no comment upon it.' In fact, she could not resist adding that '[T]he Queen always meant well, how much soever she might be blinded or misguided.'[129] One over-literal biographer has tried to calculate the number of words spoken within the time the interview had been said to take, and concluded that Sarah censored Anne's half of the dialogue.[130] This not only misses the point that Anne used her royal silence as a weapon, but seems to suggest that there is some other secret reason for the argument, as though the Grub Street stories and other slanders of lesbianism, which we can infer Sarah had spread within her own circle of friends, were not serious enough to merit it. Anne seems simply to have refused truth: her succession of intense relationships with bedchamber women – Mrs Cornwallis, Frances Apsley, Sarah (for twenty-seven years), now Abigail and, perhaps, the Duchess of Somerset.

On the other hand, Sarah's account must have been partial and Anne has left nothing to contradict it. The only clue is a comment the Queen made later to her doctor that Sarah tended to mention in her letters what Anne 'did and said, but not what the Duchess herself did and said'.[131]

The extent to which Sarah has been credited with either suffering or fury in this scene varies in accordance with different views of her character. Michael Foot doubted her claim to have wept, or thought her tears must have 'resembled drops of burning oil'.[132] One of Sarah's contemporaries, Lord Dartmouth, seems in his account to conflate this final interview with gossip that must have reached his ears about the fight over Mrs Abrahal's emoluments in February 1709:

Mrs Danvers, who was then in waiting, told me the Duchess reproached her [Anne] for above an hour . . . in so loud and shrill a voice that the footmen at the bottom of the backstairs could hear her: and all this storm was raised for the Queen's having ordered a bottle of wine a day to be allowed for her laundress without her acquainting her grace with it. The queen, seeing her so outrageous, got up to have gone out of the room: the duchess clapped her back against the door and told her that she should hear her out, for that was the least favour she could do her in return for having set and kept the crown upon her head. As soon as she had done raging, she flounced out of the room and said she did not care if she never saw her more: to which the queen replied very calmly, that she thought the seldomer the better.[133]

Sarah knew that the scene would be 'improved to a story' by her enemies, but she denied they had talked in loud voices. To say that the servants could hear them, she retorted, was 'far overdone' since the Queen's cheerless little closet had the long gallery and two further rooms between it and the place where the attendants were seated.[134] In one of her draft memoirs, furthermore, Sarah emphasised her discretion: 'I sat down in the long gallery to wipe my eyes before I came within sight of anybody.'[135] In a third version, she sat outside in the gallery to calm down, then had the nerve to go back into the chamber and ask the Queen not to dismiss her from her posts and to maintain appearances for the sake of her husband's work at the peace conference.[136]

This last example of Sarah's temerity is belied by her having written Anne another provoking letter the following day. Under the guise of warning her of a dangerous man coming to England from Vienna, Sarah complained about her treatment at the day before's meeting and said she had 'expected at least a civil if not a kind return'. Anne sent a cold note back, on which Sarah's acerbic pen has written that she must have received the sacrament that week 'more in form than true religion'. Such an intense relationship was, of course, unlikely to end in civility.

A book published by the Tory author James Ralph to answer Sarah's memoirs, entitled *The Other Side of the Question* (1742),[137] asked why the Queen should not dissolve a friendship 'without putting herself to the trouble of a formal *éclaircissement*, due only to Equals?'[138] The answer, of course, was that their sentimental friendship had been all about ignoring rank. Afterwards Sarah would complain that 'never any friend used another <u>that was their equal</u>' so badly.[139] As she faced Anne at this last meeting she found the privilege of free speech had been withdrawn and the formal power balance reasserted.

Sarah understood as well as anyone that her lobbying on behalf of the Whigs had been the original cause of Anne's resentment, yet what is remarkable from her account of their final interview is just how personal it was in tone and content. It was a scene acted out by two women who knew one another as intimately as they had known anyone in their lives, and between whom the nature of that intimacy remained a taboo subject. That the relationship ended as it did was not a miscalculation on Sarah's part, but a determination to give priority to her political principles over their relationship. It was as true of 'Queen Zarah' as it was of Anne that 'the Queen was too hard for the Friend'.[140]

8

The Good Hater

On 13 April 1710, days after Sarah's last interview with the Queen, Anne appointed the Duke of Shrewsbury as Lord Chamberlain without consulting her chief Minister. This signalled a shift of her favour from the Treasurer and the Marlboroughs towards Somerset's new grouping, the 'Juntilla' of moderate Whigs willing to work with Robert Harley. Godolphin had known Shrewsbury for over twenty years and there was little personal animosity between them, but the Treasurer feared his old colleague had been in a 'constant caballing with Mr Harley in everything'[1] and that his appointment might alarm the Dutch into making a separate peace. Shrewsbury's reasons for seeking power were principled: he believed that the Whig failure to accept a peace deal in 1709 had been profoundly wrong and his appointment encouraged the coalition in favour of an immediate end to the war. When Godolphin returned from Newmarket to discover the change made behind his back, he prophesied to Anne the country's ruin. 'We parted dryly enough,' he told Sarah.[2]

Sarah remembered that Shrewsbury tended to make 'professions in a private way to everybody that he contributed to hurt' – including her. It galled her that while he had 'made a most low and nauseous court' to Abigail[3] he was also expressing sympathy to her over Anne's betrayal. Later she would write that Shrewsbury had played 'a very dodging game'[4] under William and Mary, pretending to be Protestant while he was actually a Catholic and a Jacobite like his mother. Shrewsbury and Sir Christopher Wren had dined with her that spring and asked about her quarrel with Anne. '[B]eing naturally very plain & frank', she had told them it was not going to heal. Shrewsbury encouraged her to divulge all the particulars, flattering her by saying that the Queen had never been in better hands than hers. Sarah now concluded he had 'acted a most scandalous part, which I always wonder at more in people that seem to have good sense than in others'. She was also nettled by his personal ingratitude, especially because she had always been kind, she claimed, to his Italian wife Adelaide when she 'was the jest of all the town'.[5] Sarah was blind to any view of the war but her husband's – that it was necessary to fight until the Allies were in a position to dictate terms – and reduced her differences with Shrewsbury to the level of social rudeness.

Maynwaring was urging Sarah to return to town, but she knew from experience 'that there is more ease in forgetting my enemies than in contending with them, and I am positively resolved that I will not disturb any of their designs till I know my Lord Marlborough's resolution'.[6] She received his 'resolution' a few days later, in a reply to the letter containing her description of her last interview with Anne. Obviously shocked, Marlborough thought the scene 'so harsh that I think 240 [Sarah] should resolve never to be persuaded to expose themselves any more in speaking to 42 [Anne].'[7] He assured her he would do whatever Sunderland and Somers told him, and he foresaw further Tory attacks. He had earlier told her that nobody else was sending him any particulars of what passed at Court,[8] but neglected to mention that he was in communication with a representative of Harley and St John in Amsterdam, a Scottish merchant named John Drummond. Drummond suggested that the Tories could still be brought round to support Marlborough if only he would put a stop 'to the rage and fury of his wife'.[9] But of course Marlborough could not promise that. It was not in his power to control Sarah's politics without upsetting the delicate balance of power on which his marriage was based. St John was baffled by this deference, and for a long time failed to understand that Marlborough was inseparable from the Whigs because he was inseparable from Sarah.

Just as the Tories used Sarah's removal as code for Godolphin's dismissal, so the Whigs continued to use Abigail's removal as code for Harley's downfall. Sarah's daughter Anne, Countess of Sunderland, told her mother exactly what she wanted to hear: 'I dare say nothing will ever be right but by the removing her . . .'[10]

Sarah followed Marlborough's advice to stay away from Court, and retreated to Windsor Lodge with her daughter Henrietta, who had been given a smaller house in Sarah's grounds, and Godolphin's niece, Mrs Evelyn. Sarah was annoyed with Godolphin for not reacting more forcefully to the appointment of Shrewsbury and so would not let him visit her.[11] She sensed that the Queen was testing him with this move, and that unless he led a mass resignation of the Whig Junto in protest, his power would continue to ebb over the coming months. 'I am extremely mortified,' Godolphin told her, 'at the reproaches you make . . . of my ill returns to your long continued kindness and friendship, which I value more – and always have done – than is to be expressed in words.'[12] If he had failed to answer certain points in his previous letters it was only because he thought they should be discussed face to face.

On 1 May he wrote to Sarah again that he was sorry if 'I vexed you with what I said of 28 [Shrewsbury]. But you will have me tell you things that tis not possible to explain in a letter, with the circumstances of them, and without those circumstances tis as little possible to understand them rightly. Neither will you give me leave to come to you.' He had quoted Shrewsbury as having remarked that the break between Sarah and Anne was 'insuperable', and when Sarah took offence at this, Godolphin assured her he was merely reporting how the Whigs were lamenting the break, not blaming her for it. Many, however, did blame Sarah – the Dutch envoy de Vrijbergen wrote home to Pensioner Heinsius: 'Could the moderation of her husband and of my Lord Treasurer calm down that passion which she calls sincerity, it would be desirable indeed.'[13]

In fact, Marlborough's view was now, finally and too late, in harmony with his wife's. He predicted that when he returned from the present campaign (the siege of Douai, which was going 'scurvily')[14] they would be 'dropped by all such as will be fond of keeping their places'.[15] He spoke of their careers now as a joint endeavour ('the many troubles and dependencies we have laboured through during almost all our lifetime, for the good of our children') and reassured her that he would not betray her like Somerset and Shrewsbury by 'truckling' to Abigail, even if that might save his own neck.[16] Sarah also received supportive letters from the elder James Craggs, reflecting on the Junto's ingratitude towards her. They had, he wrote, 'seen their very best friend in danger without so much as attempting a rescue'.[17] And when Tory satirists attacked her in pieces such as the anonymous *Kiss me if you dare, OR A Royal Favourite turn'd out* (1710), the Whig hacks defended her with their own papers, such as *The Court visit; To a great lady at her country-seat, who lately remov'd her habitation because the air of St James's did not agree with her constitution* (1710).

Maynwaring referred to Abigail as a 'stinking, ugly chambermaid', and to Shrewsbury as a 'papist in masquerade'. He rightly told Sarah her story 'appears to me in a more ghastly horrid figure than it does even to you'. His imagination was enraptured by her martyrdom, the direct equation she made between her own fall and the dawning of a 'terrible national calamity'.[18] He wrote *A New Ballad to the Tune of Fair Rosamund* (1710), leaving little doubt as to the nature of the Anne/Abigail scandal:

> When as Queen Anne of great Renown
> Great Britain's Sceptre sway'd
> Besides the Church, she dearly lov'd
> A Dirty Chamber-Maid.
>
> O! Abigail that was her Name
> She stitch'd and starch'd full well
> But how she pierc'd this Royal Heart
> No Mortal Man can tell.
>
> However, for sweet Service done
> And Causes of great Weight
> Her Royal Highness made her, Oh!
> A Minister of State.

Her Secretary she was not
Because she could not write,
But had the Conduct and the Care
Of some dark Deeds at Night.

One letter from Sarah at Windsor to Maynwaring in London, dated 20 May 1710,[19] gives some sense of others that were destroyed. It is packed with political strategy and unflinching character assessments: 'I wish I may be mistaken in my opinion, but what a melancholy reflection it is for 89 [the Whigs] that now their fate depends upon gaining a man [Duke of Shrewsbury] that t'other day they would have flown over the top of the house if anybody had proposed his coming into employment.' More disillusioned with the Whig party than at any previous point in her life, she foresaw the defeat that was to come in the general election later that year.

Despite these private fears and uncertainties, Sarah still projected aggressive self-confidence to outside observers. On 28 May 1710 Martha, Lady Mansell, a Welsh Tory neighbour of Harley, wrote to him from Windsor:

I am almost fright'd to death with the threats of a great Lady who is now retired from Court . . . In a little time, she says, she shall return with as full power as ever, and that both you and every friend you have shall feel the effects of her utmost revenge. Lady Orkney is often with her, and at table begins a health to her and . . . the Duke's interest, and total destruction of those that are not for it.[20]

What they all now foresaw was the impending dismissal of Sunderland, the Marlboroughs' son-in-law. Anne had never warmed to this Whig radical who had been forced upon her Cabinet in 1706, so Marlborough told Sarah that 'When the time may be proper for the taking off of the mask, his being put out will be the first step.'[21] At the beginning of June, Godolphin reported to Sarah that moves were afoot to do just that, and that the Tories felt they had the Queen 'in a string'.[22] The prospect of this affront to her family made Sarah break silence and, on 7 June, write her first full letter to Anne since parting from her at Kensington.[23]

She began by explaining that she was reluctantly emerging from her retirement only to prevent her husband being further mortified. Quickly, however, she shifted the focus to her own martyrdom ('whoever is called your favourite will be pulled to pieces whenever the nation is dissatisfied with what you do') and returned to the old, tinderbox theme of Anne's friendship with Abigail. With the pretence that the scandal consisted of Anne's hypocrisy rather than her sexuality, Sarah mused that 'There are many people in this world that have had several passions, & if, instead of disguising your last, you had said plainly you did love her but that you would never be unjust to me, it had been a short business & you would have saved yourself a great deal of trouble . . .'

Sarah admitted that her resentment was partly due to jealousy, and compared the situation with how Anne had once felt about Sarah's relationships with Lady Fitzharding and 'The Nag's Head', Lady Bathurst. In this context, referring back to the sentimental declarations of their adolescence, Sarah described her jealousy of Abigail as 'very natural'. But, she hurried to add, 'Now I am perfectly cured.' She enclosed a private letter to her from Somerset to expose his duplicity, and explained at length why it would have been beneath her dignity to orchestrate the Parliamentary Address to remove Abigail. In one of the letter's several drafts, she referred to Anne having heard that she was the 'contriver and promoter' of the Address. These were, in fact, fitting labels for Sarah, but she denied them and claimed only to be a victim who gave Anne the 'trouble of my being much longer in the world'.

A note in Sarah's hand on the back of this extraordinary letter addresses us: 'I believe you will think upon reading my relation of the usage I had at Kensington there needs some apology for my ever writing to her again upon any occasion – but I considered her as a child in very ill hands . . .'[24] Her condescending logic unconsciously mirrored that of John Locke who had asked whether a boy-king could be said to rule over his mother.

Sarah sent Marlborough a copy of her letter, written she said with great 'care and caution'.[25] He thought it 'very reasonable and a good letter upon all accounts'.[26] The contrast usually drawn between his tactful diplomacy and Sarah's hysterical irrationality needs to take such endorsements into account. On the back of one of Godolphin's letters, Sarah also wrote a note explaining:

I used to send my Lord Godolphin my letters to the Queen before I sent them to her, to see if he would add or alter anything in them, after she came into hands that made it necessary for me to be cautious. Whoever knew him will easily believe that he could never have approved of anything from me that was disrespectful to the Queen, whatever they may think of my own passion, or unreasonableness.[27]

By the time Marlborough endorsed her 7 June letter, however, Sarah had already sent it and received back a 'short, harsh' note from Anne, telling her that she did not want to hear another word of politics from her pen: '[H]aving received assurances from yourself and the Duke of Marl that you would never speak to me of politics nor mention Masham's name again, I was very much surprised at receiving a long letter upon both.'

Sarah wrote straight back, protesting that she was only being a loyal wife: '[A]ll the politics in my letter was my concern for Lord Marlborough.'[28] For the sake of Marlborough's reputation abroad, she argued, Anne should defer the blow of Sunderland's dismissal. In an ironic jibe at her own arrogance, Sarah said that it 'brings me to beg of your Ma[jes]ty <u>upon my knees</u> that your Ma[jes]ty would only defer this thing till there is a peace or an end of the campaign, & after using this expression your Ma[jes]ty can have no doubt of my ever entering into anything that can displease you.'[29]

In a postscript to her note of 12 June, Anne had asked Sarah to return all her correspondence, dating back over twenty years. Sarah refused. Her sinister-sweet response was that if Anne would write her no more then she was obliged 'to take a little better care of the rest'. Using a phrase that suggests blackmail, she said Anne could keep the one letter Sarah had returned because 'I have drawers full of the same in every place where I have lived.'

When Marlborough heard about the plans for Sunderland's dismissal, he immediately wrote Godolphin a letter intended for the Queen's eyes, stating his hope that Sunderland's removal would be delayed until after the campaign ended. When Sarah received no answer to her second letter to Anne, Marlborough gave her clear advice: 'I think you should not be prevailed upon to write any more.'[30] He had already told Sarah to be more discreet in expressing her displeasure with the Court when in society: 'I think 11 [the Duke of Devonshire?] has given very good advice to 240 [Sarah] not to make public any harsh usage she has met with, for this is not the time to expect justice.'[31] He told Sarah to stay away from Court for her own protection,[32] saying she was 'in a country amongst tigers and wolves'.[33]

While ordering Sarah into retirement, Marlborough informed her that, for the good of 'the whole', he would not resign his commands even if sorely provoked by his son-in-law's dismissal.[34] He had just forced Douai to surrender, another hard-won victory, and believed that if he fought just a little longer France would have to make peace on British terms. Godolphin and a number of leading Whigs (Cowper, Somers, Newcastle, Devonshire, Orford, Halifax and Henry Boyle) sent him a letter persuading him to stay in place: '[W]e cannot but be extremely sensible of the great mortification this must give you at this critical juncture when you are every moment hazarding your life . . . and while the fate of Europe depends in so great a degree on your conduct.'[35] In contrast, when someone spoke to Anne of Marlborough's heroic services, she replied that every common soldier ventured his life as much as he did, which Sarah remarked, 'was certainly an expression of Abigail's'.[36]

Similarly, Godolphin wrote to Sarah to excuse himself and the Whig ministers for not flexing their muscles – by getting the City Whigs to withdraw their loans to the government, for example

– and so keep Sunderland in place. This would only vindicate the Tory claims against them in the public's eyes, he argued. He assured Sarah, however, that in her absence he was lobbying the Queen 'in such a manner as I can say has not, and will not, be said by anybody else in the world'.[37] It is hard to believe that he was using language plainer than Sarah's.

Anne disregarded all this lobbying, and replaced the 'obnoxious'[38] Sunderland with the Tory George Legge, 1st Earl of Dartmouth. She gave as her reason 'something in the Scotch business which was misrepresented to her'.[39] Sarah later told Anne that Dartmouth was simply 'a jester himself and a jest to all others'.[40]

When she looked back on the letters she had written, Sarah's evaluation was honest: 'Whether my interfering in this matter hastened the execution of the design, I cannot say. Certain it is that it did not retard it . . .'[41] She did not blame her writing style, however, but her intractable reader: 'When she had been told what she is to say, let reason and truth beat ever so hard upon her, it makes no manner of impression. You may as well speak to a tree.'[42]

Sarah observed that, as predicted, Sunderland's dismissal on 13–14 June 1710 caused 'an immediate effect on the funds and the public credit' and 'gave an alarm to all the Courts concerned in the Grand Alliance'.[43] It is true that there was a more optimistic tone in the reports of French diplomats, and celebratory articles in the *Paris Gazette*.[44] The peace negotiations fell apart in July, the French plenipotentiaries returning to Paris 'with a good deal of insolency', wrote Marlborough, who believed that they no longer credited him with the Queen's confidence.[45] The ramifications of the ministerial change were primarily symbolic – sending the Jacobites 'running to Court with faces full of business and satisfaction'[46] at the prospect of Godolphin, Sarah and the Junto losing their grip. Sarah claimed that Anne's 'evil favourites' (Abigail, Harley and the Somersets) were leading the Queen by the nose, step by step, never letting her see where she was headed.

Sarah complained furiously to anyone who would listen. She wrote to Bishop Burnet on 29 June, sounding torn between her public and private spheres, which had collided and merged in her imagination:

I think a very small dose of philosophy will serve to quiet one whenever one serves a court in which an ungrateful chambermaid has the chief influence. After the experience I have had of the world, nothing can be so agreeable to me as my own house, with family comforts, which I think of all the blessings in this world are the greatest, but if the public is not safe, how is it possible to enjoy either religion or quiet?[47]

Years later, looking back on her correspondence with the Queen and answering those who saw it as evidence of her Atossa-like temper, Sarah (through her co-author Burnet) reflected: '[P]erhaps I was too eager & too pressing of some things that went against the grain with the Queen, but in this I served no end or design of my own . . . [I]f I had more politically gone on enjoying my private favour with the advantages of it, I should have hated myself . . .'[48] She believed that Harley was responsible for having made Anne see her salutary frankness as subversive insolence, and she justified having shown her anger to the Queen by the justness of her cause. She believed one needed to control one's temper so that one 'may seem to be rather above the injury than below it'[49] but that the emotion of anger could be a heroic force when exercised with a clear conscience, defending truth. Thus Dr Johnson called Sarah 'a good hater'[50] in an age when the upper echelons of English society were defining 'politeness' as a new, particularly feminine ideal.[51] Women were increasingly perceived as placed on earth to soften the conversation of male oafs and pedants, and to soothe splenetic constitutions. Sarah, by contrast, wrote to her friend Lord Coningsby, that Sunderland's dismissal had made her plainly furious, 'for I don't pretend to be a Stoic'.[52]

Sarah's final interview with Anne – where her volubility had been met by taciturnity – set the tone for the correspondence to follow during 1710–11. In it she would pour forth her thoughts and feelings with a passion far removed from the 'polite' feminine manner, eschewing the ideal of self-restraint as if it were censorship, which in a sense it was. Sarah never repented of her own 'impolite' character, being either too old-fashioned or too modern for her own times. At the end of her life, when someone referred to two acquaintances being 'too warm', she commented, 'I own I love those that are so, and never saw much good in those that are not.'[53]

During the summer of 1710, when Sarah was unofficially expelled from Court, she began to compose a new version of her 'famous history that is to be'[54] – her memoirs about her rise and fall from favour, intended for publication. Encouraged by Maynwaring and embittered by her ostracism, she updated the story she had written in 1704 and started to defend her financial management. Her present ambiguous relation to the Court allowed her to lay claim to both the patriotic man-on-the-street's anxiety about favourites corrupting the monarch and an authoritative insider's knowledge of the characters involved. Mostly, however, these early memoirs were important as a vehicle for publishing, or threatening to publish, Anne's letters: 'I have a great many other wonderful things that may be brought in,' she told Dr David Hamilton, one of the Queen's doctors, 'but I write them generally as they happen and they are laid up very carefully, though in different places . . .'[55]

Sarah used Hamilton as an intermediary with the Queen. The doctor had a reputation for treating female disorders and had been promoted over Dr John Radcliffe who, Anne felt, did not take her obstetric problems seriously enough.[56] The association between the Queen's body and the body politic automatically made Dr Hamilton something of a political adviser.

Sarah told Hamilton that she was contemplating publishing her memoirs, her intention being to intimidate Anne into keeping her and her husband in their posts for as long as possible. On 10 July 1710, the doctor passed on Sarah's remark that 'she wondered that when Your Majesty was so much in her power, you should treat her so' and in his diary recorded Sarah's musing that 'when people are fond of one another they say many things, however indifferent, they would not desire the world to know'. Sarah clearly viewed Anne's letters as embarrassing to the Queen because of their romantic content, as much as for any other hypocrisy or faults they revealed. Later she slipped a note into the archive containing her correspondence with Hamilton, emphasising that it was he who had encouraged her to threaten the Queen with publication.[57] She knew that the doctor read aloud her letters to Anne, so she vented her feelings freely by that channel: 'I writ volumes to her to undeceive her . . .'[58]

It was also at this time that the first, rather hostile biography of Sarah, *The Life and History of Sarah, Duchess of Marlborough* (1710), was published by an anonymous Tory author. The most notable feature of this skimpy volume was its frontispiece: a woodcut portrait of Sarah looking grotesque, her face and neck covered in pockmarks that we can be fairly certain she never had. The equation between a woman's character and appearance had never been made more obvious, and Sarah was quick to see the potential in such caricatures. Apparently at about this time she said to a Mr Doddington (afterwards Baron Melcombe): 'Young man, you come from Italy. They tell me of a new invention there called caricatura drawing. Can you find somebody that will make me a caricatura of Lady Masham, describing her covered with running sores and ulcers, that I may send it to the Queen to give her a slight idea of her favourite?'[59] On another occasion, Sarah copied out a satire in the form of a horse-betting sheet on which the 'favourite' was called 'Abigail Carbunconella'.[60]

Marlborough suspected Sarah was not fully obeying his orders to stay in the country and resist communication with Anne.[61] He begged her, 'For God's sake . . . remain as quiet as is possible,'[62] and, in stronger terms than usual, 'to make no one step but my opinion shall go with you, for it is not enough, in an ungrateful age, to have reason on our side, but as things are, we must be sure to act with prudence and temper'.[63] This was precisely the distinction Sarah chose to ignore. Marlborough warned her that she did not have the right to play martyr to the truth and throw away her reputation, because her reputation, he explained, reflected on him and their children.

Many of his instructions to Sarah to keep quiet were probably written for the benefit of the Queen's spies who opened the couple's mail. But it was not just a ploy – he had never supported Sarah's vocal interventions as Godolphin, Maynwaring, Cowper and the other Whigs had. He was feeling tired and defensive, and worried about his old friend Cardonnel, who was seriously ill.[64] The last thing he needed was Sarah endangering his candidates' chances in the forthcoming elections by anything she might say or do. Though he claimed to be 'more concerned for what may vex you than anything that can happen to myself' he tended to view insults to her solely as indirect insults to him: '[A]s violencies run, I would beg of you not to be at St Albans, neither before nor at the election, fearing you might meet with some insult which would be a mortification to me . . .'[65]

On 10 August, Marlborough assessed the dangers that lay ahead: 'I am assured that the resolution is taken for the removing of 240 [Sarah], by which step they reckon upon being rid of 38 [Godolphin] and 39 [himself] also . . .'[66]

He only had the order wrong. News had not yet reached him that, on the evening of 8 August, Godolphin had been dismissed as a result of meetings between Anne, Shrewsbury and Harley. Lord Poulett would replace Godolphin as First Lord of the Treasury and Harley, it was agreed, would lead a new ministry as Chancellor of the Exchequer.

Later Sarah wrote an account of how this occurred.[67] Godolphin had been acutely aware of his lessening authority since Shrewsbury's appointment, but every time he asked the Queen whether she wanted him to continue in his post, she had said yes. Only one day after he had again asked her, 'Is it the will of Your Majesty that I should go on?' and Anne had again denied her displeasure, he received his letter of dismissal. According to Sarah, it was not even delivered into his own hands, but carried by a groom from the royal stables to Godolphin's porter. Sarah was outraged by this shabby treatment of the Lord Treasurer 'who had taught [Anne] like Mentor in "Telemachus" for more than twenty years' and had protected her with 'the care and tenderness of a father'.[68] She called Anne a hypocrite for expressing regret in the dismissal letter, and remembered Godolphin's selflessness in feeling more concern for his son's simultaneous dismissal than his own.

At this point Sarah took the widowed Godolphin, her most loyal friend whom Hamilton had described to the Queen as 'so united' with the Duchess that he would never leave her,[69] into her home as a guest. Maynwaring, the impetuous journalist so temperamentally different from Godolphin, perhaps felt some jealousy that they were now able to spend so much time together. Sarah was still beautiful at fifty, without the help of too much lye, powder or red coral paste, and her figure was flattered by the new fashion for hoop skirts. Though she was the lover of neither man, Godolphin and Maynwaring must have competed for the pleasure of her attention.

She also responded to Godolphin's dismissal by trying to protect Marlborough's now badly exposed interests. On 9 September, the Dutch envoy, de Vrijbergen, wrote back to The Hague that 'Mister Harley has influence on Her Majesty, I think because of Mrs Masham. He speaks little and is, as the English say, "behind the curtain".'[70] Despite agreeing with this assessment of the situation, Sarah tried to reassure de Vrijbergen that Marlborough still had the Queen's confidence and that the cry for peace in England would soon die down. Like Halifax, Sunderland and Godolphin, she worried that the Dutch would be alarmed into making a separate peace if they thought England's government was in Harley's hands and about to desert the Grand Alliance.[71]

When Marlborough, who was staying in an abbey near to the fighting at Saint André,[72] heard of Godolphin's dismissal, he foresaw that Sarah was the next in line: 'Nothing would please more those that wish us ill than to have a pretext for the removing of you.'[73] His army officers were beginning to head home to protect their interests in the elections, but he was obliged to remain on the Continent for at least another two months. He and Sarah agreed that Anne would probably defer her resolution to dismiss Sarah until he returned,[74] and that Louis XIV would wait to make peace until after he had seen what happened to Marlborough over the three-month winter recess from the war. Marlborough informed Sarah that, unfortunately, they could not count on George, Elector of Hanover, to defend their interests, despite his esteem for Marlborough, because he said the Elector was reluctant to 'meddle' with 'so villainous a people', as he termed the British, until he became king.

Marlborough agreed with Sarah that Somerset and Shrewsbury were being duped, 'for nobody has a real power but 256 [Mrs Masham] and 199 [Harley]', but he differed with her as to the scope for holding Anne to her old promises of friendship. He told Godolphin, 'I fear 240 [Sarah] and some of their friends judge very wrong when they think that 239 [Anne] has any difficulty as to parting with them, upon the account of their solemn promise.'[75] Despite all their rhetoric about the fatal consequences of Anne's break with their ministry, Marlborough also assured Godolphin in this letter that there was no basis for the rumour of an imminent French invasion.

On 19 September 1710, Somers, Devonshire, Henry Boyle and several other Whigs resigned from their posts in protest at the conduct of government since Godolphin's dismissal. On 21 September, Anne dissolved Parliament without consulting her Council. Later Sarah claimed to have been the only voice telling the Queen plainly that she must not 'break' Parliament,[76] and when it happened she commented acidly to a friend that 'to suffer nobody to speak makes one reflect a little upon King James [II]'s dispensing with the laws'.[77] The Whig Ministers, Lords Orford and Wharton, were forced to leave on the same day, followed by Cowper, who was invited to remain by Harley but left his post on the twenty-third. The demise of the Whig party had preceded the election, yet Sarah remained technically in charge of much of Anne's private household. In practice she was now unwelcome at Court and retaliated by withdrawing herself even further from society: she ordered her servants to deny admission to all visitors.[78]

Sarah drafted thumbnail sketches of the characters who replaced the Marlborough-Godolphin Ministry that autumn, prophesying in letters to Anne that the Marlboroughs' humiliation would 'appear amazing to posterity'.[79] She described the Duke of Buckingham as 'incapable of resisting a bribe of ten pounds', St John as having 'no principle, judgement or application', though admittedly 'able in his own profession', but saved her harshest words for Somerset: 'capricious & uncertain, lying & vain, fawning & insolent, & to avoid many words, as worthless as he is disagreeable.' Marlborough similarly told Sarah that nobody 'has shown more malice to yourself and me than this fool has done'.[80] Her awarding of positive and negative epithets worked on a simple system: those who were not for the Marlboroughs were lacking in either principle or common sense.

Sarah had once predicted that the close connection between the Whigs and 'the vast sums that had been given to support [Anne's] Crown and the liberties of Europe' would lead to disaster if her party were ousted.[81] She had stated that 'the whole interest & business of the City is now in the hands of such men as will not trust my Ld Rochester or Mr Harley with a shilling' and that if Sunderland's dismissal were followed by Godolphin's then the City would lend no more money to the government 'so that [the Queen's] army must starve'. She compared the nation's credit with a green sapling that could be blasted by a sudden north-east wind, and cited the example of Sir Godfrey Kneller ('a very unlikely man to understand the matter of parties'), who had told her that he would sell his stocks if Sunderland were put out. In the event, there had been some dip in stocks, but Godolphin, while still Treasurer, had ensured that nothing too drastic occurred on the fledgeling stock-market.

The Whig Bank of England was trying to destabilise Harley's new Ministry, but this was not an inevitable economic fact: it was a deliberate political tactic. As Defoe warned in his *Review*: 'To cry out we are all undone is to make it so . . .'.[82] Defoe had lost his employment as a propagandist when Harley fell from power in 1708, just as he had fallen on hard times with the death of his patron King William in 1702 – he and Sarah had always had exactly opposite reversals of fortune, despite their similar beliefs. Now, once again, Harley employed him to speak on behalf of the new government in his *Essay on Publick Credit* (1710), which restored a great deal of the public's faith in the credit economy. In that essay, probably unaware that she had been his patron on at least one occasion, Defoe called Sarah the 'She-Dictator', who had controlled government before Harley rescued the Queen from her clutches. Maynwaring drafted a reply in which he defended the Duchess, saying she had not had any role in government for some six months.[83] This was one of the first printed admissions, from Sarah's own 'secretary' no less, that she had previously played a significant role in politics.

At the bottom of a letter from Godolphin to Marlborough, Sarah had jotted a footnote which, unlike the rest of her letters to her husband, survived destruction in his campfire. It concerned the elections in St Albans.[84] She wanted Joshua Lommax, a Whig, to be elected. She also spent most of the month preceding the October elections with her dismissed son-in-law at Althorp, where the thought of collaborating on another political pamphlet obviously crossed her mind, as Maynwaring wrote to her at the end of September: 'Your Grace observes very right that it is too late for these elections to write anything.'[85]

Unintentionally, however, Sarah did disobey her husband's orders and interfered in the Woodstock elections. Since early September she had been fighting with Vanbrugh over the escalating construction costs at Blenheim. Godolphin reported that the architect had been complaining to Maynwaring, Manchester and other leading Whigs that Sarah was trying to ruin him.[86] After Godolphin was dismissed, Sarah was so nervous that the Treasury would withhold payments for the Blenheim works that she ordered a pre-emptive cessation of labour. This not only enraged Vanbrugh but also the unpaid workmen, and the local townspeople who had been giving the workmen credit on future wages.[87] A canon of Christ Church, Oxford, told the story of one workman who was owed six hundred pounds for limestone and brick and who had to borrow five pounds from his local MP: 'The fellow thanked him with tears and said that the money, for the present, would save him from gaol.' Sarah had to put bars and locks on Blenheim to prevent vandalism by this aggrieved man.[88]

On 14 October, Marlborough wrote to Sarah at St James's, angry that she had so undermined his interest with the Woodstock electorate and worried that the half-completed work would be left exposed to the winter weather. Already with an eye to a future court case, he urged her to make sure that all orders were seen as coming from the Treasury rather than from them personally, 'for that it is no ways proper for you or me to be giving orders for the Queen's money'.[89] (A satire had just appeared called *The Tory's Answer to the 19 Queries of the Whigs*, criticising the amounts being paid out for Blenheim at a time when there was a national money shortage.[90]) He also told her to use Maynwaring to 'manage' Vanbrugh for, as he put it, 'My temper is to quiet everybody if it were possible.'[91] While telling Sarah that he knew she was 'most reasonable' in all her actions,[92] he sent Godolphin to 'manage' her in turn and ensure construction was resumed.[93]

The October general election was a landslide for the Tories, who won a majority of two hundred in the House of Commons, including the two seats at St Albans with which Sarah had obediently not interfered. An embittered landed gentry was returned, led in spirit by Henry St John who was now noticeably to the right of Harley (and, despite Sarah calling him a crypto-Jacobite, had opposed the Occasional Conformity Bills and the Tackers). Sarah observed that 'The spirit of the nation appears to be Toryism,'[94] but wrote in her published memoirs that 'the great change of 1710' had been a tragedy mainly because it reversed all her personal achievements – that the Whigs' cause during Anne's reign 'would have been always too low to be capable of a fall, but for the zeal and diligence with which I seized every opportunity to raise and establish it'.[95]

In November Anne was quoted as saying she 'would have

my people satisfied that though I have changed my Ministers I have not altered my measures; I am still for moderation and will govern by it'.⁹⁶ She hoped Marlborough could be brought to work harmoniously alongside the now predominantly Tory Cabinet. Again, however, she underestimated his bond with the ousted Whigs through his wife, his son-in-law and Godolphin. On 29 October he told Sarah he remained loyal to the Whigs, not only from self-interest but, now that they did not have the majority necessary for voting supplies to the war, also from 'inclination and principle'.⁹⁷ Sarah's greatest lasting achievement, perhaps, was to have cornered him into this ideological position. Privately she worried, however, that what kept him from resigning was not so much principle as the desire for the Treasury to keep paying for construction at Woodstock.

Dr Francis Hare had been a close friend of and apologist for the Marlboroughs since the death of Sarah's son Jack, whom he had tutored at King's College, Cambridge. Marlborough had appointed him Chaplain-General to the Allied Forces in Flanders, from which position he hoped to witness and record a literary account of the war.⁹⁸ In July 1710, the clergyman had renewed contact with Sarah, expressing his condolences for the disloyalty of so many other old acquaintances.⁹⁹ In September, when he wrote to commiserate over the dismissal of Godolphin, she entered into a lengthy correspondence with him. He wrote that he was 'sometimes vain enough to think I could offer something that might perhaps be favourably received, but when it came to, I could not but think it too great a presumption for one who knows so little of the secret springs of affairs . . .'¹⁰⁰ He was applying to write a sympathetic biography, if Sarah would supply the material.

Now, in October, from the camp at the siege of Aire, Hare wrote again to commiserate over the election result. He saw it as the direct result of the Sacheverell trial, but did not share Sarah's certainty that the moderate Tories were aligned with the Jacobites:

*Jacobite seems to be no juster a character of a Tory as to the
body of them than Republican is of a Whig; tis the dirt each
side throws at one another, and that in such plenty as some will
stick; and the faults of a few on both sides, when the prejudices
against each other are carried to such heights, make it very hard
for either to wipe it off.*[101]

Sarah answered Hare on 31 October, and this letter is valuable
as one of her few surviving political declarations addressed to
someone other than the Queen.[102] She accepted his Jacobite/
Republican comparison as 'pretty right' but argued that the
parties were not so indistinguishable as he pretended. Judging
by actions, she said she had seen the Tories put England in danger,
whereas 'the Whigs never':

*I have known the Court since I was thirteen years old and I never
saw that the Whigs did the nation any prejudice. Tis true in some
reigns they have complied in things of no manner of consequence,
which has given handles to the Tories to say they gave up their
principles for their employments ... but for more than thirty
years I can witness for them that they complied in trifles only
to hinder (if they could) the Tories from doing all manner of
mischief, for tis unimaginable how those sort of people poison
even the Princes that have some sense with prerogatives, divine
and hereditary rights ...*

She saw all Tory voters as deceived by their own leadership,
like mini-monarchs each led astray by the lying favourites who
pretend to serve them: '[T]he design of the Tories in general do
not intend the P[rince] of W[ales]; but tis certain their leaders
do, at least after this Queen's life, and if we are to have him at
last, I can't but think it had been more for Her honour as well
as for the good of the Public that King James had never gone
away ...'

She compared a monarch and a nation to a man and his wife,
in which the man should not be unfaithful with 'little odd people
that come in the dark', and devoted the final page to worrying

how the Tories would treat Marlborough so long as he continued, against Sarah's better judgement, in their employment.

In November she sent Hare another scribbled note, obviously wanting to determine how she was portrayed in any book he planned to write:[103] 'I am not a Greek nor a Roman, nor a woman of letters that anybody can read, but I was born as I am & that is my way of thinking. I have not been corrupted by Whigs & till very lately I never conversed with anything but Tories, whose principles and practices I ever disliked . . .' At the bottom of this note, a series of words in Sarah's handwriting float at random across the page: 'Ideas, Politics, whimsicals . . . Habeas Corpus, Patriot, Jesuits, pique . . .'

That month she was again in touch with her Jacobite sister, who remained a loophole in her anti-Jacobite prejudices. Despite her own fall from favour, Sarah was still trying to help Lady Tyrconnel reclaim her possessions lost in 1688–9. She had done what she could, which was not much, to press forward her sister's petitions for a return from exile, until in the summer of 1708 Frances was allowed to move back to Dublin where she founded a Catholic convent. Marlborough helped her move from the Continent 'for she is very helpless and has a great deal of lumber with her'. In 1709 Sarah had been concerned about the rumours of a Bill to be brought into Parliament that would oblige ladies to take the oath of abjuration or forfeit their goods. 'I fancy there is nothing in it,' she had written to Lord Coningsby, but she needed to know whether it was safe to import her sister's belongings from Holland.[104] In 1710 there is also evidence that Sarah had been in correspondence, through Godolphin, with Lady Kingsland, one of Frances's three daughters by her first marriage to Sir George Hamilton, and now an Irish Catholic peeress. Sarah had written through Joseph Addison (Secretary to Lord Wharton, the Lord Lieutenant of Ireland under the Whigs) supporting her niece's decision to stay away from Court given the present circumstances.[105]

Now Sarah again enlisted Coningsby's help in having her sister better settled with a jointure.[106] On 16 November, however, she complained of an ungrateful letter from Frances, who, out of touch with events at Court, seemed to think it was still easy for Sarah to approach Anne on her behalf. Sarah asked Coningsby to investigate how difficult her sister's financial circumstances really were, remarking, '[M]y notions are so different from my sister's . . .'[107]

While Sarah's sister remained in Ireland, Abigail Masham's younger sister, Alice, was becoming the regular dinner companion of Jonathan Swift, recently returned to London.[108] Sometimes she even offered a venue for the Tory Brothers Club, which later became the famous Scriblerus Club of Swift, Pope and Matthew Prior. Swift became one of the Hill family's greatest champions, though his diaries confirm, in a sense, that Sarah's account of Abigail did not stem merely from party prejudice. In one entry, he noted how Abigail and Harley would retreat after dinner to talk business like a pair of gentlemen: '[T]is well she is not very handsome: they sit alone together, settling the nation.'[109]

Harley met Swift some time in 1710. Swift had already written *A Tale of a Tub* (1704) and *The Battle of the Books* (1704) but the clergyman was still relatively unknown as an author. Harley recruited him in 1710, causing Sarah to regard him as one of the new ministry's 'under-workmen of prostituted consciences and hardened faces'.[110] This was all very well for a woman who owned several palatial homes while Swift was paying what he considered the 'plaguey deep'[111] rent of twenty pounds a year for two rooms in Bury Street.

His first Harley-sponsored attack on the Marlboroughs appeared on 2 November 1710 in the fourteenth issue of the weekly essay-newsletter, *The Examiner*. In it he justified the 'late revolutions at Court': '[I]t was the most prudent Course imaginable in the Queen to lay hold of the Disposition of the People for changing the Parliament and Ministry at this Juncture, and extricating Herself, as soon as possible, out of the Pupilage of those who found their Accounts only in perpetuating the War.' More articulately than any author before him, Swift voiced the landed gentry's resentment against the powerful Whig 'monied interest' with which the Marlboroughs were associated: 'The Wealth of the Nation, that used to be reckoned by the value of Land, is now computed by the Rise and Fall of Stocks,' he observed, believing this a sign of national decline and instability.

This relatively mild critique was followed on 23 November by a more personal attack in *The Examiner* (no. 17), which not only repeated the insinuation that the Marlboroughs were profiteering from the war but also mocked the Duke's claim to have been treated with ingratitude. This 'Bill of British Ingratitude' not only attacked him as avaricious, corrupt and grossly ambitious, but also had words for Sarah. Swift raised the taboo subject of the Parliamentary Address against Abigail and asked, with pointed reference to Sarah's conduct, how it could be justified:

Had [Abigail] treated her Royal Mistress with insolence or neglect? Had she enriched herself by a long practice of bribery and obtaining exorbitant grants? Had she engrossed Her Majesty's favours without admitting any access but through her means? Had she heaped employments upon herself, her family and dependents? Had she an imperious, haughty behaviour? Or, after all, was it a perfect blunder and mistake of one person for another?

Finally, he took another sidelong swipe at Sarah in her role as Keeper of the Privy Purse:

A Lady of my Acquaintance appropriated twenty-six Pounds a Year out of her Allowance, for certain uses, which her Woman received and was to pay to the Lady on her Order, as it was called for. But after eight Years it appeared upon the strictest Calculation that the Woman had paid but four Pound a Year, and sunk two and twenty for her own Pocket . . .

The allegation that she had appropriated money from the Privy Purse made Sarah renew her threats to publish Anne's letters that winter.

Sarah rightly feared that, whatever the Marlboroughs' response, some of the mud from this *Examiner* article would stick. Between four and five thousand copies of that 23 November edition were

in circulation and the readership in coffee-houses was probably
far greater. Still wary, as a woman, of publishing her replies, she
sent them to Dr Hamilton and so, in effect, to the Queen, 'that
I might say what otherwise could not have been told her'.[112]

In her first letter to Hamilton/Anne[113] that winter, Sarah
enclosed a copy of *The Examiner* that had disturbed her peace of
mind: '[I]t is pretty difficult to be silent under such provocations.'
No one would bother to check the accounts to see 'whether I was
an expensive favourite', she complained, while 'to be printed and
cried about the country for a common cheat and pickpocket is
too much for human nature to bear'. She referred to the letters
and accounts in her possession, which would prove, among other
things, her financial honesty, 'since anybody that knows what
honour or a principle is would rather lose their life than be
murdered in their reputation'. She justified Marlborough's army
expenditures and listed what she had paid from her own pocket
on the leased properties at Windsor and St James's. Then came
the threat: 'I wish the same author had known my story which
I have really a mind to tell him,' she concluded, '& shall, I
believe, be tempted to it a little sooner or later, whoever's ears
may tingle . . .'

Swift's 'Bill of British Ingratitude' had been so effective because
it robbed the Whigs of their own rhetoric. Sarah herself often
remarked that there was 'a strange star for ingratitude at this
time'.[114] This was due in part to changing social relations, which
made it increasingly permissible for the Hill family and others
to fail to recompense her patronage, but on a personal level a
sense of ungrateful returns for her efforts and generosity was
one of Sarah's ruling emotions. She was constantly disappointed
in people: she held them to high standards, her standards for
herself, and when they inevitably fell short, she became bitter
and misanthropic. As bitter, one could say, as an idealistic satirist
like Swift when a Houyhnhmn turned out to be a Yahoo. Just as
Godolphin wrote to Sarah that she was 'much better tempered
than you sometimes appear to be', so Pope later wrote to Swift
saying that he would miss his company because 'I can allow for a

tenderness in your way of thinking, even when it seemed to want that tenderness.'[115]

Following Swift's lead, an anti-Marlborough satire entitled *Oliver's Pocket Looking-Glass, New Fram'd and Clean'd to give a clear view of the Great Modern Colossus* (1711) accused the couple, especially Sarah, of ingratitude:

[T]he most obliging Testimonies of Bounty, even Honour and Riches, have been swallowed by her High and Mighty Haughtiness with such an Air of Negligence, Scorn and Contempt, as if she looked upon the glorious Benefactress whose generous Hand has bestowed all this to be Debtor to her for Acceptance of such unparalleled Favours . . .[116]

In one version of her memoirs Sarah justified her outspokenness, which would culminate in publication, by the 'just indignation' she felt 'when I saw myself so oft printed as a public cheat & an insatiable, ravenous creature who set everything to sale . . .'[117] (One of her friends would later try, unsuccessfully, to console her: '[T]is only because some men are afraid of you that they take so much pains to make you seem unlovely.')[118]

Sarah's next letter to Hamilton again enclosed a newspaper, this time a Whig rag, and she suggested that she was on the verge of taking up journalism herself: 'The author of it has a very good pen but I could have mended it . . . I mean by telling him a great many things that very few know.' She also copied out a long 'Character of Marcus Antonius and his meditations', which she admired as a template for a just ruler. She concluded with the reflection that Anne would 'not make so good a figure . . . in history' as Marcus. She begged Hamilton to pass on this letter and its attachments for the Queen's moral salvation, though she questioned Anne's ability to understand it: 'I have seen people present her with books, that she would sooner read Tom Thumb.'

In the second half of the same long letter, Sarah switched from classical to scriptural reference, implying that Abigail was a new Jezebel: 'Dost thou now govern the Kingdom of Israel?' In the next instant Sarah sounds like a jealous lover; imagining herself able to address Abigail, she refers simply to 'Mrs Morley, who I did once love much more than you can do.' In the final section of this letter she returns to a crescendo of self-martyrdom, justifying the fact that she was writing such clearly offensive, self-defeating letters: '[T]hough you call me passionate . . . you might as properly have said that Socrates was passionate when he drank the cup of poison the Athenians sent him, as me, who under all these provocations have shown the terrible things of Mrs Morley to none but those I can trust with my own soul.' Again, the implication was that she could still do otherwise if she chose.

While excruciatingly self-righteous in many places, these letters are never demented. Their literary allusions pile upon each other with the clumsiness of an author new to classical education, but they are nonetheless reasonably successful in elevating the story to an epic level – where kingdoms, not just girly friendships, are at stake. They are a product of her friendship with Maynwaring; what he cited half-facetiously, Sarah regurgitated to the Queen in all earnestness.

By 6 December, Abigail's supplanting of the Marlboroughs had become public knowledge and Sarah itched to tell her side of the story. She wrote to Hamilton/Anne again, hinting that certain details of the Morley–Freeman relationship were 'very far from being public' and that she was only waiting 'till the time comes that I can make the whole world on my side'. She went on to make a statement that seems to refute the thesis that she blackmailed Anne with the accusation of lesbianism:

I fear there are some [newspapers] lately come out which they said were not fit for me to see, by which I guess they are upon a subject that you may remember I complained of to you & really it troubled me very much, upon my own account as well as others, because it was very disagreeable and what I know to be a lie, but something of that disagreeable turn there was in an odious ballad to the tune of fair Rosamond . . . [emphasis added]

In case her meaning was still unclear, Sarah explained that she meant the reference in the ballad to Abigail's 'dark deeds at night', which served as another cunning reminder to Anne that publication of her early letters might, with a little prompting, suggest lesbianism to the public imagination. That Sarah's denial should not be taken at face value is clear: she knew the ballad to have been written by Maynwaring. In this envelope she also enclosed several other anti-Abigail verses – insults to Anne, ostensibly sent as warnings – and in one case she asked to have her handwritten copy returned because she worried that it might lead someone to accuse her of being its anonymous author.

In *The Examiner* of 14 December 1710 (no. 20), Swift answered those who had leapt to the defence of the 'innocent L[a]dy' slandered in the previous edition: 'How could it be longer suffered in a free Nation that all Avenues to Preferment should be shut up, except a very few, when one or two stand Sentry, who docked all Favours they handed down; or spread a huge invisible Net between the Princess [Anne] and Subject, through which nothing of Value could pass?' This may have been briefly true in 1702–3, but not since then. Sarah was merely an easy target for those who, like Swift, had not prospered until the Whig administration. Now, cocooned at Windsor Lodge in midwinter, Sarah was far from standing sentry to anyone. On 20 December, she wrote to explain why she did not fulfil the duties of her offices, such as bringing Anne new clothes when she came out of her two years of official mourning.[119] She believed her presence at Court would only allow her enemies to find reason to dismiss her and Marlborough from their posts, 'their main point being to remove him from the Queen and not to let him serve any more, the only thing in which I ever did or ever shall agree with them'. The next day she asked for advice on this same point from Dr Hamilton: which would give less cause for complaint, her absence or her attendance?[120] Hamilton initially encouraged her to return to Court[121] but, when asked, Anne unambiguously instructed him to make sure Sarah stayed away.

On 22 December, Sarah sent Hamilton a further instalment of her notes for her own 'history' and asked him, as her surrogate for the reading public, to judge 'whether I was mercenary, corrupt or interested as some of her new Ministers have printed me to be'. In a sequel letter she continued to boast her self-restraint in having patiently suffered Somerset's lies about her for so long before daring to write to Anne on 7 June 1710, and to insist that she would never have spoken up 'if I had not been informed that the persecution against Ld Marlborough and his family was chiefly occasioned by her Majesty's displeasure and aversion to me, as having been the promoter of an Address against Mrs Masham,' which 'I had much less concern in . . . than she seemed to think.'

At last, aware that none of these letters was helping her situation, Sarah begged Anne, through Hamilton, to be allowed to leave her Court posts in 'a natural way' rather than in disgrace.

On 27 December, Hamilton recorded in his diary that Anne had said the friendship with Sarah had ended because 'the Duchess had said shocking things even to herself, *Yea as much to herself*, and afterwards in Company, as that she lied'.[122] The sad truth was that Hamilton was playing almost as much of a double game as Somerset and Shrewsbury had. He was planning to publish his own insider's account of his friendship with his royal patient, and gave chapter headings to his diary, including:[123] 'My Lady Marlborough designs to print . . . The methods I proposed to the Queen to prevent her printing . . . I caution the Queen against being too open to a Favourite from my Lady Marlborough's behaviour . . .' and 'My advice to the Queen that she should not be so much influenced by Her Favourites.'

Sarah had never entirely trusted the doctor as an intermediary, later writing that 'he pretended he would fright [Anne] about the letters I had in my power.' In fact, Hamilton was afraid of Sarah, on his sovereign's behalf, for she 'had a great Spirit, & was justly enraged to be put in print'.[124] Later Sarah was scathing that Anne was so easily persuaded to insinuate that 'there was room still for a reconciliation' only out of fear about the letters.[125]

As a Whig, Dr Hamilton's strategy was to pretend to protect Anne's health and privacy while all the time working to support

Elizabeth, Duchess of Somerset, against Abigail, especially when he found that Sarah stood no hope of recovering the Queen's lost favour for the Whig party. The doctor urged Anne to spend time with Elizabeth because it 'made her easy'.[126] Sarah described Elizabeth as 'fawning'[127] for favour – one fault of which Sarah herself could never be accused. She insinuated that Anne's growing feelings for her were of the same type as her feelings for Abigail and, by implication, other women. However, she pressed the point with far less invective in the case of a fellow duchess. The Birch Manuscript Memoranda (14 June 1754) note that a large number of letters from Anne to Elizabeth were burned at her husband's order after the death of the two women, which may be suspicious or only customary discretion. Certainly there is evidence that by the end of 1710 Elizabeth was supplanting Abigail as favourite: Abigail complained to Robert Harley that the Queen no longer listened to her.[128]

Nonetheless, Sarah and Maynwaring continued to draft letters to Anne with Abigail as their target and the accusation of lesbianism as their weapon. One draft kept among Sarah's papers was an anonymous letter from 'one of the meanest of your subjects'. It observed that the change of Ministry had proceeded 'as the world loudly talks, from an inclination that is unaccountable & from a foul polluting principle'. It was brilliantly unclear whether the pollution was being in love with a woman ('your heart is suspected to harbour secret failings & to be smitten in a weak & idle manner') or breaking promises to colleagues. It concluded with the accusation that a perceived sin was as bad as a real one – the rule of the press as spoken by Maynwaring the newspaper editor: 'Fame & honour & reputation are not naturally inherent in any person, not even a sovereign, but depend wholly on the opinion & value of the people.'

Another, later draft of the same letter separated the accusations about the Queen's political infidelity from those about her love affair, which were relegated to a long postscript. This makes it all the more clear that the reference to a 'deformity in the sight of God' meant her romantic relationship with Abigail and not merely the breaking of political allegiances.

When Marlborough returned to London in December 1710 he was greeted by cheering supporters in the streets. While gratifying, this was also rather embarrassing as it was considered dishonourable to use 'the mob' as a political lever and he did not want to confirm Tory satires that depicted him as a new Cromwell. To avoid the 'great numbers of people who flocked about him in the streets', he drove first with his son-in-law the Duke of Montagu to Montagu House rather than directly to St James's.[129] Sarah felt vindicated by the crowds, 'notwithstanding all the lies the new Ministry had spread'.[130]

On 5 January, Dr Hamilton recorded in his diary that he had spoken with Godolphin and Marlborough that evening and acquainted them, he claimed for the first time, with the content of Sarah's recent letters to himself and hence the Queen. He described the Duke as shocked at his wife's continuing references to a romantic relationship between Anne and Abigail. This might have been merely a show of surprise for the doctor's benefit, or genuine anger that Sarah had ignored his orders to remain silent. In either case, Sarah's letters stopped immediately.

She made fair copies of several of Anne's letters. 'By this time I suppose the measures had been fully concerted for turning me out of my places,' she later reflected, '[b]ut the apprehension the Queen had of my printing her letters in my own vindication was a great obstruction to it . . .'[131] She pretended the letters were only for self-vindication rather than blackmail, but told Hamilton that her daughters had better be permitted to inherit her posts or 'such things are in my power that if known by a man that would apprehend and was a right politician, might lose a crown.'[132] Several biographers have thought her threats were baseless and vaguely unhinged, not understanding that the letters revealed something more than merely what Hamilton called Anne's 'breaches of promise and asseverations'.

Shrewsbury was asked to send a servant to try to retrieve the letters, saying that the Queen 'was in the utmost pain upon this account' and it was only this, Sarah claimed, that had given her the idea of using them 'to preserve myself by them, if I could'.[133] Sarah therefore returned Shrewsbury's servant with an answer ambiguous enough to keep Anne anxious. Unfortunately, unwilling to report his failure, Shrewsbury sabotaged her blackmail by pretending to have extracted promises from Sarah that she would not publish, making Anne 'entirely easy about this matter'.

Marlborough's claim to be ignorant of Sarah's methods did not help him regain Anne's trust. Shortly after his arrival home, when he first went to pay his respects, Sarah wrote that 'nothing passed but such lively conversation as is usual with Her M[ajesty] about his journey, the ways, the weather etc . . .' She remembered that all the Ministers welcomed the returning war hero except Harley, who just sent him a cold note. Harley was reported as having said to others at Court that Sarah was 'the rock which all would break upon'.[134] Swift's diary recorded a different, less passive image of Anne at Court that day: Marlborough 'told the Queen he was neither covetous nor ambitious' and Anne later told her friends that 'if she could have conveniently turned about, she would have laughed, and could hardly forbear it in his face'.[135]

The question now was not whether Sarah had to leave her posts, but how. She did not want to go quietly unless allowed to resign in her own good time, but she had never been more powerless to act. There must also have been unadmitted pain that Marlborough was unwilling to resign on her behalf. She constantly wrote of how all the Allied leaders, such as Prince Eugene, the Whig businessmen and bankers, were begging him not to do so, while elsewhere she confessed that she 'thought using his wife so ill was as great an affront as any, but could not be sure I was not too partial in the matter'.[136]

Marlborough had forced her to write one final letter to the Queen.[137] It requested that Anne let them resign as a couple, at a time of their own choosing and, as Sarah phrased it elsewhere, 'in such a manner as to have no occasion to vindicate ourselves to the world about it'. It was signed 'with all submission & respect imaginable, your majesty's most dutiful & obedient subject & most faithful servant'.[138] In its tone of grovelling humility, it was in stark contrast to her previous letters. But Anne refused either to keep Sarah any longer or to lose Marlborough so soon. On delivering this note into the Queen's hands, Marlborough begged that Sarah should serve along with him for another nine months. He made it plain that they needed an 'honourable retreat' and, sounding more like Sarah, suggested that to do otherwise would be a slur upon Anne's own reputation as both a friend and a merciful ruler.[139]

The version of that private interview Sarah heard from him that evening was that he had pressed to know the reason for Anne's wrath against Sarah but Anne had maintained her royal silence: '[O]nly once she said to him, when he pressed her extremely upon that subject, that it was for her honour to remove the Duchess of Marl: but what that meant he could never learn . . .'

Marlborough returned to tell Sarah that she must resign immediately. He was to take the Gold Key, the totem of her power, back to the Queen within three days.[140] In a final fit of pride, determined to do it on her own terms, Sarah made him put his clothes on again and take it back immediately. When he next returned and Sarah asked him what Anne had said on receipt of the Key, he told her that the Queen had been her usual inarticulate self, barely moving her lips to 'make as if she said something when in truth no words were uttered'.

In a more analytical draft version of this story, Sarah linked her dismissal to the French funds behind Harley and the influence on Anne of the Scottish lords 'most of which were Jacobites'.[141] She claimed that Marlborough had called Anne an arbitrary ruler to her face, which does not sound like his style, and that he had knelt down before Anne to beg for a delay in Sarah's dismissal. He had once written to Sarah, 'I would go upon all-four to make it easy between you [Sarah & Anne]'[142] and now Sarah's wishful imagination had him act out this gallant expression. In this version, Sarah also noted that her dismissal was done while the Somersets were away at Petworth so that it would appear that they were not involved. She quoted a 1709 letter from Anne in which she had stated that her friend had committed no fault, and then skipped straight to the dismissal episode in 1711 as if nothing had happened in the interim: '[A]fter about forty years acquaintance, thirty years public profession of friendship and about twenty-five years faithful service ... Her M[ajest]y was prevailed upon to put me out of my employments without seeing me or giving any reason for it ...'

All Sarah's accounts of the dismissal are free of her famous temper. As if to compensate for this omission, Lord Dartmouth added a note to Burnet's *History of His Own Time* that, when Marlborough had come for her Gold Key, Sarah had torn it from her skirts and hurled it violently to the floor. Given that the Duke and Duchess were alone in the room, Dartmouth can only have had this story from a spying servant. More likely, the leitmotif of Sarah hurling things from her – the Queen's gloves, her shorn hair – was replicated by this piece of invention. In 1899, Mrs Aubrey Richardson continued the Chinese whispers by making Sarah throw the Gold Key at her husband's head.[143]

If Sarah's own accounts were confused it is hardly surprising. She had to adapt the story to fit the official version: that she had resigned voluntarily. The threat to publish Anne's letters seems to have won her at least this concession, and also prevented the government-controlled press from rejoicing too loudly at her fall. There was no mention of it in *The Examiner*. Other Tory satires did appear, however, including: *There's But One Plague in England: D[uchess] M[arlborough]* (1711), *He's Welcome Home: or, A Dialogue between John and Sarah* (1711), *S[ara]h and J[oh]n beg Pardon for What they have Done* (1711) and *A Tale of J[oh]n and S[ara]h, or Both Turn'd out of C[our]t at Last* (1711). More popular on the streets was *Sarah's Farewell to C[our]t: or, A Trip from St James's to St Albans.* To the tune of *Farewell Joy and Farewell Pleasure*, a lewd song that had been composed the year before as a prophecy of her fall:

The Good Hater

Farewell Q[ueen] my once kind Mistress
To thy Royal Love Farewell
For thou didst raise me to a Du[che]ss
But for what I ne'er could tell

Farewell to Intriguing M[asha]m
There I recommended thee
But thou hast play'd thy Cards so wisely
Now thou hast Supplanted me

Farewell P[rivy] P[ur]se, the best
Of all my P[urs]es (that was known)
My Golden K[e]y and all the rest
For I perceive they'll follow soon

Farewell Sons and Farewell Daughters
For I now do plainly see
The Tories so will manage matters
That you all may follow me

Farewell faithful wife G[odolphi]n
Always to our Int'rest true
For whilst thou rul'est the Public T[reasur]e
No one our Revenue knew

Farewell S[underlan]d and Wh[arto]n,
And to all the Dear Cabal
Was it not the Cursed'st Fortune
To be thus Thrust out of all

Farewell Royal Grotts and Bow'rs
Which Ambition did create
In rural Shades I'll pass my Hours
And forget Affairs of State

Joh[nn]y quickly haste thee over
Here we'll make a safe Retreat
No more Arms; but thus like Lovers
We'll in cool Recesses meet

Vain at Fate it is to Murmur
Long we have in Favour been
Tho by a kind of sudden Turn here
Heaven now has chang'd the scene

Hither then my Dearest Joh[nn]y
To thy Sarah's Arms Repair
We'll for St Albans quit St James's
Or for Ble[nhei]m's happier Air.

St John added his pen to the poison by publishing his *Letter to the Examiner* in which he wrote that the nation had felt the miserable consequences of subjection 'to the Caprice of an Insolent Woman. Unhappy Nation, which expecting to be Governed by the Best, fell under the Tyranny of the Worst of her Sex! But now, Thanks be to God, that Fury, who broke Loose to execute the Vengeance of Heaven on a Sinful People is restrained, and the Royal Hand is already reached out to Chain up the Plague'.

After her fall, Sarah watched the scramble for her Court places with wry amusement. The Duchess of Somerset, Lady Rochester and Abigail were the main contenders. It was soon obvious that Anne did not intend to keep the promise Sarah claimed to have extorted, that her own daughters should inherit her places.[144] Like a recording angel, Sarah noted in her draft memoirs the ingratitude of others who deserted her and now flattered the new favourites: the Duchess of Ormonde,[145] for example, and Lady Frescheville who 'spread, with a malicious zeal, all manner of the greatest falsehoods about her [Sarah]: in which laudable work the good lady had always shown a very peculiar talent and acquired an established reputation'.

The Duchess of Somerset won the post of Groom of the Stole, though Sarah believed that 'in truth the Q[ueen] never had any kindness for her but thought it a better air to have her than any other the Groom of the Stole' because of her rank and ancestry.[146] Sarah wrote bitterly that Elizabeth 'never was quite so kind as after she had taken the resolution to supplant me' – dining with her, playing cards and kissing on parting, 'which was quite new'.[147] After acquiring Sarah's post, 'she went round the town protesting that she had done nothing towards obtaining it' while dismissing all the servants appointed by the Marlboroughs, which Sarah said in her memoirs was far from customary. In another version, she remarked that Elizabeth had not at first wanted the post when she discovered it was a real job rather than a 'titular dignity' but changed her mind when she heard the salary.[148] Given that Elizabeth was the heiress to the enormous Percy estates, this might have been self-projection – though Sarah's memoirs frequently refer to having such stories from 'very good hands'.

Sarah believed Elizabeth was only a respectable screen behind which Anne could hide her relationship with Abigail, who was now appointed Keeper of the Privy Purse, a function she had been performing for some time while Sarah received the salary. However, Anne was probably trying to express her party neutrality in appointing one Whig and one Tory lady to equally powerful posts – and attemping not to repeat the mistake of cultivating a pre-eminent favourite.

Sarah was asked to submit the final accounts of her offices so that the new Ministry could study them. An external comptroller, reporting to the Treasury, had always checked that the trades-men's bills submitted by each department in Anne's household were reasonable, but Sarah was the first officeholder to have her accounts examined retrospectively.[149] The final account book is now lost, so we must take her word for its contents.

She did not try to conceal that, just before submitting the accounts, she had made herself a single payment of £18,000 from the Privy Purse, referring to it as the £2,000 per annum the Marlboroughs had refused to accept with the dukedom. She attested that the Queen's signature on the accounts was confirmation that this money was still owed in arrears. Her justification took no account of the fact that the £2,000 per annum had been intended only as compensation for an income

Marlborough had long since been granted. It seems clear that this back payment was merely a pretext: Sarah took the money so shortly after Anne's attempts to retrieve her letters that it is impossible not to regard it as the spoils of blackmail.

In her published memoirs, Sarah devoted a whole section to refuting the 'libels that I had behaved myself unworthily in my offices and been unfaithful in the trusts reposed in me'. She claimed her accounts for the Robes were exact to the nearest twenty shillings for the whole nine years of her service, and quote a letter from Harley, before they were opponents, complimenting her on her good management. She compared her modest expenditures on Anne's behalf with those of Lady Derby on behalf of Queen Mary, then justified herself against the reverse accusation of stinginess. She explained what she thought it reasonable to pay the royal tradesmen and, with her liking for hard evidence, even listed specific tradesmen and their addresses in Ludgate Hill, Covent Garden and the Strand, in case anyone should wish to cross-examine them.[150] Sarah answered the 'witty comparison that was made between me and the lady's woman who out of her mistress' pin-money of £26 put £22 into her own pocket'.[151] She justified her reclaiming of the £2,000 a year by explaining, like a guilty schoolgirl, that her friends had made her do it, telling her she need no longer be so scrupulous.

Her enemies, who must have pored over her account books in the spring of 1711, found nothing in them to leak to *The Examiner*. The specific nature of Sarah's self-defence, on the other hand, is impressive. Sometimes it even verged on the absurdly detailed, like the affidavits in a particularly nasty divorce hearing. In one draft she declared that 'I know there was never a shilling advantage made of the Lodge more than in having milk from a few cows.'[152] In another memo written on some 1709 correspondence, Sarah noted that since the bedchamber women working under her as Mistress of the Robes had been paid decent salaries, it had not been necessary for her to give them the Queen's old garments, but she had done so anyway, out of generosity. Yet the dressers 'railed at me everywhere & said I took all their clothes for myself'.[153]

In yet another version of her memoirs[154] she transferred the potential accusation of stinginess to the Queen: 'Nor did she ever give me a diamond or the value of a fan in the whole time after she was Queen, except the remainder of baskets of fruit & red deer, some seals of King Williams and an old harpsichord, which was the only thing I ever asked her for whilst I was in her service.'[155] She also remembered the 'Japan Box' Anne had offered before she became Queen but which Sarah did not take. Years later, after the arguments had begun, Sarah had seen it lying inside a wardrobe and, feeling 'less modest', went to ask Anne if she could have it. Another broken promise to add to the list: Anne agreed, Sarah wrote, 'but never gave it me'. Such self-vindications seem ridiculous unless viewed in the context of all the accusations, satirical and then finally legal, made against the Marlboroughs during 1711–12.

In a Tory satire written after Sarah's death,[156] the Marlboroughs' joint income from Queen Anne was totalled as £64,325 (the equivalent of approximately £4.6 million in today's money) – ample repayment for any services as friends or advisers. Sarah was accused of having 'possessed the Funds and governed the Wealth of the whole Nation'. This was the true complaint against Sarah: monopolisation, not corruption. Now, in 1711, that monopoly had been broken. What might be added is that transfers from the government's secret service funds to the Privy Purse account quadrupled after Abigail became its Keeper, as did large, unexplained payments from the Privy Purse to Abigail's husband.[157]

9

Banished

One morning in 1710 Lord Cowper visited the Marlboroughs at home. The couple lay in bed to receive their visitor, as was briefly the fashion, wearing cotton India gowns and tucked under 'Holland sheets'.[1] Sarah was railing against the Queen's character while her daughter Henrietta, also in the room, tearfully defended her, and Marlborough muttered an aside to Cowper that he should not mind what his wife said 'for she was used to talk at that rate when she was in a passion'.[2] A few months later, Cowper noted in his diary: 'The Duchess of M[arlborough] dined with me at Cole Green from St Albans. Her opinion that the Queen has no original thoughts on any subject, is neither good nor bad but as put into; that she has much love and passion, while pleased, for those who please, and can write pretty affectionate letters; but do nothing else well.'[3] Whether or not Sarah had spoken against Anne behind her back when she held her posts, it now seemed she spoke quite freely.

In February 1711 Marlborough sailed from Harwich to The Hague; he had been in Britain only a matter of weeks. He was now at the service of a moderate Tory Ministry, which Swift described as standing 'like an isthmus' between the Whigs and violently Tory backbenchers.[4] On 5 April he wrote Sarah a letter, which was carried to her by his friend, Ambassador Townshend,[5] urging her to stop insulting the Ministry because he knew their correspondence was opened by government spies. A little over a month later he again complained that she wrote so freely about Robert Harley that she must have 'already forgot' his request. He warned her that the government newspapers 'must be disagreeable as long as these two see and hear what 240 [Sarah] speaks and writes'[6] and 'whilst I am in the Service, I am in their powers, especially by the villainous way of printing, which stabs me to the heart.'

On 6 March 1711, Harley was almost stabbed to the heart. A French papist refugee, now government employee, named Anthonie de Guiscard, attempted to assassinate him by plunging a penknife into his chest. The minister was saved only by the protection of a thick gold brocade waistcoat. He could not have been more pleased. The fact that his attacker was a French papist undermined the Whigs' (and Sarah's) strongest charge against his predominantly Tory ministry as crypto-Catholic Jacobites. It gave him patriotic credentials. A broadsheet was promptly issued, which conveyed Parliament's congratulations on his lucky escape, and he was rewarded with the post of Lord Treasurer and the earldom of Oxford. The newly created Lord Oxford then made a gloating speech in the Commons[7] and, when Guiscard died in Newgate Prison, the gaoler arranged for the assassin's body to be pickled in a trough for people to view for tuppence a look.

Now he renewed his character assassination of the Marlboroughs. Despite her resignation, Sarah was not spared: the 'calumnies against me were so gross and yet so greedily devoured by the credulity of party rage'[8] that she found it hard to follow Maynwaring's advice and despise the malice of tongues.[9] Maynwaring also offered her Job as a dramatic role model, and among her papers she noted Job's cry when defeated by the fight against corruption: 'How long will you vex my soul & break me in pieces with words?'[10]

There was an enormous social distance between Grub Street and Sarah's world, yet in her attitudes and enthusiasms she was nearer to these writers than to many of her aristocratic friends, many of whom still believed, as the House of Commons had ruled in October 1696, that it was a breach of privilege for any peer or MP to be named in the press.[11] Only, perhaps, Maynwaring and her adversary, Lord Oxford, had equal respect for the damaging influence of the scribblers. As Charles Leslie, author of a newspaper called *The Rehearsal* wrote: '[T]he greatest part of the people do not read books, most of them cannot read at all. But they will gather together about one that can read, and listen to an *Observator* or *Review* (as I have seen them in the streets) . . .'[12] These non-voters were not supposed to be any kind of force in politics but, then, neither were women like Sarah.

Sarah saw the birth of the first distinct 'literary world', funded by publishers' sales rather than the Court. She also had the misfortune to be one of the most prominent celebrities during the establishment of the British newspaper industry. London's first daily paper had appeared as recently as 1702 (*The Daily Courant* with a circulation of only 800) but by 1712 there were twelve regular London papers and total annual sales amounted to 2.5 million copies.[13] Some of the most successful were Tory. They were filled with Court news, so that tittle-tattle about the Marlboroughs was forced down the national throat. The biggest stories of the decade were the war and the Sacheverell trial, both of which featured them and their friends at centre stage.

When Robert Harley had been allied to the Marlboroughs he had appointed the Whig Richard Steele, on Maynwaring's recommendation, as the ministry's 'Gazetteer'. Steele was dismissed in October 1710 with the change of Ministry. From this point, Harley had funded not only the official government *Gazette*, but also Defoe's *Review* and Swift's *Examiner* as a way to address specific arguments to followers of each party. Sarah was right in thinking there was a concerted campaign against the Marlboroughs, funded by the government that still employed her husband. 'I refer it to his own conscience,' she wrote of Oxford, 'to consider how much he has since contributed to raise those false & base aspersions that *The Examiner* has . . . published to the world.'[14] When someone complained to Oxford about the libels against Marlborough, she remembered that he had replied that the Duke 'must not mind them & that he himself was called dog every day in print . . . adding that "*The Examiner* himself had been upon him lately", which was so very ridiculous it made me laugh, since it is certain that all the lies in that paper are set about by himself.'[15] Elsewhere Oxford promised Marlborough that he and his colleagues in the Ministry shared his outrage at these insults: 'I abhor the practice as mean and disingenuous . . . [and] shall be very ready to take any part in suppressing them.'[16] While Marlborough was sceptical about this promise to censor, only Sarah understood Oxford's full responsibility for the libels.

Early in 1711, Swift was being invited to Oxford's 'Kitchen Cabinets' (informal dinners on Saturday nights before the real Cabinet met on Sunday) and over private drinks at the Apollo Club or the Rota they planned the next phase of the anti-Marlborough campaign. Swift was also involved in the October Club of High Church Tories. Before the 1710 elections this had been a small group that met at the Bell Tavern in King Street. Now Swift described it as 'a set of above a hundred Parliament men of the country who drink October beer at home and meet every evening at a tavern near Parliament to consult affairs and drive things to extreme against the Whigs . . .'[17] In many ways, now that Oxford was trying to build a bipartisan government, these harder-line Tory backbenchers were the greatest threat to his plans. Their chief grievance was taxation supporting the war, and St John was increasingly splitting away from Oxford to become this faction's leader.

On 1 February, *The Examiner* (no. 27) commented on some encomiums of the fallen Whigs:

When I saw the poor *Virtues* thus dealt at random, I thought the Disposers had flung their Names, like *Valentines into a Hat*, to be drawn as Fortune pleased, by the J[u]nto and their Friends. There, Crassus [Marlborough] drew *Liberality and Gratitude*; Fulvia [Sarah] *Humility* and *Gentleness* . . . the whole Set of discarded Statesmen celebrated by their judicious Hirelings for those very Qualities which their Admirers owned they chiefly wanted.

In the following week's edition,[18] Swift's 'Letter to Crassus' focused on Marlborough's perceived avarice and arrogance. Throughout February there were further passing slights against the Marlboroughs in *The Examiner* and issue 32 contained an allegory which, in allusion to the *Aeneid*'s depiction of 'Rumour' as a giant female bird of prey, depicted 'Faction' as a Whig woman who 'by her perpetual talking filled all the places with disturbance and confusion' and 'frequented Public Assemblies, where she sat in the shape of an obscene, ominous Bird, ready to prompt her Friends as they spoke'. The next substantial *Examiner* attack, however, came on 25 April 1711 (no. 38):

The Whigs are every day cursing the ungovernable rage, the haughty pride and insatiable covetousness of a certain person as the cause of their fall; and are apt to tell their thoughts, that one single removal might have set all things right. But the interests of that single person were found, upon experience, so complicated and woven with the rest, by love, by awe, by marriage, by alliance, that they would rather confound heaven and earth than dissolve such a union.

Finally, on 2 May (no. 39), Swift returned to Sarah's supposed financial corruption, referring in passing to how the misappropriation of funds had not been 'altogether neglected by the other sex; of which, on the contrary, I could produce an instance that would make ours blush to be so far outdone'.

The quality of Sarah's enemies was a perverse compliment to her, which she acknowledged in later years when she looked back and wished Swift had been recruited to write for her side.[19] When she read that he had been made a dean, she commented that he had earned it 'by the honest paper called The Examiner, which I should have thought the vilest bundle of lies that ever were invented'.[20] Oxford, however, was growing nervous of Swift's pen as he became more 'St Johnian'.[21] He was removed from editorship of *The Examiner* in June 1711.

Surprisingly, the person to whom Swift and Oxford handed over the editorship was Mrs Delariviere Manley. Her novels had long featured in the advertisements carried by the paper, with Sarah's resignation led to a 1711 reissue of *Queen Zarah* and a new volume of *The New Atalantis*. Swift had written to Joseph Addison about Mrs Manley's writing in the most insulting terms. It was, he said, 'as if she had about two thousand epithets and fine words packed up in a bag, and that she pulled them out by handfuls, and strewed them on her paper, where about once in five hundred times they happen to be right'.²² However, he later said Mrs Manley's *Examiner* attack on Sarah was by far the best edition of that paper.²³

It was published on 19 July 1711 (no. 51). It used the character Swift had given her, of Fulvia, the classical example of a wife's evil influence. In Mrs Manley's usual style, it was an imaginative scene rather than an essay, describing the 'House of Pride' (Blenheim) as an Ozymandias-style ruin, a 'dazzling, unwieldy structure . . . built amidst the Tears and Groans of a People harassed with a lingering War . . .' The author imagined herself attending the Court of the goddess Pride there, her eye caught by

a Lady, who with Precipitation broke through the Crowd and made directly to the Throne. Though past her Meridian, her Bloom was succeeded by so graceful an Air that Youth could scarce make her more desirable: Her fair hair was tucked under a Tiara of Jewels made in the fashion of a CORONET. If her Beauty prepossessed us to her Advantage, we were not less terrified in beholding the Company she was in: On one side marched Envy, lashing her with Whips and Snakes . . . Her other Supporter was Wrath . . . his Body half exposed, the rest clothed with a Robe stained with Blood, and torn by his own Fury, which was so fierce he could not restrain it sometimes from falling upon himself. His Breath was incessantly applied to the Lady's Spleen and Brain . . .

In response to *The Examiner* and other attacks, Sarah's friends – Maynwaring, Samuel Garth and Joseph Addison – founded *The Whig-Examiner*, later *The Medley*, over a meeting at White's Chocolate House or the St James's Coffee-house. Its articles consistently associated the Tories with the Pretender's return. When Garth became too busy as a physician to continue, he recommended John Oldmixon to take his place. Oldmixon later wrote *Memoirs of the Press, Historical and Political, for Thirty Years past, from 1710–1740* (1742), which he dedicated to Sarah, who had probably funded the *Whig-Examiner/Medley*, including Oldmixon's salary.²⁴ So, after June 1711, the two most prominent journals representing the Whigs and the Tories were backed and run by women –

Sarah and Mrs Manley. This was an amazing situation in an age when women were normally forbidden to be public disputants.[25] Marlborough famously snapped that he wished 'the devil had *The Medley* and *The Examiner* together',[26] but his complaints about press attacks were undermined by the fact that his own wife was invested up to her elbows in printer's ink.

When Mrs Manley had to suspend *The Examiner* temporarily at the end of July, Maynwaring stopped publishing the answering *Medley*. In the latter part of the year both editors fell seriously ill, which extended the truce. But Oxford wanted a more permanent way to silence the opposition press. There had been no effective state censorship since the lapse of the Licensing Act in 1695, despite Anne's attempts to revive it in 1702 and 1704. In 1712, therefore, he introduced the Stamp Act, to raise revenue for a new government lottery by taxing publications by the page, but incidentally outpricing certain non-governmental papers. Ultimately *The Observator* and *The Medley* would both be forced to close by this financial pressure.

On 14 May 1711, probably at Anne's request, Marlborough wrote to tell Sarah to vacate her lodgings in St James's Palace, specifically requesting she leave behind the marble fireplaces she had installed there.[27] Marlborough House was not yet ready, so Sarah moved into Montagu House with her estranged daughter Mary while awaiting its completion. Mary must have been particularly miserable to have her mother staying, given that she already had her mad mother-in-law (who believed she was the Queen of England) in the house. The Montagus were also in financial difficulty and Marlborough had recently advised them to sell up and move somewhere smaller. Luckily for the Marlboroughs, who were now without a London base, they had avoided doing this.[28]

The first hiccup in the move came when Sarah asked the Queen for somewhere to store her furniture. Anne refused, telling Sarah that she could 'take a place for ten shillings a week to put em in'.[29] 'I was forced to content myself with the small diversion of going to Mrs Cooper,' Sarah wrote, referring to one of her tenants on the land at St James's who could be relied upon to spread whatever Sarah said back to Abigail and Anne. Mischievously, Sarah described how Mrs Cooper suspected she was being teased: 'When I commended so much her Majesty's wisdom and justice, she looked as if she was not entirely convinced of that . . .' Then, when Sarah did move from the Palace lodgings, she took the door-key with her and sent back a message that they 'might have a key for ten shillings' if they wanted one.[30]

Anne accused Sarah of having 'gutted' her rooms at St James's Palace and refused to continue paying for Blenheim after such an insult. Maynwaring reported to Sarah in July on a conversation between James Craggs and Oxford in which Oxford quoted Anne as saying she would not build a house for one who had 'taken away the very slabs out of the chimneys, thrown away the keys, and said they might buy more for 10 shillings'.[31] Maynwaring suspected that this was a plot to make Marlborough blame his wife for the Treasury ceasing to pay for Blenheim.

Sarah insisted she had removed nothing 'but glasses and brass locks of my own buying and which I never heard that anybody left for those that were to come after them'. She obtained a letter from the Palace housekeeper to vouch that all was as she had found it, and so in effect won this battle. Her greater victory was in settling the matter so swiftly that *The Examiner* was unable to print the story.

Despite signed statements from impartial household servants that everything she took was her own, the story of Sarah stripping her Palace apartments has survived through history as evidence of her pettiness and greed. An undated note in Sarah's hand reflected: 'I foresee the world will interpret whatever I do that may look discontented & particular to my having lost the Queen's favour . . .'[32]

Marlborough was furious when he heard that Anne had refused to sign the warrant for continuation of the building works. Construction came to a complete halt in June 1712. Amid the incomplete 'ruins', someone scratched the following verse, a reference to the Marlboroughs' principality of Mindelheim, on a window-pane:

> A German Princess once Graced this Isle
> & now a German Princess owns this Pile.
> Alike in virtue, goodness & Estate
> And it's hoped in time, will share the other's Fate.[33]

As Christopher Wren was Oxford's friend, tensions between Sarah and her architect on Marlborough House had inevitably arisen. The Duke had written to her in early April that 'I am obliged to you for the trouble you give yourself in taking care to be as little cheated as possible. I thought you had relied so entirely on Sir Christopher Wren that you had been at ease in that point, but he is very old, and very few are to be trusted.'[34] Now in May he worried that she would move too soon into the newly built outhouses at Marlborough House, which might be damp and 'unwholesome'.[35] (The exceptionally modern plumbing of the building, which would pump Thames river water into the house at a cost of ten pounds a year, had not yet been perfected.) Sarah described what later led to her firing Wren from the project: 'I began to find that this man, from his age, was imposed upon by the workmen and that the prices for all things were much too high for ready money and sure pay, upon which I took the finishing part upon myself.'[36]

Sarah was eager to move because of growing tension between her and her daughter. In early May, while she was staying at Windsor Lodge, Sarah had received a letter informing her of a quarrel between Lady Hervey (later Lady Bristol) and Mary, of which she strongly disapproved. Lady Hervey had discovered that Mary was laughing at her behind her back. Sarah said she could not sleep for worrying about Mary's reputation after hearing this account of such rudeness 'to a woman that you & your sisters have been few days out of her house this winter'. Perhaps conscious of how the 'disagreeable noise' closely echoed that concerning her own behaviour to the Queen, Sarah stated that though she well understood the strain of being obliged to call on ladies one did not like, 'I think it has a very ill air to laugh or speak ill of anybody one is much with.'

Mary's reply was a self-vindication, much as her mother would have offered if similarly accused. Lady Hervey had started the quarrel, she protested, and if she laughed behind her back it was only to try to make light of the other's wounding aggression. However, she admitted that she had not been completely innocent and was 'mightily ashamed of quarrelling', knowing how her mother disapproved.37

Sarah showed her sensitivity to the power of gossip. Even if Mary was in the right, she wrote, 'you may assure yourself that there is not a house in town where two or three people are together but it has been the entertainment to repeat what she said of you, and there is no doubt but it is the discourse of every coffee-house . . .' The way to avoid scandal, Sarah advised, was 'not to affect to be every day of your life in a public place'. She 'tenderly' reminded Mary of the warning she gave 'when you walked every night in St James's Park with a train of fops after you' and criticised her for sitting at parties in rows of ladies 'as if it were a market for sale'. She went on, 'You should not talk as if it would kill you to be at a reasonable time of the year in the country with your children or with a mother that would always endeavour to make any place of hers easy to you . . .' The oft-remarked similarity between Mary and her mother – Queen Anne once commented that Mary was 'just like her mother'38 – comes to mind with Sarah's concluding admonishment:

[Y]ou have a way of snapping people, which makes you many enemies & that (I dare say) the best friends you have see & wish otherwise for your own sake: You have certainly a great deal of quickness & entertaining humour, and for the pleasure of that you are apt to make answers very shocking and to love to show people are in the wrong . . . and if you had a little more softness in your manner I should not wish for any other alteration in you.

Sarah kept up the family front, however, by writing to Lady

Hervey and regretting that she must break off relations with an old friend to stand by her daughter's reputation. She hinted that she thought the argument had probably started due to Mary's 'giddiness', so Mary was probably more annoyed than pleased when Sarah sent her a copy of the letter.

In July, Sarah left Montagu House to spend the rest of the summer at Holywell.39 She depicted this as a season of 'otium', her days composed of reading, contemplation and gardening. Maynwaring complimented her on having inner resources that were 'the true reason why you can better bear to be alone than anyone I ever yet knew'.40

Sarah's claims to have disavowed the gaudy town in preference for the quiet glade, however, were not entirely convincing. She was not just sitting in St Albans, reading the 'prints' over breakfast and scoffing at the puppets on the political stage like any other country lady: rather, she was using her home as headquarters of a new opposition clique. Maynwaring, Sidney and Francis Godolphin, James Craggs and his son, and the young Robert Walpole were all house guests that summer, and Sarah also saw plenty of Lord and Lady Cowper, her neighbours at Cole Green. She discussed with Maynwaring the content of each forthcoming *Medley*, supplied Bishop Burnet with material for his *History*, urged Dr Hare to write his reply to Mrs Manley's scurrilous attacks on the Marlboroughs in *The Examiner*, and continued drafting her own memoirs. Nothing could have been further from her husband's wish that she should tend the garden.

Sarah was also busy rescuing the Bank of England from Tory hands. Lord Oxford had a longstanding animosity to the Bank, based on his embarrassment at the failure of his rival project, the Land Bank, in 1696.41 Now Sarah caught wind of a Tory plan to assume directorship of the Bank of England and persuaded the shareholders to attend the meeting of directors to exercise their votes. In this way she managed to stave off the takeover, forcing Oxford to turn elsewhere for funds. One observer, Arabella Pulteney, wrote to her friend John Molesworth describing how

Sarah controlled the election of directors with her own wealth:

Upon the last election of the Governors of the Bank, [Sarah] appeared herself to bribe the electors for the persons chosen, who were most of them Whigs to her taste. But not knowing how it would go, the night before she was at the opera and had there a list brought her of the candidates' names, and those she disliked she scratched out and others nominated, and carried it by her management.[42]

By July, Sarah was so frustrated at her husband's trusting and subservient attitude towards the new Ministry (they 'must endeavour to make 'em think abroad all was well again between him and the Queen,' he said)[43] that she sent their family physician and friend, Dr Samuel Garth, over to Flanders to inform him of suspected Tory plots she dared not describe in letters. Garth was only a year younger than Sarah and, like Maynwaring, had a lively wit which, combined with a reputation for a well-developed social conscience, endeared him to her. Dr Johnson described him as 'social and liberal'[44] and, though he converted to Catholicism on his deathbed, for most of his life he was as sceptical as Sarah about organised religion. He was a member of the Kit-Cat Club, and author of a popular poem called 'The Dispensary' (1699), which satirised his medical colleagues. Like Godolphin, Garth was taken to Sarah's heart with a warmth and loyalty that he never forfeited. He once said to Lady Lechmere, one of Sarah's card-playing companions, that 'though the Duchess of Marlborough had many enemies, all of them were people who did not know her'.[45] A quick survey suggests this statement to be generally true, though by 1711 Abigail, Anne, and Sarah's daughters Henrietta and Mary were notable exceptions.

On 5 and 6 August, in a move of exceptional strategic brilliance, Marlborough wrongfooted Marshal Villars and passed the supposedly impenetrable 'Ne Plus Ultra' lines, so that he was in a position to besiege Bouchain. This final burst of military energy was belied by the doleful letters the sixty-two-year-old Duke was writing home, claiming that he wished only to 'enjoy two or three years of yours and my children's company' before he died.

While the siege was still under way, Matthew Prior was in Paris with a warrant from the Queen and Secretary St John to conduct secret unilateral peace negotiations with the French intermediary, Abbé Gaultier. They did not stay secret from the Marlboroughs for long – a customs official named John Macky discovered Prior trying to re-enter Britain undercover and sent word to Marlborough. Soon a broadsheet was published in London entitled *An excellent New Song, called Mat's Peace, or the Downfall of Trade. To the Good Old Tune of Green-sleeves* (1711), and a reference to Prior's trip was made in a pamphlet called *Bouchain* written by Francis Hare or Arthur Maynwaring. No doubt Sarah encouraged whoever wrote it, despite Marlborough's instructions for her and her clique to remain silent. It not only celebrated his military skill, but answered *The Examiner's* Fulvia attack on Sarah. Either Maynwaring or Sarah was also responsible for arranging the London publication of a sermon arguing the evil of a premature peace deal that Dr Hare had preached to Marlborough's men in the field on 9 September.[46]

By 27 September, three preliminary articles of a peace treaty had been signed, of which two were secret and contravened treaties Britain had concluded with its allies under the Whig Ministries, notably the promise to the Dutch of a fortified barrier, the 'No Peace Without Spain' principle having long been unrealistic. Philip V was recognised as King of Spain. The terms of the preliminary articles, which had originated in Whitehall but were made to appear as if they came from Versailles, seemed to Marlborough a flagrant betrayal of the Austrians, Dutch and Germans in return for commercial advantage. In one of Sarah's unpublished memoirs she drew a parallel between Anne's breaking of an international 'contract' between allies and the dissolution of the two women's 'ties' of friendship.[47] Just as Mrs Manley used private sleaze as an allegory for public betrayals, so Sarah inversely gave public actions a private moral dimension. In her published memoirs she observed that 'A peace was so necessary to the preservation of the new ministers' power that it must be had at any rate.'[48]

On 11 October,[49] Marlborough thanked Sarah for news of the peace negotiations, but asked her never again to mention this or the government in her letters, as he did not want to be associated with her complaints. This letter contained the first hint that he might choose to retire in 'a good climate' rather than in England, where Blenheim remained uninhabitable. Later that month, Sarah moved into the main building of Marlborough House.[50] Around the corner, at Leicester House, the Austrian ambassador, Count Gallas, was using his property's diplomatic immunity as cover for the printing of pamphlets and *The Daily Courant*, which were explicitly opposed to the peace talks. There was conjecture, probably well founded, that Sarah and Maynwaring were involved in this seditious activity, for which Gallas was barred from Court.[51]

Oxford and St John also banned a midnight street procession Sarah's Whig friends intended to hold on the anniversary of Elizabeth I's birthday (17 November). Traditionally a date for fervent displays of Protestant nationalism, the Tories feared that the celebrations would be hijacked and turned into a riotous demonstration and victory parade for the returning Duke of Marlborough. Mrs Manley wrote *A True Relation of the Several Facts and Circumstances of the intended Riot and Tumult on Queen Elizabeth's Birthday* (1711) to justify the government ban, describing how they knew of plans for effigies to be burned by mobs, including ones of Abigail, Sacheverell, the Pope, the Pretender and one, designed by Sarah's daughter Mary, of Henry St John. Manley referred to Sarah as the 'German Princess' responsible for funding all these preparations (in fact it was mainly the Duke of Kent's money) and ended by accusing Lord Wharton of planning a violent revolution by which Marlborough hoped to seize the Crown.

When Marlborough returned to London on 19 November 1711, he brought with him Baron von Bothmar, the unofficial representative of the Elector, the future George I. The Dutch had strengthened his resolve to oppose his own countrymen's peace deal and Bothmar's presence allowed him to stand in opposition without appearing too 'singular'. The time had come for the confrontation with his Cabinet colleagues that Sarah had always known was inevitable. Once again, her instincts about their enemies and her predictions as to their intentions proved more accurate than his. As Marlborough had once written of Sarah to Anne: 'I must do her judgement that right, as to say that she has foreseen some things which I thought would never have happened; I mean concerning the behaviour of some in your service.'[52]

St John had been soothing Marlborough with assurances that he was being kept fully informed of negotiations with the French, while all the time secretly sponsoring Swift's vilification campaign. On 27 November, Swift published *The Conduct of the Allies*, a propaganda masterpiece that made credible the charges then being investigated by the Commissioners of Public Accounts: that Marlborough was guilty of peculation – embezzlement of public funds. Swift depicted the War of Spanish Succession as pointless, and even the start of the war was attributed to the prevalence of 'private motives' (in other words, the Marlboroughs' relationship with Anne), even though St John himself had been Marlborough's aide during those early years. It showed the conflict as a conspiracy of the new City bankers whose 'perpetual harvest is war'. The article reversed some of the basic patriotic assumptions of the past decade, allowing the Tories to snatch back the rhetoric of the public interest. Sarah featured only in passing, when Anne was described as having been driven out of Windsor Castle: 'pursuant to the advice of Solomon, who tells us, *It is better to dwell in a corner of a housetop than with a brawling woman in a wide house.*'[53] For almost the first time, the true shape and scale of the conflict between Anne's female favourites was revealed to the reading public: it was about the morality of the European wars.

The Conduct of the Allies did not come out of the blue; it had a number of precursors. The Earl of Oxford was the probable co-author, with Lord Strafford, of *An Account of a Dream at Harwich* (1708),[54] which had depicted the country as drugged by the Marlboroughs, and said that if people ever dared to take their fingers out of their ears or open their eyes, the Whigs would immediately pop sugar-plums into their mouths. Sarah was described as a Medusa-witch:

[H]er chin and nose turning up, her eyes glaring like lightning, blasted all she had power over with strange diseases. Out of her nostrils came a sulphurous smoke, and out of her mouth flames of fire. Her hair was frizzled, and adorned with spoils of ruined people . . . her garment was all stained with tears and blood . . . She cast her eyes often with rage and fury on that bright appearance I have described [Anne], over whom, having no force, she tossed her head with disdain and glared about on her votaries, till we saw several possessed with [by] her.

In contrast to its precursors, *The Conduct of the Allies* was deceptively simple. It appeared merely to recount facts. When Dr Johnson later called it a 'performance of very little ability', a listener protested: 'Surely, Sir, you must allow it has strong facts.' Dr Johnson, a Tory who agreed with those 'facts', replied: 'Swift has told what he had to tell distinctly enough, but that is all. He had to count to ten, and he has counted it right.'

The Conduct of the Allies went through five editions in two months, selling at least 11,000 copies.[55] Swift took care to ensure that it was delivered into great houses across the country, to reach its natural rural supporters. Like the Sacheverell trial, this publication focused on existing resentment and roused the dormant political weight of the landed interest.

The growth of the military-fiscal State was the key political issue of Anne's reign. There was a burgeoning national debt (£50 million)[56] and the bulk of tax revenue was spent on servicing it. After 1712, most of it would be funded debt (long-term borrowing) rather than exchequer bills, and the largest category of funded debt would be fixed-term annuities held by private individuals, mostly Whigs.[57] Godolphin had floated the majority of these annuities between 1704 and 1708, and Sarah had been a major investor, benefiting from the high interest rates – up to 14 per cent – paid by the government. She and the 'monied men' did not profiteer from the war in a literal sense, but they had developed a vested interest in its continuation. While Oxford's ministry was recklessly issuing paper currency, inflation rose, and commodity taxes proliferated; an economic recession in 1710–11 escalated opposition to the war.

In truth, the burden on the landed gentry was not so great. The high rate of Land Tax mainly hit those in the south, and most landowners passed it on to their tenants.[58] Also the tax was collected by non-professionals and easily evaded. The perception among tax-paying landowners, however, was that a quarter of government revenue was spent on hiring foreign troops; that the first loan to a foreign government – a Bank of England loan to Prince Eugene – was being floated on the London market;[59] that the Whigs had sabotaged the peace talks in 1709; and that Marlborough gave little public indication of wanting the war to end. Historians today generally endorse the view that a peace deal was long overdue, and Marlborough appeared the biggest obstacle to those who believed this at the time. He had changed the cultural and religious landscape of Europe by containing French expansion and had laid the foundation for the British hegemony that would in later decades turn into a colonial empire. Even his enemies intuited the immensity of his achievement and knew that he had to be personally discredited before any peace deal would be accepted by Parliament.

The Conduct of the Allies was probably the last time that the legitimacy of public deficit spending would be questioned. It blurred the boundary between abuses of the system and a widespread distrust of the system itself, so that anxiety about a change in the role of government was converted into suspicions about Marlborough. The British public discovered that for some time Oxford had been holding charges of peculation over Marlborough's head – perhaps the true explanation of why he had not resigned earlier.

The rest of Europe was shocked at the British government's attack on its greatest hero. At first it was rumoured that Marlborough would take libel action against Swift.[60] Then it became clear he would try to fight fire with fire. On behalf of the Elector, Baron von Bothmar published an article in *The Daily Courant* supporting Marlborough and declaring the Hanoverians against the peace as a betrayal of England's Allies. It was a warning to anyone with a longer-term view and, to Marlborough's enemies, confirmation that his loyalties were focused overseas. Encouraged by Bothmar's support, and reunited among themselves, Whig MPs protested against *The Conduct of the Allies* in Parliament during early December.

The crisis of conscience for the Whig party came when it realised it could buy the support of Nottingham, the elder statesman of Toryism, by letting him pass, finally, the old Tory chestnut: an Occasional Conformity Act. The votes of his followers would tip the balance in the House of Lords, allowing rejection of the peace proposals.[61] Earlier that same year, the Whig party had rejected a Bill introduced by Oxford's ministry that obstructed the naturalisation of Protestant refugees from the Continent, but now they were willing to betray the dissenters. Like many other Whigs, Sarah must have felt torn in half by the opposition created between her two, previously compatible core beliefs: the war against the French and the principle of religious toleration. Ultimately, defence of her husband's good name tipped the balance and she celebrated the deal with Nottingham, erasing all the insults she had aimed at him in earlier drafts of her memoirs.

On 11 December, therefore, after Anne had opened the Parliamentary session with a pointed condemnation of 'those who delight in war', the lugubrious Nottingham made his speech in support of continued fighting, threatening that those who promoted a dishonourable peace would be impeached under the Hanoverians. Then Marlborough stood up to speak and called on the Queen to admit that the charges of peculation against him were slander. He stated that he, too, wanted peace and had only ever followed orders, but insisted that for Britain to make a separate deal with France now would jeopardise the 'safety and liberties of Europe'. His supporters won the vote, defeating the peace proposals by 62 votes to 54. Sarah recorded how Shrewsbury, who still pretended to Marlborough that he supported him, was conveniently ill on the day of the House of Lords' vote so did not 'declare himself one way or the other'. Similarly, she believed that Somers had betrayed Marlborough although she 'had been a martyr for him and the Whig cause'.[62]

Oxford and St John met with Swift that night at Abigail's lodgings, where they resolved that Marlborough had to be dismissed. Swift immediately published a piece of doggerel against the turncoat Nottingham, which has rightly ended up in the crowded Augustan remainder bin, but includes this on the Marlboroughs:

> The D[uke] show'd me all his fine House; and the D[uches]s
> From her Closet brought out a full Purse in her Clutches
> I talk'd of a Peace, and they both gave a start,
> His G[race] swore by [God], and her G[race] let a F[ar]t:
> My long old-fashion'd Pocket was presently crammed:
> And sooner than Vote for a Peace I'll be d[am]n'd.[63]

The charges against Marlborough consisted of two parts: first, that he had taken bribes from the army bread contractors (generally Spanish Jewish firms such as that owned by Solomon & Moses Medina – leading one satirist to refer to Marlborough's 'iniquitous Contract with a Jew')[64] and, second, misappropriating a 2.5 per cent deduction in salaries paid to foreign troops. The accusation that he had raked off a percentage of his soldiers' bread money was particularly offensive, as Marlborough prided himself on having improved his men's rations, but Sir Solomon Medina testified against him, claiming he had given Marlborough some 332,000 guilders for his own use.[65] Over a quarter of a million pounds was at stake in the second charge, but Marlborough insisted he had not pocketed this but spent it on intelligence work – a worthwhile investment, considering how much of his strategy had depended on tricking his French opponents, but it was unverifiable because he had kept no public records of this spending. In notes Sarah made on Gibson's *Memoirs of Queen*

Anne: being a complete supplement to the history of her reign . . .
(1729), she wrote that it was a blatant injustice to prosecute a man
'that had gained five battles, taken 24 strong towns besieged and
16 strong towns that surrendered without siege'[66] when the 2.5
per cent had been authorised by the Queen in a warrant dating
from July 1702, and was still being allowed to Marlborough's
successor in command, the Duke of Ormonde.

Oxford's brother and brother-in-law now held key posts in
the government auditors' office so were well placed to launch
the inquiry into Marlborough's accounts. Anne's duplicity was
evident: she claimed to deplore the investigations while actively
encouraging them.

The Commissioners' findings revealed 'huge shortfalls',[67] and
led to full impeachment proceedings. Marlborough was later
exonerated under George I[68] and today the truth remains uncertain, given these contradictory, highly partisan audits. For some
reason – perhaps a no-smoke-without-fire attitude, perhaps guilt-
by-association, given that some of Marlborough's closest colleagues did embezzle[69] – most historians have taken the earlier
conviction as the more reliable finding. In her published memoirs,
however, the later exoneration allowed Sarah to dismiss the whole
matter as having been 'a frivolous and groundless complaint'.[70]

During the winter of 1711–12, however, Sarah and her family
could not escape the humiliation of the proceedings. The Commissioners' report had been circulated just before the end of the
session, so everyone had plenty of time to gossip about it before
the trial in the new year. When Marlborough made his last visit
to Court on 30 December, 'Nobody hardly took notice of him,'
Swift wrote in his diary.[71] As for Sarah, the line between a head
held high in an effort to maintain dignity and one held high in
disdain was too fine for many observers, and her moral stamina –
or certainty in her own beliefs – made many hate her. As usual, she
regarded this season of obloquy as a time to test others' characters,
and wrote approvingly of one Whig friend: 'He owned me when
I was under a hurdle.'[72]

Marlborough's stiff upper lip and Sarah's haughty demeanour

concealed the reality of their mortification. On the streets their carriage ran the gauntlet of jeering mobs, and stones were thrown at the windows of Marlborough House. Gloating allegories began to appear on a daily basis, such as *The Ungrateful World, or; The Hard Case of a Great G[enera]l* (1712), in which they were depicted as a pair of ants, or *The Triumph of Envy: Or, The Vision of Shylock the Jew* (1712) in which the association between the Marlboroughs, the Whigs, and therefore the monied interest, including Jewish lenders and businessmen, was again turned to insult.

A performance of Farquhar's *Recruiting Officer* was interrupted by a song about Marlborough's avarice, a character trait which many attributed to Sarah's influence.[73]

An anecdote circulated about an officer who had once been despatched by the Duke in Flanders to Sarah in London to request a better commission; Sarah supposedly sent him away to find a £1,000 bribe. When Marlborough heard what had happened he apparently laughed, said he agreed to the price, and gave the man the money to go back and 'try her again'.[74] What sounds like a private joke between the couple, later twisted by Tory slander, has been repeated in biography after biography as evidence of Sarah's greed.

However, one of Sarah's biographers, Louis Kronenberger, wrote that the couple's avarice 'has only been exaggerated, not misrepresented'[75] and referred to evidence of Sarah haggling 'over every penny' at Blenheim until the work there was halted.[76] The couple shared an insecurity about money, but this was not greed. Sarah's precise financial management was merely an anomaly in an age when it was considered vulgar to be careful. Added to this was Sarah's terror of debt and bankruptcy. This was really a fear of being beholden to others and can only be explained by her wider sense that her life had been the property of others, that money alone freed her and her family from the vagaries of favour. She valued her personal assets in proportion to her own sense that her talents were undervalued.

In a note from April 1711, Sarah claimed that she had only

pushed Anne so hard in 1710, using the threat of publication of her memoirs as leverage, because she was frightened that if her husband lost his employments he would not have enough money to support so great a family,[77] this even though Marlborough's annual income was £40,000 (almost £3 million in today's money) and she herself was one of the richest private citizens in Europe.[78] It was the unreasonable extent of Sarah's worries that, understandably, made her seem miserly.

There is a long list of household goods that Sarah confiscated from a certain Mrs Reeves (perhaps a tenant) for non-payment of debts, right down to her 'pestle and mortar, a chocolate pot, two pair of snuffers', which appears ruthless in light of her own wealth.[79] On the other hand, there is ample evidence of Sarah seldom evicting a tenant for non-payment if she believed the poverty was 'honest', as during the agricultural depression of the 1730s,[80] so perhaps there was more to Mrs Reeves's story than the inventory can tell us.

Sarah annotated her household accounts to explain the reasoning behind the minutiae of her frugal spending. She listed the wages of every servant, emphasising why she had paid more than the norm in some cases and less in others. She paid the stable boys by results ('Nobody's horses look better than mine') and she noted how often the other servants had their clothing expenses repaid, adding that they should do their own laundry.[81] Elsewhere, turning the insults hurled at her against others, she accused Somerset of miserliness for giving his grandson's nurses nothing better than a sea-coal fire in winter.[82]

It was, therefore, presumably, a proper log fire into which Marlborough hurled his letter of dismissal from Anne when it arrived in January.[83] In one version of Sarah's memoirs she remarked that, upon receiving this letter, her husband's emotion broke through his usual 'unexampled calmness'.[84] At the same time, the Queen created twelve new Tory peers, including Abigail's husband, to compensate for Nottingham's switch and to allow Oxford to regain control of the House of Lords. A vote against Marlborough was held on 24 January 1712. Adam de

Cardonnell, Marlborough's Secretary, who had also been the MP for Southampton since 1701, was expelled from the House of Commons for having personally received the bribe deemed to have passed from Medina to Marlborough.

In her published memoirs, Sarah quoted in full her husband's reply to his letter of dismissal. In it he claimed to have been given no opportunity to refute the 'false and malicious' charges of the Commissioners and justified his refusal to attend Oxford's Cabinet meetings by saying that Oxford was betraying Anne to France, a nation 'destructive to your Majesty'.[85]

Prince Eugene, Marlborough's old war comrade, arrived in London too late to help him keep his post. He went to stay with Gallas at Leicester House, but appeared in public with the Marlboroughs to demonstrate his support, first at a ball held at Portland House by the son of King William's favourite. Sarah also planned a ball in the Prince's honour at Marlborough House. Like a scorned woman who wants her ex-lover to see her looking beautiful and laughing in the company of others, the intention was to appear merry and show off Sarah's new house. During this time, Lediard described Sarah as living with 'an uncommon Splendour, Liberality and Magnificence'.[86] The newspapers depicted this ball, which was scheduled to take place on Anne's birthday, as a snub to the Palace, and even hinted that it was the cover for a revolutionary plot. Sarah feared the stories aimed 'to bring a mob upon us to pull down our house' and the ball was cancelled. Instead Prince Eugene went to receive a diamond sword from the Queen. Sarah had to make do with inviting a few friends to watch her granddaughter dance, which, she wrote sarcastically to a friend, 'I believe may be done without any danger to the State.'[87]

On Grub Street it was now open season on the Marlboroughs. One anonymous work, *The Duchess of M[arlborough]'s CREED* (1712), focused on Sarah's belief in religious toleration, insulting her in terms she probably took as complimentary: 'I believe in the Assembly of Divines, in NO Catholic Church, Religions or

Ceremonies: I acknowledge Benj. H[oa]dly and G B[ur]net: I look for a Long Parliament, with the downfall of Episcopacy; Toleration without End; no Surplice; but a Cloak everlasting. Amen.'

Another anonymous broadsheet, *The Petticoat Plotters, or the D[uche]ss of M[arlboroug]h's Club* (1712), satirised a new society for Whig wives, who resolved to meet every Saturday night and chose Sarah as their figurehead, 'though they did not expect that her G[race] would honour them with her presence'. A poem called *Rufinus or the Favourite* (1712), meanwhile, depicted Sarah as a vengeful, raging monster 'With Lightning in her Eyes, and Poison in her Tongue'.

In February a fictional biography of Marlborough was published: *The History of Prince Mirabel's Infancy, Rise and Disgrace* (1712). Taking the lead from Mrs Manley, it revealed Sarah (Jenibella) as the cause of both his promotion and dismissal, but was otherwise sympathetic to Marlborough. The following month there appeared *The Perquisite-Monger; or the Rise and Fall of Ingratitude . . .* (1712),[88] ostensibly an answer to *Prince Mirabel* but actually a far more slanderous satire. Its oriental setting allowed Anne's Maids of Honour and serving women to be depicted as a lesbian seraglio, where Sarah (Zaraida): 'a Person of a mean Extraction, but who had by the Subtlety of her Mother, that was a noted humble Servant to the Pleasures of certain Great Men and her own Inclinations, so wormed herself into the Confidence of her Mistress as to be in the highest Esteem with her.'[89]

Richard Steele's defence of Marlborough, *The Englishman's Thanks to the Duke of Marlborough* (1712),[90] was immediately answered by another *Examiner*[91] attack, mocking Steele's honouring of Marlborough above the Queen herself: 'I am thinking that if the Duchess happened to be a greater Favourite to this Critic than the Duke, the Honour in the last resort must have then lain at her Grace's Feet.' The apparently derisory possibility was followed by an emotive description of the poor foot-soldiers who had risked their lives then been deprived of their pay by Marlborough.

On 27 May 1712, Earl Poulett, speaking for the Tories in the Commons, echoed Swift by suggesting that Marlborough had murdered his men for profit. Marlborough challenged him to a duel, which was only prevented when Sarah told Lord Dartmouth, who promptly arrested Poulett for his own safety.[92]

Even Daniel Defoe seemed to return to Oxford's payroll and contradict his 1711 answer to *The Conduct of the Allies* by attacking the fallen Marlboroughs. He was probably the author of *No Queen or No General* (1712),[93] which concentrated on the Whig Junto's sabotage of the peace talks in 1709. Defoe gives a first-hand account of how the Queen had wept at the failure of the negotiations, which had 'seized too much upon Her vitals', making her sick with worry about her people.

Had Sarah sought to preserve her interest with Anne, Defoe argued, no one could have supplanted her, 'and while she had kept her hold, that Ministry [Godolphin's] could never have fallen'. Blaming Sarah as 'entirely the cause of all the unhappy Breaches' in the government, Defoe depicted Anne as a pacifist wise enough to see through the oft-repeated myth that within a year the Allies would be at the gates of Paris. 'It frequently occurred to the Queen that Violence was used in several Parts of Her Kingdoms, to force Men into the Service; that Men were dragged by force out of the Arms and Embraces of their Wives and Children, who were often left in a starving Condition for want of their Labour . . .' Defoe's later *Memoirs of the Conduct of Her Late Majesty and Her last Ministry, relating to the Separate Peace with France* (1715) excused Anne and her ministers for their duplicity and blamed Sarah for the downfall of her husband in order to preserve the author's high opinion of his fallen hero. Both Whig and Tory papers thus depicted Marlborough as having been stabbed in the back by his wife, not his colleagues.

Sarah was still nervous of publishing her own self-defence, and Robert Walpole eventually persuaded her not to publish at all. Her manuscript was nevertheless circulating among an expanding circle of friends and once was almost printed without her consent. John Oldmixon read it in 1712 when it was 'surreptitiously copied' and brought to him for publication. Though he recognised it as genuine, he resisted 'trafficking with that Manuscript' and returned the bootleg copy to Sunderland.[94]

In 1712, Swift also began writing his *History of the Four Last Years of the Queen*, which Lord Oxford later persuaded him not to publish. Oxford had not let his zealous defender into all the secrets of his Ministry's dealings with France, and was probably embarrassed to read a history written in ignorance of what might later come to light. It first appeared posthumously in 1758, and taught a new generation of readers this story of Sarah:

It is to her the Duke is chiefly indebted for his greatness and his fall . . . [T]hree furies reigned in her breast, the most mortal enemies of all softer passions: which were, sordid avarice, disdainful pride, and ungovernable rage: By the last of these often breaking out in sallies of the most unpardonable sort, she had long alienated her Sovereign's mind, before it appeared to the world . . .

This lady is not without some degree of wit; and hath in her time affected the character of it, by the usual method of arguing against religion, and proving the Doctrines of Christianity to be impossible and absurd. Imagine what such a spirit irritated by the loss of power, favour and employment is capable of acting or attempting, and then I have said enough.[95]

In the summer of 1712 Sarah fed *Some hints towards a character of [Queen Anne]*[96] to Bishop Burnet. She began with Anne's taste for etiquette, suggesting that it amounted to vanity, given the Queen's place at the pinnacle of the social hierarchy: '[S]he has the greatest memory that ever was, especially for such things as are all forms and ceremonies, giving people their due ranks at Processions and their proper places at Balls . . .' More seriously, Sarah still saw her as a puppet, and a selfish one at that: '[I]n thirty years time I never knew her do a right or good thing of [by] herself. She never thought of rewarding men because they were deserving, nor of easing any people because they were miserable. All such things must be put into her mind by others, and chiefly by those she loves, who will always have the real influence . . .'

Again conflating public and private interests, Sarah wrote to the Bishop that the Queen was 'so insensible of the Public Good that once, when an express came with news of some great success [of Marlborough's] and all the family was impatient to hear it, she let the letters lie by her half an hour without opening one of them, though she was alone and had nothing in the world to do . . .'

Bitterly but brilliantly, Sarah destroyed Anne's character from every angle: '[S]he talks sometimes as if she thought herself good, and keeps a clutter with religion that would make one imagine that she had really devotion and some principles,' but 'you can never know the truth unless you happen to speak of a thing that she has not had her lesson upon, and then you may see it in her face or guess what you said was the truth by her making no answer at all . . .' Anne broke her word by pretending not to remember, 'standing as if she was recollecting and would fain remember it if she could, though she never forgot anything in her life'. Not only Anne's stubbornness but also Sarah's frustration at having been unable to trade words with someone equally articulate, are clear.

Sarah's character sketch of Anne in 1712 is no more to be trusted than a Tory description of Sarah's temper or avarice, but there is a remarkable consistency in the *Hints* and Sarah's other statements about the Queen. Two years earlier, she had written to Dr Hamilton that 'I would more willingly have confessed any fault of my own than have owned she had any weakness . . .'[97] It is hard to believe, however, that the letter to Burnet was the first time she had complained about Anne to others.

The Marlboroughs spent the summer together at Holywell. John pitched his army tent on the lawns and, treating himself like national treasure, let sightseers look at its elaborate Arras-work for an admission price of sixpence.[98] He was forced to sit back and watch the Duke of Ormonde, who had assumed active command in April, undo his victories of the past three years. But Ormonde was hemmed in by the notorious 'restraining orders' issued by Queen Anne on 10 May 1712, instructing the new Captain-General not to engage in any siege or battle so long as peace talks were in progress. This was a one-sided truce, as the French generals had no such orders and continued to attack the other Allies secure in the knowledge that the British could do nothing to help. The French therefore advanced to defeat Prince Eugene's troops and recapture the Allied bases in Douai, Le Quesnoy and Bouchain.

In September Godolphin joined the Marlboroughs at Holywell. While there, he suffered an attack of the kidney stones that had been making him seriously unwell for some years. As the only cure for this was a gruesome operation, which involved being strapped down while a surgeon, without anaesthetic, sliced between the anus and scrotum to remove the stones with a catheter,[99] it is not surprising that he decided to forgo treatment. He died, nursed by Sarah, on 15 September 1712. Sarah wondered that 'to the day of his death' he never said a disrespectful word about Anne 'though a man of his sense and honour must feel what she had done to him and his friends'.[100]

The Marlboroughs lamented the loss of their closest confidant, who had supported them with the most unwavering loyalty for almost forty years. Despite his prevarication in several political battles, Sarah had never lost respect for Godolphin's judgement and he had shown her equal respect in return – far more than Anne and perhaps even more than Marlborough. Through this friendship Sarah had achieved, by proxy or proximity, much more than she could have as merely Marlborough's wife. She wrote to Bishop Burnet to ensure that the historian would know Godolphin had been 'the best man that ever lived' with 'no sort of vanity' and to emphasise her admiration for his lack of self-interest, shown by the small estate he left to his son. She also asked Burnet's advice on the requirements for burying a Knight of the Garter at Westminster, as she wanted to avoid having attendants who were not true well-wishers.[101]

Two months after Godolphin's death, Sarah was at the bed-side of Arthur Maynwaring as he, too, lay dying. They had recently argued over the younger James Craggs, whom she had turned out of her house for trying to rape a servant girl,[102] and who therefore, Sarah believed, had written her this anonymous letter:

I will tell you what is generally thought of you: that you are madder than most of the people in Bedlam with pride and ill nature . . . You envy the little beauty your own children have (& which they are, like you, so fond of) . . . [The Queen is a] greater and a better woman than you in everything . . . In short, to finish your character, you are ridiculous in company, false and fickle in friendship, tedious and lying in the relation of your own merits . . .[103]

An ageing roué himself, Maynwaring had tried to defend Craggs and questioned that such a malicious letter could have come from his friend. Sarah forgave him for this disagreement only because he was dying of what was described as a 'venereal distemper',[104] probably syphilis. Dr Garth had treated him in August with 'a blister to his head which made a very great discharge',[105] and reported to Sarah that the patient was rambling deliriously. On 13 November, the day he died, Maynwaring was just conscious enough to recognise Sarah crying beside him. He had once told her, 'I am confident your friendship will extend beyond my life . . . a wearisome life which, without it, would be a real punishment.'[106]

Years earlier, Maynwaring had suggested to Sarah that Anne and Abigail should go into exile like the Emperor Tiberius and his favourite Sejanus in the play of that name: 'Tis pity this kingdom hath no such delicious retreat near it. What think you of the island of Silly?'[107] Later, when Sarah had fallen from her posts, and Dr Garth first spread the rumour that the Marlboroughs might go into self-imposed exile,[108] Maynwaring had lightly suggested America to them.[109] He was probably right – the New World would have suited Sarah, who in later life donated £1,000 to help Swiss peasants emigrate there[110] – but her husband had other plans.

By the autumn of 1712, the Marlboroughs were on the verge of losing everything they had worked so hard to acquire. The Duke faced impeachment and demands for repayment of the money he had been convicted of pocketing, work at Blenheim remained at a standstill and a lawsuit over a share of the building costs was looming.[111] Oxford promised that the impeachment would not be carried through and their property would be left untouched if they went abroad. The primary reason for exile was, therefore, financial. Their friends made it sound like something far more dramatic than the equivalent of tax evasion – as if it were a flight from persecution akin to that of the Protestant refugees from the Palatinate. In fact, the relatively healthy state of English civil liberties had never been more evident: in France, those convicted of war-profiteering were tortured on the wheel during Noailles' inquisitions of 1716.[112]

Darker motives for the couple's departure were hinted at in the Tory press. Two days after Maynwaring's death there had been a scandalous duel in Hyde Park between the Whig Lord Mohun and the Tory Duke of Hamilton, a self-confessed Jacobite who had recently been appointed Oxford's ambassador to France. On the morning of the intervening day, Lord Mohun and his second had paid a mysterious visit to Marlborough House. Both Mohun and Hamilton were killed, and the true reasons behind it – a dispute over an estate – became clouded by partisan press accusations. Many Tories muttered that Marlborough had put Mohun up to issuing the challenge to dispose of his old enemy Hamilton and so delay further rapprochement with France. *The Examiner* insinuated as much when it pointed out that Mohun had been Marlborough's second when the Duke had issued his challenge to Earl Poulett in May.[113] Daniel Defoe wrote *A Strict Enquiry into the Circumstances of a Late Duel* partly to clear Marlborough of this charge, but many still believed that the Marlboroughs' haste to go into exile was more than coincidence.

Whatever Marlborough's connection to the Mohun/Hamilton duel, other political reasons probably underlay his decision to go to Germany. Not only did he feel that they would be among friends there, but he certainly hoped to exert influence, via his reputation at the Allied courts, over the final outcome of the war and the peace conferences. For Sarah, the certainty that on Anne's death Britain would cave in to a Jacobite invasion overcame her reluctance to travel. The loss of Maynwaring and Godolphin, her two surest compasses, had left her feeling directionless enough to comply with whatever her husband suggested. He departed on 24 November, Sarah remaining behind to finish packing up her defeated aspirations.

During the last weeks of the year she avoided the city, staying at St Albans and coming to Marlborough House only to run errands to her banker or lawyer, and to go with her servants to the New Exchange in the Strand and stock up on supplies of English goods – tea, fabrics, wigs – that she might be unable to find on the Continent.

Her only consolation (and perhaps anxiety) that winter was the prospect of spending more time alone with her husband than she had in over a decade. She made her preparations as though she might never return, including drafting a new will. She and Marlborough transferred their properties into the care of their sons-in-law, their friend Lord Cowper, and their agent, an Exchequer official named William Clayton, and sent £50,000 to The Hague for their own use.[114] Sarah decided not to take the bulk of her savings out of England because the interest rate in Holland was only 3 per cent.[115] She appointed her friend, distant relation and lawyer, Robert Jennings, to help manage her personal fortune while she was away, and the elder James Craggs was asked to be the couple's unofficial representative in London in all other matters. Unfortunately Craggs could not prevent the cash-strapped Vanbrugh from moving himself into the Old Manor House in the grounds of Woodstock, where 'Fair Rosamund' Clifford (Henry II's mistress and one of England's most archetypal favourites, with whom Sarah was often compared by fanciful poets) had supposedly hidden. Sarah had repeatedly ordered Vanbrugh to tear it down, but instead he lived there rent-free for three years and later generously informed Sarah he did not expect her to pay for his repairs to the property.

Before she left, Sarah also disposed of her jewels. She held a raffle of her diamonds for her granddaughters – except for little Bella and Mary Montagu, who missed out due to Sarah's unimproved relations with their mother Mary. Afterwards her 1718 inventory of jewellery[116] remained extensive and most strikingly included 'One hundred and forty-seven pearls in a bracelet, with the Duke of Marlborough's picture' and four other items – rings, buckles and snuff-boxes – with his miniature in them. If she had chosen to wear them all at once she would have looked like a souvenir-seller on Westminster Bridge. She also kept with her, sentimentally, 'a little locket of crystal with my Lord Godolphin's hair'.

Even something as innocent as Sarah giving away her jewels did not go without comment. Swift wrote a story concerning a small enamelled picture of Queen Anne, rimmed with diamonds: 'When the Duchess was leaving England she took off all the diamonds & gave the picture to one Mrs Higgins (an old intriguing woman whom everybody knows) bidding her to make the best of it she could . . . Was ever such an ungrateful beast as that Duchess? Or did you ever hear such a story? I suppose the Whigs will not believe it, pray try them . . . Is she not a detestable slut?'[117] Swift had heard this titbit from Oxford, who claimed to have redeemed the picture from Mrs Higgins. When Sarah heard it, she explained she had given the old woman the picture only because she had 'nothing to eat but by a pension of the Q[ueen] that I got her', but also admitted that she took no pleasure in keeping a picture of Anne.[118]

When Sarah had had her grandchildren over to the raffle, she had let Henrietta's children drink extra cups of milky tea against their mother's orders. Just before she left the country, at a time when she expected a few kind parting words, she received a note from Henrietta complaining of this small indulgence. Her eldest daughter did not travel with her to Dover when she left but suggested that Sarah should take her thirteen-year-old daughter Harriot, a rather plain girl living in her mother's shadow at Godolphin House, away to the Continent as a travelling companion. Later, Sarah claimed that Harriot's mother had 'never loved her ... never let her eat with her and shut her up in a garret'.[119] Now she was struck by Henrietta appearing 'so desirous to part with her daughter that she thanked me for it before I had her, which was the only thanks I ever had'. Henrietta wanted the adoption to be permanent, so Sarah promised she would be 'married to [Harriot] – that was my very expression'.[120]

As Sarah sailed for Ostend aboard a packet boat, severe storms whipped the Channel and she lay seasick in her cabin among a portion of her 120 parcels of luggage.[121] An anonymous Tory poet[122] marked her departure by calling on the sea to wreck her ship: 'Ye Winds and Waves, against her Ship engage/High as her Pride and Stormy as her Rage.' But this Sarah/Sempronia, compared to Milton's fallen Archangel and the cursed Medusa, was not humbled by her banishment. She vowed to return and described her own demeanour in adversity:

> Pride brought her needful Succours to my Heart,
> Which, while it felt the Wound, disdain'd the Smart.
> Thus when Sempronia's blasted Name was Sung,
> The Jest and Sport of ev'ry idle Tongue; ...
> Then fearless, in superior Guilt [I] stood,
> And scorn'd the mean Abasement *to be Good*.

During January 1713, as Sarah travelled to meet Marlborough at Aix-la-Chapelle, she might not have been aware that he was beginning a Baroque game of conspiracy with the Allies and, simultaneously, with the Jacobites. Although he portrayed himself as a tourist, evidence has come to light that Marlborough was arranging to lead an invasion expedition into his own country. He sent William Cadogan – who had been forced to resign his offices, thanks to his friendship with Marlborough – to The Hague to present a half-baked plan to the Dutch commanders: that Hanoverian troops should be deployed in the southern Netherlands, ostensibly to garrison this region but in fact to invade England, where his son-in-law Sunderland and

General James Stanhope would simultaneously seize command. The Allies rejected this proposal for the duration of Anne's lifetime, but remained open to the possible necessity of such action if the Pretender invaded after her death.[123] In light of these proposals, Tory depictions of Marlborough as a new Cromwell appear less outlandish. Certainly both French and English spies were carefully watching the Marlborough caravan as it travelled from Allied court to court. Sarah would later commission a painting of spies with gigantic ears on the walls of her saloon at Blenheim, but she told one of her correspondents she felt secure from counterfeit at least, because no one could imitate the terrible scrawl of her handwriting.[124] All the couple's correspondence while in exile was written with a cipher which has not only driven historians mad, but which Sarah herself said she was 'very likely to mistake'. Oxford and Henry St John, who had been created Viscount Bolingbroke, pretended to the French that they had prescribed Marlborough's route to prevent his interference in the peace conferences, but this was untrue. The only hold they had over him was the threat of impeachment.[125]

Travel should theoretically have brought Sarah the wider perspective that Marlborough had gained through his career, but she found the hardships insufferable, and said only that royal courts were always full of dull company. Her unaccustomed idleness and deferment to her husband in places where he felt more at ease than she, as well as her own ill-health, all weighed on her spirits. Her daughter Anne wrote lovingly with suggested cures for rheumatism and scurvy, such as rubbing laurel leaves soaked in boiling water on the skin.[126]

As they travelled, Marlborough was receiving metaphorical laurels from grateful Continental Allies, and for the first time Sarah fully appreciated the extent of his fame. She was touched by the honours paid to him everywhere they went, which 'now, because it cannot proceed from power . . . shows he made a right use of it'.[127] She called it a 'strange paradox'[128] that the European Roman Catholics hailed him 'as if the D. of Marl. had been King'[129] while the English Protestants had driven him out of his own land.

The exiles' first stop was Aix-la-Chapelle, where Sarah could take the waters and indulge her fascination with Catholicism. She was intrigued by the serious economic consequences she attributed to it. The Church of Rome, she wrote in one letter home,

has made those atheists there are in the world, for tis impossible to see all the abuses of the priests without raising strange thoughts in one's mind . . . and I think tis unnatural for anybody to have so monstrous a notion as that there is no God if the priests (to get all the power and money themselves) did not act in the manner they do in these parts, where they have three or four parts of all the land in the country, and yet they are not contented, but squeeze the poor deluded people to get more, who are really half starved . . .[130]

Sarah did not keep most of the letters she received while travelling, but many of her own letters home have survived. Her regular correspondents were selected, it seems, for their ability to supply political gossip: Lady Cowper, Lord Sunderland, the elder James Craggs, Mrs Charlotte Clayton (wife of William Clayton), Mrs Boscawen (Godolphin's sister), her son Hugh (a Cornish MP), and Sir Gilbert Heathcote (Governor of the Bank of England). These letters have won Sarah compliments from her biographers: in them she appears calm, feminine and likeable, especially when they are compared to her correspondence with Anne, as if Sarah had changed, not the recipients and circumstances.[131]

In March 1713, the Electoral Prince presented Marlborough, through Cadogan, with the 'Bernstorff Plan' (named after a Hanoverian who would later become a Minister of George I): an invasion of England would be activated only after Anne died and Marlborough would either accompany George to London or follow him after securing key Dutch towns for the Electress Sophia.[132] Marlborough agreed to the basic plan, but hoped it would become redundant if funds were provided to bribe British

MPs to support the Hanoverian successionists, who were mainly Whigs, in the next election.

While they were in Aix, the Marlboroughs read newspaper accounts about the signing of the Treaty of Utrecht. On 31 March 1713, Britain and Holland had made peace with France and Spain. This was the long-dreaded disaster against which Marlborough had thrown all his political weight, and which Sarah believed would undo Britain. Whig historians condemned it in the belief that France could and should have been further crushed and more concessions won – Lord Chatham called it 'an indelible blot on the age'.[133] That Louis XIV sent Queen Anne six gowns and two thousand bottles of champagne afterwards was interpreted as proof that Lord Oxford had sold Britain and the Alliance cheap.[134] Trevelyan, however, admitted that Utrecht laid the groundwork for Britain's future naval empire, and condemned only the 'subservient' manner in which it had been made.

Modern historians have generally reached a more positive assessment. The Treaty, they argue, was not commensurate with England's earlier supremacy in the war, but that was the Whig Junto's fault for having thrown away the peace of 1709. Utrecht gave England and the Dutch guarantees of security (the Dutch regained the promise of a barrier, though they had lost their larger role as a world power), and it is unclear what else, apart from slightly more territory, might have been gained by pressing on to the gates of Paris. Sarah's view seemed to be that nothing but the entire destruction of France would guarantee British safety, and the revival of the French threat under Louis XV and Britain's later eighteenth-century wars with France have made this view look somewhat prophetic, but she cannot be said to have considered the final peace terms dispassionately.

From one angle it appears that the territories of Gibraltar, Nova Scotia, Minorca, St Kitts, Acadia, Newfoundland and Hudson Bay were all that Britain gained from the War of Spanish Succession. In fact, it had achieved two important British aims: it preserved the Protestant succession – France promised to expel the

Pretender from his residence in Lorraine – and Britain acquired the *Assiento*, the limited right to trade, particularly in slaves, with the ports of Peru, Chile and Mexico, which would form an important basis for future trade.[135] In terms of Britain's Allies, only Austria was left dissatisfied, although Spain ceded possessions to it in today's Italy and the Netherlands. Prussia received Guelderland, and Portugal received trading rights in the Amazon. The only real losers, in terms of their liberties, were the 'poor Catalans',[136] as Sarah called them, who were left to be persecuted by Philip V despite the British government's promises of protection, and 2,500 Gibraltarians who were thrown out of their homes at gunpoint by their new British occupiers.

When Sarah heard of the peace terms, she wrote to Lord Coningsby:[137] '[G]od knows how all this madness and infamy will end, but if it is finished as it ought to be I am sure there must be a great many hanged . . .' She told Robert Jennings that the King of France had a 'very good bargain, since tis certain that our Treaty with Spain is not yet signed, which I have always heard was the chief cause of the War'.[138] She added that '[T]hough a woman, I did all I could to prevent the mischiefs that are coming upon my country.'[139] To another friend she predicted that the Jacobites would invade after Anne's death, leading to the ruin of the nation 'or in such convulsion to prevent it as might have very dreadful consequences'.

With hindsight, however, it is clear that the Marlboroughs' fall did not have the epic consequences Sarah's self-dramatising imagination had foreseen. It is one of the traits of stage favourites that they think their personal fall will topple empires. In the Marlboroughs' case, apart from a dip in the stock-market, the immediate harm to the public good was negligible. However, the duplicitous way in which Marlborough had been undermined by his own colleagues and the manner in which the peace had been made, disregarding an agreement that all members of the Grand Alliance would seek peace together, reinforced the Hanoverians' aversion to the Tory party. George I had received his British history lessons from the Whig George Cooper, and the Marlboroughs spread the legend of Tory betrayal as they travelled across Europe during 1712–14.

On 9 April 1713, the Queen's Address to Parliament called for greater control of the press to silence Marlborough supporters critical of the peace. The following year, for example, a play at the Theatre Royal, Drury Lane, called *The Victim – A Tragedy* (1714) by Charles Johnson, would prove a popular hit with the Ministry's opponents. Its dedication to Sarah referred to 'that truly conjugal Friendship and Affection with which you accompany this Great Man in His Absence from His native Country, and share with him in all the Cares and Inquietudes his Extraordinary Merit has brought upon him.'

On 30 April, the Marlboroughs together with Harriot and their households travelled to Frankfurt, where Marlborough hoped to work with the Electoral Prince and the Austrian Emperor to elaborate a plan for Britain's defence from the Pretender. They travelled in the middle of an unseasonable blizzard and Sarah suffered from toothache but refused to be treated by any of the local doctors. Instead she chewed tobacco, which she said numbed the pain. On 14 May, she watched Prince Eugene's troops march beneath her window, a reminder of the ongoing Franco-Austrian war, by which 'I was so much animated that I wished I had been a man, that I might have ventured my life a thousand times in the glorious cause of liberty.'

Sarah also wrote to Sir Godfrey Kneller, who was estranged from Anne and the Court for his own reasons, to describe her journey through the snow-covered mountains of his native country: 'I could not help having some melancholy reflections when they told me the Duke of M. has, with so much labour and pains, carried a great army over all those barbarous countries with the hazard of his own life . . .'[140]

Sarah's favourite place on her travels was the castle of the Elector of Treves in Coblenz, with long views of joining rivers and vineyards. It was, she joked, a castle fit for Jupiter which Vanbrugh would never have been able to build, even with all the wealth of France and Spain at his disposal. Among her papers, Sarah copied this quotation from Francis Bacon: '[I]t is a pleasure . . . to stand in the window of a castle & see a battle & the adventures of it below, but no pleasure is comparable to the standing upon the vantage ground of Truth, a hill not to be commanded & where the air is always clear & serene.'[141]

She also found Frankfurt 'the best town one can be in abroad', although they had bad (unEnglish) stoves, causing her to install a new one in the house where she stayed.[142] What she did love in Germany was the food, writing home that her figure was 'a little of the fatter' for it.[143]

She described herself and Marlborough whiling away the time together in the German countryside, as if living out the pastoral idyll that so many of his letters had invoked. '[T]he D. of Marl. and I go constantly every day in the afternoon and stop the coach and go out wherever we see a place that looks hard and clean,' she told Mr Jennings. '[B]ut, though I love solitude more than ever, I would not have you think that I don't wish earnestly to see my friends and to be in a clean sweet house and garden . . .'[144]

At the end of May 1713, Marlborough left Sarah in Frankfurt with her entourage, including Harriot, to inspect his principality of Mindelheim. While he was gone, Sarah concentrated again on writing her memoirs. Her ostensible purpose was not publication, but the education of a Tory MP named Archibald Hutcheson, whom she knew to be travelling to Vienna and feared would speak ill of her there if not set straight by her version of events.

Back in December 1710, Francis Hare had written Sarah a letter of extraordinary length, which reflected back to Sarah, in even clearer outlines, her self-image as that rare creature: a virtuous favourite. '[T]hat a lady in such circumstances should adhere steadily to the principles of Whiggism, has something in it so extraordinary that it looks as if you had been born on purpose to be the guardian genius of the Queen . . .' Idealism, he argued, was the source of her own disappointments, but it was not a fault in a lobbyist as it would be in a leader, for its influence would always be counteracted by other less principled advisers.[145] He described her and her husband having dedicated their lives to 'the cause of

Europe', and was now sorry his own circumstances prevented him accompanying the couple to the Continent as a kind of Boswell. In his place he sent along the Reverend Whadcock Priest to serve as Sarah's chaplain and secretary.[146]

In the early autumn, the Marlboroughs travelled from Frankfurt to Antwerp as the Duke wanted to persuade the Dutch to support the Bernstorff Plan. They were met with a great welcoming ceremony, but Sarah was growing homesick – '[W]e are like a sort of banished People in a strange Country'[147] – and feeling the lack of a meaningful audience: 'Living abroad makes one very indifferent whether one's life be long or short.'[148] Her depression was compounded by her political pessimism: to Mrs Boscawen she described Antwerp as 'the finest old town, I believe, in the world, but grown poor & ruined for want of trade, which will be soon the decay of England'.[149] Sarah gave out a great deal of charity in these 'ruined' towns ('which I really think in all countries is the best way of employing what one can spare')[150] but always through other people so that she could remain anonymous. In Antwerp she was still collecting evidence of Catholicism's evils: she told Charlotte Clayton about mystery plays in which 'all the history of our Saviour [was] represented by trades-people of the town twice a week . . . the whole thing more impious than tis possible for anybody to imagine . . .'[151]

While in Antwerp, her diamond bracelet with the picture of Marlborough was stolen from her dressing-table. She believed that 'Ned the black footman' had taken it while helping her put on her shoes, and had her husband interrogate and arrest him. But when she heard that it was the local custom to put thieves on the rack until they confessed, then brand them on the hand, she changed her mind and had Ned discharged. She understood the ambitions that had driven him to it ('Twas a great temptation to make his fortune') and therefore only asked the elder James Craggs to search Ned on his return to England and to bar him from her houses. Later, however, Sarah discovered Ned was innocent of the theft and paid him fifty pistoles (approximately £7,400 today)[152] in compensation for her wrongful accusation.[153]

Sarah's daughter Elizabeth wrote to her mother in Antwerp, saying, 'I can't help flattering myself you will not stay long where you are, but that some good thing will happen that we may have you here soon . . .'[154] What that 'good thing' might be remained unclear. The death of the Queen or the Tory government's displacement were the only events likely to bring the Marlboroughs home, and there seemed little prospect of either, despite the competition that had erupted between old enemies in their absence. Sarah also received London gossip from young gentlemen who visited her in Antwerp – Lord Stanhope, later the Earl of Chesterfield, and Samuel Molyneux.

It seemed increasingly possible that Anne might be succeeded by her half-brother, the Pretender, so Marlborough reopened contacts with the Jacobites, using William Cadogan as an intermediary to keep his own hands clean. This was partly to glean information and partly to secure immunity from prosecution if the Pretender should return. Sarah, too, employed agents, like Molyneux, to shadow the Tory agents on the Continent. There was even evidence to suggest that Sarah's most extreme accusations had come to pass: that Abigail had met with Louis XIV's envoy after the Queen fell sick in the Christmas of 1713 in order to discuss the Pretender's return.[155] Sarah was depressed by the news, '[y]et I do believe firmly that if men that have fortunes of both parties would awake and be active that they might yet do something.'[156] On 25 December, Oxford wrote to assure Marlborough that he would not be impeached. Perhaps he was alarmed at the news of the Duke's dealings with both the Allied governments and the Jacobites, or even seeking an unlikely ally in his intensifying power struggle with Lord Bolingbroke.[157]

News of Anne's illness did not reach the Marlboroughs until early January 1714. Huddled in her chamber that winter, wearing a German cloak over her nightgown to keep out the cold (in the same style, she was told, as the Queen of Russia), Sarah wrote to her friend Charlotte Clayton: '[I]n case [Anne] should die, I shall long to hear what method the Ministers will take, for if the King of France can't send them good assistance very soon, they must be in a great deal of danger; for I reckon the City will not easily be persuaded to declare a Popish French King shall be master of all their riches . . .'

In the same letter, Sarah described how she had sat with Pensioner Buys and Lord Essex one evening and teased the Dutch Minister about how little his country had benefited from the Treaty of Utrecht. In retaliation, he asked how proud England felt of its secret peace deal, and 'this you may believe set us all laughing . . .'[158]

Marlborough and Cadogan were proposing now to go beyond the Bernstorff Plan, and use the British garrisons at Ghent, Bruges, Dunkirk and Nieuwport, all of which were personally loyal to the Captain-General, to invade England before the Queen's death. They portrayed themselves as defending the House of Hanover, rather than seizing power for themselves, yet at the same time, in March 1714, Marlborough resumed negotiations with his nephew Berwick about a pardon from the Pretender. He probably kept the Hanoverians informed about his contacts with the Jacobites – he had too much to lose to do otherwise. Sarah, however, was sheltered from these double-dealings, being too uncompromising to contemplate any flattery of the Pretender, even for self-preservation or espionage: 'That would look as if what he did in the Revolution was not for justice, as it really was, but to comply with the times . . . [I]f one must hazard, it should be in the cause of liberty, for if one was ruined for that one had the satisfaction of having performed the right part.'[159]

In mid-March 1714, a Jacobite restoration was made considerably less likely when the Pretender refused to renounce his Catholic faith, which meant that no English politician could support his cause openly. Oxford's government had split, with an opposition clique emerging that comprised Bolingbroke, Harcourt and Atterbury, supported by Abigail Masham. Oxford had quarrelled with Abigail over refusing her a share in the *Assiento* contract,[160] and with Bolingbroke over a range of other financial matters. Bolingbroke as Secretary of State continued to act as if the Hanoverians would employ High Tories: he prepared to purge the army of Whig officers and, in the summer, introduced the Schism Bill, to ban all Nonconformist teaching. Both Oxford and Bolingbroke were increasingly nervous about their futures and tried to negotiate individually with Marlborough. Oxford granted a warrant for the resumption of work at Blenheim to entice the Duke back to his side.[161]

Tory satires about the Marlboroughs continued to appear in the British press. *A Prince and no Prince OR, Mother Red-Cap's strange and wonderful Prophesy* (1714), for example, referred to the old 'war wolf' and his female mate being on the prowl. A learned astronomer (Oxford) overthrows them and forces them to flee. It ends: 'And pale-faced Death within his clutches/Will soon catch both the D[u]ke and D[uch]ess.'

In fact, their daughter Elizabeth predeceased them. She had caught smallpox, and her mother-in-law wrote to the Marlboroughs in Antwerp with the news. She consoled Sarah that 'Nobody suffered less under that disease and her death was as easy as if she had only gone to sleep.'[162] Sarah wrote to Robert Jennings, '[A]ll the arguments that I can possibly think of can't hinder me from lamenting as long as I live the loss of what I had so much reason to love . . .'[163] News quickly followed that Anne, the daughter closest to her mother's heart, was also ill. Sarah was now desperate to return to England, and said she would 'even submit to Popery' to do so.[164]

That summer, as the Queen's illness worsened, a panicking Oxford sent his cousin, Thomas Harley, to negotiate with Hanover. Meanwhile, Samuel Molyneux sent Sarah a packet of letters written by Oxford in which he stated opposition to a Hanoverian succession. It had been the Electress Sophia's last instruction on 8 June, the day before she died, that the letters should be sent to Sarah. Her trust in Sarah was well placed: no one knew better the power of incriminating letters than Sarah, nor was better connected to the Whig press. She leaked them immediately through the elder James Craggs, and they were published in London on 1 July, torpedoing the Oxford Ministry's remaining

Whig support.[165] Sarah had always threatened to bring down her enemies through the publication of letters, and now she did.

Lady Cowper described the disarray at Court to her friend in exile. Even Swift had retired and, as she put it, 'when HE complains, sure it must be very bad'.[166] A Jacobite invasion was feared, and Bolingbroke was in last-ditch negotiations with Marlborough through various intermediaries. Sarah urged her husband not to work with 'that violent wretch B' even if it was to bring down 'The Sorcerer' Oxford.[167] To Sarah, an invasion attempt in support of the Hanoverian heir and pre-empting a possible Jacobite invasion was a more honest, albeit riskier, approach. It is unclear how much she knew about the detailed plans that Marlborough had made with Cadogan. Her main worry was that the Blenheim costs should be decided upon before Anne's death: she believed that the Queen would honour the original intention that the house was a gift.[168] To Robert Jennings, she confessed: 'I believe my virtue is not like Cato's, for my concern is not for England, but for my children and a few friends and good people that are there.'[169]

On 27 July 1714, after a savage fight in the Cabinet, the now terminally ill Anne dismissed Oxford, and Bolingbroke was left effectively in charge, which again gave hope to the Jacobites. On the same day, the Marlboroughs embarked from Ostend to return home. The timing could not have been coincidental. Marlborough had waited until Parliament had been prorogued, but did not try to conceal news of his return. Swift noted that Marlborough House was being made ready, and many Marlborough veterans were talking excitedly about his return, but no one could understand why he was coming when everything remained confused, instead of waiting to see which way the dice rolled. They were expecting him to act, in other words, as the 'trimmer' he had been at the time of the Revolution, twenty years earlier, rather than as the committed Whig Sarah had, with great effort, made him. Bothmar reported to his masters: 'The impetuosity of the Duchess has probably precipitated this journey.'[170] Sarah's urging, both political and personal – a desire to see her sick daughter Anne – no doubt played a part in his decision.

As they departed, the ultra-Protestant Royal Irish Regiment quartered at Ghent came on foot to Ostend to pay their respects and wave the couple off. Sarah took this as another compliment to her husband, but did not seem to read any more seditious meaning into their coming to see if they were needed. Though they set sail in clear weather, stormclouds quickly gathered in the Channel and a day's crossing again turned into an arduous voyage of several days and nights.

Meanwhile, at Kensington, the Queen had taken to her bed and was falling in and out of consciousness. On the last night of her life she apparently stared fixedly at a clock, and suffered heated cups to be applied to the abscess in her gouty leg.[171] Her forty-nine-year-old body, battered by seventeen years of pregnancy and a lifetime of obesity, lay surrounded by few friends and no family. The Duchess of Somerset was there, but otherwise only doctors, priests and Cabinet ministers. The Dukes of Somerset, Shrewsbury and Argyll had all turned up at the Palace to outmanoeuvre Bolingbroke at the last minute. In a parody of the puppet-figure Sarah had always thought Anne to be, it was said that Lord Chancellor Harcourt had had to lift her weak arm so that she could hand over the White Staff of the Treasury to Shrewsbury.

One witness reported that at intervals of consciousness Anne asked whether the Marlboroughs had reached the British shore. The rumour circulated that she had called for Mr and Mrs Freeman to come home,[172] but in the hour of her death, Anne gave away as little as she had in life. Perhaps she was haunted by guilt at having participated in the taking of her father's crown, and hoped that her half-brother would come to claim it. Perhaps she thought of Sarah. In the last hours of her life she ordered a package of private letters to be burned, and George I was also responsible for destroying several of Anne's papers, including her will, so there is much we will never know.[173]

10

'A Kind of Author'

Queen Anne died at Kensington on the morning of 1 August 1714. Dr Hamilton recorded in his diary: 'The immediate occasion of the Queen's death proved to be the transition of the gouty humour from Her knee and foot upon Her nerves and brain. The cause of this transition was disquiet of mind.'[1] The Marlboroughs landed at Dover that afternoon. At Chatham their way was strewn with flowers.[2]

Three days later, the Marlboroughs made their triumphal entry into London, and Sarah was reunited with her daughters under the public gaze. That evening they returned with guests to Marlborough House. Sarah tried to break away from the well-wishers to have a private word with her daughter Mary, who stayed, however, in the dining room and, according to her mother, 'never said one single word to me the whole time she was there, but looked with a scornful air as if she had a mind to express that she came there to see her father and not me'.[3]

Mary's husband, the Duke of Montagu, invited his in-laws to dine at Montagu House the next day, but Sarah made her excuses, and sent a message to Mary that she would see her as seldom as possible, though often enough to avoid gossip. Montagu replied that he preferred his wife should not come at all than under those terms. 'I was prodigiously surprised & struck,' wrote Sarah, 'but did not say one harsh or angry thing, but for a quarter of an hour argued the case, in which I wetted a pocket handkerchief without making the least impression upon him.'

Henrietta's behaviour towards her mother was no warmer. Years later Sarah recalled, sadly, half forgivingly, every detail of her daughter's neglect:

I can be positive that in her whole life she never asked me once to go abroad with her, but once I desired her to carry me with her to Hyde Park, which she did in her chariot; but she had so little pleasure in it that she did not call me till it was almost dark, & I remember we met the company coming out of the Ring. However I never reproached her, loving her & seeing her of a careless temper, & we sung all the way.[4]

Mary and Henrietta attended Queen Anne's funeral at Westminster Abbey, but Sarah did not. Anne's final favourite, the Duchess of Somerset, was her chief mourner. Marlborough had been immediately reinstated as Captain-General of the Armed Forces, but to Sarah's chagrin both he and Sunderland were excluded from the list of Lord Justices overseeing the country until George, Elector of Hanover, arrived six weeks later.

Sarah was not impressed with the new King. She described him as 'not very bright, nor would have made any great figure in history' but, like Anne, reasonably well intentioned.[5] One eye-witness remembered that whenever she came to the King's drawing room in the evening he would pay her the honour of crossing directly to greet her, though neither spoke the other's language. Apparently Sarah's 'great earnestness and animation' when speaking sufficed. She and the King made bank together at cards and she was honoured with a seat next to him to watch a performance of *Twelfth Night*.[6]

As for Caroline, Princess of Wales, Sarah was flattered to receive a letter that was as obliging 'as if I had been her equal', but was nettled by the speed and confidence with which the new Court assumed its place at the head of British society and started to make its own rules of etiquette, fashion and patronage. She even found herself speaking in patriotic defence of Queen Anne and Abigail Masham when the foreigners insulted them. She felt herself included in their disdain of the previous Court and excluded – ungratefully, given that she had been such a loyal Whig – from the Hanoverian dispensation of favour.

Sarah did not wish to return to Court, but she was annoyed that

she could not obtain a better place for her son-in-law, the Earl of
Bridgwater, who was a bit of a dunce by her own admission,
than Chamberlain to the Prince of Wales. Sunderland was also
disappointed at being appointed Lord Lieutenant of Ireland,
where he had no intention of living, and Sarah pressed the
new King for his eventual promotion to Lord Privy Seal.[7] More
distressing was the way Sarah saw her husband disregarded as
too old to be politically significant and, paradoxically, distrusted
for his popularity. George I was influenced, no doubt, by some
of the pre-1711 slander against Marlborough as a would-be
Cromwell.

On 10 August, Marlborough had assured Sarah that he had
more 'real power' with the Hanoverian Prince than any other
man in England. By autumn, however, it was clear that Lord
Halifax would be the most favoured Minister. He was created
an earl and finally succeeded to the Treasury post he had always
coveted. It was reported that Sarah 'rode all about the town
triumphant; sometimes to one lady, sometimes to another; and
sometimes she would visit Lord Halifax who . . . was wont to
appease that lady's spirit with concerts of music, and poems, and
private suppers . . .'[8] At the same time, Halifax was among those
who propagated the image of Sarah as responsible for the Whig
party's fall in 1710.

Shortly after the Marlboroughs' return to London, Sarah lost
another co-author with the death of Whadcock Priest. It was
unfortunate timing, given that she felt free for the first time
to print the copious correspondence that had lain as a weapon
in her hand while Anne was alive. During 1714–15 she began
to write what became the definitive version of her memoirs.
When they were published nearly thirty years later, she wrote an
introduction explaining that her ambition for a good reputation
had 'sometimes carried me beyond the sphere to which the men
have thought proper, and perhaps, generally speaking, with good
reason, to confine our sex. I have been a kind of author'.[9]

This aspect of Sarah's life, her career as an author, has been one of the most underrated. Before she published, Dr Johnson described her as 'a woman without skill or pretensions to skill in poetry or literature'.[10] While it is true that she had no interest in writing fiction, the quantity and vibrancy of her non-imaginative writing deserves a higher reputation. Her disclaimers ('I am of the simple sex . . . I tumble my mind out on paper without any disguise') have too often been taken at face value, as if her writing were the work of hours rather than a project spanning thirty-eight years.

It was not uncommon for aristocratic women to leave collections of miscellaneous manuscripts at their deaths. Many were diaries, often destroyed either to protect family privacy or because the contents were considered immoral. Most contained a daily balance sheet of personal virtue and sin. Compared to these, Sarah's memoirs are remarkable for their lack of piety, except in reference to other people's hypocrisy. What she shared with these diarists was a seventeenth-century attitude to female authorship, that it was analogous to sexual immodesty or promiscuity. Margaret Cavendish, Duchess of Newcastle (1625–74), was one such author, accused of being a 'garrulous and self-centred eccentric'.[11] She confessed: '[M]y Ambition is restless, and not ordinary; because it would have an extraordinary fame: And since all heroic Actions, public Employments, powerful Governments, and eloquent Pleadings are denied our Sex in this age, or at least would be condemned for want of custom, is the cause I write so much.'[12]

Usually the perception of female publication as unchaste was circumvented by the author's association with some cause higher than herself. The most popular excuse was to give Christian testimony, but secular faith in various royalist causes was almost as acceptable. Women could display their commitment to the Stuarts, it was felt, without tainting themselves by the act of self-expression. The publications of the Tory writer Mary Astell (1668–1731) were therefore presented as acts of obedience to Queen Anne, and Lady Ann Halkett (1623–99) justified a book about her love affairs by including a narrative of the Duke of York's escape from St James's Palace in 1648. Sarah's far more sturdy memoirs were original in using Whig 'Revolution Principles' in the same way as this royalist ardour: to justify not only her life, but also the act of publishing.

Sarah explained to her readers how her book had begun as a letter to Elizabeth Burnet in October 1704, to convince her of Queen Mary's fallibility.[13] These origins explain the epistolary style of the memoirs, retained through many subsequent drafts. At this stage she was genuinely modest, telling Mrs Burnet that it was 'my first essay & therefore I hope you will excuse it'. This narrative, like her private letters to Queen Anne and Dr Hamilton, shows the strength of Sarah's style when it was unadulterated and unedited. It was punctuated, or punctured, by sharp images of people and their relationships. In particular, she made a point of recording stories in which men behaved as pettily as women, such as when King William would not let Prince George, the then Princess Anne's husband, wear mourning clothes for a Scandinavian relation.

Sarah next justified her authorship as self-defence: she had returned to writing only when satires began to be published 'industriously' against her. She depicted the political scene of 1710–11 as 'stormy', with herself as its only 'voice of reason'.[14] These were the years when Maynwaring was her incendiary co-author. He practised imitating Sarah's style and told her that 'I am sure nobody that were to read it would guess that it were not all writ by one person, which shows that I have not imitated your style so long quite in vain'.[15]

On the one hand, Sarah used her male co-authors to make her act of publication more respectable; on the other, she was eager to claim credit: 'Some parts of the work were of my own composition, being such passages as nobody but myself could relate with exactness.'[16] She portrayed herself as an author in character as well as action, which is rather hard to believe: 'I made it my business to observe things very exactly without being much observed myself.'[17]

The memoirs concerning her loss of Anne's favour, written

between 1710 and 1712,[18] were the first to include the graphic account of her final interview with the Queen and to describe the Hill family's ingratitude. She claimed to have written this only for the edification of Dr Hamilton and the Queen, but in fact she had a wider purpose of putting historical events on record: 'I have learnt from my dear bought experience that for one reason or another so few people relate anything exactly true, that I always have made a servant write down matter of fact as soon as anything has passed . . .'

Dr Hamilton had been struck by the pleasure Sarah took in writing: '[T]he Duchess said she took more pleasure in justifying herself than Your Majesty did in wearing your Crown.'[19] She began to keep what she referred to as her 'Brown Book', containing Anne's letters and her own explanatory narratives. She called the letters 'incontestable vouchers' that supported her arguments, and bragged, 'I know of no history but this that has vouchers.'

During 1711, when Maynwaring fell ill, Sarah had turned to Bishop Burnet as a collaborator.[20] His version of her memoirs is valuable mostly because it contains information about the early relationship between Anne and Sarah that was not published in the final version.[21] It was the first to introduce the idea of Sarah's precocious Whig instincts, her aversion to religious persecution, and her early confrontations with Lord Rochester. Burnet included extensive quotations from her private correspondence, and animated the memoir with colourful descriptions of minor characters. Nonetheless Sarah deemed his version 'not well done'.

Burnet's reason for helping Sarah with her history was self-interest: he wanted to use her recollections as material in his *History of His Own Times*, which he gave in manuscript form to her, describing it with an almost feminine modesty as a mere 'trifle'.[22] She sent him comments on his text, and charged Godolphin with delivering to him two large bundles of her own papers that might help.[23] Unsure at this stage whether she herself would dare to publish, Sarah was now able to excuse her own writing by saying that '[W]hat I write is only information to the historian, to give characters.'[24] Years later she attempted to write a more general history of England, dictating notes to one of her granddaughters, but this never took real shape.[25] However, the unpublished papers she left at her death have been a valuable source for historians, in contrast to Marlborough's diary entries – obviously by a man who disliked writing: '13 Aug 1704 – Fought the battle of Blenheim and lay in the field all night.'[26]

Burnet's version of Sarah's memoirs contains her first full apology for publishing: 'The writing of books is looked upon as an employment not fit for our sex, and if some have succeeded well in it, others have exposed themselves by it too much to encourage a woman to venture on being an author: but it will appear more unusual for one to write so copiously as I fear I may be forced to do . . .' It also promises that it will be an autobiography without reference to Sarah's family or spiritual life, or scandalous gossip, the only areas on which women were generally permitted to publish. She would only include private relationships and arguments where they were relevant to public affairs, or where they taught the reader some lesson about the morals of a public figure. In many ways this 'Vindication' was just a public continuation of Sarah's fruitless private lectures to Anne. Sarah had written to Dr Hamilton in January 1711 that she did not like 'being perpetually obliged to be vindicating my behaviour'[27] but in fact it had become her obsession.

The attacks on Sarah's name were violent enough for her high-pitched tone to be viewed as embattled rather than belligerent. She was never as thick-skinned as she pretended – Anne had once written of how she hated to see her friend 'vex and torment yourself at all the malicious stories you hear'.[28] However, if counteracting her detractors was her intention, Sarah might have been expected to portray herself as a demure wife and loyal servant. Instead, the stridency of her memoirs' tone confirmed the image of her as boldly outspoken. Nor did she make any effort to answer those who called her an atheist. She crossed out the whole final paragraph of Burnet's version of her 'Vindication', which referred to how she would turn humbly to God and away from worldly fame; she wanted to establish an identity as a disinterested politician, distinct from other royal favourites, not as a pious housewife.

In February 1713, before leaving for the Continent, Sarah had given her papers to her lawyer with orders for them all to be copied and sent to her in Frankfurt so that she could continue writing with the help of Whadcock Priest while she travelled.²⁹ This account of her life was, again, meant for private consumption – to persuade a few friends and the Hanoverians that she had been a loyal Whig.³⁰ Based on earlier drafts, including Burnet's, this version contained a literal account of her financial management and the royal bounty she had received as a favourite. While the wounds of her fall were still fresh, this version also contained some of the strongest language about Abigail, making it read less like a private complaint and more like a testimony; Sarah's accusatory finger pointing across an imagined courtroom. She portrayed Abigail's crime as epic: '[I]nstrumental in doing the greatest mischief that a nation can suffer, the reducing of it from the most flourishing to at least a very dangerous condition; & as acting the most ungratefully and injuriously to a person to whom she owes her very bread.'

So when Sarah took up her quill and another piece of her favourite thick Parisian parchment in 1715, she was not starting from scratch. This time, she approached another clergyman-cum-rationalist-scholar, her old friend Benjamin Hoadly, Bishop of Bangor, to assist her. He was a controversial Whig author in his own right, and he and Sarah together wrote the version of her memoirs that is usually referred to by its opening line: 'The Characters of Princes are hardly ever truly known . . .'³¹ In this version, Hoadly adopted the persona of an old courtier who had witnessed Sarah's career and researched 'those secret springs of action which, though they seem to be of small importance in themselves, yet produced events upon which the fate of whole nations & of posterity depends'. The third-person narrative dulls the drama of the scenes in which Sarah discovered Abigail's betrayal and confronted the Queen, but also sounds more objective. It allowed Sarah to be more fulsomely flattered than in any other version ('I know Courts too well ever to expect to see her [Sarah] equalled . . .' and 'The Duchess, in her usual way, too open & too sincere for such Politicians . . .'). Hoadly made clear that Anne had not been alienated by Sarah's insolence, but by her refusal to compromise her Whig principles. He admitted that in promoting these principles at the beginning of Anne's reign Sarah had 'argued frequently with the Queen; & sometimes not without a warmth natural to sincerity: which yet, hitherto, did not appear to leave any uneasiness behind it'. This version contains a much greater emphasis on the machinations of the Tories, the conspiracy with the French to make a secret peace, the slanders published against Sarah on the instructions of Oxford, and the trial of Dr Sacheverell as a critical turning point in the story.

Sarah circulated the text in her own handwriting to protect Hoadly's identity, a reversal of the usual trick by which a female author was protected by a male front. In a letter to her friend Lady Hardwick, for example, she pretended that her male co-author was not a real person: 'Whoever reads this Account will wonder why I put on so many masks in the history, but they were not fit to be seen from me . . .'[32]

After Sarah had read the first draft of Hoadly's version, she gave him an additional account of how Marlborough had been gradually humiliated by Anne towards the end of his service, called for a greater emphasis on people's relentless ingratitude and broken promises, and drew his attention to Godolphin's letter in answer to his dismissal, which she praised for her dead friend's prophetic accuracy.[33] She also worked on Hoadly's draft from a stylistic point of view: Hoadly had been satirised by Pope for speaking and writing in painfully long sentences, which Sarah crossed out when she found them. She also deleted an entire page about Mrs Cornwallis, to whom she had previously compared herself. It seems she no longer wished to be just one in a long line of royal favourites, or perhaps she now shied away from linking herself too closely to the scandalous implications of the

Queen's close female relationships. Certainly Hoadly toned down the part of Burnet's narrative that described the intimacy between Anne and Sarah. It remains somewhat ironic, however, that Sarah recruited so many clergymen to work on such a sexually suggestive story.

At the time Sarah was pleased with Hoadly's work, but later fell out with him:

This man I made a Bishop [of Salisbury] by my perpetual solicitation after King George came into England, gave him money when he was in distress & lived with him many years a true friend. But when times changed & he did not want me, he left off visiting me, though I never had the least quarrel with him . . . When I was out of fashion with the present King and Queen he never took any notice of me.[34]

Her next exercise in authorship was very different: in her 'Green Book' she kept narratives concerning her family.[35] For this she needed no co-authors. It was a repository for her anger and despair whenever she fought with her daughters or grandchildren, but it was also, like her other memoirs, an answer to public slander: 'I have endeavoured to hide my misfortunes from the world,' she wrote, but 'I hope nobody will blame me now for what I do, which I am forced to by them to prevent my being pointed at wherever I go.' She forced her embarrassed friends, such as Lord and Lady Bristol, to read the Green Book and 'judge of my patience and sufferings'. Though never published, it is an entertaining and original work. It is a study of a woman's resentful self-martyrdom to her family. Sarah once remarked that the story of her private troubles was so incredible that it 'sounded like . . . Robinson Crusoe'.

Throughout the 1730s, Sarah constantly reworked the Green Book, adding and deleting her complaints in accordance with family members moving in and out of her favour. She also returned to her original 1704 memoir, and had a servant copy it so that it formed a column down one side of the page, against which she could make editorial notes.[36] In this way she added some lines that do not appear in the published version, but which reveal her 'if-I-were-in-your-shoes' stance when it came to royalty: 'I was sure that had it been my own case, I should have thought it more for my honour to be easy in it than to make a dispute who should have the Crown first that was taken from her Father.' No longer addressing the long-gone Elizabeth Burnet but a wider reading public, she continually second-guesses our reactions: 'I fancy the reader has been wishing that I made some offers to the Princess [to resign] . . .'

In both her personal and political memoirs she has the same goal: to persuade her readers that she lived her life according to the dictates of morality and reason. Neither book was a work of introspection in the modern sense, but Sarah can hardly be accused of failing to examine her own actions. If she was deceiving herself, it was only the self-deception of someone who had invented a story that no other version of events could override.

In addition to the prejudices against female authorship, she was writing in a form, secular autobiography, that was relatively new. Of more than three hundred diaries and two hundred memoirs believed published in England before 1700, only twelve pre-dated Sarah's birth. Her lifetime therefore coincided with autobiography's first popularity (just as it coincided with the invention of silvered mirrors). Sarah was attracted to this form because it prided itself, as she did, on a rather rugged sincerity – there were no polished models, as in poetry, to imitate. The outstanding model of a political memoir was *The Life of Lord Clarendon (1668–72)*. This was written in the third person, straining towards objectivity, but included no information about his domestic life. Sarah was caught between emulating this model, and at the same time feeling more like Mrs Manley with her eye pressed to the Queen's keyhole. It was a contemporary of Sarah's, Mademoiselle Aïssé (1694–1733), a slave girl brought from Constantinople to Paris to be a society lady, who had coined the adage 'No one is a hero to his valet' and Sarah knew that her behind-the-scenes revelations about Queen Anne were really what made her own memoirs so intriguing.

The Countess d'Anois' *Memoirs of Her Own Life* (1715) had sparked a new fad among injured noble ladies in England for self-vindication, though these pamphlets were usually intended to correct rumours of sexual, not political, misconduct. Defoe's novels, *Moll Flanders* (1722) and *Roxana* (1724), imitated this generation of female memoirists, with mock-narrators rather like Sarah's clerical co-authors. Sarah aspired to write a much more masculine kind of memoir, yet she also played upon the frisson of sexual scandal which was inherent in autobiography when held in female hands.

Sarah freely admitted that her own style of writing was uneducated and garrulous: 'When I am writing I run on as if I were speaking . . . when at the sitting down I don't design to say very much.'[37] She scorned 'great flourishes' in writing as in architecture, preferring to ramble from one subject to another – which was exaggerated by her poor grammar and lack of paragraphs. Pope satirised compulsive women writers – specifically Anne, Countess of Winchelsea – when he invented the character of Phoebe Clinket, with pens in her hair: 'She kept writing materials in every room in case inspiration seized her, and a compliant maid followed her about with a desk strapped to her back, so that Phoebe could even write on the move.'[38]

Sarah's surviving letters, long and urgent, are inseparable from her other writing. They do not make a collection as good as Lady Mary Wortley Montagu's or Madame de Sevigné's, which Sarah had her grandson translate for her, but they do give us her distinct voice, loud and clear.

The bulk of Sarah's energy and influence had always been dedicated to her husband and family. Historians and biographers have assumed that their interests were synonymous with Sarah's own. Most of the time she herself was probably persuaded of this. But among all her achievements, the only thing Sarah ever did entirely for herself, even if sometimes she claimed to do it as a wife and mother, was to write. 'I do protest,' she wrote, 'I would not part with it [her memoir] to have Blenheim finished.'[39]

* * *

In the spring of 1715, Sarah's writing was interrupted by illness. She was struck by severe rheumatism, a bout of scurvy, which made her skin itch and her teeth fall out, and St Anthony's Fire. She was nursed by her friend Charlotte Clayton and Dr Garth. She treated the itching on her legs by rubbing them with deer suet and dabbed at her gums with laudanum, while for rheumatism she dosed herself with opium mixed with brandy and saffron.[40]

From her sickbed, she continued her arguments with her two daughters, Mary and Henrietta, who upset her most when she was physically low. Sarah needed constant demonstrations of affection, which repelled the women as adults, as when she tried to hug Henrietta, 'begging her still to love me, but all that I could get in answer to this was that she gave me a little squeeze with her hand at parting'.

On one occasion, Henrietta hit a raw nerve when she reminded her mother that there had been times Sarah had not wanted her own mother's company. Henrietta also accused her – as a family's stronger members often feel resentment on behalf of the more compliant ones – of bullying the Duke.

After one particular argument, Henrietta went running to her father, but when Marlborough heard Sarah's side he made his daughter apologise. Henrietta had said to Sarah that everyone thought she had dutiful daughters except her. To refute this, Sarah asked Francis Godolphin, Henrietta's husband, whether he thought she had been a bad mother, to which '[h]e answered with his eyes full of tears that I had been the best in the world in all respects'.[41] Sarah then wrote Henrietta a letter in which she said that she regretted having spoilt her children. She said she had never failed Henrietta 'in any one thing from your cradle', and added that though '[t]his may look like saying too much of one's self, but you have forced me to do it . . .' She ended with a flourish of self-dramatisation, extreme even by her standards, quoting from a contemporary play: 'I will trouble thee no more my child. Farewell, we shall meet sometimes I hope in a decent way. Let shame come when it will I do not call it, I do not bid the Thunderbearer strike, nor tell Tales: Mend when thou canst; be better at thy Leisure; I can be Patient.'[42]

What Sarah failed to acknowledge was that, just as much as the 'sourness and austerity of a harsh parent', her controlling, over-attentive love, or the favouritism she had lavished on her son Jack during their childhood, might have formed Henrietta's adult indifference. 'What did I ever ask of you but to live with me as a friend?' Sarah asked her daughter, but the kind of friendship she wanted was perhaps the kind she herself had grown up with – more demonstrative and possessive than her daughter could stomach. One of her friends wrote to her in the 1720s, gently trying to explain that justice, rights and duties had little to do with such intimate relationships: 'I must beg leave to dissent from you when you say you never could love anybody twenty-four hours that you thought did not love you . . . I have experience on my side that love or indifference are not voluntary and do not depend on our will . . .'[43]

Henrietta and Mary did not put on paper any justifications for their coldness towards their mother, leaving posterity as baffled as Sarah claimed to be. In Henrietta's case, at least, we can presume that her affair with William Congreve must have been part of the problem, though Sarah seldom mentioned the subject directly, even in her Green Book. Sarah had been intervening to try to end the affair since as early as 1703, promising Henrietta's husband Francis that she would never let the public discover 'a proceeding that must appear so strange & monstrous'.[44] It was the appearance of respectability that most concerned her, since in a woman's case this was the same as reality.

Perhaps guilty at having made an unhappy match, Sarah always insisted that at the time of Henrietta's marriage the girl had found it 'extremely to her own satisfaction'.[45] Now she told Hare that she had never meddled in her daughters' lives apart from 'keeping them out of bad company'[46] – her euphemism for Congreve – and when she scoffed at Henrietta's desire to be thought a wit, she was in fact expressing moral disapproval of the literati circles in which Henrietta socialised. Her daughter had 'starts of giving 100 guineas to a very low poet that will tell her she is what she knows she is not', said Sarah, and when Congreve and Vanbrugh opened their new playhouse in the Haymarket, their patron Henrietta was applauded as 'the learned Minerva'. Sarah, on the other hand, took to referring to her daughter as 'Congreve's Moll' or 'Moll Congreve'.47

Once Sarah had visited Henrietta at home to find her in the middle of a card game with Congreve and another woman. She had sensed that she was unwanted in such company, and so, she told her daughter, 'put you at ease by going away'.48 Perhaps as much as her fear of open marital infidelity besmirching the Marlborough name, it was this self-pitying sense of exclusion that made Sarah try to draw Henrietta away from the playwright and his friends.

Marlborough had grown closer to Sarah during their years in exile, and now, on the perimeters of Court politics, told her that there were 'many things of which I can open my heart to nobody but yourself'.49 One such secret might have been that he had just sent the Pretender a contribution of £4,000 towards funding a Jacobite invasion.50 There had been Jacobite riots in London since April and, on 28–9 May 1715, Abel Boyer reported that 'a large mob burnt Cromwell (some say Hoadly) in effigy' and smashed the windows of Whig merchant's shops. This was at the very time that Sarah sat with Hoadly working on her memoir. Why Marlborough sent money to the Jacobites is unclear: he was not so violently disillusioned with George I as to turn traitor, so it must have been connected with government-approved espionage. It did not, in any case, interfere with his orders to repress the Jacobite uprising when it occurred in Scotland that September and then was followed in December by an attempt of the Old Pretender to land an invasion, which failed partly due to Berwick's refusal to take part.

Marlborough had written to Sarah with advance intelligence about the invasion she had feared for so long, asking her to keep it quiet so that the stock-market remained calm. He explained

why he could not leave London, from where he commanded his
old friend Cadogan, who commanded the army, and urged her
to join him there for her own safety. When she wrote back
to excuse herself from coming immediately, not sounding in
the least frightened, he replied that she always did as she
pleased.[51]

The uprising and invasion were an utter failure, only giving the
Whigs, including Marlborough and Sunderland, increased power
and permanently dissuading George I and his son from trusting a
member of the Tory party. In the early spring of 1716, however,
the Marlboroughs and Sunderland were struck by two serious
blows, which marred enjoyment of their increased influence with
the Hanoverians.

After her return to England Sarah had visited her daughter
Anne and seen how weak she was. This did not prevent her
from reproaching Anne whenever she tried to defend her less
dutiful sisters during 1715. Anne wrote to her mother: '[W]hen
I have done anything you dislike I would go through fire and
water I had not done it, or that you would forgive it. But
if it were my last words I would say whatever fault I have
committed it did not proceed from want of love to you . . .'[52]
Sarah seems to have been sensitive about Anne laughing at
her behind her back, referring to some conversation with the
widowed Earl of Bridgwater. When Sarah finally divulged this
as the reason for her anger, Anne vehemently denied it, and the
rift was healed.[53]

Then, without warning, in the spring of 1716, Anne succumbed
to septicaemia after a bloodletting and died. Sarah was shocked
and distraught, and could only rage against the incompetence
of doctors. An obituary appeared in *The Daily Courant* of 17
April 1716,[54] between shipping news and a listing of South
Sea stock prices: 'At Two a-Clock on Sunday morning last died
the Countess of Sunderland . . . She was a faithful, submissive,
affectionate Wife, and inspected carefully all Domestic Affairs,
and yet could, in an Instant, quit all that sort of Business, to
resume her own Dignity.' When Sarah read it, she observed only

that 'much more might have been said, for she was everything that was good and everything that was charming'.

As far back as 1709, Anne had put in a letter that if she died she would leave her children to her mother's care. She must have known then that this scenario was not unlikely, and told Sarah never to mention it to her husband, who might disapprove.[55] Now Lord Sunderland found another letter his wife had left him, containing her final wishes. He passed it to Sarah. In it, Anne asked her mother to guard her daughters and any sons too young to be sent to boarding-school, 'for to be left to servants is very bad for children'. She left firm instructions with regard to the marrying and education of the children, including Lord Sunderland's daughter by his first marriage. She begged her husband not to gamble or overspend for the sake of the children's inheritance and, perhaps from experience, expressed the fear that he would neglect her children if he remarried: 'And don't be careless of the dear children as when you relied upon me to take care of them, but let them be your care, though you should marry again, for your wife may wrong them when you don't mind it.'[56]

Sarah wept over her dead daughter's fortitude and foresight. She wrote immediately to Lord Sunderland, accepting the care of her grandchildren and asking for 'some little trifle that my dear child used to wear in her pocket, or any other way', a lock of Lady Sunderland's hair and her favourite cup. She also mentioned her particular wish to care for 'dear Lady Di' – Lady Diana Spencer, the youngest of the children.

Diana would become Sarah's favourite grandchild, a beautiful girl who looked much like her mother and hence rather like the Duke. Adopted at the age of six, she was encouraged to call Sarah 'Mother' and wrote her childish letters to 'Dear Mama Duchess'.[57] At the same time, Sarah adopted Diana's slightly older cousin, Lady Anne Egerton, the child of her daughter Elizabeth, Countess of Bridgwater. Since Elizabeth's death in 1714, Anne Egerton had been living with her paternal grandmother, who was now too old to keep her. She joined Diana, as well as

Harriot Godolphin, who was still living with Sarah in keeping with Sarah's promise to Henrietta.

The children had only been in their grandmother's house for a few days when, on 28 May, Marlborough suffered his first severe stroke. Some have blamed it on his grief at seeing Diana looking so like his lost daughter, but the cause was probably less sentimental, related to the acute headaches he had suffered for decades. Sarah suddenly found herself with a fourth 'child' to care for. Experienced from having nursed her mother after paralytic strokes, Sarah devoted herself to her husband's care that summer. She accompanied him to Bath, which she loathed, and wrote minutely detailed descriptions of his health to his doctors.[58] She fed him according to his prescribed diet, 'broth made of an old cock, bruised to pieces, bones and all, now and then two eggs poached in gravy, or five or six oysters just warmed in their shells',[59] and 'codlins' (young or small cod). She even considered making him a broth of boiled vipers, sent live from Montpellier, which she had heard would do him good.

Sarah had a book of other household remedies,[60] the ingredients for which were purchased at the apothecary shops in Camomile or Bucklesbury Streets. She gave her husband either 'Russian Castor', or a mixture of root vegetables, seeds and herbs mixed up in lemon syrup, or another concoction of 'Red Cow's Milk with balm, saffron, breadcrumbs, and cinnamon syrup' for what seems to have been diabetes. In 1719 she also started treating him with something called 'Sir Walter Raleigh's Cordial'. She paid ten guineas (around £80 in today's money) to the man who dressed his blisters and smaller amounts to other servants who sat up with him at night.[61] A number of doctors and other men competed for the job of watching over the illustrious patient, in the hope that it would prove financially rewarding, but Sarah cherished her own role of nurturing martyr too much to relinquish it.

Anne Spencer's death had prompted Sarah to mend relations with her other daughters. She wrote almost immediately to Mary:

I am resolved to make one step more, which is to put you in mind that whatever differences we have had, that they did not proceed from what generally makes parents & children disagree: a desire in the first of keeping an authority over them.

All that I ever wished for was your kindness, and all that I ever complained of proceeded from the want of it, but I find I still love you too well to enter into the reproaches that I might too justly make you, & I write this only to ask you if there is any thing in the world that I can do, which can make you love me, that we may live in perfect friendship ... [B]ut if you find that you can be no otherwise to me than as formerly or what is very little better, to live in a cold uneasy ceremony, I think it is best to continue as we are, without making any new comedies for the world.[62]

Remarkably, Mary embraced this reproachful overture and came to her mother at Holywell. Sarah was so hopeful of living on better terms that she burned Mary's former letters, believing that she no longer needed to argue her case to posterity. However, as Mary was packing her coach to leave St Albans, Sarah discovered that she had in her entourage a manservant Sarah had dismissed from her own service in 1712 'for very great crimes'. She was incensed that Mary had hired this man, as if to contradict her mother's action, and had even dared to smuggle him back under Sarah's roof. In her Green Book, she was soon complaining that Mary continued to avoid her socially, never inviting her to dinner or a play or the opera, and leaving Sarah to hear from a stranger that one of her Montagu grandsons was mortally ill. But Sarah resolved to keep all these grievances to herself and her Green Book. The two continued to correspond on civil terms as Mary took her first holiday on the Continent.[63]

In October 1716, Sarah went to inspect the Blenheim building works, which had resumed in August 1714 thanks to Lord Oxford's orders. That November Marlborough's condition worsened, so Sarah summoned three doctors and both her daughters to come to the house in which they were staying at Woodstock.

It was already overstuffed with servants and isolated by bad roads. According to Sarah, Henrietta's response was to write her father a letter critical of her mother, which she ordered a servant to deliver secretly. Sarah intercepted it and the unfortunate servant was reprimanded. When Henrietta arrived after dark that night, she went directly to her father. 'Though I stood prepared to receive her,' Sarah recalled, 'she took no more notice of me than if I had been the nurse to snuff the candles.'

Sarah begged her daughter to pretend all was well between them whenever they were in front of the Duke, but Henrietta did not reply to this, and shot her mother an angry look. After dinner, Sarah wrote, 'I went through the rooms with my arm in hers to hide this matter even from the servants; & when she came into her own chamber as I was talking to her without disguise, she seemed mighty easy and indifferent & looked in the glass, upon which I said "You're extremely pretty" and so left her.'

At the building site, Sarah faced 'a chaos that turns one's brains but to think of it.'[64] Since Marlborough's stroke, she had known she would have to finish Blenheim herself, and felt a fresh urgency to do so for her husband's sake. The Marlboroughs now proposed that they would pay for all future work if the government would cover all the bills up to 1712. Vanbrugh, appointed Comptroller of His Majesty's Works and the first man to be knighted by George I, therefore had his salary paid by Sarah, which she never let him forget. The only reason she kept him on was to reassure her husband, whom she wished to shelter from worry.

In the summer of 1716 Sarah commissioned James Thornhill to paint the ceiling fresco in the Grand Hall,[65] which showed Marlborough presenting Britannia with his battle plans. Between them stood the allegorical figure of Constancy, a muscular, bearded man holding his knife over the fire. In the background was the Temple of Fame, and surrounding the scene were the four cardinal virtues: Prudence bearing a mirror, Fortitude resting on a broken pillar, Justice with a sword, and Temperance looking on. Sarah also insisted that the figures of Peace, with an olive branch, Plenty, with a cornucopia, and Humility, embracing a lamb, were included, in allegorical answer to the most common satirical attacks on her husband – his love of war, miserliness and ambition. Later Sarah dismissed Thornhill for submitting, in her opinion, unreasonable invoices in which he charged as much for painting a square yard of blue sky as for the figures. Sarah's artistic opinion, and annoyance at being fleeced, were also expressed when she took delivery of some statues for Blenheim. She wrote to the elder James Craggs: 'Though I would give £73 for a dead fly as soon as for those statues, I think the Duke of Marl is obliged to pay for them since they are done.'[66]

Sarah also had to deal with the completion of Vanbrugh's bridge. To Charlotte Clayton she complained that this preposterous folly was meant to be pretty because you would be able to sit inside one of its thirty-three rooms and watch coaches drive over your head.[67] Vanbrugh was building 'bridges in the air' just to show off, she thought, adding sourly that '[p]ainters and poets and builders have very high flights, but they must be kept down'.[68] She might have borne these imaginative extravagances if Vanbrugh had not also disobeyed her other orders: Woodstock Manor was still standing, he had built without regard for views of the grounds from the main rooms, and persisted in underestimating the time and cost of his work. 'Sir John has given Lord Marlborough an estimate in which he tells him all is to be complete for fifty-four thousand three hundred and eighty-one pounds,' Sarah wrote, 'and because I can't believe that such a sum will do all, when thirty-eight thousand so lately did nothing, I am thought by him very troublesome and quite stupid.'[69]

On 8 November 1716, Vanbrugh resigned in protest at Sarah's badgering, leaving some 1,500 men unsupervised. Many felt it was no coincidence that, the following day, Marlborough suffered his second stroke.

To Sarah's credit, she made Blenheim habitable by 1719, without hiring a replacement architect. She merely sought the assistance of a cabinet-make named James Moore, whom she described as 'a miracle of a man'[70] and very honest. She remained faithful to Vanbrugh's plans, not being so arrogant as to think she could redesign at this stage, though she neither built the grand entrance nor put the fourth wall on the front court. Later, brisk with the business of keeping Marlborough from self-pity, she finished Vanbrugh's bridge, though she simplified it considerably. She asked her husband to authorise these alterations and rose at six every morning to supervise the day's work. Sarah also used the job as a source of political leverage, writing from Windsor to her agent at Woodstock that he should employ, wherever possible, workmen who were inclined to vote against her enemies and for her candidate, a Mr Crisp.[71]

For the interiors, Sarah hired Hawksmoor, who had volunteered for the job. This was either from a desire to complete what he had started or from gratitude for Sarah's having nominated him as surveyor of London's fifty new churches.[72] He was therefore responsible for the beautiful coffered ceilings still seen today in the Long Library.

Finally, in 1719, Sarah took on Louis Laguerre, a rival of Thornhill, to decorate the Saloon walls. Perhaps inspired by the 1660s ceiling fresco in the upper chamber of the Dutch Parliament, in which representations of the four continents in contemporary dress peer down in *trompe l'œil*, Laguerre's murals depicted the four continents paying tribute to Marlborough. The Duke rides in his chariot, driven by Aurora, with Truth before him as a woman holding up a mirror. The character of Mercury is shown holding the scroll of History, and the figures of Time (Sarah's hopes for posterity) and Plenty (Sarah's munificent charity to the poor) squeezed in.

After the Duke's second stroke, Sarah was even more willing to keep the peace, or the appearance of it, with her surviving daughters. She said she never prevented them from coming to see their father, but she complained that they never came to see him in the morning when the Marlboroughs were alone, 'but at the hours when company was there, going up towards him without taking any notice of me, as if they had a pleasure in showing everybody that they insulted me. This I bore, and when any great stranger happened to be there I would ask them some common question to hide as much as I could this wonderful behaviour.' She would try to ask her daughter Henrietta civil questions when they were in the same room, but never received more than a monosyllabic response. When the only observers were close family friends, Sarah sometimes remained silent for the entire visit. 'A thousand times upon such occasions when my heart has been ready to break & the company all gone,' she wrote, 'I have gone up to the poor Duke of Marlborough with a cheerful face, hoping he might not observe always such cruelties, & talked of other things, as if I had felt nothing . . .'[73]

Despite the arguments with Henrietta, Sarah was busy working to marry her adopted granddaughter Harriot. Her first thought was Thomas Pelham-Holles, heir to the Duke of Newcastle and, before Vanbrugh's resignation, she asked him to assist in making this match. When she found Lord Stair would be more useful, she dropped the architect from the assignment and badly bruised his ego – another reason for his dislike of Sarah.[74] She then took Harriot, decked out in a set of Sarah's diamonds, to a dance at Somerset House for society's inspection. There she put a hypothetical question to the Duke of Newcastle about whether he would be interested.[75] Newcastle demanded a dowry of £40,000 as compensation for such an unattractive girl, which Sarah refused. After some negotiation he accepted a proposal of £20,000, if Sarah would throw in some jewels and pay off various mortgages. Although this remained a poor deal and another, much wealthier, suitor named Mr Wentworth was on offer, Sarah pursued it because Harriot seemed attracted to Pelham-Holles. When Harriot cried over the possibility of marrying Mr Wentworth, Sarah 'took her in my arms & assured her that she need not be in any trouble, for I would not ask her to marry the emperor of the world if she did not like him'. After further tough negotiation with Newcastle, she secured for Harriot a good amount of pin-money, a generous jointure and a country house free of taxes. Henrietta did not have to concern herself for one minute, Sarah emphasised, or pay 'the expense of a pair of gloves'.

In April 1717 there was a reception for the newlyweds at Marlborough House, and when the seventeen-year-old Harriot became mistress of her own house, Sarah wrote that she gave herself 'the trouble to sit with her in the afternoons when she received visits, finding she was very helpless among so many strangers'. They drove together to Hyde Park in the Newcastles' gold chariot, but when Sarah offered a dinner party in their honour, she felt snubbed that they declined. She retaliated by refusing to accompany Harriot to the King's drawing room, giving the excuse that she could not speak French so was not the best chaperone. After this Harriot 'came to me sometimes at the hours of company & sat in a dead way, giving me the trouble of pumping for questions'. Once again Sarah felt that a child she had raised was inexplicably rejecting her. Reading between the lines of Sarah's account, however, one suspects that Harriot was struggling with the demands of marriage to a virtual stranger, and now wanted to reclaim the affection of her glamorous mother Henrietta, with whom she was seen whispering in corners at Sarah's house, rather than spend more time nursing or being nursed by her grandmother.

When Harriot fell ill with measles in September 1718, Sarah put aside her grievances and went immediately to see the girl, finding her with a 'face as white as her sheets'. Sarah begged the Duke of Newcastle to let her give Harriot a dose of Sir Walter Raleigh's Cordial and later believed that this was what cured her. She also intervened to prevent the patient being bled, for which she was never thanked, except by the nurse. Later, when she heard that Harriot was ill with a throat infection, due to having travelled from Hampton Court by water at four in the morning, Sarah went to Claremont, the Duke of Newcastle's home near Esher in Surrey, where she found him weeping in the corridor as if Harriot were about to die. She was sent away without being allowed to see her granddaughter, and although Harriot recovered, the offence given to Sarah never healed.[76] Sarah concluded this section in her Green Book: 'These appear to be all trifling things, but there has been such a noise in the world from my silence & from worthless people talking of me, that I can't resist any longer showing how little occasion I have given for such stories.'[77]

By April 1717, Sarah and Sunderland, who had inherited Marlborough's political followers after the Duke's strokes, were now clearly aligned with George I. In opposition, a circle had formed around the Prince and Princess of Wales, Robert Walpole, and Walpole's brother-in-law, Lord Townshend. Sarah's old friend and correspondent, Charlotte Clayton, whom Sarah had introduced to the Hanoverian Court, was becoming established as Princess Caroline's favourite and joined this circle when the Prince of Wales was expelled from Court by his father that November. In this act of ingratitude to her, Sarah found in Charlotte Clayton a new Abigail. Years later, she wrote on some papers about Abigail: 'I think the mischiefs that have been done since by Q[ueen] Car[oline], assisted in all vile things by Mrs Clayton, are much greater'.[78]

In the summer of 1717, a test of political loyalties came in the form of Lord Oxford's impeachment. The defeated minister had been sitting in the Tower since July 1715: a Committee of Secrecy, appointed in March 1715 to investigate the conduct of the Utrecht peace negotiations, concluded that treachery had been involved. After having been outmanoeuvred by Somerset, Shrewsbury and Argyll on the eve of Queen Anne's death, Bolingbroke had fled to France to escape arrest and had become Secretary of State to the Old Pretender. Now Oxford himself was petitioning to be brought to trial.

Swift, never having believed that his patrons had been guilty of dealing with the Jacobites, continued to embarrass them with offers to write in their defence. He wrote to his friend Erasmus Lewis that the prosecution of Lord Oxford was 'at first the resentment of a party, but it became at last a ridiculous business weakly carried on by the impotent rage of a woman (I mean my Lady Marlborough) who is most distracted that she could not obtain her revenge'.[79]

The invalid Marlborough made his last public appearance when he struggled into the House of Lords to vote against Oxford. Sarah copied out the homily that happiness belongs to 'he that liveth to see the fall of his enemy',[80] but her exaltation turned to bitterness when she discovered that Oxford would not, after all, be brought to trial. A split amongst the Whigs resulted in his release from the Tower, to retire peacefully to Brampton Bryan until his death in 1724.[81] One story, told by a friend of Oxford to Benjamin West, President of the Royal Academy, claimed that he was released because he had blackmailed Marlborough with letters in which the Duke appeared compromised for dealing with the Jacobites.[82]

The Marlboroughs retired for the rest of the summer to Tunbridge, with their friends Mr and Mrs Robert Jennings. Henrietta visited them and again ignored her mother. On her arrival, Sarah remembered, 'I advanced two or three steps thinking to have my share in a kiss, but she went off to sit down, which made me go back.' According to Sarah, the Jenningses were shocked by such behaviour.

In 1718 Sunderland, now First Lord of the Treasury, formed a new ministry that included Stanhope and General William Cadogan, as well as the younger James Craggs. This party descended ostensibly from Marlborough's interest and was now finally coming into its own, yet Sarah had reason to be suspicious of each of these four men. She was angry that Sunderland had given the post of Captain-General to Stanhope, a man 'of a temper to be weary of any post soon after he got it', rather than letting Marlborough keep it as an honorary title until he died;[83] she had not trusted Craggs for years, especially after his attempted rape of her servant; she had quarrelled publicly with Cadogan over his mishandling of her husband's money while they had been in exile;[84] and now for the first time since their 1702 argument over the Prince's Bill, Sunderland had also fallen out with her. Since his wife's death, he had found less reason to stay on good terms with Sarah, and in the autumn of 1717 he had announced his intention to remarry. Sarah thought his choice, Judith Tichborne, improper due to her 'namelessness',[85] but also because she was only fifteen. '[H]e was marrying a kitten,' Sarah wrote, 'and really I do think it very odd for a wise man of forty-five to come out of his library to play with puss.' Sarah's main fear was that the new marriage would impoverish her Spencer grandchildren, as her daughter had feared in her deathbed letter. In fact Sunderland immediately made over the bulk of his estate to his new wife and her future children, all of whom died in infancy.

It was not a good time for Sarah to alienate her son-in-law. In 1718, the Strong family of master masons sued the Marlboroughs for their pre-1712 work at Blenheim for which the Marlboroughs held the government accountable. Sarah had to embark on a series of legal battles that would drag on until 1721.[86] Vanbrugh should have been a co-defendant, but Sarah decided to use the case as an excuse to attack him. He wrote a letter, supposedly from an anonymous gentleman who claimed to have witnessed his abuse at Sarah's hands, which was read out in court. Sarah's riposte was a sixty-nine-page memorandum of her quarrels with the architect, which she sent to her counsel, Sir Thomas Pengelly, and to anyone else she thought might bother to read it.[87] Then Vanbrugh, her match when it came to free speech, went one better: he printed and sold his reply, entitled, *Sir John Vanbrugh's Justification of what he deposed in the Duchess of Marlborough's late Trial.* The sexism that had always underlain the architect's dealings with Sarah was evident in this *Justification.* He said that Sarah's version contained 'so much honest Language in it, fair stating of Facts, and right sound Reasoning from them, that one would almost swear it had been writ by a Woman'.

Sarah attended the proceedings in person, with Lady Lechmere, wife of the Solicitor General, as her companion. When she lost, she insisted upon appealing to the House of Lords where, because of her recent fights with Sunderland, she no longer had an organised interest. The vote went against the Marlboroughs (43 to 25), a final humiliation for the retired Duke. Secretary Craggs wrote to Lord Stair that Marlborough had 'a lady who exposes and uses his name very frequently. I love him well enough to wish it were over; he is a melancholy memento'.[88]

Sarah did not let the case rest there, however: she instigated a long-running Chancery suit against the workmen themselves, naming over four hundred of them in the course of the action.[89]

Nevertheless, by August 1719, Sarah and her friend Mr Moore had completed the east wing of Blenheim sufficient to allow the Marlboroughs to move in. They threw a lavish house-warming party, which included Richard Steele and Bishop Hoadly among the guests. Dryden's *All for Love* was performed by the grandchildren for the Duke's entertainment, with Steele as stage-manager and a special prologue written by Hoadly. Lady Charlotte Maccarty, daughter of Sunderland's dead sister, who had spent the early summer with them at Windsor Lodge 'as easy as any of the children',[90] was also at this party. A few years later, Sarah would help her to arrange an advantageous marriage to the heir to Lord de la Warr.

The house guests toured and discussed the building and grounds, admiring the advanced plumbing system which included pumped water in the walnut wood water-closets and a heated plunge pool in the undercroft, reached by stairs from Sarah's bedroom.[91] Pope had written to a friend that he thought Blenheim was built 'entirely in complaisance to the taste of its owner'.[92] This was only true if that owner was taken to be Marlborough, not his wife. The building of Blenheim had cost £300,000 (almost £24 million in today's money), four-fifths of which had been paid by the State. Sarah has been criticised in numerous modern books on English architecture as tight-fisted for having thought this was an unreasonable amount for a house. 'Every friend of mine knows that I was always against building at such an expense,' Sarah wrote, 'and as long as I meddled with it at all I took as much pains to lessen the charge every day as if it had to be paid for out of the fortune that was to provide for my own children, for I always thought it too great a sum even for the Queen to pay . . .'[93]

After the guests had departed, the Marlboroughs passed their days in strolling through the gardens. Henry Wise had built a military garden for the Duke, with bastions and terraces, which was destroyed in the 1760s and replaced with a cricket pitch.[94] Indoors, they spent their time mostly in the bow-window room, the only one Sarah found cosy and convenient. It was simply furnished with some comfortable chairs, a red crimson footstool and a little stand for the tea-kettle.[95] What sunlight came through the east-facing windows was caught and reflected in the large silver mirror above the mantelpiece crafted by Mr Moore. Curtains of blue damask silk framed a view of the garden planted with roses, marigolds, black-eyed hotspurs and coxcombs.[96] For a few summers, in this room and in the gardens, Sarah gave her husband the retirement of which he had always dreamed, though he was no longer fit to enjoy it.

Sarah ruled him in his easy chair as she had ruled the invalid Queen Anne, protecting but also controlling, acting as the gatekeeper for his communication with the outside world. Dr Garth agreed that Marlborough probably lived longer due to Sarah's sustained care.[97] There is a story of Sarah trying to get her husband to take his medicine, declaring that she would 'be hanged' if it did not do him some good, and Dr Garth then joking: 'Do take it, my lord Duke, for it must be of service one way or the other.' Sarah laughed, able to take teasing from friends when it was to her face.[98]

In 1718, the Duchess of Montagu had had what Sarah described as 'a fit of decency' in so far as she wrote a six-line letter to her mother asking to be kept informed about her father's health while she was out of town. Sarah took the opportunity to complain at some length that, before leaving, Mary had come to see her father without letting her mother know that she was on the premises.[99] This was, Sarah wrote, a step beyond her usual trick of calling only when she knew Sarah to be out. The Marlboroughs went to Tunbridge Wells where they did not hear further from Mary. When they returned to London, Mary and her husband did not visit for another twenty-four hours, despite reports that Marlborough was dying, 'which I could not help thinking showed a want of tenderness even to him'. When Mary did visit, Sarah was unable to 'speak for weeping', she said, but the only enquiry Mary made was after little Diana. Sarah went on to catalogue her acute embarrassment in front of friends such as the Duchess of Monmouth whenever a servant reported that her daughter had come and gone without greeting her. She ended by hoping that Mary and Henrietta would come to understand her feelings when their own children abandoned them one day. She repeated, as if convincing herself, her certainty that she had been a good mother. Finally, almost as a postscript, she gave Mary the news she had written for: 'Your father is, with constant watching & care, generally pretty easy to himself, but I fear there is very little hope that he will ever be as he has been.'

After such an openly recriminatory letter, Sarah's denial that she was responsible for an anonymous poison-pen letter that Mary had received in the post seems credible: '[W]hatever I could have cared she should know, [I] would have signed it.'[100]

One evening that winter, Sarah came home to Marlborough House to find Henrietta sitting by a table where other visitors were playing ombre. She looked at her mother 'with a great deal of fierceness, & then took a pinch of snuff without so much as rising up to make me a curtsy'. Sarah wrote that these snubs were so hurtful and embarrassing that she started to make it a habit to go out on Sundays, when Henrietta and Mary most often visited their father. A young girl named Mary Cairnes (later Lady Blayney), whose mother had met Sarah at Blackheath soon after the Marlboroughs' return from exile and who often stayed with Sarah to keep her granddaughters company, was an impartial eye-witness to such scenes. In old age she wrote to one researcher in the Blenheim archives to assure him that she sympathised with Sarah more than with the daughters:

People have a way of saying there must be faults on both sides. Perhaps there might be some on her side, but in general the parent

Portrait of Queen Anne by Dahl, which, even taking into account the period's convention of giving ladies jowly faces, suggests her heaviness. The artist draws attention to her slender hands.

Sarah's mother and older sister, both named Frances. The portrait of her mother (*above*), attributed to Kneller, is either uncharacteristically realistic or intended to cast aspersions on the subject's morals. That of her sister (*below*), attributed to Gascars, seems to match the portrait of Sarah in which both Maids of Honour hold flowers to advertise their fertility to prospective husbands.

Sarah's four daughters: (*top left*) Elizabeth Countess of Bridgwater with her two children; (*top right*) Anne Countess of Sunderland with her daughter Diana; (*bottom left*) Mary Duchess of Montagu; and (*bottom right*) Henrietta, who inherited the Marlborough title. While Elizabeth and Anne kept in their mother's favour, Mary and Henrietta spent most of their adult lives estranged from her.

The Duke of Marlborough (*left*) with his chief engineer,
Colonel Armstrong, by Seeman, a portrait Sarah described as
being 'as like him as I ever saw'. Sarah devoted many years to
completing Blenheim Palace, shown below in a print by
Fournier, as a memorial to her husband's achievements.

Sarah's friends. *Above*: The Devil removes the rewards of
Church promotion to punish one of Sarah's co-authors,
Benjamin Hoadly, for his tolerant religious beliefs.
Below left: Arthur Maynwaring, another literary
collaborator, called Sarah 'more capable of business than
any man'. *Below right*: Sarah's long friendship with Sidney,
1st Earl of Godolphin, was as crucial to her political
influence as her relationship with Queen Anne.

Satirical images of women. (*Above*) *The Triumph of Envy*: Marlborough is surrounded by emblematic women – not only Honour and History, but also the Medusa-like Envy, with skin 'shrivelled like parchment', and Discord carrying a firebrand and blowing her own trumpet.

(*Below*) *Faction Display'd*: the Whigs and Tories accused one another of fermenting factionalism and schism, with women often depicted as driving these monsters forward by the tail.

Sarah's enemies. The portrait of Abigail Masham has been attributed as such thanks to the Whig prejudice against her as ugly. Robert Harley, 1st Earl of Oxford, was similarly described by Sarah as 'a little, shuffling wretch' after she discovered that he was advising Queen Anne to oppose her wishes.

The tomb at Blenheim, designed by William Kent under Sarah's instruction. Marlborough's body was exhumed from Westminster Abbey when Sarah died in order to join hers in Blenheim Chapel.

*has a right to a great deal from the child; we love & protect them
for so many years before it is possible for them to make the least
return & when they are old enough all we require (if we are
reasonable) is filial affection & appearance of respect . . .*[101]

Similarly, Charlotte Maccarty once wrote to Sarah: 'I have had
the opportunity of being witness to many instances of your being
ill-used from those you have had the least reason to expect it
from, which other people couldn't believe.'[102]

Another evening, when there was a masked ball at the King's
Theatre in the Haymarket, attended by one of Sarah's granddaughters and Charlotte Maccarty, a drunken group of young
masqueraders came afterwards to Marlborough House to entertain the invalid Duke with their costumes. '[A]mong which,' Sarah
believed, 'Mr Secretary Craggs came dressed as a Friar.' Craggs
sat down next to Sarah and expressed surprise that she should
agree to receive the masqueraders, for her enemies might sneak
into her house by that means. At which Sarah asked, 'Who are
my enemies?' and he answered, 'The Duchess of Montagu or
my Lady Godolphin may come and, not knowing them, you
may give them a cup of tea or a dish of coffee.' This was said,
Sarah regretted, loudly enough to be overheard by the other
amused guests.

Sarah linked her daughter Mary to this prank, perhaps because
Mary was rumoured to be having an affair with Craggs. This
gossip, at any rate, makes an appearance a decade later in
Montesquieu's commonplace book, *Le Spicilège* (1729), in which
the Frenchman recorded that the Duke of Montagu wrote to
Sarah, 'upon her daughter's F[uck]ing with M. Craggs. She
answered, "Milord, I have received your gracious letter. I am
sorry you are a cuckold, my daughter a whore . . ."'[103] Craggs
certainly kept another married woman as a mistress and was
notoriously sure of his own attractions, so it would not have
been out of character for him to seduce the young Duchess of
Montagu.

In the spring of 1719, Sarah began to involve her grandchildren in her wrangles with her daughters. She had Marlborough add a codicil to his will, which made the two grandsons who would be the main heirs – Lord Rialton (Henrietta's son, Willigo) and Lord Spencer (Anne's son, Robert) – financially independent after Marlborough's death. This detaching of children from their parents echoed the generational splits in the Hanoverian Court. The following summer, when the Marlboroughs visited the Prince and Princess of Wales at Richmond, Caroline, getting her information from Charlotte Clayton, gossiped about the Marlborough family rows. Sarah spoke with equal disapproval of the gulf between the Prince and the King. In fact Sarah ran her extended family very much like a miniature Court, in which her affection, and the wealth attached to it, were the prizes to be won. She always had favourites among her grandchildren, and her love for them was inseparable from her money. These things had always been inseparable in her own life: in Queen Anne's love for her, in her mother's and sister's demands for assistance, and in her husband's proof of his love by granting her control of her own wealth. The threat of disinheritance was an ugly tool, which Sarah wielded too often during the last decades of her life, yet it must be remembered that the money at stake was what she and her husband had earned and saved through their own efforts. In the following years, Sarah would multiply the size of her own fortune and so multiply the ways in which she could control her heirs.

During 1719, Sarah was preoccupied with marrying Lady Anne Spencer, Diana's seventeen-year-old sister, to the son of a South Sea Company director. She instructed her servants to enquire into the true size of Mr Bateman's estate before she would agree to the match. Though she found that Bateman had misrepresented it, she nevertheless agreed to the marriage, believing that he had enough for them to live on if they practised good household management: '[T]hough there must be money to make a family easy I shall always prefer sense and virtue before the greatest estates or titles,' she declared.[104] It was more difficult to force Lord Sunderland to pay some portion of his eldest daughter's dowry, when he seemed content to leave these children to the Marlboroughs' cost as well as care. Mindful of her daughter's final wishes, Sarah badgered him until he agreed to shoulder some of the responsibility. At this point, Sarah had nothing but kind words for this grand-daughter.

In early 1721, when Mary invited her father to come alone to Montagu House to play whist with Lord Sunderland, Vanbrugh and her sister Henrietta, he had replied: 'I thank you for your letter, my dear child, but I observe that you take no manner of notice of your mother. And certainly when you consider of that, you can't imagine that any company can be agreeable to me who have not a right behaviour to her.'[105] No doubt, the Marlboroughs drafted this reply together: John was so ill at that point that Sarah thought attending the game would have killed him. Mary's reply was unrepentant, referring mysteriously to 'some things she [Sarah] had done to me that were never done before by a mother, kind or unkind'. Marlborough denied that he understood his daughter's meaning, adding a postscript: 'I am not well enough to write so long a letter with my own hand; and I believe I am the worse to see my children live so ill with a mother for whom I must have the greatest tenderness and regard.' The pathos of a father pleading with his daughters to love their mother for his sake seems to have had no effect on Mary. She and Henrietta continued to visit their father approximately every ten days, always ignoring Sarah, and refusing to make even a show of reconciliation.

After Queen Anne's death, the South Sea Company set up by Lord Oxford had converted to the Hanoverian interest. The Company, with offices on the corner of Threadneedle Street and Bishopsgate, had already hit problems in 1715, because its profit was predicated on the *Assiento*. In reality, the only profit to be gained from this trade agreement was from a limited right to trade slaves. But even this agreement was never watertight: there was much competition from illegal suppliers. By far the largest investors in the Company were, separately, the Duke and

Duchess of Marlborough, with over £30,000 of Sarah's personal fortune invested in it by 1717.[106]

Women were becoming a significant minority of investors[107] and a window of opportunity opened briefly for a number of married women who could deal legally in stocks because Parliament had not yet thought to ban it.[108] Sarah had a head start in terms of experience. Since Marlborough had transferred a further portion of his fortune to his wife's control before going to war in March 1705, she had pursued an investment career. At first she was heavily dependent on friends' advice, making loans to the Treasury – that is, Godolphin – and buying £10,000 of Bank of England stock.[109] She and her husband also invested in the East India Company and the Hudson's Bay Company at that time. By 1719, Sarah was worth over £100,000 (almost £8 million today) in her own right. Her surviving correspondence is so voluminous partly because it contains many questions to dealers about dividends and stock prices, instructions to pay over specific amounts, and periodic requests to review her accounts.

Like the art of autobiography, the art of dealing in stocks was a recent innovation. The London Stock Exchange had been founded in 1697 and was unregulated when Sarah entered the market. Just when she was feeling peripheral to the Hanoverian Court, she was growing closer to this new centre of power: the City. Various handbooks had been published to educate the European public about investing, such as Joseph Penso de la Vega's *Confusion of Confusions* (1688), but Sarah had had the Lord Treasurer himself as her personal tutor. She and her husband also profited, it seems, from inside information. On 3 June 1703, for example, Marlborough had urged her to sell East India stock quickly because he was pessimistic about the course of the war in Spain; in August 1710 he had again warned her that she should sell their Bank stock before the ministerial changes; and in 1715 he had forewarned her of the Jacobite invasion partly for reasons of private financial gain. Though none of this was illegal, it might explain some of the resentment felt against the Marlboroughs as privileged profiteers.

Sarah lived in an age when a degree of shame was still associated with 'stock-jobbing'. In one *Examiner*, Swift cursed the Whig stock-jobbers who had 'brought in such a complication of knavery and cozenage, such a mystery of iniquity, and such an unintelligible jargon of terms to involve it in . . .'[110] There was a fine line between investment and the sin of gambling, which was prevalent among upper-class women. Sarah was a bad gambler, being naturally averse to risk, yet she had played cards all her life, ever since those games of piquet with Lady Fitzharding as a girl, and she still wrote, as an old woman, that she preferred the 'noise of the box and dice' to music.[111] She was not the only woman to take up the new game of stocks, but she was certainly the most powerful female player.

The fear of changeable market forces was usually expressed by representations of 'Credit' as an inconstant, wilful and gossipy woman.[112] Sarah was fascinated by the idea of credit being as subjective as a person's reputation: as Charles Davenant wrote, 'Credit was a matter of confidence and confidence was a matter of opinion.'[113] It was no coincidence that printers and booksellers worked cheek by jowl with the bankers and stock-jobbers' coffee-houses, Jonathan's and Garraway's, along the cobbled length of (Ex)Change Alley. Sarah wrote her own narrative (her 'Account') and made her own fortune – she was 'self-made' in both senses.

By May 1720, Edward Harley, Lord Oxford's brother, wrote that there were 'few in London that mind anything but the rising and falling of stocks'.[114] A plan had been launched for the South Sea Company to absorb the total national debt within twenty-five years by persuading the public to exchange government bonds for shares. The aim was to convert long-term irredeemable debts into lower-interest, redeemable stock.[115] A committee was established to lobby Parliament on behalf of the scheme and MPs, including Cabinet Ministers, were bribed with free stock to support it.

There was debate in Parliament over the scheme's monopoly and the prices paid for annuities, but objections were overridden.

Silenced by the promised rewards, nobody asked what would happen when the stock price rose above the true value of the Company.[116] The collapse of the French financial structure just before the passing of the South Sea Act seems to have made no impression in England. If the company's directors and their political allies did see any parallels, it was only in thinking that they must make sure to get out in time.

Amid the hype, Sarah was sceptical. She pulled both herself and her husband out of the scheme in May: 'I had persuaded him to sell out of the South Sea and would do all that I could to oppose his buying again.'[117] On 28 May 1720 an article appeared in *The Daily Post* stating: 'The Duke of Marlborough from £27,000 South Sea stock has made nearly £100,000 but the Duchess drew her money out of the South Sea and put it into the Bank; and on Wednesday her Grace subscribed £2,000 to the Lord Onslow's insurance of ships.' This time Sarah was not acting on inside information, but instinct. In her private letters to friends, she wrote that common sense told her it was impossible 'to carry £400,000,000 of paper credit with £15,000,000 of specie'.[118] In another letter from this period, she described the South Sea scheme as a 'gulf which has or which will swallow all things'.[119] Meanwhile, however, Sarah loaned money to friends so that they could speculate, making sure that she had firm securities for repayment, thereby cushioning her own risk. She even used what remaining influence she had with Lord Sunderland to obtain subscriptions for her friends. Sarah's sister Frances was one such petitioner, causing Sarah to write to Lord Sunderland for 'this thing which is called a favour'.[120]

When the 'bubble' burst in mid-October 1720, Sarah was one of the few who were unaffected. She watched as enemies (Vanbrugh, Prior) and friends (the Dukes of Chandos, Portland, Wharton and Bolton, to name but a few) lost their fortunes. Many aristocrats were forced to seek colonial postings to keep afloat;[121] others lost only their expected gains. The real losers were the annuitants – the owners of the government bonds who had swapped them for South Sea stock – and the middle- and working-class people who had been tempted to invest their life savings. For them, overseas exile was often a matter of escaping debtors' prison by crossing illegally to France.

In fact Sarah made a profit of over £100,000 from the calamity, which she used to furnish Blenheim, extend her art collection, and purchase estates from those now desperate enough to sell at a loss. Jonathan Swift cursed those like Sarah who profited by the burst bubble as scavengers – 'a savage race by shipwrecks fed'[122] – ironic, given that Sarah had moved her money to naval insurance.

In reality, Sarah's behaviour seems to have been astute but honourable; certainly nothing compared to that of the aristocrats in France who had profiteered from soaring inflation by stockpiling food supplies then reselling them to the poor at higher prices.[123] Evidence survives among Sarah's papers to show that she was charitable to those genuinely needy people who were ruined in the crash, especially women. She helped one Mrs Kempe, the wife of a major from Marlborough's army, to support her eight children, after receiving a letter that stated, 'If some generous hand does not rescue us from present ruin . . . all my poor children turned out to beg, I starve at home, while my poor husband to avoid a gaol perhaps dies in a ditch . . .'[124] On the other hand, Sarah did not have reason to feel overly proud of her caution and common sense, as this was only a by-product of her previous wealth. As one Mrs D'Arcy wrote enviously in December 1720: 'Independence is of immense value & that I think is your great felicity.'[125]

Despite her profits, Sarah was among the loudest of those calling for the South Sea Company's promoters to be prosecuted for criminal folly. A secret committee in the House of Commons was established to investigate over four hundred MPs and a hundred peers who were alleged to have received bribes. Robert Walpole, who had been appointed Paymaster General in June 1720, was one of the few politicians not directly involved in the scheme. What stocks he owned in the Company he had sold in March, too early to make as great a profit as Sarah but soon enough to avoid ruin.[126] After the event, in a career move more brilliant than his financial one, he chose to shield his colleagues from retribution, acting as their barrister.[127] He developed a scheme of redress, much more lenient than similar laws in France – perhaps because the aftermath of the crash was ultimately beneficial to the British government, which had rid itself of much debt.

The role Walpole played now as shield sparked off a grudge in Sarah that she would always hold against him: it made her forever suspicious of his financial probity. But it enabled him to rise to the fore of the Whig party and win the favour of the King's mistress, the Duchess of Kendal, who was heavily invested in the scheme. Walpole also saved Lord Sunderland, whose acceptance of bribes with four other Ministers, John Aislabie, Charles Stanhope and the two Craggses, was uncovered.[128]

Only Aislabie went to the Tower, but even he kept his estates and retired peacefully. The younger James Craggs, the 'wicked' rake who had provoked Sarah's anger for so many reasons since the early 1700s, also died suddenly of smallpox in February 1721, leaving his father devastated by the loss of his only son. The old man, raised by Marlborough's patronage and his own efforts from the humblest of beginnings as a local postmaster, was blamed as the *éminence grise* behind the South Sea affair, and his trial was set for 18 March 1721, but on 17 March he committed suicide with an overdose of laudanum.[129] On the back of a letter from one of her servants, Sarah noted that the South Sea scheme had been 'managed by Old Craggs, who when the villainy of it came out, poisoned himself for fear of the Parliament'.[130] She did not mention her own role in hounding him to face justice – in revenge for the way he had sided with Vanbrugh at the Blenheim trial – while he was still in the depths of profound grief.

The man most pursued by Sarah's fury, however, was her former son-in-law and political ally, Sunderland. He, in turn, was livid that she should be stirring up public anger against him, especially after he had helped her to get her friends into the Company's subscription. Lord Cadogan, taking his revenge for Sarah having earlier sued him over mishandling her husband's money, impressed upon Sunderland that Sarah was the one behind the calls for his prosecution.

One of the stranger, related stories, for which Sarah was not responsible, was the rumour that Sunderland was a homosexual who had written love letters to one Edward ('Beau') Wilson. These fictional letters were published in 1723 amid scandal and speculation over the author's identity. As a supporter of the South Sea Company, Sunderland was linked to them because the practice of stock-jobbing was seen as making profit without production, and this was linked in the public psyche with non-reproductive sex. It was for this reason that many Londoners imagined the homosexual centre of their city to be located near (Ex)Change Alley, when in fact it was more likely to be found near Lincoln's Inn Fields.[131] The slander of homosexuality was therefore a way to attack those who made 'money for nothing', an interesting variation on the old slanders against wealthy royal favourites.

Sunderland's response to Sarah's calls for his dismissal and prosecution was to summon Marlborough to his house one evening and rant about how he must control his wife's tongue. When the Duke tried to defend her, Sunderland made a stunning accusation: that Sarah 'had remitted a great sum of money when the last fright of a Scotch [Jacobite] invasion' was afoot.[132] In all probability, Sunderland had learned of the £4,000 donation during his investigations into the Atterbury Plot. (Francis Atterbury had been in correspondence with the Old Pretender in 1717 and was arrested and banished in 1723 for plotting with the Jacobites against George I.) Either this was a sideways means of threatening the Duke with what he knew, or he was misinformed that Sarah had been the donor. 'This conversation,' wrote Sarah, 'harassed the poor Duke of Marl so much that he came home half dead.' Her narrative transferred the charge of irrational temper, so often made against her, to Sunderland's shoulders. She cast herself as the gentle wife who cared for her weak husband: 'He was half dead when he came into the room, but before I knew what the occasion was of it, I revived him with a great glass of strong wine and toast . . .'[133]

In her papers Sarah described how, before their deaths, Earl Stanhope and Secretary Craggs had been part of this plot to discredit her as a Jacobite 'to frighten me from talking against the S[outh] Sea Directors'. She claimed that they showed letters to the King, forged and signed with her name, convincing George I of her treason. Having first laughed off these 'incredible' allegations, Sarah was eventually forced to take them seriously. She went twice to Court to exonerate herself via the Duchess of Kendal, accompanied by her friend Lady Blayney, but was snubbed on both occasions, which suggested to her that the Ministers' stories were believed.

Sarah's next step was to draft a letter to the King, translated into French (the common language between the King and his courtiers), protesting her innocence of the charges.[134] She delivered it in person, but went away too hastily because she was ashamed that she could not speak the language. This, she believed, gave Sunderland and the other Ministers a chance to repeat the rumours or perhaps, she guessed, to tell the King 'that I was a madwoman'.[135] Already a portrait of Sarah as an irrational old harridan was being formed to silence her.

King George's reply to her letter was unsatisfactory. It merely stated that 'I am always disposed to judge of [Marlborough] and you by the behaviour of each of you in regard to my service . . .' This might have implied that Sarah had acted without her husband's knowledge in making the donation or, as she might not have understood, the exact reverse.[136] In the middle of the King's letter, Sarah detected 'what I know to be My Lord Sunderland's style'.[137] She considered returning again to Court to clear her name, as had been her way with Queen Anne, but had the sense to realise she had no standing – and, more importantly, no language – with which to persuade.

Sarah's loyalties may also have been suspected because one of her grandsons, the Marquess of Blandford, had been to visit the Pretender in Rome and afterwards anonymously published

A Letter from an English Traveller at Rome – a skilful piece of Jacobite propaganda which was in circulation during the time of the Atterbury Plot.

In April 1722, without warning, Lord Sunderland died at the age of forty-seven. Sarah's first concern when she heard of his death was to secure his private papers on behalf of his son, Robert Spencer, now 4th Earl of Sunderland. She believed they would prove his father's guilt and her own innocence. She therefore tried to put the Marlborough seal on to his study door at Sunderland House, but government agents, eager to protect State secrets, broke through it 'in a very ill manner'.[139]

More importantly, Sarah sought control of her Spencer grandchildren. She formalised her adoption of Diana, and immediately summoned Robert Spencer home from his Grand Tour with clear instructions to visit her directly after landing at Dover. In Robert, a young man she hardly knew, Sarah hoped to find a new object for her favour, and a new means by which to play the political game vicariously.[140]

On 15 June 1722, the shadows of a warm summer evening drew in around the Lodge at Windsor Great Park, the outer calm belying the mounting tension inside the house. Three days earlier, doctors had been summoned from London with the news that the seventy-three-year-old Duke of Marlborough was dying. Sarah, who thought her soul was tearing from her body, had also summoned her daughters and grandchildren. Her account of the arguments she had with them that night is one of her most remarkable pieces of writing:

I am sure it is impossible for any tongue to express what I felt at that time; but I believe anybody that ever loved another so tenderly as I did the Duke of Marlborough may have some feeling of what it was to have one's children come in, in those last hours, who I knew did not come to comfort me, but like enemies that would report to others whatever I did in a wrong way . . . I could not say many things (which otherwise I would have) before them. Yet I would not refuse them to come in, for fear I should repent of it. Upon which I desired Mrs Kingdom [Jane Kingdom – a family friend] to go to them & tell them that I did not know what disorder it might give their father to go to him now, but I desired they would judge themselves & do as they liked, but I begged of them that they would not stay long in the room, because I could not come in while they were there, being in so much affliction. Mrs Kingdom delivered this message and she told me that the Duchess of Montagu answered that she did not understand her, but if she meant that they were not to see their mother they were very well used to that.

They stayed a great while (as I thought) and not being able to be out of the room longer from him, I went in though they were there and kneeled down by him: They rose up when I came in, and made curtsies, but did not speak to me, and after some time I called for prayers. When they were over, I asked the Duke of Marlborough if he heard them well and he answered Yes & he had joined in them.

After that he took several things & when it was almost dark, these ladies being all the time present, I said, I believe he would be easier in his bed, the couch being too narrow & asked him if he liked to go to bed. He said Yes, so we carried him upon the couch into his own room.

When his blisters & inflammation upon his back were dressed & he was in bed, to my great surprise the Duchess of Montagu & Lady Godolphin came in & some time after that the Duchess of Newcastle and stayed there a great while after the candles were brought in. The room not being very large was pretty full with d[octo]rs, surgeons, apothecaries & servants, so I went myself to my Lord Sunderland [Robert Spencer] and desired him to go away and send Lady Egerton, Di and her two brothers out of the room.

Sarah, again waiting outside the room, then repeatedly asked her two daughters and granddaughter Harriot to leave it so that she could lie down beside her husband. They refused, Mary answering:

Will our being here hinder her from lying down? Then I sent Grace [Ridley – her servant] to her again, to ask If she had such an affliction

& was in my condition, whether she would like to have me with her? She said No, but did not go out until I sent to her a third time.

At this point Harriot left the Lodge, while Henrietta and Mary stayed in the drawing room until four in the morning. This was the hour when Marlborough died of a final cerebral stroke – if not peacefully, then at least in his own bed and with Sarah at his side.

II

Dowager

After the long night of Marlborough's death, Sarah almost never saw her daughters in private again. She believed that, as soon as they returned to London, they immediately thrust a private matter into the public light, claiming that she had ordered her servants not to give them food or drink then to throw them out in the middle of the night.[1] Later she organised a reconstruction of the deathbed scene at Windsor Lodge so that servants and other witnesses, including 'Little Di', could disprove her daughters' version of events. She also sat down to write the scene, to 'vindicate myself to a few friends'. She concluded: 'I wish that I may be forever miserable if I ever loved anything the hundredth part so well as I did all my children (except the Duke of Marl) till they used me so cruelly, and tis not to be expressed how much I have suffered before I could overcome the tenderness I had in my heart for them . . .'

What has lasted in posterity is the impression that Sarah's maternal love came a very distant second to her marital love. When Mary read the narrative Sarah had sent her, she apparently replied that it was 'not for her to contradict what her mother said'. Sarah scoffed at this, claiming there was no answer Mary could dare to make because 'there were at least 8 people in the room' who had seen and heard what happened.[2] But when one of these eight, Jane Kingdom, did not definitively contradict her daughters, Sarah accused her of spreading slander and declared, 'It is not my fault – I was not the aggressor & am the mother.'[3] What Sarah never addressed were the emotional causes of her daughters' actions: how it felt for their mother to be jealous of their relationship with their father.

Sarah wrote to Charlotte Clayton, with whom she was intermittently reconciled, that she had given up on Henrietta: 'I am just now before her picture when a child, which has a gentle good natured look as ever I saw & it amazes me to think that such a face . . . could be made by ill company such a creature as she is now . . . I am sure there can never be any alteration in her for the better after so many years.'4 According to another friend, Sarah 'used to say she had made them all such great ladies that it turned their heads'.5 When Sarah ejected her husband's paunchy chaplain, Dean Barzillai Jones, from her home for having spread a rumour that she was trying to make the government pay for the Duke's funeral, Henrietta immediately sent him a hundred pounds as compensation. Sarah discovered this insult when his note of thanks was misdelivered to her as the 'Duchess of Marlborough' instead of 'Dowager Duchess'.6 There was no easier way for people to flatter the new Duchess than by insulting her mother and much of this mail landed accidentally in Sarah's hands. When Sarah freed a debtor because he 'had but half clothes to cover him, that his shirt was as black as ink, that he was all over Lice & must perish in a very short time if he was not taken out', malicious gossip said that she had hired a servant who had stolen from Henrietta as revenge for Henrietta's gift to Dean Jones.7

It was to answer these insults and accusations from her daughters after Marlborough's death that Sarah had started to write the Green Book. With time, it evolved into a kind of 'how-not-to' portrait of a dysfunctional family, an unintentional parody of the period's preachy advice books for wives and children. It opens with an expression of reluctance to say a word against her own flesh and blood, yet goes on to fill hundreds of large, dense pages. When, years later, Sarah would send the book to Alexander Pope, his reply was both bluntly true and subtly double-edged: 'I wish everybody you love may love you, and am sorry for everyone that does not.'8

When not re-enacting her husband's last day or arranging for the rooms at Marlborough House to be draped in black cloth, Sarah sought solitude. We know that she read Bishop Hopkins' *Death Disarmed of Its Sting* but it is unlikely that she found much consolation in its pious pages.

If it was true that Sarah had lost much of her natural humour and gaiety after the death of her son Jack, she had now lost the only person who had known her gentler, more vulnerable side. As a woman's character was believed to be only as good as her reputation, so a side of Sarah vanished when no one was left to see it.

Meanwhile, Marlborough's embalmed body lay in state in Westminster Abbey. Admission to see it was by ticket only, and Mr Pulteney asked Sarah for the honour of sculpting some copper medals to be sold as souvenirs.[9] For weeks the streets were packed with mourners, honouring the Captain-General in a way that he had not been honoured for over a decade. The funeral took place on 9 August, which, in accordance with custom, Sarah did not attend. Henrietta did attend, having turned up at the rehearsals with Congreve and John Gay.[10] She had chosen the music for the service – a piece by Giovanni Bononcini – and even this was a calculated insult to her mother. The women had extended their feud into supporting opposing sides in the musical rivalry between Bononcini and Handel. Henrietta was a patron of the former, which prompted Sarah to send support to Handel, who is said to have played the organ at Woodstock Church for her.[11]

Concerned with conducting herself so as to avoid journalistic slanders about the Marlboroughs rivalling the pomp of royalty, Sarah worried about including the Chelsea pensioners in the procession: 'I suppose them to be miserable spectacles from their wounds in the war & I am doubtful whether the wicked enemies of the poor Duke of Marlborough might not say something disagreeable upon that . . .'[12] The spectacle of the funeral was described to her by friends, and inspired Defoe, remembering his old hero, to write his essay 'The Instability of Human Greatness'.

In the month after Marlborough's death, Sarah received few visitors. Sir Gilbert Heathcote, founder and Governor of the Bank of England, and Sir Nathaniel Gould, an East India Company director who had joined Sarah in calling for the South Sea directors to be punished, came to pay their condolences. This was a tribute to Sarah's newly inherited financial power. In Marlborough's last will,[13] Sarah had been made the chief of seven executors. He had deliberately signed it in public, in the middle of a dinner party at Windsor Lodge, so that it could never be said he was not in his right mind or had been forced to sign it by his wife. Just as wills made by wealthy women in this period were usually contested on the basis that women were scarcely rational creatures, Marlborough had had the foresight to know that his daughters and sons-in-law would challenge Sarah as his primary beneficiary.

It was customary for a widow to receive a third of her husband's property, another third to be divided among the children, and the final third only to be decided by the will.[14] (When Robert Jennings died intestate in 1726, Sarah was kind enough to call together her best lawyers to advise his less worldly widow on her rights.)[15] According to Marlborough's will, however, Sarah received the outright ownership of Marlborough House, the right to use Blenheim for life and, apart from the funds in excess of £1 million she controlled as chief executor, a personal jointure of £20,000. The wording was unambiguous: all this was given by Marlborough 'out of the tender affection, great respect and gratitude which I have and bear to her'.

The will also favoured Henrietta's son Willigo, now Marquess of Blandford, who was made independent of his parents. Henrietta complained of this divisiveness, and of not receiving enough money as the present holder of the title. In early 1723 she persuaded her husband and the other sons-in-law, Montagu and Bridgwater, to challenge the will. Sarah shrugged at their efforts: she would have benefited if the will had been overturned as she would then have been given a third of her husband's estate outright, but she respected Marlborough's wishes too much to seek this reversal, and valued her place as chief executor more than the money. When Montagu insisted on seeing the will, she took it to the lawyers for examination. When they found that their clients would be worse off under the terms of the previous

1712 will, Sarah wrote that '[t]he lawyers of those Dukes seemed themselves to be ashamed of this proceeding'.[16]

Sarah said she had 'nothing left but money, which from my humour I don't want much of'.[17] This was only half true: she valued not the money itself but the power it gave her, which, as she acknowledged, made her situation 'in many things different from other women's'.[18] Most importantly, her approval was required for her husband's trust to reinvest in the short-term loans that were essential to the economic stability of the government of which Robert Walpole was now Prime Minister (the term was just coming into use). Sarah wrote, 'I lent such sums to the government as reduced the interest from six percent to four percent . . . thinking it would have a good effect for the security of the nation; and at that time [Walpole] could not have compassed such sums without me.'[19] It was true that Sarah's loans towards the Land Tax, and the trust's loans towards the malt and salt duties, were indispensable to the government in the 1720s,[20] but less fair for her to take the credit for the nation's low interest rates, to which she in fact objected, having grown accustomed to inflated wartime rates. Together, Sarah and the trust were also the largest investors in the East India Company in 1723/4 – the trust invested £83,355 and Sarah £25,280 – and Sarah was one of only four women proprietors of the Company, holding over twice as much stock as any of the other three.[21]

Sarah's animosity towards Walpole had been born during the South Sea crisis, but was greatly aggravated by their first meeting after Marlborough's death. Walpole no doubt shared the general assumption that women had less business acumen than men, and had never taken Sarah seriously as a Whig lobbyist under Queen Anne – his letters to her in 1709 had told her to 'behave as you should do' in pushing for Whig promotions, as if she were only following orders.[22] This was despite the fact that Sarah had been responsible for Walpole's first political appointment, as Treasurer to the Navy.[23] Most people have blamed their arguments throughout the 1720s and 1730s on Sarah's inability to accept that this once lowly clerk was now Prime Minister, rather than

listening to her explanation that Walpole was ungrateful and
needlessly patronising. He was, after all, the one who came to
her to re-borrow the £200,000 the government needed from the
trust, and who tried to pretend that the lower interest rate he was
offering would be advantageous. When Sarah took offence at his
manner, which implied that his visit was just a formality, she
reminded him of his obligations to her. He laughed, she thought
contemptuously, so Sarah ended the interview.[24]

Francis Godolphin, however, pressed Sarah to accept the terms
of the loan. Sarah thought he was more gullible than she, while
in fact there were probably few other places to invest such an
enormous sum. Reluctantly she agreed, but later felt that her
fears of being duped were proved correct.[25]

In a period of single-party government, Whig factionalism
had come to replace the Whig/Tory divide. Sarah quickly joined
with the so-called 'Country Party' (Patriots or Old Whigs) in
opposition to Walpole and his 'Court Party'. During the years of
his Ministry, she became genuinely disillusioned for the first time
in her life and, in a way, this was a vindication of Marlborough's
and Queen Anne's predictions that one day the Whigs would
disappoint her.

Sarah's critique of Walpole, however, came more from anger
at his policy of appeasement towards France than from any
new leaning towards Toryism. It was also based on a financial
rectitude that was neither Whig nor Tory. Incensed by his use
of bribery to maintain his political majority, Sarah could not
understand how a politician could disown the old rhetoric of
disinterest as Walpole did, ridiculing 'all notions of public virtue
and the love of one's country, calling them the chimerical school-
boy flights of classical learning, declaring himself at the same
time no saint, no Spartan, no reformer'.[26]

Over the years, other explanations of Sarah's hatred for Walpole
accumulated: for example, his taxation of the Marlborough
House grant; his refusal to extend Sarah's lease at Windsor;
his refusal to permit her to drive through St James's Park (while
allowing the Duke of St Albans to drive through her park); and

even his government's mismanagement of the post office, which continually confused her with Henrietta.[27] As usual, Sarah was in the right in many of these disputes, but Walpole did not share her belief that he should serve her out of gratitude for earlier favours.[28]

It was certainly distrust of Walpole, as much as distrust of stocks after the South Sea crash, that led Sarah to invest in land after 1722. She withdrew an enormous lump sum from her banker Mr Burton[29] to bid in the property auctions of those ruined by the crash. Her agents laid out over £150,000, mostly on estates for renting, but also on a fifth residence at Wimbledon Park in Surrey owned by one of the bankrupted South Sea directors. The thirty properties Sarah bought gave her, above all, power at the polling booths. She wrote to her tenants with instructions on how to vote, always against Walpole's candidates, and so came to control several opposition seats in the House of Commons.

Shortly after her husband's death, Sarah found herself with several suitors. Part of the attraction was her immense wealth, but also her enduring beauty and, historically obscured, charm. Lord Coningsby made a badly timed proposal in 1722, while she was still deep in grief for Marlborough, causing her to break off their correspondence.[30] Then, in 1723, she began to receive attentions from a most unlikely source: the Duke of Somerset, whose wife Elizabeth, Queen Anne's last favourite, had died just a few months after Marlborough. He had betrayed Sarah politically, and she had always detested his arrogance about his ancestry, but now he claimed he had always secretly adored Sarah and wanted her companionship in old age. No doubt she enjoyed his flattery, but she rejected him, and also it was rumoured Lord Harcourt, for one reason: she did not want to lose her freedom – and she had no incentive to remarry. In his novel *Roxana* (1724), Defoe depicted his beautiful old heroine, a contemporary of Sarah and just as gutsy and sharp-tongued, as refusing to marry a Dutch merchant because 'it was my opinion a woman was fit to govern and enjoy her own estate' and 'seeing liberty seemed to be the man's property, I would be a man-woman'. So too Sarah's self-sufficiency, the basic trait that made her both so alluring and so unlovable, came into its own in her widowhood.

Somerset pursued her until the autumn of 1726 when she finally helped him to marry a less difficult quarry. She must have been relieved to have him off her hands, as London was starting to laugh at their elderly courtship. She also went back through her memoirs and crossed out her most damning criticisms of his earlier conduct.³¹ From then until he died, she could rely on Somerset to support her in politics.

One private family matter on which Sarah solicited his vote in the House of Lords was the battle over the marriage portion for her granddaughter Lady Anne Egerton. In her Green Book, Sarah digresses to give a long list of the amounts of pin-money left by mothers to their daughters which unscrupulous fathers then try to pocket for themselves, as if she were a kind of ombudsman defending young ladies' rights.³² Anne Egerton had been left £20,000 by the Duke of Marlborough, £10,000 by her mother Elizabeth³³ and £300 a year pin-money. Sarah believed that Scrope Egerton, Lord Bridgwater, now wished to reclaim custody of his daughter only to solve his own financial problems with this money.

Anne Egerton was sixteen and had lived with her grandmother for six years. A portrait of her by Charles Jervas shows her at about this age in Turkish dress, with a black servant holding her parasol.³⁴ The young Wriothesley Russell, 3rd Duke of Bedford, recommended himself to Sarah as a prospective grandson-in-law because of his opposition to Walpole's government, but she hoped that he would marry her favourite Diana. Bedford's mother had even promised her son's hand for this younger granddaughter, while Sarah had the Duke of Chandos's son, Lord Carnarvon, in mind for Anne. Bridgwater had remarried in 1722 and his new wife, Lady Rachel Russell, might have persuaded him to bring the disposal of Anne's dowry under his own control. He had therefore sent for his daughter to visit him where he lived at Ashridge, ending his invitation with a strong hint that she should come unchaperoned by Sarah: '[Y]ou are so discreet a woman that I can trust you to come alone'.35

Anne replied that she could not leave Windsor Lodge because of an earache, which Bridgwater disbelieved, jumping to the conclusion that Sarah was trying to stop him seeing his daughter. He came to the Lodge where he made, according to Sarah, 'something which was supposed to be some compliment, but as it is hard to understand what he says, it is impossible to repeat it', and then argued with her for three-quarters of a hour about whether he could take Anne away. Anne herself came down to dinner in a flannel nightdress and nightcap, looking ill. Bridgwater gave way and left without her.36

The following year, 1723, Bridgwater sent Anne an order to pack her belongings and move to his house the following morning. Sarah described Anne in tears at this, adding that he seemed very well informed on the details of her packing though he had given her nothing in eight years 'but a box of Shrewsbury cakes, a hat & a whip, and a little string of diamonds that was her mother's which (when he sent it) he took care to say he only lent it'.37 Elsewhere Sarah added that she would have sent the Shrewsbury cakes back to him with the other items 'but that they were eat'.

Sarah wrote back on Anne's behalf that he had given too little notice for this demand, that Anne did not want to go and, in any case, was again too sick to be moved. On receiving this reply, Bridgwater turned up in the forecourt of Marlborough House at midnight, with his steward and two footmen carrying lanterns and candles, and wearing 'a footman's coat upon him, with an air of being quite mad'. Faced with this crew, as she stood in her hall in her nightclothes, Sarah was forced to let Anne leave, 'upon which my Lord ordered Lady Anne's woman to pack up all her things, foul as well as clean'. The patient was dragged from her bed, bundled into a shawl and handed over to her father. In conclusion to this section of the Green Book, Sarah described Bridgwater as 'so contemptible' that he did not deserve to be written of, except to justify his deletion from her will.38

On Christmas Day 1724, Sarah wrote to Anne complaining

that she had made no effort to see or write to her since she was snatched from Marlborough House. Rather than suppose that Bridgwater had prohibited contact, she blamed her grand-daughter, signing, 'I was, as long as it was possible, your most affectionate grandmother.'[39] Bridgwater replied to her that there would be no further correspondence.

In 1725, Sarah received an unexpected letter from the Duke of Bedford, who had become a legal ward of Bridgwater – as the younger brother of Bridgwater's new wife – telling her that he and Anne had escaped from Bridgwater's house and gone to Woburn to be married. He said that they had had to elope because of 'the violence of his passion if he should come to know it'.[40] Sarah realised that she should have guessed that Anne's previous silence had been enforced, and forgave her, despite her annoyance that her own plan to marry Bedford to Diana had been scuppered by the elopement. At least Bedford was now in the family.

Bedford entertained Sarah with political gossip. They sent one another copies of satires against Walpole, whom Bedford described sarcastically as Sarah's 'friend'. In May, he wrote to tell her that Anne's father had demanded the return of some jewels, with which Bedford complied although he did not believe it was right. Anne herself still seldom wrote to her grandmother, and her few letters contained long excuses for why she could not visit.[41] One note from Anne apologised for bothering Sarah with so many questions about how she should furnish her new home, Southampton House, which had sat unoccupied in Bloomsbury Square for some years.[42] Sarah spent the summer of 1725 ener-getically helping the young couple with their furnishing, even upholstering their conjugal bed by hand. She hunted in antiques shops and auction houses in a town which, as another lady of the time wrote to Swift, had 'grown to such an enormous size that above half the day must be spent in the streets in going from one place to another.'[43] Despite the building boom, which had greatly extended the city within Sarah's lifetime, street numbers were still uncommon, houses and shops being located in relation to landmarks such as Montagu or Marlborough House. Now

Sarah was trying to set the stage for a new landmark family, the Bedfords as a branch of the Marlboroughs.

Sadly, Sarah's hopes, both for Bedford as a political ally and for her bedroom upholstery, were dashed: the young Duke soon declined into alcoholism and gambling, and there are several hints that this was due to his marriage's sexual failure. Sarah said she had never seen worse behaviour in public than Bedford's, but added that his drinking 'perhaps might not have been so bad if he had not had a great aversion to his wife'.[44] Lady Mary Wortley Montagu gossiped that he 'pukes at the very name of her, and determines to let his estate go to his brother rather than go through the filthy drudgery of getting an heir to it . . . This comes of living till sixteen without a competent knowledge of either practical or speculative anatomy, and literally thinking fine ladies composed of lilies and roses.'[45] Sarah tried her best to help, recruiting the Duke of Devonshire to have a man-to-man talk with Bedford,[46] but the Bedfords would not divulge the precise nature of their problem to anyone. 'I that was a grandmother did not know the secrets between them,' wrote Sarah.[47]

Sarah's advice, however, was certainly biased against the possibility of separation or divorce. When Anne left Bedford briefly in 1726 Sarah told her to go back and submit as far as necessary ('to live well with the Duke of Bedford is the best thing that anybody can advise, & in any way that he shall insist on'),[48] just as she had ordered her daughters, Mary and Henrietta, to submit to their marriages for the good of their reputations. She was offended when Anne did not take her advice and still begged her grandmother's permission to leave her husband, even threatening to throw herself on her father's mercy, though both women knew that Bridgwater would never have had her back.

In mid-August 1723 Sarah returned to Blenheim. She had been back the previous year, just after Marlborough's death, accompanied by Robert, Lord Sunderland, and Mr and Mrs John West (Charlotte Maccarty and her husband). She had planted an orchard as her husband had always wanted: '100 of the very best Paradise stocks that can be got, all Golden Pippens; 31 Dwarf Cherry trees, 10 of which must be Morellos, 15 of Duke Cherries and 6 of White Hearts'.[49] The apples would come in the autumn, the cherries in early summer, so Sarah could have the fruit sent to her in both seasons. For the first time, Sarah began to like the house she had built: '[T]here has been a great waste and many faults, but altogether I believe there is no place so fine.'[50] This time she was accompanied by the young connoisseur and architect Lord Burlington, and by Hawksmoor. She showed off the house, took their advice on the bridge, and discussed with them the erection of a 'column of victory' in honour of her husband. This last was not completed until 1728 – Sarah searched for many years for an adequate inscription.[51] Amazingly, she chose one written by her old enemy Lord Bolingbroke, who had returned to England from exile in 1726. She had not forgiven his character, but recognised his literary talent and wept when she read the wording he suggested. Around the base of the obelisk were inscribed the Acts of Parliament that had promised to fund the building of Blenheim, Sarah's memorial to her own struggle to have them honoured.

The Chancery suit over the costs of Blenheim continued until 1725, depleting the Marlborough trust. Vanbrugh complained of it often in his letters, calling Sarah 'that B.B.B.B. old B. the Duchess of Marlbh' and wondering why 'her family don't agree to lock her up'. In one letter, however, he admitted that Sarah was 'though a worse thing, not a fool'.[52] She had banned the architect from ever entering the grounds of Blenheim, but in 1725 he attempted to visit with his wife and Lord Carlisle. Sarah's gardener wrote to describe how, as ordered, the architect's party was barred entry but had sneaked back on horseback that night to peek 'over the wall to see the water'.[53] Eventually Vanbrugh, by the intervention of Walpole, received full payment for his work on Blenheim, 'in spite of the hussy's teeth'. He died six months later.

The end of the Blenheim suit did not leave Sarah without the pleasure of litigation. She had launched a lawsuit in 1724 against William Guidott MP, a fellow trustee and nephew of her old friend and lawyer Anthony Guidott.[54] She accused him of fraud with regard to the Marlborough trust, and in 1727 published a narrative of the case revealing the close link between legal and literary argument in her mind.[55] Francis Godolphin and the other trustees wearied of Sarah's litigious nature, and her unwillingness to overlook anything she knew to be wrong. She had once written to Lady Cowper, 'You know I pretend to be a great lawyer'[56] breaking yet another rule of her sex. As Margaret Cavendish had once put it, 'Women had become Pleaders, Attorneys, Petitioners . . . thus Trafficking with idle words . . .'[57]

Sarah did not tire of the law courts until 1741: 'I sometimes think that where the right is ever so strong, it is better to yield than to go into Westminster Hall, where, after twenty years' vexation, you may lose your suit from the partiality or ignorance of a judge.'[58] She would never tire, on the other hand, of trafficking with 'idle words'.

In 1726, Sarah received a long letter from her old friend Dr Francis Hare,[59] who had decided, as Robert Walpole's friend also, to try to reconcile the two. Walpole, Hare promised her, 'thought himself obliged to you for the credit and service you had done the government by lending for several years so great a sum to it, so he was always desirous to serve you'. With regard to the taxes on Windsor Park and the dispute over driving through St James's Park, Hare excused Walpole as having done his best to end her inconveniences. Hare told her that Francis Godolphin shared his opinion that all her resentments were 'ill-founded' and appealed to Sarah's rationality, while implying her tendency towards the reverse: 'Ill-grounded suspicions, violent passions, and a boundless liberty of expressing resentments of persons without distinction from the Prince downwards, and that in the most public manner, and before servants, are certainly blemishes, and not only so, but attended with great inconveniences . . .' He was clever enough to know that he could only tell Sarah such home truths if he framed them according to a narrative she understood, so he told her that she now suffered the 'fate of great persons', as Queen Anne once had, that nobody would tell them their faults.

Sarah responded in good humour to Hare's letter,[60] saying that she loved him for his plain-speaking. At the same time as she admitted to her 'blemishes', however, Sarah added that she would never consciously have a 'great fault'. She reminded him that he had only heard Walpole's side of the story, and went on to explain how the Prime Minister always treated her like an idiot while taking her money. He had dragged his feet over 'trifles' that she had requested, she said, such as helping a good man 'who only sold nails' to find a job as a postmaster.

With regard to the Windsor taxes, Sarah made a reasonable counter-argument, saying that she should not pay them, 'no more than I could expect my servants should pay out of their salary the taxes at [her property in] St Albans', and citing historical precedents that no Ranger had ever contributed to royal taxes at Windsor before. She estimated that she paid out more to maintain Windsor Great Park than she was reimbursed by the Crown ('I make no advantage of the park but to eat sometimes a few little Welsh runts'), and complained that all the servants thought it belonged to the King so 'that they have a right to get all they can' out of the land. Sarah explained that she had only troubled the Prime Minister with such a minor matter 'to save me from the uneasiness of having the officers for the taxes at Windsor coming to me perpetually to tell me they would seize my goods at the Lodge'.

She answered the quarrel about driving through St James's Park less effectively. In this instance she merely felt snubbed that the Duchess of Buckingham should have this dispensation while she did not. She assured Hare she was not and never had been in a passion about any of these matters, and had done her best moral trick of imagining another person in her shoes and herself in the Prime Minister's. '[I]f I could have so sweet a temper as you wish me,' she continued, 'I can't see that it would be of any use to me, for all the good wishes that I have made for this government (not to mention some services) can't make the Ministers treat me with common decency . . .' She drew a distinction between being free to dislike people, as she was, and being in a 'passion', which she denied.

In Hare's reply[61] he regretted sending his earlier letter. It seemed only to have involved him in his friends' argument while she had missed the message that Walpole would welcome a reconciliation. But Hare missed Sarah's point that what she resented was being treated as insignificant. While he did not disagree with her right to dislike whomever she pleased, he told her that she took these resentments too far and cited both scriptural and classical sources which recommended 'the government of the tongue'.

Universally applied, Sarah's level of candour would 'destroy society', Dr Hare lectured. He dared tell her that this was indeed a great fault, not a minor imperfection, and cast her falling out with Queen Anne in this light, holding up her husband and Sidney Godolphin in contrast as models of discretion: '[W]here L[or]d G[odolphin] said ten words at table, before servants or in mixed company, your Grace will give me leave to believe you say ten thousand.' He overlooked the extent to which these two politicians had hidden behind Sarah's ungovernable tongue when it suited them. As an afterthought, he added, 'It is as impossible for your Grace to converse without warmth & force as it is for you to be dull or ugly . . . and as long as you have fire & vivacity they will show themselves in resentments.' With regard to his earlier accusation of Sarah's 'passion', Hare corrects himself: 'I acquit your Grace of that charge and do admit that your Grace can speak with as much warmth out of passion as most people can do in it.'

The right of free speech, he said in another letter, did not apply to private relationships. Specifically, he mentioned his surprise at her harsh reply to a submissive letter from her daughter Mary, which, he now revealed, Marlborough and Godolphin had drafted.[62]

When Sarah wrote back, both amused and upset, she told Hare

that since Marlborough had seen and approved every letter she sent to her daughters, it would have been absurd for him also to draft Mary's replies. She suggested wittily that Hare's own letters were examples of affronts she should take his counsel and ignore. 'I have read most of the books you mention & I like them extremely, but I never found in any of those books that great faults were the result of great virtues, & all the philosophers that I have been fond of prefer Truth better than anything.' She concluded curtly that this was the last reply she would bother writing to his 'attacks'.[63]

On the outside of the envelope, Sarah later wrote of Dr Hare: 'As bad a man as ever was born. He had great obligations to me as well as to the Duke of Marl; I remember that Robert Walpole once told me that Doctor Hare had no more religion than the devil, but after that made him a bishop, having some talents to write for him. I believe he has some learning, but he has not one good quality besides.'[64]

Despite Hare's efforts, the arguments with Walpole soon worsened. Sarah's hopes for his downfall were briefly raised by the death, in June 1727, of George I, with whom she had not been on good terms since the accusations made against her by Sunderland. Walpole had lost the Prince of Wales' favour when he was brought into the King's government, leading to warmer relations, in turn, between Sarah and the Prince. She had invited the Prince and Princess to Blenheim earlier that year to celebrate the end of her 'labour of 22 years', with Vanbrugh's bridge finally finished and the Chancery case closed. There is no record of them taking up the invitation. Now she was invited to George II's coronation. She was sixty-seven and one of the few women present who could boast of having attended five. Several observers remarked on her still outstanding beauty, especially her 'most expressive eyes'. In part this was because Sarah continued to dress with plain, late-seventeenth-century elegance, with a simple neckline and diamonds, while other ageing women in the procession had been tempted to try the more exaggerated eighteenth-century fashions.[65]

Sarah drew attention to herself at the coronation, rather as she had at the Sacheverell trial, by deciding to sit down halfway through the procession. She called on one of the army drummers and plumped herself down on his drum outside Westminster Abbey, to the delight of the crowd.[66] She also left the Abbey early, too fatigued to wait to receive one of the medals struck as souvenirs for peeresses.[67]

To Sarah's annoyance, however, Walpole was not displaced: Queen Caroline gave him her support, and as she had great influence over her husband, Walpole stayed. If anything, his power was enhanced by this feat of survival. He rewarded the King and Queen with Parliamentary votes of large incomes.[68] In the 1730s there would be a revival of plays about Elizabethan and Jacobean royal favourites, and Walpole came to be denigrated in the same terms: for his 'vast wealth' of land in Norfolk and in Bank of England stock, for example (despite the fact that he died in debt).[69] Sarah herself turned the Queen Zarah trick against her enemy, remarking that Sir Robert was 'in reality King'.[70]

His survival turned Sarah sharply against Caroline, who was far more educated and cultured than she, but similarly progressive on religion and every bit as interested in politics. She used Walpole and the King much as Sarah had used Marlborough and Godolphin, though with a discretion her enemies saw as sinister, talking privately to each man but retiring whenever the King and Prime Minister met. The two women should, by rights, have appreciated one another's intelligence, but a series of quarrels made this impossible. When the Queen denied Sarah permission to drive out of her back door through St James's Park, Sarah tried to prevent the Queen driving across her property at Wimbledon. Caroline then appears to have attempted to force Sarah to sell two acres of ground at Wimbledon to the Crown for enclosure. When Sarah refused, Caroline threatened to stop Crown payment of the taxes on her grant at Windsor.[71] Sarah relented over access across the Wimbledon property, with the proviso that Caroline would pay an amount of money to the poor tenants who used the common land.[72] She also sent Caroline a copy of the Windsor grant as proof of her rights, including the direct employment of all Rangers: 'I have had the direction of this Park this eight and twenty years . . .'[73] Sarah was not foolish enough to take Walpole and Caroline to court and in the end paid out the Windsor taxes. Her only satisfaction was in sending the worst cuts of venison back to the Queen.[74]

In the summer of 1727, Voltaire visited Sarah at Blenheim. He was in exile, having been released from the Bastille in May on condition he left France. He came to hear Sarah's recollections of Marlborough's views on King Charles XII during his diplomatic missions to Sweden.[75] Sarah was happy to oblige. In return, she asked him to look at the memoirs she was again thinking of publishing. Oliver Goldsmith tells us that Voltaire's reaction was negative – not because the memoirs lacked literary or historical merit, but because he thought it improper to publish Queen Anne's private letters: '[H]e gravely assured her that the publication of secrets which were communicated under the seal of friendship would give the world no high opinion of her morals.'[76] Goldsmith himself had no high opinion of Sarah's writing, commenting in his *Life of Richard Nash* (1762) that she 'seems to have been not a much better writer than Mr Nash; but she was worth many hundred thousand pounds and that might console her'.[77] Another unsympathetic author's anecdote of the Voltaire visit has Sarah listening to the Frenchman's recital of all Marlborough's achievements until, 'apprehending, as he went on, that his eloquence was like to be confined to the Duke only, the spirit which had ever possessed [her] could not help bursting out – "All this is true, Sir: But you forget that all this and much more is owing to ME."'[78]

Voltaire's assessment of Sarah's influence on English politics was generous. He described an incident that is either apocryphal, appears nowhere else, or was intended only metaphorically: 'If the Duchess of Marlborough had not thrown a glass of water in the face of Lady Masham, and some drops on Queen Anne, the Queen would not have thrown herself into the hands of the Tories and would not have given to France a peace without which France could not have sustained itself.'[79] This thrown water – rather like the apocryphal gloves thrown to the ground in disgust – was enough to inspire Eugène Scribe in 1900 to write an entire play about Sarah called *Le Verre d'eau ou les effets et les causes.*[80]

Another literary visitor to Blenheim was Sarah's friend Lady Mary Wortley Montagu, who had a standing invitation to come every summer.[81] She had returned from Constantinople in 1718 and was crusading to introduce smallpox vaccination into Britain. Sarah had taken an instant liking to Lady Mary, although she was more of a *belle esprit* than was usually to Sarah's taste. According to her granddaughter, Lady Mary was 'Whig to the teeth – *Whigissima*',[82] so they had this in common, as well as a 'slightly soured worldliness'[83] and a self-reliance that each appreciated in the other. Sarah told Lady Mary that she had 'one advantage that few of our sex has in an equal degree, which is that you can be alone and entertain yourself at least as well as any company can do it'. For her own part, Sarah said she agreed with the philosophers that 'a quiet kind of life, spent in reflection & improvement of the mind was not only more pleasing but most fit to be pursued'.[84] She went on to admit, however, that lately she had not been reading philosophy so much as readying Blenheim for visitors. In such ways, Sarah both imitated and laughed off the intellectual pretensions of Lady Mary and her 'blue-stocking' friends, among whom she must have felt slightly out of her depth. She sometimes took a defensive pride in her lack of education – 'I am no scholar . . . nor a wit, I thank God,' she had once written to Maynwaring – but the mere fact that she played hostess to this circle belied her ostensible lack of interest in scholarship.

The debate of the period was not yet about the rights of women, but rather about the relative moral and intellectual capacities of the sexes. Both Lady Mary and Sarah shared contempt for the majority of women. 'To say truth,' admitted Lady Mary, 'I have never had any great esteem for the generality of the fair sex, and my only consolation for being of that gender has been the assurance it gave me of never being married to any one amongst them.'[85]

Though Sarah's old friend, the 1st Lord Hervey, had once complimented her on having 'a most acute and elevated understanding, equally partaking of the solid as well as the shining faculty',[86] the truth was that her intellect was more 'solid' than otherwise. Sarah was not very in touch with the intangibles – spiritual questions, imaginative literature or aesthetics detached from function – and tended to read books only to reinforce what she already believed, politically and morally. Since 1709, Maynwaring had supplied her with Seneca and Descartes, but always in summary so that she did not have to struggle through the originals, and by September 1719 her library included Burnet's and Clarendon's histories, Milton, Dryden and Spenser.[87] In 1721, her house at St Albans also contained Shakespeare, Jonson, Montaigne, Cowley's poems, Waller, Saint-Evrémond, Plutarch, Epictetus in translation, Swift's novels, Addison's essays, Congreve's plays, *Don Quixote* and numerous volumes on architecture. While she was no blue-stocking, these were not the shelves of a philistine.

Between the 1720s and 1740s Sarah vastly expanded her collection of art with her profits from the South Sea Company. Her knowledge of her own pictures was not always impressive – on an inventory of the paintings at Blenheim and Marlborough House, she listed several merely by their content ('A woman's head in a round gilt frame', 'a fruit piece', or 'a small dark battle piece'), yet William Hazlitt, writing in 1843, complimented her on having had a collection of Rubens' showing that 'she understood the master's genius well'.[88] She kept a Rubens of 'a woman taken in adultery' in her bow-window room at Blenheim, and two madonnas over her bedroom doors, one by Rubens and one by Van Dyck. She also purchased Van Dyck's *Portrait of Lady Mary Villiers with Lord Arran*, which is still owned by the Marlborough estate. Over the fireplace in her bedroom she hung a full-length Kneller portrait of Marlborough and over a guest bedroom fireplace she kept a full-length portrait of Queen Anne, 'bought by the Duchess of M[arlborough] of one Lely, a painter in York Buildings'. She also collected many pictures by Bruegel and Rottenhammer, probably first seen while travelling in Flanders in 1712–14, and hung the long gallery at Blenheim with exquisite Titians. This included the remarkable painting known as 'Roman Charity', which depicts a woman feeding an old, shackled prisoner from her breast. Sarah had bought it from Lord Portland's auction after he lost his money in the South Sea bubble and moved to Jamaica.[89] She would probably have preferred this image of a woman's self-sacrifice to the image of herself as a strident intellectual. She was certainly more conscious of her sacrifices than confident of her accomplishments.

In 1729, while she was convalescing from an illness serious enough to have appeared in the newspapers, Sarah embarked upon another grand building project: a new house on her Wimbledon estate, a convenient hour south of London. She intended to give it eventually to her granddaughter Diana, whom she loved dearly. 'Happiness in life depends much on natural temper,' Sarah told her. 'You are luckier in that than most people I ever knew.'[90]

Sarah designed Wimbledon House herself, but based it on a model by the Earl of Burlington. She enlisted the assistance of Lord Henry Herbert, 9th Earl of Pembroke, and Roger Morris, both neo-Palladians. In 1712, the 3rd Earl of Shaftesbury's *Letter Concerning Design* had called for a new architecture founded on 'truth and nature' rather than 'fancy',[91] attacking the French and Gothic styles and seeming to refer to Blenheim as 'a false and counterfeit Piece of Magnificence as can be justly arraigned for its Deformity by so many knowing Men in Art, and by the whole People ...' This was followed in 1715 by Colen Campbell's *Vitruvius Britannicus*, the neo-Palladian manifesto which Whig grandees observed religiously during the 1720s and which Sarah had among her books. She thought that neo-Palladian houses designed like villas were as good as follies, and preferred the long ranges of interconnecting rooms – the traditional 'great house' layout – with which she had grown up. As it was unusual for

Herbert and Morris to build anything other than villas, Sarah's influence on the Wimbledon design is clear.[92]

Once again, Sarah supervised every detail of the construction, writing to Lady Cowper: 'I find one can't be long from any building without the danger of having a window or a door or something or other that one does not like & yet I think I am in the best hands we have. But their rules do not always agree with my fancy & I am forced to be perpetually on the watch.'[93] As ever, she dismissed the architects before the end of the project and completed it herself.

Lady Mary Wortley Montagu might have been referring to Wimbledon rather than Blenheim when she wrote: 'The D[uchess] of Marlborough used . . . [to say] one might always live upon other people's follies, yet you see she built the most ridiculous house I ever saw, since it really is not habitable from the excessive damps.'[94] This was unfair: the only 'ridiculous' part of the house was perhaps the front staircase, which made it look, Sarah later admitted, as if the house were squatting. The point about the damp, regrettably, was true.

During the same period, Sarah also completed the chapel at Blenheim, according to her own design, again with the emphasis on simple elegance. She would have been horrified at its later eighteenth- and nineteenth-century ornamentation. She had written to a friend in May 1732: '[C]onsidering how many wonderful figures and whirligigs I have seen architects finish a chapel withal, that are no manner of use but to laugh at, I must confess I cannot help thinking that what I have designed for this chapel may as reasonably be called finishing of it . . .'[95]

Other letters from the early 1730s are crammed with architectural observations and opinions. That same May of 1732, for example, she had written to compliment her grandson on the upkeep of Althorp, approving the renovations he had undertaken on what had always been her favourite English house. The previous month she had written to Diana from Cheam, expressing the hope that her brother would not buy a house that Sarah had just inspected, built in the 'Versailles style' she thought absurd.

She laughed at triangular doorjambs, and one wall between an upstairs room and a passageway made of 'glass the same as in windows from the ceiling to the floor ... And this I must acknowledge is extremely new.' Sarah peered closely at a 'broken misshaped stone', placed on a pedestal, which she was told was very valuable but which she suggested to the owner could be found lying anywhere on the ground if he needed another. Finally, she saw the hall full of statues of noble ancestors, 'but I durst not ask who those heads represented, being resolved to observe the Spanish proverb and not to laugh till I turned the street'.[96]

That summer, Sarah went to take the spa waters at Scarborough, stopping to see Woburn Abbey on the way, which she complimented for the delicate fretwork of its ceilings.[97] She also stopped in York to see the cathedral and to condemn the poor design of the town's assembly room with, she thought, superfluous pillars obstructing one's view and windows as high as in a prison.[98]

When Wimbledon House was finally finished in the mid-1730s, Sarah, both envying and despising the professional architects, told Diana that it was done well enough, but would have been better built only by bricklayers following her orders.[99] Despite its unorthodox layout for a neo-Palladian home, it featured in the fifth edition of *Vitruvius Britannicus*.

12

A Dozen Heirs

Sarah had planned to leave the bulk of her fortune to Robert Spencer, Earl of Sunderland, with the proviso that he would never support Walpole. However, in September 1729, while Robert was in Paris, Sarah heard that he had caught a fever. Before there was time for her to pack her apothecary's bag and cross the Channel, he had died, unmarried and heirless.[1] As Sarah remarked the following year, she had lost 'about a dozen' heirs.[2] Now she was forced to try to forge stronger relations with Henrietta's son Willigo, Marquess of Blandford, and the twenty-three-year-old Charles Spencer, now 5th Earl of Sunderland.

Sarah had paid careful attention to all her grandsons' education, taking them out of Eton and finding them a private tutor soon after her husband's death. She had been concerned that the tutor should teach mathematics, 'which is one of the main points', and also Latin and history. 'I think it is more likely to find a proper man for this business that is <u>not a clergyman</u>,' she emphasised. Eventually she had appointed James Stephens, a brilliant mathematician who later qualified as a physician and became one of her most trusted friends.

In 1725, she had kept an eye on Willigo and the sixteen-year-old John Spencer when they were together in Paris under the supervision of Mr Fyshe. Sarah sent weekly letters to Willigo, so lengthy that one of his friends who read them compared her to 'some animal that stifles her young with too much fondling'.[3] The letters were not without sharpness: when the young men sent Sarah and Diana mantillas from Paris with instructions on how to wear them, Sarah thanked them ironically for the 'directions how to dress myself'.[4]

Partly to avoid his grandmother's 'stifling' and match-making,

Willigo had floated around the Continent for several years. Then, in the summer of 1727, he informed her that he was planning to marry a Utrecht burgomaster's daughter named Marie de Jonge with whom he had fallen in love. They were married in July 1729. Sarah had disapproved of the match with an untitled foreigner, but after Robert's death, she wrote in forgiveness to Willigo, made a new will and urged him to return home: '[T]hink how odd it must appear to all people to have such a man live, as you do, at Utrecht, from all your relations or friends that are of value.'⁵

Sarah knew one reason why Willigo had stayed so long overseas. In 1723, according to Boswell, his mother Henrietta had given birth to an illegitimate daughter by Congreve, christened Mary Godolphin. Lady Mary Wortley Montagu recorded the scandal of the birth: 'My poor friend the young D[uchess] of Marlborough, I'm afraid, has exposed herself to a most violent ridicule; she is as much embarrassed with the loss of her big belly, and as much ashamed of it, as ever dairy maid was with the getting one.'⁶ To Sarah's eye, this child was dangerously close to inheriting the Marlborough title, and this social 'ridicule' was also a major reason why Willigo, financially independent thanks to Marlborough's will, had decided to live in Holland.

The previous year, in January 1729, Congreve had died at his lodgings in Surrey Street with Henrietta sitting vigil. It was this death, as much as Robert Spencer's, that now freed Willigo to come home.

Willigo's father was more forgiving than his son or mother-in-law. Congreve had left the bulk of his estate to Henrietta for 'her Sole and Separate Use' but 'in Confidence of the Honesty and Justice of him the said Francis, Earl of Godolphin, I do hereby constitute and appoint him the sole Executor of this my Will, in Trust for his said Wife . . .'⁷ Some were shocked that Congreve had left so much to Henrietta, who was already wealthy enough, but clearly it had been agreed between them that Henrietta should spend his money on a diamond necklace for their daughter. His initials were engraved on the back of each stone.⁸ When the playwright's body was taken to Westminster Abbey,

Francis Godolphin was among the pallbearers, and this tolerant husband not only executed the will in good faith, but also raised Mary as his own, even after Henrietta's death. This technical respectability of birth allowed her later to marry the Duke of Leeds, and at the very end of her life Sarah was reconciled with her illegitimate granddaughter.

The slurs against Henrietta and the Marlborough name, which Sarah had always feared, came only after Congreve's death. A story appeared in *The Daily Post* that Henrietta had bought a full-size wax model of her dead lover because:

> She something more of Substance wants;
> Something that she might with her Arm
> Stroke o'er and finger every Charm;
> Might privately survey the Part
> That made the Conquest of her Heart.[9]

Wax or clay figures of great personages were often displayed in Westminster Abbey after their deaths, models for the tombs to be built, which might have been the one Henrietta was reported to have purchased. (Or the wax Congreve might have come from Mrs Salmon's Waxworks in Fleet Street, the precursor to Madame Tussaud's, which included models of hundreds of famous people of the day.) The monument to Congreve in the Abbey referred to the happiness and honour Henrietta had enjoyed in his company, and caused Sarah to comment acerbically: 'I know not what happiness she might have had in his company but I am sure it was no honour.'[10]

Sarah spent the next several years striving unsuccessfully to suppress other publications that alluded to her daughter's affair, such as Edmund Curll's *Memoirs of the life, writings and amours of William Congreve* (1730) and a satire called *The Secret History of Henrada Maria Teresa* (1733), which not only retold the love affair of Henrietta and Congreve but also took the opportunity to recall the sexually ambiguous relationship between Sarah and Anne.

So, in comparison to Henrietta's social disgrace, Willigo's

marriage to a Dutch nobody paled into insignificance. Sarah welcomed the Blandfords home in 1730, though at first meeting Willigo's wife, she wrote nastily that 'If anybody saw her by chance, they would be ready to ask her to show them what lace she had to sell.'[11]

It had been rumoured in the drawing rooms of London that Frederick Louis, Prince of Wales, had had an affair, like Congreve, with Henrietta. Either unaware of this gossip, or disregarding it, Sarah tried to arrange an engagement between her granddaughter Diana and the Prince. At least this was the story according to Horace Walpole who, however, had reasons for inventing it – not only as an insult to Sarah's blind ambition but as a compliment to his father, Robert, for having prevented the match, winning the thanks of George II and Queen Caroline. No other proof of the story's truth exists, although the Prince of Wales's visit to Windsor Castle in September 1730 corresponded with a period that Sarah and Diana spent at the Lodge, and Diana was sometimes invited to join the royal party for dinner, a hunt or to play cards in the evening.[12]

During the summer, Sarah had been more concerned with Diana's relationship with a female friend. This was Lady Elizabeth Rich, wife of Sir Robert Rich, who had fought under Marlborough (and daughter of Edward Griffith, the widower of Sarah's dead sister Barbara, and his second wife, Elizabeth 'Duck' Griffith, later Lady Mohun). Lady Mohun had written Sarah adoring letters during the years when they and their husbands had shared Lord Oxford as a political adversary. Sarah had been generous to her, but eventually wearied of making loans on which the only return was more flattery.[13] Lady Mohun had died in 1725, and it was probably after this that Sarah befriended her daughter as a companion for Lady Diana.

Brought up in the shelter of her grandmother's constant supervision, Diana must have found Elizabeth, though middle-aged, a breath of fresh air. They seized every opportunity to spend time together, promenading in the royal parks between five and seven every evening, or one and three in the wintertime. The Serpentine had just been dug in Hyde Park, and they could chat while driving around it in a carriage, or go together to a play or dinner.

By 1729, however, Sarah disapproved of the friendship, which was, she said, creating a 'great noise in the town'. The women wrote to one another almost every day, in language that can only be described as romantic, filling small sheets of notepaper until it hurt their eyes. Sarah was too aware of how any hint of lesbianism could be used as slander, having been both the object and spreader of it herself. She whisked Diana off to Tunbridge Wells and pointedly did not invite Lady Rich, who wrote plaintive letters expressing her misery at Diana's absence.[14]

The following August, saddened by their separation and blinded by headaches, Elizabeth declared to Diana, 'Never believe anybody can love you more than I do,' and warned that she would not be able to stop herself deliberately annoying Sarah when she next saw her. Sarah's note on the back explains: 'This letter was given to Di before me. I ask[ed] to see it. She told me she had writ to Lady Rich upon my having told her that there was a great noise in the town about her writing so very often to her, who had not a character good enough for her to have such a violent friendship with, but it was best to let it drop by degrees & I would be always very civil to her myself.'[15]

Lady Rich and her husband together wrote to Sarah, telling her that she was listening to lies. Sarah received this letter on the road returning from her summer at Windsor, and sent her answer promptly to the Riches' house in Grosvenor Street. She quoted back to them the lines of Elizabeth's that had recently caused her such offence and reiterated that there could be 'no other construction put upon it than as I took it'. She declared: '[N]obody can believe that any child was ever more dear to a mother than Di is to me.' She dismissed the women's love as 'ridiculous' but did not mention her fear for her granddaughter's reputation because of the same-sex friendship. She insisted she did not mean to make a drama out of the situation, only for the relationship to become less intense.[16] Elizabeth backed off.[17]

Determined that Diana, now in her twenties, should marry soon and so put an end to such 'comedies for the world' – by which she also meant flirtations with young men, such as a certain captain from the Royal Irish Fusiliers[18] – Sarah held a ball for her granddaughter at Marlborough House on 5 February 1731. The aim was to find the bright and beautiful Diana a suitable husband. Henry Pelham, later to become Prime Minister, was among the suitor guests. A Mr Fielding, possibly the future novelist recently returned from his studies in Leiden, also attended. Sarah tried to arrange a match between Diana and the Duke of Dorset's son, though it was far from the most financially advantageous. She advertised Diana's dowry and inheritance: 'I said very frankly that she should have fifty thousand pounds down, & that accidents might happen, not very unlikely, that would add vastly to her fortune.' Yet Sarah was so dissatisfied with the jointure offered in return that she dropped the plan as soon as Diana expressed her lack of interest in the young man.[19]

Sarah's next idea, though morbid, was far more to her granddaughter's liking. Having failed to marry Diana to the Duke of Bedford, Sarah looked towards his younger brother, Lord John Russell, a worthy match only if the Duke of Bedford was indeed dying, as Sarah suspected. Anne Egerton had taken her husband to their country seat at Woburn Abbey so that he would not be tempted to drink or fall prey to the card-sharps at White's Chocolate House or in Newmarket. But even there, she complained, he was losing money at whist, for 'he now knows no other way to divert himself, which is a melancholy thing to think of'. Sarah was equally baffled by him. '[T]here is nothing so amazing to me as to see a man that seems to have so much good sense and yet to have made a havoc of his constitution and of his estate.'[20] When Sarah went to visit him she saw his poor health at first hand. As he showed her the property, she felt herself stronger on her legs than the twenty-four-year-old Duke. After he had taken her to see the pictures in the Long Gallery along the west front of the house, Sarah wrote to Diana, 'He sat down very often, which I conclude proceeded from weakness. I made him as easy as

I could in everything, for I find he cannot endure to be thought ill, and therefore did not take any notice that I saw it but contrived to sit down often as we talked over the pictures . . .'[21]

The Duke, knowing what Sarah's interest in his younger brother signified, was generous enough to support the match-making, and when the deal was done, Sarah was delighted. Anne Egerton, trapped in her unhappy marriage and looking forward to widow-hood, was also pleased that the girl with whom she had grown up as a sister was marrying her brother-in-law. In December 1731, after Diana and Lord John had been married a few months and were living together in Cheam, Anne wrote to Sarah to express how relieved she was to hear that they seemed happy together, 'having so great an affection for them both'.[22]

However, one of Diana's first actions as soon as she was married and independent of Sarah's direct control was to renew her friendship with Elizabeth Rich.

Accomplishing Diana's marriage gave Sarah a manic cheerfulness despite two sad events. In 1731 her sister Frances, whom she had not seen since 1708, had died aged eighty-two, and in the summer, Sarah lost another male heir. Willigo collapsed suddenly from over-drinking at the annual meeting of the High Borlase Club at Balliol College, Oxford. While Sarah went into mourning, Willigo's mother, Henrietta, was reported to continue throwing parties at Godolphin House. Marie, Willigo's Dutch wife, was devastated, but remarried several years later, with Sarah's approval. Lady Mary Wortley Montagu remarked to Sarah that she thought the girl was throwing away her only chance of freedom.[23]

Willigo's death meant that his cousin Charles Spencer would inherit the Marlborough income and title after Henrietta's death. According to the terms of the Duke's will, this meant that he had to give up his claim to Althorp, passing it to his younger brother John Spencer. Charles was happy to forgo this side of his inheritance, however, as the Marlborough income would free him, as his friend Lord John Hervey (son of the peer

Sarah had nominated) put it, from 'that unloving, capricious, extravagant old fury of a grandmother'.[24] Hervey, however, was one of the mythologisers of Sarah's fiery temper (he nicknamed her 'Mount Aetna'), so he might well have put these words into Charles's mouth. Sarah returned Hervey's insults in posterity, describing him as 'the most wretched, profligate man that ever was born, besides ridiculous; a painted face and not a tooth in his head.'[25] Their mutual animosity was largely political fencing: Sarah opposed the 'favourite of a favourite' – Hervey was a prominent supporter of Walpole and Queen Caroline.

There must have been some truth in Charles's relief at becoming independent of Sarah, however, as he quickly took the risk of offending her. Before the end of his first year as the Marlborough heir, Charles sent her notice that he was planning to marry and, to Sarah's horror, his choice was Elizabeth Trevor. She was the daughter of the Duke of Marlborough's old enemy Thomas Trevor (Baron of Broham, Bedfordshire), one of the peers created by Queen Anne to pass the peace preliminaries in 1711. Sarah described it as 'a contemptible family, the chief of which cheated his grandfather by a false mortgage of 10,000 pounds'.[26] On the same passage, Charles later wrote in the manuscript's margin: 'All lies'.

The most offensive part of this *fait accompli*, however, was that Sarah felt displaced as head of the family by the intervention of Lady Bateman, the eldest Spencer grandchild, now living in Soho Square. Lady Bateman's marriage, to the son of the South Sea director, had proved loveless and she turned to her brothers for sympathy. With her natural taste for political metaphor, Sarah thought that Lady Bateman was trying to become 'a great Minister' within the family by managing her brothers' interests.[27] Painted as having an angular profile to match her strong character, Anne Bateman was also aligned with the Court and Walpole's Whigs; once again, private and public life, friendships and favour became entangled in Sarah's life.

In May 1732, Sarah sent Charles a shrill letter, demanding that he break off his engagement for the sake of his grand-father's honour, and informing him that she had just altered her will to disinherit him. Charles replied, with obvious pleasure in his new-found independence, that she had offered no rational arguments against the match 'unless invectives are to be looked on as arguments'. He assured her that the choice was his, not his 'overbearing sister's (as you are pleased to call her)' and he ended icily: 'As for putting me out of your will, it is some time since I neither expected or desired to be in it. I have nothing more to add but to assure Your Grace that this is the last time I shall ever trouble you by letter or conversation. I am Your Grace's grandson, Sunderland.'[28]

Sarah instructed the other Spencer grandchildren, John and Diana, that they had to choose between their elder siblings or their duty to her. John decided to ignore Sarah's implied threats of disinheritance, and attended his brother's wedding that summer, although Diana did not. It seems as if the Spencer grandchildren had privately agreed that at least one of them should hold on to Sarah's favour, and Diana was naturally disinclined to desert her doting grandmother.

This was the summer Sarah had spent at Scarborough spa, inspecting the latest architectural styles while she took the waters. She had all but given up on doctors, remarking to Diana that '[t]hey only guess and one can tell oneself best what one feels, and try such things as are safe'.[29] She was not so feeble that she could not eat pigeons (plural) and drink three glasses of champagne at a single meal.[30] She suspected that the average alcoholic intake of the mid-eighteenth century was not ideal ('I am convinced that the less wine or malt drink young people take, it is much the better. But for the people of my age that have been used to drink wine, one can only lessen it by mixing it with water'),[31] and appreciated the air and mineral waters of the spa, though the primitive facilities of the town appalled her.[32] She wrote to Diana every day, bored by endless card games with dull company. 'Your desiring me to take care of myself for your sake is very kind,' she told her, 'and I return it by assuring you that I desire to live only for you.'[33]

When she heard of John Spencer's attendance at the Sunderlands' wedding, Sarah did disinherit him and banned him from visiting Windsor Lodge. An anonymous letter she received in November 1732 survives, calling her 'mad' and attacking her for having split asunder a family 'that you pretend to espouse' by turning everyone against Lady Bateman. 'Is it not enough for you to exercise your petty temper yourself?' the anonymous author asked, '& for some atonement to your family, entail your money without your wickedness & die as soon as you can.'[34] It seems that Sarah was proving no more successful in managing her heirs than she had been in managing Queen Anne.

Sarah observed Anne Bateman and her new sister-in-law holding hands in public, which she read as a sinister sign of Lady Bateman's 'management' of Charles,[35] as well as politicians paying court to her as a means of influencing her brother's vote in the House of Lords.[36] Sarah told Diana she must drop all contact with the Batemans; she would, she said, accept no 'trimming' in the matter.[37]

Lady Bateman later fell out with the Trevor and Spencer families and lost her influence over her brothers, so Sarah remained the 'governing person' of the family.[38] Sarah's anger at Charles's betrayal, however, remained. Several years later, when she was involved in a court case over the Duke of Marlborough's trust, defending herself from the charge of having pocketed about £40,000, Sarah wrote a long narrative of her relationship with Charles.[39] She sent it to the Lord Chancellor, although she knew it was not legal evidence, 'no more than reading a newspaper'.

First she described Charles's appearance: 'His person is very well if he had a mask on, but he has something extremely unmeaning in his face, and his eyes so dead and disagreeable, that though he is very well-made and genteel, the countenance already described makes it impossible for anybody to like him.' Then she condemned him as charmless, unprincipled, easily led astray, and ill-tempered when contradicted, just like his father 'who was famous for it'. He also had a vain love of fashion 'which is the simplest of all faults, but his exceeds anything of that nature that ever was heard of before'.

Sarah remembered when Charles had been a little boy at school in Hampstead and caught smallpox. He was put in quarantine in a cold outbuilding of the school and left without medical attention. His mother was dead and his father cared nothing for him, so Sarah had gone to fetch him, 'wrapped him up in blankets and with a great deal of care brought him to London where he was near all the help he could want,' and nursed him back to health. Similarly, when he went to Eton and fell sick with a fever, she had transported him to Windsor Lodge 'where I got a very good tutor to look after him, and he continued in my several houses till I sent him beyond sea, finding he learnt nothing at all'. She had managed his money for him, often giving from her own pocket. When she sent him to college in Geneva, the sixteen-year-old dandy bought himself finely embroidered clothes though it was against the law there to wear anything but black silk suits. His other extravagances included keeping boats on the Thames, renovating rented houses that the landlords then took back, renting an overpriced house at Blackheath, pulling down the best buildings at Althorp and ruining the layout of its parkland, even when Sarah had bribed him to leave it alone. This list was only to explain to the Chancellor why Charles found himself in such debt. Through all of it she said she had tried to live with him 'as well . . . as if I had depended upon him for a jointure'.

Returning to the reasons for his immense debts, Sarah criticised his love, like Henrietta's, of literary dedications, buying them where Sarah said she would have paid good money not to be mentioned. 'He buys up all the toyshops in town to make presents of snuffboxes', and paid prostitutes and other women to keep him company.

Finally, Sarah accounted for her handling of the Duke's trust with as much precision as she had shown in her accounts for the

Privy Purse. She listed the exact dates and sums loaned to Charles over the years, then went on to explain how his father had not supported the Marlboroughs in various legal cases during the last years of his life and so cost them money. The son, she ended, was 'a backwarder plant than the father' but otherwise of an identical species.

During the summer of Charles's wedding, Sarah had to continue dealing with the Bedfords' hopeless marriage. Anne's husband had forbidden her to be in London at the same time as he was, and so, as she was embarrassed for them to be seen avoiding one another, she could not visit Marlborough House.⁴⁰ Bedford had left Anne without horses and a coach with broken windows. More worrying was that he had been advised by doctors to travel south, and was planning to tour Lisbon, Naples and Turin. His wife did not want to leave England and claimed travelling would do her own fragile health fatal damage.⁴¹

Bedford's main concern was to avoid the expense of two households, one in England and one abroad. Sarah advised her granddaughter, in May 1732, that if she were in her shoes she would disobey her husband, '[a]nd whether the law will give him power to force her away against her will is the question. I know nothing of that but I will enquire about it.'⁴² Sarah's enquiries into women's rights were vaguely reassuring. Anne wrote to Sarah that she was glad to hear 'there can be so much favour in the law for a woman as to hinder his taking me by force, but it would be a terrible thing to have another open quarrel with him'. She had her doctors testify that she should not travel, and eventually Sarah solved the problem of the expense by offering to take Anne back into her own household. She was given apartments in Marlborough House where, according to Sarah, they 'lived like sisters' for several months.⁴³

When the Duke of Bedford died at sea in November that year, Sarah resettled Anne in her own house in Pall Mall. Over-excited by her sudden freedom, Anne rushed to engage herself to William Villiers, 3rd Earl of Jersey, after only a fortnight's acquaintance.⁴⁴ Her grandmother heard about this through a mutual friend, and disapproved, although she did not even know the groom's first name. At least it was better than another rumour she had heard – that Anne hoped to marry her cousin John Spencer. Sarah tried to persuade Anne to make a good financial settlement for herself when she married Jersey, but eventually had to step in to handle the negotiations. She gave her support to the marriage in January 1733,[45] when Anne herself seemed penitent for her haste: 'I have not done an ill thing, though I have done a very foolish one & for which I never more shall have any ease.'[46]

Bedford's death meant that Anne's cousin Diana Spencer became the Duchess of Bedford. At the time, she was heavily pregnant with her first child, and busy furnishing her townhouse, with advice from Sarah tactfully accepted and declined. (Sarah teased her that her marriage bed was so big that she and her husband could sleep with their pet spaniel, named Duchess, comfortably between them.)[47] Sadly, shortly after they had inherited the dukedom, the Bedfords lost their baby on the day of its birth. Remembering the loss of her own first-born, Sarah ordered that another baby – probably a servant's – be laid beside the exhausted mother until she was more able to 'hear the truth and be told that it was only a Pretender'.[48]

Later Sarah provided refuge for another granddaughter, Bella, daughter of Mary Duchess of Montagu, who had been forced into an early marriage. The twenty-three-year-old 2nd Duke of Manchester had fallen passionately in love with her. He made a habit of locking himself in a room with two loaded pistols, saying he would kill himself if she refused to marry him. On one occasion he actually shot out his right eye, along with some of his skull, and on a second shot shattered his jaw. Next he tried to hang himself, at which point servants broke down the door and saved him. After all this, Bella was persuaded to accept him, though she never loved him and received a long line of suitors throughout her marriage.[49]

Sarah wrote that her daughter Mary had 'longed to be rid of' Bella so married her to Manchester even though he was obviously unstable, had a relatively small estate, and 'in half an hour's conversation with him the Duchess of Montagu must know that a woman that had sense must be very miserable with him'. Bella had complained to Sarah that her mother had had 'strange fancies and suspicions' about her, thinking she was glad when her brother died so that she could become the primary Montagu heir. Sarah herself witnessed that Mary had lost all protective interest in her daughter after she had married her off, which she compared to releasing a caged bird when it did not know how to survive in the wild.[50]

The Duke of Manchester died thankfully young in 1739, but left Bella only an old sedan chair and half a year's pin-money (as he had left each servant half a year's wages). Sarah therefore took her in and bought her a fully furnished house on Dover Street.

Perhaps Mary's rejection of Bella had more to do with her closeness to Sarah. Bella was frequently turned away by the porter at Montagu House when she went to enquire after her mother, and wrote letters seeking reconciliation that went unanswered. Sarah exclaimed, 'How cruel must a heart be, not to be reconciled to a child that had made such submissions!' However, Sarah's pity for Bella did not last long.

Bella's desirability was, like Sarah's, mixed with an outspokenness that became known as temper. Hervey nicknamed her the 'She-tiger' and wondered whether she had 'swallowed or spit out again the tips of all the noses she has bit off'.[51] Sarah, on the other hand, described her granddaughter as 'the most disinterested creature that I ever knew in my life'.[52] Later, after she herself had argued with Bella, she admitted that although Bella had much wit she also had 'a very unfortunate temper, which she cannot help. And though she is sometimes extremely agreeable in conversation, that humour comes upon her like a fit of a fever . . .' Time after time Sarah forgave her for these tantrums, but after one argument, Sarah quoted to her from Brutus' speech on how Cassius had inherited his mother's humour, 'to which the Duchess of Manchester answered "I had my ill humours from my mother and she had hers from you."' This was not something wisely said to Sarah's face. She stormed from the room and refused to speak to Bella again.

With so few grandchildren left in Sarah's good books, she increasingly looked for alternative places to leave her money. In 1732, when she had disinherited Charles Spencer, she had decided to found some almshouses in St Albans. She wrote to Sir Philip Yorke with regard to the construction of a hospital for army officers' widows and other 'distressed people'. It was to be built during her lifetime, but endowed by her will.[53] She also mentioned it in a letter to Diana in July 1732, where the project sounds as much an excuse for her architectural interest as charity.[54] In an age where there was limited parish provision for the poor, however, private almshouses were vital for the public welfare. The Marlborough Almshouses on Hatfield Road cost around £50,000 (over £4 million in today's money) and housed between thirty and forty people. They are still being used today as semi-institutional housing for elderly residents.

The founding of the almshouses has been cynically attributed to Sarah's wish to spite her heirs. In fact, the reasons for the bequest were plain enough: war veterans and their widows appealed constantly to the Captain-General's widow, and Sarah often responded to them, especially when the shadow of debtors' prison loomed. One Catherine Holford wrote in gratitude: '[T]o your Grace I owe my deliverance out of prison, for without this assistance your Grace has been so charitable to give me, it would have been impossible for me to compass it. Your Grace is not only my deliverer but the saver of my life for I have suffered so much here that it has impaired my health . . .'[55]

A letter from Elizabeth Maccarty, a relative of Charlotte, had begged for a charitable income of £100 a year, describing herself as pursued by creditors, living on bread and water, and in fear of being 'dragged to prison'.[56] The almshouses gave Sarah a way to justify refusals of *ad hoc* charity, made the Marlborough family look good in the eyes of St Albans' voters, and also brought the satisfaction of building another monument to her husband's memory. Furthermore, Sarah may have enjoyed the private joke of disproving a Tory satire published back in 1713, which had included her building hospitals among a list of absurd impossibilities.[57]

As Sarah knowingly preserved only correspondence that related to her arguments, it is fair to assume that the above letters of thanks are indicative of others. Benjamin Hoadly had once written to her, after she had granted some help to a poor man, that he could not 'but take notice of the great difference I have experienced between Your Grace, & other great persons – So much readiness to oblige, so much zeal to carry it through, so much goodness as even to go beyond the desires of the petitioner . . .'[58] His flattery warrants only partial scepticism.

By 1733, John Spencer had returned penitently to his grand-mother, tempted by all he stood to inherit if he could find his way back into her will. Sarah began to take an interest in arranging his marriage.[59] A possibly apocryphal anecdote has it that she sent him an alphabetical list of the women she considered suitable, and he simply picked the first name on the list.[60] On 14 February of the following year, he married Georgiana Carteret, a match that pleased Sarah because Lord Carteret (alongside her friends Lords Marchmont, Chesterfield and Stair) was a member of William Pulteney's anti-Walpole opposition. This 'Country Party' was an extraordinary coalition of Tories and disaffected Whigs. It was odd that Sarah's enmity to Walpole should have led her to befriend so many who had been enemies since 1688, given that she had far less at stake than she had in 1710 when she refused to support Lord Bolingbroke or other Tories in their opposition to Lord Oxford. The only explanation is that Sarah assessed her level of influence and found it necessary to ally in the 1730s as she had not in 1710. She confessed to one friend that she had 'no real interest at Court' and had not 'seen a Minister but in the streets this many years'.[61] Many others, faced with Walpole's complete domination of Parliament, were in a similar position.

Sarah remarked to Diana that John Spencer had a 'frankness in his temper which I love' and only needed the guidance of a politically sound father-in-law.[62] Yet she was still sharp enough to know that this grandson's dutiful behaviour was mercenary. In October 1734, she visited him at Maidenhead unannounced, and found herself unwelcome among the young holiday crowd. He did not change his plans for her, but Sarah boasted that she had managed to hide her resentment.[63] There is also an anecdote of Sarah declaring at some large family gathering that it was 'a glorious sight . . . to see such a number of branches flourishing from the same root' and John muttering under his breath: 'Alas, the branches would flourish far better if the root were underground.'[64] By the end of 1735, John and Georgiana had given her her first two great-grandchildren.

At this stage in her life, Sarah knew what it was to be wished dead. Her old sensitivity to being excluded and unloved by those she cherished re-emerged in the form of depression as she felt her grandchildren growing away from her. She now felt patronised for her age, as she had always been for her gender, and could not bear to think that her grandchildren took her for a fool. On 2 August 1733, for example, she had written to Diana reproaching her for preferring to visit her Windsor neighbour, Jane Kingdom: 'A great while after you had left me, I went out in my coach to take the air and saw your coaches standing at her door, in a violent rain, though you were in so much haste to leave me.'[65] Diana was uniquely talented at soothing her grandmother, perhaps because her love and respect were genuine, and managed to explain away what Sarah had seen.

That summer Sarah heard that her daughter Henrietta, Duchess of Marlborough, was dying.[66] Despite Sarah's last-minute attempts at reconciliation, Henrietta died without seeing her, on 24 October 1733, and the Marlborough title passed to the Spencer/Sunderland branch of the family. Sarah wrote to Diana: 'You have judged very right in thinking that . . . I should feel much more than I imagined formerly I could ever do.' Yet Sarah's final verdict on her eldest daughter was unsentimental: '[S]he had many good things in her, with some oddnesses,' but she was 'a cruel daughter and mother'.[67]

Several days later, Sarah wrote: 'I am so humbled and worn out with continual afflictions and disappointments . . . I grow fond of entertaining myself with my own melancholy . . .' She was by now in constant pain, able only to 'crawl about sometimes with the help of two sticks',[68] and increasingly aware of the emptiness of all but the handful of relationships in her life that were truly mutual: 'I have always thought that the greatest happiness of life was to love and value somebody extremely that returned it, and to see them often . . .'[69] Diana sent her grandmother a goose pie, for which Sarah thanked her 'because it shows you think of me'.[70]

The average life expectancy of the period was only thirty-five, though women who survived past thirty were likely to live ten years longer in 1730 than they had in 1680; Sarah was now seventy-three. She used only one room in each of her grand houses, demanding complete silence from 11 p.m. until seven or eight in the morning.[71] She found insomnia the worst of her complaints, the next being that she could no longer hold a pen, her arthritic right hand wrapped always in a flannel.[72] In the summer of 1733 she went to Tunbridge Wells again for the waters, and felt slightly better, although 'I am sure, whatever I do, I can never be well. And at my age, as Sir William Temple says, the play is not worth the candles.'[73] She compared herself, in these moods, to the martyred Job, though now her worst enemies were not politicians but loneliness and old age.

Her depression, however, never lasted for more than a few weeks, and her servant and friend James Stephens was soon reporting to Diana that 'when she is employed about anything that engages her attention, she can talk with as much vigour as ever I remember her.'[74] Sarah also had the ability to attract the brightest of the younger generation to her side: she did not live in the past, or even the present, but had an eye to the future, knowing that her reputation in posterity would be in the hands of the younger historians and politicians who could claim to have known her – men like Marchmont, Chesterfield and Carteret.

After losing Henrietta, Sarah was moved to reconcile with Charles, now 3rd Duke of Marlborough. Whatever else she might think of his wife, Sarah admitted she did 'have sense' – Sarah's basic criterion for women.[75] For his part, Charles's debts were increasing by the day, so he was willing, even after the bridge-burning letter he had written Sarah in 1732, to come crawling back. On a visit to Windsor Lodge he was charming, agreed to repay his debts to his brother John, and to comply with her political wishes.[76] This last was a difficult choice of Sarah's patronage over advancement under Walpole. Where Sarah would have chosen power, her heirs tended to choose money.

She had successfully promoted her grandsons and her agents in the 1727 and 1730 elections. Having failed to secure a seat for John Spencer at St Albans in 1730, Sarah had him nominated at Woodstock in 1732. He won his seat after she set up a charity to clothe eighty poor men and women of the town.[77]

The spring of 1733 had seen Walpole's introduction of an excise scheme that promised revenues from Customs and Excise to bring down the Land Tax to one shilling in the pound. This benefited the landed aristocracy, but hurt traders and hence the growing middle classes. It faced an unexpectedly wide opposition when the Country Party exaggerated the extent of the excise Walpole was planning, and so almost brought down Walpole's government in the elections of 1734.[78] Through Sarah's involvement – in Woodstock, St Albans, Bedfordshire and Surrey – the opposition won several marginal seats. One grateful opponent to the excise scheme wrote to her: 'We owe to your Grace's influence that this [Excise] Bill, big with mischiefs to our trade and liberties, was thrown out of the House of Commons . . .'[79]

In December 1733, the Duke of Bedford had proposed that John Spencer should stand with him in Bedfordshire, to which Sarah agreed, on condition that John also came to Woodstock to electioneer for her interest there. Both seats were won, though Sarah did not think she had John Spencer to thank for it: 'I had a vast deal of trouble and I verily believe I should not have carried the election, though it cost me a great deal of money, if it had not been for the pains which Mr Plummer [Walter Plummer, Sarah's electoral adviser] took in it . . .'[80] Nor did she have much to say for Bedford's political ability, describing him as barely capable of getting 'some words by heart when dictated to him' and as having manners that 'tired one to death'.[81] It is hard not to feel sorry for her: she had poor surrogate material to work with in this generation of grandsons and male in-laws.

Still in the mindset of the old wars, Sarah complained that 'Sir Robert has been making France strong some years and spent as much of the English money in the time of peace as if the King of France could be depended upon as a friend.'[82] Sarah also believed that the recent 'great fall of stocks', in which she and the trust had lost 'a vast sum', were due to Walpole's mismanagement. To Diana, she condemned the expense of the royal wedding (between the Princess Royal and the Prince of Orange) as an insult to the people of Britain at such a time of economic depression. On 11 November, Sarah wrote a description of the marriage between her carter and her kitchen maid, intended as a kind of burlesque on the royal wedding preparations.[83] This was part of her self-image in her seventies, as just one of the people, speaking up patriotically against the Court and its corrupt favourites.

She was deeply involved in the 1734 general election, her last great political stand. John Spencer had to decide which of his seats, Bedfordshire or Woodstock, to defend and which to give up. To the Duke of Bedford's fury, Sarah persuaded him to choose Woodstock, where Walpole was mounting a concerted opposition. Throughout August, Sarah canvassed with pen and ink, dictating letters to her friends and tenants throughout the country. She was a good landlady: in 1726, she had written to the Earl of Lichfield, telling him not to encroach upon her lands at Woodstock because she would 'stand by' her tenants there, who all had common access to her property. She eventually had to threaten him with legal action to defend these rights. One tenant, Humphrey Bradford, is on record as having sent her two brace of cocks, nine brace of snipe and two dozen larks as thanks for her help in finding his brother a job.[84] Now she expected her tenants' votes in return. She also acted as a *de facto* whip for the Country Party, bringing on board influential friends and using as leverage her control over the Marlborough trust's estates.

In November 1734, Sarah received a letter from William Pulteney with regard to the appointment of Fellows at King's College, Cambridge, which in turn would affect the election of the MPs for Cambridge. He urged Sarah not to retire from politics but to continue working for his Country Party. 'Believe me, Madam,' he wrote, 'no-one living is of more consequence than you are; you have friends, you have credit, you have talents, you have power & you have spirits still to do an infinite deal of service if you please to exert them, & why you should lock yourself up I cannot conceive.'[85]

The strange alliances formed by the anti-Walpole opposition meant that Sarah even received a letter of encouragement directly from the Pretender,[86] and considered supporting the son of her old rival Abigail Masham 'to get one vote for the public' – in other words, against Walpole.[87] This has led one of Sarah's biographers to accuse her of being 'no longer in any sense a Whig'[88] during the 1730s. This is unfair. Sarah, like Pulteney, saw Walpole as perverting original Whig principles: he had failed to push through the repeal of the Test Acts, relying only on non-enforcement of this legislation to protect religious freedoms, and reducing Britain's stature overseas – for example, by persuading George II to stay neutral in the War of Polish Succession. Walpole's supporters dubbed Sarah's friends 'mock-patriots'[89] and contrasted the relatively minor complaints of the times with the threats to English liberties that were rife before the Revolution. Sarah was one of the few who could remember that more clear-cut age: when she had been young, politicians were frequently executed for their beliefs; now they held their necks as a joking gesture in Parliament. Sarah had not mellowed with age, lambasting her political enemies with all her old energy, but the times themselves were less desperate. When she wrote to Bella's husband, the Duke of Manchester, that 'we have nothing to keep us from slavery but a wise and honest House of Commons',[90] she was using language from another era.

In the 1734 elections Walpole retained a strong majority, but the opposition was strengthened and large enough to keep him on his toes. For this Sarah deserves a share of the credit. Her financing (such as a beer hall opened to woo votes in St Albans) had made possible certain key opposition victories.

A story was long in circulation that in 1734 Sarah had also single-handedly rescued Child's Bank. The Bank of England was supposedly trying to foreclose on the smaller bank by collecting notes and bringing them all in for payment at once. Sarah was said to have written Mr Child a Bank of England cheque for £100,000 to cover the payments, thereby destabilising it in turn. According to one of Child's archivists, however, this story is, like so many of the best stories about Sarah, apocryphal.[91]

In the summer of 1734, Sarah was writing often to Diana with advice about the renovation of Bedford House, strongly suggesting that the front steps be widened like those at Marlborough House.[92] Again, Diana seemed able to say no to her grandmother without giving offence, and to see the more positive side of her interferences. That July, for example, when Diana's cousin Lady de la Warr (as Charlotte Maccarty was titled after 1724) fell seriously ill following childbirth, Sarah rushed to her old friend's bedside and nursed her to health, though she remained covered from head to toe in spots from 'something that I cannot write', presumably a venereal disease.[93]

Sarah also sent orders to the Bedfords as to how she would like their portrait to be painted for her, having little confidence in the painter's talent or honesty. 'You will not forget to make a bargain with Mr Whood,' she advised, 'since most people as well as he are apt to overvalue their work.'[94] Sarah's ability to bargain had not diminished with age. When visiting Althorp the following summer, she quizzed a servant about what he charged for making hay, in order to compare it to the rate charged by workmen at other houses.'[95] Charles, her heir, was still frittering money away, and Sarah was forgoing her jointure payments from the trust to keep him afloat. This generosity has usually been overlooked and her meddling in Charles's housekeeping condemned. 'I am labouring like a packhorse every day to save him from the cheats,' she wrote to Diana.

Sarah's own estates, while good investments, required a great deal of management and laid her open to dishonest brokers. She kept in employment her under-ranger at Windsor, a man named Chris Loft, after she found he was cheating, and promised not to 'hurt his credit' so long as he promised to bring her all bills for inspection in future. She had supported Loft and his family while he studied law, 'when otherwise he would have been a beggar, and could not have been taught to read', yet he continued to cheat her. 'One thing he has said of me to a great number of people that I was as mad as anybody in Bedlam & thought I had no memory nor did not know what I did.' She worried that he might be a dangerous witness if he ever said this in litigation concerning her will after her death.[96]

In 1735 she made a new will, in which she bequeathed the house at Wimbledon to Diana, whom she had nicknamed 'Cordelia',[97] and attached Marlborough House to the Marlborough title. When Walpole was finally forced into war against France and Spain, Sarah's fears were confirmed. If England was invaded, she wrote, 'We must bid farewell to Althorp, Blenheim, and to all property, and to conclude, be entire slaves.'[98] In her imagination the national good and her private good were still inextricably linked, as they were on the stock-market.

Sarah's letters in the late summer of 1735 show her concern for Diana's health during what both women must have assumed were the early stages of pregnancy – even though Diana reported that 'Lady Charlotte' had visited her twice since she became sick.[99] They are filled with practical advice, the most common way in which Sarah expressed love. On 16 August, she offered Diana Marlborough's old campaigning tent so that she could sit on the lawns at Woburn and take fresh air while remaining in the shade.

Nothing had prepared her, however, for seeing death in Diana's twenty-five-year-old face when she went to visit her shortly after this. She was shocked to find that Diana had consumption, which was too far advanced for her nursing to help, and railed against Bedford for having kept her granddaughter in the country with useless doctors.[100] She immediately moved Diana to the Bedfords' house on the north of Bloomsbury Square, and brought in better physicians, including James Stephens. She ordered them not to give up on their young patient, but also demanded that they tell Diana she was dying so that she could make arrangements, as was her right.

When Diana was told she had little time left, she made several verbal legacies to her friends and servants. She was suspicious that her husband would not respect her wishes, and so begged Sarah to be her defender after she was gone. On the final day of her life, 27 September 1735, Sarah fought with Bedford and was excluded, by his order, from the sickroom. 'I sat silently in outward rooms, bathed in tears; and I own I flattered you,' she later wrote to the widower, 'which was out of fear that . . . you would order the porter not to let me in,'[101] as indeed he had. It was perhaps the first time in her entire life that Sarah had been reduced to conscious flattery, but it was too late.

In the heat of her grief, Sarah burned all the letters she had received from Diana.[102] In her Green Book, she recorded only her fights with Bedford about petty material matters, though each was invested with sentimental meaning – the distribution of Diana's jewels, the return of Marlborough's tent, and the giving of a legacy to a nursemaid as Diana had wanted. She also condemned Bedford for being inappropriately sociable too soon after Diana's death. Sarah was again trying to dictate how others grieved, implying that their love had been shallow. She even went so far as to tell him that he had 'murdered his wife for want of common care'. Bedford had 'often made speeches like a philosopher, how he would behave when she [Diana] was dead', she wrote, while in fact 'there is nothing so silent as true grief.'[103]

What Sarah kept silent (until Frances Harris's biography finally unearthed the scene) was that, soon after Diana's death, she was found by a visitor to Marlborough House lying prostrate on the floor of a darkened room. She explained to the visitor that she had been praying, 'and that she lay thus upon the ground, being too wicked to kneel'.[104]

13
'A Flight for Fame'

In 1735, at a low point in George II's popularity, Sarah commemorated Queen Anne with a tenderness absent from her *Hints on the Character of Queen Anne* (1712) by erecting a statue of her at Blenheim. She told one granddaughter, 'I have a satisfaction in showing this respect to her, because her kindness to me was real'[1] – not, it should be noted, because she had been a wise queen. Henry Fielding called the monument 'an Instance of the Goodness and Gratitude' of Sarah's character.[2] Since her husband's death she had also commissioned three works – the sepulchre in the chapel, the column of victory, and the triumphal arch – to commemorate her late husband. After all were complete, she wrote that she did not 'design to see Blenheim again'.[3]

The sepulchre, designed by William Kent and sculpted by Michael Rysbrack, is particularly expressive of Sarah's heart and mind. The effigial grouping includes her two dead sons (portrayed at the ages of their deaths) and none of her daughters. The boys were probably modelled from paintings and Sarah's memory. Above them their father stands in the pose of a Roman senator. Sarah herself sits on a large throne-like chair, wearing her ducal coronet. Her son Charles, aged two, is pushing against her knees trying to gain her attention, echoing Catholic images of Jesus and Mary, but Sarah is focused on Marlborough. Her lower level in the composition should have symbolised her subordinate role in the family. In fact, Sarah is restless, as if trying to jump to her feet. As Charles grabs at her, so she gestures towards John, like the traditional emblem of Discord, a woman grabbing at someone's legs. The symbolic figures of Fame with his trumpet (on the left) and History with his pen (on the right) join the family members, making Sarah the sole woman in the group. These figures did not represent Marlborough's inner qualities, but rather his public image. This choice of symbolism combined with realistic portraits was highly innovative, expressing not only the love of a widow but also Sarah's vision of her family as central to England's destiny as the New Rome.

Underneath the sarcophagus is carved a dragon-like creature, the size of a lapdog. Some have interpreted it as a symbol of Chaos, Malice or Envy, being squashed by the solid block of Truth. A proposed inscription for the tomb mentioned Marlborough conquering Envy, but the creature in the finished sculpture does not seem to be dying. If anything it seems to be slipping out, away from Truth. Others have suggested that it could merely be the wyvern on the Marlborough family coat-of-arms.

The triumphal arch was modelled by Hawksmoor on the Arch of Titus in Rome, or at least on bad drawings of it that Hawksmoor had seen, and the inscription again said as much of Sarah's labours as the Duke's: 'This gate was built the year after the death of the most illustrious John Duke of Marlborough by order of Sarah his most beloved wife, to whom he left the sole direction of the many things that remained unfinished of this fabric . . .' Horace Walpole described Blenheim as decorated with inscriptions in honour of the Duke but with Sarah herself 'mentioned, as putting 'em up, in almost all of 'em'.[4]

Among her notes, Sarah copied from Ecclesiastes: 'A good name is better than precious ointment,'[5] and in a sense the final decade of her life was devoted to healing the wounds inflicted on Marlborough's reputation between 1710 and 1714. She strongly believed that 'when once the madness of passion shall cease with time; & personal malice be wearied & appeased', truth would triumph.[6] She believed in history's redemptive power far more than in any religious salvation. Disappointed by most of those who surrounded her, she turned to posterity as though it were an alternative circle of friends, or a jury.

As late as 1742, Sarah was commissioning additional busts of Marlborough and Godolphin, taken from their portraits.[7] However, her true monument to these men would be made not of stone but of words. She had always paid close attention to what would survive on paper. One letter, dated 9 September 1710, for example, is partially obliterated because, Sarah noted in later years, 'What I have put out was not proper to the past.' There is also an anecdote, told by Lord Oxford's grandson, that after Oxford's death, the elderly widow managed to obtain and destroy the document that suggested Marlborough had dealings with the Jacobites.[8] She wanted as much surviving evidence as possible to be under her control before she died.

Now Sarah devoted herself to the herculean task of editing her papers. As she sorted through them, her annotations second-guess the reader at every stage: 'If you should think upon reading any of these papers that I took too much liberty with Mrs Morley . . .' or 'I fear after such usage you will think I say too much, but let your next thought be that it was for the sake of my friends, & there is nothing false in this letter, though I think [it] too submissive.'[9] Her two favourite amanuenses, Charles Hodges and Judith Foster, spent endless hours recopying letters she was determined to preserve.

In 1735 she had asked Alexander Pope to help her prepare her memoirs for publication, but he had tactfully declined. It was not until 1740 that she was introduced to his friend, Nathaniel Hooke, who became the co-author finally to bring them to press. Lord Chesterfield wrote to the Earl of Marchmont: 'I have brought Mr Hooke and her together, and having done that will leave the rest to them, not caring to meddle myself in an affair which I am sure will not turn out at last to her satisfaction, though I hope, and believe, it will be to his advantage.'[10] Chesterfield was too pessimistic: though Sarah argued with Hooke when he foolishly tried to convert her to Catholicism, she was satisfied with his literary work and paid him £5,000.

One contemporary remembered that on her better days, 'though oppressed with the infirmities of age, and almost bed-rid, she would continue speaking for six hours together; she delivered to [Hooke], without any notes, her account in the most lively as well as the most connected manner'.[11] Hooke's role in the final book has usually been overestimated: he merely improved the style as Sarah dictated the content, drawing upon previous drafts.

The book was entitled *An Account of the Conduct of the Dowager Duchess of Marlborough – From her first coming to Court to the Year 1710 – In a letter from Herself to My Lord —*, an unintentionally ironic allusion to the 'conduct literature' for women which Sarah's whole life had disregarded. It was published by James Bettenham for George Hawkins,[12] a printer on the Strand whose offices overlooked the four half-constructed arches of Westminster Bridge.

Publication gave Sarah a boost of energy late in life and a great deal of pride. In one edition, the story of her favour, her rise and fall, stood monumentally alone. One reader wrote to Sarah that it would be a monument to Queen Anne's weakness that would 'probably outlast that of marble which you have generously raised to her virtues'.[13] In another edition, intended perhaps for a smaller audience of friends and acquaintances, she also included the long narrative of her acrimonious dealings with the 3rd Duke of Marlborough.

The dedication at the front of Sarah's *Conduct* has usually been misattributed. One of her later editors, William King, imagined that the 'noble Lord' whose name began with 'Ch' was George, 3rd Earl of Cholmondeley, the son-in-law of Sir Robert Walpole. Why Sarah would have chosen him for such an honour is wholly unclear. It is far more likely to have been Chesterfield, as thanks for introducing her to Hooke.

Sarah's aim in publishing was defensive. Her husband could let others speak for his actions, but as biographies of women's lives were rare, Sarah had to speak for herself. The first line of the published *Conduct* confesses to this vanity: 'I have been often told, that there is a sort of philosophy, by which people have brought themselves to be indifferent, not only whether they be at all remembered after death, but whether in case their names should survive them, they be mentioned with praise or infamy.' Very soon, she wrote, nothing would remain of her 'but a *name*' and she could not help but be concerned that those who 'begin with forming to themselves characters . . . upon slight and idle reports, by which they admit or reject whatever they afterwards hear' should be 'undeceived' as to the character that went with the name of Sarah Churchill, Duchess of Marlborough. This went beyond the version written with Bishop Burnet, in which she claimed only to address her descendants: '[S]ince I am likely to leave behind me a posterity that is already distinguished by rank & estate, and that may branch out into more families, I am under some obligation to let them know by what principles and measures I governed myself . . .'[14]

Sarah cut from the published version a highly rhetorical paragraph regarding posterity's judgement on Queen Anne:

When posterity comes to be assured of this [Anne's behaviour to Marlborough] will it not shake & surprise them? And will not many be apt to ask what part her justice had in this procedure? What her pity, what her gratitude, what her honour, what her faith & what her constancy? I will give no further answer . . . Facts speak too plainly to be denied.[15]

She also omitted several descriptions of her own emotions during the central crises of her life, criticisms of secondary characters with whom she had since reconciled or towards whom her heart had softened after their deaths, as well as several explicit condemnations of Anne's motives. She added further details of a general historical nature, explaining her role in the battles over occasional conformity and her career as a lobbyist for the Whigs. She was playful with her own biases ('I am perhaps too much concerned in the affair to be a proper judge of this letter'), and moralised only occasionally, as when she mentioned forgiving trespasses as we expect to be forgiven. Her deterministic attitude, however, was that not of a Christian but that of a writer. She saw her trials and tribulations in terms of a narrative pattern, where portents had meaning within the arc of the story and where characters received their just deserts at the nib of her pen, not in another world.

Before the end of the year, five or six reactions to the *Conduct* had been published. The most substantial and engaging was

The Other Side of the Question (1742)[16] by James Ralph, an American friend of Benjamin Franklin, Congreve and Vanbrugh. Curiously, he posed as an anonymous 'Woman of Quality' when he answered Sarah, but then objected when her memoir descended to 'the Flats and Marshes of Family Affairs',[17] missing the point that the story of the Hill family's ingratitude was important to Sarah precisely because it had higher, political ramifications in the world of men. He failed to understand the complex and symbolic meanings behind the fall of a royal favourite: 'One would almost think the Fate of an Empire was depending, or even that the good Genius of the World was taking its Final Leave,' he scoffed.[18]

James Ralph told Sarah that her fault was not malice but egotism; she made herself the 'little Hero of each Tale'.[19] He was shocked at her insolence in using the Queen as a foil to display her virtues, and took the conventional line that the truly virtuous had no need to blow their own trumpet. He told her that the public 'expected a History of your own Times, not an Apology for your own Conduct'[20] and sneered at her for choosing a subjective literary form.[21] Ralph concluded that 'It was shrewdly said by a certain noble Lord that your Book was an Answer to itself',[22] but failed to recognise this insult as also a compliment to Sarah's critical intelligence. Her version of events is coherent and, ultimately, more convincing than the Other Side as presented by Ralph.

Even less convincing was the anonymous reply entitled Her Grace of Marlborough's Party-Gibberish explained (1742), which marvelled at an uneducated woman's admission of having meddled in politics. The author doubted that, as a woman, Sarah had the intellect to examine 'titles to estates, bills in Chancery, and accounts'.[23]

Dr Johnson, writing in the Gentleman's Magazine (1742), reviewed Sarah's book more favourably.[24] He pondered the popularity of political memoirs in general: '[W]e consider the writer as indubitably possessed of the ability to give us just representations, and do not always reflect that, very often, proportionate to the opportunities of knowing the truth, are the temptations to disguise it.' He saw clearly what motivated Sarah as much as any male author: '[T]he parent of all memoirs is the ambition of being distinguished from the herd of mankind.'

Though his politics were not hers, he complimented her as a historian on her generous use of letters as unmediated evidence, and on her 'unaffected dignity of style' and 'artful simplicity of narration'. He remarked on how she blackened the characters of William and Mary – it was the first time that this popular and pious Queen had been so criticised – and he seemed willing to believe, at least in part, Sarah's criticisms. As for Queen Anne, he wrote that her letters convicted her of having had a real 'tenderness of affection' but, on the other hand, a 'helpless dependence on the affection of others'. He called her intelligent but not regal, 'born for friendship not for government'. The published letters, he presumed, were selected by Sarah 'with some regard to respect and ceremony' and showed that Anne 'was what she has been represented, little more than the slave of the Marlborough family'. After her death, Johnson again mentioned Sarah's memoirs in one of his *Rambler* essays, describing her as 'a late female Minister of State' but also calling her 'shameless' and guilty of peddling sophistries about the duty of friendship.[25]

In the anonymous poem *The Old Wife's Tale: or, E[dwar]d's Wish* (1742) Sarah was again attacked as a witch, a boozing old crone, 'wrapt in Flannel, Cloth and Fur ... tott'ring in her Wicker-Chair/With Half-shut Eyes and cunning Leer'. She launches into a political prophecy, which the poet suggests is a product of her drunken senility: 'Of nut-brown Nappy [she] took a Tip/And grumbled out what's underwrit . . .' Similarly, in *The Sarah-Ad: or, a Flight for Fame* (1742), her memoirs were retold as burlesque, the plot of party rivalry transferred to two clubs fighting over the use of a dining room above a pub of which Anne is the landlady. Sarah was depicted as an 'arrant Authoress' whose apologies for the indecent act of self-publication are parodied: 'Excuse the Theme, the Style the same / You know tis all a Flight for Fame.'

A *Review of a Late Treatise* (1742) attacked Sarah's *Conduct* because in it she tried only to prove that she was 'ever in the Right' and 'never once in the Wrong'. The anonymous author accused her of thoroughly distorting the truth, while admitting that hers was not a book 'sent into the world . . . to spread Slander'. Like James Ralph, however, this author failed to replace Sarah's version of events with another, equally convincing account.

Sarah's main defence came from Henry Fielding. She is said to have hired the novelist to reply to her hostile reviewers,[26] though there is no hard evidence that *A Full Vindication of the Dowager Duchess of Marlborough* (1742) did not appear spontaneously.[27] Fielding's father had fought under Marlborough, his sister was a friend of Benjamin Hoadly, the Fielding name had appeared on various of Sarah's party invitation lists, and he was on her side against Walpole's government. Fielding referred to her generosity as a patron, but in its choice of arguments *A Full Vindication* seems to have been written without her direction.

Fielding admitted that Sarah was 'indeed rich and if her Enemies accuse her of that I believe she must plead guilty,'[28] but asserted that her wealth could be fully accounted for by honest gain. He catalogued the slurs on her character: she had been accused of insolence, rapaciousness, lying, affectation, lacking forgiveness, indecency, ingratitude, cant, and portrayed as 'a Tyrant . . . charged with Ill-nature and governing her Husband'. He was offended both on her behalf and for the sake of what 'all Europe' owed to Marlborough. He replied to the common assumption that Sarah was a woman 'of great Pride and Haughtiness' by stating 'that her Grace is superior to all Meanness, that she knows her own great Consequence, that her vast Abilities are no more hid from herself than from those who have the Honour of her Conversation', but that she was pure affability to those beneath her in rank, fortune or abilities.[29]

A few years after her death, Horace Walpole included Sarah in his *Catalogue of Royal and Noble Authors* (1758), giving her a surprising amount of credit as a literary figure. This royal favourite, he wrote:

wound up her capricious life with an apology for her conduct. The piece, though weakened by the prudence of those who were to correct it, though maimed by her Grace's own corrections, and though a great part of it is rather the annals of a wardrobe than of a reign, yet has still curious anecdotes, and a few of those sallies of wit which fourscore years of arrogance could not fail to produce in so fantastic an understanding.[30]

In a letter to a friend, however, Horace Walpole revealed his true prejudice against female authorship, remarking that Nathaniel Hooke's materials had been 'so womanish that I am sure the man might sooner have made a gown and petticoat with them'.[31]

In 1734 Sarah had been pleased to see the opposition win 204 seats, but attributed it cynically to politicians' anticipation of a change of ministry with the death of King George II. In 1737 she gossiped about the rows between Frederick Louis, Prince of Wales, and his father, and in July her friendship with the Prince was such that, when he left the Court with his wife and newborn baby, she offered Marlborough House as a refuge. He did not accept but moved instead to Leicester House, where the government opposition swarmed around this rival Court. When Queen Caroline died in November, Sarah scoffed at her for leaving debts to the King and stated without apology that she was glad the woman who supported Walpole 'in all his arbitrary injustice' was finally gone.

She was also scathing about the government's claim to be paying off the national debt, unable to understand how, despite the money coming in from the civil list, Ireland and Scotland, overseas plantations, and the taxes on malt in the Gin Act, the debt did not substantially decrease. In a narrative that resembles a draft for a political pamphlet, she included such detailed items as the cost of the King travelling back and forth to Hanover, the amounts given by various companies and corporations for political favours, and other revenues taken from 'the honest Creditors of the Public'. Her interest in economics shines through this essay, though she was always more perceptive about how government policy was reducing her own income as a stockholder than about what was fiscally beneficial for the country as a whole. Walpole taught the country that it could be stable, even prosperous, under the shadow of a national debt, but Sarah was perhaps too old to be taught this new trick and never gave Walpole credit for the fact that the debt had not continued to rise:

Four and a half percent is allowed for circulating exchequer bills which, I am persuaded, is not lent by the Bank. And this at the same time that the property of people's money, which was lent upon Parliament security, is reduced by their own consent from six to four, for the good of the nation to sink the public debt, which is very little lessened.

Also apparent is her taste for political rhetoric: 'Query: Whether any man that is concerned for his country, his posterity or for himself, if he has any estate, can with a good conscience or common sense, assist in starving so many people, only to give their money to Ministers?'[32]

In the spring, Sarah again sold her stocks and bought more land, but the truth was, now that the Exchequer could get the funds from elsewhere, Walpole was refusing her loans from the Marlborough trust. This was a serious blow since there was nowhere else that such large sums could be as safely and profitably invested.

Sarah made notes on the lists of MPs for the Committees of Enquiry into Walpole's administration, showing she was still an agitator for greater transparency and accountability in government.[33] She held evening salons for the opposition leaders at Marlborough House, but was discontented to see them so disunited and the Tories not wary of the danger she perceived from Franco-Jacobite invasion. In one diary entry she remarked modestly that '[M]y own opinion may possibly be very wrong, for it is only from what I think I see, putting things together, for nobody tells me anything that I can depend upon.'[34] The truth was, for a woman of seventy-seven, she was still remarkably well connected. When Lord Grimston stood for a seat at St Albans that year, she found a copy of an embarrassing play that he had written when he was thirteen, *The Lawyer's Fortune, or Love in a Hollow Tree* (1705), and had a new edition printed at her own expense. She sold it to the voters of St Albans to persuade them not to elect him. When he tried to buy up all the copies, she had another edition printed in Holland and imported.[35]

The year 1738 brought Sarah one terrible shock. Without warning, the 3rd Duke of Marlborough, Charles Spencer, defected from Prince Frederick's side to that of the Court Party because, he claimed, he was appalled by the Prince's callous attitude to his mother's death. In fact, Charles was so desperate for money that he had had to take Court employment and accept the command of a West Indies regiment, despite risking Sarah's ire. Sarah believed, probably correctly, that his friend Henry Fox was responsible for Charles's decision. She also, again, blamed Lady Bateman who 'imagined she should be a sort of Madame Mant[enon] and govern all'.[36] A story circulated that Sarah scrawled in black paint over a portrait of Lady Bateman and left it hanging in the dining room at Marlborough House for the world to see. One version of the story had her screaming that Bateman was 'the vilest woman I ever knew in my life; and deserves to be burnt,'[37] while another had her writing on the bottom of the picture that her granddaughter was 'blacker within'.[38] The picture, if it ever existed, has not survived, so the story, which portrays Sarah as a prisoner of her own foolish, impotent temper, cannot be verified. After a lifetime of being told she was an unstable, irrational creature, Sarah perhaps chose to avenge herself in old age by becoming one.

Sarah cancelled the will in which she had left Marlborough House to Charles, and also ordered him to vacate the smaller Lodge at Windsor. In strange parallel to the story told against her when she moved out of St James's Palace, he pulled out all of the fixtures and, Sarah claimed, deliberately damaged the floors. She laughed at such pettiness, given that it was not she but his brother John who was to move into the house. The Duchess of Portland told the story from a different angle: 'The Duke of Marlborough has the Lodge in the Little Park and he has made very great improvements there and great plantations . . . The old Duchess came there a little while ago and brought a great many men from London to destroy everything that had been done, pulled up the trees and cut and hacked at everything she came near.'[39]

In her new will, John Spencer, whom she now discovered was also in debt, became Sarah's primary heir, on condition that he did not accept any Court or government post. Sarah believed that it was in revenge for this new will that Charles subsequently brought a Chancery case against her for mismanagement of the trust, which was heard in June 1740. In the final stages of the hearing, Sarah pleaded her own case, not incompetently.[40] The judge found no fault with her management of the trust, but tried to give her grandsons as much income from it as possible.

Sarah continued to record in her notes her despair about the fate of the nation under Walpole: 'I think one can't leave the world at a better time than now, when there is no such thing as real friendships, truth, justice, honour, or indeed anything that is agreeable in life' and 'I compare our situation to a ship near sinking . . .'[41] She pretended to fear that half of her property was tied up in government funds that could be 'spunged off', but comforted herself that she would not starve so long as she had cows on her land. She concealed her frustration at Walpole's rejection of her loans by buying Lord Yarmouth's estate because 'land will be the last thing that will be taken from us'. Some years later, when she was permitted to reinvest in government stock, she offered exactly the reverse logic: '[W]hen I have any money I had rather avoid the troubles of land & have it where I can easily get at it, that I may give it away when I see the storm near.'[42]

She saw the army as incompetent ('throwing away all the Duke of Marlborough's successes and giving us up to France') and the opposition as little better, corrupted by the desperation of being so long out of power. In February 1739, she recorded the battle in the House of Lords over Walpole's Convention of El Prado with Spain, the text of which was found among her papers.[43] The opposition thought that Walpole was giving away English shipping rights, but lost the vote in the House of Commons, causing Sarah's hopes for a change of Ministry to flag once again. Women were excluded from the gallery for the course of the debate, but the Duchess of Queensberry led ten other opposition ladies (a 'tribe of dames') in thumping on the doors until they were opened, then charging in. Bedridden at home, Sarah must have envied them as they jeered and hooted at Lord Hervey's speech for the government.[44]

In 1740, when the Ministry was forced by public jingoism to enter the War of Austrian Succession with Spain and France, Sarah indulged in many 'melancholy' moods about the army's lack of preparedness, fearing that Jamaica would be lost, and that Parliament 'would sell their country & all that is valuable' until they realised that they were on the verge of ruin. Her hopes were invested in Lords Chesterfield and Marchmont, to whom she was in the habit of sending clippings from the newspapers, the one small assistance she could offer them apart from funds. She also sent clippings to Sir Hynde Cotton, a Tory friend and fellow member of the Country Party with whom she corresponded regularly, apologising for her own outside position: 'I can't pretend to send you any news but what is in the prints.'[45] To him she joked about campaigning like a man: 'I am sure if you were to stand to be elected, I should be tempted to get on horseback myself.'[46]

She scowled at having seen Walpole laughing in public, 'not decent at this time, when so great a country, once happy, is just sinking' and feared the worst on the home front: 'Tis said by a great many people in town that there is to be an invasion in three places. And I can see no General worth naming for us.' None of the present officers, she wrote, had seen more action than play-battles on the Serpentine, and she bemoaned the lack of a defence force because the ships were too far away to be called back.[47] On 11 October 1740, she wrote offering 'to give security for six and twenty Scotch Members that will vote for the true Interest of England' and urged Cotton to help her lobby before the next significant vote.[48] Two days later she wrote again that if the House of Lords would not desert Walpole during the war, then 'nothing can do good I think but a majority in Parliament for the security of England, which would bring things right at once, notwithstanding all the corruption & folly that has been committed; which I pray heartily for & that you would pardon my writing so much upon politics, who could not see anything if it were not very plain'.[49]

In the 1741 general election Sarah again wrote to her stewards with voting instructions although she had less vigour for campaigning than in earlier years. When Lord Sandwich requested that she join him in the election of some men in the county of Huntingdon who were not of the Country Party but who would undermine one of her enemies, she refused, saying, 'I always like to go in a straight line.'[50]

Finally Walpole lost real ground in these elections, though the Duke of Marlborough, to Sarah's continuing disgust, was one of his few remaining supporters. Her mood was expressed in a poetic pamphlet titled *The Year Forty-One: Carmen Seculare* (1741), which was dedicated to her for 'bravely standing up to stem that Torrent of public Enormities'. It described the people of England becoming isolationists, with their soldiers at home in 'sloth and riot', without exports, too much consumption, and corrupted by 'Such Treating, Voting, Swearing, Bribing, Biting/ Such Dearth of Learning, yet such Crops of Writing'.

In November 1741, Sarah wrote to the Bank of England, wearily accepting that its stock would continue to fall, and adding that 'I am so near fourscore that whatever happens it can't signify much to me.'[51] By 1742, she had lived to see Walpole fall – though without the hard landing she might have wished for. The popularity of the war had made his isolationist policies appear outdated, and it was the King's prerogative to ask for the First Minister's resignation after twenty-one years at

Downing Street. Several of her friends, such as Lord Stair, were brought into the new Ministry.

Shortly after breaking with her granddaughter Bella, Sarah was coaxed into seeking a reconciliation with her last surviving child, Mary. The intermediary was a kindly, not very bright woman named Jane Hammond, whom Lady Mary Wortley Montagu had watched displace another friend – Elizabeth Dunch – as the favourite 'in the D[uchess] of Marbro's Court'.[52]

Mary, Duchess of Montagu, was now in her fifties and going blind.[53] In May 1739, Mrs Hammond committed what Sarah called a 'pious fraud' in pretending to each woman that the other had made the first step.[54] However, Sarah would not forgive Mary until she received an admission from her daughter that she had been in the wrong. From Wimbledon she sent her daughter a long narrative from her Green Book, containing all Mary's 'monstrous behaviour' towards her. 'I cannot give any good reason for writing all this, which, if a stranger ever happens to read, they will think a Romance,' she wrote to Mary. 'I believe you may not remember many things in it yourself, for your passions are too strong to let you reflect.'[55] She did not expect the letter to have any effect on her daughter, she confided, 'but I had a mind that she should not continue in her notion that she had done nothing wrong or unbecoming in a child'.[56]

Mary replied with a short, rather formal apology, which Mrs Hammond thought was 'a great deal for one of her spirit to say' although Sarah thought 'twas no more than if she had trod by chance upon my toe'.[57] Then Mrs Hammond suggested that Sarah should write an example of what kind of letter would satisfy her, at which Sarah remembered that 'I could not help laughing very much, saying that it was surprisingly new that I should dictate a letter to myself from a daughter that had used me in such a manner for so many years.'[58] When Mrs Hammond promised to present it to Mary as her own composition, however, Sarah's curiosity prompted her to see whether Mary would return it.

By November there was still no progress. Sarah described Mary as a woman of sense but with a 'hardness of her heart'. When a fuller letter of apology eventually came, Sarah underlined the phrases that to her mind did not go far enough: 'that in <u>some</u> <u>things</u> I have wronged you'/ 'for any faults I <u>may</u> have been guilty of . . .' She wrote a lengthy analysis to Mrs Hammond, complimenting the letter's 'dexterous' style, but refusing to see or accept the kind intention behind the words. Mary commented that she wished her mother 'had been less pleased with the style of my last letter and more so with the matter'.

The following month, when Sarah received another apology from Mary, her response was still cynical and wary. She told Mrs Hammond that the new warmth of Mary's tone 'puts me in mind of myself, when I have gone to a shop and they have asked too much I have gone away without buying it, and afterwards gone again, and because 'twas of use to me, given their high price'. She said that she had forgiven Mary in her heart but could not bear to see her, explaining with her usual candour:

I am what is called bedridden and dying. And though I believe her wit entertaining, I can read that out of any book, and am content with the very few friends I keep company with when I am out of pain. And, at my age, tis impossible to love anybody with passion, as I did her a great while, but I own that has been long burnt out. And I have nothing to do but be as quiet as I can.[59]

Two years later, however, Sarah was persuaded to write words of forgiveness to her daughter. Characteristically it was also a self-vindication; she protested that she had never loved Mary less than her sister Anne or her brothers. She confessed that she had hoped, upon sending Mary the Green Book's 'Tragical Account' of their relationship, that Mary would rush over to Wimbledon and beg forgiveness. She took pride in never having embarrassed her children with any immodest behaviour in her whole life, while Mary had sometimes 'kept very bad company' – again, her euphemism for marital infidelity. This letter, she wrote, was intended as her last words to her last child.[60]

Mary immediately wrote back, grateful for the expressions of forgiveness but longing, she said, to see her mother and beg for forgiveness on her knees. Sarah recorded how pleased she was to receive this letter, the first in thirty years to answer hers with any warmth, she felt. Yet she claimed she did not really want Mary to prostrate herself, and replied that a visit 'would give no satisfaction to me who never wished anything from you but your heart in return for mine'. Besides, Mary would find her 'very stupid company'. She had long wished herself out of the world, but wished her daughter a long and happy life. Mary told her mother that all her faults 'came from my head, not my heart, & that I have been so far from not having loved you for thirty years that I have not in my life been so many days without knowing that I loved you'. Shortly afterwards, Mary made a private visit to Sarah at Marlborough House; no record of their conversation survives.

Sidney Godolphin once warned Sarah that 'old age betrays one's nature as much as wine',[61] yet Sarah remained sharp until the end. Lady Mary Wortley Montagu, when she herself had grown old, wrote to her sister: 'I think my time better employed in reading the adventures of imaginary people than the Duchess of Marlborough's, who passed the latter years of her life in paddling with her will, and contriving schemes of plaguing some and extracting praise from others, to no purpose, eternally disappointed and eternally fretting.'[62] Yet this harsh verdict cannot have been the whole story of Sarah's octogenarian personality, since she was one of the last people to whom Lady Mary bade a tearful farewell before she fled England with her lover Algarotti in 1739. Lady Mary had always competed with Sarah as to who was the greater cynic, elsewhere writing:

Public Life is what I was never fond of . . . I have always been amazed at the passion for it continuing as in the late Duchess of Marlborough, and can only attribute it to the flatterers round her, who nourished in her that desire of applause which is as vain as the endeavours of children that run to catch the rainbow.[63]

In fact we know that, besides 'paddling with her will', Sarah spent a good deal of time in reading. She was so taken with the fourth part of *Gulliver's Travels* that she forgave Swift 'all the slaps he has given me and the Duke of M'.[64] Her friend Mr Lewis wrote to her in August 1742 to suggest that 'since your Grace seems at present to be in a humour to read grave books', she should add Boethius to her library of philosophy. Yet, despite this evidence of contemplative pursuits, her reputation in old age has been reduced to that of a childish, cantankerous, quarrelsome nuisance. Speaker Onslow, for example, on reading Burnet's *History*, wrote that after sensible men stopped controlling her, Sarah's 'talk and actings in the latter part of her life were like the rage of madness . . . She had no true wisdom or greatness of mind, and was in truth a very weak passionate woman.'[65]

Sarah's temper had always been a cover for pain and power-lessness. For most of her life she did not sit and marinate in her anger, but used it as fuel for action and, above all, for writing. Only in the final years of her life was she forced to sit alone with it. She hated staying in London all year, as 'one is always in dread of seeing those one wishes never to see, or in expectation of seeing some few that are generally better employed than to come',[66] and copied the line from Francis Bacon: 'A crowd is not company & faces are but a gallery of pictures & talk but a tinkling cymbal where there is no love.'[67]

The Dukes of Marlborough and Bedford, and John Spencer, were united against her now, counting the weeks until she died. Their mutual friend, a man named Robert Maccarty, 5th Earl of Clancarty, Charlotte Maccarty's brother, was her main channel of communication with them.[68] In the 1730s, Sarah had tried to help him recover the estates confiscated in 1697 from his Jacobite father, and Clancarty, who had Jacobite sympathies himself, was united with Sarah by his resentment against Walpole for denying these claims. At the same time he was a friend of Charles Spencer, and therefore became a neutral intermediary when, in 1741, Sarah threatened Charles with another lawsuit unless she and Francis Godolphin were paid their jointures from the trust, and unless the £3,000 he had borrowed from her was repaid.[69] Charles could not pay up; rather, he was borrowing small sums (£500–£1,000) on the credit of what he stood to inherit when Sarah died. Sarah heard that these promissory notes were 'sold in the alleys like South Sea stock'.[70]

In July 1742, Sarah lost the final Chancery case against the workmen at Blenheim. This experience did not deter her from threatening legal action against Lord Cornbury that same month when he sent her some rotten venison. She wrote that she wanted a refund of eleven shillings. When he teased her for having the energy to pursue such trivia at her advanced age, she justified her general interest in seeing people act as responsible trustees to their estates. Lord Cornbury wrote a sarcastic reply, hoping that they would not have to resort to the law, but pleased if they did so to be contributing to her amusement. Sarah wrote back thanking him for the amusement he afforded, insisting that she preferred to deal with disputes through lawyers these days than to quarrel in person.

Horace Walpole supplied another story about Sarah in these final years, that she feigned unconsciousness to eavesdrop on what her doctors and servants said about her. With her eyes shut, unmoving and unresponsive, she listened for several days until she heard one doctor opine, 'She must be blistered, or she will die', at which she snapped open her eyes and declared, 'I won't be blistered and I won't die.'[71]

The story parodied her continued preoccupation with what would be said about her and her family after her death. She had once declared that she would give £500 to anyone who could compass the character of her late husband in six lines, and paid up in good humour when a friend wrote:

> Five hundred pounds!
> Too small a Boon
> To put the Poet's Muse in tune
> That nothing may escape her
> Of the Illustrious Churchill's glory
> It would not buy the paper.[72]

More seriously, she searched for official biographers for her husband. Her first choice, Richard Steele, disgraced himself by pawning the papers Sarah gave to him.[73] The next was Viscount Molesworth, Marlborough's old aide-de-camp who had fought at Blenheim and saved the Duke's life at Ramillies.[74] Finally, however, she decided on Richard Glover and David Mallet. Glover was a West India merchant as well as an author, with whom she had long corresponded about foreign news, considering him 'a very honest man'.[75] He had flattered Sarah that she was one who had 'trod firm on the most slippery paths, while everyone about her has fallen in her sight; in fine, who after so much experience and such severe trials in a bad world, can say with truth I *have* done well'.[76] As for Mallet, he had already written a biography of Francis Bacon which recommended him to her.

Sarah sent a five-page list of her own papers[77] to where Mallet was staying near Chiswick. In return he sent her an apple, in imitation, he explained, of a Russian cobbler who presented a turnip to the Tsar. He promised her that the documents she sent him would be kept under lock and key, and that he would 'throw all other business aside' to work on the biography. Though it was to be about Marlborough, Sarah also sent the author material relating more to her own career: 'A folio book bound in parchment, relating to the differences between Queen Mary and the Princess of Denmark',[78] 'How the Duchess of Marlborough escaped the South Sea Scheme', and the 'Case of Blenheim, writ by me'.[79]

In her instructions to the two biographers, Sarah was clear about what she wanted. '[I]t will require no Flourishes to set it off, but short plain Facts,'[80] she wrote, and ordered that it should contain no poetry. She drew this little character sketch of her dead husband to point them in the right direction: 'Vigilance, Sobriety, Regularity, Humility, Presence of Mind, void of Capriciousness, execution of orders well given, Health proceeding from temperance, Early up, Never taken at a Why Not.'[81]

Sarah's bedchamber at Marlborough House had been moved, according to the modern fashion, upstairs to the first floor. Her bed and windows were draped with crimson damask, which had been there since the house was first built but was now worn thin and faded. As Sarah became bedridden, the rest of the house became the domain of her servants: the butler Mr Griffiths; her old friend and secretary, James Stephens; the housekeeper Mrs Loft and her husband; Anne Patten; the groom of the chambers Mr Lewis; and her longest-serving companion, head chambermaid Grace Ridley. There were other under-servants, laundry maids, porters, and handymen who stopped by to maintain the property, but these were her core staff and now some of her most trusted friends.

The house was dark – few candles lit for few visitors. The entrance hall, with Laguerre's realistic mural of the battle of Malplaquet, soldiers wet in mud up to their shins and women stripping the mangled corpses to resell the uniforms; the royal staircase with its mural of the battle of Ramillies, a dead horse painted with its beady eye on the slippery marble steps up to Sarah's room; the drawing room dominated by the Closterman group portrait of Sarah's young family; the dining room encircled by the characters of the Marlboroughs' careers, Sidney Godolphin, Prince Eugene and Queen Anne[82] – all lay unused as Georgian London spun by on the Mall outside her windows.

A penny-post letter, purportedly from one of Sarah's maids, said that its writer was going to have to resign if the old woman did not stop teasing her maliciously, and included the line, 'I went to see Charles Churchill last night but did not stay long, you know why.'[83] Though this letter from a possible 'spy' in Sarah's house seems genuine, it lies in the archives beside many others suggesting that Sarah was in fact a kind employer. Dr Johnson wrote that 'more knowledge may be gained of a man's real character by a short conversation with one of his servants than from a formal and studied narrative begun with his pedigree and ended with his funeral.'[84] Sarah's servants would have spoken fondly of her.

Sarah's longevity meant that she saw Henry Pelham, the Duke of Newcastle's brother and a man she believed naturally honest, become Prime Minister. As she tried to order all her business affairs before she died, she wrote to him on 11 September 1744 with a request concerning taxes on her property at Windsor Great Park, adding, 'I desire no favour, but only sheer justice.'[85] The Secretary to the Treasury, John Scrope MP, replied on Pelham's behalf, assuring her that the new Ministry understood how important she had been to the Country Party and promising to honour her with as much assistance as she needed:

[H]ow Your Grace could think yourself insignificant I can't imagine. You can despise your enemies (if any such you have), you can laugh at fools who have authority only in their own imagination, and Your Grace hath not only the power, but a pleasure, in doing good to everyone who is honoured with your friendship and compassion. Who can be more significant? This will make you always esteemed and admired by everyone that hath any sense of virtue, charity, humanity.[86]

Warmed by such a respectful letter, Sarah replied to Scrope that same day to thank the Prime Minister. She added that she had 'entered into new business which entertains me extremely: tying up great bundles of papers to enable two very able historians to write the Duke of Marlborough's History . . .'[87]

Every day, when she woke from a few hard-won hours of rest, Sarah would have her husband's and Godolphin's correspondence read aloud to her by James Stephens or Grace Ridley. Macaulay once described her in her later years as 'lamentably deficient in memory', but nothing could have been further from the truth: she was still able to dictate from memory the entire inventory of Blenheim, right down to 809 napkins and 91 tablecloths,[88] and she was still annotating her husband's letters to help Mallet and Glover understand the codes and the Westminster intrigues of thirty years past. Humane and commonsensical, Sarah's notes put flesh on the dry bones of political history – for example, when she remembered the confusion in the Duke of York's household in Scotland when a letter had arrived from Louis XIV 'which put all the family into a great disorder, for nobody could read it'.[89] She was still, as Robert Harley had once called her, 'that busy woman'.[90]

As she lay dying, Sarah never reneged on her earlier scepticism about the authority of the Church. She was no atheist – some time after Marlborough's death she had written that though she was 'not fond of those that keep a great chatter about religion', she could not understand atheism.[91] However, rather than speculating on an afterlife, she told Scrope that she only hoped the final stroke of death 'may not be very painful'. One day, when her servants had forced her to have her bedroom chimney swept, a little boy in rags came to do the job. When she saw him, Sarah ordered that he be fed and reclothed. The incident prompted her to write playfully to her friend the Earl of Marchmont: 'I find you are as ignorant of the soul as I am. I do think there must be rewards and punishments after this life, and I have a great mind to believe that Kings' and First Ministers' souls when they die go into chimney-sweeps.'[92]

When Queen Anne's mother and Sarah's first mistress, the Duchess of York, lay dying and was asked if she was still a Protestant and continued 'in the truth', she had replied, 'What is truth?': (an evasive answer because of her recent conversion to Catholicism).[93] Sarah was untormented by this question, having had an enviable certainty about her own life and its meaning from beginning to end. However, in late September she had written to Scrope with a long account of how she had managed Queen Anne's Privy Purse and dwelt for some time on the one thing that obviously still preyed on her conscience: the money withdrawn through blackmail in 1711. 'I apprehend that you will think I was in the wrong to put her [Anne] in mind of the £18,000,' she wrote, 'as I did myself, I confess it.'[94]

It was fitting that her final confession should have been made to the Secretary to the Treasury rather than to a priest. Scrope came to Marlborough House to pay his and Prime Minister Pelham's respects to Sarah four days before she died. There is no record of the meeting, though we can guess she had words of advice for the inexperienced Ministers.

Sarah passed into history at nine in the morning on 18 October 1744. At her side were Grace Ridley, Anne Patten, James Stephens, the Earl of Clancarty and her grandson John Spencer.

14
Afterlife

According to Tobias Smollett, Sarah's death 'was very little regretted, either by her own family or the world in general'.[1] Apart from the handful at her bedside, few friends or family were alive to mourn her. She had directed that her funeral should be 'private, with no more expense than decency requires',[2] and in this way she was buried in the Blenheim Chapel tomb. Four days later, her late husband's remains, wrapped in a woollen shroud, were exhumed from Westminster Abbey and driven to Blenheim to be laid beside her 'as was always intended'.[3] Henrietta Godolphin's will had specifically forbidden that her body be buried alongside her mother's.

An anonymous satirical epitaph promptly appeared on Sarah's tomb:[4]

> Beneath this monumental Bust,
> Here lies entombed Dame Sarah's Dust,
> Relict of hero John the Brave,
> To gainful Loans and Funds a slave;
> Midst heap of Gold laid up in Store,
> Extremely rich, extremely poor;
> On whims and various humours bent,
> And yet, by fits, magnificent;
> Though fat with Royal favours grown,
> Yet no Great Friend to G[eorge]'s throne;
> In former Courts polite and gay,
> And still a Beauty in Decay.
> Go mourn in Form, yet shed no tears,
> Such falls give life to Happy Heirs;
> Who can lament a full Ripe Death,
> When 85 Resigns its breath . . . ?

The playwright and theatre-manager Thomas Odell, however, published a more respectful *Elegiac Ode*⁵ that doubled as an attack on the Hanoverians. It envisaged Sarah being carried to heaven to be greeted by Britannia and congratulated on having made Queen Anne's reign so glorious, then by Godolphin and the entire Whig Junto, including those who, like Lord Sunderland, had died her sworn enemies. Odell equated Sarah's dismissal from her Court posts with the end of Britain's golden age. Unusually, he also credited her with having other successful dimensions to her life:

> But SARAH still in private Life,
> The mournful Widow, dut'ous Wife,
> The Mother or the Friend;
> Her Duties all discharg'd so well,
> In ev'ry State did so excel,
> That all must mourn her End.

Simple notices in seven or eight newspapers reported her death, but there was no obituary in the modern sense.⁶ Lady Mary Wortley Montagu wrote from Avignon that she had seen the Dowager's death reported 'in the Dutch prints . . . with a very imperfect account of her will'.⁷

Sarah's final will, the last of twenty-six, was dated 11 August 1744, with a codicil of 15 August.⁸ It was published in full in the *London Magazine* in 1745, as well as in book form – a trend popularised by Edmund Curll to feed a growing public interest in the use of self-made fortunes. Unreconciled with Charles Spencer, who had thrown away 'not much less than half a million', Sarah died having named his younger brother, John, her main heir. John died of alcoholism just two years after Sarah, thereby leaving an eleven-year-old boy to inherit 'th'unguarded store' mentioned in Pope's portrait of Atossa. Luckily Sarah had appointed a number of solid trustees for the boy: James Stephens, Lord Chesterfield and William Pitt.

Lord Chesterfield was entrusted with Sarah's papers and asked to supervise the Duke's biography, for which task she left him a legacy of £20,000 as well as her 'best and largest diamond ring'.

Unfortunately neither of the appointed biographers earned the £500 advance (plus sales profits) that Sarah left to them – Glover declined the job and Mallet never started. The Marlboroughs' papers were returned to Blenheim.

Sarah had spotted the talent of the young William Pitt, grandson of her old friend Lady Grandison, so he received £10,000 which allowed him to embark upon his political career. A little anonymous ditty called 'On the Duchess of Marlborough's Will' appeared in the paper in 1746 as a satire on Pitt:

> Piqued at the Court she knew not why,
> & Ostentatious of her plenty,
> Old Sarah, when she came to die
> Bequeathed her Thousands, Ten & Twenty;
> Not that or Chesterfield or Pitt
> She valued farther than their name,
> But hoped the Orator & Wit
> Would leave her twice as much in Fame . . .[9]

Sarah owned twenty-seven estates at the time of her death,[10] leading someone who wrote a preface to her will to joke that the readers should count themselves lucky that she had died when she had or she would have purchased all England. She left a number of these estates to Marchmont and to Beversham Filmer, two of her executors alongside the Bishop of Oxford, and James Stephens.

When Charles Spencer died, heavily in debt, his son, the 4th Duke of Marlborough still inherited a sizeable fortune thanks to Sarah's strenuous efforts to protect the Marlborough trust from Charles's spending habits. Then, having served its purpose, the trust was dissolved.

A quotation in Sarah's hand, copied from Francis Bacon, declared, '[D]efer not charity till death: for certainly if a man weigh it rightly he that doth so is rather liberal of another man's than of his own.'[11] This perhaps explains why Sarah left only £300 to the poor of Woodstock village and little else to charity, apart from the endowment of her almshouses in St Albans. Many regarded this as confirmation of her avarice. They ignored the fact that Sarah had left annuities to nearly all of her servants, making them not just comfortable but very wealthy. Her favourite, Grace Ridley, who had been paid a salary of only ten pounds a year while Sarah was alive,[12] received £16,000 (approximately £1,320,000 today), two paintings (one of Sarah 'by Sir Godfrey Kneller which is only a head') and half of Sarah's clothing. Her daughter Ann Ridley also received a substantial sum. Such generosity to servants was far from customary.

In June 1751, Lady Mary Wortley Montagu wrote to her sister Lady Bute that '[O]ur most serious projects have scarce more foundation than those edifices that your little ones raise in cards. You see to what period the vast fortunes of the Duke and D[uchess] of Marlbro . . . are soon arrived?'[13] While the Marlborough fortune might have been depleted, Sarah's properties stood long after her death. The exceptions are the Lodge at Windsor, of which little or nothing remains, and the house at Wimbledon, burned to dust in 1785. Holywell House, her birthplace and favourite retreat, was destroyed in 1827, though just about everything else in St Albans is still named after the Marlboroughs, thanks to Sarah.

Blenheim Palace, of course, stands as a national treasure, opened to the public in 1950 by the present Duke's father and his wife Mary (a descendant of Marlborough's old Quartermaster General, William Cadogan). Today the tour guides barely mention Sarah's central role in the building of the property; its existence is entirely credited to the Duke's military heroism and Vanbrugh's designs. The text of the official booklet – though it opens with a full-page portrait of Sarah – only blames her for 'teasing and tormenting' the Queen until the Crown refused to pay for the house. Sarah's favourite bow-window room is now plump with Colefax & Fowler fabrics; William Congreve's eight-day timepiece sits on the mantel. The servants' quarters are now administrative offices, their occupants grateful no doubt for the extra light let in by the windows that Sarah insisted on enlarging. The present 11th Duke, John Spencer-Churchill, and his third wife, Rosita Douglas, a painter, now spend their summers at a house of more manageable proportions in Charlbury, eight miles away, while the tourists ride through the grounds on the miniature train to visit the butterfly house, the adventure playground or the putting green, or hire rowboats on the lake (which in the 1760s was made proportionate to Vanbrugh's folly-bridge by Capability Brown's decision to flood it from the river Glyme). Sarah's monuments to her husband – the column, the triumphal arch, the Blenheim tomb – remain intact, while Sarah herself is remembered only for her parsimony.

Marlborough House stood virtually empty for fourteen years after Sarah's death, the solitary occupant her friend and executor James Stephens. The 4th Duke took it over in 1758, when Stephens died, and it remained in the family until 1817, at which point the land reverted to the Crown. Edward, Prince of Wales, and his wife Alexandra moved into it in 1863, and it was in one of the ground-floor drawing rooms that, in 1936, Edward VIII informed his mother he was planning to abdicate. During the Second World War it was used to house refugees, and afterwards the dowager Queen Mary lived there until her death in 1953.

In 1959 Marlborough House was given by the Crown to the Commonwealth Secretariat, and today the upstairs bedchamber in which Sarah is believed to have died is the office of the Secretary General. The central dining room holds what must be the largest conference table known to man and looks out on gardens that have retained their plainness, save for the Victorian addition of a pet cemetery. A Jervas portrait of Sarah reclining in a red dress hangs in one of the downstairs reception rooms, although most of Sarah's art collection was moved to either Althorp or Blenheim. Outside, around Pall Mall, the streets bear the names of Sarah's friends, enemies and descendants. Marlborough Road tube station was closed in 1939.

Sarah once remarked that she was 'lucky in having so much that every knave may have a bit of me'.[14] This was as true of her character and reputation as of her fortune. On 3 December

1744, an advertisement appeared for a new edition of Sarah's memoirs with the printer assuring the public 'that whatever Accounts of her Grace may be published in numbers by any other persons are spurious and a great imposition'.[15] Then, in the new year (in which, had she lived to see it, an attempted Jacobite rebellion would have vindicated her political forebodings), the first anti-Sarah satire was published to which she could no longer reply. It was called *A Dialogue in the Shades: Between Mrs Morley and Mrs Freeman. Containing a Review of all the most material incidents in their past lives* (1745) and described Sarah's ghost pursuing Queen Anne's into the 'shades' of Elysium. This satire is, in effect, a chance for Queen Anne to answer back. She becomes the warm and loquacious one, while the Duchess is forced to listen quietly. She accuses Sarah of having an instinct for factionalism and cliques, and blames herself for having been ruled by a favourite because of a virtuously feminine 'distrust of my own capacity'.[16] She blames Sarah for having teased her relentlessly 'on a subject which must of Necessity make me uneasy as often as it is named' (in other words, Abigail).[17] Abigail is there in the next world too, smiling at Sarah with infuriating indifference.

Another satire in the same genre was published over a decade later, where Sarah's ghost was 'hackneyed out' – as one reviewer put it – to argue the case against an alliance between England and Prussia. *A Letter from The Duchess of M[a]r[lborou]gh, in the Shades, to The Great Man* (1759)[18] was supposedly addressed by Sarah to William Pitt. Even in death, it seems, she could not put down her pen or leave the political arena. *The Monitor, or British Freeholder* complained about this use of a 'turbulent old woman who was hated in her lifetime' as a totem to champion any cause.

Sarah had lived her life as a mediated woman, and after her death this tradition continued. Sarah has been the subject of some twenty-five biographies in the past 250 years (the term 'biographer' was first used in 1715), and has featured as a major character in over twenty other histories, historical novels, television series and plays. She is a bit-part player in hundreds more.

The myths surrounding her have hardened, while at the same time she shimmers in the confusion of contradictory testimony. Swift, Mrs Manley, Lord Dartmouth and Horace Walpole described a Sarah who bore little resemblance to the Sarah portrayed by Bishop Burnet, Maynwaring, Henry Fielding or the other Whig cheerleaders.

Sarah believed that it was possible for posterity to know the facts, separated from 'the affections and passions of writers'.[19] In his review of Sarah's *Conduct*, Dr Johnson was less optimistic: he asked whether the subjectivity of biography meant that we had to give up on truth and 'live in perpetual negligence of past events; or, what is still more disagreeable, in perpetual suspense?'.[20] One history of the biographical form admitted that, in the case of the Marlboroughs, it 'affords little more than a forum for displaying debating skill in the successive black or white lives of the Duke and the Duchess'.[21] More than most historical figures, more than most royal favourites, Sarah's afterlife has resembled a courtroom debate.

After Lord Chesterfield returned Sarah's papers, they were held by the Spencer family until Lord Marchmont obtained a legal opinion that they belonged with the Marlborough estate.[22] General James Cunningham went 'rummaging' through the Blenheim papers in 1777,[23] but the family's first professional archivist, in the mid-nineteenth century, was Marlborough's biographer and the tutor of Sarah's great-grandson John Spencer, Archdeacon William Coxe. He disregarded Sarah's attempts at arrangement, removed enclosures from letters and generally brought as much confusion as order to the collection. In 1815 a closet full of Sarah's draft memoirs was opened for the first time, and in 1842, a trunk of Marlborough's papers was discovered during repairs. The days of such discoveries are now over, unless, by some miracle, Marlborough did not burn but hid all of Sarah's letters written to him when he was in Europe.

Twentieth-century archivists have included Sarah's biographer Stuart J. Reid and, in the 1970s–80s, J. P. Hudson.[24] The papers were acquired by the nation in 1973, in lieu of estate duty.[25]

Today they are primarily held in the British Library, where Dr Frances Harris, Sarah's 1991 biographer, is the present expert curator. Other manuscripts have travelled as far afield as New York, where the Pierpont Morgan Library acquired a box, and Los Angeles, where in 1921 the Huntington Library acquired Sarah's correspondence with the Duke of Chandos. Such libraries now guard Sarah's 'vouchers' of truth.

The first biography of Sarah, in 1710,[26] was, despite its Tory author and extreme brevity, one of the most objective ever published. It fell into the usual trap of digressing at length into her husband's life, as though his successes and failures were the same as Sarah's. Sarah next featured, as a very minor character indeed, in Thomas Lediard's *Life of John, Duke of Marlborough* (1736). Though a household name during her lifetime, Sarah therefore received the least attention during the years immediately after her death. Horace Walpole wrote in 1748 that 'Lord Bolingbroke, Sarah Malcolm [a murderess] and Old Marlborough [Sarah] are never mentioned but by elderly folks to their grandchildren, who had never heard of them.'[27] He seemed to launch a concerted, one-man campaign to rectify this situation by recording a glut of insulting anecdotes about Sarah in his letters and memoirs. He claimed, for example, that she was 'too cheap to dot her "i"s', preferring to save the ink – which is ironic, given the vast amount of paper and ink she obviously got through.

In the 1750s and 1760s, Jonathan Swift's two histories of Queen Anne's reign were published for the first time, each containing negative portraits of Sarah. Even in the early, reprinted Whig histories Sarah's supposed faults were only softened, not questioned. The analysis spread by Lord Halifax, that Sarah was at least partially to blame for the fall of her husband, Godolphin and the Junto, became the orthodoxy, causing the Duke of Wellington to defend Marlborough on the basis that 'his errors were due to his wife'.[28]

In 1818, William Coxe's *Memoirs of John, Duke of Marlborough* portrayed Sarah as interfering, bad-tempered, the source of Marlborough's problems, and as having achieved nothing in her own right. The clergyman seems to have been somewhat terrified by Sarah, baffled by her mood swings. Then, in 1839, the first scholarly biographical attempt to understand Sarah was made by Mrs A. T. Thomson,[29] who expressed amazement that in the ninety-six years since Sarah's death there had been 'no complete account of her singular career, no memoirs of her as a private individual'. Yet Mrs Thomson disclaimed the right to invigilate in past politics: 'From a sense of her own incompetency, the Authoress has, therefore, abstained as much as possible from political discussions . . .' Like Queen Anne and Marlborough, Mrs Thomson viewed party politics as a travesty of government, best ignored. Her verdict on Sarah's life, therefore, was that she had behaved like 'a spoiled child'[30] and that she took only a 'trivial share' in public life.[31] She did defend Sarah, however, from Mrs Manley's charge of having had an affair with Godolphin on the basis that Sarah's household management did not seem to deteriorate, apparently 'the first signal of a woman's ruin'.[32]

In 1852, Thackeray published his historical novel *The History of Henry Esmond* which portrayed Sarah as a crotchety old woman boxing children's ears. In 1855, in his *History of England*,[33] Macaulay took his image of Sarah straight from Pope's Atossa: 'an ancient crone at war with her whole kind', although he also attempted to explain this character, saying that she had been 'ulcerated by disasters and mortifications' over the years.[34] On the whole, however, he continued the tradition of judging Sarah as a failure as a woman: 'She had little of that tact which is the characteristic talent of her sex . . .' while half admiring her sexual dominance:

Though it is impossible to discover in anything she ever did, said or wrote, any indication of superior understanding, her fierce passions and strong will enabled her to rule a husband who was born to rule grave senates and mighty armies. His courage . . . failed him when he had to encounter his Sarah's ready tears and voluble reproaches, the poutings of her lip and the tossings of her head.[35]

Aside from biographies and histories, Sarah also became known through her collected writings. Lord Hailes is suspected of being the anonymous editor of a volume of Sarah's *Opinions* (1788). This was an odd miscellany, organised in alphabetical subject order, so that her political views on the 'Duke of Argyle' and 'Queen Caroline' were followed by wistful reflections on 'Dogs/ My Entail/ Forebodings'. Then, in 1836–8, the two-volume edition of Sarah's *Private Correspondence* was compiled and published. The editor was possibly Lord John Russell, using Coxe's sometimes faulty transcripts. In 1875, another anonymous compiler published *Letters of Sarah Duchess of Marlborough, now first published from the original manuscripts at Madresfield Court*. This selection contained those letters written while in exile in 1712–14 and a few after her return. The editor seems surprised to find him or herself in sympathy with the author of the letters, referring to how his reading made him feel that a 'wrong twist' had been given to everything in Sarah's life, and observing:

Making all due allowance for the suspicion of partiality, in being a witness in her own cause, it would not seem unreasonable to conclude, after an unprejudiced perusal of these Letters, that, with all her faults, Sarah Duchess of Marlborough was not deserving of much of the obloquy that was so persistently cast upon her, not only during her lifetime but for a long while afterwards.

The 'wrong twist' continued, however, when Agnes Strickland published her pro-Tory biography of Queen Anne in 1884 and damned Sarah with apocryphal anecdotes. In 1894, Viscount Wolseley's incomplete biography of Marlborough was first published, again regurgitating the Atossa myth, 'Unlovable in character as she was lovely in face, her life was one long war with the world . . .' and the opinions of the Tory satirists of the 1700s: 'Her obstinacy was a species of insanity, and her masculine determination aggravated her feminine faults of suspicion and jealousy . . . her whole character was, as it were, a freak of nature.'[36] In 1899, Mrs Aubrey Richardson's *Famous Ladies of the English Court* continued the Victorian condemnation of

Sarah's 'rank individualism and lack of all reverence for dignities' towards her monarch.[37] Mrs Richardson's account was imbued with snobbery, seeing Sarah's behaviour as 'vulgarity' and describing her as 'made of coarse stuff'.[38] She saw Sarah and Anne's relationship purely as a private matter, but could not bear to have Sarah displaced by someone as humble as Abigail so she condensed the story and made the Duchess of Somerset the one to have toppled her.

Both Fitzgerald Molloy (in 1901) and Mrs Colville (in 1904) produced biographies of Sarah lengthened by a large amount of background social history. Mrs Arthur Colville published under her married name, indicative of the fact that she would concentrate on Sarah as Marlborough's wife and, again, stay away from politics. She was a distant descendant of Sarah, and at least seemed to take a to-know-is-to-forgive approach to her subject.[39]

Then, in 1914, Stuart J. Reid published a joint biography of the Marlboroughs.[40] He had been working on it since 1889, engaged by the 8th Duke of Marlborough to archive the Blenheim papers, and regarded it as his task to 'vindicate' the couple. In practice, this meant vindicating Marlborough by perpetuating the old image of Sarah dragging him down with her. If she had only preserved her friendship with Queen Anne, Reid wrote, 'Godolphin might have died Prime Minister and the Duke's military career would not have ended under a cloud. As it was, she brought about the undoing of a statesman who held her in chivalrous respect, and of the man who, with an undivided heart, adored her.'[41] Reid admitted that she was a great businesswoman, 'alert, sagacious and practical to the last degree'.[42] Uniquely, he also gave her credit for her charity, stating that 'few people in that hard century troubled themselves at all deeply with the social condition of the poor. The Duchess of Marlborough was an exception to this rule.'[43] He did not, on the other hand, have much time for her memoirs, finding them vicious and inaccurate, as if drafted for the first time in her eighties 'when her judgment was warped and her powers were failing'.[44]

In 1924, Benjamin Bathurst's *Letters of Two Queens* accused

Sarah of causing the rift between Anne and Mary in the 1690s, and Macaulay's great-nephew, G. M. Trevelyan, the last historian in the Whig tradition to regard William as the unquestioned saviour of English freedom, defended Marlborough from many Tory accusations while making no similar attempt to rescue Sarah. In 1930, Philip W. Sergeant's reproving yet admiring book entitled *Dominant Women*, influenced by the nascent feminism of the 1920s, included a chapter on Sarah, recognising her political ambition and placing her in the formidable company of Cleopatra and Catherine the Great.

Two years later, Kathleen Campbell described herself as joining the 'moth-like tribe' of Sarah's biographers. Hers was the first biography to be influenced by Freud, and she diagnosed Sarah with clinical paranoia.[45] Making a case for the defence almost worse than the charge, she pointed out that the fights with Queen Anne started just when Sarah was at an age – forty-eight to fifty – when 'mental instability would inevitably have increased'. She saw the quantity of self-justifying letters as a pathological symptom of inherited mental disorder rather than entertaining the possibility that Sarah perhaps took pleasure in writing. She was sympathetic, if pitying, towards the Duke of Marlborough whose 'lifelong homage and undimmed devotion' rested 'like a crown upon the head of Sarah Churchill, his wife'.[46]

Both Campbell and Frank Chancellor, who also published a biography of Sarah in 1932, were denied access to the Blenheim archives while Winston Churchill, their proprietor, was working on a biography of his ancestor Marlborough. Campbell remarked bitingly that 'Perhaps when Mr Winston Churchill has found time to make use of them, the embargo at present placed on them may be removed and they may be available to other scholars.'[47] Churchill published the first volume of his tour-de-force military history and biography, somewhat justifying his selfishness, in the following year.[48]

The representations of Sarah since her death are like rings in the wood of an old tree, or a geographical sample taken from the earth, in which we can compare not only British society's changing views of women, but also a range of other attitudes held by her biographers. Most moving are the biographies written in the 1930s, which reflect the pacifist attitudes between the two world wars in their portrayal of Marlborough's campaigns in the War of Spanish Succession. Churchill's final volume of Marlborough's life was not published until six months after the *Anschluss*. In it, he drew obvious parallels between the threat from Louis XIV's France and Hitler's Germany, describing Europe in the early 1700s as impotent without British aid. The Treaty of Versailles was clearly in his mind as he analysed the Treaty of Utrecht, and as he judged the Whigs – and hence Sarah – on their desire not only to liberate Europe but also to crush France remorselessly.

Churchill admired much about Sarah, but believed that politics should be the business of 'grave, independent men who gave lifelong thought to doctrine and policy' and who transacted that business 'by long personal letters, laboriously composed, in which every word was weighed'[49] – in sharp contrast to Sarah's flowing diatribes. Yet he could not overlook the evidence in the archives of Sarah's independent importance during the period of Queen Anne's reign. Behind Marlborough, Churchill wrote, 'stood his beloved wife, and in a sense Cabinet colleague, Sarah, whose intimate relations with the Queen at times vastly helped and at others vastly hindered harmonious action'.[50]

Like the Victorians, however, Churchill was squeamish about looking at the sexual undertones in the relationship between the Queen and her female favourites. Sarah's 'salt common sense, her pithy conversation, and her pungent judgment of men, women, and politics, had long fascinated, fleetingly convinced, and at times terrified the Queen,' he wrote. 'The two women had hitherto lived in the most sincere and natural comradeship possible between persons of the same sex.'[51] He half mocked his own priggishness when having to admit that Marlborough had had a pre-marital affair with Barbara Castlemaine ('Our readers must now brace themselves for what will inevitably be a painful interlude . . .')[52] and he was one of the first to try to acquit the Duke of Sarah's accusations of infidelity, blaming all the couple's quarrels on Sarah's paranoia. He also continued the tradition of dismissing Sarah's literary efforts, saying that her memoirs proved her 'as wrong-headed in defending her case to posterity as in pleading it with Queen Anne'.53 None of these criticisms, however, deterred him from naming his own daughter, who later became the great statesman's own biographer, Sarah Churchill.

The 1930s also saw the first stage play to tell Sarah's story, written by Norman Ginsbury and produced by Tyrone Guthrie.54 *Viceroy Sarah* was most recently performed in the mid-1980s in the walled gardens designed by Sarah at Chilworth Manor, one of her properties in Surrey. It was one of the first to retell the battle between Sarah and Vanbrugh over the costs of Blenheim, with Sarah asking, 'Are you supposed to be building us a house or a war-god's pagoda?' and Vanbrugh complaining, 'You've been letting off your crackers at my tail ever since the foundation stone was laid.' In Act Three, Sarah's temper flares at her daughter Elizabeth: 'That's right – make the easy assumption that I forced a quarrel on her [Queen Anne]. Believe all the idle tittle-tattle you hear . . . Lord knows what the history books will have to say about me.'

A popular historical novel appeared in 1950, retelling the story from Abigail Masham's perspective. *That Enchantress*, by Doris Leslie, opens with the dramatic contrast of the Duchess sweeping in on the Hill family, living in penury, her silk stockings tiptoeing through the rubbish to their hovel's door. With godlike arrogance she disposes of their fates, separating the poor orphans to their various jobs. Only Abigail feels a secret pride to match Sarah's own and mimics her wealthy relation behind her back. The twentieth-century reader's sympathy is solicited on behalf of Abigail as a representative of the common people, and Sarah's fall from favour is depicted merely as backdrop to Abigail's rise.

Edith Sitwell was one of the first to compliment Sarah on her 'soldierly courage and honesty' and to recognise that she was a woman of contradictions, not only in how others perceived her but in being torn between her idealistic beliefs and her personal ambitions. Sitwell's collection of biographical essays, *English Women* (1942), put Sarah in the company of Elizabeth I, George Eliot, Florence Nightingale and Christina Rossetti. However, it was not until 1957 that Sarah found another worthy defender in Michael Foot, with his brilliant book about the battles between Swift and the Marlboroughs, *The Pen and the Sword*. Foot was the first to question whether it was really Sarah's primary duty to mollify Queen Anne rather than to express her own deeply held views. '[U]nfortunately for her political reputation, her letters have been destroyed, and Marlborough's biographers, notably Sir Winston Churchill, invite us to accept at every move the superior wisdom of the Duke,'[55] he observed. 'She stands exposed as a rancorous old woman, while the proofs of her foresight as the leader of the Whigs in her greatest days are lost in obscurity.'[56]

The next full biography of Sarah, by Louis Kronenberger, a friend of W. H. Auden, was a step backwards: *Marlborough's Duchess – A Study in Worldliness* (1958) conveyed by its very title a certain approbation of seventeenth-century attitudes to the subordination of women. Kronenberger portrayed Sarah as merely a bystander who occasionally, inexplicably, was addressed on important matters by the key players. He concluded that she 'was not at all . . . a great woman, but by any standards she must rank with the very greatest personalities'.[57]

In the 1960s, Bonamy Dobrée wrote several short biographies of Sarah, again concentrating on her immense energy rather than on her intelligence or bravery. *As Their Friends Saw Them* (1967) and *Three Eighteenth Century Figures* (1962) both described Sarah's ambition in life to be 'a worldly end, a shallow one if you will' – the accumulation of wealth and power – while admitting that 'For sheer work done, for crude horse-power, she has no equal of her sex in English History except Queen Elizabeth [I].'[58] A more comprehensive and entertaining biography published in 1967 by David Brontë Green, a friend of the 10th Duke of Marlborough and a *Country Life* journalist, reached a similar, ambivalent conclusion: 'But was she great? If toughness is greatness she was.'[59]

This same year (1967) also saw the publication of Iris Butler's *Rule of Three*, which took the traditional line that petticoat politics were to blame for the divisions between the men, suggesting that Marlborough and Lord Oxford could have worked together happily for the national good if Sarah had not pursued a vendetta against Abigail Masham and the Tories.[60] Sarah and Anne, Butler regretted to say, 'demonstrated some very adolescent attitudes . . . At one time this would have been attributed to their sex. Now we can judge it as their lack of education and experience.'[61] She did, however, think that Sarah 'succeeded in the most satisfying purpose of a woman's life – a complete relationship with a man'.[62]

Both she and Dobrée dismissed Sarah and Anne's relationship as nothing more than a phase and credited them with an undeserved naïvety. 'Female society was more separated from male than it has since become,' Dobrée explained, 'and it is as though some of the girls had to play the male part in these friendships.'[63] Butler remarked, with distaste, that it was currently 'fashionable to look for abnormal emotional relationships in every close friendship between people of the same sex . . . If there was any such situation both were entirely unconscious of it.'[64]

The fictionalisation of Sarah continued in the 1960s with Jean Plaidy's novel, *The Queen's Favourites* (1966). Facts taken from schoolbook history lie like uncrushed pills in the jam of this romantic fiction, heavy with forebodings of disaster and clunking dialogue. ('"One would think that you were the royal Princess – Her Highness, your servant," said Barbara. "You ought to take care, Sarah Churchill . . ."')

In 1969, A. L. Rowse's history *The First Churchills* was adapted by Donald Wilson into a BBC costume drama, lavish for its day, but to our taste drily educational and theatrical. Susan Hampshire played Sarah, and described her in an interview as 'in her own way a monster'.[65] What was most striking about the series was its failure to give Sarah's temper a psychological motive. According to tradition, Sarah was shown throwing things – wine into the face of the Duchess of Cleveland, or her shorn hair to the ground – and the only explanation offered was that these tempers afflicted her during pregnancy. Abigail, meanwhile, is shown eavesdropping at doors, ever-ready to massage the Queen's shoulders after a stressful argument with the Duchess, applying pressure to the Queen's mind as she applies poultices to her legs.

A feminist revolution occurred between the publication of Iris Butler's *Rule of Three* and that of Dr Frances Harris's masterly academic biography, *A Passion for Government* (1991), in which she set out to prove that a political biography could be written about Sarah's career, just as for Marlborough, Godolphin, Oxford or Walpole. In striving to counter-balance the myth that Sarah was motivated mainly by jealousy, Harris probably went too far in erasing the sexual and emotional ambiguities in her relationship with Queen Anne, and in recognising the extent of Sarah's political activity, she also showed the extent of Sarah's failure ('[I]n her more honest moments she had to acknowledge that . . . her personal contribution had counted for very little').[66] However, with a true historian's reluctance to impose modern standards upon the past, she continued to blame Sarah, rather than seventeenth- or eighteenth-century society's sexism, for these disappointments.

Events in the late 1990s refocused attention on Sarah. The death of Diana, Princess of Wales, in 1997, was partly what prompted two books, *The Spencer Family* (1999) by Earl Spencer, and *Blood Royal* (1999) by John Pearson, both featuring Sarah as the founder of the Spencer-Churchill dynasty. The refounding of an independent Scottish Parliament also focused interest on the reign of Queen Anne and the signing of the Act of Union. A BBC radio play in June 1999, *An End to Auld An Sang*,[67] for example, dramatised Sarah lobbying for the Union.

In the United States, the Artemis Theater Company remembered Sarah in a one-act play performed in 1996. In the summer of 1998, in New York's West Village, a two-queen drag show re-created the catfights between Sarah and Anne with extra sequins sprinkled on top. The gay history website 'QueerHis' confidently lists Anne and Sarah as an early lesbian couple, and the editor of *The Lesbian Pillow Book*[68] describes Princess

Anne as 'part of a friendship circle of physically loving girls and young women.' In 1976, a collection of *Lesbian Lives* included Anne and Sarah, stating with absolute certainty that they had a physical relationship after 1692, if not before, and hinting that the enormous legacy Sarah left to Grace Ridley could only have had one explanation.[69]

In 2000, Profile Books published a self-help book for businessmen called *The 48 Laws of Power*,[70] which offered anecdotes about Sarah to exemplify the type of person the author termed a 'financial sadist'.[71] Uncritically accepting Vanbrugh's account of his torture at Sarah's hands, the author recorded that the Duchess 'quibbled over every cartload of stone and bushel of lime, counted every extra yard of iron railing or foot of wainscot, hurling abuse at the wasteful workmen, contractors and surveyors'. The conclusion of the case study was that 'the powerful must have grandeur of spirit' and you should 'never let financial details blind you to the bigger picture of how people perceive you'. This was, in fact, the very lesson Sarah taught in her *Conduct*,[72] when she described King William dismissing the Duke of Gloucester's servants, without compensation, when the boy died and so showing 'a diligence of frugality which was surely not very decent in a king'.

Now, a wave of biographers of eighteenth-century women, written mainly by women, are showing that private and public lives often intertwined. Ironically, this can sometimes mean retrieving the supposedly more 'feminine' materials of the Victorian biographers – the private gossip, the risks of childbirth, the strains on family finances – but putting them in the context of a woman's other achievements and ambitions, and finding deeper social meanings hidden beneath apparently shallow stories. As the biographer Robert Skidelsky has said, the achievement of a life is now merely the living of it. The University of East Anglia has founded Britain's first course in 'comparative biography' and no one could make a better subject for such study than Sarah Churchill: her traducers and defenders, slanderers and hagiographers ranged through the centuries.

One hostile reviewer of Sarah's *Conduct*[73] said that she had too high a sense of her own merit to be treated gently by posterity, which is perhaps fair comment. Few people have lived their lives with such self-conscious concern for how future generations would judge them, and what have sometimes been heard as the screams of Sarah falling into the 'bottomless abyss' of lost favour[74] are in fact the arguments of her self-defence continuing to make themselves heard above every criticism.

On 18 October 1994, a service of commemoration was held at Althorp Chapel to mark the 250th anniversary of Sarah's death. The Spencers' chaplain, Canon Jim Richardson, told the small family congregation that they were gathered to honour Sarah's 'dedication to the causes in which she so firmly believed' and her 'character, insight, energy and remarkable ability'. He went on to explain that they honoured 'the unique and personal contribution she made to the house of Spencer through her grandson John, which led to the creation of his son as the first Earl Spencer, and the beginning of this family's distinguished service to the nation and beyond . . . But,' he concluded, 'there is no moral person, no matter how high, who can live or die without the need of God's loving mercy and forgiveness . . .' And so they recited the Lord's Prayer for Sarah's soul. The present Earl, who had suggested the service, read the lesson from Proverbs:

The day is short and the work is great. A woman of worth, who can find? For her place is far above rubies. She stretches out her hand to the poor – yea, she puts forth her hands to the needy. Strength and wisdom and the law of loving kindness is on her tongue. Her children rise up and call her happy – Her husband also and praises her saying 'Many daughters have done worthily, but you excel them all'. Give her the fruit of her hands and let her works praise her in the gates.

Dr Frances Harris gave an address, including a quotation from the character portrait drawn of Sarah by her old Whig friend

Elizabeth Burnet, stating that Sarah was 'sincere because she could not be otherwise', that she served the Queen 'with more truth and zeal than favourites generally practise', and concluding that 'If ever any lady had a just claim to a great genius, it is the Duchess of Marlborough.' Music by Sarah's favourite Handel was performed, and the most patriotic selection of British hymns – 'Jerusalem' and 'I Vow to Thee my Country' – was sung, before the chaplain sent the family away with the blessing to 'have courage'.

Almost no house holds so much of Sarah's spirit as Althorp, thanks both to the huge number of portraits of her and her immediate family that hang throughout its public rooms and to the present Earl's veneration for this ancestor he believes provided the genetic 'blueprint for the second half of the Spencer family history'.[75] He has compared Sarah's flight from England in 1712 to his sister's having been hounded out of the country by the English press in the 1990s,[76] and has pointed out that the prohibition in Sarah's will against John Spencer entering politics was not against a career in the House of Commons but specifically against 'any employment or Pension from the Crown'.[77] Sarah undermined Anne by revealing the Queen's flawed humanity, refusing to treat her as beyond rational argument or reciprocal obligation, and extended this healthy scepticism about the Royal Family to the Hanoverians. However, in refusing to admit her own weaknesses – to make her own memoirs confessional or apologetic – Sarah never managed to win the popularity that should have rightly come with such a democratic stance. The Spencer descendant who would have made Sarah most proud was probably John Charles, Viscount Althorp, who in 1830 became the leader of the Whigs in the House of Commons and then Chancellor of the Exchequer, guiding the Reform Bill through the House of Lords.

Sarah was fortunate to have had a husband who allowed her great latitude, immense and independent wealth, and male friends and relatives who also allowed her to work through them; nevertheless, her career was fundamentally constrained because she was a woman. While she never explicitly complained about less able men succeeding where she could not, her bitter little character sketches of some Junto members and the Tories who came to power in 1710 hint at these frustrations.

The greatest political victories of Sarah's life were probably the softening of Anne's views on occasional conformity and of Godolphin's and Marlborough's views of the Whigs, the appointment of Cowper as Lord Keeper in 1705, and, above all, the appointment of Sunderland as Secretary of State in 1706. But despite her long list of other achievements – the buildings, the memoirs – Sarah spent a large part of her time feeling fundamentally thwarted, patronised and under-appreciated. As much as she sublimated her own ambition into her husband's career, as much as she immodestly pointed out her supportive role, and as tantalisingly close as she got to the centre of power, Sarah's taste for it remained ultimately unsatisfied. When one wonders whether she merits all the biographies written about her, or whether she really achieved anything lasting with all her energy and brains, one is only asking the question that must have haunted her as she lay awake with insomnia in old age. Her infamous anger had often been an expression of these feelings of irrelevance, which for many years she could hardly articulate, even to herself.

Sarah's faults were a product not only of her natural warmth, as frequently observed, but also of her extreme rationality. Her critics have believed that being kind is more important than being right – the platitude Sarah always rejected. She had a remarkably fixed character from the age of fifteen onwards, so could never understand other people's changeability or inconsistencies. She believed that she could collect love as she collected a debt, and that her life was a predestined narrative, in which she was often the victim, told in the context of a just and rational universe.

The artificiality that biography is often accused of giving to a life was given to Sarah's by Sarah herself. She was also the first royal favourite to become her sovereign's critical biographer. In the satire *A Dialogue in the Shades*, Mrs Freeman 'in consideration of her having been a biographer' was doomed to have 'no other Conversation than that of Archilocus who wrote his Father Lycambes to Death'. As she herself lay dying, preparing the materials for her husband's biographers, she wrote to Mr Scrope at the Treasury:

I am satisfied that what will be proved to be true will make it the most charming history that has ever yet been writ in any country, and I had rather, if I were a man, have deserved to have such an account certified of me . . . than have the greatest pension or estate.[78]

Notes

Prologue

1. Warburton, quoted in Spence, Joseph, *Observation, Anecdotes and Characters of Books and Men*, ed. James M. Osborn (2 vols), Oxford, 1963, p. 166.
2. Campbell, Kathleen, *Sarah, Duchess of Marlborough*, London, 1932, p. 278.
3. Sherburn, George (ed.), *The Correspondence of Alexander Pope*, vol. IV, Oxford, 1956, p. 459: letter to Lord Marchmont.
4. Selina, Countess of Huntington's letters, a source that has had its authenticity questioned. Quoted in Green, David Brontë, *Sarah Duchess of Marlborough*, London, 1967, p. 325.
5. Quoted in Hailes, Lord (ed.), *The Opinions of Sarah Duchess-Dowager of Marlborough*, London, 1788.
6. *Ibid.*

1. Miss Jennings

1. Harris, Frances, *A Passion for Government*, London, 1991, p. 9.
2. Churchill, Sir Winston, *Marlborough: His Life and Times*, Edinburgh, 1947, vol. 1, p. 35.
3. Add MS 61423.
4. Chancellor, Frank, *Sarah Churchill*, London, 1932, p. 6.
5. Letter, S to sister Frances, quoted in Green, David Brontë, *Sarah Duchess of Marlborough*, London, 1967, p. 38.
6. Defoe, Daniel, *Journal of the Plague Year*, 1722.
7. De Beer, Esmond, *John Evelyn Diaries*, 1955, vol. 3, p. 453.
8. Harris, 1991, chapter 1.
9. Lever, Sir T., *Godolphin*, London, 1952, p. 17.
10. Add MS 61453, folios 25–26.
11. Bathurst, Benjamin, *Letters of Two Queens*, London, 1924, p. 41.
12. Add MS 61453.
13. *The Perquisite-Monger; or the Rise and Fall of Ingratitude (being one of the stories which the Monks of Godstow were formerly wont to divert Fair Rosamond with, and which may serve to clear up several Absurdities in the History of Prince Mirabel)*, March 1712, p. 10.
14. 'The Murmur of the Oak', MS Rawl poet 181, folio 70.

15. Harley MS 6913.
16. Quoted in Hopkins, Graham, *Nell Gwynne – A Passionate Life*, London, 2000, p. 225.
17. See Herbst, Katrin, *Schönheit als Tugend – Sir Godfrey Kneller und die Englische Portraetmalerei um 1700*, PhD thesis, Free University of Berlin, March 2002.
18. See De Beer, Esmond (ed.), *John Evelyn Diaries*, 6 vols, Oxford, 1955; Evelyn, John, *The Life of Mrs Godolphin*, Samuel Lord Bishop of Oxford (ed.), London, 1847; Boswell, Eleanore, *The Restoration of the Court Stage*, Harvard, 1932.
19. Sitwell, Edith, *English Women*, London, 1942, p. 12.
20. Add MS 61426, 'Characters of Princes'.
21. Gregg, Edward, *Queen Anne*, London, 1980, p. 7.
22. Fea, A., *The Loyal Wentworths*, London, 1928, p. 172.
23. Add MS 33388, folio 158.
24. Pepys, quoted in Stone, Lawrence, *The Family, Sex and Marriage in England 1550–1800*, London, 1982, p. 328.
25. Evelyn, John, *A Character of England as it was lately presented in a letter to a Noble Man of France*, London, 1659.
26. Thomson, A. T., *Memoirs of Sarah, Duchess of Marlborough*, London, 1839, vol. 1, p. 72.
27. Add MS 61423, Burnet's 'Vindication'.
28. Add MS 61474, S to Lady Cowper, 3 September 1716.
29. Quoted in Harris, 1991, p. 16.
30. De Beer, 1955, vol. 4, p. 79.
31. Hamilton, Anthony, *Memoirs of Count de Grammont*, trans. Horace Walpole, London, 1965, p. 171.
32. *Ibid.*, p. 200.
33. Thomson, 1839, p. 74.
34. Harris, 1991, p. 22.
35. S to Mr Mallet, on reading Lediard's *History of the Duke*, quoted in Butler, Iris, *Rule of Three: Sarah, Duchess of Marlborough and Her Companions in Power*, London, 1967, p. 171.
36. Sicco van Goslinga, quoted in Barnett, Corelli, *Marlborough*, London, 1999, p. 11.
37. Paglia, Camille, *Sexual Personae*, Yale, 1990, p. 521.
38. Hamilton, 1965, pp. 220–1.
39. Weil, Rachel Judith, *Sexual Ideology & Political Propaganda in England 1680–1714*, PhD thesis, Princeton University, 1991, p. 297.
40. Burnet, Gilbert (Bishop), *History of His Own Time*, 1715, Everyman edition, p. 101.
41. Harley MS 6913.
42. Pinto, Vivian De Sola, *Restoration Carnival – Five Courtier Poets*, London, 1954, p. 141.
43. Harris, 1991, p. 22.

44. Add MS 61427.
45. Harris, 1991, p. 20.
46. Dobrée, Bonamy (ed.), *The Letters of Philip Dormer Stanhope, 4th Earl of Chesterfield*, London, 1932, vol. IV, p. 1262; (Letter to his Son, no. 1601).
47. Add MS 61427.

2. 'Flames of Extravagant Passion'

1. Add MS 61421, S's 'True account of the ill & undeserved treatment of the Princess Anne of Denmark by King William and Queen Mary her sister, contrived & carried on by the Earl of Rochester', Windsor Lodge, 13 November 1704.
2. Burnet, Gilbert (Bishop), *History of His Own Time*, 1715, p. 157.
3. Add MSS 61423, Burnet's 'Vindication'.
4. Nick Fielding, quoting Newton in *Sunday Times* article, 'Isaac Newton archive goes on the internet', 31 October 1999.
5. Add MSS 61423, Burnet's 'Vindication'.
6. Thomson, Gladys Scott (ed.), *Letters of a Grandmother 1732–35*, London, 1943, p. 172: S to Lady Diana Spencer, 25 August 1735.
7. Add MS 61427.
8. *Ibid.*
9. *Oxford Dictionary of Quotations*, citing oral tradition.
10. Waller, Maureen, *1700: Scenes from London Life*, London, 2000, p. 3.
11. Add MS 61454, Edward Griffith to S.
12. Add MS 61427.
13. Historian Robert Chambers quoted in Gleeson, Janet, *The Moneymaker*, London, 1999, p. 29.
14. Burnet, *History*, pp. 185 and 209.
15. Churchill, Sir Winston, *Marlborough: His Life and Times*, Edinburgh, 1947, vol. I, p. 154.
16. Add MS 61426, 'Characters of Princes'.
17. Churchill, Sarah, and Hooke, Nathaniel, *An Account of the Conduct of the Dowager Duchess of Marlborough*, 1742, p. 125.
18. Burnet, *History*, p. 103.
19. S to Lady Bathurst; quoted in Harris, Frances, *A Passion for Government*, Oxford, 1991, p. 100.
20. William Denton to Sir Ralph Verney, 13 November 1682, Verney Papers.
21. John Verney to Sir Ralph Verney, 9 November 1682, Verney Papers.
22. Gregg, Edward, *Queen Anne*, London, 1980, p. 28.
23. Add MS 61416, Queen Anne to S, 9 June 1703.
24. Add MS 61426.
25. Quoted in Green, David Brontë, *Sarah Duchess of Marlborough*, London, 1967, p. 32.

26. Add MS 61426.
27. *Ibid.*
28. *Ibid.*
29. Harris, 1991, pp. 32–3.
30. Add MS 61426, 'Characters of Princes'.
31. Add MS 61474, Lady Cornwallis to S, 4 March 1703.
32. Bathurst, Benjamin, *Letters of Two Queens*, London, 1924, p. 29.
33. Quoted in Kronenberger, Louis, *Marlborough's Duchess*, London, 1958, p. 56.
34. Bathurst (1924), pp. 60–1.
35. *Ibid.*, p. 122, Mary to Frances, 23 July (c.1680).
36. Boswell, Eleanore, *The Restoration Court Stage*, Harvard, 1932, pp. 130–1.
37. Bathurst, 1924, p. 165.
38. Hamilton, Anthony, *Memoirs of Count de Grammont*, trans. Horace Walpole, London, 1965, p. 171.
39. *Ibid.*, p. 175.
40. Green, 1967, p. 31.
41. Kronenberger, 1958, p. 56.
42. Add MS 61414.
43. Add MS 61426, 'Characters of Princes'.
44. Add MS 61422.
45. Add MS 61421, 'True account'.
46. Add MS 61418, 23 April 1711.
47. Gregg, 1980, p. 35.
48. Add MS 61426, 'Characters of Princes'; Add MS 61422, 'Narratives and correspondence relating to the Duchess's removal from her St James' lodgings, May–June 1711'.
49. Burnet, *History*, p. 202.
50. Add MS 61423, Burnet's 'Vindication'.
51. Add MS 61414.
52. Harris, 1991, p. 37.
53. Add MS 61427.
54. Quoted in Barnett, Corelli, *Marlborough*, Wordsworth Military Library, London, 1999, p. 180.
55. Defoe, Daniel, *A Short Narrative of the Life and Actions of his Grace John, Duke of Marlborough*, 1711, p. 45.
56. Add MS 61423.
57. S to Duke of Bedford, 5 May 1725, quoted in Harris, 1991, p. 6.
58. For example, Add MS 61427, 23 July 1702.
59. Add MS 61474, Lady Fitzharding to S.
60. S to Lady Diana Spencer, 11 July 1732, quoted in Thomson, Gladys Scott, *Letters of a Grandmother*, London, 1943, p. 45.
61. Add MS 61427.
62. Add MS 61448 – S to Lady Diana Spencer, 13 May 1732.

63. Add MS 61414.
64. De Beer, Esmond (ed.), *John Evelyn Diaries*, London, 1955, vol. 4, p. 361, entry for 24 January 1684.
65. Harris, 1991, p. 38.
66. Add MS 61442.
67. *Ibid.*
68. Anne to S, 1691, quoted in Gregg, 1980, p. 81.
69. Add MS 61426, 'Characters of Princes'.
70. Add MS 61474, Burnet's 'Vindication'.
71. Add MS 61426, 'Characters of Princes'.
72. Churchill and Hooke, *Conduct*, p. 53.
73. *Ibid.*, p. 13.
74. Dobrée, Bonamy (ed.), *Three Eighteenth Century Figures*, Oxford, 1962, p. 35.
75. S to Mallet, October 1744, Althorp Papers.
76. Add MS 61442.
77. Wolseley, Lord, *Marlborough*, London, 1894, vol. I, p. 304.
78. Add MS 61415.
79. Gregg, 1980, p. 101.
80. Churchill and Hooke, *Conduct*, p. 150.
81. Add MS 61414.
82. Kishlansky, Mark, *A Monarchy Transformed: Britain 1603–1714*, London, 1997, p. 272.
83. Add MS 61474, Burnet's 'Vindication'.
84. Trevelyan, G. M., *England Under Queen Anne*, London, 1930, p. 127.
85. Burnet, *History*, p. 238.
86. Quoted in Churchill, 1947, vol. 1, p. 219.
87. Harris, 1991, p. 46.
88. Quoted in Gregg, 1980, p. 50.
89. Add MS 61479.
90. Churchill and Hooke, *Conduct*, p. 18.
91. Add MS 61421.
92. As of 8 December 1688; Dickson, P. G. M., *The Financial Revolution in England*, London, 1967, p. 431.
93. Add MS 61421, 'True account'.
94. Add MS 61464, correspondence with Francis Hare (folios 1–94).
95. Add MS 61421.
96. Churchill and Hooke, *Conduct*, p. 17.
97. Add MS 61421, 'True account'.
98. Add MS 61426, 'Character of Princes'.
99. Ralph, James, *The Other Side of the Question*, London, 1742, p. 17.
100. Lediard, Thomas, *The Life of John, Duke of Marlborough*, 1736, vol. 1, p. 80.
101. Add MS 61421, 'True account'.

102. Churchill and Hooke, *Conduct*, p. 18.
103. Bathurst, 1924, p. 218.
104. Burnet, *History*, p. 275.
105. Quoted in Dobrée, 1962, p. 14.
106. Add MS 61426.
107. Letter from Pepys to Lord Dartmouth, 26 November 1688, quoted in Bathurst, 1924, p. 220.
108. Harris, 1991, p. 51.
109. Add MS 61423, S to Burnet.
110. Add MS 61474, Burnet's 'Vindication'.
111. *Ibid.*
112. Roy Jenkins quoted in *Observer* article, 'Long to reign over us' by Geoffrey Wheatcroft, 30 July 2000.
113. Add MS 61421, 'True account'.
114. Hailes, Lord (ed.), *The Opinions of Sarah, Duchess-Dowager of Marlborough*, London, 1788, section on 'Kings'.
115. Add MS 61426, 'Characters of Princes'.
116. 'The Revolution of 1688–9 and the English republican tradition' by Blair Worden, in Israel, Jonathan I. (ed.), *The Anglo-Dutch Moment: Essays on the Glorious Revolution and Its World Impact*, Cambridge, 1991, pp. 241–77.
117. 'The Character and Principles of the Present Set of Whigs', 1711, quoted in Kenyon, J. P., *Revolution Principles – The Politics of Party 1689–1720*, Cambridge, 1977, p. 160.
118. Churchill and Hooke, *Conduct*, p. 21.
119. *Ibid.*, p. 20.
120. Doebner, R. (ed.), *Memoirs of Mary, Queen of England 1689–1693*, Leipzig, 1886.
121. Add MS 61421.
122. Campbell, Kathleen, *Sarah, Duchess of Marlborough*, London, 1932, p. 98.
123. Add MS 61474, Burnet's 'Vindication'.
124. Anon., *A Dialogue in the Shades between Mrs Morley and Mrs Freeman*, 1745, p. 18; and Ralph, 1742, p. 48.
125. Add MS 61421, 'True account'.
126. Add MS 61414, Queen Anne to S, early 1691.
127. Add MS 61426, 'Characters of Princes'.
128. Ralph, 1742, p. 40.
129. Churchill and Hooke, *Conduct*, p. 29.
130. *Ibid.*, p. 25.
131. *Ibid.*, p. 115.
132. *Dictionary of National Biography*: Frances Jennings.
133. Harris, 1991, p. 58.
134. Add MS 61427.
135. MS Lister 2–4, Bodleian Library, 2 March [no year].

136. *Memorials of an Ancient House: A History of the Family of Lister or Lyster*, Denny, Rev. Henry Lyttleton Lyster, 1913.
137. Harris, 1991, p. 58.
138. Records of St Albans' School, quoted in Harris, 1991, p. 60.
139. Add MS 61426, 'Characters of Princes'.
140. Add MS 61474, Burnet's 'Vindication'.
141. Churchill and Hooke, *Conduct*, pp. 177–80.
142. Quoted in Green, 1967, p. 122.
143. Quoted in Dobrée, 1962, p. 26.
144. Add MS 61461, Maynwaring to S, November 1709.

3: The Cockpit Circle

1. Churchill, Sarah, and Hooke, Nathaniel, *An Account of the Conduct of the Dowager Duchess of Marlborough*, 1742, pp. 14–15.
2. Add MS 61415.
3. Add MS 61426.
4. Defoe, Daniel, *Conjugal Lewdness*, 1727, p. 25.
5. Churchill, Sir Winston, *Marlborough: His Life and Times*, Edinburgh, 1947, vol. 1, p. 324.
6. *Ibid.*, p. 328.
7. Add MS 61474.
8. Hailes, Lord (ed.), *The Opinions of Sarah, Duchess-Dowager of Marlborough*, London, 1788, pp. 73–4.
9. Burnet, Gilbert (Bishop), *History of His Own Time*, 1715, p. 315.
10. 8 February 1692, quoted in Churchill, Sir Winston, vol. 1, pp. 343–4.
11. Add MS 61421.
12. Churchill and Hooke, *Conduct*, p. 41.
13. *Ibid.*
14. Add MS 61414.
15. Churchill and Hooke, *Conduct*, p. 25.
16. *Ibid.*, p. 23.
17. *Ibid.*, p. 56.
18. Add MS 61414.
19. Add MS 61421, 'True account of the ill & undeserved treatment of the Princess Anne of Denmark by King William and Queen Mary her sister, contrived & carried on by the Earl of Rochester', Windsor Lodge, 13 November 1704.
20. Harris, Frances, *A Passion for Government*, Oxford, 1991, p. 65.
21. Add MS 61421, 'True account'.
22. *Ibid.*
23. *Ibid.*
24. Horace Walpole's letter to Sir Horace Mann, quoted in Toynbee, Paget (ed.), *Letters of Horace Walpole*, Oxford, 1903–5.
25. Add MS 61414, 1692.

26. Add MS 61414, January 1693.
27. Quoted in Churchill, Sir Winston, 1947, p. 348.
28. Wilson, John Harold, *Court Satires of the Restoration*, Ohio, 1976, p. 290.
29. Add MS 61474.
30. Add MS 61421.
31. Add MS 61414.
32. Churchill and Hooke, *Conduct*, p. 30.
33. Add MS 61421.
34. Add MS 61474.
35. Burnet, *History*, p. 295.
36. Kronenberger, Louis, *Marlborough's Duchess*, London, 1958, p. 61.
37. Quoted in Glendinning, Victoria, *Jonathan Swift*, London, 1998, p. 46.
38. Brantome, Pierre de Bourdeille, *The Lives of Gallant Ladies*, trans. Alec Brown, 1961.
39. Glendinning, 1998, p. 208.
40. Quoted in Faderman, Lillian, *Surpassing the Love of Men*, New York, 1981, p. 68.
41. Add MS 61479.
42. Quoted in Glendinning, 1998, p. 259.
43. Harris, 1991, p. 67.
44. Add MS 61414.
45. Churchill and Hooke, *Conduct*, p. 62.
46. *Ibid.*, p. 87.
47. Add MS 61421, 'True account'.
48. Churchill and Hooke, *Conduct*, p. 21.
49. *Ibid.*, p. 70.
50. Add MS 61454.
51. Churchill and Hooke, *Conduct*, p. 103.
52. *Ibid.*, pp. 97–8.
53. Add MS 61415.
54. Spencer, Charles, *The Spencer Family*, London, 1999, p. 39.
55. Churchill and Hooke, *Conduct*, p. 111.
56. Add MS 61415.
57. Add MS 61475.
58. PRO PROB 11/418/12: Will of Frances Jenyns, 1692.
59. Fielding, Henry, *A Full Vindication of the Dowager Duchess of Marlborough*, 1742, p. 23.
60. Add MS 61415.
61. Churchill and Hooke, *Conduct*, p. 256.
62. *Ibid.*, p. 112.
63. MS Rawl D.361, folio 346.
64. Porter, Roy, and Rousseau, G. S., *Gout – The Patrician Malady*, Yale, 1998, p. 239.

65. West, Richard, *The Life and Strange Adventures of Daniel Defoe*, London, 1998, p. 195.
66. Monod, Paul, *Jacobitism and the English People 1688–1788*, Cambridge, 1989, p. 167.
67. Lever, Sir T., *Godolphin*, London, 1952, p. 14.
68. Swift, Jonathan, *History of the Four Last Years of the Queen*, London, 1712, p. 12.
69. Add MS 61442.
70. Add MS 61418.
71. Pearson, John, *Blood Royal – The Story of the Spencers and the Royals*, London, 1999, p. 45.
72. Add MS 61415.
73. Anon., *The Sarah-ad or, A Flight for Fame*, 1742.
74. Gregg, Edward, *Queen Anne*, London, 1980, p. 109.
75. Add MS 61415.
76. Add MS 61480.
77. Add MS 61456.
78. Pearson, 1999, p. 46.
79. 25 October 1708, quoted in Snyder, Henry L. (ed.), *The Marlborough–Godolphin Correspondence*, Oxford, 1975, vol. II, p. 1138.
80. Churchill and Hooke, *Conduct*, p. 120.
81. Churchill, Sir Winston, 1947, vol. 1, p. 16.
82. Add MS 61427.
83. Weightman, Christine B., *A Short History of The Hague*, Schiedam, 1973.
84. Stanhope to Harley, 15/26 December 1704; PRO SO 84/227.
85. Add MS 61472.
86. Add MS 61421, 'True account'.
87. Commons Journals, vol. 10.
88. Dispatches of Count Wratislaw, 11 March; quoted in Churchill, Sir Winston, 1947, p. 499.
89. Add MS 61464, correspondence with Francis Hare.
90. For example, letter from May 1710, in Add MS 61475.
91. Quoted in Weil, Rachel Judith, *Sexual Ideology and Political Propaganda in England, 1680–1714*, PhD thesis, Princeton University, 1991, p. 232.
92. 'The Queen's Famous Progress, or Her Majesty's Royal Journey to Bath and Happy Return', quoted in Gregg, 1980, p. 162.

4: The Glass Ceiling

1. Anon., *A Dialogue in the Shades*, 1745, p. 36.
2. Ralph, James, *The Other Side of the Question*, 1742, p. 149.
3. Churchill, Sarah, and Hooke, Nathaniel, *An Account of the Conduct of the Dowager Duchess Marlborough*, 1742, p. 121.

4. Add MS 61444, S to Humphrey Fyshe, 4 July 1727.
5. Bucholz, R. O., *The Augustan Court: Queen Anne and the Decline of Court Culture*, Stanford, 1993, p. 39.
6. *Ibid.*, p. 83.
7. Harris, Frances, *A Passion for Government*, Oxford, 1991, p. 87.
8. Add MS 61479, notes by S on *Memoirs of Queen Anne: being a compleat supplement to the history of her reign* by Gibson, 1729.
9. Gregg, Edward, *Queen Anne*, London, 1980, p. 194.
10. Add MS 61416.
11. Add MS 61427.
12. Add MS 61427, 12/23 July 1702 (concerning petition of James Dayrolle, Secretary to Alexander Stanhope).
13. Veenendaal, A. J., *De Briefwisseling van Anthonie Heinsius*, The Hague, 1976–2001, vol. I (158RGP): 1702.
14. Add MS 61427, 23 July 1702.
15. Add MS 61421.
16. Add MS 61421, 'True account'.
17. Anon. [Cunningham?], *Review of a Late Treatise entitled 'An Account of the Conduct of the Dowager Duchess of Marlborough'*, 1742.
18. Add MS 61421.
19. Spencer, Charles, *The Spencer Family*, London, 1999, p. 80; Kronenberger, Louis, *Marlborough's Duchess*, London, 1958, p. 277; Harris, 1991, p. 84.
20. Spencer, 1999, p. 80.
21. Add MS 61416.
22. De Beer, Esmond (ed.), *John Evelyn Diaries*, Oxford, 1955, vol. 5, pp. 523–6: entry for 30 December 1702.
23. Add MS 61425.
24. Add MS 61426.
25. Ralph, 1742, p. 199.
26. Add MS 61464, Francis Hare, December 1710.
27. Churchill and Hooke, *Conduct*, p. 123.
28. *Ibid.*, p. 130.
29. Add MS 61416.
30. Add MS 61474.
31. Add MS 61442.
32. Swift, Jonathan, *History of the Four Last Years of the Queen*, London, 1712.
33. Churchill and Hooke, *Conduct*, p. 145.
34. Gregg, 1980, p. 223.
35. Rawl poet 169, folio 31.
36. Rawl.D.383, folio 118.
37. S from Antwerp, quoted in Green, David Brontë, *Sarah Duchess of Marlborough*, London, 1967, pp. 188–9.
38. Add MS 61423, S to Bishop Burnet.

39. Trevelyan, G. M., *The England of Queen Anne*, London, 1959, p. 167.
40. Add MS 61421.
41. Add MS 61418, April 1697.
42. Add MS 61416, 29 June 1703.
43. Add MS 61433, Godolphin to S, 4 June 1705.
44. Add MS 61449.
45. De Beer, vol. 5, p. 525.
46. Add MS 61416, Queen Anne to S, 31 May 1703.
47. Harris, Frances, 'The Honourable Sisterhood' in *British Library Journal*, XIX, 1993, no. 2, pp. 181–98.
48. Add MS 61474.
49. *Ibid.*
50. *Ibid.*
51. Add MS 61455.
52. Add MSS 61425, drafts co-authored by Whadcock Priest.
53. Add MS 61424, drafts co-authored by Arthur Maynwaring.
54. Quoted in Moore, Lucy, *Amphibious Thing*, London, 2000, p. 184.
55. Harris, 1991, p. 94.
56. Add MS 61479.
57. Add MS 61427.
58. Add MS 61414.
59. Harris, 1991, p. 98.
60. Anon. (ed.), *Letters of Sarah Duchess of Marlborough, now first published from the original manuscripts at Madresfield Court*, London, 1875, p. 36.
61. Harris, 1991, p. 99.
62. Quoted in Thomson, A. T., *Memoirs of Sarah Duchess of Marlborough*, London, 1839, vol. 1, p. 426.
63. *The Tears of Amaryllis for Amyntas – A Pastoral. Lamenting the Death of Lord Marquis of Blandford, Inscrib'd to the Right Hon. the Lord Godolphin*, 1703.
64. Egerton MS 1695, folio 1.
65. Add MS 61425, drafts co-authored by Whadcock Priest.
66. Snyder (ed.), 1975, vol. 1, p. 166, Marlborough to Godolphin, 9/20 April 1703.
67. Add MS 61427.
68. *Ibid.*
69. *Ibid.*
70. Add MS 61451.
71. Add MS 61450.
72. Add MS 61427, Marlborough to S, 17/28 May 1703.
73. Add MS 61427, 13 May 1703.
74. Add MS 61433, 13/24 May 1703.
75. *Ibid.*, S to Godolphin (from Margate) 19 May 1702.
76. Add MS 61427, Marlborough to S, 10/21 June 1703.

77. Churchill and Hooke, *Conduct*, p. 137.
78. Add MS 61451.
79. Add MS 61433, Godolphin to S, 12 June 1703.
80. Add MS 61427, 24 May/4 June 1703.
81. *Ibid.*, 10/21 July 1703.
82. *Ibid.*, 2/13 August 1703.
83. *Ibid.*, 5/16 August 1703.
84. For example: Churchill, Sir Winston, *Marlborough: His Life and Times*, Edinburgh, 1947, vol. 1, p. 722; Gregg, 1980, p. 169.
85. 'A Rational Account of the Natural Weaknesses of Women and of Secret Distempers Peculiarly Incident to Them', 1727, quoted in Greer, Germaine, *The Change*, London, 1991, p. 227.
86. Add MS 61449; Add MS 61466.
87. Wagstaffe, William, *The Story of the St Albans Ghost*, London, 1712, p. 13.
88. Brewer, John, *The Sinews of Power: War, Money and the English State 1688–1783*, London 1989, p. xix.
89. Defoe, Daniel, *The Storm: or a Collection of the most Remarkable Casualties and Disasters which Happened in the late dreadful Tempest both by Sea and Land.*
90. Plaidy, Jean, *The Queen's Favourites*, London, 1966, p. 163.
91. Harley MS 6914, vol. II, folio 106.
92. Add MS 61427.
93. Add MS 61458.
94. Add MS 61428.
95. Butler, Iris, *Rule of Three: Sarah, Duchess of Marlborough and Her Companions in Power*, London, 1967, p. 162.
96. Quoted in Green, David Brontë, *Sarah Duchess of Marlborough*, London, 1967, p. 95; and *Blenheim*, London, 1974, p. 20.
97. Snyder, Henry L. (ed.), *The Marlborough–Godolphin Correspondence*, Oxford, 1975, vol. 1, p. 272.
98. Add MS 61428, 11/22 April 1704.
99. *Ibid.*, 14 April 1704.
100. *Ibid.*, 18/29 April 1704.
101. *Ibid.*, 21 April/2 May 1704.
102. *Ibid.*, 24 April/5 May 1704.
103. Add MS 61433, 26 April 1704.
104. *Ibid.*, Godolphin to S, 24 April 1704.

5. 'Driving the Nail'

1. Add MS 61416, Queen Anne to S, 17 May 1704.
2. Quoted in Holmes, Geoffrey, *The Trial of Dr Sacheverell*, London, 1973, p. 31.
3. Add MS 61416, Queen Anne to S, 24 May 1704.

4. *Ibid.*, 26 May 1704.
5. *Ibid.*, 21 November 1704; quoted in Gregg, Edward, *Queen Anne*, London, 1980, p. 193.
6. Harris, Frances, *A Passion for Government*, London, 1991, p. 109.
7. Add MS 61428, 28 May/8 June 1704.
8. *Ibid.*, 5/16 July 1704.
9. For example, in Add MS 61479.
10. Churchill, Sarah, and Hooke, Nathaniel, *An Account of the Conduct of the Dowager Duchess of Marlborough*, 1742, p. 147.
11. Add MS 61423.
12. Churchill and Hooke, *Conduct*, p. 183.
13. Add MS 61414.
14. Churchill and Hooke, *Conduct*, p. 147.
15. Add MS 61416, 9/20 October 1704.
16. *Ibid.*, 23 October/3 November 1704.
17. Add MS 61428, 5 and 7 November 1704.
18. Gregg, 1980, p. 182.
19. Swift, Jonathan, *Memoirs Relating to that Change which happened in the Queen's Ministry in the Year 1710*, 1714.
20. Add MS 61428, 14/25 November 1704.
21. Snyder, Henry L. (ed.), *The Marlborough–Godolphin Correspondence*, Oxford, 1975, vol. 1, p. 274: Marlborough to Godolphin, 8 April 1704.
22. Quoted in Churchill and Hooke, *Conduct*, p. 155
23. Churchill, Sir Winston, *Marlborough: His Life and Times*, Edinburgh, 1947, vol 2, p. 915.
24. Szpila, Kathleen H., *Sarah Duchess of Marlborough as Patron of the Arts*, PhD thesis, Temple University, 1997, p. 104.
25. Green, David Brontë, *Sarah Duchess of Marlborough*, London, 1967, p. 105.
26. Szpila, 1997, pp. 119–20.
27. Add MS 61450.
28. Add MS 61434, Godolphin to S, 28 February 1705.
29. Add MS 61451.
30. Add MS 61427, Marlborough to S, 8/19 July 1703.
31. Add MS 61450.
32. Dobrée, Bonamy, *Three Eighteenth Century Figures*, Oxford, 1962, p. 29.
33. Lee, Christopher, *This Sceptred Isle*, London, 1997.
34. Add MS 61451.
35. Dobrée, 1962, p. 61.
36. Add MS 61428, Marlborough to S, 10/21 April 1705.
37. *Ibid.*, 21 November/2 December 1704.
38. Sir Charles Lyttelton to Viscount Hatton, 21 September 1702, quoted in Sergeant, Philip, *Dominant Women*, London, 1930, p. 575.
39. Add MS 61428, Marlborough to S, 10/21 April 1705.

40. Harris, 1991, p. 117.
41. Add MS 61474.
42. Add MS 61434, Godolphin to S, 18 May 1705.
43. Harris, Frances, 'The Electioneering of Sarah, Duchess of Marlborough', in *Parliamentary History*, 1983, 2, p. 74.
44. Campbell, Kathleen, *Sarah Duchess of Marlborough*, London, 1932, p. 167.
45. Add MS 61474.
46. Anon. (ed.), *Letters of Sarah Duchess of Marlborough, now first published from the original manuscripts at Madresfield Court*, London, 1875, p. 37.
47. Add MS 61423.
48. Add MS 61475; 1712–13, Mr Bernard Wilson to S.
49. Snyder, Henry L., 'Daniel Defoe, the Duchess of Marlborough and the Advice to the Electors', *Huntington Library Quarterly*, 1965–6, vol. 29, no. 1, pp. 53–62.
50. Add MS 61429, Marlborough to S, 9/20 May 1706.
51. Hopkins, Graham, *Nell Gwynne – A Passionate Life*, London, 2000, p. 255.
52. MS Rawl C. 986; Harley 6914, vol. II, folio 106.
53. MS Rawl C. 986.
54. Add MS 61474.
55. Add MS 61451, folio 107ff.
56. Willis, Deborah, *Malevolent Nature: Witch-hunting and Maternal Power in Early Modern England*, Cornell, 1995, p. 43.
57. Add MS 61428, 5/16 June 1705.
58. *Ibid.*, 7/18 June 1705.
59. *Ibid.*, 23 July/3 August 1705.
60. *Ibid.*, 7/18 July 1705.
61. Add MS 61474.
62. Green, David Brontë, *Blenheim*, London, 1974, p. 54.
63. Snyder, 1975, vol. 1, p. 474; Marlborough to Godolphin, 13/24 August 1705.
64. Add MS 61428, see enclosures in letters of 18 July, 1 August and 14 August 1705.
65. Downie, J. A., *Robert Harley and the Press*, Cambridge, 1979, p. 13.
66. Add MS 61428, Marlborough to S, 16 August 1703.
67. *Ibid.*, 25 June/6 July 1704.
68. Rosenberg, Albert, 'Prior's Feud with the Duchess of Marlborough. With a Further Note on Prior and Faction Display by H. Bunker White', *Journal of English and Germanic Philology*, January 1953, vol. LII, no. 1, pp. 27–31.
69. Quoted in Brown, Richard, *The Role of the Duchess of Marlborough in Augustan Literature*, PhD thesis, Rochester University, 1972, p. 146.
70. Add MS 61429, Marlborough to S, 10/21 July 1707.

71. Brown, 1972, p. 147.
72. Add MS 61426, 'Characters of Princes'.
73. Add MS 61414.
74. Churchill and Hooke, *Conduct*, p. 147.
75. *Ibid.*, p. 148.
76. Add MS 61443, Charles Spencer to S, 8/19 September 1705.
77. Snyder, 1975, p. 271.
78. Add MS 61428, Marlborough to S, 11/22 September 1705.
79. *Ibid.*, 27 August/7 September 1705.
80. Add MS 61434, Godolphin to S, 13 September 1705.
81. Harris, 1991, p. 120.
82. Add MS 61426, 'Characters of Princes'.
83. Churchill and Hooke, *Conduct*, p. 150.
84. *Ibid.*, p. 159.
85. *Ibid.*, p. 161.
86. Add MS 61118.
87. Quoted in Harris, 1991, p. 125.
88. Add MS 61428, Marlborough to S, 1/12 February 1704.
89. Add MS 61429, Marlborough to S, 20 June/1 July 1706.
90. *Ibid.*, 18/29 July 1706.
91. Snyder, 1975, p. 638.
92. *Ibid.*
93. Add MS 61417.
94. Add MS 61429, Marlborough to S, 13/24 May 1706.
95. Churchill and Hooke, *Conduct*, p. 170.
96. Gregg, 1980, p. 231.
97. Add MS 61417.
98. Add MS 61429, Marlborough to S, 12/23 August 1706.
99. Add MS 61423, S to Sir David Hamilton, 3 December 1710 from Windsor.
100. Quoted in Green, 1967, p. 167.
101. Add MS 61417, S to Queen Anne, 27 August 1706.
102. Add MS 61434, Godolphin to S, 7 September 1706.
103. *Ibid.*, 1 September 1706.
104. Quoted in Churchill and Hooke, *Conduct*, p. 165.
105. Add MS 61434, Godolphin to S, 14 September 1706.
106. *Ibid.*, 18 September 1706.
107. Snyder, 1975, vol. 1, p. 675; Godolphin to Marlborough, 10 September 1706.
108. Add MS 61429, Marlborough to S, 29 August/9 September 1706.
109. *Ibid.*, Marlborough to S, 23 September/4 October 1706.
110. Add MS 61434, Godolphin to S, 17 September 1706.
111. Snyder, 1975, vol. I, p. 714; Godolphin to Marlborough, 18 October 1706.
112. Downie, 1979, p. 20.

113. Add MS 61428, Marlborough to S, 30 July/10 August 1705.
114. Churchill and Hooke, *Conduct*, p. 171.
115. Osborn MS fc/10/I/89, anonymous letter by S to Mrs Masham.
116. Add MS 61418, S to Queen Anne, 1711.
117. Add MS 61417, S and Maynwaring to Queen Anne, 12/13 March 1708.
118. Quoted in Cowles, Virginia, *The Great Swindle: The Story of the South Sea Bubble*, London, 1960, p. 10.
119. Churchill and Hooke, *Conduct*, pp. 261–2.
120. Add MS 61474.
121. Downie, 1979, pp. 68 and 74.
122. *Review*, vol. III, nos 244, 278.
123. Churchill and Hooke, *Conduct*, p. 191.
124. Churchill, 1947, vol. 3, p. 33.
125. Add MS 61417, S to Queen Anne, 20 October 1706.
126. Gregg, 1980, p. 315.
127. Add MS 61423, S to Burnet.
128. Queen Anne to Marlborough, 22 June 1708.
129. Churchill and Hooke, *Conduct*, p. 160.

6: 'Raised from the Dust'

1. Add MS 61429, Marlborough to S, 5/16 August 1706.
2. Szpila, Kathleen H., *Sarah Duchess of Marlborough as Patron of the Arts*, PhD thesis, Temple University, 1997, p. 136.
3. Quoted in Campbell, Kathleen, *Sarah, Duchess of Marlborough*, London, 1932, p. 232.
4. Szpila, 1997, p. 141.
5. Add MS 61434, Godolphin to S, 9 November 1706.
6. Add MS 61426, 'Characters of Princes'; Churchill, Sarah, and Hooke, Nathaniel, *An Account of the Conduct of the Dowager Duchess of Marlborough*, 1742, p. 175.
7. Add MS 61417.
8. Quoted in Churchill, Sir Winston, *Marlborough: His Life and Times*, Edinburgh, 1947, vol. 2, p. 422.
9. Add MS 61417.
10. Butler, Iris, *Rule of Three: Sarah Duchess of Marlborough and Her Companions in Power*, London, 1967, p. 188.
11. Burnet, Gilbert (Bishop), *History of His Own Time*, 1715, p. 391.
12. Add MS 61423, Burnet's 'Vindication'.
13. Colley, Linda, *Forging the Nation*, London, 1992, p. 11.
14. For example, Add MS 61434, Godolphin to S, 18 October 1706.
15. Snyder, 1975, vol. 2, p. 629; Godolphin to Marlborough, 22 July 1706.
16. Quoted in Harris, Frances, *A Passion for Government*, Oxford, 1991, p. 31.
17. Snyder, 1975, vol. 2, p. 791; Godolphin to Marlborough, 25 May 1707.

18. Russell, Lord John (ed.), *Private Correspondence of Sarah, Duchess of Marlborough*, London, 1838, pp. 395 and 69.
19. Add MS 61417.
20. Add MS 61429, Marlborough to S, 22 May/2 June 1707.
21. Add MS 61454, folios 198–216b; correspondence with Abigail.
22. Sir John Clerk, quoted in Gregg, Edward, *Queen Anne*, London, 1980, p. 232.
23. Churchill and Hooke, *Conduct*, p. 182.
24. Butler, 1967, p. 190.
25. Churchill and Hooke, *Conduct*, pp. 182–3.
26. Add MS 61426, 'Characters of Princes'.
27. Bucholz, R. O., *The Augustan Court: Queen Anne and the Decline of Court Culture*, Stanford, 1993, p. 137.
28. Churchill and Hooke, *Conduct*, p. 184.
29. Add MS 61422, 'Account of discovery of Abigail's favour with Anne'.
30. Add MS 61423, S to Burnet.
31. Quoted in Gregg, 1980, p. 234.
32. Mesnager, Nicolas, *Minutes of the Negotiations*, 1717, p. 290.
33. Quoted in Gregg, 1980, p. 234.
34. Add MS 61422, 'An account of the Duchess's relations with the Hill family'.
35. Add MS 61422, 'Account of discovery of Abigail's favour with Anne'.
36. Add MS 61426.
37. Dr Arbuthnot to Henrietta Howard, May 1728; quoted in Bucholz, 1993, p. 123.
38. Richardson, Aubrey, *Famous Ladies of the English Court*, London, 1899, p. 333.
39. OSB MSS 'm' #9877–9938: 9912, S to Mr Cooke of Newington, 6 April 1742.
40. Add MS 61417.
41. Churchill and Hooke, *Conduct*, p. 213.
42. Add MS 61417.
43. Green, 1967, p. 152.
44. Add MS 61417, S to Queen Anne, 21 July 1707 (?).
45. Quoted in Gregg, 1980, p. 246.
46. Add MS 61429, Marlborough to S, 4/15 August 1707.
47. Add MS 61429, Marlborough to S, June 1707.
48. Snyder, 1975, vol. 2, p. 884; Godolphin to Marlborough, 16 August 1707.
49. Chamberlain, Henry, *History of England*, London, 1770, p. 172.
50. Add MS 61451.
51. Add MS 61442.
52. Add MS 61429, Marlborough to S, 18/29 August 1707.
53. Add MS 61417, Queen Anne to S, 1 September 1707(?).
54. Add MS 61429, Marlborough to S, 4/15 September 1707.

55. Add MS 61429, Marlborough to S, 18/29 September 1707.
56. Churchill and Hooke, *Conduct*, p. 186; Add MS 61454, folios 198–216b, correspondence with Abigail Masham.
57. Churchill and Hooke, *Conduct*, p. 187.
58. *Ibid.*; Add MS 61454, folios 198–216b, correspondence with Abigail Masham.
59. Add MS 61454, S to Abigail Masham (copy), 27 September 1707.
60. Churchill and Hooke, *Conduct*, p. 203.
61. Harley MS, 29 September 1707, quoted in Gregg, 1980, p. 247.
62. Add MS 61454, folios 198–216b, correspondence with Abigail Masham.
63. Elliot, J. H., and Brockliss, L. W. B., *The World of the Favourite*, Yale, 1999, n.33.
64. Add MS 61417, S to Queen Anne, 20 October 1706.
65. Gregg, 1980, p. 261; Harris, 1991, p. 147.
66. Quoted in Gregg, 1980, p. 279.
67. Dr Arbuthnot to Henrietta Howard, May 1728, quoted in Bucholz, 1993, p. 123.
68. Anon., *The Perquisite-Monger; or the Rise and Fall of Ingratitude*, March 1712.
69. Add MS 61423, Burnet's 'Vindication'.
70. Add MS 61423, Burnet's 'Vindication'.
71. Add MS 61429, Marlborough to S, 28 October/8 November 1707.
72. Dating given by Gregg, 1980, p. 252.
73. Add MS 61423, Burnet's 'Vindication'; Churchill and Hooke, *Conduct*, p. 207.
74. Churchill and Hooke, *Conduct*, p. 208 ff; Add MS 61417, 27 December 1707.
75. Jonathan Swift quoted in Dobrée, Bonamy, *Three Eighteenth Century Figures*, Oxford, 1962, p. 36.
76. Add MS 61479.
77. Add MS 61474.
78. *Ibid.*
79. Harris, Frances, 1991, p. 142.
80. Add MS 61475.
81. Osborn MS 'm' 9883, 17 September 1709, S to Lord Coningsby.
82. Churchill and Hooke, *Conduct*, p. 212.
83. Add MS 61474.
84. Add MS 61426, 'Character of Princes'.
85. *Ibid.*
86. Daniel Defoe quoted in Bucholz, 1993, p. 156.
87. Gregg, 1980, pp. 188–9.
88. I. A. A. Thompson quoted in Elliot and Brockliss, 1999, p. 19.
89. Greer, Germaine, *The Change*, London, 1991, p. 416.

90. Hailes, Lord (ed.), *The Opinion of Sarah, Duchess-Dowager of Marlborough*, London, 1788, p. 120.
91. Churchill and Hooke, *Conduct*, p. 11.
92. *Ibid.*, p. 12.
93. Add MS 61426, 'Characters of Princes'.
94. Add MS 61450.
95. Arthur Maynwaring quoted in Green, David Brontë, *Sarah Duchess of Marlborough*, London, 1967, p. 133.
96. Add MS 61461.
97. Russell (ed.), 1838, p. 146.
98. Add MS 61417.
99. Add MS 61454.
100. Add MS 61426, 'Characters of Princes'.
101. Add MS 61422, 'An Account of Mrs Masham's taking the Duchess of Marlborough's lodgings at Kensington in 1708'.
102. Add MS 61423, Burnet's 'Vindication'.
103. Add MS 61425, draft co-authored by Whadcock Priest.
104. Green, 1967, p. 130; Reid, Stuart J., *John and Sarah, Duke and Duchess of Marlborough*, London, 1914, pp. 275–6.
105. Add MS 61417.
106. *Ibid.*
107. Quoted in Monod, Paul, *Jacobitism and the English People 1688–1788*, Cambridge, 1989, p. 287.
108. Add MS 61417.
109. Russell (ed.), *Private Correspondence*, 1838, p. 104.
110. Thomson, Gladys Scott, *Letters of a Grandmother 1732–1735*, London, 1943, p. 105, S to Lady Diana Spencer, 8 November 1733.
111. Add MS 61429, Marlborough to S, 9/20 April 1708.
112. James Thompson to Dr Cranston in 1725, quoted in Cohen, S. J., 'Hester Santlow', *New York Public Library Bulletin*, 1980, pp. 95–106.
113. Lord Wharncliffe, *The Letters and Works of Lady Mary Wortley Montagu*, London, 1887, vol. 1, p. 10.
114. Add MS 61466.
115. Add MS 61429, Marlborough to S, 11/22 April 1708.
116. Add MS 61118, 22 May 1708: Anne to Sidney Godolphin.
117. Add MS 61118, note by S.
118. Add MS 61429, Marlborough to S, 13/24 May 1708.
119. *Ibid.*, ?17/28 June 1708.
120. *Ibid.*, 24 May/4 June 1708.
121. *Ibid.*, 27 May/7 June 1708.
122. Add MS 61430, Marlborough to S, 1/12 July 1708.
123. Russell (ed.), 1838, p. 132.
124. *Ibid.*, p. 136.
125. *Ibid.*, p. 139.
126. Add MS 61422, 'An account of a conversation with the Queen [in

September 1709], when she refused to give me an inconsiderable lodging, to make a clean way to mine'.

127. Add MS 61417.
128. *Ibid.*
129. Add MS 61430, Marlborough to S, 8/19 July 1708.
130. *Ibid.*, 12/23 July 1708.
131. *Ibid.*, 15/26 July 1708.
132. *Ibid.*, 22 July/2 August 1708.
133. Add MS 61417.
134. Vanbrugh to Earl of Manchester, 27 July 1708, quoted in *Historical Manuscripts Commission 8th Report*, Appendix II, 'Court and Society from Elizabeth to Anne', vol. II, p. 377.
135. Churchill and Hooke, *Conduct.*
136. Massey, Victoria, *The First Lady Diana*, London, 1999, p. 27.
137. Add MS 61462, 'A Ballad on Mrs Abigail. To the Tune of the Dame of Honour', attributed to Arthur Maynwaring, 1708.
138. Gregg, 1980, p. 237.
139. Russell (ed.), 1838, pp. 415–16.
140. Add MS 61430, Marlborough to S, 12/23 August 1708.
141. *Ibid.*, 9/20 August 1708.
142. Add MS 61417, S to Queen Anne, 16 August 1708.
143. Churchill and Hooke, *Conduct*, p. 219.
144. Churchill, 1947, vol. 3, p. 417.
145. Ackroyd, Peter, *London*, London, 2001, p. 361.
146. Add MS 61417; Churchill and Hooke, *Conduct*, p. 220.
147. Snyder, 1975, vol. 2, p. 1064: Marlborough to Anne, 28 August/8 September 1708.
148. Add MS 61430, Marlborough to S, 6/17 September 1708.
149. Add MS 61425, draft co-authored by Whadcock Priest.
150. Churchill and Hooke, *Conduct*, p. 263.
151. Add MS 61430, Marlborough to S, 3/14 June 1708.
152. *Ibid.*, 20 June/1 July 1708.
153. *Ibid.*, 28 September/9 October 1708.
154. Harris, 1991, p. 154.
155. Earle, P., *A City Full of People: Men and Women of London 1650–1750*, London, 1994, pp. 7–16.
156. Thomson, 1943, S to Lady Diana Spencer, 19 April 1733, 24 June 1734.
157. Arthur Maynwaring quoted in Green, 1967, p. 145.
158. 'The Seasonable Caution', MS Rawl Poet 181, folio 70.
159. Add MS 61459.
160. Campbell, 1932, p. 201.
161. Add MS 61430, Marlborough to S, 11/22 July 1709.
162. Bodleian Library, MS Add.A.191, S to Bishop Burnet. Bodleian, MS Add.A.191, June 1710, S to Bishop Burnet.

163. Manley, Delariviere, *The New Atalantis*, London, 1710, p. 204.
164. Add MS 61474.
165. 'W. Seward's Anecdotes', 1795, quoted in Churchill, 1947, vol. 3, p. 411.
166. Add MS 61479, notes by S on *Memoirs of Queen Anne: being a compleat supplement to the history of her reign* by Gibson, 1729, p. 47.
167. Wharton's essay on Pope, quoted in Thomson, A. T., *Memoirs of Sarah, Duchess of Marlborough*, 1839, vol. 2, p. 347.
168. Ralph, James, *The Other Side of the Question*, 1742, p. 171.
169. Add MS 61425, draft co-authored by Whadcock Priest.
170. Add MS 61430, Marlborough to S, 13/24 September 1708.
171. *Ibid.*, 20 September/1 October 1708.
172. Churchill and Hooke, *Conduct*, p. 222.
173. Churchill, 1947, vol 3, p. 478.
174. Add MS 61422, 'An Account of the Closet where she [Anne] saw Mrs Masham & of what passed at the Princes' death'.
175. Add MS 61426, 'Characters of Princes'.
176. Add MS 61417.
177. Quoted in Gregg, 1980, p. 290.

7: 'Noise of the Town'

1. Russell, Lord John (ed.), The *Private Correspondence of Sarah, Duchess of Marlborough*, London, 1838, p. 249.
2. Add MS 61422, 'An Account of Charles Seymour, 6th Duke of Somerset and his wife'.
3. Russell (ed.), 1838, p. 265.
4. Add MS 61434, Godolphin to S, 17 October 1708.
5. Add MS 61430, Marlborough to S, 14/25 November 1708.
6. *Ibid.*, 22 November/3 December 1708.
7. Add MS 61459, 23 November 1708.
8. Add MS 61430, Marlborough to S, 24 January/4 February 1709.
9. For example, Add MS 61430, Marlborough to S, 8–9 May 1709.
10. Add MS 61430, Marlborough to S, 27 December 1708/7 January 1709.
11. Osborn MS 'm' 9885, 30 June 1709.
12. Bucholz, R. O., *The Augustan Court: Queen Anne and the Decline of Court Culture*, Stanford, 1993, p. 77.
13. Add MS 61430, Marlborough to S, 24 May/4 June 1709.
14. *Ibid.*, 27 May/7 June 1709.
15. Add MS 61417, S to Queen Anne, 29 July 1709.
16. Add MS 61417, written on back of letter from Queen Anne to S, August 1703.
17. Add MS 61417, S to Queen Anne, 29 July 1709.
18. Add MS 61430, Marlborough to S, 8/19 August 1709.
19. *Ibid.*, 15/26 August 1709.

20. Add MS 61434, Godolphin to S, 19 August 1709.
21. *Ibid.*
22. Russell (ed.), 1838, p. 255.
23. Add MS 61430, Marlborough to S, 29 August/9 September 1709.
24. *Ibid.*, same letter continued on 31 August/11 September 1709.
25. *Review*, 12 January 1712.
26. Brewer, John, *The Sinews of Power: War, Money and the English State 1688–1783*, London, 1989, p. 165.
27. Add MS 61611, Edward Tennison, Rector of Sundridge to 3rd Earl of Sunderland.
28. Osborn MSS 'm' #9877–9938: 9883, S to Lord Coningsby, 17 September 1709.
29. Add MS 61422, 'An account of a conversation with the Queen [in September 1709], when she refused to give me an inconsiderable lodging, to make a clean way to mine'.
30. Add MS 61430, Marlborough to S, 12/23 September 1709.
31. Add MS 61101, Marlborough to Queen Anne, 29 September/ 10 October 1709.
32. Add MS 61430, Marlborough to S, 7/18 October 1709.
33. *Ibid.*, 10/21 October 1709.
34. Add MS 61418, final letters to Queen Anne.
35. Churchill, Sarah, and Hooke, Nathaniel, *An Account of the Conduct of the Dowager Duchess of Marlborough*, 1742, p. 224.
36. *Ibid.*, p. 225.
37. Add MS 61101.
38. Add MS 61418, S to Queen Anne, 29 October 1709.
39. Add MS 61426, 'Characters of Princes'.
40. Russell (ed.), 1838, p. 259.
41. 1709 peace proposal, Articles IV and XXXVII.
42. Add MS 61430, Marlborough to S, 3/14 October 1709.
43. Add MS 61418, S to Queen Anne, early November 1709.
44. Russell (ed.), 1838, p. 226.
45. Manley, Delariviere, *The Adventures of Rivella*, 1714, p. 7.
46. Manley, Delariviere, *The New Atalantis*, 1709, p. 20.
47. Manley, *Rivella*, p. 114.
48. Baker, Ernest A., *The History of the English Novel*, London, 1929, vol. III.
49. Russell (ed.), 1838, p. 228.
50. Needham, Gwendolyn B., 'Mary de La Riviere Marley, Tory Defender', in *Huntington Library Quarterly*, May 1949, vol. 12, p. 266.
51. Add MS 61418.
52. Add MS 61425, draft co-authored by Whadcock Priest.
53. Ackroyd, Peter, *London*, London, 2001, p. 133.
54. Maynwaring, Arthur, *The Rival Dutchess: Or, Court Incendiary*.

In a Dialogue between Madam Maintenon and Madam M[asham],
London, 1708.

55. Quoted in Green, David Brontë, *Sarah, Duchess of Marlborough*,
London, 1967, p. 297.
56. Churchill and Hooke, *Conduct*, p. 228.
57. Add MS 61422, 'Accounts of a dispute between Queen Anne and
Marlborough over the disposal of the regiment of Algernon Capell, 2nd
Earl of Essex in Jan 1710; 14 Feb 1710 with later additions', and copy
variant by Maynwaring.
58. Churchill and Hooke, *Conduct*, p. 228.
59. *Ibid.*, p. 180.
60. Add MS 61423, S to Sir David Hamilton.
61. Add MS 61422, 'Accounts of a dispute between Queen Anne and
Marlborough'.
62. Harris, Frances, 'The Honourable Sisterhood', in *British Library
Journal*, vol. 19, no. 2, 1993, p. 193.
63. Churchill and Hooke, *Conduct*, p. 234.
64. Add MS 61418.
65. Add MS 61422, 'An account of a conversation with her Majesty [in
February 1710] when it appear'd plainly that she did not intend to keep
her promise to the Duchess of Marlborough in letting her resign her
employments to her children'.
66. Churchill and Hooke, *Conduct*, p. 235.
67. Holmes, Geoffrey, *The Trial of Doctor Sacheverell*, London, 1973,
p. 123.
68. Maynwaring, Arthur, *Four Letters to a Friend in North Britain – Upon
the Publishing the Trial of Dr Sacheverell*, 1710.
69. Add MS 61426, 'Characters of Princes'.
70. Maynwaring, *Four Letters to a Friend*.
71. Holmes, 1973, p. 128.
72. Filmer, Robert, *Patriarchia, Or the Natural Power of Kings*, 1690.
73. Quoted in Kenyon, J. P., *Revolution Principles – The Politics of Party
1689–1720*, Cambridge, 1977, p. 128.
74. For example, Alexander Cunningham, *History of Great Britain*, 1787.
75. Add MS 61433, Godolphin to S, 8 October 1702.
76. Quoted in King, William (ed.), *Memoirs of Sarah, Duchess of
Marlborough*, London 1930, p. 14.
77. Holmes, 1973, pp. 83–6.
78. Add MS 61426, 'Characters of Princes'.
79. Churchill and Hooke, *Conduct*, p. 247.
80. Holmes, 1973, p. 132.
81. *Ibid.*, p. 115.
82. Quoted in Kronenberger, Louis, *Marlborough's Duchess*, 1958, p. 184.
83. *Review*, 9 May 1710, quoted in West, Richard, 1998, p. 157.
84. Quoted in Holmes, 1973, p. 127.

85. Article 1, in defence of the Revolution and legal resistance; Article 2, framed to assert supremacy of civil over ecclesiastical power; Article 3, the 'Church in Danger', suggested that Sacheverell had slandered the Queen; Article 4, slanders against the government and incitement of public to treason.
86. Holmes, 1973, p. 129.
87. Add MS 61423, S to Sir David Hamilton.
88. Add MS 61422, 'An account of a stratagem of the Duke and Duchess of Somerset at Doctor Sacheverell's trial'.
89. Richardson, Aubrey, *Famous Ladies of the English Court*, London, 1899, p. 337.
90. Bodleian Ref: 75/459, microfilm no. 740, *Mrs Caesar's Diary 1724–41*.
91. Holmes, 1973, p. 116.
92. Abigail Masham to Robert Harley, February 1710, quoted in Gregg, Edward, *Queen Anne*, London, 1980, p. 306.
93. Snyder, 1975, vol. 3, p. 1453: Godolphin to Marlborough, with postscript by S, 4 April 1710.
94. Add MS 61431, Marlborough to S, 8/19 March 1710.
95. Holmes, 1973, p. 135.
96. Cholmondeley (Houghton) MS no. 67.
97. Holmes, 1973, p. 150.
98. *Ibid.*, p. 161.
99. Veenendaal, A. J., *De Briefwisseling van Anthonie Hensius*, The Hague, 1976–2001, Saunière to Heinsius, 1 March 1710.
100. Holmes, 1973, p. 156.
101. Add MS 61426, 'Characters of Princes'.
102. Holmes, 1973, pp. 169–70.
103. *Review*, 8, 10 and 22 December 1710.
104. Bodleian Ref: 75/459, microfilm no. 740, *Mrs Caesar's Diary 1724–41*.
105. Maynwaring, *Four Letters to a Friend*.
106. Holmes, 1973, p. 201.
107. Add MS 61426, 'Characters of Princes'.
108. Add MS 61431, Marlborough to S, 14/25 March 1710.
109. *Ibid.*, 24 March/4 April 1710.
110. Add MS 61422, 'An Account of Charles Talbot, Duke of Shrewsbury and his wife'.
111. Maynwaring, *Four Letters to a Friend*.
112. Oldmixon, John, *Memoirs of the Press, Historical and Political from 1710–1740*, 1742, p. 6.
113. Quoted in Kenyon, 1977, p. 151.
114. Snyder, Henry L., 'Daniel Defoe, Arthur Maynwaring, Robert Walpole and Abel Boyer: Some considerations of authorship', in *Huntington Library Quarterly*, 1970, XXXIII, p. 133.
115. Maynwaring, *Four Letters to a Friend*.
116. Add MS 61461, S to Maynwaring, 30 June 1710.

117. Add MS 61431, Marlborough to S, 31 July/11 August 1710.
118. Add MS 61422, November 1710, S's notes on Simon Clement's *Faults on Both Sides*.
119. Add MS 61464, correspondence with Francis Hare.
120. Add MS 61418.
121. Add MS 61422, 'An account of a stratagem of the Duke and Duchess of Somerset'.
122. Russell (ed.), 1838, p. 242.
123. Coxe, quoted in Campbell, Kathleen, *Sarah, Duchess of Marlborough*, London, 1932, pp. 186–7.
124. Add MS 61426, 'Characters of Princes'.
125. Churchill and Hooke, *Conduct*, pp. 239ff.
126. Add MS 61422, 'The account of the conversation with the Queen upon Good Friday 1710'.
127. Add MS 61418, final letters to Queen Anne.
128. Add MS 61426, 'Character of Princes'.
129. Churchill and Hooke, *Conduct*, p. 244.
130. Green, 1967, p. 152.
131. Add MS 61423, table of contents of Hamilton's diary.
132. Foot, Michael, *The Pen and the Sword*, London, 1957, p. 101.
133. Lord Dartmouth, quoted in Barnett, Corelli, *Marlborough*, London, 1999, p. 246.
134. Add MS 61425, drafts co-authored by Whadcock Priest.
135. Quoted in Kronenberger, 1958, p. 188.
136. Add MS 61425, folio 132; Roberts, Philip (ed.), *Diary of Sir David Hamilton 1710–1714*, Oxford, 1975, p. 28.
137. Ralph, James, *The Other Side of the Question*, London, 1742, p. 300.
138. *Ibid.*, pp. 396–7.
139. King, William (ed.), *Memoirs of Sarah, Duchess of Marlborough*, London, 1930, p. 255.
140. Add MS 61426, 'Characters of Princes'.

8: The Good Hater

1. Sidney Godolphin quoted in Churchill, Sarah, and Hooke, Nathaniel, *An Account of the Conduct of the Dowager Duchess of Marlborough*, 1742, p. 250.
2. Add MS 61434, Godolphin to S, 17 April 1710.
3. Add MS 61422, 'An Account of Charles Talbot, Duke of Shrewsbury and his wife'.
4. Add MS 61425, drafts co-authored by Whadcock Priest.
5. *Ibid.*
6. Add MS 61461, S to Maynwaring, 28 April 1710.
7. Add MS 61431, Marlborough to S, 24 April/5 May 1710.
8. *Ibid.*, 8/19 April 1710.

9. Quoted in Barnett, Corelli, *Marlborough*, London, 1999, p. 255.
10. Add MS 61442.
11. Add MS 61434, Godolphin to S, 30 April 1710.
12. *Ibid.*, 29 April 1710.
13. Veenendaal, A. J., De *Briefwisseling van Anthonie Heinsius*, The Hague, 20 vols, 1976–2001, Vrijbergen to Heinsius, 16 May 1710.
14. Add MS 61431, Marlborough to S, 22 May/2 June 1710.
15. *Ibid.*, 8/19 May 1710.
16. *Ibid.*, 18/29 May 1710.
17. Add MS 61475, Mr Craggs to S, 18 May 1710.
18. Russell, Lord John (ed.), *Private Correspondence of Sarah, Duchess of Marlborough*, London, 1838, vol. 1, p. 390.
19. *Ibid.*, p. 709.
20. *Ibid.*, p. 715.
21. Add MS 61431, Marlborough to S, 18/29 May 1710.
22. Add MS 61434, Godolphin to S, 1 June 1710.
23. Add MS 61418.
24. Add MS 61418, note of 23 April 1711.
25. Add MS 61425, draft co-authored by Whadcock Priest.
26. Add MS 61431, Marlborough to S, 15 June 1710.
27. Snyder, Henry L. (ed.), *The Marlborough–Godolphin Correspondence*, Oxford, 1995, vol. 3, p. 1687.
28. Quoted in Churchill and Hooke, *Conduct*, p. 356.
29. Add MS 61423, S to Sir David Hamilton, December 1710.
30. Add MS 61431, Marlborough to S, 19/30 June 1710.
31. *Ibid.*, 1/12 June 1710.
32. *Ibid.*, 26 June/7 July 1710.
33. *Ibid.*, 22 June/3 July 1710.
34. *Ibid.*
35. Add MS 61422, 'Accounts and correspondence relating to the dismissal in 1710 of Charles Spencer, 3rd Earl of Sunderland, as Secretary of State, and Adam Cardonnell as Secretary at War'.
36. *Ibid.*
37. Add MS 61434, Godolphin to S, 26 June 1710.
38. Queen Anne to Godolphin, 13 June 1710, quoted in Add MS 61422.
39. Add MS 61418, note of 23 April 1711.
40. Add MS 61418.
41. Churchill and Hooke, *Conduct*, p. 257.
42. Add MS 61422, 'Accounts and correspondence . . . Charles Spenser'.
43. Churchill and Hooke, *Conduct*, p. 259.
44. Add MS 61431, Marlborough to S, 13/24 July 1710.
45. *Ibid.*, 17/28 July 1710.
46. Add MS 61426, 'Characters of Princes'.
47. MS Add.A.191, S to Burnet, 29 June 1710.
48. Add MS 61423, Burnet's 'Vindication'.

49. Add MS 61479, S's notes from Sir Francis Bacon.
50. Dr Johnson quoted in Thomson, A. T., *Memoirs of Sarah, Duchess of Marlborough*, London, 1839, vol. 1, p. 312.
51. See Langford, Paul, *Polite and Commercial People: England 1727–1783*, Oxford, 1998.
52. Osborn MSS 'm' #9877–9938: 9885, S to Lord Coningsby, 30 June 1710.
53. Hailes, Lord (ed.), *The Opinions of Sarah, Duchess Dowager of Marlborough*, London, 1788, p. 72.
54. Add MS 61423, S to Sir David Hamilton.
55. *Ibid.*
56. Bucholz, R. O., *The Augustan Court: Queen Anne and the Decline of Court Culture*, Stanford,1993, p. 90.
57. Add MS 61423, S to Sir David Hamilton.
58. Add MS 61423, Burnet's 'Vindication'.
59. S to George Bubb Doddington, quoted in Lynch, Bohun, *A History of Caricature*, London, 1926, p. 46.
60. Add MS 61423, S to Sir David Hamilton.
61. Add MS 61431, Marlborough to S, 6/17 July 1710.
62. *Ibid.*, 10/21 July 1710.
63. *Ibid.*, 20/31 July 1710.
64. *Ibid.*, 22 July/2 August 1710.
65. *Ibid.*, 14/25 August 1710.
66. *Ibid.*, 10/21 August 1710.
67. Add MS 61422, 'An account of the dismissal of Sidney Godolphin, 1st Earl of Godolphin, as Treasurer in August 1710, and of the mediation of Sir David Hamilton between Queen Anne and the Duchess'.
68. Churchill, Sir Winston, *Marlborough: His Life and Times*, Edinburgh, 1947, vol. 4, p. 974.
69. Roberts, Philip (ed.), *Diary of Sir David Hamilton 1710–1714*, Oxford, 1975: entry for 16 May 1710.
70. Veenendaal, 1976–2001, Vrijbergen to Heinsius, 9 September 1710.
71. *Ibid.*, 12 August 1710.
72. Add MS 61431, Marlborough to S, 24 August/4 September 1710.
73. *Ibid.*, 19/30 August 1710.
74. Marlborough to S, 2/13 September 1710.
75. Snyder, 1975, vol. 3, p. 1628; Marlborough to Godolphin, 7/18 September 1710.
76. Add MS 61418.
77. Osborn MSS 'm' #9877–9938: 9891, S to Lord Coningsby, 23 September 1710.
78. Osborn MSS 'm' #9877–9938, S to Lord Coningsby, 6 October 1710.
79. Add MS 61418.
80. Add MS 61431, Marlborough to S, 8/19 May 1710.
81. Add MS 61418.

82. Downie, J. A., *Robert Harley and the Press*, Cambridge, 1979, p. 125.
83. *Medley*, no. 1, 5 October 1710.
84. Snyder, 1975, vol. 3, p. 1634; Godolphin to Marlborough, 12 September 1710.
85. Russell, (ed.), 1838, vol. 1, p. 392.
86. Add MS 61434, Godolphin to S, 8 September 1710.
87. Harris, Frances, 'The Electioneering of Sarah, Duchess of Marlborough', in *Parliamentary History* (1983), 2, pp. 71–92.
88. Quoted in Fowler, Marian, *Blenheim, Biography of a Palace*, London, 1989, p. 59.
89. Add MS 61431, Marlborough to S, 14/25 Oct 1710.
90. Add MS 61464.
91. Add MS 61431, Marlborough to S, 29 October/9 November 1710.
92. *Ibid.*, 13/24 November 1710.
93. Snyder, 1975, vol. 3, p. 1645; Marlborough to Godolphin, 14/25 October 1710.
94. S to Lady Cowper, quoted in Harris, Frances, *A Passion for Government*, Oxford, 1991, p. 174.
95. Churchill and Hooke, *Conduct*, p. 122.
96. Queen Anne to Sir Peter King, quoted in Holmes, Geoffrey, *The Trial of Dr Sacheverell*, London, 1973, p. 272.
97. Add MS 61431, Marlborough to S, 29 October/9 November 1710.
98. Reid, Stuart J., *John and Sarah, Duke and Duchess of Marlborough 1660–1744*, London, 1914, p. 123.
99. Add MS 61464, correspondence with Francis Hare, 13/24 July 1710.
100. *Ibid.*, correspondence with Francis Hare, September 1710.
101. *Ibid.*, correspondence with Francis Hare, October 1710.
102. *Ibid.*, correspondence with Francis Hare, 31 October 1710.
103. *Ibid.*, correspondence with Francis Hare, November 1710.
104. Osborn MSS 'm' 9880, S to Lord Coningsby, May 1709.
105. Add MS 61434, Godolphin to S, 28 April 1710.
106. Osborn MSS 'm' 9895, S to Lord Coningsby, 13 November 1710.
107. Osborn MSS 'm' 9896, S to Lord Coningsby, 16 November 1710.
108. Glendinning, Victoria, *Jonathan Swift*, London, 1998, p. 110.
109. Swift's diary (14 November 1711), quoted in Bucholz, 1993, p. 164.
110. Add MS 61426, 'Characters of Princes'.
111. Earle, P., *A City Full of People: Men and Women of London 1650–1750*, London, 1994, p. 168.
112. Add MS 61422, 'An account of the dismissal of Sidney Godolphin'.
113. Add MS 61423, S to Sir David Hamilton.
114. *Ibid.*
115. Glendinning, 1998, p. 177.
116. Anon., *Oliver's Pocket Looking-Glass New Fram'd and Clean'd*, 1711, p. 42.
117. Add MS 61423, Burnet's 'Vindication'.

118. Add MS 61464, Francis Hare to S, 29 January 1713.
119. Add MS 61423, S to Sir David Hamilton.
120. *Ibid.*, 21 December 1710.
121. Churchill and Hooke, *Conduct*, 1742, p. 263–4.
122. Roberts (ed.), 1975, p. 22.
123. *Ibid.*, pp. 115–26.
124. Add MS 61422, 'An account of the dismissal of Sidney Godolphin'.
125. *Ibid.*
126. Quoted in Weil, Rachel J., *Sexual Ideology and Political Propaganda in England 1680–1714*, PhD thesis, Princeton University, 1991, p. 247.
127. Add MS 61426, 'Characters of Princes'.
128. Portland Papers, quoted in Bucholz, 1993, p. 163.
129. Add MS 61422, 'Accounts of the Duchess's resignation from her Court offices and other events in January 1711'.
130. Add MS 61425, drafts co-authored by Whadcock Priest.
131. *Ibid.*
132. Roberts (ed.), 1975, p. 26, 10 January 1711.
133. Add MS 61425.
134. Add MS 61422, 'Accounts of the Duchess's resignation'.
135. Williams, Harold (ed.), *Journal to Stella*, Oxford, 1948, p. 145: entry for 31 December 1710.
136. Add MS 61422.
137. Add MS 61418.
138. Add MS 61425, draft co-authored by Whadcock Priest.
139. Add MS 61422, 'Accounts of the Duchess's resignation'.
140. Harris, 1991, p. 178.
141. Add MS 61425, draft co-authored by Whadcock Priest.
142. Quoted in Churchill, Sir Winston, *Marlborough: His Life and Times*, Edinburgh, 1947, vol. 4, p. 650.
143. Richardson, Aubrey, *Famous Ladies of the English Court*, London, 1899, p. 342.
144. Add MS 61422, 'An account of a conversation with her Majesty [in February 1710] when it appear'd plainly that she did not intend to keep her promise to the Duchess of Marlborough in letting her resign her employments to her children'.
145. Add MS 61426, 'Characters of Princes'.
146. Add MS 61422, 'An Account of the events before and after Marlborough's dismissal in Dec 1711'.
147. Add MS 61422, 'An Account of Charles Seymour, 6th Duke of Somerset and his wife'.
148. Add MS 61423, Burnet's 'Vindication'.
149. Bucholz, 1993, p. 43.
150. Churchill and Hooke, *Conduct*, p. 281.
151. *Ibid.*, p. 293.
152. Add MS 61424, 2nd Letter to a Friend.

153. Add MS 61417, note by S on letters from *c.* 1709.
154. Add MS 61425, draft co-authored by Whadcock Priest.
155. *Ibid.*
156. Anon., *Review of a Late Treatise entitled 'An Account of the Conduct of the Dowager Duchess of Marlborough' by a Defender of William & Mary*, London, 1742.
157. Glendinning, 1998, p. 104.

9: Banished

1. Add MS 61472, Household Accounts.
2. Lord Dartmouth quoted in Butler, Iris, *Rule of Three: Sarah, Duchess of Marlborough and Her Companions in Power*, London, 1967, p. 251.
3. 14 October 1710, diary of Lord Cowper, quoted in Campbell, Kathleen, *Sarah, Duchess of Marlborough*, London, 1932, p. 207.
4. *Examiner*, 4 March 1711.
5. Add MS 61431, Marlborough to S, 5/16 April 1711.
6. *Ibid.*, 14/25 May 1711.
7. Add MS 61422, 'Accounts of parliamentary proceedings'.
8. Churchill, Sarah, and Hooke, Nathaniel, *An Account of the Conduct of the Dowager Duchess of Marlborough*, 1742, p. 272.
9. Russell, Lord John (ed.) *The Private Correspondence of Sarah, Duchess of Marlborough*, London, 1838, p. 409.
10. Add MS 61479.
11. Hanson, Laurence, *The Government and the Press 1695–1763*, Oxford, 1936, p. 33.
12. Charles Leslie quoted in Downie, J. A., *Robert Harley and the Press*, Cambridge, 1979, p. 6.
13. Black, Jeremy, *The English Press*, London, 2001, p. 12.
14. Add MS 61423, Burnet's 'Vindication'.
15. Add MS 61422, 'Narratives and correspondence relating to the Duchess's removal from her St James' lodgings, May–June 1711'.
16. Foot, Michael, *The Pen and the Sword*, London, 1957, p. 275.
17. Lever, Sir. T., *Godolphin*, London, 1952, p. 245.
18. *Examiner*, no. 28, 8 February 1711.
19. Hailes, Lord (ed.), *The Opinions of Sarah, Duchess-Dowager of Marlborough*, London, 1788, pp. 79–81.
20. Osborn MSS 'm' #9877–9938: 9900.
21. Downie, 1979, p. 135.
22. Swift to Addison, 22 August 1710, quoted in Stauffer, Donald A., *English Biography Before 1700*, New York, 1990, p. 72.
23. Needham, Gwendolyn B., 'Mary de La Riviere Manley, Tory Defender', in *Huntington Literary Quarterly*, May 1949, vol. 12, p. 273.
24. Snyder, Henry L., 'Arthur Maynwaring and the Whig Press 1710–12',

in Haas, Rudolf *et al*, (eds), *Literatur als Kritik des Lebens*, Heidelberg, 1977.

25. McDowell, Paula, *The Women of Grub Street – Press, Politics and Gender in the London Literary Marketplace, 1678–1730*, Oxford, 1998, pp. 6–7.
26. Quoted in Foot, 1957, p. 239.
27. Add MS 61431, Marlborough to S, 14/25 May 1711.
28. *Ibid.*, 27 March/7 April 1711.
29. Add MS 61422.
30. *Ibid.*
31. Russell (ed.), 1838, vol. 2, p. 77.
32. Add MS 61478.
33. Rawl D.383, folio 118.
34. Add MS 61431, Marlborough to S, 3/14 April 1711.
35. *Ibid.*, 28 May/8 June 1711.
36. Quoted in 'Blenheim Palace' article in *Country Life* (1951).
37. Add MS 61451.
38. Add MS 61423, table of contents of Hamilton's Diary.
39. Harris, Francis, *A Passion for Government*, Oxford, 1991, p. 185.
40. Quoted in Green, David Brontë, *Sarah, Duchess of Marlborough*, London, 1967, p. 215.
41. Cowles, Virginia, *The Great Swindle: the Story of the South Sea Bubble*, London, 1960, pp. 23–4.
42. Arabella Pulteney to Mr John Molesworth, quoted in Campbell, 1932, p. 223.
43. Add MS 61422, 'An account of a conversation with her Majesty [in February 1710] when it appear'd plainly that she did not intend to keep her promise to the Duchess of Marlborough in letting her resign her employments to her children'.
44. Quoted in Brown, Richard G., *The Role of the Duchess of Marlborough in Augustan Literature*, PhD thesis, Rochester University, 1972, p. 150.
45. Quoted in Reid, Stuart J., *John and Sarah, Duke and Duchess of Marlborough 1660–1774*, London, 1914, p. 444.
46. Needham, Gwendolyn B., 'Mary de la Riviere Manley, Tory Defender', in *Huntington Library Quarterly*, May 1949, vol. 12, p. 275.
47. Add MS 61426, 'Characters of Princes'.
48. Churchill and Hooke, *Conduct*, pp. 265–6.
49. Add MS 61431, Marlborough to S, 11/22 October 1711.
50. Add Ch. 76137, Plan of Marlborough House (1744).
51. Foot, 1957, p. 277.
52. Snyder, 1975, vol. 2, p. 873: Marlborough to Queen Anne, 4/15 September 1707.
53. Swift, Jonathan, *The Conduct of the Allies*, 1711, p. 34.
54. Downie, 1979, pp. 105–7.
55. *Ibid.*, p. 11.

56. Gregg, Edward, *Queen Anne*, London, 1980, p. 298.
57. Brewer, John, *The Sinews of Power: War, Money and the English State 1688–1783*, London, 1989, p. 122.
58. *Ibid.*, p. 200–1.
59. Carswell, John, *The South Sea Bubble*, London, 1960, p. 37.
60. Foot, 1957, p. 356.
61. Kenyon, J. P., *Revolution Principles – The Politics of Party 1689–1720*, Cambridge, 1977, p. 178.
62. Add MS 61422, 'An Account of the events before and after Marlborough's dismissal in December 1711'.
63. Firth-b-21/94, doggerel by Swift (*c.* 1708–11).
64. Anon., *A Dialogue in the Shades: Between Mrs Morley and Mrs Freeman*, London, 1745, p. 44.
65. Churchill, Sir Winston, *Marlborough: His Life and Time*, Edinburgh, 1947, vol. 3, p. 894.
66. Add MS 61479.
67. Kishlansky, Mark, *A Monarchy Transformed: Britain 1603–1714*, London, 1997, p. 333.
68. See Churchill, 1947, vol. 4, chapter 31.
69. Carswell, 1960, p. 21.
70. Churchill and Hooke, *Conduct*, p. 266.
71. Williams, Harold (ed.), *Journal to Stella*, Oxford, 1948, pp. 451–2: entry for 30 December 1711.
72. Quoted in Kronenberger, Louis, *Marlborough's Duchess*, London, 1958, p. 190.
73. Trevelyan, G. M., *The England of Queen Anne*, London, 1959, p. 149.
74. *Dialogue in the Shades*, 1745, p. 47; Thomson, A. T., *Memoirs of Sarah, Duchess of Marlborough*, London, 1839, vol. 2, p. 349.
75. Kronenberger, 1958, p. 104.
76. *Ibid.*, p. 203.
77. Add MS 61418, note to the reader in S's hand, dated 23 April 1711.
78. Dickson, P. G. M., *The Financial Revolution in England: A Study in the Development of Public Credit 1688–1756*, London, 1967, p. 431.
79. Add MS 61472, Household Accounts and Financial Correspondence.
80. Pierpont Morgan MS: letter from S, 31 January 1740.
81. Add MS 61472, Household Accounts and Financial Correspondence.
82. Add MS 61434, S to Godolphin, 17 October 1710.
83. Add MS 61467, S to John Scrope MP, Secretary to the Treasury 1742–4, 20 September 1744.
84. Add MS 61426, 'Characters of Princes'.
85. Churchill and Hooke, *Conduct*, p. 267–9.
86. Lediard, Thomas, *The Life of John, Duke of Marlborough*, London, 1736, vol. 3, p. 104.
87. S to Lady Cowper, quoted in Harris, 1991, p. 188.

88. Anon., *The Perquisite-Monger, or the Rise and Fall of Ingratitude*, March 1712.
89. *Ibid.*, p. 10.
90. *Spectator*, January 1712.
91. *Examiner*, 10 January 1712 vol. II, no. 6.
92. Reid, 1914, p. 373; Russell (ed.), 1838 vol. 2, pp. 68, 71, 76, 314.
93. Defoe, Daniel, *No Queen or No General. An Argument proving the Necessity Her Majesty was in, as well as the safety of Her Person, as of Her Authority, to Displace the D[uke] of M[arl]borough*, 1712.
94. Oldmixon, John, *Memoirs of the Press, Historical and Political, from 1710–1740*, 1742.
95. Swift, Jonathan, *History of the Four Last Years of the Queen*, London, 1712.
96. Add MS 61422.
97. Add MS 61423, S to Sir David Hamilton.
98. Churchill, 1947, vol. 4, p. 968.
99. West, Richard, *The Life and Strange Adventures of Daniel Defoe*, London, 1998, p. 388.
100. Add MS 61118, notes on Sidney Godolphin's character.
101. Bodleian Library: MS Add.A.191 – S to Bishop Burnet, 25 September 1711.
102. Harris, 1991, p. 190.
103. Add MS 61475.
104. Brown, 1972, p. 135.
105. Add MS 61475.
106. Quoted in Green, 1967, p. 180.
107. *Ibid.*, p. 164.
108. Russell (ed.), 1838, vol. 2, p. 62.
109. *Ibid.*, vol. 2, p. 182.
110. Chancellor, Frank, *Sarah Churchill*, London, 1932, p. 232.
111. Churchill, 1947, vol. 4, p. 971.
112. Gleeson, Janet, *The Moneymaker*, London, 1999, p. 100.
113. Stater, Victor, *High Life, Low Morals: The Duel That Shook Stuart Society*, London, 1999, pp. 246 and 251–2.
114. Gregg, Edward, 'Marlborough in Exile 1712–14', in *Historical Journal*, 1972, vol. XV, no. 4, p. 596.
115. Campbell, Kathleen, *Sarah, Duchess of Marlborough*, London, 1932, p. 316.
116. Thomson, 1839, appendix to vol. 1.
117. Williams, Harold (ed.), *Journal to Stella*, Oxford, 1948, pp. 658–9.
118. Stowe MS 751, S to Mr Craggs, 4 June 1714.
119. Quoted in Massey, Victoria, *The First Lady Diana*, London, 1999, p. 50.
120. Add MS 61451.
121. Green, 1967, p. 183.

122. Anon., *An Epistle from Sempronia to Cethegus. TO which is added Cethegus's Reply*, London, 1713.
123. Gregg, Edward, 'Marlborough in Exile 1712–14', in *Historical Journal* (1972), p. 599.
124. Green, David Brontë, *Blenheim*, 1974, p. 19.
125. Gregg, 'Marlborough in Exile 1712–14', p. 595.
126. Butler, 1967, p. 283.
127. Anon. (ed.), *Letters*, 1875, S to Robert Jennings, 12 February 1712/13.
128. Add MS 61475, S to Sir Godfrey Kneller, Frankfurt, May 1713.
129. Anon. (ed.), *Letters*, 1875, p. 31, S to Robert Jennings, 14 May 1713.
130. *Ibid.*, p. 27ff, S to Robert Jennings.
131. Butler, 1967, p. 271.
132. Gregg, 'Marlborough in Exile 1712–14', p. 601.
133. Quoted in Cowles, 1960, p. 32.
134. Reid, 1914, p. 394.
135. Brewer, 1989, p. 172.
136. Osborn MSS 'm' 9900, letter from S, May 1713.
137. Osborn MSS 'm' 9898, letter from S, March 1713.
138. Anon. (ed.), *Letters*, 1875, p. 46.
139. *Ibid.*, pp. 37 and 41.
140. Add MS 61475, S to Sir Godfrey Kneller, Frankfurt, May 1713.
141. Add MS 61479.
142. Green, 1967, p. 187.
143. Osborn MS 'm' 9900, letter from S, Frankfurt, May 1713.
144. Anon. (ed.), *Letters*, 1875, p. 34, S to Robert Jennings, 16 May 1713.
145. Add MS 61464.
146. *Ibid.*
147. Anon. (ed.), *Letters*, 1875, p. 72, S to Robert Jennings.
148. *Ibid.*, p. 66, S to Robert Jennings.
149. S to Mrs Boscawen, quoted in Harris, 1991, p. 197.
150. Anon. (ed.), *Letters*, 1875, p. 68, S to Robert Jennings, 9 July 1713.
151. S to Mrs Clayton, quoted in Green, 1967, p. 189; Osborn MS f.c.110/I.
152. 1712: 1 pistole = 17s.1d.
153. Stowe MS 751.
154. Add MS 61449.
155. Butler, 1967, p. 269.
156. Anon. (ed.), *Letters*, 1875, p. 81, S to Robert Jennings, 28 December 1713.
157. Gregg, 'Marlborough in Exile 1712–14', p. 606.
158. Osborn MS f.c.110/1/2–87: letters from S to Mrs Clayton.
159. Anon. (ed.), *Letters*, 1875, p. 69, S to Robert Jennings, 9 July 1713.
160. Churchill, 1947, vol. 4, p. 1000.
161. *Ibid.*, p. 1003.
162. Add MS 61449, letters from her daughter Elizabeth; March 1714?: letter of condolence from Bridgwater's mother.

163. Anon. (ed.), *Letters*, 1875, pp. 93–4.
164. Kronenberger, 1958, p. 218.
165. Gregg, 'Marlborough in Exile 1712–14', pp. 613–14.
166. Russell (ed.), 1838, vol. 2, p. 103, Lady Cowper to S in exile, June 1714.
167. Stowe MS 751, folios 48–51, S to Mr Craggs.
168. *Ibid.*
169. Anon. (ed.), *Letters*, 1875, p. 72.
170. Churchill, 1947, vol. 4, p. 1004.
171. Chancellor, 1932, p. 198.
172. Gregg, 'Marlborough in Exile 1712–14', p. 615.
173. Green, 1967, p. 194.

10: 'A Kind of Author'

1. Roberts, Philip (ed.), *The Diary of Sir David Hamilton 1709–1714*, Oxford 1975, p. 115.
2. Kronenberger, Louis, *Marlborough's Duchess*, London, 1958, p. 233.
3. Add MS 61451.
4. *Ibid.*
5. Longleat Portland MSS Box 1 on BL microfilm 921.
6. Add MS 61466, letters of Mary Cairnes.
7. Massey, Victoria *The First Lady Diana*, London, 1999, p. 44.
8. Quoted in Thomson, A. T., *Memoirs of Sarah Duchess of Marlborough*, 1839, vol. 2, p. 65.
9. Churchill, Sarah, and Hooke, Nathaniel, *An Account of the Conduct of the Dowager Duchess of Marlborough*, 1742, p. 5.
10. Quoted in Brown, Richard G., *The Role of the Duchess of Marlborough in Augustan Literature*, PhD thesis, Rochester University, 1972, p. 85.
11. Delaney, Paul, *British Autobiography in the Seventeenth Century*, London, 1969, p. 160.
12. Cavendish, Margaret, *Nature's Pictures Drawn by Fancies Pencil to the Life*, 1656.
13. Add MS 61421, 'True account of the ill & undeserved treatment of the Princess Anne of Denmark by King William and Queen Mary her sister, contrived & carried on by the Earl of Rochester', 1704.
14. Churchill and Hooke, *Conduct*, p. 6.
15. Quoted in Green, David Brontë, *Sarah Duchess of Marlborough*, London, 1967, p. 133.
16. Churchill and Hooke, *Conduct*, pp. 6–7.
17. Quoted in Green, 1967, p. 30.
18. Add MS 61422.
19. Roberts (ed.), 1975, p. 12.
20. Harris, Frances, 'Accounts of the Conduct of Sarah, Duchess

of Marlborough 1704–1742', in *British Library Journal*, 1982, vol. 8, p. 16.

21. Add MS 61423, Burnet's 'Vindication'.
22. Osborn MSS, f.c. 110/II/316: Bishop Burnet to Mrs Clayton.
23. Bodleian Library, MS Add.A.191, 13 June 1711.
24. King, William (ed.), *Memoirs of Sarah, Duchess of Marlborough*, London, 1930, p. 269.
25. Quoted in Green, 1967, p. 42.
26. Green, David Brontë, *Blenheim*, London, 1974, p. 121.
27. Add MS 61423, S to Sir David Hamilton, January 1711.
28. Add MS 61414.
29. Harris, 'Accounts of the Conduct of Sarah, Duchess of Marlborough 1704–1742', p. 17.
30. Add MS 61425, draft co-authored by Whadcock Priest.
31. Add MS 61426, 'Characters of Princes'.
32. Add MS 35853.
33. Add MS 61426.
34. Add MS 61464, correspondence with Hoadly.
35. Add MS 61451.
36. Add MS 61421, 'True account of the ill & undeserved treatment of the Princess Anne of Denmark'.
37. Add MS 61423, S to Sir David Hamilton.
38. Gay, John & Pope, Alexander, *Three Hours after Marriage. A Comedy*, 1717.
39. Stowe MS 751.
40. Add MS 61479.
41. Add MS 61451.
42. Quoted in Kronenberger, 1958, p. 78.
43. Add MS 61466, Marie La Vie to S, 1720s.
44. Add MS 61451.
45. *Ibid.*
46. Add MS 61464, S to Francis Hare, October 1726.
47. *Ibid.*
48. Add MS 61451.
49. Add MS 61431.
50. Gregg, Edward, 'Marlborough in Exile 1712–14', in *Historical Journal*, 1972, vol. XV, no. 4, p. 617.
51. Add MS 61431.
52. Add MS 61442.
53. *Ibid.*
54. *Daily Courant*, no. 4522.
55. Add MS 61442.
56. *Ibid.*
57. Massey, 1999, p. 54.
58. Green, 1967, p. 200.

59. Kronenberger, 1958, p. 238.
60. Add MS 61479.
61. Add MS 61472, Household Accounts and Financial Correspondence.
62. Add MS 61450.
63. *Ibid.*
64. Quoted in Coxe, William, *Memoirs of John, Duke of Marlborough*, 1820, vol. 6, p. 372.
65. Szpila, Kathleen H., *Sarah Duchess of Marlborough as Patron of the Arts*, PhD thesis, Temple University, 1997, p. 266.
66. Stowe MS 751.
67. S to Mrs Clayton, quoted in Campbell, Kathleen, *Sarah, Duchess of Marlborough*, London, 1932, p. 247.
68. Quoted in Kronenberger, 1958, p. 241.
69. S to Mrs Clayton, quoted in Campbell, 1932, p. 247.
70. Anon. (ed.), *Letters of Sarah Duchess of Marlborough, now first published from the original manuscripts at Madresfield Court*, London, 1875, p. 107.
71. S to Mr Townshend from Windsor, 1721, BL Longleat Microfilm.
72. Szpila, 1997, p. 308.
73. Add MS 61451.
74. Add MS 61427.
75. Add MS 61451.
76. Add MS 61475.
77. Add MS 61451.
78. Add MS 61462.
79. Williams, Harold (ed.), *The Correspondence of Jonathan Swift*, Oxford, 1965, vol. 3, p. 103.
80. Add MS 61479.
81. Downie, J. A., *Robert Harley and the Press*, Cambridge, 1979, pp. 188–9.
82. Quoted in Thomson, 1839, pp. 306–7.
83. Add MS 61451.
84. Reid, Stuart J., *John and Sarah, Duke and Duchess of Marlborough*, London, 1914, p. 378.
85. Green, 1967, p. 208.
86. PRO, E 134/11 Geol/Mich 27 and East 7 (case of Edward Strong *v.* SM).
87. Campbell, Kathleen, *Sarah, Duchess of Marlborough*, London, 1932, p. 246.
88. James Craggs (Jnr) to Lord Stair, 11 May 1718, quoted in Harris, Frances, *A Passion for Government*, Oxford, 1991, p. 221.
89. Hibbert, Christopher, *The Marlboroughs: John and Sarah Churchill 1650–1744*, London, 2001, p. 338.
90. Add MS 61466.
91. Fowler, Marian, *Blenheim: Biography of a Palace*, London, 1989, p. 53.

92. Sherburn, George (ed.), *The Correspondence of Alexander Pope*, Oxford, 1956, vol. 1, p. 432.
93. Quoted in Chancellor, Frank, *Sarah Churchill*, London, 1932, pp. 128–9.
94. Green, *Blenheim*, 1974, p. 136.
95. Green, 1967, p. 104; Add MS 61473.
96. Fowler, 1989, p. 29.
97. Add MS 61475.
98. Chancellor, 1932, p. 207.
99. 24 July 1718 from Windsor Lodge, quoted in Add MS 61451.
100. Add MS 61451, 107ff, copy of Green Book with additions to 1739.
101. Add MS 61466, letters of Mary Cairnes.
102. Add MS 61443, Lady de la Warr to S, July 1723.
103. Baron de Montesquieu, Charles de Secondat, '*Le Spicilège*', Paris, 1729, no. 625.
104. Add MS 61475.
105. Add MS 61541.
106. Harris, 1991, p. 282.
107. Dickson, P. G. M., *The Financial Revolution in England: A Study in the Development of Public Credit 1688–1756*, London, 1967, pp. 280–1.
108. Carswell, J., *The South Sea Bubble*, London, 1960, p. 144.
109. Add MS 61472, Household Accounts and Financial Correspondence, 18 March 1704/5, note re money loaned the Treasury (Godolphin), bank stock bought in men's names.
110. *Examiner*, 2 November 1710, no. 14.
111. Campbell, 1932, p. 250.
112. Nicholson, Colin, *Writing and the Rise of Finance – Capital Satires of the Early Eighteenth Century*, Cambridge, 1994, p. 1.
113. Brewer, John, *The Sinews of Power: War, Money and the English State 1688–1783*, London, 1989, p. 187.
114. Cowles, Virginia, *The Great Swindle: the Story of the South Sea Bubble*, London, 1960, p. 119.
115. Brewer, 1989, p. 125.
116. Cowles, 1960, pp. 84, 86–7.
117. Quoted in Green, 1967, p. 218.
118. Cowles, 1960, p. 135.
119. Add MS 61475.
120. Add MS 61443.
121. Cowles, 1960, p. 148.
122. Swift quoted in Ackroyd, Peter, *London*, London, 2001, p. 292.
123. Gleeson, Janet, *The Moneymaker*, London, 1999, p. 198.
124. Add MS 61476.
125. Add MS 61475, Mrs D'Arcy to S, December 1720.
126. Plumb, J. H., *The Life of Sir Robert Walpole*, London, 1956, pp. 306–7.

127. Langford, Paul, *A Polite and Commercial People: England 1727–1783*, London, 1998, p. 22.
128. Cowles, 1960, p. 164.
129. Carswell, 1960, p. 200.
130. Add MS 61475.
131. McFarlane, Cameron, *The Sodomite in Fiction and Satire 1660–1750*, New York, 1997, pp. 93–5.
132. Add MS 61451.
133. Add MS 61418, 'An Account of my Lord Sunderland's Proceedings with the Duke and Duchess of Marlborough in 1720'.
134. Osborn MS, f.c. 110/I/97: S to King George I.
135. Add MS 61418, 'An Account of my Lord Sunderland's Proceedings'.
136. Add MS 61418.
137. Quoted in Green, 1967, p. 220.
138. See: Sedgwick, Romney (ed.), *The House of Commons 1715–54*, London 1970, vol. II, pp. 66–7.
139. Add MS 61475.
140. Harris, 1991, p. 241.

11: *Dowager*

1. Add MS 61451; Churchill, Sir Winston, *Marlborough: His Life and Times*, Edinburgh, 1947, vol. 4, p. 1037.
2. Add MS 61451, 107ff, copy of Green Book with additions to 1739.
3. Quoted in Green, David Brontë, *Sarah Duchess of Marlborough*, London, 1967, p. 233.
4. *Ibid.*, p. 235, S to Mrs Clayton, 9 October 1722.
5. Add MS 61466, letters of Mary Cairnes.
6. Green, 1967, p. 227.
7. Add MS 61451.
8. Quoted in Green, 1967, p. 304.
9. Add MS 61476.
10. Massey, Victoria, *The First Lady Diana*, London, 1999, p. 87.
11. Campbell, Kathleen, *Sarah, Duchess of Marlborough*, London, 1932, p. 254.
12. Pierpont Morgan MS, S to Dr Clarke in 1722.
13. Add MS 61409.
14. Waller, Maureen, *1700: Scenes from London Life*, London, 2000, p. 120.
15. Anon., *Letters of Sarah Duchess of Marlborough, now first published from the original manuscripts at Madresfield Court*, London, 1875, p. 143.
16. Add MS 61451, 107ff, copy of Green Book, with additions to 1739.
17. Pearson, John, *Blood Royal*, London, 1999, p. 69.

18. S to Somerset, August 1723, quoted in Harris, Frances, *A Passion for Government*, London, p. 253.
19. King, William (ed.), *Memoirs of Sarah, Duchess of Marlborough*, London, 1930, p. 299.
20. Dickson, P. G. M., *The Financial Revolution in England: A Study in the Development of Public Credit 1688–1756*, London, 1967, p. 433.
21. *Ibid.*, p. 279.
22. Plumb, J. H., *The Life of Sir Robert Walpole*, London, 1956, p. 142.
23. Kronenberger, Louis, *Marlborough's Duchess*, London, 1958, p. 250.
24. Thomson, A. T., *Memoirs of Sarah Duchess of Marlborough*, London, vol. II, p. 385.
25. *Ibid.*, p. 388.
26. *Ibid.*, p. 380.
27. Green, 1967, p. 267.
28. Add MS 61463.
29. Add MS 61476, S to her banker Mr Burton at Leicester Street.
30. Churchill, 1947, vol. 4, p. 1038.
31. Add MS 61426, 'Characters of Princes'.
32. Add MS 61451.
33. Add MS 61466, letters of Mary Cairnes.
34. Reproduced in Thomson, Gladys Scott (ed.), *Letters of a Grandmother 1732–1735*, London, 1943.
35. Add MS 61449.
36. *Ibid.*
37. *Ibid.*
38. Add MS 61451.
39. Add MS 61449.
40. *Ibid.*
41. *Ibid.*
42. *Ibid.*
43. Williams, Harold (ed.), *The Correspondence of Jonathan Swift*, Oxford, 1965, vol. 4, p. 475: Mrs Pendarves to Swift in 1736.
44. Add MS 61451.
45. Quoted in Blakiston, Georgiana, *Woburn and the Russells*, London, 1980, p. 91.
46. Add MS 61476.
47. Add MS 61451.
48. Add MS 61449.
49. Add MS 61472, Household Accounts and Financial Correspondence.
50. Add MS 61466.
51. Add MS 38056.
52. Quoted in Kronenberger, 1958, p. 245.
53. Add MS 61476.
54. Add MS 38056; Add MS 61466.
55. Churchill, Sarah, and Maynwaring, Arthur, *An Account of Mr Guidott's*

Proceedings; which occasion'd the late trial between the late Duke of Marlborough's executors and the said Mr Guidott, London, 1727.

56. S to Lady Cowper, quoted in Green, 1967, p. 269.
57. Cavendish, Margaret, *Nature's Pictures Drawn by Fancies Pencil to the Life*, 1671, p. 380.
58. S to Mr Cook at Bank of England, 26 November 1741, quoted in Butler, Iris, *Rule of Three: Sarah Duchess of Marlborough and Her Companions in Power*, London, 1967, pp. 338–40.
59. Add MS 61464, Francis Hare to S, 26 August 1726.
60. *Ibid.*
61. *Ibid.*, 24 September (?) 1726.
62. *Ibid.*, 26 August 1726.
63. *Ibid.*
64. *Ibid.*
65. Lady Mary Wortley Montagu to Lady Mar, October 1727, Halsband, Robert (ed.), *The Complete Letters of Lady Mary Wortley Montagu*, Oxford, 1965, vol. 2, p. 85.
66. Cesar de Saussure, *A Foreign View of England*, quoted in Kronenberger, 1958, p. 274.
67. Add MS 61476, Mr Methuen to S, 13 October 1727.
68. Kronenberger, 1958, p. 271.
69. Hailes, Lord (ed.), *The Opinions of Sarah, Duchess-Dowager of Marlborough*, London, 1788, pp. 100–12.
70. *Ibid.*
71. Add MS 61467.
72. Chancellor, Frank, *Sarah Churchill*, London, 1932, p. 230.
73. Add MS 61418.
74. Chancellor, 1932, p. 230.
75. Reid, Stuart J., *John and Sarah, Duke and Duchess of Marlborough 1660–1744*, London, 1914, pp. 455–6.
76. Quoted in Brown, Richard G., *The Role of the Duchess of Marlborough in Augustan Literature*, PhD thesis, Rochester University, 1972, p. 193.
77. Goldsmith, Oliver, *The Life of Richard Nash Esq.*, 1762, p. 97.
78. Ralph, James, *The Other Side of the Question*, London, 1742, p. 466.
79. Voltaire, F. M. A., *Siècle de Louis XIV*, in Moland, Louis (ed.), *Oeuvres Completès de Voltaire*, Paris, 1878, vol. XIV, p. 546.
80. Scribe, Eugène, *Le Verre d'eau ou les effets et les causes*, New York, 1900.
81. Pierpont Morgan MS, 18 September 1731.
82. Grundy, Isobel, *Lady Mary Wortley Montagu*, Oxford, 1999, p. 3 n. 12.
83. Kronenberger, 1958, p. 275.
84. Pierpont Morgan MS, letter to Lady Mary Wortley Montagu, 12 March 1721.
85. Quoted in Redford, Bruce, *The Converse of the Pen – Acts of*

Intimacy in the Eighteenth Century Familiar Letter, Chicago, 1986, chapter 1.

86. Lord Hervey to Sir R. Cocks, July 1704, quoted in Trevelyan, G. M., *England under Queen Anne*, London, 1930, p. 5n.
87. Green, 1967, p. 171, list of S's books, dated September 1719, now at Althorp.
88. Quoted in Campbell, 1932, p. 261.
89. Add MS 61473.
90. Thomson, 1943, S to Lady Diana Spencer, 20 July 1734.
91. Worsley, Giles, *Classical Architecture in Britain – The Heroic Age*, Yale, 1995, p. 103.
92. *Ibid.*, p. 113.
93. S to Lady Cowper, quoted in Green, 1967, p. 264.
94. Halsband (ed.), 1965, p. 211.
95. Add MS 61477, S to Sir Philip Yorke, 24 May 1732.
96. Thomson, 1943, S to Lady Diana Spencer, from Cheam, 2 April 1732.
97. *Ibid.*, 4 July 1732, from Leicester.
98. *Ibid.*, 9 July 1732, from Scarborough Spa.
99. *Ibid.*, 5 August 1734.

12: A Dozen Heirs

1. Harris, Frances, *A Passion for Government*, Oxford, 1991, p. 275.
2. Quoted in Green, David Brontë, *Sarah Duchess of Marlborough*, London, 1967, p. 284.
3. Quoted in Harris, 1991, p. 263.
4. Quoted in Green, 1967, p. 283.
5. Add MS 61440, S to Blandford, 8 February 1730.
6. Halsband, Robert (ed.), *The Complete Letters of Lady Mary Wortley Montagu*, Oxford, 1965, p. 30.
7. Wilson, Charles, *Memoirs of the Life, Writings and Amours of William Congreve Esq.*, London, 1730.
8. Thomas, David, *William Congreve*, London, 1992, p. 12.
9. Anon., *The Amorous D[uc]h[e]ss: or, Her G[race] Grateful*, London, 1733.
10. Quoted in Dobrée, Bonamy, *Three Eighteenth Century Figures*, Oxford, 1962, p. 60.
11. Add MS 61440.
12. Hervey to Stephen Fox, 9 September 1730, quoted in Massey, Victoria, *The First Lady Diana*, London, 1999, p. 138.
13. Stater, Victor, *High Life, Low Morals: The Duel That Shook Stuart Society*, London, 1999, p. 264.
14. Massey, 1999, p. 130.
15. Add MS 61454, Lady Diana Spencer's Correspondence with Lady Rich (August–September 1730).

16. *Ibid.*
17. *Ibid.*
18. Massey, 1999, p. 137.
19. Add MS 61477.
20. Quoted in Blakiston, Georgiana, *Woburn and the Russells*, London, 1980, p. 101.
21. Thomson, Gladys Scott, *Life in a Noble Household 1641–1700*, Ann Arbor, 1959, p. 280.
22. Add MS 61449.
23. Quoted in Grundy, I., and Wiseman, S., *Women, Writing, History 1640–1740*, London, 1992, p. 307.
24. Lord Ilchester (ed.), *Lord Hervey and His Friends*, London, 1950, p. 80: Lord John Hervey to Stephen Fox.
25. Hailes, Lord (ed.), *The Opinions of Sarah, Duchess-Dowager of Marlborough*, London, 1788, pp. 42–4.
26. Quoted in Masters, Brian, *The Dukes*, London, 2001, p. 200.
27. Add MS 61451.
28. Add MS 61446, Sunderland to S, May 1732.
29. Thomson, 1943, S to Lady Diana Spencer, 8 August 1732.
30. *Ibid.*, 2 April 1732.
31. *Ibid.*, 30 July 1732.
32. *Ibid.*, 11 July 1732, from Scarborough Spa.
33. *Ibid.*, 25 July 1732, from Scarborough Spa.
34. Add MS 61447, anon. letter to S, November 1732.
35. Thomson, 1943, S to Lady Diana Spencer, 9 July 1732, from Scarborough Spa.
36. *Ibid.*, S to Lady Diana Spencer, 3 January 1733.
37. *Ibid.*, late November/early December 1732.
38. Add MS 61451, folios 141–196b, narratives re Charles 3rd Duke of Marlborough, prompted by the Chancery Suit 1738–44.
39. *Ibid.*
40. Add MS 61449.
41. *Ibid.*
42. Thomson, 1943, S to Lady Diana Spencer, 13 May 1732.
43. Add MS 61451.
44. *Ibid.*
45. Thomson, 1943, S to Lady Diana Spencer, 3 January 1733.
46. Add MS 61449.
47. Thomson, 1943, S to Lady Diana Spencer, 25 September 1732.
48. *Ibid.*, 18 November 1732: S to Lady Diana Spencer; Massey, 1999, p. 178.
49. Masters, 2001, pp. 337–8.
50. Add MS 61451, 107ff, copy of Green Book, with additions to 1739.
51. Quoted in Masters, 2001, pp. 337–8.
52. Add MS 61451, 107ff, copy of Green Book, with additions to 1739.

53. Add MS 61477, S to Sir Philip Yorke, May 1732.
54. Thomson, 1943, S to Lady Diana Spencer, 21 July 1732, from Scarborough Spa.
55. Add MS 61475, undated letter from one Cath. Holford writing from Fleet Prison.
56. Add MS 61475.
57. Anon., *An Epistle from Sempronia to Cethegus. TO which is added Cethegus's Reply*, 1713.
58. Add MS 61464, correspondence with Hoadly.
59. Thomson, 1943, S to Lady Diana Spencer, 3 January 1733 and 6 November 1733.
60. Spencer, Charles, *The Spencer Family*, London, 1999, p. 100.
61. S to Fyshe in July 1727, quoted in Rowse, A. L., *The Later Churchills*, London, 1958, p. 14.
62. Thomson, 1943, S to Lady Diana Spencer, 25 December 1733.
63. *Ibid.*, 21 October 1734.
64. Reid, Stuart J., *John and Sarah, Duke and Duchess of Marlborough, 1660–1744*, London, 1914, p. 437.
65. Thomson, 1943, S to Lady Diana Spencer, 2 August 1733, from Windsor.
66. *Ibid.*, 29 June 1733.
67. *Ibid.*, October 1733.
68. *Ibid.*, September 1733.
69. Hailes, (ed.), 1788, p. 57.
70. Thomson, 1943, S to Lady Diana Spencer, 8 November 1733.
71. Thomson, 1943, September 1733.
72. Thomson, 1943, S to Lady Diana Spencer, 1 November 1733, from Windsor.
73. *Ibid.*, 24 September 1734.
74. Quoted in Harris, 1991, p. 295.
75. Thomson, 1943, S to Lady Diana Spencer, 21 July 1732, from Scarborough Spa.
76. *Ibid.*, 1 November, from Windsor.
77. Add MS 61438.
78. Langford, Paul, *A Polite and Commercial People: England 1727–1783*, Oxford, 1998, p. 28.
79. Add MSS 61477, letter from William Chapman, August 1733.
80. Pierpont Morgan MS, Rulers of England XI, Duchess of Marlborough Letters, no. 15, to Sir John Hynde Cotton, 13 September 1740.
81. Add MS 61451.
82. Thomson, 1943, S to Lady Diana Spencer, 5 November 1733, from Windsor.
83. *Ibid.*, 11 November 1733, from Windsor.
84. Add MS 61477.
85. Add MS 61477, Pulteney to S, 24 November 1734.

86. Harris, 1991, p. 298.
87. Harris, Frances, 'The Electioneering of Sarah, Duchess of Marlborough', in *Parliamentary History*, vol. 2, p. 88.
88. Kronenberger, Louis, *Marlborough's Duchess*, London, 1958, p. 270.
89. Hervey, John, *The Publick Virtue of Former Times, and the Present Age Compared*, 1732.
90. Add MS 61450, S to the Duke of Manchester, 1733.
91. Archivist named Mr Shelton, in Brown, Richard G., *The Role of the Duchess of Marlborough in Augustan Literature*, PhD thesis, Rochester University, 1972, p. 118; Campbell, Kathleen, *Sarah, Duchess of Marlborough*, London, 1932, p. 267.
92. Thomson, 1943, S to Lady Diana Spencer, 21 June 1734.
93. Thomson, 1943, S to Lady Diana Spencer, 20 July 1734.
94. *Ibid.*, 13 July 1734.
95. *Ibid.*, 18 July 1734.
96. Add MS 61472, Household Accounts and Financial Correspondence.
97. Thomson, 1943, S to Lady Diana Spencer, 5 June 1735.
98. Quoted in Harris, 1991, p. 310.
99. Add MS 61448.
100. Add MS 61451.
101. Quoted in Green, 1967, p. 273.
102. Spencer, 1999, p. 92.
103. Add MS 61451.
104. Quoted in Harris, 1991, p. 312.

13: 'A Flight for Fame'

1. Quoted in Harris, Frances, 'Accounts of the Conduct of Sarah, Duchess of Marlborough', in *British Library Journal*, 1982, vol. 8, pp. 7–35.
2. Fielding, *A Full Vindication of the Duchess Dowager of Marlborough*, London, 1742, pp. 14–15.
3. Hailes, Lord (ed.), *The Opinions of Sarah, Duchess-Dowager of Marlborough*, London, 1788, pp. 82–4.
4. Horace Walpole to George Montagu, 6 May 1736, in Toynbee, Paget (ed.), *Letters of Horace Walpole*, Oxford, 1903, vol. 1, p. 15.
5. Add MS 61479.
6. Add MS 61426, 'Characters of Princes'.
7. Add MS 61478, Rysbrack to S, November 1742.
8. Sir John Dalrymple quotes Lord Oxford's grandson, quoted in turn in Churchill, Sir Winston, *Marlborough, His Life and Times*, Edinburgh, 1947, vol. 1, p. 377.
9. Add MS 61418, 23 April 1711 and 12/13 June 1711.
10. Dobrée, Bonamy (ed.), *The Letters of Philip Dormer Stanhope, 4th Earl of Chesterfield*, London, 1932, vol. 2, p. 449: Chesterfield to Marchmont, 24 April 1741.

11. Quoted in Chancellor, Frank, *John Churchill*, London, 1932, p. 248.
12. Harris, 1982, pp. 7–35.
13. Add MS 61478, Dr Doddridge to S, 3 April 1742.
14. Add MS 61423, Burnet's 'Vindication'.
15. Quoted in Green, David Brontë, *Sarah Duchess of Marlborough*, London, 1967, pp. 176–7.
16. Ralph, James, *The Other Side of the Question*, London, 1742.
17. *Ibid.*, p. 301.
18. *Ibid.*, p. 80.
19. *Ibid.*, p. 3.
20. *Ibid.*, p. 5.
21. *Ibid.*, p. 90.
22. *Ibid.*, p. 141.
23. North, Roger, *Her Grace of Marlborough's Party-Gibberish Explained and the True Sons of the Church Vindicated*, London, 1742, p. 5.
24. 'Review of the Account of the Conduct of the Duchess of Marlborough', *Gentleman's Magazine*, 1742, quoted in Murphy, Arthur (ed.), *Dr Johnson's Works*, Oxford, 1825, vol. 6, p. 4.
25. *Rambler*, 1 May 1750, no. 13, in Murphy (ed.), 1825, vol. 2, p. 63.
26. Campbell, Kathleen, *Sarah, Duchess of Marlborough*, London, 1932, p. 293; Thomson, Gladys Scott (ed.), *Letters of a Grandmother 1732–1735*, London, 1943, p. xi.
27. Fielding, 1742.
28. *Ibid.*, p. 37.
29. *Ibid.*, p. 40.
30. Walpole, Horace, *Catalogue of Royal and Noble Authors*, 1758, vol. 1, p. 179.
31. Toynbee (ed.), 1903, vol. 1, pp. 100–12.
32. Add MS 61479, 'Accounts relating to the public debts and civil list, with comments by the Duchess', 1739.
33. Add MS 61479.
34. Hailes (ed.), 1788, p. 139.
35. Langford, Paul, *Public Life and the Propertied Englishman 1689–1798*, Oxford, 1991, pp. 555–6.
36. Add MS 61451, folios 141–196b, narratives re Charles 3rd Duke of Marlborough, prompted by the Chancery suit 1738–44.
37. Quoted in Pearson, John, *Blood Royal*, London, 1999, p. 83.
38. Quoted in Dobrée, Bonamy (ed.), *Three Eighteenth Century Figures*, Oxford, 1962, p. 62. (NB: misapplied to Lady Anne Egerton in this source.)
39. Duchess of Portland to Lady Llanover, quoted in Rowse, A. L., *The Later Churchills*, London, 1958, p. 37.
40. Harris, Frances, *A Passion for Government*, Oxford, 1991, p. 328.
41. Hailes (ed.), 1778, p. 27.
42. S to John Spencer, 1742, quoted in Green, 1967, p. 295.

43. Add MS 61478.
44. Halsband, Robert (ed.), *The Complete Letters of Lady Mary Wortley Montagu*, Oxford, 1965, vol. 2, pp. 135–6.
45. Pierpont Morgan MS, S to Sir Hynde Cotton, 20 September 1740.
46. *Ibid.*, 13 September 1740.
47. *Ibid.*, 20 September 1740.
48. *Ibid.*, 11 October 1740.
49. *Ibid.*, 13 October 1740.
50. Add MS 61478.
51. S to Mr Cook at Bank of England, 26 November 1741, quoted in Butler, Iris, *Rule of Three: Sarah, Duchess of Marlborough and Her Companions in Power*, London, 1967, pp. 338–40.
52. Halsband (ed.), 1965, vol. 2, p. 244.
53. *Ibid.*, p. 479n.
54. Add MS 61451.
55. *Ibid.*
56. Add MS 61450.
57. Add MS 61451.
58. Add MS 61450.
59. Add MS 61450, S to Mrs Hammond, December 1739.
60. *Ibid.*, January 1741.
61. Add MS 61434, Godolphin to S, 18 September 1706.
62. Halsband (ed.), 1965, vol. 3, p. 134.
63. *Ibid.*, p. 453.
64. Kronenberger, Louis, *Marlborough's Duchess*, London, 1958, p. 288.
65. Quoted in Butler, 1967, p. 191.
66. Quoted in Green, 1967, p. 20.
67. Add MS 61479.
68. Harris, 1991, p. 347.
69. Rowse, 1958, p. 53.
70. *Ibid.*, p. 54.
71. Horace Walpole to Sir Horace Man, quoted in Dobree, 1962, p. 67.
72. Bodleian Library, MS Ballard 29, folio 110.
73. Steele to Dr Johnson, quoted in Reid, Stuart J., *John and Sarah, Duke and Duchess of Marlborough 1660–1774*, London, 1914, p. 477.
74. Reid, 1914, p. 477.
75. *A True Copy of the Last Will & Testament of Her Grace Sarah, late Duchess Dowager of Marlborough*, 1745.
76. Add MS 61478, Richard Glover to S.
77. Add MS 61479.
78. Add MS 61478.
79. Add MS 61418.
80. Churchill, Sir Winston, *Marlborough: His Life and Times*, Edinburgh, 1947, Appendix II, pp. 998–9.
81. Quoted in Butler, 1967, p. 264.

82. Add MS 61473.
83. Add MS 61478.
84. *Rambler*, no. 60, 'Dignity & Uses of Biography' in Murphy(ed.), 1825.
85. Add MS 61467.
86. Add MS 61467, John Scrope MP to S, 13 September 1744.
87. *Ibid.*
88. Add MS 61473.
89. Quoted in Churchill, 1947, vol. 1, pp. 149–50.
90. Quoted in Thomson, A. T., *Memoirs of Sarah Duchess of Marlborough*, London, 1839, vol. 2, p. 63.
91. Add MS 61478.
92. Letter to Hugh, Earl of Marchmont, quoted in Campbell, 1932, p. 292.
93. Burnet, Gilbert (Bishop), *History of His Own Time*, 1715, Everyman edition, p. 113.
94. Add MS 61467, S to John Scrope MP, 22 September 1744.

14: Afterlife

1. Quoted in Pearson, John, *Blood Royal*, London, 1999, p. 89.
2. *A True Copy of the Last Will & Testament of Her Grace Sarah, late Duchess Dowager of Marlborough*, 1745.
3. *Ibid.*; Churchill, Sir Winston, *Marlborough: His Life and Times*, Edinburgh, 1947, vol. 4, p. 1040.
4. Stowe MS 751.
5. Odell, Thomas, *An Elegiac Ode – Sacred to the Memory of The Most Noble Her Grace The Late Duchess Dowager of Marlborough*, London, 1744.
6. *General Advertiser*, 19 October 1744, 'Yesterday morning, at 9 o'clock died at her house in St James Park, Her Grace the Dowager Duchess of Marlborough in the 85th year of her age'; also, *Penny London Post*, or *Morning Advertiser*, 24 October 1744, no. 233; *Craftsman*, 20 October 1744; *London Evening Post*, 20 October 1744, no. 2645; *Daily Post*, 19 October 1744; *Daily Advertiser*, 23 October 1744, no. 4368.
7. Halsband, Robert (ed.), *The Complete Letters of Lady Mary Wortley Montagu*, Oxford, 1965, vol. 2, p. 347.
8. British Library ref: 292.i.12.
9. Printed Book Firth b.22 – folio 49: 'On the Duchess of Marlborough's Will', 1746.
10. Harris, Frances, *A Passion for Government*, Oxford, 1991, Appendix II.
11. Add MS 61479.
12. Add MS 61472, Household Accounts and Financial Correspondence.
13. Halsband (ed.), 1965, vol. 2, p. 484.
14. Quoted in Green, David Brontë, *Sarah Duchess of Marlborough*, London, 1967, pp. 308–9.
15. British Library ref: 1850.C.10.

16. Anon., A *Dialogue in the Shades: Between Mrs Morley and Mrs Freeman*, London, 1745, p. 27.
17. *Ibid.*, p. 54.
18. British Library ref: 1103.d.17.
19. Add MS 61426, 'Characters of Princes'.
20. 'Review of the Account of the Conduct of the Duchess of Marlborough', *Gentleman's Magazine*, 1742, quoted in Murphy (ed.), 1825, vol. 6, p. 4.
21. Stauffer, Donald A., *The Art of Biography in Eighteenth Century England*, Princeton, 1970, p. 332.
22. Harris, 1991, p. 350.
23. Add MS 61466.
24. Hudson, J. P ., 'The Blenheim Papers', in *British Library Journal*, 1982, vol. 8, no. 1, pp. 1–6.
25. Public Record Office IR 40/18181.
26. Anon., *Life and History of Sarah, Duchess of Marlborough*, London, 1710: Bodleian Library Vet A3 e.237(14).
27. Toynbee, Paget (ed.), *Letters of Horace Walpole*, Oxford, 1901, vol. 2, p. 302.
28. Masters, Brian, *The Dukes*, London, 2001, p. 198.
29. Thomson, A. T., *Memoirs of Sarah, Duchess of Marlborough*, London, 1839.
30. *Ibid.*, vol. 2, p. 481.
31. *Ibid.*, vol. 2, p. 493.
32. *Ibid.*, vol. 1, p. 231.
33. Macaulay, T. B., *History of England*, London, 1931, vol. II, p. 221.
34. *Ibid.*, vol II, p. 221.
35. *Ibid.*, vol. III, pp. 484–5.
36. Wolseley, Lord, *Marlborough*, London, 1894.
37. Richardson, Aubrey, *Famous Ladies of the English Court*, London, 1899, p. 344.
38. *Ibid.*, p. 300.
39. Colville, A., *Duchess Sarah*, London, 1904.
40. Reid, Stuart J., *John and Sarah, Duke and Duchess of Marlborough 1660–1744*, London, 1914.
41. *Ibid.*, p. 273.
42. *Ibid.*, p. ix.
43. *Ibid.*, p. 476.
44. *Ibid.*, p. 471.
45. Campbell, Kathleen, *Sarah, Duchess of Marlborough*, London 1932, p. 309.
46. *Ibid.*, p. 30.
47. *Ibid.*, p. 11.
48. Churchill, Sir Winston, *Marlborough: His Life and Times*, Edinburgh, 1947.

49. *Ibid.*, vol. 1, p. 42.
50. *Ibid.*, vol. 2, pp. 494–5.
51. *Ibid.*, vol. 2, p. 508.
52. *Ibid.*, vol. 1, p. 39.
53. *Ibid.*, vol. 4, p. 651.
54. Ginsbury, Norman, *Viceroy Sarah*, 1935. First performed by the Arts Theatre Club on 27 May 1934.
55. Foot, Michael, *The Pen and the Sword*, London, 1957, p. 51.
56. *Ibid.*, p. 369.
57. Kronenberger, Louis, *Marlborough's Duchess*, 1958, p. 314.
58. Dobrée, Bonamy, *Three Eighteenth Century Figures*, Oxford, 1962, p. 66.
59. Green, David Brontë, *Sarah Duchess of Marlborough*, London, 1967, p. 22.
60. Butler, Iris, *Rule of Three: Sarah Duchess of Marlborough and Her Companions in Power*, London, 1967, p. 217.
61. *Ibid.*, p. 99.
62. *Ibid.*, p. 31.
63. Dobrée, 1962, p. 12.
64. Butler, 1967, p. 200.
65. Interview with Susan Hampshire, *Sunday Telegraph*, 31 December 2000.
66. Harris, 1991, p. 122.
67. Radio 4, 30 June 1999, Douglas Young, *An End to Auld An Sang*.
68. Hennegan, Alison (ed.), *The Lesbian Pillow Book*, London, 2000.
69. Grier, Barbara, and Reid, Coletta (eds), *Women, Writing, History 1640–1740*, London, 1976, pp. 213–15.
70. Greene, Robert, *The 48 Laws of Power*, London, 2000.
71. *Ibid.*, pp. 337–8.
72. Churchill, Sarah, and Hooke, Nathaniel, *An Account of the Conduct of the Dowager Duchess of Marlborough*, 1742, p. 120.
73. Anon., *Review of a Late Treatise entitled 'An Account of the Conduct of the Dowager Duchess of Marlborough'*, 1742.
74. Kishlansky, Mark, *A Monarchy Transformed: Britain 1603–1714*, London, 1997, pp. 319–20.
75. Spencer, Charles, *The Spencer Family*, London, 1999, p. 70.
76. *Ibid.*, p. 84.
77. *Ibid.*, p. 106.
78. Add MS 61467, S to John Scrope MP, 13 September 1744.

Bibliography

Manuscript Sources

THE BRITISH LIBRARY, LONDON
Additional Manuscripts (Add MSS): the Blenheim Papers – particularly 'Part B:
   The Correspondence and Papers of Sarah, Duchess of Marlborough'
Stowe MS 751
Egerton MS 2678
Longleat microfilms, nos 863, 921, 904
Verney Papers
Althorp Papers
Add Ch. 76137, Plan of Marlborough House (1744)

PIERPONT MORGAN LIBRARY, NEW YORK
Letters to, *inter alia*, Lady Mary Wortley Montagu, Mr Townshend, Dr Clarke,
   Sir Hynde Cotton

BENEIKE LIBRARY, YALE UNIVERSITY
Osborn Manuscripts: 'm' 9877–9938

BODLEIAN LIBRARY, OXFORD
MS Lister 2–4: letters from Sarah to her uncle, M. Lister
MS Add.A.191: letters to Bishop Burnet
MS Rawl D.1208 (folio 153)
MS Rawl C.986
MS Carte: Nairne's Papers 208
MS Carte: Nairne's Papers 210
Rawl D. 383: folio 118
MS Ballard 29: folio 110
MS Rawl D.361: folio 345
Pr.Bk. Firth b.22: folio 49
MS Rawl poet 181: folio 70
Firth-b-21/94
Microfilm no. 740: 'Mrs Caesar's Diary'

CAMBRIDGE UNIVERSITY LIBRARY
Cholmondeley (Houghton) MSS: papers of Sir Robert Walpole

Bibliography

HUNTINGTON LIBRARY, SAN MARINO, CALIFORNIA
Ellesmere (Bridgwater) MSS
Hastings (Huntington) MSS
HM 16600–16635: letters of Sarah to her lawyer
HM 44710: letters to Hanover (1713)
Loudoun MSS
Stowe (Brydges) MSS
RB 284482

PUBLIC RECORD OFFICE, KEW, UK
AO 1/2067/103, 104 and 105 (Privy Purse accounts)
E 134/11 Geo1/Mich 27 and East 7 (Case of Edward Strong *v.* SM)

Printed Primary Sources

GENERAL BACKGROUND
Addison, Joseph, *Cato* (first performed 10 April 1713)
Anon., *Out with em while you are about it, OR A Great Change at Court* (1710)
Anon., *Kiss me if you dare, OR A Royal Favourite turn'd out* (1710)
Anon., *The Bubbler's Medley or a Sketch of the Times* (1720)
Anon., *The Prophesy OR M[asha]m's Lamentation for H[arle]y* (1710)
Baglivi, G., *The Practice of Physick* (1704)
Bathurst, Benjamin, *Letters of Two Queens* (London, 1924)
Bolingbroke, Lord, 'Remarks on the History of England', and 'A Dissertation on Parties', in *The Works of Lord Bolingbroke*, 4 vols (Philadelphia, 1841)
Brantome, Pierre de Bourdeille, *The Lives of Gallant Ladies*, trans. Alec Brown (London, 1961)
Brown, B. C. (ed.), *The Letters and Diplomatic Instructions of Queen Anne* (London, 1968)
Burnet, Gilbert (Bishop), *History of His Own Time* (1715)
  An Enquiry into the Measures of Submission (c. 1688)
Cavendish, Margaret, *Nature's Pictures Drawn by Fancies Pencil to the Life* (1656)
Cibber, C., *An Apology for the Life of Mr Colley Cibber*, 2nd edition (London, 1740)
Commons Journals 1547–, vol. 10
Coxe, William, *Shrewsbury Correspondence, Private and Original* (London, 1821)
Crouch, Nathaniel, *The Unfortunate Court-Favourites of England, exemplified in some remarks . . .* (1695)
Crowne, John, *Calisto, or The Chaste Nymph* (1675)
Dartmouth, Lord, *Bishop Burnet's History of the Reign of King James the Second. Notes by the Earl of Dartmouth, Speaker Onslow, and Dean Swift* (Oxford, 1852)
Davenant, Charles, *True Portrait of a Modern Whig* (1701)

Davis, Herbert (ed.), *Pope – Poetical Works* (Oxford, 1989)

Davis, H. J., and Ehrenpreis, I., *Jonathan Swift: Prose Works – Political Tracts 1713–19*, 15 vols (Oxford, 1939–74)

De Beer, Esmond (ed.), *John Evelyn Diaries*, 6 vols (Oxford, 1955)

Defoe, Daniel, *The Trueborn Englishman & Other Writings* (1705)

    The Conduct of the Parties (1708)

    A Speech without Doors (1710)

    The Secret History of the White Staff (1714)

    The Family Instructor (1715)

    Memoirs of the Conduct of Her Late Majesty and Her last Ministry, relating to the Separate Peace with France. By the Right Hon the Countess of — (1715)

    Memoirs of Public Transactions in the Life and Ministry of His Grace the Duke of Shrewsbury (1718)

    The South-Sea Scheme examin'd & the reasonableness thereof demonstrated (1720)

    Journal of the Plague Year (1722)

    Moll Flanders (1722)

    Roxana (1724)

    Tour Through the Whole Island of Great Britain (1724–6)

    Conjugal Lewdness (1727)

Dobrée, Bonamy, (ed.), *The Letters of Philip Dormer Stanhope, 4ᵗʰ Earl of Chesterfield*, 6 vols (London, 1932)

Doebner, R. (ed.), *Memoirs of Mary, Queen of England 1689–1693* (Leipzig, 1886)

D'Uffey, *The Hubble Bubbles* (1720)

Evelyn, John, *A Character of England, as it was lately presented in a letter to a Noble Man of France* (London, 1659)

    The Life of Mrs Godolphin (London, 1847)

Fielding, Henry, *Joseph Andrews* (London, 1742)

Filmer, Robert, *Patriarcha, Or the Natural Power of Kings* (1690)

Gay, John (and Pope and Arbuthnot), *Three Hours After Marriage. A Comedy* (1717)

Goldsmith, Oliver, *The Life of Richard Nash Esq.* (1762)

Grimston, Lord, *The Lawyer's Fortune, or Love in a Hollow Tree. A Comedy* (1705)

Halsband, Robert (ed.), *Complete Letters of Lady Mary Wortley Montagu* (Oxford, 1965)

Hamilton, Anthony, *Memoirs of Count de Grammont*, trans. Horace Walpole (Folio Society, 1965)

Hawtrey, E.C. (ed.), *Private Diary of William, First Earl Cowper* (Eton, 1833)

Hervey, John, *The Publick Virtue of Former Times, and the Present Age Compared* (1732)

Hervey, Sydenham H. A. (ed.), *The Letter-Books of John Hervey, first Earl of Bristol*, 3 vols (Suffolk, 1894)

Hoadly, Benjamin, *Thoughts of an Honest Tory upon the present proceedings of that party* (1710)

Bibliography

Latham, R., and Matthews, W., *The Diary of Samuel Pepys*, 11 vols (London, 1985)

Lee, Nathaniel, *Mithridates, King of Pontus – A Tragedy* (1678)

Marvell, Andrew, *Account of the Growth of Popery and Arbitrary Government* (1677)

Maynwaring, Arthur, *Four Letters to a Friend in North Britain – upon the Publishing the Trial of Dr Sacheverell* (1710)

Mesnager, Nicolas, *Minutes of the Negotiations* (1717)

Moland, Louis (ed.), *Oeuvres Complètes de Voltaire* (Paris, 1877–85)

Montesquieu Baron de, Charles de Secondat, *Le Spicilège* (Paris, 1729)

Murphy, Arthur (ed.), *Dr Johnson's Works*, 11 vols (Oxford, 1825)

Oldmixon, John, *Arthur Maynwaring – Life and Posthumous Works* (1715)
    Memoirs of the Press, Historical and Political, for Thirty Years past, from 1710–1740 (1742)

Prior, Matthew, *History of His Own Time* (1740)

Roberts, Philip (ed.), *Diary of Sir David Hamilton 1709–1714* (Oxford, 1975)

Sedgwick, R. (ed.), *Memoirs of John Hervey*, 3 vols (London, 1931/1963)
    The House of Commons 1715–54 (London, 1970)

Sherburn, George (ed.), *The Correspondence of Alexander Pope*, 5 vols (Oxford, 1956)

Singer, W., (ed.), *The Diary of Lord Clarendon 1687–1690*, 2 vols (London, 1828)

Swift, Jonathan, *The Furniture of a Woman's Mind* (London, 1750)

Toynbee, Paget, ed., *Letters of Horace Walpole* (Oxford, 1903)

Trapp, Joseph, *The Character and Principles of the Present Set of Whigs* (1711)

Wharncliffe, Lord (ed.), *The Letters & Works of Lady Mary Wortley Montagu*, 2 vols (London, 1887)

Williams, Harold (ed.), *Journal to Stella* (Oxford, 1948)
    The Correspondence of Jonathan Swift, 5 vols (Oxford, 1965)

NEWSPAPERS

Court, City and Country Magazine; Craftsman; Examiner; Gazette; Gentleman's Magazine; Medley; Observator; Review; Spectator; Tatler

ON FEMALE FRIENDSHIP / LESBIANISM

Anon., *The Sappho-An. An Heroic Poem of three Cantos in the Ovidian Style, Describing the Pleasures which the Fair Sex Enjoy with Each Other. According to the Modern and Most Polite Taste. Found amongst the Papers of a Lady of Quality, a great Promoter of Jacobitism* (1749)

Anon., *Venus in the Cloyster: Or, the Nun in her Smock – Translated from the French by a person of honour* (London, 1725)

Anon., 'Of the Game of Flats', in *Plain Reasons for the Growth of Sodomy in England* (London, 1728)

Anon., *Satan's Harvest Home: or the Present State of Whorecraft, Adultery, Fornication, Procuring, Pimping etc. in Great Britain* (1749)

Anon., *An epistle from Signora F—a to a lady* (1727)
Dunton, John, *King Abigail: or, The Secret Reign of the She-Favourite, Detected, and Applied; In a Sermon upon these words, 'AND WOMEN RULE OVER THEM' Isa.3.12* (1715)
Fielding, Henry, *The Female Husband: or, the Surprising History of Mrs Mary, alias Mr George Hamilton* (1746)
King, William, *The Toast – an Heroick Poem in four Books, written originally in Latin by Frederick Scheffer: Now done into English . . . by Peregrine Odonald* (1736)
Jones, Erasmus [Father Poussin], *Pretty Doings in a Protestant Nation* (1734)
Maynwaring, Arthur, *The Rival Dutchess: Or, Court-Incendiary. In a Dialogue between Madam Maintenon and Madam M[asham]* (London, 1708)
Walsh, William, *A Dialogue Concerning Women, Being a Defence of the Sex – Written to Eugenia* (London, 1691)

REPRESENTATIONS/PUBLICATIONS OF SARAH DUCHESS OF MARLBOROUGH
Anon., *Remarks upon the account of the conduct of a certain duchess: in a letter from a member of the last Parliament in the reign of Queen Anne, to a young nobleman* (London, 1742)
Anon. [Cunningham?], *A Review of a Late Treatise entitled 'An Account of the Conduct of the Dowager Duchess of Marlborough' by a Defender of William & Mary* (London, 1742)
Anon., *The History of Prince Mirabel's Infancy, Rise and Disgrace* (London, 1712)
Anon., *The Duke of M[arlboroug]h's Vindication: In answer to a pamphlet falsely so called* (London, 1712)
Anon., *Verses on the founding of a hospital for incurables in Dublin* (1744)
Anon., *The Age of Wonders – To the tune of Chivy Chase* (London, 1710)
Anon., *A Prince or no Prince OR, Mother Red-Cap's strange and wonderful Prophesy* (London, 1714)
Anon., *The Duchess of M[arlborough]'s CREED'* (London, 1712)
Anon. [Harley, Robert], *An Account of a Dream at Harwich* (1708)
Anon., *A Speech of Caius Memmius, Tribune, to the People of Rome* (1709)
Anon., *The Court visit; To a great lady at her country-seat, who lately remov'd her habitation because the air of St James's did not agree with her constitution* (1710)
Anon., *A Ballad on the Junto (to the tune of Lilly bullero)* (1710)
Anon., *Sarah's Farewell to C[our]t: or, A Trip from St James's to St Albans. To the tune of Farewell joy and Farewell Pleasure* (London, 1710)
Anon., *The Sarah-Ad: or, a Flight for Fame* (1742)
Anon., *A Tale of J[oh]n and S[ara]h or, Both Turned out of C[our]t at Last* (London, 1711)
Anon., *There's But One Plague in England: D[uchess] M[arlborough]* (London, 1711)

Bibliography

Anon., *The Glory of England* (1739/40)

Anon., *He's Welcome Home: or, A Dialogue between John and Sarah* (London, 1711)

Anon., *An Epistle from Sempronia to Cethegus. TO which is added Cethegus's Reply* (1713)

Anon., *The Old Wife's Tale: or, E[dwar]d's Wish. A Satire. Humbly inscribed to her grace the Dowager Duchess of M[arlborough]* (1742)

Anon., *The Beasts in Power, or ROBIN's Song: with An Old Cat's Prophecy* (1709)

Anon., *The Eagle and the Robin* (1709)

Anon., *The Perquisite-Monger; or the Rise and Fall of Ingratitude* (1712)

Anon., *The Birth, Parentage and Rise of J[ohn] D[uke] of M[arlborough]* (1712)

Anon., *The Ungrateful World, or; The Hard Case of a Great G[enera]l* (London, 1712)

Anon., *The Triumph of Envy: Or, The Vision of Shylock the Jew* (London, 1712)

Anon., *The Secret History of Henrada Maria Teresa* (London, 1733)

Anon., *Upon a Great Lady's Visiting the Tomb of Humphrey the Good, Duke of Gloucester, at St Albans*

Anon., *The Seasonable Caution*

Anon., *Rufinus or the Favourite, a Poem translated from Claudian* (1712)

Anon., *Our Ancestors as Wise as We: Or, Ancient Precedents for Modern Facts in Answer to a Letter from a Noble Lord* (London, 1712)

Anon., *Oliver's Pocket Looking-Glass New Fram'd and Clean'd to give a clear view of the Great Modern Colossus* (1711)

Anon., *The Consultation* (London, 1712)

Anon., *On the Great Storm, 26 Nov 1703* (1703)

Anon., *When a Church on a Hill . . .* (1704)

Anon., *Bellisarius, a Great Commander, and Zariana, his Lady: A dialogue* (London, 1710)

Anon., *S[ara]h and J[oh]n beg Pardon for What they have Done* (London, 1711)

Anon., *A Dialogue in the Shades: Between Mrs Morley and Mrs Freeman. Containing a Review of all the most material incidents in their past lives* (London, 1745)

Anon., *A Letter from the Duchess of M[arlbo]r[ou]gh, in the Shades, to The Great Man* (London, 1759)

Anon., *Life and History of Sarah, Duchess of Marlborough* (c. 1710)

Anon., *A Brief Discovery of the True Mother of the Pretended Prince of Wales* (1696, 1702)

Anon., *The Duchess of Marlborough's Vision* (London, 1711)

Anon., *The Amorous D[uc]h[e]ss: or Her G[race] Grateful* (London, 1733)

Anon., *The Petticoat Plotters, or the D[uche]ss of M[arlboroug]h's Club* (London, 1712)

Anon., *To the Duke of Marlborough on the Taking of Bouchain* (1711)

Churchill, Sarah, and Hooke, Nathaniel, *An Account of the Conduct of the*

Dowager Duchess of Marlborough – From her first coming to Court to the Year 1710 – In a letter from Herself to My Lord — (1742)

A True Copy of the Last Will & Testament of Her Grace Sarah, late Duchess Dowager of Marlborough: with the Codicil thereto annexed (1745)

Churchill, Sarah, and Maynwaring, Arthur, *Advice to the Electors of Great Britain: Occasioned by the Intended Invasion of France* (1708)

An Account of Mr Guidott's proceedings; which occasion'd the late trial between the late Duke of Marlborough's executors and the said Mr Guidott (London, 1727)

Clement, Simon, *Faults on Both Sides* (London, 1710)

Congreve, William, *The Tears of Amaryllis for Amyntas – A Pastoral Lamenting the Death of Lord Marquis of Blandford, Inscrib'd to the Right Hon. the Lord Godolphin* (London, 1703)

Defoe, Daniel, *Hymn to Victory* (1705)

The Double Welcome (1705)

No Queen: or No General. An Argument proving the Necessity Her Majesty was in, as well as the safety of Her Person, as of Her Authority, to Displace the D[uchess] of M[arl]borough (1712)

A Short Narrative of the Life and Actions of His Grace John, Duke of Marlborough (1711)

Dunton, John, *Petticoat Government. In a letter to the Court Ladies* (1702)

Fielding, Henry, *A Full Vindication of the Dutchess Dowager of Marlborough – Both with regard to the Account lately published by her Grace, and to Her Character in general; Against the base and malicious Invectives contained in a late scurrilous Pamphlet entitled Remarks on the Account etc. In a Letter to the Noble Author of those Remarks* (London, 1742)

Hare, Francis, *The Charge of God to Joshua: In a sermon preach'd before His Grace the Duke of Marlborough at Avenes le Sec, September 9, 1711 . . .* (1711)

Johnson, Charles, *The Victim* (London, 1714)

Manley, Mary Delariviere, *The Secret History of Queen Zarah and the Zarazians: Being a Looking-glass for S[arah] Ch[urchi]ll in the Kingdom of Albigion* (London, 1705)

Secret Memoirs and Manners of several Persons of Quality of Both Sexes. From the New Atalantis, an Island in the Mediterranean (London, 1709–11)

Memoirs of Europe . . . (London, 1710)

The Adventures of Rivella (London, 1714)

Miller, James, *The Year Forty-One: Carmen Seculare – Dedicated to Her Grace the Duchess Dowager of Marlborough* (London, 1741)

Neale, Thomas, *Ode (in imitation of Horace) on Ramellies* (London, 1706)

North, Roger, (published anon.), *Her Grace of Marlborough's Party-Gibberish explained, and the True Sons of the Church Vindicated* (London, 1742)

Odell, Thomas, *An Elegiac Ode – Sacred to the Memory of The Most Noble Her Grace The Late Duchess Dowager of Marlborough* (London, 1744)

Oldisworth, William, *The British Court: A Poem describing the Most Celebrated Beauties at St James's, The Park and The Mall* (May 1707)

Bibliography

Pope, Alexander (as Edras Barnivelt), *A Key to the Lock, Or, A Treatise proving, beyond all contradiction, the Dangerous Tendency of a late Poem, entitled the Rape of the Lock, to Government and Religion* (London, 1715)

    Epistle to a Lady [containing: 'Verses upon the late D[uche]ss of M[arlborough] by Mr P[ope]'] (1746)

Ralph, James, *The Other Side of the Question: OR an Attempt to Refine the Characters of the Two Royal Sisters Q Mary and Q Anne, Out of the Hands of the D[uches]s D[owager] of [Marlborough] in which all the remarkables in her Grace's late Account are stated in their full Strength and fully answered; the Conduct of Several Noble Persons is justified; and all necessary Lights are thrown on our Court-History from the Revolution to the Change of the Ministry in 1710. In a Letter to Her Grace by A Woman of Quality* (London, 1742)

Shippen, William, *Faction Display'd* (1704)

    Moderation Display'd (1705)

Swift, Jonathan, *The Conduct of the Allies* (London, 1711)

    Memoirs Relating to that Change which happened in the Queen's Ministry in the Year 1710 (London, 1714)

Vanbrugh, Sir John, *A Justification of what he depos'd in the Duke of Marlborough's late Trial* (1718)

Wagstaffe, William, *The Story of the St Albans Ghost OR The Apparition of Mother Haggy* (4th edition, London, 1712)

Walpole, Horace, *Catalogue of Royal and Noble Authors*, vol. IV (1758)

Wilson, Charles, *Memoirs of the Life, Writings and Amours of William Congreve* (London, 1730)

Secondary Sources

GENERAL BACKGROUND

Ackroyd, Peter, *London* (London, 2001)

Adair, Richard, *Courtship, Illegitimacy and Marriage in Early Modern England* (Manchester, 1996)

Amussen, S., *An Ordered Society – Class and Gender in Early Modern England* (Oxford, 1988)

Archer, John, 'Character in English Architectural Design', in *Eighteenth Century Studies* (Spring 1979), vol. 12, no.3, pp. 339–71

Ashton, J., *Social Life in the Reign of Queen Anne* (London, 1882)

Backscheider, P. and Richetti, J. J., *Popular Fiction by Women 1660–1730: An Anthology* (Oxford, 1996)

Ballard, George, *Memoirs of Several Ladies of Great Britain . . .* (Oxford, 1752)

Ballaster, Ros, *Seductive Forms: Women's Amatory Fiction from 1684 to 1740* (Oxford, 1992)

Barker, Francis *et al.*, *1642: Literature and Power in the 17th Century* (Colchester, 1981)

Barker, H., and Chalus, E., *Gender in 18ᵗʰ Century England – Roles, Representations and Responsibilities* (London, 1997)

Beckett, J. V., *The Aristocracy in England 1660–1914* (Oxford, 1986)

Black, Jeremy, *The English Press in the Eighteenth Century* (Aldershot, 1991)
  The English Press 1621–1861 (London, 2001)

Bostridge, Ian, *Witchcraft and Its Transformations c.1650–c.1750* (Oxford, 1997)

Boswell, Eleanore, *The Restoration Court Stage* (Harvard, 1932)

Brewer, John, *The Sinews of Power: War, Money and the English State 1688–1783* (London, 1989)

Brodzki, B., and Schenck, C., *Life Lines – Theorizing Women's Autobiography* (Cornell, 1988)

Brown, Irene Q., 'Domesticity, Feminism and Friendship: Female Aristocratic Culture and Marriage in England (1660–1760)', in *Journal of Family History* (Winter 1982), vol. 7, no. 4, pp. 406–24.

Brown, Laura, *Ends of Empire: Women and Ideology in Early Eighteenth Century Literature* (Cornell, 1993)

Bucholz, R. O., *The Augustan Court: Queen Anne & the Decline of Court Culture* (Stanford, 1993)

Carswell, J., *The South Sea Bubble* (London, 1960)

Chalmers, Hero A., *The Feminine Subject in Women's Printed Writings, 1653–1689*, PhD thesis (Oxford University, May 1993)

Chamberlain, Henry, *History of England* (London, 1770)

Cohen, Murray, *Sensible Words: Linguistic Practice in England 1640–1785* (Baltimore, 1977)

Colley, Linda, *Forging the Nation 1707–1837* (London, 1992)

Cowles, Virginia, *The Great Swindle: the Story of the South Sea Bubble* (London, 1960)

Delaney, Paul, *British Autobiography in the Seventeenth Century* (London, 1969)

Denny, Rev. Henry Lyttleton Lyster, *Memorials of an Ancient House: A History of the Family of Lister or Lyster* (London, 1913)

Dickinson, H. T., *Liberty and Property: Political Ideology in Eighteenth Century Britain* (London, 1977)

Dickson, P. G. M., *The Financial Revolution in England: A Study in the Development of Public Credit 1688–1756* (London, 1967)

  Dictionary of National Biography

Downes, K., *English Baroque Architecture* (London, 1966)

Downie, J. A., *Robert Harley and the Press* (Cambridge, 1979)

Earle, P., *A City Full of People: Men and Women of London 1650–1750* (London, 1994)

Elliot, J. H., and Brockliss, L. W. B., *The World of the Favourite* (Yale, 1999)

Faderman, Lillian, *Surpassing the Love of Men* (New York, 1981)

Foot, M., *The Pen and the Sword* (London, 1957)

Foucault, Michel, *The History of Sexuality*, 3 vols (London, 1981)

Fowler, Marian, *Blenheim: Biography of a Palace* (London, 1989)

Foxon, D., *Libertine Literature in England 1660–1745* (London, 1964)

Fraser, Antonia, *The Weaker Vessel* (London, 1984)

Garber, D., and Ayers, M., *The Cambridge History of 17ᵗʰ Century Philosophy* (Cambridge, 1998)

George, M., *Women in the First Capitalist Society: Experiences in 17ᵗʰ Century England* (Brighton, 1988)

Green, David Brontë, *Blenheim* (London, 1974)

Greer, Germaine, *The Change* (London, 1991)

Grier, Barbara, and Reid, Coletta (eds), *Lesbian Lives* (Oakland, California, 1976)

Grundy, I., and Wiseman, S., *Women, Writing, History 1640–1740* (London, 1992)

Hamilton, Ian, *Keepers of the Flame – Literary Estates and the Rise of Biography* (London, 1992)

Hanson, L., *The Government and the Press 1695–1763* (Oxford, 1936)

Harris, Frances, 'The Honourable Sisterhood', in *British Library Journal* (1993), XIX, no. 2, pp. 181–98.

Hennegan, Alison (ed.), *The Lesbian Pillow Book* (London, 2000)

Herbst, Katrin, *Schönheit als Tugend – Sir Godfrey Kneller und die Englische Portraetmalerei um 1700*, PhD thesis (Free University of Berlin, March 2002)

Hill, Christopher, *England's Turning Point: Essays on 17ᵗʰ Century English History* (London, 1998)

Holmes, Geoffrey, *The Trial of Dr Sacheverell* (London, 1973)
  British Politics in the Age of Anne (London, 1987)
  The Making of a Great Power: England 1660–1722 (London, 1993)

Hudson, J. P., 'The Blenheim Papers', in *British Library Journal* (1982), vol. 8, no. 1, pp. 1–6.

Hufton, Olwen, 'Women without Men: Widows and Spinsters in Britain and France in the 18ᵗʰ century', in *Journal of Family History* (Winter 1984), 9.

Israel, Jonathan (ed.), *The Anglo-Dutch Moment: Essays on the Glorious Revolution and Its World Impact* (Cambridge, 1991)

Jack, Ian, *Augustan Satire: Intention and Idiom in English Poetry 1660–1750* (Oxford, 1952)

Jones, D. W., *War & Economy in the Age of William III & Marlborough* (Oxford, 1988)

Jones, J. R., *Britain and the World, 1649–1815* (Sussex, 1980)

Kenyon, J. P., *Revolution Principles – The Politics of Party 1689–1720* (Cambridge, 1977)

Kishlansky, Mark, *A Monarchy Transformed: Britain 1603–1714* (London, 1997)

Langford, Paul, *Public Life and the Propertied Englishman 1689–1798* (Oxford, 1991)
  A Polite and Commercial People: England 1727–1783 (Oxford, 1998)
  Englishness Identified: Manners and Character 1650–1850 (Oxford, 2000)

Lee, Christopher, *This Sceptred Isle* (London, 1997)

Lonsdale, Roger, *Eighteenth Century Women Poets* (Oxford, 1990)

Lowe, Robert W., *Their Majesties' Servants – Annals of the English Stage* (London, 1888)

Lynch, Bohun, *A History of Caricature* (London, 1926)

Macaulay, T. B., *History of England*, vols III and IV (London, 1855)

Maccubbin, Robert Purks, *Tis Nature's Fault: Unauthorised Sexuality during the Enlightenment* (Cambridge, 1985)

McFarlane, Cameron, *The Sodomite in Fiction and Satire 1660–1750* (New York, 1997)

McKay, D., and Scott, H. M., *The Rise of the Great Powers 1648–1815* (London, 1983)

McDowell, Paula, *The Women of Grub Street – Press, Politics and Gender in the London Literary Marketplace 1678–1730* (Oxford, 1998)

Mendelson, S., *The Mental World of Stuart Women: Three Studies* (Reading, 1987)

Monod, Paul, *Jacobitism & the English People 1688–1788* (Cambridge, 1989)

Montagu of Beaulieu, Lord, *Wheels Within Wheels* (London, 2001)

Mullan, John, *Sentiment and Sociability – The Language of Feeling in the Eighteenth Century* (Oxford, 1988)

Myers, S. H., *The Bluestocking Circle – Women, Friendship and the Life of the Mind in 18th Century England* (Oxford, 1990)

Nicholson, Colin, *Writing and the Rise of Finance – Capital Satires of the Early Eighteenth Century* (Cambridge, 1994)

Nussbaum, Felicity A., *The Brink of All We Hate: English Satires on Women 1660–1750* (Kentucky, 1984)

Pinto, Vivian De Sola, *Restoration Carnival – Five Courtier Poets* (London, 1954)

Pipes, Richard, *Property and Freedom* (London, 1999)

Pocock, J. G. A., *The Machiavellian Moment* (Princeton, 1975)
    Three British Revolutions: 1641, 1688, 1776 (Princeton, 1980)

Porter, Roy, *English Society in the Eighteenth Century* (Harmondsworth, 1990)
    and Tomaselli, S., *The Dialectics of Friendship* (London, 1989)
    and Rousseau, G. S., *Gout – The Patrician Malady* (Yale, 1998)

Prior, Mary, *Women in English Society 1500–1800* (London, 1985)

Redford, Bruce, *The Converse of the Pen – Acts of Intimacy in the Eighteenth Century Familiar Letter* (Chicago, 1986)

Riley, John, 'Portraiture in the Age of Kneller and His Immediate Successors', in Waterhouse, Ellis, *Painting in Britain 1530–1790* (Yale, 1994)

Rogers, Pat, *Hacks and Dunces – Pope, Swift and Grub Street* (London, 1972)

Rose, Mary Beth, 'Gender, Genre and History – Seventeenth Century English Women and the Art of Autobiography', in Rose, Mary Beth, *Women in the Middle Ages and Renaissance* (New York, 1986)

Roseveare, Henry, *The Financial Revolution 1660–1750* (London, 1991)

Saxonhouse, Arlene W., *Women in the History of Political Thought – Ancient Greece to Machiavelli* (New York, 1985)

Bibliography

Schama, Simon, *The Embarrassment of Riches – An Interpretation of Dutch Culture in the Golden Age* (London, 1991)

Sewter, A. C., 'Kneller & the English Augustan Portrait', in *Burlington Magazine* (1940), vol. 77

Stater, Victor, *High Life, Low Morals: The Duel that Shook Stuart Society* (London, 1999)

Snyder, Henry L., 'Daniel Defoe, Arthur Maynwaring, Robert Walpole and Abel Boyer: Some considerations of authorship', in *Huntington Library Quarterly* (1969–70), XXXIII, pp. 133–53

    'Arthur Maynwaring and the Whig Press 1710–12' in Haas, Rudolf *et al.* (eds), *Literatur als Kritik des Lebens* (Heidelberg, 1977)

Speck, W. A., *Stability and Strife: England 1714–1760* (London, 1977)

    Literature and Society – Ideology, Politics & Culture 1680–1820 (London, 1998)

Spence, Joseph, *Observations, Anecdotes and Characters of Books and Men*, ed. James M. Osborn, 2 vols (Oxford, 1963)

Stauffer, Donald A., *English Biography Before 1700* (New York, 1964)

    The Art of Biography in Eighteenth Century England, 2 vols (Princeton, 1970)

Stewart, J. Douglas, *Sir Godfrey Kneller* (National Portrait Gallery Catalogue, London, 1971)

    Sir Godfrey Kneller and the English Baroque Portrait (Oxford, 1983)

Stone, Lawrence, *The Family, Sex and Marriage in England 1550–1800* (London, 1982)

Summerson, John, *The Unromantic Castle and Other Essays* (London, 1990)

Thompson, Roger, *Unfit for Modest Ears: A Study of Pornographic, Obscene and Bawdy Works Written or Published in England in the Second Half of the Seventeenth Century* (London, 1979)

Thomson, Gladys Scott, *Life in a Noble Household 1641–1700* (Ann Arbor, 1959)

Thorold, Peter, *The London Rich: The Creation of a Great City from 1666 to the Present* (London, 1999)

Todd, J., *Women's Friendship in Literature* (New York, 1980)

Trevelyan, G. M., *History of England* (London, 1926)

    England Under Queen Anne, 3 vols (London, 1930)

Utter, R. P., and Needham, G. B., *Pamela's Daughters* (New York, 1937)

Veenendaal, A. J., *De Briefwisseling van Anthonie Heinsius*, 20 vols (The Hague, 1976–2001)

Vickery, Amanda, *The Gentleman's Daughter – Women's Lives in Georgian England* (Yale, 1998)

Waller, Maureen, *1700: Scenes from London Life* (London, 2000)

Waterhouse, Ellis (ed.), *Painting in Britain 1530 to 1790* (Yale, 1994)

Weightman, Christine B., *A Short History of The Hague* (Schiedam, 1973)

Weil, Rachel Judith, *Sexual Ideology and Political Propaganda in England 1680–1714*, PhD thesis, (Princeton University, 1991)

Wendorf, Richard, *The Elements of Life: Biography and Portrait Painting in Stuart and Georgian England* (Oxford, 1990)

White, T. H., *The Age of Scandal* (Folio Society, 1993)

Wildeblood, Joan, *The Polite World: A Guide to the Deportment of the English in Former Times* (London, 1973)

Willis, Deborah, *Malevolent Nature: Witch-hunting and Maternal Power in Early Modern England* (Cornell, 1995)

Willis, John E., *1688: A Global History* (London, 2000)

Wilson, John Harold, *Court Satires of the Restoration* (Ohio, 1976)

Worsley, Giles, *Classical Architecture in Britain – The Heroic Age* (Yale, 1995)

REPRESENTATIONS/BIOGRAPHIES/PUBLICATIONS OF SARAH, DUCHESS OF MARLBOROUGH

Anon., *Life of Sarah Duchess of Marlborough* (London, 1745)

Anon. (ed.), *Letters of Sarah Duchess of Marlborough, now first published from the original manuscripts at Madresfield Court* (London, 1875)

Barnett, Corelli, *Marlborough* (Wordsworth Military Library, London, 1999)

Brown, Beatrice Curtis, 'Sarah, Duchess of Marlborough', in Dobrée, Bonamy (ed.), *Six Brilliant English Women* (London, 1930)

Brown, Richard Grant, *The Role of the Duchess of Marlborough in Augustan Literature*, PhD thesis (University of Rochester, 1972)

Burnet, Gilbert (Bishop), *History of His Own Time* (Everyman, 1991)

Butler, Iris, *Rule of Three: Sarah, Duchess of Marlborough and Her Companions in Power* (London, 1967)

Campbell, Kathleen, *Sarah, Duchess of Marlborough* (London, 1932)

Carter, Winifred, *Sarah* (London, 1943)

Chancellor, Frank, *Sarah Churchill* (London, 1932)

Chandler, David G., *Marlborough as Military Commander* (London, 2001)

Churchill, Sir Winston, *Marlborough: His Life and Times*, 2 vols (Edinburgh, 1947)

Colville, A., *Duchess Sarah* (London, 1904)

Cowles, Virginia, *The Great Marlborough and His Duchess* (London, 1983)

Coxe, William, *Memoirs of John, Duke of Marlborough*, 6 vols (London, 1820)

Dobrée, Bonamy (ed.), *Six Brilliant English Women* (1930)

  Three Eighteenth Century Figures (Oxford, 1962)

  As Their Friends Saw Them (London, 1933)

Ginsbury, Norman, *Viceroy Sarah* (London, 1935)

Green, David Brontë, *Sarah Duchess of Marlborough* (London, 1967)

Greene, Robert, *The 48 Laws of Power* (London, 2000)

Gregg, E., 'Marlborough in Exile 1712–1714', in *Historical Journal* (1972), XV, no. 4, pp. 593–618

Hailes (ed.), Lord, *The Opinions of Sarah, Duchess-Dowager of Marlborough: Published from the Original Manuscripts* (London, 1788)

Harris, Frances, 'Accounts of the Conduct of Sarah, Duchess of Marlborough', in *British Library Journal* (1982), VIII, pp. 7–35

Bibliography

'The Electioneering of Sarah, Duchess of Marlborough', in *Parliamentary History* 2 (1983), pp. 71–92

A Passion for Government (Oxford, 1991)

Hibbert, Christopher, *The Marlboroughs: John and Sarah Churchill 1650–1744* (London, 2001)

Horn, Robert Dewey, *Marlborough: A Survey; panegyrics, satires and biographical writings 1688–1788* (Folkestone, 1975)

King, William (ed.), *Memoirs of Sarah, Duchess of Marlborough* (London, 1930)

Kronenberger, Louis, *Marlborough's Duchess* (London, 1958)

Lediard, Thomas, *The Life of John, Duke of Marlborough*, 3 vols (London, 1746)

Leslie, Doris, *That Enchantress* (London, 1950)

Molloy, J. F., *The Queen's Comrade: The Life and Times of Sarah, Duchess of Marlborough* (London, 1901)

Pearson, John, *Blood Royal – The Story of the Spencers and the Royals* (London, 1999)

Plaidy, Jean, *The Queen's Favourites* (London, 1966)

Reid, Stuart J., *John and Sarah, Duke and Duchess of Marlborough 1660–1744* (London, 1914)

Richardson, Aubrey, *Famous Ladies of the English Court* (London, 1899)

Rosenberg, A., and Bunker, H., 'Prior's Feud with the Duchess of Marlborough', in *Journal of English and Germanic Philology*, (January 1953), LII, no. 1

Rowse, A. L., *The Later Churchills* (London, 1958)

The First Churchills (BBC Television, 1969)

Russell, Lord John (ed.), *Private Correspondence of Sarah, Duchess of Marlborough*, 2 vols (London, 1838)

Saunders, Beatrice, *Sarah Duchess of Marlborough: Her Life and Times* (London, 1985)

Scribe, Eugène, *Le Verre d'eau ou les effets et les causes*, Eggert, Charles A. (ed.) (New York, 1900)

Sergeant, Philip W., 'Duchess Sarah', in *Dominant Women* (London, 1930)

Sitwell, Edith, *English Women* (London, 1942)

Snyder, Henry L. (ed.), *The Marlborough–Godolphin Correspondence* 3 vols (Oxford, 1975)

'Daniel Defoe, the Duchess of Marlborough and the Advice to the Electors of Great Britain', in *Huntington Library Quarterly* (1965–6), vol. 29

Spencer, Charles, *The Spencer Family* (London, 1999)

Swift, Jonathan, *History of the Four Last Years of the Queen* (London, 1712)

Thackeray, W. M., *Henry Esmond* (London, 1852)

Thomson, A. T., *Memoirs of Sarah Duchess of Marlborough*, 2 vols (London, 1839)

Thomson, Gladys Scott (ed.), *Letters of a Grandmother 1732–1735* (London, 1943)

Wolseley, Lord, *Marlborough*, 2 vols (London, 1894)

Young, Douglas, *An End to Auld An Sang* (BBC Radio 4, 30 June 1999)

BIOGRAPHIES OF SARAH'S FRIENDS AND CONTEMPORARIES

Blakiston, Georgiana, *Woburn and the Russells* (London, 1980)

Cohen, S. J., 'Hester Santlow', in *NY Public Library Bulletin* (1980) vol. 64

Dickinson, H. T., *Bolingbroke* (London, 1970)

Dickinson, W. C., *Sidney Godolphin, Lord Treasurer, 1702–1710* (London, 1990)

Earle, P., *The World of Defoe* (London, 1976)

Fea, A., *The Loyal Wentworths* (London, 1928)

Fraser, Antonia, *King Charles II* (London, 1997)

Glendinning, Victoria, *Jonathan Swift* (London, 1998)

Gregg, Edward, *Queen Anne* (London, 1980)

Grew, Marion E., *William Bentinck & William III* (London, 1924)

Grundy, Isobel, *Lady Mary Wortley Montagu* (Oxford, 1999)

Hamilton, Elizabeth, *The Illustrious Lady – A Biography of Barbara Villiers, Countess of Castlemaine and Duchess of Cleveland* (London, 1980)

Hill, Brian W., *Robert Harley – Speaker, Secretary of State and Premier Minister* (Yale, 1988)

Hopkins, Graham, *Nell Gwynne – A Passionate Life* (London, 2000)

Killanin, Lord, *Sir Godfrey Kneller and His Times 1646–1723* (London, 1948)

Kramnick, Isaac, *Bolingbroke and his Circle: The Politics of Nostalgia in the Age of Walpole* (Oxford, 1968)

Kronenberger, Louis, *Kings and Desperate Men* (London, 1942)

Laslett, Peter, 'Masham of Otes: The Rise and Fall of an English Family', in *History Today* (1953), vol. 3

Lever, Sir T., *Godolphin* (London, 1952)

Massey, Victoria, *The First Lady Diana* (London, 1999)

Masters, Brian, *The Mistresses of Charles II* (London, 1997)
    The Dukes (London, 2001)

Moore, Lucy, *Amphibious Thing* (London, 2000)

Needham, Gwendolyn B., 'Mary de la Riviere Manley, Tory Defender', in *Huntington Library Quarterly* (May 1949), vol. 12

Plumb, J. H., *The Life of Sir Robert Walpole* (London, 1956)

Sergeant, P. W., *My Lady Castlemaine* (London, 1912)
    Little Jennings & Fighting Dick Talbot (London, 1913)

Strickland, Agnes, *Lives of the Queens of England* (London, 1878)

Szpila, Kathleen Helen, *Sarah Duchess of Marlborough as Patron of the Arts*, PhD thesis (Temple University, 1997)

West, Richard, *The Life and Strange Adventures of Daniel Defoe* (London, 1998)

Whistler, Laurence, *Sir John Vanbrugh: Architect and Dramatist 1664–1726* (London, 1938)

Index

'S' indicates Sarah, Duchess of Marlborough and 'M' the 1st Duke of Marlborough.